Learning to Teach

TENTH EDITION

Richard I. Arends

Seattle University

Mc
Graw
Hill
Education

LEARNING TO TEACH, TENTH EDITION

Published by McGraw-Hill Education, 2 Penn Plaza, New York, NY 10121. Copyright © 2015 by McGraw-Hill Education. All rights reserved. Printed in the United States of America. Previous editions © 2012, 2009, and 2007. No part of this publication may be reproduced or distributed in any form or by any means, or stored in a database or retrieval system, without the prior written consent of McGraw-Hill Education, including, but not limited to, in any network or other electronic storage or transmission, or broadcast for distance learning.

Some ancillaries, including electronic and print components, may not be available to customers outside the United States.

This book is printed on acid-free paper.

1 2 3 4 5 6 7 8 9 0 DOW/DOW 1 0 9 8 7 6 5 4

ISBN 978-1-260-78143-4
MHID 1-260-78143-7

Senior Vice President, Products & Markets: *Kurt L. Strand*
Vice President, General Manager, Products & Markets: *Michael Ryan*
Vice President, Content Production & Technology Services: *Kimberly Meriwether David*
Managing Editor: *Penina Braffman*
Marketing Specialist: *Alexandra Schultz*
Director, Content Production: *Terri Schiesl*
Content Project Manager: *Heather Ervolino*
Buyer: *Susan K. Culbertson*
Cover Designer: *Studio Montage, St. Louis, MO*
Cover Image: *Image Source/Getty Images*
Media Project Manager: *Jennifer Bartell*
Compositor: *Laserwords Private Limited*
Typeface: *9.5/12 Palatino LT std*
Printer: *R. R. Donnelley*

All credits appearing on page or at the end of the book are considered to be an extension of the copyright   page.

Library of Congress Cataloging-in-Publication Data

Arends, Richard
  Learning to teach/Richard I. Arends.—Tenth edition.
    pages cm
  ISBN 978-0-07-811030-6 (alk. paper)
  1. Teaching—Textbooks. 2. Effective teaching—Textbooks. I. Title.
  LB1025.3.A74 2014
  371.102—dc23

                                    2013042979

www.mhhe.com

About the Author

Richard I. Arends is currently a Visiting Professor at Seattle University and Professor of Educational Leadership and Dean Emeritus at Central Connecticut State University, where he served as Dean of the School of Education and Interim Provost of Academic Affairs from 1991 to 2004. Before going to Connecticut, he was on the faculty and chaired the Department of Curriculum and Instruction at the University of Maryland, College Park. He received his Ph.D. from the University of Oregon, where he also served on the faculty. A former elementary, middle school, and high school teacher, his special interests are teaching, teacher education, organization development, and school improvement.

Professor Arends has authored or contributed to over a dozen books on education, including the *Second Handbook of Organization Development in Schools, Systems Strategies in Education, Exploring Teaching, Teaching for Student Learning,* and *Learning to Teach.* The latter is now in its tenth edition and has been translated into several foreign languages. He has worked widely with schools and universities throughout North America, in Jamaica, and in the Pacific Rim, including Australia, Samoa, Palau, and Saipan.

The recipient of numerous awards, Professor Arends was selected in 1989 as the outstanding teacher educator in Maryland and in 1990 received the Judith Ruskin Award for outstanding research in education. From 1995 to 1997, Professor Arends held the William Allen (Boeing) Endowed Chair in the School of Education at Seattle University. Currently, he is retired in Seattle, Washington, where he teaches, pursues his favorite projects and continues to write.

Brief Contents

Contents

Part 2

The Leadership Aspects of Teaching   93

Chapter 3

Teacher Planning   94

Chapter 4

Learning Communities and Student Motivation   136

Chapter 10

Cooperative Learning   368

Chapter 11

Problem-Based Learning   404

Chapter 12

Classroom Discussion   436

Chapter 13

Using Multiple Approaches to Teaching and Differentiation   470

Part 5

The Organizational Aspects of Teaching   497

Chapter 14

School Leadership and Collaboration   498

Resource Handbook

Preface

Learning to be a teacher is a long and complex journey full of excitement and challenge. It begins with the many experiences we have with our parents and siblings; it continues as we observe teacher after teacher through sixteen to twenty years of schooling; and it culminates, formally, with professional training, but continues through a lifetime of teaching experiences.

Purpose and Audience

This is the tenth edition of *Learning to Teach*. It is intended for teacher candidates taking a course commonly labeled General Methods of Teaching, and offered through the elementary, secondary, or general education programs. A variety of other course titles—Analysis of Teaching, Study of Teaching, Principles and Practices of Teaching, or Strategies of Teaching—are sometimes used. Whatever its title, the course's content normally focuses on general models, strategies, and tactics that apply to teaching in all subject areas and at all grade levels.

Although these courses vary somewhat among institutions, most of them share the following general goals. Most instructors want their students to

- develop a repertoire of basic teaching approaches, strategies, and tactics.
- understand the theoretical foundations behind teaching and student learning.
- understand the dynamics of teaching, both inside and outside the classroom.
- develop an awareness and appreciation of the knowledge base that supports current practices in teaching.
- appreciate the opportunities and challenges of teaching in classrooms characterized by diversity.
- develop understandings and skills for assessing and evaluating student learning.
- know how to adapt instruction to meet the needs of all learners and to guarantee their success.
- acquire skills with which to observe, record, and reflect on teaching.

Organization and Content of the Tenth Edition

The tenth edition of *Learning to Teach* provides a comprehensive and balanced view of teaching. To accomplish this, the book is organized into five parts. Part 1 introduces the book, explores the meaning of effective teaching, and considers the processes and stages that beginning teachers go through on the way to becoming accomplished teachers. It also lays out the major themes of the book as well as the contemporary social context of teaching—a context characterized by student diversity and societal demands that teachers help all students realize their learning potentials.

Parts 2, 3, 4, and 5, the heart of the book, are organized around concepts of what teachers do. These sections assume that all teachers have three important responsibilities: (1) They lead a group of students—the *leadership aspects of teaching;* (2) they provide students with direct, face-to-face instruction—the *interactive aspects of teaching;* and (3) they work with colleagues and parents to perform the *organizational aspects of teaching.* The interactive aspects of teaching have been divided into two parts. Part 3 (Chapters 7–8) describes the more traditional and teacher-centered and transmission approaches to instruction, whereas Part 4 (Chapters 9–13) focuses specifically on contemporary student-centered constructivist approaches as well as on ways to use various approaches together or in tandem to meet a variety of instructional goals.

Research Applied to the Practical Problems of Teaching

To be successful, teachers must have a solid understanding of the research evidence that supports and defines effective teaching practices. They must also command a deep practical knowledge about students, how they learn, and about the strategies that promote student learning. With this belief, *Learning to Teach* emphasizes how important research is to teaching and learning and shows how ideas from research can be applied to the practical problems faced daily by teachers.

The Research, Evidence-Based Side of Teaching

Much progress has been made over the past fifty years in clarifying and organizing the knowledge base on teaching and learning. It is important for teachers in the twenty-first century to have a command of the specialized knowledge that has accumulated over the past half-century and more. This knowledge will set teachers apart from the average person and provide them, as professionals, with some guarantees that they are using best practice.

Theory to Practice Connections.   *Learning to Teach* strives to provide readers with the theory and rationale that underlie and support specific principles and practices. Each chapter has a Theoretical and Empirical Support section that provides a sampling of the research that is the basis of particular practices followed by explanation of why a recommended practice or procedure works the way it does.

Research Summary Boxes.   Each chapter contains a boxed Research Summary of an important research study pertaining to the chapter topic. The studies have been selected to illustrate not only some aspect of the knowledge base that supports the topics under discussion, but also particular modes of inquiry practiced by educational researchers. Some of the studies are more traditional empirical studies, whereas others represent contemporary qualitative approaches. Many of the studies are considered classics, and together they cover almost fifty years of educational research. Although highly compressed, these summaries are true to the investigators' methods and conclusions.

Resource Handbook Reading and Using Research,   found at the end of the text contains a succinct guide to reading and understanding the research literature available through professional journals. This handbook provides an introduction to consuming literature—an ability any serious student of teaching must develop.

The Applied and Practical Side of Teaching

Although teaching is based on knowledge derived from theory and educational research, it also has an important applied and practical side. The content in *Learning to Teach* has been organized to help address many of the everyday problems faced by teachers. It takes those who are learning to teach behind, instead of in front of, the teacher's desk to provide a practical and realistic view of what teaching is all about. Chapters provide concrete guidance on how to plan and conduct a variety of lessons, how to assess and evaluate student learning, and how to create and manage a productive learning environment. The organization of the text and its approach are designed to provide readers with specific understandings and skills so they can apply these understandings to concrete classroom situations.

Multiple Approaches to Teaching and Differentiation.   While *Learning to Teach* discusses various approaches and models of teaching independently in order to provide a comprehensive, research-based discussion of each, the reality is that teachers rarely use a particular approach alone. They generally use several in any given lesson or unit. In this edition, a chapter describes how to use multiple approaches in a lesson or unit and how to differentiate instruction to support individual student learning.

Diversity and Differentiation.   The discussion of diversity and differentiation is one that spans the entire text. It begins in Chapter 2 and focuses on student learning in diverse classrooms. The discussion started in Chapter 2 is continued through the rest of the text in sections that focus on diversity and differentiation for student learning in relation to the topic at hand. These special sections describe how teachers can adapt or differentiate their instructional practices to the wide range of abilities, diverse cultural backgrounds, and various special needs they face in their classrooms.

Enhancing Teaching and Learning with Technology.   It is important for beginning teachers to step into the classroom ready to use computers, digital technology, and the Internet and social media in support of their teaching and to enhance student learning. A boxed feature, Enhancing Teaching and Learning with Technology, can be found in most chapters to help accomplish this goal. Computer and digital technologies pertaining to a particular chapter topic are highlighted and how these technologies are influencing education today and in the future is discussed.

Home and School.   An increasing amount of evidence suggests that home, family, and community matter a lot in what students learn. This feature was introduced in the eighth edition of *Learning to Teach* and expanded in the current edition. It emphasizes the importance of developing family partnerships and for staying connected to the students' homes and communities. This feature is included in chapters as appropriate, and it provides beginning teachers with concrete guidance on how to work with families and how to involve the community.

Support for Student Learning

Learning to Teach has several features created to support learning and to help readers access and learn information from the text.

- **Learning Goals.** Each chapter begins with Learning Goals that focus the student on key aspects of the chapter.

- **Check, Extend, Explore.** Each major chapter section concludes with "Check" questions to help the reader review the content covered, "Extend" questions that prompt reflection and also ask poll questions that the reader can respond to on the Online Learning Center, and "Explore" listings of related Web site topics that can be linked to through the Online Learning Center.
- **Marginal Notes.** Throughout the chapters, marginal notes highlight main ideas and define important concepts.
- **Summary.** Tied to the chapter-opening Learning Goals, the summary provides a point-by-point review of the chapter's content.
- **Key Terms.** Key terms with page references are listed at the end of each chapter. Definitions are listed in the book-ending Glossary.
- **Books for the Professional.** At the end of each chapter a list of books deemed important for further exploration of the chapter's topics is provided. These have been carefully vetted for relevancy and accuracy.

Application and Interactive Opportunities

Although many aspects of teaching can be guided by the knowledge base, many others can be looked at from more than one point of view and require problem solving and reflection on the part of teachers. *Learning to Teach* includes several applied features that allow teacher candidates to reflect on important issues, compare their ideas and opinions to those of experienced teachers, and practice what they are learning.

- *Reflecting On . . .* Each chapter begins with a short scenario and series of questions designed to prompt readers to reflect on their own lives and classroom experiences to prepare them for the content to follow. Readers can respond to the questions through the Online Learning Center.
- *Reflections from the Classroom*—**Case Study.** Each chapter concludes with a classroom case or teaching situation that is followed by reactions to the scenario from two experienced classroom teachers.
- *Portfolio and Field Experience Activities.* Organized by *Learning to Teach* chapters, these activities constitute a field guide that assists teacher candidates in gathering and interpreting data, examining their own experiences, and developing a professional portfolio. The activities are on the Online Learning Center and each is matched to one or more of the InTASC Standards.
- **Lesson Planning Exercises and Practice Activities.** The Online Learning Center includes two types of interactive activities that were designed to help teacher candidates apply what they are learning by giving them the opportunity to plan lessons and engage in a variety of practice activities. The *Lesson Planning Exercises* walk the student through planning a lesson based on particular approaches to teaching. The student is given a task and the tools (background information about a real classroom, student descriptions, video clips, sample lesson plans, etc.) to complete it. Each task constitutes one step in planning a lesson based on a particular approach to teaching. The stand-alone *Practice Activities* allow the student to complete an activity that a teacher would typically do.
- **Portfolio Resources.** Many teacher candidates today are required to have a professional portfolio. To help students with the construction of portfolios, the *Portfolio and Field Experience Activities* section of the Online Learning Center includes

an introduction to portfolios as well as many activities that can become portfolio artifacts. Additionally, many of the text features can guide portfolio exhibit development.

New in the Tenth Edition

As with previous editions, revisions for this edition were based on my own experiences in schools as well as on systematically gathered feedback from users and colleagues across the country. Although the general goals, themes, and features of the previous editions have remained constant, many revisions have been made in response to user feedback, as well as to developments in the expanding knowledge base on teaching and learning and to recent changes in the societal and policy environments.

Based on reviewer comments and on developments in the field, this edition includes new or expanded content on the following topics:

- Continued coverage of the cognitive/constructivist views of teaching and learning, including the growing importance of the neurosciences for understanding human motivation and learning.
- Increased coverage and emphasis on the impact of digital technologies, social media, and global communication on the context of teaching and learning, and their impact on the lives of students.
- Expanded coverage of standards-based education along with challenges and opportunities created as a result of the Common Core Standards that are beginning to be implemented as this edition of *Leaning to Teach* is revised.
- New discussion in Chapter 5 (classroom management) with more attention to strategies for secondary teachers and ways to motivate and work with students who are seriously disengaged. A new section on how to deal with "bullying" has also been included, along with a new technology box on "cyberbullying."
- Continued emphasis on the importance of diversity in today's classroom and the importance for teachers to be culturally competent.
- Continued emphasis on the importance of formative assessment for enhancing student learning.

The tenth edition also includes important updates and perspectives of the Enhancing Teaching and Learning with Technology feature. This feature has been updated to include new developments in technology and social media and its use in the classroom, as well as a description of the Net generation of students found in today's classrooms. Additionally, more than 100 new references have been added to ensure the currency of the knowledge base on teaching and learning.

Supplements

This edition of *Learning to Teach* is accompanied by a wealth of supplemental resources and learning aids for both instructors and students.

For the Instructor

- **Instructor's Online Learning Center at www.mhhe.com/arends10e.** The password-protected instructor's section of the Online Learning Center contains the Instructor's Manual, PowerPoint slides, and a Test Bank along with access to the online student resources. Contact your local sales representative for log-in instructions.

- *Teaching Methods in the Classroom.* This original video includes twelve segments that show teachers implementing the various approaches and strategies described in the text as well as other important teaching processes.
- **PowerPoints.** A complete package of PowerPoint slides for each chapter is available for instructors. It can be found in the Online Learning Center.

For the Student

- **Student Online Learning Center at www.mhhe.com/arends10e.** The Student Online Learning Center contains Lesson Planning Exercises and Practice Activities, Portfolio and Field Experience activities, the *Teachers on Teaching* audio clips referenced in the text, resources for using *Learning to Teach* to prepare for the PRAXIS II™ exam, an Action Research Handbook, the Lesson Plan Builder, and a rich set of student study guide materials. Among the study guide materials are self-grading practice quizzes with feedback, key word flashcards, chapter outlines, and links to outside Web sites for further study. Students can also use the Online Learning Center to respond to the *Reflecting On . . .* and *Extend* poll questions posed in the text and compare their answers to a pool of students nationwide.

Student and Instructor Feedback

As with previous editions, I encourage students to provide feedback about any and all aspects of the text. Please e-mail me at arends@ccsu.edu.

CourseSmart eTextbooks

This text is available as an eTextbook from CourseSmart, a new way for faculty to find and review eTextbooks. It's also a great option for students who are interested in accessing their course materials digitally and saving money. CourseSmart offers thousands of the most commonly adopted textbooks across hundreds of courses from a wide variety of higher education publishers. It is the only place for faculty to review and compare the full text of a textbook online, providing immediate access without the environmental impact of requesting a print exam copy. At CourseSmart, students can save up to 50 percent off the cost of a print book, reduce their impact on the environment, and gain access to powerful Web tools for learning including full text search, notes and highlighting, and e-mail tools for sharing notes between classmates. For further details, contact your sales representative or go to www.coursesmart.com.

McGraw-Hill Create
www.mcgrawhillcreate.com

Craft your teaching resources to match the way you teach! With McGraw-Hill Create, you can easily rearrange chapters, combine material from other content sources, and quickly upload content you have written, such as your course syllabus or teaching notes. Find the content you need in Create by searching through thousands of leading McGraw-Hill textbooks. Arrange your book to fit your teaching style. Create even allows you to personalize your book's appearance by selecting the cover and adding your name, school, and course information. Order a Create book and you'll receive a complimentary print review copy in three to five business days or a complimentary electronic review copy (eComp) via e-mail in about one hour. Go to www.mcgrawhillcreate.com today and register. Experience how McGraw-Hill Create empowers you to teach *your* students *your* way.

Acknowledgments

Because the field of teaching and learning is becoming so comprehensive and so complex, I have relied on colleagues to assist in writing about topics outside my own area of expertise. Outstanding contributions were made in previous editions by chapter authors Dr. Richard Jantz, Dr. Virginia Richardson, and the late Dr. Nancy Winitzky.

I also want to acknowledge and extend my thanks to the many co-teachers and colleagues from over the years. Drs. Hilda Borko, Sharon Castle, Pat Christensen, Lenore Cohen, Neil Davidson, Margaret Ferrara, Jim Henkelman, Nancy Hoffman, Shelley Ingram, Paulette Lemma, Frank Lyman, Linda Mauro, Joe McCaleb, Ronald Moss, Karen Riem, Kathy Rockwood, Susan Seider, Carole Shmurak, and Roger Zieger have not only been a source of support but have provided important input for early versions of the manuscript as well as for this revision.

I want to extend a special thanks to Dr. Sharon Castle, a colleague from George Mason University, who was the primary developer of the case exercises and practice activities. Dr. Castle was also responsible for much of the early development and editing of the audio and video clips. Finally, a very, very special thanks to two Vicki's. The first to my wife, Vicki Foreman, who assisted with many final editing tasks, double-checked all the references, and helped me think through my discussions about the Visible Thinking Program and how best to teach students how to think. The second to Vicki Butler, a teacher and IT coordinator at the Seattle Academy, who was so gracious with her time to teach me about how technology can be used to enhance student learning.

The Reflections from the Classroom and Teachers on Teaching features are brought to life by the following classroom teachers who shared their experiences. Thank you.

Angela Adams	Kendra Ganzer
Faye Airey	Mike Girard
Ian Call	Dennis Holt
Amy Callen	Patricia Merkel
Diane Caruso	Jason O'Brien
Lynn Ciotti	Jennifer Patterson
Ellen Covell	Addie Stein
Sandra Frederick	Vickie Williams

Many reviewers also contributed useful reactions and critiques that have resulted in a much-improved text. I would like to extend a special thanks to the reviewers who provided feedback during the revision of the ninth and tenth editions:

Judith Barbour, *Eastern Illinois University*
Wendy Burke, *Eastern Michigan University*
Richard Cangro, *Western Illinois University*
Patricia Hewitt, *The University of Tennessee at Martin*
Laura Hopfer, *Lincoln Memorial University*

Deborah MacCullough, *Philadelphia Biblical University*
Wendy McCarty, *University of Nebraska at Kearney*
Jane Murphy, *Middlesex Community College*
Leonard Parker, *Liberty University*
Michal Larraine Rosenberger, *Concordia University Texas*
Donald Shepson, *Montreat College*
Annette Smith, *South Plains College*
Robert Townsend, *Indiana Wesleyan University*
Eileen Lorraine Yantz, *Gaston College*

Thanks to the editorial and production team whose work has supported the book's development, production, and marketing: Craig Leonard, Freelance Developmental Editor; Penina Braffman, Managing Editor; Alexandra Schultz, Marketing Specialist; Heather Ervolino, Content Project Manager; Susan K. Culbertson, Buyer; Marian John Paul, Full-Service Project Manager; and Jennifer Bartell, Media Project Manager.

PART 1 Teaching and Learning in Today's Classrooms

Part 1 of *Learning to Teach* is about teachers and teaching, students and learning. The chapters in Part 1 are designed to provide you with background information about teaching and learning that will serve as a foundation for understanding later chapters that describe a variety of teaching approaches, strategies, and tactics.

Chapter 1, The Scientific Basis for the Art of Teaching, provides a brief historical perspective on teaching from colonial times to the present and strives to show how expectations for teachers have been characterized by both constancy and change. As you will read, some aspects of teaching are not much different than they were one hundred years ago. Others have changed dramatically over the past two decades, particularly those aspects of the role needed to address new and important teaching challenges of the twenty-first century.

Most important, Chapter 1 outlines the overall perspective on the purposes and conceptions of effective teaching that has influenced the plan and content of *Learning to Teach.* This perspective holds that teaching is both an art and a science and that effective teachers base their practices on both traditions. On one hand, effective teachers use research on teaching and learning to select practices known to enhance students' learning. On the other hand, teaching has an artistic side that rests on the collective wisdom of experienced teachers. Experienced teachers know that there is no one best way to teach in all situations. Instead, effective teachers have repertoires of practices known to stimulate student motivation and to enhance student learning. Particular practices are selected depending on the goals teachers are trying to achieve, the characteristics of particular learners, and community values and expectations.

Chapter 2, Student Learning in Diverse Classrooms, tackles one of the most difficult challenges faced by teachers today: how to ensure that every child reaches his or her potential regardless of the abilities or backgrounds each brings to school. This chapter examines the challenges and opportunities diversity presents and describes how, unlike in earlier times, today's classrooms are characterized by many different kinds of students and are governed by societal beliefs that the learning potential of all children must be realized: "No child can be left behind." The chapter describes diversity at both ends of the spectrum of students labeled exceptional—those with learning disabilities and those who are gifted. Similarly, differences in race, ethnicity, culture, religion, language, and gender are also described in some detail. The chapter introduces several new conceptions of diversity and provides extensive discussion about strategies and guidelines for teaching and working with diverse groups of students in inclusive classrooms.

CHAPTER 1
The Scientific Basis for the Art of Teaching

Learning Goals

After studying this chapter you should be able to

The Scientific Basis for the Art of Teaching	Explain the meaning of the "scientific basis for the art of teaching."
Historical Perspective on Teaching	Describe how perspectives on effective teaching have changed over time and how teachers' roles have changed as a result of historical and demographic forces.
A Perspective on Effective Teaching for the Twenty-First Century	Identify and discuss the essential attributes of the effective teacher for twenty-first-century schools.
Learning to Teach	Explain how learning to teach is a developmental process and describe the flexible stages teachers go through as they progress from novice to expert status.

 ## Reflecting on Learning to Teach

If you are like many individuals, you begin this book and this course with a sense of excitement and challenge, perhaps also some concerns. You have decided you want to be a teacher, but you also know some of the challenges teachers face today, and you know you have a lot to learn if you are going to meet these challenges. Before you read this chapter, take a few minutes to think about teachers, teaching, and education today.

- Think about the best teachers you have had. Do you still know their names? Why were they good teachers? How did they influence your life?

- Think about teachers you didn't think were very good. Why didn't you consider them good teachers? Regardless of how good they were, what kind of influences did they have on your life?

- Which aspects of teaching do you look forward to the most? Which aspects give you the greatest concern? What do you see as the major challenges facing teachers today?

- Think about education in general. Do you believe most schools are doing a good job? Or do you believe schools are in lots of trouble and need serious reform? Do you see yourself as a person who can help schools become better?

 Go to the Online Learning Center at www.mhhe.com/arends10e to respond to these questions.

Teaching offers a bright and rewarding career for those who can meet the intellectual and social challenges of the job. Despite the spate of reports over the years critical of schools and teachers, most citizens continue to support schools and express their faith in education. The task of teaching the young is simply too important and complex to be handled entirely by parents or through the informal structures of earlier eras. Modern society needs schools staffed with professional teachers to provide instruction and to care for children while parents work.

In our society, teachers are given professional status. As professionals, they are expected to use **best practice** to help students learn essential skills and attitudes. It is no longer sufficient for teachers to be warm and loving toward children, nor is it sufficient for them to employ teaching practices based solely on intuition, personal preference, or conventional wisdom. Contemporary teachers are held accountable for using teaching practices that have been shown to be effective, just as members of other professions, such as medicine, law, and architecture, are held to acceptable standards of practice. This book is about how to learn and to use best practice—practice that has a **scientific basis.** It is aimed at helping beginning teachers master the knowledge base and the skills required of professionals whose job it is to help students learn.

This book also explores another side of teaching: the **art of teaching.** Like most human endeavors, teaching has aspects that cannot be codified or guided by scientific knowledge alone but instead depend on a complex set of individual judgments based on personal experiences. Nathaniel Gage (1984), one of the United States' foremost educational researchers, some years ago described the art of teaching as "an instrumental or practical art, not a fine art aimed at creating beauty for its own sake":

> As an instrumental art, teaching is something that departs from recipes, formulas, or algorithms. It requires improvisation, spontaneity, the handling of hosts of considerations of form, style, pace, rhythm, and appropriateness in ways so complex that even computers must, in principle, fall behind, just as they cannot achieve what a mother does with her five-year-old or what a lover says at any given moment to his or her beloved. (p. 6)

Carol Ann Tomlinson and Amy Germundson (2007) have also written about the nonscientific aspect of teaching and compared teaching to creating jazz. They write:

> Teaching well . . . is like creating jazz. Jazz blends musical sounds from one tradition with theories from another. . . . It incorporates polyrhythm. It uses call-and-response, in which one person comments on the expression of another. And, it invites improvisation. (p. 7)

Notice some of the words used by Gage and by Tomlinson and Germundson to describe teaching—*form, spontaneity, pace, polyrhythm, call-and-response, improvisation.* These words describe aspects of teaching that research cannot measure very well but that are nonetheless important characteristics of best practice and are contained in the wisdom of experienced teachers. This book strives to show the complexity of teaching— the dilemmas faced by teachers and the artistic choices that effective teachers make as they perform their daily work. It also presents an integrated view of teaching as a science and as an art, and emphasizes that what we know about teaching does not translate into easy prescriptions or simple recipes.

This chapter begins with a brief historical sketch of teaching, because the basic patterns of teaching today are intertwined in the web of history and culture, which impact the processes of learning to teach. This introduction is followed by the perspective on effective teaching that has guided the design and writing of *Learning to Teach*. The final section of the chapter describes a portion of what is known about the processes of learning to teach. It tells how beginners can start the process of becoming effective

Teaching has a scientific basis—its practices are based on research and scientific evidence.

Teaching is also an art based on teachers' experiences and the wisdom of practice.

"The dream begins with a teacher who believes in you, who tugs and pushes and leads you onto the next plateau."

Dan Rather

Vast changes in the nineteenth century determined many elements of the educational system we have today.

teachers by learning to access the knowledge base on teaching, accumulating the wisdom of practice, and reflecting on their experiences.

Historical Perspective on Teaching

Conceptions of teaching reflect the values and social philosophy of the larger society, and as these elements change, so, too, does society's view of its teachers. To understand the role of the teacher in today's society requires a brief historical review of some of the important changes that have taken place in teaching and schooling over the past three centuries.

Role Expectations in Earlier Times

The role of teacher, as we understand it today, did not exist in the colonial period of our national history. Initially, literate individuals, often young men studying for the ministry, were hired on a part-time basis to tutor or teach the children of the wealthier families in a community. Even when schools started to emerge in the eighteenth century, the teachers selected by local communities did not have any special training, and they were mainly middle-class men who chose to teach while they prepared for a more lucrative line of work.

Common, or public, schools came into existence in the United States between 1825 and 1850. During this era and for most of the nineteenth century, the purposes of schools were few and a teacher's role rather simple, compared to today. Basic literacy and numeracy skills were the primary goals of nineteenth-century education, with the curriculum dominated by what later came to be called the three Rs: reading, writing, and arithmetic. Most young people were not required (or expected) to attend school,

Standards for teachers in the nineteenth century emphasized the conduct of their personal lives over their professional abilities or abilities to accomplish student learning.

Figure 1.1 *Sample Nineteenth-Century Teacher Contract*

I promise to take a vital interest in all phases of Sunday-school work, donating of my time, service and money without stint for the benefit and uplift of the community.

I promise to abstain from dancing, immodest dressing, and any other conduct unbecoming a teacher and a lady.

I promise not to go out with any young man except as it may be necessary to stimulate Sunday-school work.

I promise not to fall in love, to become engaged or secretly married.

I promise to remain in the dormitory or on the school grounds when not actively engaged in school or church work elsewhere.

I promise not to encourage or tolerate the least familiarity on the part of any of my boy pupils.

I promise to sleep eight hours a night, eat carefully...

Source: Brenton (1970), p. 74.

and those who did so remained for relatively brief periods of time. Other institutions in society—family, church, and work organizations—held the major responsibility for child rearing and helping youth make the transition from family to work.

Teachers were recruited mainly from their local communities. Professional training of teachers was not deemed important, nor was teaching necessarily considered a career. Teachers by this time were likely to be young women who had obtained a measure of literacy themselves and were willing to "keep" school until something else came along. Standards governing teaching practice were almost nonexistent, although rules and regulations governing teachers' personal lives and moral conduct could, in some communities, be quite strict. Take, for example, the set of promises, illustrated in Figure 1.1, that women teachers were required to sign in one community in North Carolina. This list may be more stringent than many others in use at the time, but it gives a clear indication of nineteenth-century concern for teachers' moral character and conduct and apparent lack of concern for teachers' pedagogical abilities.

Twentieth-Century Role Expectations

By the late nineteenth and early twentieth centuries, the purposes of education were expanding rapidly, and teachers' roles took on added dimensions. Comprehensive high schools as we know them today were created, most states passed compulsory attendance laws that required all students to be in school until age 16, and the goals of education moved beyond the narrow purposes of basic literacy. Vast economic changes during these years outmoded the apprentice system that had existed in the workplace, and much of the responsibility for helping youth to make the transition from family to work fell to the schools. Also, the arrival of immigrants from other countries, plus new migration patterns from rural areas into the cities, created large, diverse student populations with more extensive needs than simple literacy instruction. Look, for example, at the seven goals for high school education issued by a committee appointed by the National Education Association in 1918, and notice how much these goals exceed the focus on the three Rs of earlier eras:

1. Health
2. Command of fundamental processes
3. Worthy home membership
4. Vocational preparation
5. Citizenship
6. Worthy use of leisure time
7. Ethical character

Such broad and diverse goals made twentieth-century schools much more comprehensive institutions as well as places for addressing some of the societal problems and reforms that characterized the twentieth century. Schools increasingly became instruments of opportunity, first for immigrants from Europe and later for African Americans, Hispanics, Asians, and other minority groups who had been denied access to education in earlier times. Expanding their functions beyond academic learning, schools began providing such services as health care, transportation, extended day care, and breakfasts and lunches. Schools also took on various counseling and mental health functions—duties that earlier belonged to the family or the church—to help ensure the psychological and emotional well-being of youth.

Obviously, expanded purposes for schooling had an impact on the role expectations for teachers. Most states and localities began setting standards for teachers that later became requirements for certification. Special schools were created to train teachers in the subject matters they were expected to teach and to ensure that they knew something about **pedagogy.** By the early twentieth century, teachers were expected to have two years of college preparation; by the middle of the century, most held bachelor's degrees. Teaching gradually came to be viewed as a career, and professional organizations for teachers, such as the National Education Association (NEA) and the American Federation of Teachers (AFT), took on growing importance, both for defining the profession and for influencing educational policy. Teaching practices of the time, however, were rarely supported by research, and teachers, although expected to teach well, were judged by vague global criteria, such as "knows subject matter," "acts in a professional manner," "has good rapport," and "dresses appropriately." However, progress was made during this period, particularly in curriculum development for all the major subject areas, such as reading, mathematics, social studies, and science. Also, major work was accomplished in helping to understand human development and potential as well as how students learn.

> The study of the art and science of teaching is called pedagogy.

Teaching Challenges for the Twenty-First Century

No crystal ball can let us look fully into the future. Certain trends, however, are likely to continue, and some aspects of education and teaching will remain the same, while others may change rather dramatically (see Figure 1.2). On one hand, the tremendous changes occurring in the way information is stored and accessed with computers and digital technologies holds the potential to change many aspects of education. The Internet has already demonstrated its potential of connecting students to a vast array of resources not previously available as well as to other people around the world. Many believe that the Internet will become, if it hasn't already, the primary medium for information and will substantially redefine other forms of print and visual publications. Several commentators, such as Friedman (2005), Gore (2007), Tapscott (2008), and West (2012), have observed that the Internet has replaced television as the primary means for political and social dialogue and has become the "intellectual commons" for globalwide collaborative communities. Obviously, this has important implications for education and the goals and curricula we devise.

On the other hand, it is likely, at least in the immediate future, that society will continue to require young people to go to school. Education will remain committed to a variety of goals and some new ones may be added, but **academic learning** will remain the most important. Also, it is *not* likely that the physical space called *school* will change drastically in the foreseeable future. Organizing and accounting for instruction will change, online education and virtual schooling will expand, but if history is a guide, this change will come slowly. Schools will likely continue to be based in communities, and teachers will continue to provide instruction to groups of children in rectangular rooms.

> Academic learning is likely to remain the most important purpose of schooling.

Contemporary reform efforts show the potential of bringing new and radical perspectives about what academic learning means and how it can best be achieved. New

Figure 1.2 *Challenges for Twenty-First-Century Teachers*

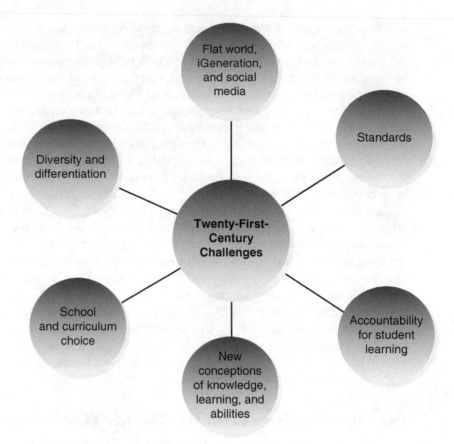

perspectives also are emerging as to what constitutes *community* and its relationship to the common school. The nature of the student population and the expectations for teachers are additional factors that likely will change in the decades ahead.

Flat World, the iGeneration, and Social Media. In a very interesting book, Thomas Friedman (2005) almost a decade ago described how technology has flattened our world and reshaped our lives in rather dramatic ways. By "flattened," he means that technological advances have provided greater access to information and jobs and that information has become global and instantaneous. Worldwide Internet access makes services and products available to just about anyone, anywhere, and events in one place on the globe affect not only that place, but every other place as well.

As U.S. society completes the transition into the information age described by Friedman, teaching and schools will be required to change, just as they did when we moved from an agrarian to an industrial society in the late nineteenth century. Learning in a flat world, according to Friedman, has become easier for students, but it has also made education more difficult and complex. Students today, including most of you as you were growing up, have had access to information unknown to earlier generations, and the Internet and social media have captured everyone's attention. At the same time, these elements pose difficulties in determining the validity and reliability of information and have caused some students to become completely turned off to more traditional in-school learning. Tapscott (2010), Rosen (2010), and Giant (2013) have referred to today's students as the *Net generation* or the *iGeneration*. They argue that tomorrow's teachers will need to move away from an outdated, broadcast-style pedagogy (i.e., lecture and drilling) toward student-focused, multimodal pedagogy, where "the teacher is no longer in the transmission of data business, . . . [but rather] in the customizing-learning-experiences-for-students business" (Tapscott, 2010, p. 1). The practice of "flipping classrooms" (Honeycutt, 2013; Sams & Bergmann, 2013), described in more detail later, is one example of how teachers are moving away from the transmission mode.

We don't know exactly how schools will look by the middle of the twenty-first century. Futurists, however, have argued that formal schooling as currently conceived and practiced will be as out-of-date in the system of learning as the horse and buggy are in the modern transportation system. The fact that over fifteen million K–12 students are currently involved in some form of online education or e-learning is evidence that education is changing.

Integrating technology into teaching is such a critical challenge for twenty-first-century teachers that we have included a special feature in *Learning to Teach* labeled Enhancing Teaching and Learning with Technology. This feature consists of box inserts in every chapter to help you see how teaching today is influenced by technology, how technology impacts the lives of students, and how the use of technology can enhance student engagement and learning. The Enhancing Teaching and Learning with Technology box for Chapter 1 provides an overall perspective about technology and poses the question: Can technology transform education? Later chapters will highlight particular aspects of technology related to the chapter's content. For instance, effective use of the Web to assist student investigations will be discussed in Chapter 10 on problem-based learning. The concept of "flipping classrooms" as a technological alternative to in-class presentations or demonstrations will be described in Chapter 7. For the most part, the Enhancing Teaching and Learning with Technology feature will not provide a lengthy list of specific resources, such as Web sites or computer software, currently available for teachers to use; there are simply too many and they represent too much diversity to be effectively reviewed in a book like *Learning to Teach*. Instead we will strive to highlight a few resources, describe trends in the use of technology to enhance teaching and learning, and provide road maps for those of you who want to learn more.

Diversity. One of the most complex challenges facing twenty-first-century teachers has been how to transform schools and approaches to teaching that were created in the late nineteenth and early twentieth centuries, a time when most of the students in schools had Western European backgrounds and spoke English, to the schools and approaches required today to meet the needs of a much more diverse student population. Schools in the United States have been experiencing a major demographic shock over the past forty years, a shift that will affect schools and teachers well into the twenty-first century. The most important demographic shift involves the increasing number of students who have non-European ethnic or racial heritages, who speak English as a second language, and/or who live in poverty.

We live in a global, multicultural society; it is a condition of our culture.

As will be described in more detail in Chapter 2, almost 15 percent of students in schools today have disabilities and receive services under the Individuals with Disabilities Act (IDEA). More than one-third of students have non-European heritage, up from one-fifth in 1970. By 2020, it is predicted that as many as one-half to two-thirds of students in public schools will have Latina/Latino, Asian, or African American backgrounds (*The Condition of Education*, 2009, 2012). Similarly, linguistic diversity constitutes a rapidly growing shift as an increasing number of non-English-speaking children attend the public schools. The number of English language learners (ELLs) has more than doubled over the past thirty years. Today they represent more than

Today, 20 percent of children in school are English language learners.

Enhancing Teaching and Learning with Technology

Will Technology Transform Education?

We introduced the feature Enhancing Teaching and Learning with Technology in an edition of *Learning to Teach* that appeared in the early 1990s. At that time, our goals were quite narrow—to discuss ways teachers could use technology to enhance student learning and to describe available computer-related resources. We focused mainly on the use of personal computers. Computers at that time were coming down in price, and schools were starting to purchase a few and place them in centralized computer labs. Although the Internet was starting to be used in some sectors of society, in 1994 fewer than 5 percent of the U.S. schools had Internet access. *Education Week* introduced its "Technology Counts Report" in 1996 and wrote proudly that "billions of dollars are being spent to prepare schools and students for tomorrow's technological demands and challenges" (2007, p. 8).

In our first Enhancing Teaching and Learning with Technology we featured L. Perelman's book *School's Out: Hyperlearning, the New Technology, and the End of Education* (1992). Perelman argued at that time that the new technologies of that day would bring about the end of schools as we knew them and that computers, information networks, and multimedia would give everyone in society access to learning, something not possible when schools were created in the late nineteenth century. Instead of learning occurring within the "classroom box," learning in the future, according to Perelman, would permeate every form of social activity. Instead of learning being confined to children, it would be the province of everyone at every age. In 1992, Perelman argued that it made no sense to reform schools, and that reform efforts such as school choice or higher standards served only as a diversion from the main things he predicted would happen:

- Complete privatization of education
- Replacement of school buildings with learning channels and information superhighways
- Abolition of all credentialing systems (including those for teachers), which he believed choked progress
- Creation of national technological schools that would exist without campuses or formal faculty

Two decades later, some of Perelman's predictions seem to have been quite accurate. Today, home schooling, **e-learning,** and blended learning, as described elsewhere in this chapter, have grown substantially across the country, and the so-called **iGeneration,** of which many of you are members, use the Internet, social networks, and an array of digital devices for learning what you want to learn, when you want to learn it. Compared to two decades ago, computers are now found in every classroom and many schools provide every student with a laptop computer or tablet. Currently, almost all schools have high-speed Internet access, although a "digital divide" exists, making access more limited in many poorer communities and neighborhoods. Similarly, the past decade has seen an explosion in all kinds of new digital technologies. Many students (perhaps most) have their own MP3 players, smartphones, and tablets. Most households have access to digital cameras and video recorders, and students participate regularly in making movies and sharing photos and videos on Facebook and YouTube. Interactive features such as blogs, podcasts, and social networks allow students to post their journals and media presentations on the Internet and to interact with their peers worldwide.

Online education was almost nonexistent a decade ago. Today, many approaches to online or e-learning are available, ranging from virtual schools found in over 40 states where students are enrolled full time to more modest arrangements that allow students to remain in their regular, more traditional classrooms but to enroll in a few online classes. Barth (2013) reported that virtual schools enrolled 275,000 students in 2012 and that 55 percent of school districts had some students enrolled in at least one online course.

So, with all this activity where are we today and where are we going? At first blush, one might conclude that technology is currently in wide use and has had an *immense* impact on education. However, closer inspection reveals that this is not necessarily the case, and reviews on the effects of technology on schools, youth, and learning have revealed both positive and negative results.

On the negative side, some argue that we haven't come all that far. Even though many school districts have found a mix of face-to-face and e-learning classes to be effective, several states have attempted to establish e-learning enrollment caps. In addition, although many teachers make use of computers, digital devices, and social networking resources, Collins and Halverson (2009) and West (2012) believe that schools have kept digital technologies on the "periphery" of their core academic practices. Again it has been observed that many young people's reliance on digital technology outside of school is much different than their use in school. Take for instance these student comments about the difference between their high-tech personal lives and their low-tech school lives:

"I absolutely hate school. They make me sit and listen as some old, stuffy teacher drones on and on about stuff from a book written in the dark ages. We have to read pages of facts in college. Oh sure, they (the books) have pictures, but they are so one-dimensional. Geez, pictures? Don't they know anything about video and what kids like to do. We get to the computer lab once a week for an hour—if that—and even then most of what I want to do is blocked. I can't wait to get out of this place and go to college . . . [where they] know how to treat wired kids like me." (Rosen, 2010, p. 1)

"The biggest challenge is that [students] are growing up as digital natives, but when they get to the school door, they leave that at the door." (Elliott, 2013, p. A8)

"You [teachers] think of technology as a tool . . . we [students] think of it as a foundation; it underlies everything we do." (Prensky, 2013, p. 23)

Finally, Trotter (2007) a few years ago and West (2012) more recently have pointed out that many schools use digital resources primarily to provide drill-and-practice opportunities for students and to keep track of standardized test scores, but that beyond that digital tools have not caught on with many teachers and that real innovation has been neglected. Studies by the Educational Testing Service have also concluded that young people's use of technology is only "skin deep." Many high school students cannot correctly judge the objectivity of a Web site or use multiple terms in a Web search.

Perhaps this shouldn't surprise us. Several years ago, David Tyack and Larry Cuban (2000) argued that computers, telecommunications, and emerging digital technologies would have a significant impact on teaching partly because they have become so pervasive in other aspects of the lives of youth and also because they hold the potential of having important advantages over other educational tools. However, they warned that many claims about the effectiveness of educational technology had been overstated and that we should not expect an "educational moonshot" through technology. More recently, Cuban (2013) repeated this warning when he reported that since the time of the introduction of the typewriter Americans have had great faith that each new piece of technology—radio, television, etc.—would revolutionize education. To date that hasn't happened.

On the positive side some observers believe that the use of technology has had considerable positive effects. West (2012), for example, reports that there are many tech-savvy teachers who have fully integrated technology into their classroom instruction and have demonstrated some "amazing practices." They know that multimedia presentations using interactive whiteboards are more interesting and effective than scratching a few words on the chalkboard. They know that an array of Web sites can enrich students' understanding of things far away and in the distant past far better than can printed words on paper. They know that using blogs, wikis, and social media can be valuable tools for intellectual and social development. Perhaps most important, the generation preparing for teaching today (your generation) has grown up with digital technology. Maybe it will be your generation that realizes technology's full potential for teaching and student learning in the information age.

400 languages and approximately 10 percent of the school population (*The Condition of Education*, 2012). A majority of these students speak Spanish (80 percent), but other languages represented include Arabic, Vietnamese, Russian, and Tagalog.

A trend throughout the history of American schools has been to extend educational opportunities to more and more students. Compulsory attendance laws enacted early in the twentieth century opened the doors to poor white children; the now-famous Supreme Court decision, *Brown v. Board of Education of Topeka* (1954), extended educational opportunities to African American children. The Education for All Handicapped Children Act of 1975, now called the Individuals with Disabilities Education Act (IDEA), brought an end to policies that prevented children with disabilities from getting an education and changed the enrollment patterns in schools significantly. For example, in the mid-1970s, when IDEA was passed, only about 8 percent of children in schools were identified and were served for their disability, whereas today this statistic has risen to almost 15 percent (*The Condition of Education*, 2009, 2012). In addition, today more and more students with disabilities are also being educated in regular classrooms rather than special education classes or separate schools.

Another demographic factor that affects schools and teachers is that many children who attend public schools today live in poverty, currently as high as 22 percent, up from 12 percent in 2000. In fact, some observers argue that poverty and social class have replaced race as the most urgent issue facing the nation and that poverty is at the core of most school failure (*A Broader, Bolder Approach to Education*, 2008; Children's Defense Fund, 2012). Child poverty is defined as children who live in families with incomes below the federal poverty level and is measured by identifying students who qualify for free or reduced-price lunches. Child poverty is most pronounced among African American, Latino, and American Indian children and children who live in the South. Poverty rates vary from a low of 9 percent in New Hampshire to a high of 31 percent in Mississippi (*The Condition of Education*, 2012).

Today's schools require teachers who have a repertoire of effective teaching strategies so the needs of all children can be met.

These demographic realities have significance for teaching and for those preparing to teach in at least three important ways. First, for both social and economic reasons, many people in the larger society will remain committed to providing educational opportunities to all children. Society will also demand that minorities and students with disabilities do well in school. Some of these students will come from homes of poverty; others will come from homes in which parents do not speak English; some will be emotionally or physically different from their classmates. These students will experience school differently than those whose parents were educated in public schools and who have prepared their children for them. Working with youth from diverse cultural backgrounds and with various special needs will necessitate that teachers have a repertoire of effective strategies and methods far beyond those required previously. Teachers will also need skills to differentiate curriculum and instruction to make these suitable to a wide range of students who may find school devastatingly difficult or irrelevant to their lives.

It is likely that schools will continue to be scrutinized for racial and ethnic balance, although the more traditional means of balancing race, such as having racial quotas, will likely no longer be used because of the Supreme Court decisions that the use of race to achieve diversity violates the Equal Protection Clause of the Fourteenth Amendment. However, teachers can expect to experience complex social and organizational arrangements in which school enrollment boundaries will be changed and efforts will

Schools today must accommodate a wide variety of learning and cultural differences.

be made to diversify student populations. Schools today must accommodate a wide variety of learning and cultural differences through open enrollment and magnet school programs, and teachers themselves may be moved from school to school more often than in the past, particularly if they teach in schools that have been identified as failing. Finally, and perhaps most important, the voices of minority and immigrant communities and those who are English language learners will no longer be ignored. Parents of these children will no longer tolerate schools with inadequate materials and untrained teachers. They will not allow their children to be automatically grouped by ability and placed in non-college-bound tracks. They will demand a curriculum and approaches to teaching that will ensure the same academic and social success for their children as for children in the mainstream. Listening to the voices of a multicultural community and providing effective learning experiences for all students will be the most difficult, but also the most interesting, challenge of your generation of teachers.

Standards, the Common Core, and Accountability. A new system of schooling, called "standards-based education," has emerged in the United States, Canada, and most developed countries. The key features of this new system consist of (1) acceptance of a common set of standards (currently called the **Common Core**) that define what students should know and be able to do; (2) a belief that every child and youth can meet these standards; (3) insistence that teachers use evidence-based practices; and (4) accountability, consisting mainly, at the present time, of using standardized tests to assess student learning. This view of schooling differs in some important ways from the textbook-based and norm-referenced perspectives of the nineteenth and twentieth centuries and poses important challenges to teachers. It alters what students are expected to learn and proficiency levels they are expected to attain. Students are expected to meet agreed-upon standards instead of working only "for a grade," and these standards are held for all students rather than only a few of the most capable. This view of schooling requires new and different practices for teachers. As Schalock and his colleagues (2007) have pointed out, this system of schooling demands "the alignment of instruction with standards; the integration of curriculum, instruction and assessment; and the differentiation of instruction to accommodate the learning histories and needs of individual students" (p. 2). Alignment, integration, and differentiation become the core of teachers' work in a standards-based system of schooling.

This conception of schooling didn't appear overnight, but instead evolved over a number of years. Some aspects of the standards movement that characterizes today's schools date back to the early part of the twentieth century when standardized tests were first introduced to measure students' abilities and achievement. In 1983, a national report, *A Nation at Risk: The Imperative of Educational Reform*, encouraged schools to set higher and more rigorous standards at all levels of education and to implement the use of standardized tests to measure student achievement. A decade later, Congress passed the Goals 2000 Act of 1994. This legislation promised that by the year 2000 several goals for education would be achieved, including making sure that all students entered school ready to learn and guaranteeing a 90 percent graduation rate. Although the recommendations outlined in *A Nation at Risk* and the lofty aims of Goals 2000 were never realized, they did bring about a fundamental change in the way we thought about education and provided a prelude to the passage of the No Child Left Behind Act (NCLB) in 2002 and more recent Race to the Top efforts. These federal initiatives required alignment of classroom instruction to prescribed standards, yearly testing to hold schools accountable for student learning, and sanctions on schools that failed.

The latest effort to expand a standards-based educational system has been the development of Common Core State Standards, a collaborative effort among the states under the leadership of the National Governors Association for Best Practices (NGA Center) and the Council of Chief State School Officers (CCSS). Established and started in 2009 then and released in 2010, Common Core Standards in language arts and literacy and mathematics have been adopted by forty-six states. As of 2013, other subject area standards are in the planning stages. The Common Core Standards attempt to define in great detail the knowledge and skills required of students to find success in academic college courses or in career training programs. Even though most states have adopted Common Core Standards at the time of this writing, some states are rethinking their initial commitments. More detail about the Common Core will be provided in Chapter 3. The Common Core Standards can be downloaded from the Common Core Web site (www.corestandards.org).

This view of schooling is embraced by many educators today although others maintain reservations. For instance, the standards-based movement has produced an array of standards and has led to demands by governing agencies, in the name of being more rigorous, to require more and more courses for graduation. This strategy has not produced as much in the way of results as some envisioned. For instance, increases in scores on the National Assessment of Educational Progress have been very modest over the past decade and many students who start ninth grade do not graduate from high school. For instance, reading scores in 2009 were only one point higher than in 2007 and four points higher than in 1992 (Gewertz, 2010). The latest results from the Program of International Assessment (PISA) showed that the performance of American 15-year olds has remained flat in reading literacy and science and has lagged behind in mathematics as compared to students in 65 other countries and school systems. (First look at PISA 2012). Landsberg (2008) reported that the California Dropout Research Project found declining graduation rates (at the time below 50 percent) in Los Angeles public schools. According to the study, this decline started when California raised standards and began requiring students to pass an exit exam prior to receiving a diploma. Finally, longtime NCLB supporter Diane Ravitch has written (Ravitch, 2010, 2013) how she has lost faith with federal reform policies because they have led to too much federal interference into areas that should be controlled by state and local agencies. And, as discussed in more detail in later chapters, fewer and fewer students are reporting that they are finding their schoolwork meaningful and important. Regardless of these weaknesses, the standards-based conception of schooling has become an important part of the policy context that affects teaching and learning. It is likely to have a great deal of influence in the immediate future and will continue to present a set of challenging issues for teachers in the twenty-first century.

School and Curriculum Choice. Alternatives to the standard school are found in many areas of the country today. These alternatives consist of magnet or special-focus schools, where curriculum is designed around the performing arts or science and technology. This type of alternative is financed by public funds, but students and their parents can choose the alternative over other, more traditional schools in their community. Between 1993 and 2007, the percentage of students attending a school of their or their parents' choice increased from 11 to 15 percent. The percentage of students attending private schools also increased by approximately 1 percent between 1993 and 2007, but then started to decrease in 2010, when 10 percent of elementary and secondary students were enrolled in private schools. The largest proportion were enrolled in Catholic or Conservative Christian schools (*The Condition of Education*, 2012). It appears that although many parents still prefer neighborhood schools, nearly 50 percent reported that they had the opportunity to send their children to a chosen public school (*The Condition of Education*, 2012). This trend toward choice will continue, and the number of public school alternatives in the future will likely be significantly greater.

A trend in schools situated in the larger cities in the United States, where student populations are most diverse and where resources to support public education are scarcest, is privatization. For instance, several large city school systems from Florida to California have contracted with private firms to run some of their schools, with the intent of making a profit. For-profit online education companies are also making an impact, and many parents take advantage of the wide range of options currently available. These for-profit companies tailor curriculum to particular states, and they design and deliver through e-mail lessons and lesson plans to teachers and parents. Some of these companies monitor attendance and assignments online, including required field trips.

Schools of choice have been popular in urban areas, whereas "virtual" schools cater mostly to students in rural and hard-to-reach parts of the country. The results of this type of education remain unknown. Some observers, Barth (2013), for instance, are skeptical about the effectiveness of e-learning, and others contend that for-profit education is contrary to the nation's resolve to maintain a system of strong public schooling. Public charter schools have also come under attack in some parts of the country. Their critics argue that a two-tiered system has been created with serious demographic and economic disparities. District-sponsored charter and magnet schools create a system of publicly funded private schools favoring well-off families who can search out educational options and provide their own transportation. The more able and well-off subsequently attend the charter or magnet schools, leaving the neighborhood schools populated by students mainly from low-income families.

Another trend related to choice over the past decade has been the home schooling movement. Parents have taken on the responsibility of educating their own children for a variety of reasons. Some belong to fundamentalist religious groups who fear that the secular nature of public schools will dilute their children's faith. Others are concerned about the school environment and want to keep their children separated from youth culture and the drugs and violence perceived to characterize the public schools in their communities. Still others want to express their right to have their children experience a "monocultural" rather than a multicultural community. According to the National Center for Education Statistics (*The Condition of Education*, 2012), in 2003, the number of students who were being home schooled was 1.1 million, an increase from 850,000 in 1999. In 2007, about 1.5 million, or 2.9 percent, of school-age children were home schooled.

The latest trend in school choice has been the charter school movement. Charter schools are publicly funded schools conceived and started by parents, citizens, or teachers; in some ways, they operate like private schools in that they are independent of the local public school districts and exempt from many of the local and state regulations imposed on public schools. After individuals or groups obtain a charter from a school district or the state government, they are then given public monies to operate the school and are held accountable by the chartering agency for meeting prespecified standards. These schools are normally smaller than their public school counterparts, enroll a larger proportion of black and Hispanic students, but also have fewer students eligible for free or reduced lunch. The National Center for Education Statistics reported that between 1999 and 2010 the number of students enrolled in public charter schools increased from 0.3 million to 1.6 million students and that in 2010 about 5 percent of all public schools were charter schools (*The Condition of Education*, 2012).

Giving parents a choice in the schools their children attend challenges the traditional concept of the standardized public school.

It appears that parents who choose charter, choice, or home schooling do so for different reasons. Minority parents and parents in the more urban areas see charter and schools of choice as a way to allow their children to escape what they perceive as racially segregated and often failing neighborhood schools. White middle-class parents, in contrast, choose charter schools that more closely reflect their more liberal values about child rearing and education. Parents who choose to home school their children do so because they are concerned about the environments in public schools and/or because they want to provide religious and moral instruction for their children.

School choice and privatization have their critics as well as their advocates. Advocates maintain that charter, private, and profit-driven schools will introduce an element of competition into the educational system and that schools, once freed from the bureaucratic structures and political processes that have come to characterize many large city schools, will provide superior education for students for the same or lower cost through innovative programming and more effective use of human resources. Many people are willing to allow these experiments to proceed because of beliefs that the public schools simply are not functioning as they should.

However, many educators and concerned citizens worry that private schools and schools of choice will not accept the more difficult-to-teach students, thus making the public schools more and more the home for the most helpless and hopeless young people in our society (Merrow, 2009). Others are concerned about the values and moral system reflected, either formally or informally, in for-profit schools. Still others are afraid that the best teachers in the country will be drawn to the charter and for-profit schools, leaving the less capable to teach those students who need good teachers the most (Ravitch, 2010, 2013; Wolk, 2011).

Finally, offering choice from the standard school, as with constructivist perspectives, may be working at cross-purposes with efforts to create a standards-based educational system with a common core. This raises many questions. For example, do all students need to be exposed to the same ideas in particular subjects, at the same time, and in the same manner? Should all students be required to go to the same type of school with the same curriculum and for the same length of time? Should all students be expected to achieve the same standards and reach the same level? It is interesting to note that an increasing number of policymakers, parents, and educators are saying no to these types of questions while at the same time embracing standards-based education.

New Conceptions of Knowledge, Learning, and Abilities. Our educational system, including standards-based education, has its roots in an **objectivist perspective** about knowing and learning. Knowledge from this perspective is conceived as being somewhat constant and unchanging. Teaching consists of transmitting known knowledge to students in the form of facts, concepts, and principles. Because knowledge is known and fixed (relatively speaking), it is possible to establish a core curriculum and set of standards for all students to meet. This perspective led to the statewide testing movement, to No Child Left Behind (NCLB), Race to the Top, and the Common Core.

An alternative to the objectivist perspective, and one that has gained respectability in educational circles over the past two decades, is known as **constructivism.** Rather than viewing knowledge as fully known, fixed, and transmittable, the **constructivist perspective** holds that knowledge is somewhat personal, and meaning is constructed by the learner through experience. Learning is a social and cultural activity in which learners construct meaning that is influenced by the interaction of prior knowledge and new learning events.

> The traditional view of knowledge holds that there are "truths" and an objective reality that humans have access to and can learn through discovery.

> A constructivist perspective holds that learning is a social and cultural activity, that knowledge is somewhat personal, and that learners construct meaning through interaction with others.

From a constructivist perspective, learning is viewed not as students passively receiving information from the teacher but rather as students actively engaging in relevant experiences and having opportunities for dialogue so that meaning can evolve and be constructed. Learning takes place not in passive classrooms but in learning communities characterized by high levels of participation and engagement. In *Learning to Teach*, we will repeatedly come back to the idea that learning is the process of making sense out of experience, and you will come to see that teaching for active learning will require drastic changes in teacher behavior as contrasted to many of the teachers you have observed for most of your life.

Traditional theories and practices have held that individuals have specific mental abilities. At the turn of the nineteenth century, psychologists such as Alfred Binet in France and Lewis Terman at Stanford University in the United States developed tests aimed at measuring human intelligence and abilities. These tests were used widely in Europe to determine who could benefit from advanced schooling. In the United States, they were soon employed to help place students in instructional groups based on their abilities as well as to help determine who was fit to serve in the army and go on to higher education. Even though IQ tests have fallen into disfavor over the past half century, tests of basic skills and those that measure more general knowledge, such as the Scholastic Assessment Test (SAT), have replaced them and are used widely to make decisions about where students should be placed in school and where they can go to college. Over a century of work has left us with three unresolved questions: Is intelligence one or many things? Is intelligence inherited? And, can intelligence be accurately measured?

Many practicing educators today believe that IQ tests and tests of general knowledge have little to do with an individual's ability or capacity for learning but instead reflect one's social and cultural background. Children from families and communities that reflect the cultural mainstream, for instance, do better on these tests than the children of parents who live in poverty or who just immigrated to the United States and speak little English.

The best teachers show concern for their students and assume responsibility for their learning.

Today's teachers are held accountable for their teaching practices and for what their students learn.

Check, Extend, Explore

Check

- How have teacher roles evolved over the years, and what forces have contributed to these changes?
- What demographic shifts have led to changes in the student population, and how have these trends impacted schools and teachers?
- What are major teaching challenges of the twenty-first century?

Extend

- What revisions to schooling do you foresee in the next ten years? Twenty years?
- Do you agree or disagree that it is fair to hold teachers accountable for the learning of every student? Why? Go to "Extend Question Poll" on the Online Learning Center to respond.

Explore

- Go to the Online Learning Center at www.mhhe.com/ arends10e and link to the Web site for the National Board for Professional Teaching Standards or link to the National Center for Education Statistics for current data about the conditions of education in the United States. Go to the Common Core Web site and explore the latest developments.

Finally, some contemporary psychologists, such as Howard Gardner (1983, 2011) and Robert Sternberg (1985, 2009), among others, have challenged the idea that there is a general intelligence. Instead, they theorize that intelligence and abilities are much more than language usage and logical thinking as measured by most intelligence and aptitude tests but instead are multifaceted, hierarchical, and consist of many different abilities (Kanazawa, 2010). We will come back to theories of intelligence in Chapter 2.

Accountability for Student Learning. Until very recently, teachers had minimal preparation and there were few expectations as to their performance. However, the twentieth-century standards movement began to emphasize liberal arts preparation and some exposure to pedagogy. During the early part of the twenty-first century, this trend is accelerating rather dramatically. Beginning teachers will increasingly be required to demonstrate their knowledge of pedagogy and subject matter prior to certification. They will be held **accountable** for using best practice throughout their careers and to assume responsibility for student learning. For instance, today all states require some type of testing before issuing an initial certificate to teach, and student performance on standardized tests is being used in the evaluation of teachers. Most states are using the Praxis tests developed by the Educational Testing Service (ETS), but alternative and more performance-based tests are currently being considered in a number of states.

Before getting a license to teach, you may be required to demonstrate through examination your knowledge and skill in teaching. Competency in academic subject matter will no longer be sufficient, particularly for teaching in classrooms that are culturally diverse and contain students with various special needs. Neither will liking children, in and of itself, be enough for tomorrow's teachers. Twenty-first-century teachers will be required to have a command of various knowledge bases (academic, pedagogical, social, and cultural) and to be reflective, problem-solving professionals. Writing for the National Academy of Education, Linda Darling-Hammond and John Bransford (2005) used the following words to describe what teachers should know and be able to do:

> in addition to strong subject matter knowledge, all new teachers (should) have a basic understanding of how people learn and develop, as well as how children acquire and use language, which is the currency of education. In addition . . . teaching professionals must be able to apply that knowledge in developing curriculum that attends to students' needs, the demands of the content, and the social purposes of education: in specific subject matter to diverse students, in managing the classroom, assessing student performance, and using technology in the classroom. (inside cover)

In 1986, the Carnegie Task Force on Teaching as a Profession recommended establishing a career ladder for teachers and the creation of a National Board for Professional Teaching Standards (NBPTS). NBPTS was formed the following year and is currently governed by a sixty-three-member board of directors, mostly K–12 teachers but also including administrators, curriculum specialists, state and local officials, union and business leaders, and college and university professors. The National Board has designed procedures to assess the competence of experienced teachers, and it issues a national teaching certificate to those who meet its rigorous standards. National certification is voluntary, and the national certificate is not intended to replace the continuing or advanced certificate offered by the states.

A Perspective on Effective Teaching for the Twenty-First Century

Central to the process of learning to teach are views about how children learn, the primary goals of education, and definitions of an effective teacher. The goals of education in a complex society are diverse, and trying to define an effective teacher has long occupied the thoughts of many. For example, in the media we have traditional images of effective teachers, such as the kindly Miss Dove and the bumbling but caring Mr. Chips. More recently, the effectiveness of the rigid and authoritarian Joe Clark has been described, as has that of James Escalante of *Stand and Deliver* fame, who was able to get his low-achieving Latino students in Los Angeles to learn advanced algebra and accomplish extraordinary feats. Dave Holland of *Mr. Holland's Opus* is another example of how an ordinary person can be an extraordinary teacher by helping his students achieve their goals through music. Professor Melvin B. Tolson, played by Denzel Washington in *The Great Debater,* showed how a passionate teacher with a cause could get his students to do extraordinary things.

Within the educational community there has been a remarkable diversity in the definition of effective teaching. Some have argued that an effective teacher is one who can establish rapport with students and who can create a nurturing, caring classroom environment. Others have defined an effective teacher as a person who has a love for learning, a superior command of a particular academic subject, and an ability to transmit his or her subject effectively to students. Still others argue that an effective teacher is one who can activate student energy to work toward a more just and humane social order. Many citizens and policymakers have taken the position that effective teachers are those who can accomplish student learning as measured primarily by yearly progress on standardized tests.

The content of a teacher education curriculum is itself a statement about what effective teachers need to know. Clinical experiences and tests for certification, such as Praxis I or Praxis II, make similar statements, as do the assessment systems used in schools to evaluate and mentor beginning teachers.

The purposes of education and conceptions of the effective teacher are also central to writing a book about teaching, and influence its plan, its organization and unifying themes, and the choice of topics to include. The following sections describe the point of view of *Learning to Teach* on these matters.

> Central to learning to be a teacher are views about how children learn and definitions of the effective teacher.

The Ultimate Goal of Teaching

Citizens in a diverse and complex society such as ours expect their schools to accomplish many different goals. For example, here are a few that appear regularly in the popular press: teach basic academic skills, build student self-esteem, prepare students for college, promote global understanding, prepare students for work, transmit cultural heritage. The multiple purposes of education can become overwhelming unless teachers can focus their teaching goals. *Learning to Teach* takes the position that the ultimate purpose of teaching is *to assist students to become independent and self-regulated learners.* This purpose does not negate other purposes of education, but instead it serves as an overarching goal under which all other goals and teacher activities can be placed. This primary purpose stems from two underlying assumptions. One is the contemporary view that knowledge is not entirely fixed and transmittable but is something that all individuals, students and adults alike, actively construct through

> The ultimate purpose of education is to help students become independent and self-regulated learners.

personal and social experiences, including important experiences over the Internet and social media. The second is the perspective that the most important thing that students should learn is *how to learn.*

A View of the Effective Teacher

The concept of effective teaching that has guided the planning and writing of *Learning to Teach* does not include any of the stereotypes embodied in Mr. Chips, Joe Clark, or Mr. Holland; neither does it include an argument about whether academic competence is more important than nurturance or vice versa. Effective teaching requires at its baseline individuals who are academically able, who have command of the subjects they are required to teach, and who care about the well-being of children and youth. It also requires individuals who can produce results, mainly those of student academic and social learning. These characteristics are prerequisites for teaching, but they are insufficient without five higher-level attributes:

1. Effective teachers have *personal qualities* that allow them to develop **authentic** and caring human relationships with their students, parents, and colleagues.
2. Effective teachers can create classrooms that model **social justice** for children and adolescents in a democratic society.
3. Effective teachers have positive dispositions toward knowledge. They have command of at least three, broad **knowledge bases** that deal with subject matter, human development and learning, and pedagogy. They use this knowledge to guide the science and art of their teaching practice.
4. Effective teachers command a **repertoire** of effective teaching practices known to stimulate student motivation, to enhance student achievement of basic skills, to develop higher-level thinking, and to produce self-regulated learners.
5. Effective teachers are personally disposed toward **reflection** and problem solving. They consider learning to teach a *lifelong process,* and they can diagnose situations and adapt and use their professional knowledge appropriately to enhance student learning and to improve schools.

These attributes of effective teachers are illustrated in Figure 1.3. Jigsaw diagrams are used here to illustrate twenty-first-century educational challenges and later to communicate views about effective teaching and the interrelationships among teachers' work and student learning. These are used to illustrate that no single aspect of education or teaching is discrete or exists independently. Instead, as with a jigsaw puzzle, the whole is realized only after all the independent pieces are successfully fitted together.

In *Learning to Teach,* these attributes of an effective teacher are crucial themes and have been woven into each of the chapters in the book. Just as theme songs are used in Broadway musicals to highlight main ideas and characters, you will find the themes summarized below referred to again and again throughout the book.

Personal Qualities for Developing Authentic Relationships

For many years, people believed that a teacher's personal qualities were the most important attributes for effective teaching. In general, teachers who were warm and loving were thought to be more effective than those who were perceived to be cold and aloof. Like most beliefs, this one had a measure of truth to it. It also left an incomplete picture, because effective teaching requires much more than being warm and loving toward children.

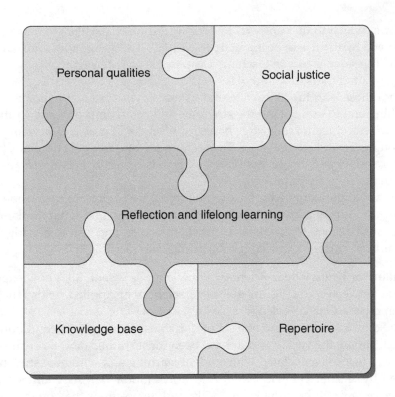

Figure 1.3 *A View of Effective Teachers*

However, it is very important for teachers to have caring dispositions toward children and to possess sufficient interpersonal and group skills to establish authentic relationships with their students and their colleagues. They must also have a "passion" for learning that can be translated into inspiration for their students to learn. Horace Mann said it a long time ago, "a teacher who is attempting to teach without inspiring the pupil with a desire to learn is hammering on cold iron." Similarly, it is from authentic relationships with colleagues and passion that schoolwide goals are developed and accomplished.

> Establishing authentic relationships with students and teaching with passion are prerequisites to everything else in teaching.

Democratic and Socially Just Classrooms

Classrooms are mirrors of the larger society. Students learn about people different from themselves and about equity and fairness in their classrooms at a young age. These lessons stay with them into adulthood. To be effective, teachers must be able to create classroom learning communities that are democratic and socially just and where high expectations are held for all students. As will be described in later chapters, too often teachers do not hold high expectations for all students. Instead, they have perceptions that some students, mainly those from non-mainstream cultures, are less capable of learning. As a result of these faulty perceptions and expectations, students' opportunities to learn are severely restricted. It is critical for the cycle of failure built into our educational system to come to an end in the twenty-first century.

> Effective teaching requires abilities to create democratic and socially just classrooms.

Knowledge Base to Guide the Art of Practice

Effective teachers have control over a knowledge base that guides what they do as teachers, both in and out of the classroom. In fact, professionals by definition have control over information (the knowledge base) that allows them to deal with certain matters more insightfully and more effectively than the average person. At the same time, no professionals, including doctors, engineers, and lawyers, have a complete knowledge base from which to find answers to every question or problem. Not every problem can be solved by the use of best practice—patients die, design ideas fail, and legal cases are lost. The same is true in teaching. Despite the use of best practice, some students do not learn and others drop out of school.

It is important for those learning to teach to understand what is meant by the *knowledge bases* for teaching and to understand the strengths and limitations of the scientific research that informs the current knowledge bases for teachers. It is also important to point out that, though the knowledge bases for teaching are still not yet complete, in contrast to the fragmentary and inconsistent knowledge bases of two or three decades ago, the situation today is vastly improved.

Three questions about the knowledge base for teaching are important to consider: (1) What does it mean to have a knowledge base about teaching, and what domains of knowledge are most relevant? (2) How do teachers access and use knowledge? (3) What are the limits of current knowledge on teaching and learning?

There are several domains of knowledge that inform teaching, some of which stem from research and others from the experiences of practicing teachers.

Nature and Domains of Knowledge. Scientific knowledge is essentially knowledge about relationships between variables. In the social sciences or applied fields (such as education), this means that knowledge exists about how one variable is related to another and, in some instances, how one set of variables under certain conditions affects others. In education, the variables that have been most studied, and those most relevant to teaching, are those associated with student learning and with how student learning is affected by teacher behavior. John Bransford, Linda Darling-Hammond, and Pamela LePage organized the knowledge, skills, and dispositions that are important for all teachers into three general domains:

1. Knowledge of *learners and their development* in social context. This includes what is known about learning and human development in general and more specifically language development over a lifetime.
2. Conceptions of *subject matter and curriculum* goals. This includes understanding of the subject matter and skills to be taught and how these relate to the school's curriculum and social purposes of education.
3. An understanding of teaching in relation to content and the learners to be taught. This includes pedagogy related to particular content areas, the role of assessment, and classroom management in diverse classrooms (adapted from Bransford, Darling-Hammond, & LePage, 2005, p. 10).

Evidence-based practices are teaching practices in which evidence from research has shown them to be effective in producing student learning.

Figure 1.4 highlights these three domains of knowledge. *Learning to Teach* synthesizes and describes the enormous body of knowledge that has been created in the past half century and informs our understanding of how students learn; the factors that motivate learning; how leadership can be provided to manage complex instructional settings; and, specifically, the links that have been found between teacher expectations and behaviors and student achievement. It also describes and summarizes "evidence-based" programs and practices that are available today. These are programs and practices that research evidence has shown to be effective in producing high levels of student achievement and social learning. At one time what we knew about relationships and **evidence-based practices** was very limited. Currently, we can be confident of considerable knowledge in several areas, some of which have been validated experimentally and replicated under varying conditions.

A practical argument is the reasoning, based on knowledge and beliefs, that is used by teachers as they make pedagogical decisions.

Teacher Use of Knowledge. Educational philosopher Gary Fenstermacher (1986) proposed that the major value of educational research for teachers is that it can lead to the improvement of their **practical arguments.** His argument for this position goes something like the following.

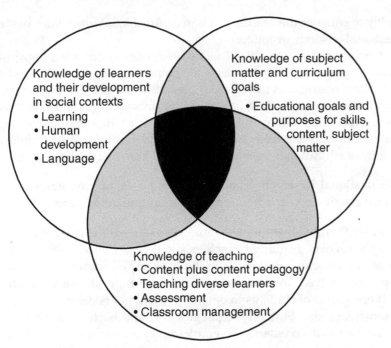

Figure 1.4
*Knowledge Base for
Teaching and
Learning*

Source: Adapted from Bransford, Darling-Hammond, and LePage (2005), p. 11.

The knowledge and beliefs that teachers, as well as other professional practitioners, hold are important not only for their own sake but also because they prompt and guide action. Actions taken by practitioners are guided by a number of premises—beliefs held to be just and true and linked together in some logical format. Sometimes these premises and the underlying logic have been made explicit by the practitioner; many times, however, they are not consciously aware of their practical arguments. Fenstermacher (1986) provided the following example of a teacher's practical argument used to support the methods she used to teach reading:

1. It is extremely important for children to know how to read.
2. Children who do not know how to read are best begun with primers.
3. All nonreaders will proceed through the primers at the same rate (the importance of learning to read justifies this standardization).
4. The skills of reading are most likely to be mastered by choral reading of the primers, combined with random calling of individual students.
5. This is a group of nonreaders for whom I am the designated teacher.

Action: (I am distributing primers and preparing the class to respond in unison to me) (p. 46).

In this example, premise 1 is a statement of value, on which most people concur. Premise 5 is a statement of fact, presumed to be accurate. Premises 2, 3, and 4, however, are beliefs held by the teacher about how children learn and about pedagogy. These beliefs influence the actions of using primers and choral reading. In this particular instance, these beliefs are simply not supported by the research on reading instruction.

Fenstermacher pointed out that the results of research, and knowledge of "best" practice, if known, could lead this teacher to doubt his or her beliefs and subsequently rethink the premises undergirding the pedagogical behavior and instructional practices. Knowing about and using research becomes a process of understanding, doubting, and challenging the beliefs we hold about how children learn and about the best practices to employ to enhance this learning. It is in contrast to taking actions based on tradition, conventional wisdom, or folklore.

Research on teaching, then, can dispel old wives' tales about teaching, just as other research can dispel myths about aspects of the physical and social world outside education. For this reason, it is important for teachers to have a firm grasp of the knowledge base on teaching, including its application in various settings. Everyone, however, should be cautious and remember that teaching is a tremendously complex process that continually departs from fixed recipes and formulas. We should also remember the limits of educational research and current knowledge about teaching.

The Limits of Educational Research. There are several reasons why evidence from research can inform classroom practice in some instances and not in others.

> There are no easy prescriptions or simple recipes for teaching effectively.

No Fast Formulas or Recipes. Even though principles and guidelines for best practice exist for today's teachers, beginning teachers should not jump to the conclusion that principles based on research will work all the time, for all students, or in all settings. That simply is not true. Instead, teaching and learning are very situational. What works with one group of students in one setting will not necessarily work with another group someplace else. Similarly, strategies and approaches used by expert, experienced teachers cannot necessarily be emulated by a novice teacher. Teachers must take explanations and principles and apply them within the capacity of their own abilities and skills and within the contextual confines of particular groups of students, classrooms, and communities.

> Societal views and community values influence what and how teachers teach.

Explanations Are Not Automatically Recommendations. Practicing teachers often ask researchers to make recommendations based on their research. Some examples of the types of questions they ask include: Should we use ability groupings in third-grade classrooms? What are the best concepts to teach in tenth-grade social studies? How can I motivate John, who comes to school tired every morning? The reply to such questions has to be that research alone cannot provide answers to such specific practical problems. For example, take the question about what to teach in tenth-grade social studies. Even though a researcher might provide information about what other school districts teach in the tenth grade or about the abilities of most 15-year-olds to understand historical concepts, this would not tell a teacher what concepts to teach, given a particular group of students, the goals of a particular social studies curriculum or teacher, and the community values—all crucial factors to consider.

Explanations Are Not Inventions. A final limitation is that, for the most part, research evidence focuses on existing practice. The descriptions and explanations about what teachers currently do are valuable but should not preclude the invention or use of new practices. The two examples that follow may help to highlight the importance of this point.

Many of the research-based practices for classroom management stem from studies in which researchers compared the classroom management procedures used by researcher-defined effective teachers with those used by less-effective teachers. From this research, patterns of effective classroom management practices have emerged. However, these results do not mean that better practices are not to be invented. It simply means that compared to the range of current practices, we can say that some classroom management procedures are better than others under certain conditions.

Along the same line, much of the research on effective teaching has been done in classrooms that represent the more traditional patterns of teaching—a single teacher working with whole groups of students for the purpose of achieving traditional learning objectives—student acquisition of basic information and skills. Although this research, like the classroom management research, can inform us about best practices within the confines of the traditional paradigm, it does not tell us very much about worthwhile innovations and new paradigms that may exist in the future.

As Duffy and Kear (2007) have so aptly argued, the profession should continue to encourage teachers to use research-based practices, but we should also encourage them to feel free to adapt these practices to meet the needs of their particular teaching situations. We should also remain aware of the comment "research says" when it has been made by policymakers, who all too often cite only the research that supports their point of view. Finally, as teachers we should strive to keep parents and the larger public informed that research today is often commercialized and that they should be cautious of accepting quick fixes promised by gurus looking to make a profit.

Repertoire of Effective Practice

Effective teachers have a repertoire of effective practices. *Repertoire* is a word used mainly by people in the performing arts to refer to the number of pieces (such as readings, operas, musical numbers) a person is prepared to perform. Obviously, more experienced and expert performers have larger, more diverse repertoires than novices do. This is also true for teachers.

This book emphasizes that effective teachers have diverse repertoires and are not restricted to a few pet practices. This is in contrast to some arguments from earlier eras intended to prove the superiority of one approach to another—for example, inductive versus deductive teaching, the lecture versus discussion method, or the use of phonics to teach reading versus a balanced literacy approach. This debate is futile and misdirected. No single approach is consistently superior to any other in all situations. Instead, many teaching approaches are appropriate, and the selection of a particular model depends on a teacher's goals, the characteristics of a specific group of learners, and community values and expectations.

The teaching practices described in this book comprise a minimum number of models, strategies, and procedures that should be in a beginning teacher's repertoire. Some are large and complex models of teaching; others are rather simple procedures and techniques. The practices described are obviously not all that exist; effective teachers add to their repertoires throughout their careers.

The concept of repertoire carries with it the idea that a course of action is linked to various aspects of the job. To use the performing arts analogy again, an accomplished musician may have one repertoire for performances of classical music, one for appearances in nightclubs or pop concerts, and perhaps another for family get-togethers. Just as this text was designed around a particular perspective on teaching, so too was it constructed around a conception of what teachers do and the repertoire required in three domains of their work.

Teachers, regardless of their grade levels, their subject areas, or the types of schools in which they teach, are asked to perform three important jobs. They provide leadership to a group of students, they provide direct instruction to students, and they work within an organizational setting consisting of colleagues, parents, and others for the purpose of improving classrooms and schools. These three aspects of teachers' work are illustrated in Figure 1.5. Obviously, these aspects are not always discrete, nor does the teacher always perform one aspect of the job independently of the others. These labels, however, are convenient organizers for helping you make sense out of the bewildering array of events associated with teaching in a complex school setting.

Figure 1.5 *Three Big Jobs of Teaching*

Teachers provide leadership to their students through planning, motivation, and the facilitation of learning.

Leadership. In many ways, a contemporary teacher's role is similar to those of leaders who work in other types of organizations. Leaders are expected to plan, to motivate others, to coordinate work so individuals can work interdependently, and to help formulate and assess important goals.

The **leadership** view of teaching has sometimes been criticized. Critics argue that it grew out of the industrial age concept of the efficient manager and that this image makes people think about schools the same way they think about factories and, thus, overemphasizes the technical and skill side of teaching. The "teacher as leader" metaphor can also lead to excessive attention to control, orderliness, and efficiency at the expense of creativity and spontaneity.

Regardless of past misuse of the "teacher as leader" metaphor, there are indeed many parallels between the work performed by both teachers and leaders in other fields. *Learning to Teach* presents these leadership skills in a manner that does not violate the artistic side of teaching—that is, teacher creativity and spontaneity.

The most important aspect of teachers' work is providing direct instruction to students in classrooms.

Instructional. When most people think about what teachers do, they think of the day-by-day **instruction** of students. The overall framework for thinking about this aspect of teaching comes mainly from three sources: (1) the models or approaches to teaching, such as those developed by Bruce Joyce and Marsha Weil (1972) and Joyce, Weil, and Calhoun (2003); (2) the teaching strategies and procedures that have resulted from the research on teaching over the past forty years (Gage, 1963; Richardson, 2001; Travers, 1973; Wittrock, 1986); and (3) the wisdom of practice contained in the repertoire of experienced teachers (Shulman, 2004).

Over the years, many different teaching approaches have been created. Some were developed by educational researchers investigating how children learn and how teaching behavior affects student learning. Others were developed by classroom teachers experimenting with their own teaching in order to solve specific classroom problems.

Table 1.1 *Classification of Six Models or Approaches to Teaching*

Traditional, More Teacher-Centered	Constructivist, More Learner-Centered
Lecture/presentation	Cooperative learning
Direct instruction	Problem-based learning
Concept and inquiry-based teaching	Classroom discussion

Still others were invented by psychologists, industrial trainers, and even philosophers such as Socrates.

A model or approach, as defined here, is more than a specific method or strategy. It is an overall plan, or pattern, for helping students to learn specific kinds of knowledge, attitudes, or skills. A teaching model or approach, as you will learn later, has a theoretical basis or philosophy behind it and encompasses specific teaching steps designed to accomplish desired educational outcomes.

Teachers need many approaches to meet their goals with a diverse population of students. A single approach or method is no longer adequate. With sufficient choices, teachers can select the approach that best achieves a particular objective, the approach that best suits a particular class of students, or the models that can be used in tandem to promote student motivation, involvement, and achievement.

Literally dozens of models and approaches to teaching have been identified, but how many of these should be in a beginning teacher's repertoire? Obviously, it is unrealistic to ask a beginner to master all the models—that is a lifelong process. To require command of only a single model is equally unrealistic. It seems fair and practical to ask beginning teachers to acquire a modest repertoire during the initial stages of their career. Therefore, we have selected six models that, if learned well, can meet the needs of most teachers. These are presentation, direct instruction, concept and inquiry-based teaching, cooperative learning, problem-based learning, and classroom discussion. In Table 1.1, you will find that the first three teaching approaches—presentation, direct instruction, and concept and inquiry-based—stem from more traditional perspectives about student learning and rest on more teacher-centered principles of instruction. Cooperative learning, problem-based instruction, and discussion, on the other hand, stem from more constructivist perspectives of learning and more learner-centered approaches to teaching (Donovan & Bransford, 2005; Pelech & Pieper, 2010; Tobias & Duffy, 2009).

Another way of classifying various approaches to teaching is to consider the types of learning outcomes each has been designed to achieve. Table 1.2 shows these comparisons.

Table 1.2 *Comparison of Approaches to Teaching and the Learning Outcomes They Were Designed to Achieve*

Teaching Model or Approach	Type of Learning Outcome
Presentation and direct instruction	Develop basic skills and knowledge
Concept and inquiry-based teaching	Extend basic knowledge and develop thinking, reasoning, and inquiry skills
Cooperative and problem-based teaching and discussion	Develop personal, social, and problem-solving skills

Working with other teachers is an important aspect of a teacher's job.

In addition to working with students, teachers today are expected to work with other adults in the school setting and with parents for the purpose of schoolwide planning and coordination.

Student learning not only depends on what teachers do in their classrooms; it is also strongly influenced by what teachers and parents in particular schools do in concert.

Organizational Engagement.   The common view of teaching focuses mostly on classroom interactions between teachers and students, and as such it is insufficient for understanding the reality of teaching in contemporary schools. Teachers not only plan and deliver instruction to their students but also serve as **organizational** members and leaders in a complex work environment.

Schools are places where children learn; they are also places where adults carry out a variety of educational roles—principal, teacher, resource specialist, aide, and so forth. Schools are both similar to and different from other workplaces. Similarities include the ways coordination systems are designed to get the work of the school accomplished. Beginning teachers will find that adults who work in schools are pretty much like adults who work in any other organization. They strive to satisfy their own personal needs and motives in addition to achieving the mission of the school. At the same time, those of you who have worked in other organizations (perhaps during the summer or in a previous career) will find some unique aspects of the school workplace: Norms give teachers a great deal of autonomy in their work but often isolate them from their colleagues; clients (students) do not always participate voluntarily in the organization; and because the school is highly visible politically, diverse and unclear goals exist that reflect the multiple values and beliefs of contemporary multicultural society.

Schools are also places, like other organizations, that need to be changed as the larger society changes around them. Many people preparing to teach have strong idealistic drives to make education and schools better. This idealism, however, is not always supported with sound strategies for putting good ideas into practice, even though the knowledge base on educational change and school improvement has increased substantially over the past two decades. A knowledge base now exists to explain why many earlier education reform efforts failed, and this knowledge can be applied to school improvement ideas you may want to implement.

Building a repertoire of organizational skills is important for two reasons. First, your ability to perform organizational roles and to provide leadership within the school as well as the classroom will greatly influence your career. It is through performing organizational roles well that beginning teachers become known to other teachers, to their principals, and to parents. For example, all too often colleagues do not observe a teacher's classroom while he or she is teaching. However, they have many opportunities to see the teacher speak up in faculty meetings, volunteer for important committee work, and interact with parents in open houses or meetings of the Parent-Teacher Association. Through these opportunities, teachers become influential professionally with their colleagues and beyond the confines of their schools. Conversely, a beginning teacher's inability to perform organizational functions effectively is the most likely reason for dismissal. Many teachers who are terminated in their early years are dismissed not for instructional incompetence but for their inability to relate to others or to attend to their own personal growth and psychological well-being within a complex organizational setting.

A second reason for learning organizational skills is because researchers and educators understand that student learning is related not only to what a particular teacher does but also to what teachers within a school do in concert. To work toward schoolwide effectiveness requires such organizational skills as developing good relationships with colleagues and parents, engaging in cooperative planning, and agreeing on common goals and common means for achieving those goals. The effective and successful teacher is one who has a repertoire for entering into schoolwide and communitywide dialogue about important educational issues and one who can join with colleagues for the purpose of enhancing student learning.

Reflection and Problem Solving

Many of the problems faced by teachers are situational and characterized by their uniqueness. Unique and situational cases call for "an art of practice," something that cannot be learned very well from reading books. Instead, effective teachers learn to approach unique situations with a problem-solving orientation and learn the *art of teaching* through experimentation with reflection on their own practice.

In addition, many of the problems facing teachers become problems of values and priorities that scientific knowledge can help explain but cannot help decide. An observation from Schön (1983) a number of years ago underscores the value-laden world of practicing teachers:

> Practitioners are frequently embroiled in conflicts of values, goals, purposes and interests. Teachers are faced with pressure for increased efficiency in the context of contracting budgets, demands that they rigorously "teach the basics," exhortation to encourage creativity, build citizenship, and help students to examine their values. (p. 17)

Lampert (2001) made similar observations about the complexity of teaching and why reflection and problem solving are so important:

> One reason teaching is a complex practice is that many of the problems a teacher must address to get students to learn occur simultaneously, not one after another. Because of simultaneity, several different problems must be addressed in a single action. And a teacher's actions are taken independently; there are interactions with students, individually and as a group. A teacher acts in different time frames and at different levels of ideas with individuals, groups and the class to make each lesson coherent. (p. 32)

If knowledge cannot provide a complete guide for effective practice, how do practitioners become skilled and competent in what they do? Again Schön (1983) provided

Check, Extend, Explore

Check
- What are the major characteristics of effective teachers?
- What specific personal qualities are typically exhibited by effective teachers?
- Why should a teacher's repertoire of strategies be as diverse and flexible as possible?
- What are the three major aspects of a teacher's job?

Extend
- At this stage in your development, do you think you will tend to use mainly teacher-centered or student-centered approaches? Go to "Extend Question Poll" on the Online Learning Center to respond.
- What views do you hold about the organizational aspects of a teacher's job? Do you value these? Why or why not?

Explore
- Go to the Online Learning Center at www.mhhe.com/arends10e and listen to audio clips of Amy Callen and Ronald Moss as they talk about what it means to be an effective teacher today.

Explore
- Go to the Online Learning Center and view the "Dennett" and "Carol" video clips and listen to what they say about having high expectations for students.

valuable insights. He argued that there is an irreducible element in the art of professional practice and that gifted practitioners, whether they are engineers, scientists, managers, or teachers, display their artistry in their day-to-day practice. And, though we don't always know how to teach the art of practice, we do know that for some individuals it is learnable.

Learning to Teach strives to present its textual information in such a way as to alert you to the areas of teaching where our knowledge is fragmented and incomplete and to possible teaching situations in which you will be required to exhibit individual problem solving and reflection. Many of the learning aids found in the Online Learning Center (OLC) will assist you in becoming problem-oriented and reflective about your teaching practice. Reflection and problem solving are complex dispositions and skills and are not easily learned. However, as you read previously, the art of professional practice is learnable, and it is experience, coupled with careful analysis and reflection, that produces results.

Learning to Teach

Some teachers, like fine wines, keep getting better with age. Others do not improve their skills even after years of practice and remain at about the same skill level they possessed the day they walked into their first classroom. Why is it that some teachers approach the act of teaching critically and reflectively; are innovative, open, and altruistic; are willing to take risks with themselves and their students; and are capable of critical judgment about their own work? Conversely, why do others exhibit exactly the opposite traits?

Becoming a truly accomplished teacher takes a long time, fueled by an attitude that learning to teach is a lifelong process.

Becoming truly accomplished in almost any human endeavor takes a long time. Many professional athletes, for example, display raw talent at a very early age, but they do not reach their athletic prime until their late twenties and early thirties and then only after many years of dedicated learning and practice. Many great novelists write their best pieces in their later years only after producing several inferior and amateurish works. The biographies of talented musicians and artists often describe years of pain and dedication before the subjects reached artistic maturity. Becoming a truly accomplished teacher is no different. It takes purposeful actions fueled by the desire for excellence; it takes an attitude that learning to teach is a lifelong developmental process in which one gradually discovers one's own best style through reflection and critical inquiry.

This section describes some of the things we know about the process of learning to teach and emphasizes that learning to teach is a lifelong and developmental process, not one limited to the period of time between the first methods class and the date a teaching license is acquired. Few effective teachers are born effective. Rather, they become increasingly effective through attention to their own learning and development of their own particular attributes and skills.

Models of Teacher Development

As you will read later, contemporary views about how children learn also apply to how teachers learn. As applied to teaching, it means that individuals develop cognitively and affectively through stages. As we learn to teach, we process experiences through our existing cognitive structures. Obviously, individuals entering teaching have a rather complex cognitive structure about teaching because they have spent so many hours observing teachers during their years in school. As we gain new experiences, growth occurs and we progress to a more complex stage. Growth, however, is not automatic and occurs only when appropriate experiences provide a stimulus to a person's cognitive and emotional growth. When environmental conditions are not optimal—that is, too simple or too complex—then learning is retarded. In other words, as people learning to teach become more complex themselves, their environments must also become correspondingly more complex if they are to continue developing at an optimal rate. Although it is not possible to readily change many of the environments you will experience as you learn to teach, you can, nonetheless, try to seek out environments and experiences that will match your level of concern and development as a teacher.

What this means is that becoming a teacher, like becoming anything else, is a process in which development progresses rather systematically through stages with a chance of growth remaining static unless appropriate experiences occur. The following are specific developmental theories about how people learn to teach.

Stages of Development and Concern. The late Frances Fuller (1969) studied student teachers, beginning teachers, and more experienced teachers at the University of Texas in the late 1960s. During the 1980s and 1990s, Sharon Feiman-Nemser and her colleagues (1983) and Richardson and Placier (2001) also described processes that teachers experience as they move from **novice** to **expert** status. The stages initially observed by Fuller and later defined by Feiman-Nemser have stood the test of time and have been confirmed by more recent research (Conway & Clark, 2003, for example). The phases or **stages of teacher development** are summarized below.

> Novice teachers go through rather predictable stages in the process of becoming accomplished.

1. *Survival stage.* When people first begin thinking about teaching and when they have their first classroom encounters with children from in front of rather than behind the desk, they are most concerned about their own personal survival. They wonder and worry about their interpersonal adequacy and whether or not their students and their supervisors are going to like them. Also, they are very concerned about classroom control and worry about things getting out of hand. In fact, many beginning teachers in this initial stage have nightmares about students getting out of control.

2. *Teaching situation stage.* At some point, however—and this varies for different individuals—beginning teachers start feeling more adequate and pass beyond the survival stage. Various aspects of controlling and interacting with students become somewhat routinized. At this stage, teachers begin shifting their attention and energy to the teaching situation itself. They start dealing with the time pressures of teaching and with some of the stark realities of the classroom, such as too many students, inappropriate instructional materials, and perhaps their own meager repertoire of teaching strategies.

3. *Student results and mastery stage.* Eventually, individuals mature as teachers and find ways of coping or dealing with survival and situational concerns. During this stage, teachers master the fundamentals of teaching and classroom management. These become effective and routine. It is only then that teachers reach for higher-level issues and start asking questions about the social and emotional needs of students, being fair, and the match between the teaching strategies and materials and pupil needs. Most importantly, it is during this stage that teachers have concern and assume responsibility for *student learning*.

This final stage is where teachers develop what some have labeled *expertise.* Unlike novice teachers, experts have command of knowledge about their subjects and about pedagogy so they know when and why to use particular aspects of their wide repertoire in a variety of teaching situations (Bransford, Brown, & Cocking, 2000). They are also able to observe patterns in what is going on in the classroom that may appear to be chaos to the novice teacher (see Darling-Hammond & Bransford, 2005; Hammerness et al., 2005; Sabers, Cushing, & Berliner, 1991).

Over the past few years there has been a gradual shift away from the stage theory described above and toward a more flexible view about how teacher development occurs (Conway & Clark, 2003; Richardson & Placier, 2001). This more flexible perspective posits that developmental processes for teachers are evolutionary and gradual and not as precise as suggested in the Fuller and Feiman-Nemser model. However, the Fuller and Feiman-Nemser model is useful for thinking about the process of learning to teach. Their principles help to put present concerns in perspective and to prepare beginners to move on to the next and higher level of concern. For example, a beginning teacher who is overly worried about personal concerns might seek out experiences and training that build confidence and independence. If class control takes too much mental and emotional energy, a beginning teacher can find ways to modify that situation. A questionnaire to measure your concerns at this point in your career is included in the Online Learning Center.

Implications of Developmental Models for Learning to Teach. As beginning teachers go through the process of learning to teach, the developmental models have numerous implications. First, these models suggest that learning to teach is a developmental process in which each individual moves through stages that are simple and concrete at first and later more complex and abstract. Developmental models thus provide a framework for viewing one's growth.

Second, you can use the models to diagnose your own level of concern and development. This knowledge can help you to accept the anxiety and concerns of the beginning years and, most important, to plan learning experiences that will facilitate growth to more mature and complex levels of functioning.

Early Influences on Teaching

Our parents and teachers have had important influences on our desire to teach and on our perspectives about what constitutes effective teaching.

It appears that some aspects of learning to teach are influenced by the experiences that people have with important adult figures, particularly teachers, as they grow up and go through school. In the early 1970s, Dan Lortie, a sociologist at the University of Chicago, spent several years studying why people become teachers, what kind of a profession teaching is, and what experiences affect learning to teach. As part of his study, he interviewed a rather large sample of teachers and asked them what experiences most influenced their teaching. Many experienced teachers told Lortie that early authority figures, such as parents and teachers, greatly influenced their concepts of teaching and their subsequent decision to enter the field. Many studies since Lortie's have confirmed that particular teachers and the act of observing teachers teach when we are students help shape the views we have as adults about effective teaching and the "good teacher" as illustrated in the research study for this chapter.

This is the first example of research summary boxes you will find in each chapter of *Learning to Teach*. These summaries are included to help you get a feel for some of the research that has been carried out in education and to help you develop an appreciation for the knowledge base on teaching. The boxed research summaries were chosen either because they are considered *classics* in particular fields or because they illustrate the variety and richness of the research methods found in educational research.

The format used to present this chapter's Research Summary is one that will be followed throughout the book when research reports are summarized. The

Research Summary
The Good Teacher and Good Teaching

Murphy, P. K., Delli, L. M., & Edwards, M. N. (2004). The good teacher and good teaching: Comparing beliefs of second-grade students, preservice teachers, and inservice teachers. *Journal of Experimental Education, 72(2), 69–93.*

Problem and Approach: Most students, parents, and teachers want good teachers, and teacher education programs strive to teach individuals how to be good teachers. However, what exactly are the characteristics that define good teaching, and what type of consensus exists among various educational stakeholders? In a unique and interesting study, Karen Murphy and her colleagues explored individual beliefs about the characteristics of good teaching and compared the beliefs held by second-grade students, college students preparing to teach, and experienced teachers.

Sample: The researcher chose three groups (second-grade students, preservice teachers, and experienced teachers) to participate in the study. The second-graders consisted of thirty-two girls and twenty-eight boys in a midwestern elementary school. The sixty-one preservice teachers (fifty women and eleven men) were enrolled in a master's level teacher preparation program at a large university in the Midwest. Twenty-two

(nineteen female and three male) elementary and middle school teachers from midwestern urban and suburban schools formed the sample of experienced teachers.

Methods and Procedures: The Tuckman Teacher Feedback Form (Tuckman, 1995) was used to measure beliefs about good teaching. This instrument presents a list of characteristics, and respondents are asked to rate the extent to which a particular characteristic contributes to good teaching. Characteristics believed not to be understandable to the second-graders were deleted from the original questionnaire. The 4-point Likert scale for the adults was modified using "smiley faces" for the second-grade version. In addition, all three groups were asked to draw a picture of good teachers and good teaching.

Pointers for Reading Research: The data presented in Table 1.3 are typical of what a data table looks like in educational research. The researchers have compared the means and standard deviations of the three groups studied. If you go to the Resource Handbook at the end of this book you will find that a **mean score** is the arithmetic average of a group of scores and that **standard deviation (SD)** is a measure that shows the spread of a set of scores from the mean.

Table 1.3 *Means and Standard Deviations of the Good Teacher Characteristics, by Group*

Characteristic	Overall M	SD	Second-Graders M	SD	Group Preservice Teachers M	SD	Inservice Teachers M	SD
Caring	1.08	0.44	1.05	0.39	1.10	0.47	1.14	0.47
Patient	1.20	0.58	1.27	0.58	1.13	0.56	1.18	0.66
Boring*	1.21	0.59	1.10	0.44	1.25	0.65	1.41	0.73
Polite	1.27	0.58	1.12	0.37	1.36	0.66	1.41	0.73
Organized	1.36	0.65	1.25	0.51	1.39	0.69	1.59	0.80
Unclear*	1.51	0.79	1.37	0.69	1.64	0.86	1.55	0.86
Likeable	1.61	0.68	1.20	0.55	1.93	0.63	1.82	0.59
Forgetful*	1.62	0.89	1.62	0.94	1.54	0.83	1.86	0.89
Shy	1.67	0.77	1.45	0.77	1.74	0.70	2.09	0.75
Softspoken	2.13	0.80	1.93	1.06	2.25	0.54	2.32	0.48
Ordinary	2.32	0.97	1.97	1.16	2.64	0.68	2.41	0.73
Strict	2.57	0.93	2.93	1.21	2.38	0.52	2.14	0.56

*These negative characteristics were reverse-scored to be compared with the other positive characteristics.

Figure 1.6 *Drawing by an Inservice Teacher of a Class Being Held Outdoors*

Figure 1.7 *Classroom Drawn by a Second-Grader from a Bird's-Eye Perspective in Which the Teacher Is Proportionately Larger than the Students*

Results: The first step by the researchers was to analyze the data from the Tuckman Teacher Feedback Form. These data are presented in Table 1.3.

As can be observed, all three groups were in agreement that good teachers were "caring" and "patient." However, more advanced statistical analysis of data displayed in Table 1.3 found some differences between the three groups. The second-graders believed that "likeable," "shy," and "ordinary" were more important characteristics than did preservice or experienced teachers and "not surprisingly, the second graders . . . believed that it was less important to be 'strict'" (p. 80) than did the preservice or experienced teachers.

When the researchers analyzed the "good teacher" drawings displayed in Figures 1.6 and 1.7, they found something very interesting. The majority of second-graders (60 percent) and preservice teachers (72 percent) drew the teachers in the pictures as much larger than the students whereas experienced teachers drew pictures where teachers and students were more evenly proportioned.

The researchers suggested the reason for this difference was that the second-graders and preservice teachers emphasized the power differences between teachers and students, whereas this difference was deemphasized by the experienced teachers. In addition, researchers found that most second-graders (68 percent) drew pictures showing teachers doing whole-group instruction. By comparison a majority of preservice

teachers (65 percent) and experienced teachers (64 percent) showed small-group instruction. When the respondents were asked to describe what the teachers were doing in the pictures, similar descriptions were found across all three groups. According to the researchers, the "good teacher was taking part in active teaching of content (i.e., facilitating, guiding, challenging, thinking) and trying to communicate with students" (p. 84). One area of difference was found. Unlike second-graders or experienced teachers, the preservice teachers (40 percent) said the teacher was taking part in some classroom management issue. This is not surprising because, as will be described in Chapters 4 and 5, preservice teachers are often preoccupied with management concerns.

Discussion and Implications   There is nothing surprising in the idea that good teachers are supposed to be caring, polite, not boring, and active in their engagement with students. These characteristics have popped up in the literature over a long time. However, what is interesting is that belief systems about good teaching seem to begin assembling at an early age, which confirms that when individuals enter teacher preparation programs they come with beliefs "that have accumulated over a decade" (p. 88). It also confirms that individuals preparing to teach hold beliefs that mirror those held by experienced teachers. An important implication of this study for teacher educators and for those learning to teach is that beliefs formed as early as the second grade and reinforced over the years may be difficult to change.

problem the researcher addressed is presented first, followed by brief descriptions of who was studied and the types of procedures used. When needed, pointers are provided to help you read the research. Each Research Summary concludes with a description of important findings and statements about the implications of the research for teaching.

This format is used because it is important that you become knowledgeable about the research base on teaching and learning, and it is equally important that you learn how to read, critique, and use research. At the end of this book is a special section called Reading and Using Research. This section provides further insight into the nature of research on teaching and a practice exercise for reading research; you may want to read it before going on.

A great deal is known about the process of learning to teach that goes beyond the scope of this chapter. However, by way of summary, those learning to teach should enter the process valuing the experiences they have had and recognize that they already know a lot about teaching. At the same time, they should also accept that they have much to learn. Effective teachers must learn to execute complex and particularly effective procedures and methods. They must also challenge their existing perceptions and learn how to think like experienced teachers. This is not always easy because expert and novice teachers think differently. Mastering the behaviors and thought processes of teaching are among the most important challenges of learning to teach and, when accomplished, can bring the most cherished rewards.

Check, Extend, Explore

Check

- What are the stages that teachers typically go through during the process of becoming an effective teacher?
- What forces seem to influence many teachers when they initially make the decision to enter the profession? What are the advantages and disadvantages of this situation?

Extend

- Think about your own experiences. What individuals or forces influenced you to enter teaching? How did they influence your views about teaching?
- Have you ever had teachers who did not continue to develop and grow? Why do you think this happens to some teachers? What safeguards can you take to make sure it doesn't happen to you?

Explore

- Visit the National Board for Professional Teaching Standards (NBPTS) Web site to see how this group defines effective teaching and compare their definition with the one provided in *Learning to Teach*.
- There are literally thousands of teacher blogs on the Internet. Visit a few to get ideas about what teachers are thinking and talking about. Start your own blog on teaching.
- Go to the Council of Chief State School Officers (CCSSO) Web site and listen to its "Teachers of the Year" answer the question "Why do I teach?"

 Reflections **from the** *Classroom*

You have just completed your first year of teaching, and the professor at the local university from which you graduated has asked you to provide your perspective on *effective teaching* to her teaching strategies class. You feel honored that the professor has asked you to do this. At the same time, you know that coming up with a definitive answer about what constitutes effective teaching is no easy task. So, you start asking yourself, What is the perspective that guided my actions while I was student teaching? During my first year of teaching? How were my teaching practices tied to my views about student learning? How were my teaching practices influenced by research? How did my own experiences or those of my cooperating teachers or teacher colleagues influence my practice? How has my practice changed over the past year?

Reflect on answers to these questions as you prepare your presentation and compare them to the following views expressed by experienced teachers. Approach this situation from the perspective closest to the grade level or subject area you are preparing to teach. You may want to turn your presentation into a reflective essay and an exhibit on effective teaching for your portfolio.

Diane Caruso

Saltonstall School, 4th and 5th Grade
Salem, MA

Effective teaching and best practices are phrases that have been essential components of my planning and teaching for years. Reflection of my own teaching, that of my colleagues, and of research is a constant, necessary element of my continuous growth as a teacher. When mentoring new teachers, I always stress that, although there are certain qualities and skills that will always be part of effective teaching, in order to encourage the success and welfare of our students, our own fulfillment, and to counteract the many frustrations teachers face on a daily basis, we must remain lifelong learners.

As I reflect upon the philosophy that has guided my teaching over the past twenty-five years, it includes certain qualities and skills such as dedication, sensitivity, inquiry, literacy, logic, and many more. The basic belief that all children can learn, and that they can experience success and a sense of self-worth while enjoying the process that leads to those goals remains consistent. I believe good teachers make sincere efforts to communicate with students, parents, colleagues, and administrators, as well as with their network of educational professionals. They also strive to provide their students with the most rewarding educational experience possible.

In summary, I would advise the members of a teaching strategies class that effective teaching involves:

1. Holding the belief that every child can learn and experience success;

2. Remaining open to new ideas and techniques through professional development opportunities and lifelong learning; and

3. Communicating effectively at all levels. Perhaps, most of all, teachers must be willing to learn from their students. Learn who they are, what they're about (personally and culturally), what their needs are, and what excites their thirst for knowledge.

Theresa Carter

10th Grade

If I were asked to provide students in a methods class my perspective on effective teaching, I would emphasize two important things: knowledge and passion for my subject, and ability to relate to students. Mainly, I hold a constructivist perspective about how students learn. This means that it is not enough merely to present information to students, have them take notes, and then give it back to me on a test. I want students to build and develop their own knowledge and meaning. This requires that I know my subject well enough so I understand the nuances of the field and so I can create lessons that connect new subject matter to what my students already know. Also, I need to be able to explain things in response to student questions and in ways they understand.

I think effective teachers must also show students that they really care about them as individuals. It is the kind of caring where teachers hold high expectations for the student's work, where they take the time to provide each student with in-depth and constructive feedback, and where they pay attention to what students are doing in aspects of their lives that extend beyond the classroom.

Summary

Explain the meaning of the "scientific basis for the art of teaching."

- Teaching has a scientific basis that can guide its practice; it also has an artistic side. Mastery of both is required for effective teaching.

Describe how perspectives on effective teaching have changed over time and how teachers' roles have changed as a result of historical and demographic forces.

- The role of the teacher is a complex one that has been shaped by historical and contemporary forces. Expectations for teachers have changed. In the eighteenth and nineteenth centuries, the primary concern was the teacher's moral character, whereas today we are more concerned about the teacher's pedagogical abilities.

- Today, a large percentage of students in schools come from non–Western European backgrounds, many are English language learners, and many of them are poor. These three factors in combination have reshaped the teacher's role. Teachers are expected to work in complex multicultural educational settings, to provide good educational experiences for all children, and to take responsibility for their learning.
- Teachers today are expected to help students construct their own knowledge and to be actively involved in their own learning.
- Increasingly, teachers are expected to have advanced preparation and to demonstrate their knowledge of both subject matter and pedagogy.

Identify and discuss the essential attributes of the effective teacher for twenty-first-century schools.

- Effective teachers possess personal qualities for developing authentic relationships with their students, are committed to social justice, understand the knowledge base on teaching and learning, can execute a repertoire of best practices, have attitudes and skills necessary for reflection and problem solving, and consider learning to teach a lifelong process.
- The scientific basis of teaching is learned mainly through studying research and the wisdom of practice accumulated by the profession. From scientific knowledge certain teaching principles and propositions have been derived that can inform best teaching practices.
- Principles based on research, however, cannot be translated directly into fixed recipes and formulas that will work all the time. This is true because teaching is situational, and the characteristics of particular students, classrooms, schools, and communities affect what works and what doesn't.

- *Repertoire* refers to the number of strategies and processes teachers are prepared to use. Effective teachers develop a repertoire of methods and skills to successfully carry out various aspects of their work.
- A teacher's work can be divided into three main areas: leadership, instruction, and organizational engagement.
- The leadership aspects of teaching refer to the leadership roles teachers are expected to play in their classrooms, such as providing motivation, planning, and allocating scarce resources.
- The instructional aspects of teaching refer to methods and processes teachers employ as they provide day-by-day instruction to students.
- The organizational aspects of teaching refer to teachers' work in the school community, including work with colleagues, parents, and school leadership personnel.
- Effective practice includes abilities to approach classroom situations in reflective and problem-solving ways.

Explain how learning to teach is a developmental process and describe the flexible stages teachers go through as they progress from novice to expert status.

- Learning to teach is developmental and a lifelong process. Teachers go through predictable although flexible stages. At first they are concerned about survival, later about their teaching situation, and finally about the social and academic needs of their pupils.
- Parents and teachers often influence a person's decision to enter teaching and affect a teacher's vision of teaching. Memories of favorite teachers, however, may not be the best models for developing one's own teaching style, because these teachers may not have been as effective as they seemed.
- Learning to teach is a complex process, and information that is useful to experienced teachers may not have the same value for beginners.

Key Terms

academic learning 7
accountable 18
art of teaching 4
authentic relationship 20
best practice 4
Common Core 13
constructivism 16
constructivist perspective 16
e-learning 10

evidence-based practice 22
expert teachers 31
iGeneration 10
instructional aspects of teaching 26
knowledge bases 20
leadership aspects of teaching 26
mean score 33
novice teachers 31
objectivist perspective 16

organizational aspects of teaching 28
pedagogy 7
practical arguments 22
reflection 20
repertoire 20
scientific basis of teaching 4
social justice 20
stages of teacher development 31
standard deviation 33

Interactive and Applied Learning

Study and Explore

- Access your Study Guide, which includes practice quizzes, from the Online Learning Center.

Observe and Practice

- Listen to audio clips on the Online Learning Center of Amy Callen (fourth/fifth grade) and Ronald Moss (twelfth-grade social studies) talking about what it means to be an effective teacher in the *Teachers on Teaching* area.

Complete the following **Practice Exercises** that accompany Chapter 1:
- Practice Exercise 1.1: Implications of Twenty-First-Century Challenges for Teachers
- Practice Exercise 1.2: Twenty-First-Century Trends and Effective Teaching
- Practice Exercise 1.3: Analyzing Effective Teaching

Portfolio and Field Experience Activities

Some aspects of teaching can be learned in college classrooms and by reading. Many others, however, can be learned only through experience and "doing." This feature at the end of each chapter has been designed to help you learn from your field experiences and to assist you in the preparation of artifacts for your professional portfolio on topics and standards associated with Chapter 1. Many teacher preparation programs require or encourage teacher candidates to design portfolio activities to show how particular program standards are met and to demonstrate that they have aligned their program standards to those developed by the CCSSO and found in the organization's "Model Core Teaching Standards" (InTASC, 2011). We show how specific portfolio activities are connected to InTASC standards and provide the actual materials you will need to complete the activities. These are found in the *Portfolio and Field Experience Activities* area in the Online Learning Center.

1. Complete the Reflections from the Classroom exercise for this chapter and use the recommended presentation or reflective essay as an exhibit of your views of effective teaching. **(InTASC Standard 9: Professional Learning and Professional Practice)**

2. **Activity 1.1: Assessing My Efforts for Learning to Teach.** Assess your current efforts at learning to be a teacher. Summarize the results as an exhibit for your portfolio. **(InTASC Standard 9: Professional Learning and Professional Practice)**

3. **Activity 1.2: Assessing My Teaching Concerns.** Assess your current level of concern about teaching. **(InTASC Standard 9: Professional Learning and Professional Practice)**

4. **Activity 1.3: Interviewing Teachers about the Scientific Basis of the Art of Teaching.** Find out about their perceptions of the scientific basis of the art of teaching. **(InTASC Standard 9: Professional Learning and Professional Practice)**

5. **Activity 1.4: Portfolio: My Teaching Platform.** Develop a "teaching platform" that describes your current thinking about teaching and learning. **(InTASC Standard 9: Professional Learning and Professional Practice)**

Books for the Professional

Barnett, B. (2011). *Teaching 2030: What we must do for our students and our public schools—now and in the future.* New York: Teachers College Press.

Collins, A., & Halverson, R. (2009). *Rethinking education in the age of technology: The digital revolutions and schooling in America.* New York: Teachers College Press.

Danielson, C. (2007). *Enhancing professional practice: A framework for teaching* (2nd ed.). Alexandria, VA: Association for Supervision and Curriculum Development.

Darling-Hammond, L., & Bransford, J. (Eds.). (2005). *Preparing teachers for a changing world: What teachers should learn and be able to do.* San Francisco: Jossey-Bass.

Kumashiro, K. (2012). *Bad teacher! How blaming teachers distorts the bigger picture.* New York: Teachers College Press.

Marzano, R. (2007). *The art and science of teaching: A comprehensive framework for effective instruction.* Alexandria, VA: Association for Supervision and Curriculum Development.

Pelech, J., & Pieper, G. (2010). *The comprehensive handbook of constructivist teaching: From theory to practice.* Charlotte, NC: Information Age.

Ravitch, D. (2010). *The death of and life of the great American school system: How testing and choice are undermining education.* New York: Basic Books.

Tobias, S., & Duffy, T. (Eds.). (2009). *Constructivist instruction: Success or failure?* New York: Routledge.

West, D. (2012). *Digital schools: How technology can transform education.* Washington, DC: Brookings Institution.

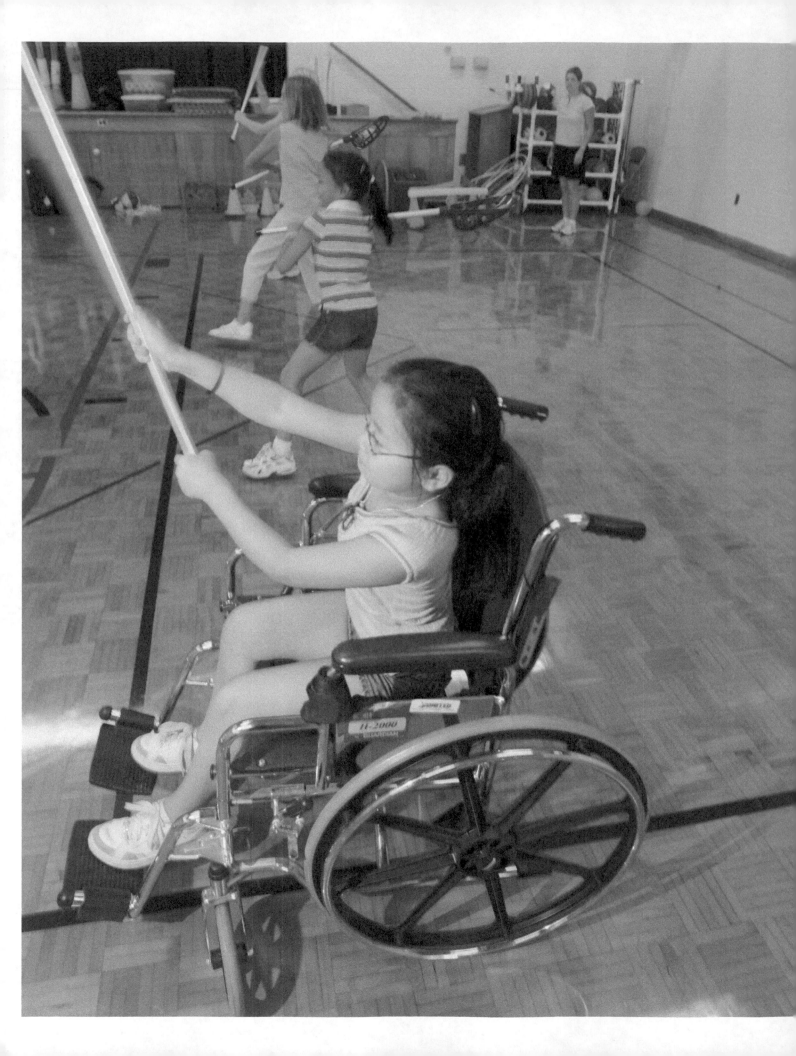

CHAPTER 2
Student Learning in Diverse Classrooms

Learning Goals

After studying this chapter you should be able to

Perspective and Overview	Describe the changes that have occurred in the demographics of schooling and discuss why it is important for teachers to be able to help all students learn.
Theoretical and Empirical Support	Discuss how the concepts of equity, differential treatment, and variations in learning abilities are of central concern in regard to student learning.
Exceptionalities	Discuss how students with disabilities and students who are gifted are to be educated today and describe how teachers can best work with these students.
Culture, Ethnicity, and Race	Describe contemporary perspectives on culture and race, compare these with views from earlier times, and explain what effective teachers do to enhance learning for all students in culturally and racially diverse classrooms.
Religious Diversity	Describe the religious diversity that exists in today's schools and the actions teachers can take to recognize and deal with religious differences among students.
Language Diversity	Discuss the significance of language diversity in today's classrooms and describe effective strategies to use with English language learners.
Gender Differences	Describe the importance of gender differences in today's classrooms and discuss how effective teachers work with these differences.
Social Class Differences and Poverty	Describe the characteristics of low-SES students, explain the special needs they have, and discuss effective strategies for working with them.
Some Final Thoughts and Schoolwide Issues	Explain why schoolwide actions are required to ensure success for all students.

Reflecting on Student Learning in Diverse Classrooms

As a teacher, it will be your responsibility to respond positively and effectively to cultural, gender, linguistic, and socioeconomic diversity as well as to students with special needs. Before you read this chapter, respond showing the extent to which you "strongly agree," "agree," "disagree," or "strongly disagree" with the following statements:

- I have an understanding of the cultures that may be represented in my classroom.
- I am aware of culture-based learning styles.
- I have high expectations for all students regardless of culture.
- I make conscious efforts to engage all students in learning activities.
- I make conscious efforts to give equivalent attention and encouragement to all students, including those with special needs.
- I have participated in programs that help people better understand diversity.
- I am open to identifying racial and cultural biases in myself, in my students, and in my curriculum materials.
- I know how to use methods that foster inclusion (for example, cooperative learning).
- My instruction and methods will not conflict with the cultural beliefs of some students in my classroom.
- I know how to use a variety of tasks, measures, and materials in assessing student competencies to avoid inadvertent bias in assessment.

Source: Based on original ideas from Sara LaBrec, *How to Respond to a Culturally Diverse Student Population* (Alexandria, VA: Association for Supervision and Curriculum Development, 1994).

 Go to the Online Learning Center at www.mhhe.com/arends10e to respond to these questions.

Perspective and Overview

Schools, as we have come to know them in the twenty-first century, were created at a time when most students were of Western European heritage, spoke English, and only a small portion of them attended school at all. Immigrant and farm children were expected to work or help their families. Children who were physically challenged and those with severe learning problems either stayed home or were taught in special schools. Girls, until the post–World War II era, were *not* expected to finish high school or go to college. The monocultural schools created in the nineteenth and early twentieth centuries suffered under the assumption that learning potential was genetically and culturally derived, that teachers were relatively powerless to do anything about these conditions, and that society could tolerate low levels of achievement by some students.

Today, as you know, this has all changed. All children are expected to be in school. These children and youth bring with them a wide range of cultural backgrounds, talents, and needs. Many come from homes where support and encouragement are in short supply. This is true for impoverished and wealthy homes alike. Some students are learning disabled; others are gifted. It is no longer acceptable to allow some students to be placed in special classrooms, to let others drop out, or to allow still others to pass from grade to grade without having mastered basic knowledge and skills needed to be successful in college or work. Instead, schools belong to all children, and the learning potential of each child must be realized. Diversity in classrooms is no longer a question of policy, values, or personal preferences. It is a fact!

Recognizing the diversity among students and understanding how different students learn are among the most important challenges you will face as a teacher. Fortunately, you will be assisted with a growing knowledge base about how different students learn and how teachers can create culturally responsive classrooms where every student is respected and where every student can succeed.

Understanding students and how they learn in a diverse classroom is one of the most important challenges in teaching.

The primary goal of this chapter is to help you understand how students learn in today's diverse classrooms so you can meet the diversity challenge. Let's begin by looking into an experienced teacher's classroom and the students she meets every day.

Ms. Caliendo loves her seventh-grade science class. In her fifth year of teaching, she has been highly successful in raising her students' achievement and is considered one of the best teachers in the school. Part of her success stems from her understanding of her students and her unrelenting respect for each one of them. Ms. Caliendo has spent hours in the community attending cultural events and meeting with parents. This is no small feat when one observes the diversity found in her classroom, as portrayed in Table 2.1.

Ms. Caliendo has firm understandings of and keen sensitivities to the various cultures and native languages her students bring with them to school. She strives to make her

Table 2.1 *A Sample of Students in Ms. Caliendo's Seventh-Grade Science Class*

Name	Ethnicity	First Language	Father's Occupation	Mother's Occupation
Tyler	Caucasian	English	Auto mechanic	Retail clerk
Olivia	African American	English	Educator	Social worker
Han	Asian American	Cantonese	Restaurant owner	Waitress
Maria	Latino	Spanish	Landscaper	Health aide
Noah	Caucasian	English	Not available	Cleaning lady
Maya	Latino	Spanish	Migrant laborer	Migrant laborer
Elias	Alaskan Native	Inuit	Student	Day care worker
Alani	Pacific Islander	English	Software developer	Banker
Juan	Latino	Spanish	Medical technician	Hairdresser
Aadan	African (Somali)	Arabic	Taxi driver	Homemaker
Sophia	Caucasian	English	Attorney	Dental hygienist

Source: Adapted from Cushner, McClelland, and Safford (2005).

curriculum and pedagogy culturally relevant. She is careful to never silence any student's voice and to always make all students feel comfortable while expressing themselves regardless of their language skills. Most important, Ms. Caliendo has created a community of learners and has made deep and meaningful connections to each of her students.

The variety of students found in Ms. Caliendo's class is not an exception; it is the norm. Likely it is similar to the classroom you were in when you were in school. Working with them as Ms. Caliendo does is not something that happens automatically either. Instead, her teaching practices result from a deep understanding of diversity and how students learn. This chapter introduces you to the diversity found in classrooms like Ms. Caliendo's and to the understandings and skills she has for working successfully in this type of classroom. The first two sections examine the nature of today's classrooms, the challenges and opportunities diversity presents, and a theoretical framework for understanding these challenges. The third section describes differences found at both ends of the spectrum of those students labeled as *exceptional*—students who have learning disabilities as well as those who are gifted and have exceptional talents. Later sections describe other kinds of differences found in classrooms: differences in *race, ethnicity, culture, religion, language, gender,* and *social class.* Each of these sections will present the best scientific knowledge about the differences that exist and provide guidelines for teaching and working with diverse groups of students. The chapter concludes with a very important discussion pointing out how teachers by themselves *cannot* solve all student learning problems and how schoolwide and societal reform are required.

The categories in which we place individuals are social constructions and culturally influenced.

It is important to note that the categories used to organize this chapter are social constructions that are culturally determined. Although membership in any one category may be based on physical characteristics such as skin color or disability, they are categories we have devised. The characteristics of people in various categories may take on more or less significance in different cultures. For example, in the United States, a person with any African ancestry is usually considered black; in Puerto Rico,

Today's classrooms are characterized by great diversity.

however, the same person may be classified as white if his or her social standing is high. A disability may or may not constitute a limitation depending on social factors. Ease in manipulating symbols, for example, is important in technological societies but less so in agrarian communities; a person lacking this skill is considered learning disabled in one society but not in another. Similarly, no individual exists in a single category. We are not just men or women, black or white, affluent or poor. In real life, we are members of many groups.

Finally, it is important to learn how to use the right language when discussing diversity and when referring to racial groups or to students with special needs. This has become increasingly significant as our society becomes more sensitive to individuals with different heritages and disabilities. It is very important to use "African American" when referring to students whose parents have African heritage and to use correct language in describing students with Hispanic or Asian backgrounds. We also need to be aware of regional differences and group preferences that influence the words we use to describe particular groups. For example, people from Puerto Rico who live mainly on the East Coast prefer to be called Puerto Rican instead of Hispanic. On the West Coast, people from Mexico sometimes prefer Chicano. Latino is also used to describe individuals of Spanish-speaking descent who are American citizens or residents of Latin America. Most people today believe that it is not appropriate to refer to someone as "handicapped" because of the term's evolution. At one time, according to Friend and Bursuck (2012), people with disabilities had to resort to begging and were referred to as "cap-in-handers." Later, they were called "hand-in-cappers," a term obviously similar to the contemporary term **handicapped.** Some prefer the term **challenged** or *differently abled* instead of **disability** when referring to students with special needs. For example, a person who cannot walk might be said to be *physically challenged;* a student with learning disabilities could be referred to as *cognitively challenged.* Some hold this preference because the term *challenge* communicates an obstacle that can be overcome, whereas *disability* seems to convey a condition that is permanent. The term *disability,* however, still remains acceptable, and you will find it used in many textbooks and a variety of documents. *Special needs* is a more current term. *Learning to Teach* will use all three terms—*disability, challenged,* and *special needs*—depending upon the situation.

Theoretical and Empirical Support

Values, philosophical perspectives, and politics influence teaching practices in diverse classrooms, and these are matters with which beginning teachers need to be concerned. At the same time, teachers must pay attention to a substantial knowledge base that describes what actually happens to children who have special needs and those from diverse cultures when they attend school, as well as the best practices for working with these children and youth. Equity and the differential treatment of children have provided the impetus for much of the research on diversity. Similarly, a substantial knowledge base exists about the nature of students' learning abilities and their learning styles and preferences. These topics will be discussed in this section.

Lack of Equity

Historically, equitable conditions have not existed in our schools. Even at the end of the first decade of the twenty-first century, many students have restricted opportunities and experience lack of **equity.** Textbook shortages exist in many schools,

Check, Extend, Explore

Check
- How have society's expectations changed over the past century in regard to who should be educated?
- Why is using the right language important when discussing differences and referring to students' backgrounds and abilities?

Extend
- Think back to your own schooling. What kind of diversity existed in your classrooms? How did you respond to this situation as a student?

Explore
- Go to the Online Learning Center at www.mhhe.com/arends10e for links to Web sites related to *perspectives on diversity*.

Using appropriate language when discussing diversity or referring to students' backgrounds and abilities is critical.

A serious and troubling gap continues to exist between the achievement of white middle-class students and that of students from other racial groups and those who live in poverty.

and some schools attended by African American and Latino students still have limited access to computers, the Internet, and advanced courses required for college (*The Condition of Education*, 2009, 2012; Oakes, Joseph, & Muir, 2004; Oakes, Lipton, Anderson, & Stillman, 2012; Oakes & Saunders, 2002). Teachers in schools attended by minority students too often focus on basic skill instruction instead of developing inquiry and problem-solving skills. Teachers in these schools are also likely to be less qualified—some lack degrees or majors in education or in the subjects they teach (Banks et al., 2005; Darling-Hammond, 2010; Darling-Hammond & Bransford, 2005).

Most important, however, is the fact that minority students do less well in school than do students from European backgrounds, and the achievement gap between African American students and Hispanic students and their white peers has existed for years. Although SAT averages have risen for most racial and ethnic groups over the past twenty years, they still lag behind white and Asian students by more than 20 points on the National Assessment of Educational Progress's math and reading assessments. They also lag behind on most state mastery or achievement tests. (Achievement Gap, 2011; *The Condition of Education*, 2011, 2012). Although more African American and Hispanic students are completing high school and going to college than ever before, an important gap remains (*The Condition of Education*, 2009, 2012; Rothstein, 2004) between them and their white peers. Similar gaps have been identified with regard to the type of courses minority students take in high school, their graduation rates, and their college attendance.

This achievement gap has been one of the driving forces behind twenty-first-century standards-based reform efforts such as No Child Left Behind, Race to the Top, and the Common Core Standards. This persistent and troubling gap has existed for a long time, actually as long ago as the Coleman Report (1966) that identified in-school, family, and community factors that contribute to student performance. Many observers today (Hawley & Nieto, 2010) argue that socioeconomic conditions are the most important factors influencing achievement in schools and that these factors lead to schools in low-income neighborhoods that lack the resources found in more affluent and middle-class neighborhoods. More about these conditions will be discussed later in the chapter.

A final set of inequity issues include the uneven placement of minority students into remedial classes and disparities in the way discipline is handed out in schools. For example, some report that African American and Latino students are identified and placed in special education classes in K–12 schools at a higher rate than their white or Asian peers. Similarly, independent studies at Teachers College, Columbia University, and the Harvard Graduate School of Education found that the way colleges use standardized placement tests often misidentifies students. This results in placing them in remedial classes they don't actually need. A higher proportion of African American students are placed in these classes as compared to their peers from other races (Sparks, 2013).

As this chapter is being written (March 2013), the U.S. Department of Education's Office for Civil Rights has filed complaints against several school districts over disparities in discipline policies. For example, in Seattle (where the author lives) during the 2011–2012 school year 27.2 percent of black middle school students received suspensions, as compared to 7 percent of white students. For high school students the same figures were 12.9 and 3.8 percent (Ervin & Long, 2013). The reasons used to explain these disparities in discipline vary. Some have argued that disparities are the result of poverty, racism, and a lack of diversity among the teaching profession. Others point to strict discipline policies adopted by many school districts over the past few years that have led principals to zealously punish students for every minor infraction.

Poverty is another problem. The United States and other parts of the world experienced great economic prosperity in the 1990s and early years of the twenty-first century. However, all individuals and groups did not advance equally. The overall poverty rate has been increasing, and the middle class is shrinking. Although there are different ways to calculate poverty, the National Poverty Center, using data from the Bureau of the Census, estimates that approximately 49 million Americans (15.1 percent) live below the poverty line. This is up from previous years, and many of those living in poverty are children, with 16.4 million (22 percent) being under 18. Many students living in poverty are also homeless. In some cases, life events, such as having to take a job or to care for family members, cause them to drop out of school. Child poverty is most pronounced among African American, Latino, and American Indian children and among children living in the South. As described in Chapter 1, the lowest poverty rates are in the North and Midwest. Across the fifty states the percentage of children living in poverty ranges from 9 percent in New Hampshire to 31 percent in Mississippi (*The Condition of Education*, 2012; National Center for Children in Poverty, 2013).

Many prominent educators (*A Broader, Bolder Approach to Education*, 2008; Noguera, 2011) maintain that poverty and social disadvantage are the fundamental challenges facing education, and that until these factors are addressed other efforts at school reform will fail.

Some of you may be asking why teachers should concern themselves with the larger social problem of equity. It may be unfair, even unrealistic, to expect teachers and schools to remedy inequities that have existed in the larger society for a long time. At least two arguments can be advanced in response: The first is that these issues should be of major concern to every citizen—it is incumbent on us as citizens to work toward the public good by trying to ameliorate these problems. As educators, we can all do our part by ensuring that every young person gets equal opportunities to learn and that each person achieves to his or her highest potential. The second argument is that Americans have a strong belief in the power of education as the route to later success in life—economically, politically, and culturally. This belief is supported by research, which consistently shows that education is related to income and accomplishments. The argument has intuitive appeal as well, in that educated people are equipped with the tools to escape from poverty and to participate fully in our economic, social, and political systems. As teachers, it is part of our responsibility to help them secure their escape.

> In a multicultural and diverse world, teachers really have no choice but to create classrooms that are inclusive and equitable.

Differential Treatment of Students

Whereas one body of research has documented the inequities that exist in education as a whole, another has documented the **differential treatment** of students by teachers within classrooms. Differential treatment occurs partially because teachers, consciously or unconsciously, have different expectations for some students as contrasted to others. Let's look at how this works.

> Differential treatment refers to the differences between educational experiences of the majority race, class, culture, or gender and those of minorities.

Self-Fulfilling Prophecy. In 1968, Robert Rosenthal and Lenore Jacobson published *Pygmalion in the Classroom*. This book, instantly popular with professional and lay audiences, introduced the concept of the **self-fulfilling prophecy** and the effects of teacher expectations on student achievement and self-esteem. In their research,

Rosenthal and Jacobson provided teachers in a particular elementary school information about several students in each of their classes. They told teachers that a few students had been identified through a new test as "bloomers" and that they could expect these students to make large achievement gains during the coming year. In fact, these students had been identified at random—no special test information existed. As the year progressed, however, the identified bloomers, particularly those in the early grades, made significant gains in achievement. Rosenthal and Jacobson argued that these gains could be attributed to the differential treatment received from the teachers as a result of their false expectations—thus, the self-fulfilling prophecy, a situation in which inaccurate perceptions of students' abilities and subsequent acting on these perceptions make them come true.

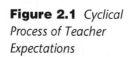

Self-fulfilling prophecy refers to situations in which teachers' expectations and predictions about student behavior or learning cause the behavior to happen.

Teacher Expectations. Rosenthal and Jacobson's study, although faulted at the time because of its methodological weaknesses (see Brophy & Good, 1974; Claiborn, 1969), aroused the interest of the research community about the effects of **teacher expectations** on student achievement. Over the past several decades, researchers have found that although the effects of teacher expectations on students are not quite so straightforward as suggested in the Rosenthal–Jacobson study, they are, nonetheless, real. Expectations create a cyclical pattern of behaviors on the part of both teachers and students. Drawing from the work of Good and Brophy (2008), Oakes (1985), Oakes and Lipton (2006), and Oakes, Lipton, Anderson, and Stillman (2012), this cyclical process is illustrated in Figure 2.1.

There are two important questions to ask about this process: How are expectations created in the first place? How do they get communicated to students?

In the classroom, as in all other aspects of life, people make impressions on us. The way students dress, the language they use, their physical features, as well as their interpersonal skills influence teachers. Information about a student's family or information gleaned from the school's records can also create impressions and expectations, even before the teacher meets the student. As long as initial impressions are accurate, there is no problem. But when initial impressions are translated into inaccurate expectations about students and then used in differential treatment toward them, there is a problem.

Once expectations (positive or negative) are formed, they are communicated to students in numerous ways. You can probably recall several instances when a

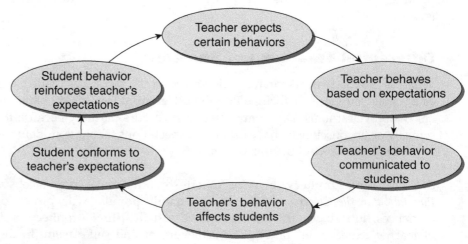

Figure 2.1 *Cyclical Process of Teacher Expectations*

particular teacher communicated expectations to you that influenced your attitude and work in his or her class. You may remember high expectations a teacher held for you. From the first day of class, she chose to single you out for important assignments; she wrote positive comments on your papers; and she called on you to answer difficult questions. It is likely that you worked hard for this teacher, perhaps even beyond your potential. Or you may remember an instance when a teacher had low expectations for you. He seldom acknowledged your work publicly, and even though you raised your hand, he seldom called on you. If this teacher's behavior persisted, it is likely that you started to ignore your work in his class and concentrated your energies elsewhere.

Table 2.2 shows some of the ways that teachers communicate their expectations to students and how they behave differentially toward those for whom they hold high and low expectations.

The discussion up to this point has focused on expectations in situations wherein teachers hold inaccurate beliefs about particular students. There is actually a second expectation effect that is called the **sustaining expectation effect.** This effect exists when a teacher accurately reads a student's ability and behaves accordingly toward the student but does not alter the expectation when the student improves or regresses over time. Again, you can probably recall instances of this happening to you in classrooms as well as in other places. Perhaps you were an excellent English student. The essays you wrote for the teacher were always meticulous. You wrote with clarity, you showed considerable creativity, and you depicted beautiful images with words. You always received an A for your effort. One week, however, you were recovering from

Sustaining expectation effect occurs when teachers do not change their expectations about a student, even after the student's performance has changed.

Table 2.2 *How Teachers and Schools Communicate Differential Expectations to Students*

Teaching or School Practice	For Students Perceived to Be More Capable	For Students Perceived to Be Less Capable
Curriculum, procedures, pacing, qualities of the environment	More opportunities to perform publicly on tasks; more enrichment and resources; more opportunities to think	Less opportunity to perform publicly on meaningful tasks; fewer enrichment opportunities; less opportunity to think; work aimed at practice
Grouping practices	Assigned to higher-ability groups with assignments aimed at understanding	Assigned to lower-ability groups with more worksheet and drill-like assignments
Responsibility for learning	More autonomy and more choices	Less autonomy and frequent teacher direction and monitoring
Feedback and evaluation practices	More opportunity for self-feedback and evaluation	Less opportunity for self-evaluation
Motivational strategies	More honest, direct, and contingent feedback	Less honest and more gratuitous feedback
Teacher quality	More qualified and experienced teachers	More uncertified and inexperienced teachers
Quality of teacher relationships	More respect for learners as individuals with unique needs	Less respect for learners as individuals with unique needs

Sources: Adapted from Good and Brophy (2008), Good and Weinstein (1986), and Oakes and Lipton (2006).

the flu and were overwhelmed with other schoolwork. You had to write your essay in haste and with little thought or care. When the paper was returned marked with an A and a comment from the teacher, "Another superb piece of writing," you knew that your work had been judged not on its current value but on your previous history of producing good essays.

You can also probably think of instances when the sustaining expectation effect worked the other way. Perhaps you were notorious for not keeping up with your reading assignments in history. Every time the teacher called on you, you answered with silly and careless answers. This behavior made your classmates laugh and covered up your unpreparedness. You decided one day to stop this behavior. You started to read your assignments very carefully, and you came prepared to discuss your ideas in class. You raised your hand in response to the teacher's questions over and over, but someone else was always selected to recite. When you did get your chance, everyone started to laugh, including the teacher, before you could complete your point. You had changed your behavior, but the teacher and other students sustained their past expectations.

Tracking (formal or informal) limits educational opportunities for students placed in the lower tracks.

Tracking and Ability Grouping. Differential treatment also results from ability grouping and tracking (Banks et al., 2005; Hallinan, 2003; Oakes, 1985, 2005). Low-socioeconomic-status (SES) and minority students are disproportionately placed in low-ability groups and low-track classes. Instructional quality is often poorer in these groups than in the higher groups. The criteria used to guide placement decisions are sometimes of dubious merit. Those used most often are standardized aptitude test scores (the type administered in large groups, deemed least valid by test developers) and teachers' judgments. Unfortunately, teachers' judgments are influenced by race and class, and even when ability and teacher recommendations are equivalent, race and class are often the most likely determining factors in placing children.

In the 1980s and 1990s, tracking and ability grouping, as it had been used historically, fell out of favor. However, recent reports (Loveless, 2013a, b; Toppo, 2013) suggest that there has been a resurgence of ability grouping in the last decade. This trend may be explained by the pressures put on teachers by No Child Left Behind regulations that pay particular attention to students who are "below proficiency levels." Current grouping practices, as you will read about in Chapter 13, are more flexible than they once were and are used to enhance the achievement of all students. However, teachers and all educators should remain concerned if current practices cause possible differential treatment of some students regardless of good intentions. Loveless (2013a, b) has raised a number of good questions about current trends: Does tracking and differential treatment in math and advanced placement courses in middle and high schools have harmful effects on other students? What will be the effect of the Common Core Standards on grouping practices? What will happen to students who have already met Common Core grade-level standards? Will they be placed in special classes? What about those who lag behind?

Learning Abilities, Styles, and Preferences

A third major theoretical perspective about diversity that classroom teachers need to consider is the differences observed in student abilities, their talents, and their learning styles and preferences. This section explores how learner abilities are defined and how students will vary widely in different kinds of abilities. It also discusses how students may vary in their approaches to learning and in how they process cognitive and emotional information.

Learner Abilities and Intelligence. The belief that people vary in their ability to learn is not new. In fact, the early Greeks puzzled over these differences, as have many others over the past several thousand years. One important step in understanding students and learning in diverse classrooms is to understand differences in **learning abilities** and how these abilities have been defined and measured.

General Intelligence. Traditional theories held that individuals have specific **mental abilities** as measured by performance on particular cognitive tasks such as analyzing word associations, doing mathematical problems, and solving certain kinds of riddles. At the turn of the twentieth century, psychologists such as Alfred Binet in France and Lewis Terman in the United States developed the first tests aimed at measuring human intelligence. These theorists saw **intelligence** as having a single dimension that would predict future performance. Binet, for example, wanted to find ways to measure learning ability so children could be provided special help rather than being dismissed from school, as was the practice in France and other European countries at that time. Out of Binet's work came the idea of **mental age.** A child who could pass the same number of test items as passed by other children in the child's age group would have the mental age of that age group. The concept of **intelligence quotient (IQ),** according to Woolfolk (2010), was added after Binet's test was brought to the United States. An IQ score became the computation of a person's mental age divided by his or her chronological age and multiplied by 100, as in the following example:

> Intelligence refers to the ability or abilities to solve problems and adapt to the physical and social environments.

$$\text{Intelligence quotient} = \frac{\text{Mental age (10)}}{\text{Chronological age (10)}} \times 100 = 100$$

Performance on a variety of intelligence tests designed during the first two decades of the twentieth century was highly correlated and thus offered support to the single ability theory. These tests were used widely in Europe to determine who could benefit from advanced schooling. In the United States, they were soon employed to help place students in instructional groups, to determine who was best fit to serve in the army, and who should go to college. Even though IQ tests have fallen into disfavor, tests of academic achievement and those that measure more general knowledge, such as the Scholastic Assessment Test (SAT), have replaced them and are used widely to make decisions about where students should be placed in school and where they can go to college.

Multiple Intelligences. Over the past three decades, contemporary psychologists such as Howard Gardner (1983, 1993, 2011) and Robert Sternberg (1985, 1999a, 2009) have challenged the idea that there is general or singular intelligence. Instead, they theorize that intelligence and ability are much more than the dimensions of logical thinking and use of language. Sternberg maintains that we should be teaching for what he has labeled **successful intelligence,** an intelligence that involves three kinds of processes: analytical, creative, and practical. **Analytical intelligence** involves an individual's cognitive processes. **Creative intelligence** is an individual's insight for coping with new experiences. **Practical intelligence** is an individual's ability to adapt and reshape his or her environment. Sternberg argues that "intelligent behavior" may vary from one occasion or setting to another. It depends on the environmental context, one's prior experiences, and particular cognitive processes required of the task or setting. Success in life, according to Sternberg, depends not on how much of each of the three intelligences individuals have, but on understandings individuals have of their own

Table 2.3 *Gardner's Eight Types of Intelligence*

Type	Description
Logical-mathematical	Ability to discern logical and numerical patterns and to manage long chains of reasoning
Linguistic	Sensitivity to the sounds, rhythms, and meanings of words and to the different functions of language
Musical	Ability to produce and appreciate pitch, timbre, rhythm, and the different forms of musical expression
Spatial	Ability to perceive the visual-spatial world accurately and to perform transformations on one's perceptions, both mentally and in the world
Bodily-kinesthetic	Ability to exert great control over physical movements and to handle objects skillfully
Interpersonal	Capacity to discern and respond appropriately to the moods, temperaments, motivations, and desires of others
Intrapersonal	Perceptiveness about one's own emotional state and knowledge of one's own strengths and weaknesses
Naturalist	Ability to discriminate among living things and sensitivity to features of the natural world

strengths and weaknesses, how to use their strengths to an advantage, and how to compensate for their weaknesses. Success also depends on individuals drawing from their past experiences to deal with new situations and adapting their behavior appropriately to fit particular environments. In some instances, intelligent behavior requires finding an environment conducive to a particular individual's success. This latter idea helps explain why individuals are highly successful in one college and fail in another or succeed in one job and not another.

> **Sternberg and Gardner have posited the view that intelligence is more than a single ability but instead encompasses many abilities and talents and is contextual.**

Howard Gardner is the best-known contemporary theorist who believes that intelligence is more than a singular ability. Gardner's theory of **multiple intelligences** proposes eight separate intelligences: logical-mathematical, linguistic, musical, spatial, bodily-kinesthetic, interpersonal, intrapersonal, and naturalist. These different intelligences and their attributes are displayed in Table 2.3. According to Gardner, individuals differ in their strengths in the various intelligences. Some may be strong in logical and mathematical reasoning, whereas others may have exceptional musical talent or physical dexterity. Recently, Gardner (2009) further expanded the kinds of mental abilities that are important for the information-rich environment of the twenty-first century. He described five abilities (minds) and labeled them the disciplined, synthesizing, creating, respective, and ethical minds. He has described how these minds can be used and cultivated in schools and other places in the environment. Gardner, Sternberg, and their disciples believe that teachers and schools should expand the range of abilities they value and teach in ways that accommodate different kinds of intelligence. Unfortunately, many schools today and the society at large continue to emphasize success as determined by language and mathematical abilities and largely ignore the other forms of intelligence. According to Sternberg and his colleagues, one reason that ideas associated with multiple intelligence are not more widely reflected in the ways teachers teach is that until late they have not been supported by evidence obtained from empirical research. To correct this situation, Sternberg and his colleagues (Sternberg & Grigorenko, 2004; Sternberg, Torff, & Grigorenko, 1998) conducted experiments comparing students taught using traditional (memory-based) instructional strategies to those using strategies that emphasized analytical, creative, and practical intelligences. These studies produced some rather convincing evidence that using strategies associated with successful intelligence and assessments that measured analytical, creative, and practical achievements produce higher student learning in all three of these dimensions as well as higher achievement in recall of factual information.

Emotional Intelligence. A final type of intelligence of interest to teachers is **emotional intelligence (EQ)** (Goleman, 1995, 2006). EQ is the ability to recognize and manage one's own emotions, to recognize emotions in others, and to handle relationships. This concept has become quite popular in the preparation of leaders in all types of fields; evidence shows that leader success is perhaps more dependent on EQ than on cognitive skills (Goleman, McKee, & Bayatzis, 2002) The field that interprets brain research for classroom practice (Sousa, 2006; Willis, 2006; Zull, 2002) has also recognized the interaction between the cognitive and the emotional in all matters of human functioning. The important thing about EQ for teachers is to recognize emotion as an ability and realize that it can be influenced like other abilities. Teaching students to be in touch and to manage strong emotions such as anger provides the focus for many human relations lessons. Teaching students to work toward desired goals rather than act on emotional impulse is another example of how EQ has become part of the schools' curriculum.

> **Emotions interact with human cognition in all matters of human functioning, including how students learn in school.**

Nature or Nurture? A debate has existed for years over whether intelligence(s) (result) from heredity (nature) or from the environment (nurture). On one side of the argument are those who believe that we are born with a set amount of intelligence that can be unfolded but not exceeded (Herrnstein & Murray, 1994). On the other side are those such as Perkins (1992, 1995) and Okagaki (2000) who view intelligence as a "capacity to learn" that is mostly environmentally determined. Most psychologists today (Miller, 2011) take a middle road and view intelligence as resulting from both heredity and the environment. Heredity establishes a range of abilities, but environment heavily influences what individuals do with it.

> **Most psychologists believe that one's intelligence and capacity to learn result from both inherited traits and environmental influences.**

Many practicing educators today believe that the results of IQ tests and tests of general knowledge have little to do with an individual's ability or capacity to learn, but instead reflect one's social and cultural background. Children from families and communities that reflect the cultural mainstream, for instance, do better on these tests than do the children of parents who live in poverty, those who recently immigrated to the United States, or those who are English language learners. It is important for teachers to remember that all understandings and skills are improvable and that

"Well, Dad, my guess would be that heredity played a part in those bad grades."

© Adam Stoller. Reprinted with permission.

many differences, particularly those among older students, result from what and how students have been taught in schools.

Differences in Cognitive and Learning Styles. Another especially important area for teacher awareness is cognitive and learning style variations, mainly in the ways that students perceive their world and in how they process and reflect on information. Some of these variations seem to be caused by differences in the brain, others by individual preferences, and still others by culture. Many different cognitive and learning styles and preferences have been described; a few of these follow.

Cognitive Styles. For a long time, psychologists have observed that people differ in how they perceive and process information (Wapner & Kemick, 1991). Some individuals appear to be **field dependent**—they perceive situations "as a whole" rather than "in parts." They are likely to see the big picture in most problem situations. Other people are **field independent**—they tend to see the separate parts of the whole instead of the whole itself. In general, field-dependent individuals are more people-oriented; social relationships are important to them, and they work well in groups. Individuals who are field independent, on the other hand, have strong analytical abilities and are more likely to monitor their information processing rather than their relationships with others. The classroom implications are obvious. It is likely that field-independent students will need assistance in seeing the "big picture" and may prefer working alone, whereas field-dependent students will prefer working on longer-term and problem-based assignments. Others, such as Mayer (2011) and Mayer and Massa (2003), have focused on cognitive styles in regard to how people think and learn information. They identify two important differences: verbal learners and visual learners. Verbal learners are more comfortable learning from words and verbal information, whereas visual learners think and learn using images and information presented in visual form. This is the style that has most empirical support.

Learning Styles. Individuals also approach learning in different ways. One important **learning style** difference has been labeled "in-context" and "out-of-context" style. These differences appear, to some extent, to be culturally influenced. In some cultures and domestic subcultures, teaching and learning are conducted **in-context,** whereas in mainstream American schools, the predominant mode is **out-of-context.** What does "in-context learning" mean? It means that children acquire skills and knowledge at the point that they are needed and in real-life situations. For example, children may learn to use a paring knife in the context of helping their parents prepare meals, or they may learn how to multiply fractions in the context of doubling a recipe when company is coming. "Out-of-context" learning means that learning is unconnected to a real, immediate need. When parents play "what's this" games with infants or when math is broken down into discrete algorithms, each drilled separately before application to real math problems, then out-of-context learning is happening. Both kinds of teaching and learning are important, and both can clearly "work," but children accustomed to in-context learning are often confused by out-of-context teaching so dominant in schools.

Learning Preferences. Finally, some evidence suggests that students have preferences for particular kinds of learning environments and modalities. A widely popular conceptualization of **learning preferences** was developed some years ago by Dunn and Dunn (1978, 1993). Gregorc (1982) has also developed a learning preference model. They argue that students differ in preferred learning environments (sound, light, seating patterns), in the amount of required emotional support, and in the degree of structure and peer interaction. Learners, according to the Dunns, also differ in their preferred learning modality. Some students are more visually oriented, whereas others prefer to obtain information through auditory channels.

Obviously, it is important for teachers to recognize that students differ in the ways they process information and in their preferred ways of learning. They should make an effort to adapt their instruction to the ways their students learn and to how the brain works (Kotulak, 1996; Wolfe, 2001). Successful, experienced teachers have known this for a long time. However, three caveats are in order for beginners: (1) At the present time, there is no consensus about which of the several cognitive and learning styles are most important for teachers to pay attention to, and some researchers (Brody, 2001; Coffield et al., 2004; Stahl, 2002) have argued that the research base on learning styles and preferences is inadequate. (2) Some students may communicate that their preferred learning style is the one that is easiest for them or one for which they have no alternative. They may have to be helped to develop a repertoire of learning styles and taught how to select the most appropriate one for particular learning situations. And, finally (3) there are real drawbacks to planning completely around learning style differences. The number of different styles sometimes is too varied to make it practical for teachers to accommodate every student's style. However, that doesn't mean that teachers shouldn't attend to differences in the ways students learn and strive to diversify and differentiate strategies to meet the varying needs of students. This issue will return in Chapter 13.

Exceptionalities

Student **exceptionalities** account for some of the greatest diversity found in today's classrooms. In any one classroom, teachers find students with severe learning disabilities or other special needs as well as students who are gifted and possess special talents. This section describes students who have disabilities and those who are gifted. It also provides you with strategies for working with all kinds of exceptionalities.

Students with Disabilities

Students who have learning disabilities or who are challenged have special needs that must be met if they are to function successfully in and out of school. Before the post–World War II era, not much attention was paid to this group, and those who did receive an education were more likely to do so in special schools. This has changed dramatically over the past forty years as a result of legislation and court action. The landmark event was the passage of Public Law 94-142, the Education for All Handicapped Children Act in 1975. Now called the Individuals with Disabilities Education Act (IDEA), this law has been amended and reauthorized every session of Congress since that time. IDEA now protects the rights of all individuals with cognitive, emotional, or physical disabilities from birth to age 21. These laws, along with numerous court decisions, were enacted in response to inequalities and discrimination in services provided to children and adults with disabilities and special needs. In the case of education, some jurisdictions had barred children from attending school because of their special needs; in others, the education such children received was often segregated and inferior. This situation has changed dramatically. As shown in Figure 2.2, there has been a significant increase in the number of children with disabilities who

Check, Extend, Explore

Check
- Why should teachers be concerned about classrooms that are inclusive and equitable?
- Contrast "self-fulfilling prophecy" with the "sustaining expectation effect."
- Give some examples of how teachers treat students for whom they hold high expectations as compared to those for whom they hold low expectations.
- Contrast the traditional definition of IQ with the views held by Robert Sternberg and Howard Gardner.
- Why are the concepts of cognitive and learning styles important when thinking about diverse classrooms?

Extend
- Think of situations in your own schooling when teachers had inaccurate expectations about you. Why did they hold these expectations? How did you respond?
- What proportion of ability do you think results from nature? From nurture? Go to "Extend Question Poll" on the Online Learning Center to respond.

Explore
- Go to the Online Learning Center at www.mhhe.com/arends10e or to the Internet and search for Web sites related to multiple intelligences and learning preferences.

Figure 2.2 *Percentage of Children Receiving Services under the Individuals with Disabilities Act from 1976–1977 through 2009–2010*

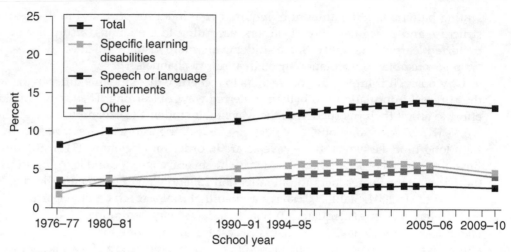

Source: *The Condition of Education* (2012).

were served by federally supported programs between 1976–1977 and 2009–2010, the latest date for which data are available.

Features of Special Education. The aim of the Individuals with Disabilities Education Act was to ensure a free and appropriate public education for all children in a setting that was most suitable for their needs. It also guaranteed due process. This legislation introduced the concept of **mainstreaming**, a strategy to move children out of special education and into regular classrooms (the mainstream) to the degree possible. At first, only children who had mild disabilities were placed in regular classrooms. The concept of **inclusion** followed on the heels of mainstreaming and promoted a wider goal—including all students, even those with severe disabilities, in regular classrooms. Unlike mainstreaming, inclusion begins with students in regular classrooms and makes provisions for pulling them out for services as needed.

> Inclusion is the practice of placing students with mild and somewhat severe disabilities into regular classrooms and pulling them into special classrooms only as needed.

Mainstreaming and inclusion would be important even if law did not mandate them. Other educational benefits accrue in addition to alleviating discrimination. For example, children with special needs in regular classrooms have the opportunity to learn appropriate social and academic behaviors by observing and modeling other children. Children without disabilities also benefit by seeing firsthand the strengths and potential contributions, as well as the limitations, of their peers with disabilities. The school environment and society at large are thereby enriched.

Public Law 94-142 and subsequent IDEA rest on four premises: (1) students should be educated in the least restrictive environment; (2) each child with a special need should have an individualized education plan (IEP); (3) evaluation procedures should be fair and nondiscriminatory; and (4) rights should be guaranteed through due process.

> Least restrictive environment refers to the placement setting for students with disabilities that is most like the regular classroom.

Children are to be educated within the **least restrictive environment.** This means that to the extent possible, children with disabilities should be included in the regular classroom. Today, approximately 95 percent of school-age children and youth served by IDEA are enrolled in regular classrooms (*The Condition of Education,* 2012). Those with very mild physical, emotional, and learning disabilities are to spend their entire school day in the regular classroom. Those with slightly more serious problems are to receive extra assistance from a special educator, either in or out of regular classrooms. As the disabilities grow more serious, the responsibility of the regular classroom teacher normally is reduced, and the child receives a larger portion of his or her education in more specialized settings. In practice, the majority of children with learning or physical disabilities attend regular classes for at least part of the day.

Each child with a disability is to have an **individualized education plan (IEP).** IEPs are developed by a committee composed of the regular classroom teacher, the child's parents, the special education teacher, and other staff who may be helpful, such as psychologists, speech therapists, or medical personnel. IEPs describe the child's current level of academic performance and set goals for future development. The IEP, and the teacher's role in the process, will be described in more detail in the next section of this chapter.

In 2004 the reauthorization of IDEA established a new process for working with children who have difficulty with school. The legislation created a process called "Response to Intervention" (RTI) that was designed to provide services to struggling students as early as possible. The key features of RTI are summarized below based on the work of Bradley, Danielson, and Doolittle (2005) and Klotz and Canter (2013):

- *Universal screening* performed by school personnel early in every school year to ensure that struggling students get instruction and support as early as possible.
- Use of high-quality, *research-based* instructional strategies and approaches.
- *Monitoring the progress* of interventions and assessing their effectiveness on achievement and performances.
- Use of a *multiple-level* intervention system by increasing intervention intensity starting with general interventions; moving to secondary interventions, perhaps in small groups; and then offering individualized and intensive services.
- *Careful documentation* of parent involvement throughout the process.

School systems receive special federal funds for each child with a disability, so the process of categorizing looms large in schools. Controversy reigns, however, about the desirability of labeling per se and the validity of current means for evaluating

Diagnosis and evaluation are important aspects of the IEP process.

exceptionality. Advocates of labeling contend that it helps educators meet the special needs of the student and brings additional funding to bear where it is most needed. While they acknowledge the weaknesses of the current system of evaluation and placement, they argue that eliminating labeling amounts to throwing the baby out with the bathwater.

Opponents counter that labeling creates some serious problems. For example, questions about equity arise because of the differential placement of boys, students of lower socioeconomic status, and minorities into special education programs and because the incidence of disabilities varies widely from state to state. Opponents also contend that labeling causes teachers to view problem behaviors as deficiencies that are inherent in the child; teachers who hold this view could overlook deficiencies in the learning environment. Finally, labels can become permanent once students are placed in a special education program, and they may end up staying there. Regardless of the problems involved in identifying students with disabilities, few parents or educators would prefer going back to the days when students with disabilities and their education were not protected under the law.

Working with Students Who Are Learning-Challenged. Most beginning teachers worry about what they can do in the classroom to assist students who are challenged. They can take several steps. First, it is important for beginning teachers to know district policies pertaining to students with special needs and the teacher's role in the referral, screening, and IEP process. Familiarize yourself with district policies and procedures for referral and screening. Be alert for students with problems or special potential. Do you have any students whose academic work is well below or well above grade level? Do you have students whose behavior is well below or above the maturity level of their age mates? Do any of your students demonstrate especially low or high persistence at learning tasks? Typically, districts expect teachers to refer students who exhibit these characteristics—unusual academic performance, behavior or emotional problems, lack of persistence—to appropriate colleagues for further evaluation.

A student's individualized education plan (IEP) specifies his or her functioning, long- and short-term goals, and how the student will be evaluated.

Also, teachers need to be aware of the specific categories of disabilities as prescribed by federal law. Students who have one of the disabilities described in Table 2.4 are eligible for special education services. Schools are required to have an individualized education plan (IEP) for each student identified with a disability. In most school districts, IEPs are developed by a committee composed of the regular classroom teacher, the child's parents, the special education teacher, and any other staff who may be helpful. IEPs should contain information about the child's current level of academic performance, a statement of both long- and short-term educational goals, a plan for how these goals will be achieved, the amount of time the child will spend in the regular class, and an evaluation plan. The IEP is revised annually.

Evaluation procedures used to assess students with special needs are tied to the IEP process and, by law, must be nondiscriminatory. In screening a child for special services, school officials are required to use a variety of tests and must consider the child's cultural background and language. The involvement of parents in the evaluation process is mandated, and no major educational decisions may be made without their written consent. Parents must be informed of intended school actions in their own language.

For specific lessons, teachers can develop learning materials and activities commensurate with the abilities of children with special needs, much as they adapt lessons

Table 2.4 *Summary of Federal Disability Categories*

Federal Disability Category	Characteristics
Developmental disability or delay	Developmental delays in one or more of the following areas: physical development, cognitive development, communication development, social or emotional development, or adaptive development. Includes autism.
Deaf-blindness	Concomitant hearing and visual impairment; amount can vary.
Deafness	Hearing impairment that is severe.
Emotional disturbance (ED)	Difficulties in social and emotional areas; trouble with social relationships.
Hearing impairment	Significant hearing loss; amount can vary.
Mental retardation	Significant, below-average mental functioning and cognitive abilities.
Multiple disabilities	Two or more interwoven disabilities.
Orthopedic impairment	Serious physical disabilities; impaired ability to move around.
Other health impairments	Conditions resulting from chronic health problems or disease.
Specific learning disability	Disorder in one or more psychological processes in understanding or using language.
Speech or language impairment	Communication disorder such as stuttering or impaired articulation.
Traumatic brain injury (TBI)	Intellectual and physical impairments resulting from brain injury.
Visual impairment	Significant vision loss; amount can vary.

Sources: Adapted from data from U.S. Department of Education (2010); and Turnbull, Turnbull, and Wehmeyer (2010).

to the individual differences of all students. In doing so, they should expect to work closely with resource teachers and other support personnel. Most schools have such support services readily available. Cooperative learning strategies can also be used often, both to facilitate achievement and to help exceptional and regular students accept and appreciate each other.

Two perspectives currently exist about the best approach to use with students most likely to be included in regular classrooms—students who are mildly learning disabled and behaviorally or emotionally disabled. Turnbull and colleagues (2010), Swanson (2005), and Tomlinson (2004), who favor a somewhat structured and direct instruction approach, offer the following recommendations:

- Use highly structured materials. Tell students exactly what is expected. Avoid distractions.
- Allow alternatives to the use of written language, such as tape recorders or oral tests.
- Expect improvement on a long-term basis.
- Reinforce appropriate behavior. Model and explain what constitutes appropriate behavior.
- Provide immediate feedback and ample opportunities for drill and practice.

As you will see, these practices are *not* very different from many of the effective teaching behaviors described in Chapter 8.

Not all agree, however, that these are the only effective teaching strategies for this population. Many, such as Cohen and Lotan (2004), Haberman (1991), Hawley and Nieto (2010), and Villegas and Lucas (2002), believe that instruction for students with disabilities should stem from their interests and that strategies used by teachers should not emphasize basic information but should instead promote the student's ability to solve problems and think critically. They recommend strategies that resemble those recommended for gifted children—group investigation, community problem solving, problem-based learning, and activities that emphasize cooperative and active learning. Approaches such as cooperative learning and reciprocal teaching convey to all students that they can learn, that all students can make a contribution to the learning process, and that all perspectives are valued.

Teachers also need to carefully think through the physical layout of their classrooms and make any changes that will facilitate easy movement for all students, particularly those who require wheelchairs or special walking devices. They need to consider scheduling and time constraints and how these might affect students with special needs—for example, the transition time between lessons may need to be extended for a student who is physically disabled. Teachers also need to consider how to manage the downtime created for the students without disabilities—highly able students will accomplish learning tasks very quickly, and thought must be given to how they can use their extra time meaningfully. Routines and procedures for such contingencies must be planned and taught to the whole class. Teachers may also be called upon to assist students with special equipment, a topic that is highlighted in this chapter's Enhancing Teaching and Learning with Technology box.

Teachers must accommodate individual differences and maintain communication with parents. They must help exceptional and regular students work and play together. Like all students, students with special needs model their teachers' intended and unintended behaviors, and they often live up to teachers' expectations, whether positive or negative. Positive, even-handed regard for exceptional students is a prerequisite for effective teaching, as are making the curriculum relevant, employing strategies known to work with students who have special needs, and using the resources of special education teachers and personnel. It is important to remember that although students with disabilities may have trouble with a variety of academic tasks, they, like any group of students, are not all alike, and their needs will vary.

Gifted and Talented Students

In addition to students who are challenged and need special help to meet regular curricular expectations, teachers will also have students in their classrooms who have exceptional abilities. **Gifted and talented** students demonstrate above-average talent in a variety of areas, including those defined by the Gifted and Talented Students Education Act passed by Congress in 1988: intellectual ability, creativity, leadership, and special talents in the visual or performing arts.

There is less support and consensus for how gifted students should be served than there is for serving students with disabilities. Several reasons account for this. Some people believe that having special classes or providing extra support for gifted students is undemocratic and elitist and that it takes scarce resources from students of lesser abilities who need them the most. This is compounded by the fact that many gifted students go unnoticed in schools (Gallagher & Gallagher, 1994; Winner, 2000). Students may hide their talents because they fear ridicule from peers or, in some

There is less consensus for how gifted students should be served than there is for serving students with disabilities.

Enhancing Teaching and Learning with Technology

Using Assistive Technology

The Individuals with Disabilities Education Act (IDEA) requires that schools provide appropriate **assistive technologies** to special education students who can benefit from them. These technologies help students with special needs learn to perform tasks associated with learning and daily living. Some assistive technologies make it possible for students with disabilities to have access to computers; others make available a wide variety of educational opportunities not previously offered. Below are a few examples from a wide array of assistive technologies currently available.*

Assistive Technologies for Students Who Are Blind or Have Low Vision

- Computer-assisted large print and Braille translations that can assist communication for students who have visual impairments. Braille translation software can convert text into correctly formatted Braille.
- Screen-magnification software that increases the size of text and graphics, similar to captioning and real-time graphic display on television, which relays the dialogue and action in television programs and movies via printed text.
- Talking calculators and calculators with extra-large displays.

Assistive Technologies for Students Who Have Trouble Communicating Effectively

- Computer speech synthesizers that can generate spoken words artificially.
- Speech-recognition software that can assist students who can speak only a few sounds to perform a variety of tasks. An individual is taught a few "token" sounds that can be responded to by a specially programmed computer. The computer recognizes the sounds and performs everyday and school-based functions, such as turning on the TV, starting a video, or accessing appropriate school curriculum on CD-ROM.
- Software that allows communication via pictures and symbols.

Assistive Technologies for Students Who Have Difficulty Accessing Communication, Learning Devices, or Regular Classroom Activities

- Keyboards that can be modified so one-handed or one-fingered typists can use them.
- Voice-recognition programs that allow students with physical disabilities to input text into a computer by speaking.

- Joysticks, foot pedals, or similar devices that allow individuals to control the computer by pointing with their chin, head, or feet.
- Computer speech synthesizers that can generate spoken words artificially.
- Computerized "gait trainers" that can help individuals with poor balance or those who lack control of their bodies learn how to walk.
- Radio-controlled devices to open doors and operate telephone answering machines.

Assistive Technologies for Students Who Are Deaf or Hearing Impaired

- Hearing aids and special communication boards.
- Closed captioning for television and video.
- Bluetooth for phone service and amplified listening devices.

Assistive Technologies for Students Who Have Learning, Behavioral, or Cognitive Disabilities

- Software programs that are engaging and provide tutoring and practice opportunities in such subjects as math and spelling.
- Software programs, such as Teachtown, that have been designed to heighten the attention span of students with autism.
- Advanced devices that react to brain signals and translate them into digital commands and actions.

A particularly interesting piece of technology has been designed for students who are sick and must be hospitalized. Through Starlight-Starbright's PC Pals, special computers and software can be made available. These services provide entertainment and educational software and Internet access so hospitalized students can keep up with their schoolwork and maintain contact with their friends.

Special Web sites have been created that are noted for their ease of use for students with disabilities. The most prominent are those developed and promoted by the Center for Applied Special Technology (CAST), an organization whose mission is to expand opportunities for people with disabilities through the use of computers and assistive technologies. CAST offers Web sites and software such as Thinking Reading, Wiggle-Works, Bobby, and Universal Design for Learning.

Because more and more students with disabilities are being included in regular classrooms, it is very likely that you will encounter students who require the use of assistive technology.

*Category scheme following one provided by the North Central Regional Educational Laboratory.

You will not be alone, however, in making decisions about the appropriate technologies to use. Schools are required to assist individuals with disabilities to identify, obtain, and learn how to use appropriate assistive devices. Schools are assisted in identifying resources through the use of assistive technology loan libraries, something that is required in every state by the Assistive Technologies Act of 2004. Assistive devices are identified during the development of a student's IEP, which is explained elsewhere in this chapter. You will be expected to work with appropriate personnel in the school to develop the IEP. Once the student is provided with an assistive device, you and others will be expected to help the student use it appropriately.

instances, because they prefer *not* to have the additional work that may come with harder challenges. Also, many gifted students, particularly those who are at risk or those who are culturally different, are often underidentified because of bias in teacher expectations.

There is also a lack of consensus among educators about who should be identified as gifted and talented. At one time, gifted students were identified primarily through traditional IQ scores. Those with scores above 125–130 were perceived to have advanced cognitive functioning and, thus, were considered "gifted." However, as you read earlier, researchers and theorists such as Sternberg (1985, 2002) and Gardner (1983, 2011) have questioned the singularity of intelligence and have proposed instead the idea of multiple intelligences, thus raising the question of whether gifted students should be identified in each of the domains of multiple intelligences.

Some aspects of giftedness are culturally defined.

Finally, giftedness is culturally defined and may take different forms in different cultures. For example, very talented athletes are not identified in most schools for "gifted and talented" classes, yet special academies have been established for them in some countries, such as India. Students who have special interpersonal skills or sensitivities are normally not identified as gifted in American schools, but these attributes are valued highly in some Native American and African cultures.

Characteristics of Gifted and Talented Students. Students who are gifted and talented can have a wide range of characteristics, particularly if we accept the concept of multiple intelligences. These include extraordinary cognitive functioning, the ability to retain lots of information, flexible thought processes, creative problem-solving skills, large vocabularies, extensive knowledge of particular subjects, advanced artistic or physical talents, excellent metacognitive skills, and high standards for performance. Turnbull and colleagues (2012) organize these characteristics into five categories to provide teachers with clues about what to watch for in identifying gifted students who may be in their classes:

- *General intellect.* Students with above-average general intellect can grasp complex and abstract concepts readily. They often have advanced vocabularies, ask lots of questions, and approach problems in unique and creative ways.
- *Specific academic ability.* Gifted students often have information and skills in particular academic subjects well in advance of their peers. They normally acquire this advanced understanding in mathematical reasoning, scientific inquiry, or writing because they are avid readers and have been reading adult materials from an early age.
- *Creative productive thinking.* Gifted students are often highly creative. This quality demonstrates itself in traits that are intuitive, insightful, curious, and flexible.

Students come up with original ideas and see relationships often missed by others. Their creativity may express itself in risk taking and sometimes in an extraordinary sense of humor.
- *Leadership ability.* Gifted individuals sometimes display advanced inter- and intra-personal skills along with the ability to motivate and lead others.
- *Visual or performing artistry.* Some gifted students have advanced visual, physical, or performing arts talents. They master physical and artistic skills quickly and well ahead of their peers. Students with certain cognitive, emotional, or physical disabilities may have very highly developed visual or performing arts skills. You know of

Home and School

Parent and Family Involvement Improve Student Learning and Success

The Individuals with Disabilities Education Act (IDEA) requires parents to help plan, implement, and make decisions about the education of their children. And, as you have read, most observers believe that the education of ELLs and other minorities who experience discontinuity between home and school are greatly enhanced by strengthening parent and family involvement.

This has led us to include a feature in *Learning to Teach* called **Home and School.** In this feature, found in most chapters, we describe how teachers can partner with parents, maintain communication, and work with them effectively. Working and involving parents is important for several reasons. One, as Rothstein-Fisch and Trumbull (2008) have observed, "families set the context of children's cognitive and social development . . . and orientation to the classroom" (p. 48). Families thus become an important source of information for understanding their children and youth. Two, involved parents and family members can become important partners in helping their children (your students) find success.

Several guidelines help teachers partner with families who have children who are disabled or who are disconnected from the school because of cultural or social-class differences. These are listed briefly below. Some will become items for more in-depth discussion in later chapters.

Communicating and Building Relationships with Parents*

- Strive to keep parents informed in a variety of ways: telephone, Web sites, newsletters, notes home.

- Use informal meetings at the bus stop or school door to build relationships and to help validate families' cultures.
- Show that you believe that families can contribute to educational decisions about their child. Avoid exerting "expert power" ("I am the teacher and I know best").
- Never adopt the attitude that a parent does not care about his or her child. Recognize that almost all parents have "dreams for their children," and that as teachers we can learn much even from parents who may be relatively uneducated.
- Seek information from parents about their child (e.g., favorite things, what he or she likes to do, etc.).

Conferencing and Meeting with Parents

- Interact in ways that make parents feel welcome in your classroom.
- Always be prepared and communicate clear purposes.
- Let parents know ahead of time about purposes and how they might prepare. Listen to their concerns.
- Keep good records of the conference.

We will expand our discussion about how to conference with parents in Chapter 14.

Finally, as beginning teachers it will be important to familiarize yourself with the cultures and backgrounds of your students and reach out to people in the community and try to understand their points of view. Talk to your students and get to know them. When students and parents observe your efforts, they will feel that you do, indeed, value their experience and respect their uniqueness.

*Today many students live in homes headed by adoptive parents. Many also live with foster parents or in living situations where a variety of childcare providers provide parental functions. We will refer to these various types of child providers sometimes as parents and sometimes as families, depending on the situation.

many examples: the musician Stevie Wonder, the artist Vincent van Gogh, and John Nash, the Nobel Prize winner in economics depicted in the award-winning movie, *A Beautiful Mind.*

Gifted and talented individuals vary widely in their emotional and social skills as they are growing up. Some are very popular, are well-balanced emotionally, and are school leaders. Other gifted individuals lack social skills and may have serious emotional problems. They may see themselves as different and may be reluctant to join with others for social events or classroom group lessons. This lack of social skills and/or emotional maturity can sometimes mask the exceptional talents some students possess—another reason many go unnoticed. Many gifted individuals do poorly in school and are not popular with their teachers, and only as adults are their talents recognized—well-known historical examples include Edison, Einstein, Mozart, and Gandhi.

Working with Gifted and Talented Students. Guidelines and programs for working with gifted and talented students vary enormously from district to district and from state to state. Some states identify large portions (as many as 10 percent) of their students as gifted, whereas other states may identify less than 1 percent. Some districts have extensive programs for students who are gifted and talented; other districts have none. Districts that have such programs normally employ three types of strategies: acceleration, enrichment, and creative explorations.

The following are some examples of these types of strategies.

- *Acceleration.* Using curriculum to allow students to advance beyond regular students, such as taking algebra early or enrolling in college classes while still in high school.
- *Enrichment.* Encouraging students to elaborate on the standard curriculum, such as performing advanced experiments in chemistry or writing a research paper in history using original sources.
- *Creative explorations.* Encouraging students to explore standard curriculum in alternative and creative ways, such as creating a multimedia presentation on a topic of interest, teaching a topic to younger students, or creating a Web site demonstrating how people in some future society will live.

On a day-to-day basis, particularly in districts or schools where special programs do not exist, it is the classroom teacher who must remain alert for students with special talents, identify these talents, and find ways to meet their special needs. Unfortunately, this doesn't always happen, as shown in the following case reported by Gardner (1983):

> People like me are aware of their so-called genius at ten, eight, nine . . . I always wondered, "Why has nobody discovered me? In school, didn't they see that I'm more clever than anybody in school? That the teachers are stupid, too? That all they had was information I didn't need?" It was obvious to me. Why didn't they put me in art school? Why didn't they train me? I was different, I was always different. Why didn't anybody notice me? (p. 115)

Regardless of districtwide programs, there are numerous strategies teachers can use to meet the needs of gifted and talented students in their own classrooms.

Differentiate Instruction for Gifted Students. Instruction or curriculum that has been modified to meet the needs of particular students is called **differentiation**

Differentiation refers to instruction that has been modified from a standard approach to meet the needs of particular students.

(Gregory & Chapman, 2002; Tomlinson, 1999, 2004; Tomlinson & Imbeau, 2010). Most often this occurs when teachers modify particular standard lessons or their curriculum to accommodate students with learning disabilities. However, differentiation is also an effective means for working with gifted and talented students. In her book on differentiated instruction, Carol Ann Tomlinson (1999) wrote that teachers need to be "aware that human beings share the same basic needs for nourishment, shelter, safety, belonging, achievement, contribution, and fulfillment":

> [They] also know that human beings find those things in different fields of endeavor, according to different timetables, and through different paths. [They] understand that by attending to human differences (they) can best help individuals address their common needs. . . . In the differentiated classroom, the teacher unconditionally accepts students as they are, and . . . expects them to become all they can be.

We will come back to the topic of differentiation in more detail in Chapter 13.

Hold Gifted Students to High Standards. All students need the teacher's help in setting standards appropriate to their needs. This is particularly true for students who have special talents. Even though these students may be capable of high performance and achievement, they will not automatically set high goals for themselves—nor, in some instances, will their peers or families. Teachers can assist these students by showing them what a truly outstanding performance is in a particular field. Teachers can encourage students to aim for an outstanding level of performance rather than be content with a level that may be seen in their peers or that will merely earn a passing grade.

Culture, Ethnicity, and Race

The United States has a rich history of cultural diversity and interaction among cultural groups. This interaction started when the first European settlers made contact with Native American populations and continued with each new wave of immigrants in the four centuries that followed. Currently, we are experiencing an increased movement of diverse groups of people into the United States, and we have become more aware and sensitive to the impact of cultural diversity for both newcomers and the groups who have been here for a long time. As can be observed in Figure 2.3, today one-third of students in public schools represent minority or nonwhite race or ethnicity. The predominant minority student populations in today's schools are African Americans and Hispanics, although Asians and children of immigrants from all over the world are present in large numbers. Diversity in culture, ethnicity, and race present instructional challenges for teachers, particularly because the racial and ethnic inequalities and issues of intolerance that persist in society are mirrored in schools and classrooms. As described earlier, accumulated evidence has shown that many minority students receive a lower-quality education as a result of differing enrollment patterns, an unequal curriculum, tracking, and differential classroom interactions with teachers. Cultural and ethnic diversity in classrooms also provides teachers with important opportunities. Every day, it presents opportunities to teach students about diversity and the importance of understanding different values and ways of doing things. It opens doors for discussion and exploration of the realities students will face in today's world.

Check, Extend, Explore

Check
- What are the main features of inclusion as defined by legislation and judicial decisions over the past half century?
- What is an IEP and what are features of the IEP process?
- What strategies can teachers use when working with students with disabilities?
- What characteristics are often observed in gifted students?
- What strategies can teachers use when working with gifted and talented students?

Extend
- What are your views about placing children with learning disabilities in regular classrooms?
- Do you think scarce resources should be used on students who are gifted and talented? Go to "Extend Question Poll" on the Online Learning Center to respond.

Explore
- Go to the Online Learning Center and listen to Diane Caruso in the Teachers on Teaching area discuss students with disabilities in her classrooms. Search the Internet for Web sites related to special education or gifted education.

Culture refers to the way members of groups think about social action and problem resolution. **Ethnicity** refers to groups that have a common heritage. **Race** refers to groups that have common biological traits.

Figure 2.3 *Percentage Distribution of Public School Students Enrolled in Prekindergarten through Twelfth Grade, by Race/Ethnicity: Selected Years, October 1972–October 2010*

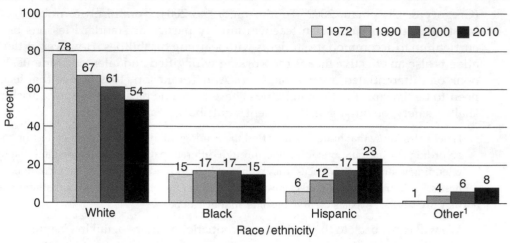

[1]*Other* includes all students who identified themselves as being Asian, Native Hawaiian, Alaska Native, Pacific Islander, American Indian, or two or more races.

Sources: U.S. Department of Commerce, Census Bureau, Current Population Survey (CPS), October Supplement, 1990, 2000, and 2010; and as reported in *The Condition of Education* 2010 and 2012.

Perspectives on Culture, Ethnicity, and Race

Although culture, ethnicity, and race are treated together in this section, it is important to point out that these terms do not mean the same thing. **Culture,** as used here, is a term that describes a group's total way of life—its histories, traditions, attitudes, and values. "Culture" is how members of a group think and the ways they go about resolving problems in collective life. Culture is learned and is ever changing; it is not static. In the United States, we belong to all kinds of groups that have distinctive cultures—racial, ethnic, religious, social class. Organizations, such as schools and businesses, also have cultures. Cultures are not groups; they are created by groups.

Ethnicity, in contrast, refers to groups that have common language and identities such as nationality. Individuals of Polish, Irish, or Italian descent, for instance, may be classified as ethnic groups even though they are a subset of a larger Western European culture. **Race** is a term reserved for groups that have common biological traits. We all belong to many different groups and are influenced by many different cultures, as illustrated in Figure 2.4. We are influenced the most by those groups with which we have the closest identification. It is important to point out that all three of these terms are socially constructed and their use can sometimes be controversial.

Figure 2.4 *Multigroup Membership in the United States*

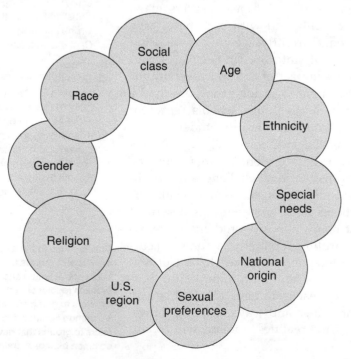

Melting Pot or Salad Bowl? The United States has always been a land of immigrants. It is likely that many of your parents or grandparents came to the United States in the late nineteenth or early twentieth centuries. Immigration from many countries continues today, and indeed some of you may be new to the United States. At one time the

melting pot was the metaphor often used to describe this blending process. Today, however, many prefer the concept of **cultural pluralism,** a perspective that acknowledges the existence of a dominant American culture but also recognizes the permanence of diversity. This view normally purports that each cultural, racial, or ethnic group will accept some of the common elements of the dominant culture as it interacts with that culture, but will also inject into the culture new elements for the benefit of all. Thus, the "melting pot" metaphor, with its implications of homogeneity, has been replaced with the "salad bowl" metaphor, in which each ingredient is distinct and valued by itself, while at the same time contributing to the whole and binding to others with a common dressing—that is, the dominant culture.

> **Today we prefer the "salad bowl" metaphor to think about cultural pluralism, a situation wherein each ingredient is valued for itself but also binds with others to make something different.**

Cultural Deficits versus Cultural Differences. For a long time, students who did not become fully blended or assimilated were often considered to be culturally disadvantaged. Differences in achievement between minority and majority students were accounted for by the **cultural deficit theory.** Various deficit theories have been posited. Minorities were said to be genetically deficient in intelligence or they had some other inherent defect (dysfunctional family, poor nutrition) that interfered with their ability to be successful in school. For example, Harvard psychologist Arthur Jensen (1969) argued that children who came from poor families were intellectually inferior. A quarter of a century later, Herrnstein and Murray (1994) wrote *The Bell Curve: Intelligence and Class Structure in American Life,* a book that argued that African Americans inherited lower IQs than whites.

For the most part, these theories have been discredited, partly because of analyses done by a variety of scholars over the past decade. For example, Gould (1996), in *The Mismeasure of Man,* points out the statistical flaws in IQ testing. Jerome Bruner, in *Acts of Meaning* (1990) and *The Culture of Education* (1996), has shown how learning is social and cultural and how intelligence grows as people interact with one another in society. As described in the previous section, Robert Sternberg and Howard Gardner have provided important perspectives on how individuals, regardless of race or culture, possess many different abilities rather than the one or two measured by the more traditional aptitude tests.

Also in the 1990s, Villegas (1991) elaborated on what he labeled the **cultural difference theory** to account for the achievement difficulties experienced by minority students in schools. He maintained that language is the vehicle for interaction in school, and if language is used by a subculture in ways different from the mainstream, then members of the subculture are at a disadvantage. Villegas explained:

> **Cultural difference theory holds that low achievement of minorities is explained by the discontinuity between home culture and school culture and not by some cultural defect.**

> Children whose language use at home corresponds to what is expected in the classroom have an advantage in the learning process. For these students, prior experience transfers to the classroom and facilitates their academic performance. In contrast, minority children frequently experience discontinuity in the use of language at home and at school. They are often misunderstood when applying prior knowledge to classroom tasks. (p. 7)

Using the cultural differences perspective rather than cultural deficits has led policymakers and educators to consider that the problem of student failure has not been the fault of minority students or their families, but rather disjunctures between home and school and the negative relationships between school and society. From this perspective, solutions will require finding more culturally sensitive political links among the school, its communities, and the larger society.

> **Cultural discontinuity exists when the values and beliefs of one culture call for a different set of behaviors than another culture calls for.**

Cultural Discontinuity. Teachers and their students often occupy different cultures, each with unique beliefs and values and different ways of communicating. This leads to **discontinuity** and miscommunication between the home and the school. For example, forty years ago Phillips (1972) studied how Native American children learned at home and compared it to the way they were expected to learn in school. She observed that these children were silent in classroom lessons, sometimes even when asked a direct question by the teacher. Most Americans would assume that these children were extremely shy or that they had learning or linguistic disabilities—in the latter case, referring them to low-ability or special classes would make sense. However, Native American children are expected to learn by watching adults, not by interacting with them. Their culture instructs them to turn to older siblings, not adults, when they need assistance; and they are accustomed to a great deal more self-determination at home than is permissible in the school environment. In light of this information, their classroom behavior can be properly interpreted as an example of cross-cultural discontinuity rather than a deficiency.

Another example of cultural discontinuity and miscommunication comes from a landmark study by Heath (1983), who documented the diverging communicative styles of working-class African Americans, middle-class African Americans, and Euro-Americans in the Piedmont region of the Carolinas. One of the many cultural differences she found involved the use of questions. At home, working-class African American adults didn't ask children very many questions, and when they did, they were *real* questions—really seeking information that the adult didn't have. In school, however, teachers expected children to answer questions all the time, and the questions themselves were artificial in that the adults already knew the answer. From the students' perspective, these questions didn't make any sense at all, and there was difficulty bridging the cultural gap.

These results have been replicated many times over the past decade.

Working with Students in Racially and Culturally Diverse Classrooms

Beginning teachers worry a lot about what they can do in the classroom to work effectively with a culturally diverse group of students. Fortunately, numerous strategies are available for developing classrooms that respond to the needs of students, regardless of their racial or ethnic backgrounds. Beginning teachers are encouraged to work first on their own knowledge and attitudes and to battle biases, stereotypes, and myths they may hold. Equally important, teachers need to make sure their curriculum is fair and culturally relevant and that they are using teaching strategies known to be effective and culturally responsive.

> Perhaps the most important thing teachers do to work successfully with minority children is to have deep cultural understandings and sensitivities.

Developing Cultural Competence. The first step teachers can take to prepare to work in culturally diverse classrooms is to develop an awareness of their own culture and understanding, sensitivity, and respect for the cultures represented in their classroom. Some multicultural experts (Sue & Sue, 2007) refer to this as acquiring **cultural competence.** They write that a culturally competent professional is one who:

- is in the process of becoming aware of his or her own assumptions about human behavior, values, biases, preconceived notions, and personal limitations.
- actively attempts to understand the worldview of culturally diverse populations.
- is in the process of actively developing and practicing appropriate, relevant, and sensitive skills in working with culturally diverse students, families, communities, and colleagues (cited in *Equity and Race Relations: What Is Cultural Competence?* 2010).

Cultural competence is important because, as observed by Ritchhart (2002), beginning teachers are often startled by some of their unconscious beliefs and misconceptions about students who come from cultures different from their own and about the capacity of these students to learn.

Hawley and Nieto (2010) have observed that an important first step is to examine some of the beliefs we hold. These beliefs, although they may seem sensible, can actually be unproductive and serve to undermine students' opportunities to learn. Here are some examples of unproductive beliefs and alternatives paraphrased from Hawley and Neito (p. 68):

- *Belief:* To ensure fairness, teachers should be color-blind and ignore racial differences.
- *Alternative:* Teachers need to recognize, respect, and build on differences.
- *Belief:* Teachers can enhance students' self-esteem by reducing rigor.
- *Alternative:* Teachers should hold high expectations and provide needed support to all students.
- *Belief:* Teaching should be adapted to students' learning styles.
- *Alternative:* Teachers should recognize that although students learn in different ways and differentiation is important, differences exist among all students, not just minorities.
- *Belief:* Teachers assume that students must have good basic skills before they can engage in more complex activity.
- *Alternative:* Teachers recognize that all students can explore complex ideas and materials as they learn basic skills.

Cultural competence also means coming to understand what schools and classrooms look like to members of a minority culture. A Navajo woman described her first school experience:

> Well, my first deal is just getting to school. Just when you live all Navajo culture and you first start school and first see the brick buildings, you don't know what's inside them buildings. Especially when you've only been to trading post twice in your life before school. It's when you get there you see these long lines of kids with their mamas. All the kids throwing fits and cryin, hangin onto their mom. And your mom's standin there beside you sayin, "You can't be like them. You can't cry cause you're big girl now. You gotta go to school. Don't, don't shame me at the beginning. You gotta make me proud" . . .
>
> So she took all of us to school, and she dropped me off there. . . . The ceilings were so high, and the rooms so big and empty. It was so cold. There was no warmth. Not as far as "brrr I'm cold," but in a sense of emotional cold. Kind of an emptiness, when you're hanging onto your mom's skirt and tryin so hard not to cry. And you know it just seems so lonely and so empty. Then when you get up to your turn, she thumbprints the paper and she leaves and you watch her go out the big, metal doors. The whole thing was a cold experience. The doors were metal and they even had this big window, wires running through it. And these women didn't smile or nothin. You watch your mama go down the sidewalk, actually it's the first time I seen a sidewalk, and you see her get in the truck, walk down the sidewalks. You see her get in the truck and the truck starts moving and all the home smell goes with it. You see it all leaving. (McLaughlin, 1996, pp. 13–14)

An educational anthropologist's description of elementary classrooms in Mexico can provide insights into the culture of many Hispanic students:

> Characteristic of instruction in the *Primaria* was its oral, group interactive quality. . . .
> Students talk throughout the class period; teachers are always available to repeat, explain,

and motivate; silent seat work is rare; and often a crescendo of sound . . . is indicative of instructional activity. The following observation of a first-grade classroom illustrates this pattern of verbal and physical activity:

> As she instructs children to glue sheets of paper in their books and write several consonant-vowel pairs, the teacher sometimes shouts her directions to compete with the clamor of kids asking for glue, repeating instructions to each other, sharing small toys, sharpening pencils, asking to go to the bathroom, etc. This activity and "noise" is compounded by the large number in the classroom, 35, but things somehow seem to get done by some, if not all, students. Then teacher has the children recite the word pairs taped to the chalkboard. They shout these out loudly as a group as she points to each combination with an old broken broom handle. Sometimes she calls out the pairs in order; other times, out of order to check their attention. Then she calls individual children to the board, gives them the stick, they choose a pair of sounds, but then have to pronounce them loudly and quickly as she presses them for correct responses. (Macias, 1990, p. 304)

Teachers need to be sensitive to the basis of cultural differences and how they can affect a student's classroom behavior.

There are a number of areas of cultural difference that seem to consistently cause trouble. Beginning teachers need to be alert to these. Cultures differ, for instance, in their attitudes toward work and the appropriate balance between being on task and socializing. Middle-class American culture tends to be very task-oriented, but many other cultures give more attention to social interaction. Cultures also vary in their sense of time. For many Americans, punctuality is an unquestioned virtue, and children in school are penalized for tardiness, turning work in late, and so on. But in many non-Western cultures, people are more relaxed about time—they do not regard punctuality as particularly sacred and do not pay strict attention to deadlines. The amount of physical space deemed proper between people who are conversing and norms about making eye contact are other key areas of difference.

Another area of possible misunderstanding is the relative weight put on the needs of the group versus the needs of the individual. American culture is very oriented to the individual, whereas Japanese and some Native American and Hispanic cultures place more emphasis on the group. Many Native American children, for example, do not want to be singled out for praise and attention—a situation that can be very disconcerting to their teachers.

Cultures also differ in their attributions, or judgments, about the causes of behavior. A polite smile that conveys friendliness in one culture may constitute a cold rebuff in another. Giving a friend academic assistance can mean helpfulness to one person and cheating to another. Erroneous attributions can obviously hinder the development of rapport among people of different cultures.

Finally, people of different cultures categorize and differentiate information differently—that is, they chunk information, combining and separating bits, in a variety of ways. A simple example comes from language comparisons. In English, there are the separate verbs *to like* and *to love,* while in French, one word, *aimer,* means both, and in Italian, no verb meaning *to like* exists. Speakers of these different languages categorize and differentiate experiences differently. It is easy to imagine the difficulties in communicating clearly when the interacting parties, even though both may be speaking English, are relying on such divergent conceptions.

Reaching out to parents and others in the school's communuity is an important avenue for understanding students and their cultural differences.

With so many areas of divergence, it is easy to see how students and teachers from different cultures could come into conflict and have misunderstandings. Simply being aware of these potential sources of misunderstanding will reduce the risk that miscommunication will occur.

Creating a Culturally Relevant Curriculum. In addition to attending to their own understandings and sensitivities, beginning teachers need to be prepared to make curriculum decisions that will help their classrooms be culturally relevant and multicultural. It is beyond the scope of this book on teaching strategies to go into depth about cultural relevancy and multicultural education. However, in general, **multicultural education** is defined as curriculum and pedagogical approaches that teach students to *respect and value diversity.*

Multicultural education has a wide variety of meanings and approaches. The approaches below are summarized from Banks (1993, 2007) and Grant and Sleeter (2011). James Banks offers a perspective that includes several approaches:

- The *contribution* approach consists of devoting lessons to the heroes of various cultures; celebrating holidays of various cultures; and recognizing the art, music, literature, cuisine, and language of different cultures.
- The *ethnic* or *single group* approach sets aside lessons or units on specific groups or cultures or brings in literature or books that convey different cultural perspectives. Although these can be very worthwhile educational activities, both the contribution and additive approaches have limitations. They emphasize differences between groups, not similarities, and they may have the undesired side effect of widening cultural gaps rather than bringing cultures closer together.
- A third approach is called *transformational.* When teachers use this approach, they strive to transform the curriculum by incorporating a series of concepts associated with cultural pluralism into ongoing lessons. With this approach, teachers identify important concepts (for example, pluralism, interdependence, or communication) appropriate to a particular subject or grade level and then use those concepts as the basis for lessons to promote understanding of cultural diversity.
- A final approach defined by Banks is the *social action* approach, which encourages students not only to examine problems associated with diversity, but also to pursue projects that hold potential for taking action and promoting social justice.

No matter which approach is used, teachers need to review their curricular decisions to ensure that they demonstrate to their students they are valued people and that they provide a complex curriculum—one that is challenging and culturally relevant to students. A **culturally relevant curriculum** (Gay, 2010; Howard, 2003) includes everyone and provides the voices of diverse people, particularly those who have been traditionally left out. For young black or Latino students, a curriculum lacking black or brown faces, traditions, literature, or music tells them that they don't count; it gives students from other groups the same message. Culturally relevant curricula, on the other hand, convey both value and challenge. They are often thematic, integrating subject areas from diverse traditions and, most important, they arise out of students' own questions and experiences.

A final aspect of creating a culturally relevant and multicultural curriculum is to ensure that the curriculum is free of bias. Much of a school's curriculum is communicated through textbooks and other print materials. Researchers have identified curricular bias in many of the materials traditionally used in classrooms. Although progress has been made in eliminating bias over the past three decades, teachers nonetheless need to be on the lookout and ensure that the materials they use are free of bias and stereotyping.

Using Culturally Relevant Pedagogies. The heart of working with cultural diversity is the teacher's ability to *connect the world of his or her students and their cultures to*

It is important for teachers to connect to the world of their students' culture.

Check, Extend, Explore

Check
- Contrast the meanings of the terms *culture*, *ethnicity*, and *race*.
- How do the "melting pot" and "cultural pluralism" perspectives differ?
- Contrast the theory of cultural deficits with the cultural differences and assets theory.
- Describe actions teachers can take to develop cultural understandings of the students in their classrooms.
- Why is it important for teachers to be culturally competent and to use culturally relevant pedagogies?

Extend
- What are your own personal views about the cultural deficit as contrasted to the cultural difference theory?
- Some have argued that teachers and students must be of the same race to work effectively together. Do you agree or disagree with this view? Go to the "Extend Question Poll" on the Online Learning Center to respond.

Explore
- Go to the Online Learning Center at www.mhhe.com/arends10e and listen to Jennifer Patterson in the Teachers on Teaching area discuss cultural diversity in her classroom. Search the Internet for Web sites related to cultural diversity and multicultural education or read a review of *The Dreamkeepers*.

the world of the school and the classroom. It is finding ways to embed the culture of the student into every lesson and every act. The strategies described in Part 2 of *Learning to Teach* form the basis for teaching in culturally diverse classrooms. For example, direct instruction has been used widely and found effective for teaching basic skills to students with special needs. Cooperative learning has been shown to be effective in all kinds of urban classrooms with diverse student populations and in changing the attitudes of students of different cultures positively toward their peers. Therefore, attention here is on instructional strategies that are aimed particularly at culturally diverse classrooms. The discussion draws heavily on the work of Gloria Ladson-Billings (1995a, 1995b, 2009), Lisa Delpit (1995), Geneva Gay (2010), and Jeannie Oakes and Martin Lipton (2006). All of these educators have argued for a curriculum and a pedagogy that is culturally relevant and committed to social justice. This chapter's Research Summary, *The Dreamkeepers*, is a very important study conducted by Gloria Ladson-Billings, and it speaks directly to what teachers do to make their curriculum and instruction culturally relevant.

Making Connections to Prior Knowledge. Teachers can anchor instruction in students' prior knowledge and help them construct links between what they know and what they are to learn. By doing this, teachers help students see commonalities and differences among cultures and assist students in developing multicultural awareness. To do this effectively, though, teachers must actively seek out information about students' prior knowledge. They must spend time understanding their students' cultures and sizing up what they know and what they don't know.

Using Flexible Grouping. When teachers group students for instructional purposes, they can lean heavily on heterogeneous grouping and minimize ability grouping. The deleterious effects of tracking and the poor-quality instruction generally found in lower-ability groups and classes are well documented (see Oakes, 1985; Oakes & Lipton, 2006). Membership in ability groups should be flexible; group composition should change as students progress or as new and different needs are identified. Much more will be said about the appropriate use of grouping in Chapter 13.

Differentiating Instruction and Attending to Learner Differences. Teachers can differentiate curriculum and learning activities that mesh with a variety of learning differences. As described earlier, teachers can vary their instruction along several dimensions. One route is to incorporate visual, auditory, tactile, and kinesthetic modalities into lessons. Teachers can also apply cooperative as well as individualistic task-and-reward structures. Further, teachers can vary their lessons by making them more or less concrete or abstract and more or less formal or informal and by emphasizing in-context as well as out-of-context learning.

Several theorists, including Irvine and York (1995), Dilworth and Brown (2004), and Mayer (2011), have argued that certain kinds of students display preferences in the way they learn. Examples include:

- Response to things in whole rather than in parts
- Preference for visual rather than verbal instruction
- Preference for group learning situations
- Preference to learn privately rather than in public

However, it is important to point out again that there is a great deal of variation in regard to learning preferences within any group and that styles and preferences can be

Research Summary

How Do Successful Teachers Work with African American Children?

Ladson-Billings, G. (1994, 2009). The dreamkeepers: Successful teachers of African American children (1st and 2nd eds.). San Francisco: Jossey-Bass.

Of the many challenges facing education, none has been more difficult than improving the academic achievement of African American students. Everyone seems to agree that success requires "culturally relevant teaching." However, there has been a paucity of research-based knowledge about what this entails. Gloria Ladson-Billings's study, highlighted here, went a long way in helping us understand culturally relevant teaching practices. Ladson-Billings's work is interesting for two reasons: for the insights it provides and for the research methods she used. *The Dreamkeepers* represents a very nice piece of qualitative research that breaks with a scholarly convention: *objectivity*. In addition to her study of successful teachers of African American children, Ladson-Billings takes the liberty as a researcher to write and provide insights into the problem gleaned from her own life experiences and her memories of being an African American student.

Problem and Approach: The purpose of Ladson-Billings's study was to describe the practices of "highly effective teachers of African American students." The study was based on three premises: (1) effective teachers are capable of describing their practice, contrary to the belief held by some that they operate intuitively; (2) African American students and their parents act rationally and normatively; and (3) it was OK for the researcher (Ladson-Billings) to insert her own beliefs and experiences into the research process.

Methods: This was an ethnographic study with four components: teacher selection, teacher interviews, classroom observations and videotaping, and collective interpretation and analysis.

Teacher Selection: The teachers who participated in the study were selected through a "nomination" process. Community members were asked to nominate teachers they believed worked effectively with their children. Seventeen teachers were nominated. To cross-check community members' perceptions, Ladson-Billings consulted with several elementary school principals and teachers. They were asked the same question: "Who works effectively with African American students?" The principals and teachers identified twenty-two individuals. Nine teachers who were nominated by both groups were selected to participate in the study; one declined to participate. Of the eight teachers in the final study, five were African American and three were white. All were experienced, ranging from twelve to forty years in the classroom.

Interviews: Ladson-Billings interviewed each teacher with a set of predetermined questions. She reported, however, that she allowed teachers to converse freely about their concerns and their teaching practices. Interviews were taped and transcribed.

Classroom Observations and Videotaping: Over a two-year period, Ladson-Billings visited and observed the teachers' classrooms for ninety minutes to two hours once a week. She reported that she visited each classroom over thirty times. She audiotaped and wrote notes during the visits. During some visits, she also functioned as a participant-observer—in addition to observing the class, Ladson-Billings also participated as a tutor, a teacher's aide, and sometimes as a member of a student group. Many ethnographers like to engage in this type of participation because it helps them build rapport with the people they are studying and they learn things they seldom learn in an observer-only role. During the end of the first year, each teacher was videotaped.

Collective Interpretation and Analysis: Ladson-Billings met with the eight teachers and worked collectively with them to analyze and interpret their interview data and the audio- and video-tapes collected in their classrooms. Together, they developed their model of "culturally relevant teaching practices." Involving participants this way is also quite unique in educational research.

Results: An abbreviated description of the results of Ladson-Billings's study cannot do justice to the rich ethnographic data described in the full study. If you are interested, you should obtain *Dreamkeepers* and read the whole book.

However, following are some of the main ideas and conclusions reached by Ladson-Billings and her eight teachers. These conclusions are broken down into the four categories found in the study, which later became chapter titles for her book.

1. *"Seeing Color, Seeing Culture."* The successful teachers in Ladson-Billings's study rejected the "equity of sameness." They *saw and valued* their students' racial and ethnic differences. They loved their work and saw themselves as part of the community. These teachers helped students see themselves as members of the community, but also helped them make connections to larger national and global communities. They believed strongly that all students can *succeed.*

2. *Developing "We Are Family."* The successful teachers in Ladson-Billings's culturally responsive classrooms encouraged a *community of learners.* They made deep and flexible connections with each of their students and cultivated relationships beyond the boundaries of the classroom. They encouraged students to learn cooperatively and to teach and take responsibility for each other's learning.

3. *Having Passion for Knowledge.* The successful teachers held a constructivist view about knowledge and the curriculum—a view that knowledge is not static but instead is continuously evolving and changing. Teachers were *passionate* about their content, but also viewed excellence as a complex standard in which student differences were taken into account. These teachers spent lots of time helping students develop learning skills and building *scaffolds* for bridging the curriculum of the school and the knowledge students brought with them from home.

4. *Focusing on Literacy and Numeracy.* The teachers in Ladson-Billings's study had strong literacy and math programs. These programs did not use the more traditional "drill-and-practice" approaches, but instead emphasized communal activities and ways to make learning to read, write, and compute meaningful for African American students. Students were apprenticed in the community, and their real-life experiences were "legitimized" as part of the officialcurriculum. Students in these classrooms were treated as competent and were moved from "what they know" to what they need to know.

Discussion and Implications Ladson-Billings's study tells the story of eight teachers who were successful in one of the most difficult challenges in education: improving the academic achievement of African American students. It has a happy ending. Teachers who engage in culturally responsive practices—recognizing and valuing the racial and ethnic backgrounds of their students, creating vibrant learning communities characterized by mutual respect and collaboration, and having a passion for knowledge—can produce great results. The significant question that stems from this study is "How do we get all teachers who work with African American students (and all students, for that matter) to use the practices found to be so successful in the classrooms of the eight teachers in Ladson-Billings's study?"

Your Reflections Which of the findings from Ladson-Billings's study are congruent with beliefs you already hold? Which are new or incongruent? Do you think it is possible to get all teachers to teach the way the teachers in Ladson-Billings's study taught? Why or why not?

learned and unlearned. When preferences such as those listed above are discovered, it is important to not let them become reasons for stereotyping students.

Employing Strategy Instruction. Strategy instruction is an instructional element that should be an important part of teaching. One of the characteristics that distinguishes good learners from poor learners is their ability to use a variety of **learning strategies** to read and write, to solve problems involving numbers, and to learn successfully. When teachers help at-risk students acquire the strategies they need to learn effectively, they give them the tools for school success. Many programs are available to support teachers in this goal. Palincsar (1986) and Palincsar and Brown (1989) have documented the effectiveness of reciprocal teaching—an approach to reading instruction used in both elementary and secondary classrooms in which peer teaching is used to help students master basic reading skills and become better strategic readers. More about strategy instruction will be provided in later chapters.

Religious Diversity

As with their cultural and ethnic backgrounds, students also come to schools, as they should in a free society, with a variety of religious beliefs ranging from atheism to deep and observant faith. These beliefs are not left at the schoolhouse door. Religious groups in the United States once consisted mainly of members of the various Protestant denominations, Catholics, and Jews—all with beliefs within the larger Judeo-Christian tradition. Major issues were characterized by conflicts over separation of church and state and the teaching of "evolution" in science classes. Today, however, most communities include members of a growing number of religions that were unfamiliar to most Americans a few years ago, including Islam, Buddhism, and other faiths from Asia and the Middle East. Conservatives and fundamentalists from all religions are also more prevalent today, as are members of several New Age religions.

The Constitution regulates the place of religion in schools, although interpretations of what separation of church and state means remain controversial. For instance, in 2005 the Supreme Court issued split decisions on whether the Ten Commandments could be posted on courthouse lawns or school properties. The role of religious holidays in schools is also often contentious. Most schools today do not have Christmas pageants or Christmas and Easter vacations. Instead, they celebrate winter or spring and release students for holiday breaks. Issues have arisen about whether or not students can hold prayer or devotional meetings on school property during the lunch hour or after school. Finally, religious differences can erupt in serious conflict and violence as they did in a Jersey City high school where age-old strife among Muslims and Christians of Egyptian descent surfaced, and students fought one another in reaction to the killing of four community members allegedly because of their religious affiliation.

Larger policies about the role of religion in particular schools are beyond the influence of a single teacher. However, teachers can make their voices heard and help focus policy debates. Haynes (2013), for instance, has pointed out that too often schools have failed to come up with effective policies. They have gone from one extreme of having practices that favor only one religion (Christianity) to the other extreme of making schools entirely free of all religion. A successful policy, according to Haynes (2013), would be one where schools recognize and treat all religions with fairness and respect, teach about religions, and make sure that students from minority religions are not marginalized.

It is in pursuing the goals associated with this set of policies that teachers can play the largest role. Teachers can help students gain what Kunzman (2012) has labeled "fluency" in talking about religion and its role in society. They can teach and discuss the ideas, beliefs, and traditions of various religions in fair and intellectually honest ways. They can model respect by:

- having students consider how understanding the beliefs of others does not mean endorsement of their ideas.
- accepting student absences for observing their own particular religious holidays and by stopping ridicule by students who hold different beliefs.
- not debating the truth about particular religious beliefs but instead discussing how particular beliefs affect individuals and public life.

Finally, teachers can find ways to bring students of different faiths together, as Beauchamp (2013) did by using videoconferencing to connect students from around the world to discuss their religious traditions.

Language Diversity

As described in Chapter 1, language diversity represents one of the significant shifts in the demographics of schools. In 2009–2010, an estimated 4.7 million students were English language learners. This represents approximately 10 percent of the public school enrollment, ranging from highs in urban areas of 18 percent to 4 percent in rural areas. In New York City, at least half of the students have one foreign-born parent. More than 400 languages are spoken in the United States. A large proportion (80 % of ELLs) speak Spanish. However, the influx of immigrants in recent years has added many other languages. In addition to English and Spanish, the most frequently spoken languages in the United States are French, German, Italian, Russian, and several Asian languages (*The Condition of Education,* 2012).

Students for whom English is a second language are referred to as **English language learners (ELLs).** On almost all measures of academic achievement they lag well behind their English-speaking peers. Because language is such a big factor in student learning, it is important to develop effective ways to work with students who do not have standard English as their first language.

Second-Language Acquisition

How do ELLs approach the problem of learning English? It is not an easy task, as you know if you have ever tried to learn a foreign language. Communicative competence in any language consists of more than simply knowing its phonology (pronunciation), morphology (word formation), syntax (grammar), and lexicon (vocabulary). The speaker also must understand how to organize speech beyond the level of single sentences; know how to make and interpret appropriate gestures and facial expressions; understand the norms surrounding use of the language in accordance with roles, social status, and in different situations; and, finally, know how to use the language to acquire academic knowledge.

In first-language learning, these abilities are acquired over an extended period of time and in meaningful social interaction with others. It is estimated that non-English speakers require two years to attain basic communication skills but need five to seven years to develop academic language proficiency. Children can get along on the playground and in social situations very readily, but they need much more time to become skillful in learning academic content in the medium of English. It appears that the task of learning a second language is a creative one. Second-language learners do not passively soak up a new language—they must listen attentively, rely on social and other context cues to help them make guesses about how to use the language, test out their guesses, and revise accordingly. Regardless of what some policymakers say, *all of this takes time.*

Working with Language Diversity in the Classroom

The submersion approach is the practice of placing LEP students in regular classrooms and expecting them to pick up English on their own.

Schools are legally required to assist English language learners. Bilingual education, as it is sometimes called, gained support when Congress passed the Bilingual Education Act in 1972. Instruction for language-different students gained further ground as a result of the 1974 Supreme Court ruling in *Lau v. Nichols,* a class action suit brought by Chinese students in San Francisco against the school district. The Court reasoned that instruction presented in a language students could not understand amounted to denying them equal access to the educational system. The district's practice, common to many districts, had been simply to place ELL students in regular classrooms with native speakers. This **submersion approach,** allowing language-minority students to sink or swim on their own, is no longer permissible.

Schools have responded to the *Lau v. Nichols* mandate plus an array of laws and other court actions in a variety of ways. One approach has been to provide ESL instruction in pullout programs that place ESL students in regular classrooms for most of the day but in separate classes in English instruction for part of the day. Another approach has been to provide a **transitional bilingual program** for English language learners. In these programs, instruction is initially provided in the native language, with gradual increases in English usage until the student is proficient. **Full bilingual programs,** in which the goal is full oral proficiency and literacy in both languages, have been used in some places, but these remain fairly rare.

The whole topic of how best to educate ELLs has been very controversial, and student learning often has taken a back seat to political pressures. Many citizens and policymakers have been against bilingual programs because they believe that this approach hinders children's progress in learning English. Some states have passed legislation restricting bilingual programs and the use of students' native languages in schools, replacing them with programs that emphasize English and provide less transition time.

When politics can be set aside, however, there is actually a pretty good knowledge base that can provide guidelines for best practices to use with English language learners. The following current best practices are summarized from a variety of sources (Goldenberg, 2008; Lessow-Hurley, 2003; Rolstad, Mahoney, & Glass, 2005):

- *Program effectiveness:* Bilingual education has been shown consistently to be more effective as compared to the all-English approaches. Bilingual programs enhance academic effectiveness, and teaching students to read in their first language promotes higher levels of reading achievement in English.
- *Curriculum and instruction:* Goldenberg (2008) has observed that what we know about "good instruction and curriculum in general holds true for English language learners" (p. 8). Much of what we know has been summarized in *Learning to Teach.* Several things, however, stand out for ELLs. Like non-ELLs, English language learners benefit from clear goals and learning objectives; challenging and motivating materials; and active involvement and engagement and structured lessons with opportunities for guided and independent practice followed by specific, meaningful, and frequent feedback.
- *Modification and support for ELLs:* As described in previous sections on working with students with special needs, instructing English language learners requires modifying instruction to meet the special needs of language limitations. Appropriate modifications include using materials with content that is familiar to students; spending additional time helping ELLs build vocabulary; making English comprehensible by keeping the learners' needs in mind; providing structures and scaffolds to link new materials to prior knowledge; and using students' first language when appropriate.
- *Community and family understanding and support:* Recommendations provided earlier in regard to working with racially and culturally different students holds true for ELLs. It is important for teachers to become familiar with the students' communities and language patterns and to incorporate these patterns when appropriate. It is equally important to know the families of ELLs and help them celebrate their first language by using it when appropriate.

Check, Extend, Explore

Check

- What types of language diversity are teachers likely to find in their classrooms?
- Why is it critical that teachers be supportive of language differences?
- How do children approach the problem of learning English if it is not their native language?
- Contrast transitional bilingual programs with full bilingual programs.

Extend

- In some states, legislation has been passed that limits how much instruction can be provided to students in their native language. What do you think of this type of legislation?
- Suppose that all of the students in a school in Los Angeles spoke Spanish as their first language. Should the school provide all instruction in Spanish? Go to "Extend Question Poll" on the Online Learning Center to respond.

Explore

- Search the Internet for Web sites related to language diversity and English language learners.
- Go to the National Center for Education Statistics' Web site for current data on the number and type of English language learners found in schools in your region.

Dialect Differences

In addition to many major languages, the United States also enjoys a rich diversity of dialects. Black English, or **Ebonics;** Hawaiian Creole; and Spanglish are a few of the major indigenous dialects. In the past, these and other dialects often were considered "substandard" languages and their use was cited as a reason for children's poor academic performance (another manifestation of the cultural deficit theory). The school's remedy was to attempt to eliminate the use of the home dialect. This approach has not worked very well; children do not improve academically when their language is suppressed or when the language of their family is degraded.

The issue of the use of dialects in schools can become politically charged, as evidenced when a few years ago the Oakland, California, school board made Ebonics an accepted language of instruction. The board later rescinded this policy and then introduced it again, but only after considerable debate and cultural warfare. The important thing for teachers to remember is to be sensitive and not to make negative judgments about students' abilities based on their use of particular dialects. Teachers should not assume that students whose language is different from standard English lack the intellectual capital to be academically successful. One teacher chose to deal with the language her students brought with them to school in the following way:

> I vowed never to deliberately silence my students' voices. This vow is not easy to keep; it is something I struggle with daily. I am committed to creating a safe environment within my classroom, where my students feel comfortable expressing themselves regardless of the language that they bring with them, be it Ebonics, Spanglish, or other English dialects. But, to facilitate my students' acquisition of mainstream English, all of their assignments must be written in "standard" English. The majority of the time, I communicate with my students using standard English, but I feel that it is also necessary to model code switching in the classroom. I validate my students' primary language, but I do not feel the need to teach it. They come to class equipped with this language. (Oakes & Lipton, 2006, p. 27)

Gender Differences

Gender represents another set of differences found in diverse classrooms. Traditionally, concerns about gender focused on **gender bias** against girls, how boys and girls are socialized, differences between boys and girls in verbal and mathematical abilities, and whether these differences are the result of nature or differential treatment. However, within the last decade concerns have shifted to boys and how they may be lagging behind in their verbal skills and college attendance as a result of what happens to them in school.

Nature of Gender Differences

One important question for teachers and many others in society has been how do boys and girls, men and women, differ? This question has been thoroughly investigated over a long period of time, and though disagreements exist, some general results have emerged. According to Halpern and LaMay (2000), most studies have *not* found major, inherent differences between boys and girls in general cognitive abilities. In a persuasive meta-analysis (a technique for synthesizing and summarizing results from many individual studies), Linn and Hyde (1989) concluded that differences between boys and girls "were always small, that they have declined in the last two decades, that differences arise in some contexts and situations but not in others, and that educational programs can influence when differences arise" (p. 17). In the past, some researchers, such as Pollard (1998) and Gurian (2002), proposed that the brains of boys and girls differed. However, Eliot (2010), a neuroscientist, has concluded that the "neurosciences have identified very few differences between boys and girls' brains" (p. 32) and that in the three areas of performance that were identified the differences were actually very small:

- Baby boys are modestly more physically active than girls.
- Toddler girls talk, on average, one month earlier than boys.
- Boys are more spatially aware.

In terms of personality and physical features, differences are more pronounced, and the research is quite consistent. Men appear to be more assertive and active and have higher self-esteem as compared to women, who are more open and trusting. Three decades ago, Carol Gilligan's (1982) landmark study described the drop of self-esteem in girls during their adolescent years and how they became less intellectually and socially confident, primarily as the result of socialization. Obviously, men and women differ in physical features. Girls reach puberty before boys. Boys grow taller and have more muscle tissue than girls.

Ormrod (2008) summarized over thirty years of research on gender differences and the implication of this research for teachers. Table 2.5 summarizes the result of her work along with Eliot's work cited above.

Origins of Gender Differences

A second important question about gender differences is their origins. The nature-nurture debate described earlier in the chapter to explain differences in ability also applies to explaining gender differences and gender role identity. The best evidence is that biology and hormones (nature) affect the kinds of play and activities pursued by young children, with boys preferring more active play (Eliot, 2010). At the same time, studies have shown that both mothers and fathers play more roughly (socialization) with their sons than with their daughters (Lytton & Romney, 1991). Other adults in a child's life—neighbors, siblings, teachers—also hold beliefs about what it means to be a man or a woman, and they act on these beliefs and act differently toward girls than boys. For example, boys are given more freedom and independence; girls are provided more protection. Brannon (2007) found that men in media are more often heard in narrator roles and voices of authority compared to women. So, what may have started as small biological differences soon are influenced significantly by the socialization process as children interact with their parents, their peers, and other adults. An important perspective for teachers about the origin of gender differences is that though some small gender differences may exist early on in a child's life they are not fixed and can be changed by experience. They may also be situational and change over time. For example, studies done in the 1980s and 1990s about gender expectations and gender bias might show different results if they were repeated today. However, stereotyping and differential treatment are still important topics for teachers to understand.

Stereotyping and Differential Treatment

Boys and girls learn about becoming men and women in school just as they do in their families. For many years, curriculum materials fostered a gender bias by portraying

Table 2.5 *Gender Differences and Educational Implications*

Features	Differences/Similarities	Education Implications
Cognitive and academic abilities	On average, boys and girls perform similarly on tests of general intelligence and have similar cognitive and academic abilities. Boys do slightly better on visual-spatial tasks, and girls are slightly better at verbal tasks. Girls consistently earn higher grades in school.	Expect boys and girls to have similar cognitive and academic abilities.
Physical activity and motor skills	After puberty, boys have an advantage in height and muscle strength and they tend to develop their physical skills more than girls. Boys are temperamentally predisposed to be more active than girls.	Assume both genders have potential for developing physical and motor skills. Expect boys to have difficulty sitting still for long periods or enjoying sedentary activity such as reading.
Motivation	Girls, in general, are more concerned about doing well in school. They tend to work harder but take fewer risks.	Expect boys and girls to excel in all subjects; avoid stereotyping.
Career aspirations	Girls tend to see themselves as college-bound more than boys. Boys have higher long-term expectations for themselves in stereotypically "masculine" areas.	Expose all students to successful male and female models. Encourage boys to aspire to go to college and show girls people who juggle careers and families.
Interpersonal relationships	Boys tend to exhibit more physical aggression; girls tend to be more affiliative. Boys feel more comfortable in competitive situations; girls prefer cooperative environments.	Teach both genders less aggressive ways to interact and provide a cooperative environment for all.

Sources: Adapted from Olmrod (2000, 2008) and Eliot (2010).

men and women in stereotyped roles. Studies (Sadker, Sadker, & Klein, 1991; Women on Words and Images, 1975) found that men were more likely to be portrayed in active and professional roles while women were seen more often in passive and homemaker roles. Similarly, a series of studies spread over two decades (Baker, 1986; Sadker & Sadker, 1994; Serbin & O'Leary, 1975) showed that teachers interact differently with boys than they do with girls. They ask boys more questions, give them more praise, and allow them to use equipment in science labs more frequently. The reason behind differential treatment is complex. Some argue that it results from gender stereotyping (AAUW, 1992), while others maintain that teachers pay more attention to boys than girls because boys are more active and more likely to cause trouble if left unattended. (See David's action research study in the Handbook on Action Research in the Online Learning Center.)

Gender bias and differential treatment of girls may still be a problem. However, there have also been some successes over the past thirty years. Eccles (1989) and Ormrod (2008) report that schools and teachers have increasingly strived to treat boys and girls the same. Today, boys' and girls' sports receive equal financial support, and in some regions of the country they receive equal publicity in the local media. Since 1971, girls have made definite strides in terms of graduating from high school and attending and graduating from college. In 1971, only about 78 percent of girls finished high school compared to almost 90 percent of boys. Today, this figure had essentially been reversed. Also, in 1971, less than 40 percent of women had completed one year of college and less than 20 percent had graduated. Compare these data to undergraduate enrollments projected to 2016 illustrated in Figure 2.5, and observe that currently many more women than men are enrolled in college.

A number of educators (Jha & Kelleher, 2007; Neu & Weinfeld, 2006) have written about the problems experienced by boys and young men in school. Hallinan (2003) pointed out that the majority of students who are referred to special education are boys. Boys have a higher dropout rate as compared to girls, and they are more likely to fall behind in verbal skills and college attendance, as described in Figure 2.5.

A variety of reasons have been given for the problems boys experience in school. Kleinfield (1999) argued that the attention paid to girls since the passage of Title IX in 1972 has resulted in the neglect of boys, especially African American and Latino boys. Others (Gurian, 2002; Husband, 2012; Sax, 2009; Tyre, 2006, 2008) say that the ways in which schools are structured are inconsistent with the ways boys learn and the ways they behave. Tyre (2006) believes that teachers emphasize language and sitting quietly, two traits that girls do better than boys. The result has been for "girl behavior" to become the gold standard and for boys to be treated as "defective girls."

The idea that there is a "boys' crisis," according to Strauss (2008), has not gone unchallenged. In 2008, the American Association of University Women issued a report that concluded that the "boys' crisis" is a myth (Corbett, Hill, & St. Rose, 2008). The report argued that the huge discrepancies in achievement are not between boys and girls, but rather differences that can be accounted for by the divisions among race/ethnicity and family income level.

It is likely that this debate will continue for some time. Advice for teachers is to recognize that differential treatment in schools of either girls or boys (or both) is a troubling concern. Effective teachers are knowledgeable of this situation and strive to be sensitive to the unique needs of *all* students.

Figure 2.5 *Undergraduate Enrollment by Gender between 1970 and 2016*

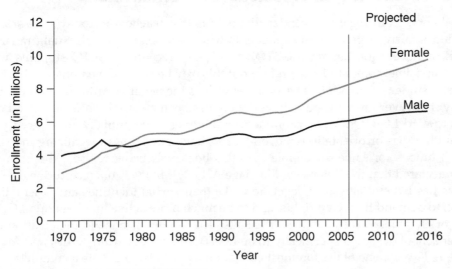

Source: *The Condition of Education* (2007, 2009).

Check, Extend, Explore

Check

- How is gender bias still a problem in the classroom?
- Discuss gender differences in regard to personality and abilities.
- Contrast gender differences attributed to nature as compared to socialization.
- What kinds of differential treatment in regard to gender are most likely to be found in schools?

Extend

- Some have argued for same-sex schooling as a way to reduce gender bias and to enhance the self-esteem of girls. Others have argued the same for African American boys.
- Do you agree or disagree with having same-sex or same-race schools? Go to "Extend Question Poll" on the Online Learning Center to respond.

Explore

- Search the Internet for Web sites related to gender differences.
- Google "Title IX" and read the history and success of this piece of legislation.

Working with Gender Differences in the Classroom

Many of the guidelines provided for teachers who work with students of various races and ethnic groups or students with special needs also apply to working with boys and girls, and young men and young women:

1. *Be aware of your own beliefs and behavior.* Sometimes, particularly in mathematics, boys are the norm to which girls must catch up. Reject this idea—it is the same as the cultural deficit theory described earlier. If assignments are differentiated, make sure they are based on the needs of particular students and not on gender stereotyping.
2. *Monitor the frequency and nature of your verbal interaction.* Treat boys and girls the same in your expectations, questioning, and praise. More about discourse patterns and the use of questioning and praise will be provided in Chapter 12.
3. *Make sure your language and curriculum materials are gender-free and balanced.* Today, most current curriculum materials have been scrutinized for sexual stereotyping. However, it is still a good idea to submit all materials and your own speech to scrutiny regarding what was described in the previous section as "linguistic gender bias." Do not use masculine pronouns to refer to all people. Make sure boys and girls and men and women are portrayed in a variety of active and positive ways that show career and parenting roles equally.
4. Assign classroom chores to children in an equitable fashion and find ways for boys and girls to play together in quiet and active ways. These informal acts can provide models for students to follow.
5. Encourage students to be reflective about their own work and attitudes and discuss sex-role stereotyping with students.
6. Remain sensitive to classroom or teaching situations that may be inconsistent with the learning preferences and emotional needs of boys or girls.
7. *Show respect for all students and challenge both boys and girls appropriately.* As with matters of race and ethnicity, all students should be shown respect and given the sense they are valued. All teacher actions should show both boys and girls that you have confidence in their abilities and have high expectations for all aspects of their work.

Sexual Identities, Expressions, and Orientations

A final concern in regard to gender diversity is that teachers in today's classrooms will find a fairly large number of students who are lesbian, gay, bisexual, transgendered, or queer/questioning (LGBTQ). Until very recently, LGBTQ students were mainly invisible; some students preferred it this way because of the homophobia held by many students and adults in schools as well as the negative attitudes in the larger society. However, over the past decade there has been a seismic shift in societal attitudes toward LGBTQs. Many prominent individuals have publicly announced their sexual identities or orientations. Several states have passed laws legalizing marriage or civil unions for same-sex couples. As this book was being revised, the Supreme Court declared that the Defense of Marriage Act (DOMA) was unconstitutional.

This has led students at all levels to make their sexual identities and orientations public, to demand their civil rights, and to be much more active in organizing LGBTQ clubs or chapters in their schools. It has also led in one instance to the creation of a charter school designed specifically to be LGBTQ-friendly (Pardini, 2013) and for the *Phi Delta Kappan,* one of the foremost educational journals, to devote a complete issue to "sex in the schools," with several articles on LGBTQs [*Phi Delta Kappan,* 2013, 94(5)].

It is important for teachers to be aware that they will have LGBTQ students in their classrooms and to take several steps to show them respect and concern. One important action is to get the terminology right. For example:

- *Gender identity* refers to how persons think about themselves.
- *Gender expression* refers to how persons might demonstrate or express their gender.
- *Sexual orientation* is to whom a person is physically and emotionally attracted. See Killerman (2013) and Slesaransky-Poe (2013) for expanded definitions.

It is also important for teachers to recognize that even though advances have been made, LGTBQ students still face difficulties in life and in schools. Many do not fully understand their sexual identities or orientations and may suffer from mental health issues, depression, anxiety, and substance abuse. According to the Gay, Lesbian, and Straight Education Network (2011), 85 percent of LGBTQ students have heard "gay" used in a negative way; 71 percent have heard homophobic remarks such as "dyke" or "faggot"; 81 percent reported having been verbally harassed; and 18 percent said they had been physically assaulted.

Teachers should monitor situations where they see students or faculty making jokes about individuals with sexual identities and orientations different from their own and to encourage and model respect for tolerance. Teachers should also become aware of counseling and educational programs in their districts for LGBTQ students as well as workshops for teachers aimed at equal treatment and opportunity for all students regardless of their sexual identities, expressions, or orientations.

Finally, below is a set of guidelines adapted from McGarry (2013) for teachers who want to make LGBTQ students feel included and respected:

- Make sure that any analogies used don't express heterosexuality as a given.
- Use inclusive language when referring to students' families and others outside the classroom.
- Use students' preferred names and gender pronouns.
- Build knowledge of vocabulary such as *ally, respect,* and *diversity.*
- Use gender-neutral language, such as *partner.*
- Consider and control how stereotypes are perpetuated. Intervene when necessary.

Social Class Differences and Poverty

For a long time, social scientists have studied variations among individuals with regard to wealth, status, power, and prestige. As you likely know, they use the term **socioeconomic status (SES)** to refer to these differences and have categorized individuals in Western societies into four socioeconomic classes: upper class, middle class, working class, and lower class. Several characteristics account for an individual's social class identification: occupation, income, political power, education, neighborhood, and, sometimes, family background. Boundaries between SES lines, however, are not always clearly defined. An individual may be high in one characteristic and not so high in another. College professors and teachers have fairly high status as a result of their occupation, but they may have low incomes, relatively speaking. A representative in Congress may have a substantial amount of power, but not very much money. A successful entrepreneur may be very wealthy, live in an elite neighborhood, and yet lack formal education.

The fact that an individual's socioeconomic status overlaps with race and ethnicity further complicates efforts at defining precise SES categories. For example, middle-class whites and middle-class African Americans often have more in common than they do with lower-class members of their own race. Educated, working-class Americans may live in the same community and find they have much in common with their middle-class neighbors. Because of the legacy of discrimination in the United States, low-SES African Americans and Hispanics may be treated differently and exhibit different values and behaviors than do low-SES individuals who have not experienced racial or ethnic discrimination.

Characteristics, Performance, and Differential Treatment of Low-SES Students

Many children of working-class parents and almost all children of low-SES families live in poverty. Today it is estimated that one in every five children in public schools in the United States lives in poverty (Children's Defense Fund, 2010; *The Condition of Education,* 2012). Some are raised in single-parent households by an adult who lacks education, language proficiency, and job skills. Many low-SES children of poverty are also children of first-generation immigrants who are likely to have limited formal education and, perhaps, limited command of either English or their native language. Many suffer from malnutrition and poor health. Often, these are the children who come to school without breakfast, wearing old clothes, and speaking a language different from the one used in school.

Most important, there is an achievement gap between low-SES and middle-class students. Just as in the case of racial and ethnic minority students, low-SES students, regardless of race, show less achievement than their high-SES peers and they often suffer under unequal curriculum, tracking, and differential classroom interactions with teachers. They, too, are underenrolled in college preparatory courses and are less likely to go to college. Research, three decades ago, demonstrated dramatically the differences that SES can have on school learning. Cazden (1972) examined speech patterns, specifically sentence length, under differing contexts for a working-class (low-SES) child and a middle-class (middle-SES) child. She found that while all the children gave their shortest utterances in the same context—an arithmetic game—their longest sentence context varied. The middle-class child, for example, spoke more extensively during a formal, story-retelling situation. The working-class child, however, spoke longer during informal, out-of-school conversations.

Hart and Risley (1995) found large differences between the amount of language 3-year-old children from welfare families had been exposed to compared to the amount children from middle-class, professional families had been exposed to. This language exposure was linked to superior language (particularly vocabulary) development on the part of the children from the professional families. In the past decade, many researchers, such as Eamon (2002), Noguera (2011), and Payne (2008), have found similar relationships between poverty and achievement.

Differential treatment provides one explanation of the lower achievement of low-SES students. Teachers may hold low expectations for these children and stereotype their abilities because of the clothes they wear or their use of language. As described earlier, teachers' low expectations for students can lead to the children's low self-esteem and low expectations for their own work.

Perhaps the most serious problem for low-SES students is ability grouping and tracking. Traditionally, low-SES students have been disproportionately placed in low-ability groups and low-track classes where instructional quality is poorer than in the

Socioeconomic status (SES) refers to variations among people based on income, family background, and relative prestige within society.

higher groups. The criteria used to guide placement decisions are sometimes of dubious merit, as described in a landmark study by Ray Rist (1970) over forty years ago. Rist studied a single class of children in an urban area over a three-year period. He documented that kindergarten teachers used nonacademic data—namely, who was on welfare, a behavioral questionnaire completed by the children's mothers, teachers' own experiences with and other teachers' reports about siblings, and the children's dress—to make initial ability grouping decisions. The teacher used this information to place children in low-, middle-, and high-ability groups on the eighth day of kindergarten. Children of like "ability" were seated together and received like instruction throughout the year. The teacher gave more positive attention to the children in the high-ability group and spent more instructional time with them. She reprimanded the children in the low-ability group more often.

When the students entered first grade, their new teacher also divided them into low-, middle-, and high-ability groups and seated them together. All the kindergarten highs became first-grade highs (group A), the former middle and low children became middle children (group B), and children who were repeating first grade constituted the new low group (group C). Only the group-A children had completed the kindergarten curriculum and were able to start right away with the first-grade material. Groups B and C children spent the early part of their first-grade year completing kindergarten lessons.

The second-grade teacher continued the low-middle-high grouping practice. Group A students became "Tigers," group B and C students became "Cardinals," and repeating second-graders became "Clowns." Thus, low children were locked into the low group, making it nearly impossible to advance into the higher group. Rist summed up his results with this statement: *"The child's journey through the early grades of school at one reading level and in one social grouping appeared to be pre-ordained from the eighth day of kindergarten"* (p. 435).

Rist's findings shocked the educational community at the time. He had demonstrated that teachers' expectations and instructional decisions and actions were profoundly influenced by the social-class characteristics of children and that children who did not fit the middle-class mold suffered academically and emotionally. In the forty years since the publication of Rist's study, other researchers (Anyon, 1980; Goodlad, 1984; Hallinan & Sorensen, 1983; Oakes, 1985; Oakes & Lipton, 2012; Sorensen & Hallinan, 1986) have corroborated his disturbing findings. However, recent experiments by Robert Slavin and his colleagues have demonstrated that schools and classrooms can be organized with programs and processes that offset the impact of poverty and social class (Stevens & Slavin, 1995). Similarly, as ability grouping has fallen out of accepted practice, it is being replaced with **flexible grouping**, a practice that consists of putting students in groups for specific subjects or activities (most often reading or mathematics) but considering these groups to be only temporary, where membership can change as targeted content and skills are accomplished. Much more detail about flexible grouping will be provided in Chapter 13.

Working with Low-SES Students in the Classroom

Many of the strategies recommended for working with students from different racial or ethnic backgrounds or for dealing with gender or language differences are appropriate for working with low-SES students. They, too, respond to teachers who show respect for them regardless of their dress and language patterns. They, too, benefit from challenge rather than low expectations and from instruction that is differentiated

Check, Extend, Explore

Check
- How do social scientists define the term *socioeconomic status (SES)*?
- What specific problems are faced by students of low economic status and poverty? Out of school? In school?
- How can teachers prevent the negative situations described in the Rist study?

Extend
- Some teachers believe they can teach students better if students are placed in ability groups. Do you agree or disagree? Go to "Extend Question Poll" on the Online Learning Center to respond.

Explore
- Go to the Online Learning Center at www.mhhe.com/arends10e for links to Web sites related to *social class and education.*
- Use Google to search the topic "diversity in the classroom." You will find thousands of Web sites devoted to this topic. Look at two or three and learn about the resources and tools available for teachers.

according to their unique needs and aspirations. Effective teachers strive to help low-SES students improve their thinking and language skills and find ways to assign competence to strengths that they do possess.

In many schools, low-SES students (unless they have been identified as troublemakers) are nearly invisible. They are unlikely to participate in extracurricular activities and special programs that exist for identified racial groups or for girls. Low-SES students can benefit schoolwide when teachers pay attention to them, help them become involved, and advocate for their rights to get an equal education.

Some Final Thoughts and Schoolwide Issues

We conclude with an admonition that all problems regarding diversity cannot be solved by teachers working alone. Instead, schoolwide and societal actions are required that will make schooling more sensitive to students from diverse backgrounds and those with special needs. A number of approaches hold promise.

Most schools offer free and reduced-price lunches for students to help offset the negative impact of poverty.

One of the most consistent findings from research is that tracking by ability or retention does not promote achievement. Further, it has damaging consequences for minority students. A good place to start reform, then, is to reduce inappropriate tracking and grouping practices. Many schools are beginning to experiment with reorganizing into teams of teachers and students. Some schools are developing interdisciplinary curricula, relying heavily on cooperative learning in heterogeneous groups, alternatives to standardized testing, and flexible grouping.

There are also school-level actions that can be taken to address the difficult life circumstances of students considered "at risk" due to poverty. Most schools offer free and reduced-price lunches and in some cases breakfasts for students. The connection between student learning and basic nutrition is not only self-evident, but also well documented, so it behooves schools and districts that lack these basic programs to implement them.

School programs that target early intervention are also helpful. The effectiveness of one such program—Head Start—is well established. For every dollar invested in Head Start, many more are saved later on in reduced need for discipline and remediation, welfare, and criminal justice. Currently, it appears that these programs are going to be expanded, yet not all eligible children are served. The process of establishing a Head Start center is long and complex, but as a beginning teacher, you can lend your support to existing centers by promoting awareness among colleagues and parents and by lobbying for increased funding so that more low-income children can be served.

As described in this chapter's Home and School feature, an extremely important avenue for improving the educational outcomes of all students is parent and community involvement. When families and other community members are involved in the life of the school through tutoring programs, mentoring programs, school improvement committees, parent education, site-based governance, or other activities, students benefit (Epstein, 1995, 2001; Epstein, Sanders, et al., 2002; Nettles, 1991). This is a topic that will receive more attention in Chapter 14.

Underlying all the recommendations made in this chapter is the importance of teachers individually and collectively valuing each and every student and challenging them to reach their highest potential. Some years ago Claude Steele (1992) highlighted the themes of value and challenge: "If what is meaningful and important to a teacher is to become meaningful and important to a student, the student must feel valued by the teacher for his or her potential and as a person." If anything going on in the school—curriculum cast as remediation, or instruction cast as the pedagogy of poverty—diminishes students' sense of themselves as valued people, students will be disinclined to identify with the goals of the school. Intellectual challenge goes hand in hand with valuing. "A valuing teacher-student relationship goes nowhere without challenge, and challenge will always be resisted outside a valuing relationship" (p. 78).

Reflections **from the** *Classroom*

Student Tensions

During your first year of teaching, you have been assigned to the school's interdisciplinary team (this could be in either a middle or high school). With one other teacher, you are responsible for teaching literature, writing, and history to a group of forty-seven students. You meet with your students in eighty-minute blocks of time three times a week.

You like this assignment, but it presents you with some real challenges. Students in your classroom are about equally mixed among three racial and ethnic groups. In the larger community, these groups have traditionally *not* gotten along very well with each other. In addition, three of your students have been diagnosed as having behavior disorders; two have learning disabilities; and one student has a physical disability.

The major problem you face is that the students just don't seem to get along with one another. Students from the three racial and ethnic groups hang out mostly with members of their own group. It's not that they are impolite to one another—they simply ignore anyone outside their own group. From time to time, some students make fun of the students with behavior disorders. Although things are not out of control from a classroom management perspective,

the overall climate is not positive. It is not the type of learning environment you or your colleague want for your classroom.

What would you do to make the learning environment more productive and to help students in your group get along better? Where would you start? Which of your actions would involve instruction? Group development? Are there outside resources that you might call upon? Write a reflective essay for your portfolio on this problem and then compare what you write to what the following experienced teachers have said they would do. Approach this situation from the perspective closest to the grade level or subject area you are preparing to teach.

Cassandra Garcia
5th and 6th Grade

This is the type of situation that demands action on two fronts, one short term, the other more long term. For the short term, I would have some of the special education and counseling personnel provide human relations training for students in the class. I would want them to emphasize how to get along with one another, how to communicate in positive ways, and how to resolve conflict situations without resorting to anger or force. I would also like them to provide students with experiences through which they would get to know each other on a personal level. I think this would help students listen to each other a little better and display less indifference toward one another.

On a longer-term basis, I would work to establish an environment of trust between the students and myself and among the various groups of students. I would use "classroom meetings" to help students discuss their problems and differences. I would start using cooperative learning groups on a regular basis. I would make sure that each group had representatives from the three racial and ethnic groups and that each group had one of the special-needs students. I would make sure that all assignments were set up in such a way that students had to work together and each student's success was tied to the group's accomplishments and to individual growth.

I know that it will take a long time to develop the type of learning environment I envision. I will have to remain patient and to expect many setbacks along the way.

Dennis Holt

**Tampa Bay Technical High School, 11th and 12th Grade
Hillsborough, FL**

I teach in the most ethnically diverse high school in my district so I understand classrooms made up of students from a variety of racial and ethnic backgrounds and with any number of behavioral/learning disabilities. It is important at the beginning of the year to mold these students into an academic team. A first-step that I have found to be successful is to focus on identifying the variety of learning styles and multiple intelligences evident among my students. The theory of multiple intelligences is based on the work of Howard Gardner and suggests that individuals have eight different intelligences. Also, I have utilized a number of learning style inventories that are readily available via the Internet or through commercial sources. Since learning styles cut across racial, ethnic, and gender boundaries, students quickly comprehend that a variety of different learning styles are evident among members of "their" group and that they share similar learning styles with members of other groups. It is fun for me to become aware, along with my students, that the girl who had been tapping her pencil on the desk is primarily a musical-rhythmic learner and that the body-kinesthetically inclined "dumb jock" is not so dumb after all. I never hesitate to share my own primary visual-spatial learning style with my students. This exercise in self-analysis and appreciation of diverse learning styles has been a valuable first-step in team building. The next step is to assign students to mixed race/gender/learning-style teams of four to five to engage in cooperative work or problem-solving activities. I would suggest that the group work be something that the students consider to be "fun" as well as academic. Remember, at this point the idea is to build a sense of "team" among your students. Once a cooperative atmosphere is established in your classroom more intense academic work will follow. Establishing a team-oriented classroom is so important that I suggest you consider devoting as much time as you need to team-building activities. I have begun my school year this way for several years now and have found this method to be very successful. Good luck.

Summary

Describe the changes that have occurred in the demographics of schooling and discuss why it is important for teachers to be able to help all students learn.

- Over the past half century, the student population in American schools has changed dramatically. Understanding diversity and helping each student learn are the major teaching challenges of the twenty-first century.
- Using appropriate language when discussing diversity or referring to students' backgrounds and abilities is critical.

Discuss how the concepts of equity, differential treatment, and variations in learning abilities are of central concern in regard to student learning.

- Much of the research and concern with diversity has focused on three topics: equity, differential treatment, and variations in the learning abilities of students.
- Equity refers to making the conditions in schools impartial and equal for everyone. Historically, equal conditions have not existed. Some students have been provided restricted opportunities because of their race, social class, or abilities.

- Differential treatment refers to the differences between educational experiences of the majority race, class, culture, and gender and those of minorities.
- Studies over the years have shown that minority students receive a lower-quality education as a result of enrollment patterns, tracking and grouping patterns, and differential interactions with teachers.
- Teachers' expectations affect relationships with students, what they learn, and students' perceptions of their own abilities. Teachers can learn to be aware of and minimize their biases about students of different backgrounds.
- Students vary in their abilities to learn. For many years, human intelligence was conceived of as a single ability.
- Modern theorists view ability and intelligence as more than a single ability and propose theories of multiple intelligences.
- Debates have existed for a long time over whether ability to learn is inherited (nature) or is a result of the environment (nurture). Today, most psychologists believe it is a combination of both and also recognize that an individual's capacity to learn reflects cultural backgrounds.

Discuss how students with disabilities and students who are gifted are to be educated today and describe how teachers can best work with these students.

- Students who have learning disabilities have special needs that must be met if they are to successfully function in and out of school. Traditionally, these students have received an inferior education. Current efforts to mainstream and include students with special needs are aimed at correcting this situation.
- Inclusion is an effort to extend regular classroom educational opportunities to students with special needs, a group that traditionally has been segregated and has received inferior educational opportunities.
- Public Law 94-142 and IDEA specified that students with disabilities must be educated in the least restrictive environment and that each must have an individualized education plan (IEP).
- Teachers' responsibilities for working with students who have special needs include helping with the IEP process and adapting instruction and other aspects of teaching so all students can learn.
- Perspectives differ on how best to work with students with disabilities. Some advocate highly structured approaches, whereas others argue that instruction should stem from the student's interest and emphasize problem solving and critical thinking. A combination of both is likely to prove to be the most effective.
- There is lack of consensus about how to identify and educate students who have special gifts and talents. Some believe that paying attention to gifted students takes resources away from students who need them more.
- Characteristics of gifted students can include extraordinary cognitive functioning, the ability to retain lots of information, flexible and creative thought processes, large vocabularies, and advanced artistic talents.
- Effective strategies for working with gifted students include differentiating instruction, creating rich learning environments, using flexible groupings, compacting curriculum and instruction, using independent study, and helping gifted students set high standards for themselves.

Describe contemporary perspectives on culture and race, compare these with views from earlier times, and explain what effective teachers do to enhance learning for all students in culturally and racially diverse classrooms.

- Contemporary perspectives reject ideas about cultural deficits and instead embrace theories of cultural assets and differences and cultural discontinuity to account for the difficulties minority students experience in school.
- To work effectively with students in culturally and racially diverse classrooms, teachers must recognize, understand, and appreciate cultural groups, whether based on racial, ethnic, language, gender, or other differences.
- Becoming aware of one's own bias and developing understandings and sensitivities of students' cultures is an important first step for successful teaching in culturally diverse classrooms.
- Effective teachers of racially and culturally different students know how to create culturally relevant and multicultural curricula and how to use culturally relevant pedagogies.
- Specific teaching models and strategies available to accomplish multicultural learning goals include direct instruction, cooperative learning, and reciprocal teaching.

Describe the religious diversity that exists in today's schools and the actions teachers can take to recognize and deal with religious differences among students.

- Teachers will find considerable religious diversity in their classrooms, including not only students who hold more traditional Judeo-Christian beliefs, but also students who hold beliefs associated with Islam, Buddhism, and various fundamentalist and New Age religions.
- The U.S. Constitution regulates the place of religion in schools; Supreme Court interpretations of what separation of church and state means vary and often are controversial.
- Teachers can teach students about various religions and model respect and tolerance for various religious beliefs.

Discuss the significance of language diversity in today's classrooms and describe effective strategies to use with English language learners.

- Teachers will find significant language diversity in today's classrooms. This includes diversity in dialects spoken by native speakers as well as many students who speak English as their second language.
- Second-language acquisition is a difficult and long-term process for students. It includes not only learning phonology, morphology, syntax, and vocabulary, but also learning to interpret gestures and facial expressions, learning the norms that surround language usage, and using language to acquire cognitive knowledge.
- Language diversity must be respected and bilingual skills must be encouraged and developed for students who are English language learners.

Describe the importance of gender differences in today's classrooms and discuss how effective teachers work with these differences.

- Even though teaching has been a field dominated by women, gender bias and differential treatment of girls have traditionally been problems in schools.
- Most studies show that there are few major, inherent differences between the abilities of men and women.

- Although some aspects of female and male personality and behavior can be attributed to nature, socialization also plays an important role in role identity.
- Traditionally, teachers have interacted differently with boys and girls. They ask boys more questions, give them more praise, and afford them greater independence.
- Today, more women than men attend and graduate from college and many are concerned that boys are perhaps now being left behind as girls were for so many years.
- Effective teachers are aware of their own possible gender bias, show respect, challenge all students, and make sure their language and curriculum materials are gender-free and balanced.
- Today students are making known their sexual identities, expressions, and orientations. It is important for teachers to show respect and concern for gay, lesbian, bisexual, transgendered, and queer students.

Describe the characteristics of low-SES students, explain the special needs they have, and discuss effective strategies for working with them.

- Low-SES students, for the most part, come from families who have limited formal education and often speak English as a second language. They come to school in poor health, with old clothes, and speak a language other than English.
- Socioeconomic status has rather dramatic effects on school learning, mainly because of tracking and grouping and because of differential treatment.
- Low-SES students respond to teachers who show them respect, who challenge them by holding high expectations for their academic learning, and who will be advocates for their rights to an equal education.

Explain why schoolwide actions are required to ensure success for all students.

- Teachers alone cannot solve all the problems faced by schools today. Many of the challenges of providing equal opportunities can be met only through community and schoolwide actions and reform.

Key Terms

analytical intelligence 51	ethnicity 66	least restrictive environment 56
assistive technologies 61	exceptionalities 55	mainstreaming 56
challenged 45	field dependent 54	melting pot 67
creative intelligence 51	field independent 54	mental abilities 51
cultural competence 68	flexible grouping 85	mental age 51
cultural deficit theory 67	full bilingual programs 77	multicultural education 71
cultural difference theory 67	gender bias 78	multiple intelligences 52
culturally relevant curriculum 71	gifted and talented 60	out-of-context learning style 54
cultural pluralism 67	handicapped 45	practical intelligence 51
culture 66	inclusion 56	race 66
differential treatment 47	in-context learning style 54	self-fulfilling prophecy 47
differentiation 64	individualized education plan (IEP) 57	socioeconomic status (SES) 83
disability 45	intelligence 51	submersion approach 77
discontinuity 68	intelligence quotient (IQ) 51	successful intelligence 51
Ebonics 78	learning abilities 51	sustaining expectation effect 49
emotional intelligence (EQ) 53	learning preferences 54	teacher expectations 48
English language learners (ELLs) 76	learning strategies 74	transitional bilingual program 77
equity 45	learning styles 54	

Interactive and Applied Learning

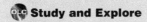 Study and Explore

- Access your Study Guide, which includes practice quizzes, from the Online Learning Center.

Observe and Practice

- Listen to audio clips on the Online Learning Center of Diane Caruso (fourth/fifth grade) and Jennifer Patterson (eighth-grade American history) talking about the diversity of their students in the *Teachers on Teaching* area.

Complete the following **Practice Exercises** that accompany Chapter 2:
- Practice Exercise 2.1: Teacher Expectations
- Practice Exercise 2.2: Multiple Intelligences
- Practice Exercise 2.3: Planning Instruction for a Gifted Student
- Practice Exercise 2.4: Analyzing and Teaching for Classroom Diversity

Portfolio and Field Experience Activities

Expand your understanding of the content and processes of this chapter through the following field experiences and portfolio activities. Support materials to complete the activities are in the *Portfolio and Field Experience Activities* area in the Online Learning Center.

1. Complete the Reflections from the Classroom exercise for this chapter. The essay will provide insight into your views about diversity and strategies you might use to resolve student conflicts and tensions that may arise in diverse classrooms.

2. **Activity 2.1: Assessing My Skills for Promoting Student Learning in Diverse Classrooms.** Check your abilities to develop a classroom where children will respect one another and where all will be successful. **(InTASC Standard 2: Learning Differences)**

3. **Activity 2.2: Observing and Interviewing Teachers with Special-Needs and Culturally Diverse Students.** Find out how experienced teachers teach and manage special-needs and culturally diverse students. **(InTASC Standard 2: Learning Differences)**

4. **Activity 2.3: Interviewing a Student from a Different Culture.** Gain knowledge about people different from you. **(InTASC Standard 2: Learning Differences)**

5. **Activity 2.4: Portfolio: My Understanding of Policies Related to Student Learning, Diversity, and Inclusion.** Gather materials and artifacts for your portfolio by completing the tasks called for in this activity. **(InTASC Standard 3: Learning Differences; InTASC Standard 9: Professional Learning and Ethical Practice)**

Books for the Professional

Cushner, K., McClelland, A., & Safford, P. (2011). *Human diversity in education: An integrative approach* (7th ed.). New York: McGraw-Hill.

Friend, M., & Bursuck, W. (2012). *Including students with special needs: A practical guide for classroom teachers* (6th ed.). Boston: Allyn & Bacon.

Gay, G. (2010). *Culturally responsive teaching* (2nd ed.). New York: Teachers College Press.

Howard, T. (2010). *Why race and culture matter in school: Closing the achievement gap in America's classrooms.* New York: Teachers College Press.

Howe, W., & Lisi, P. (2013). *Becoming a multicultural educator: Developing awareness, gaining skills, and taking action.* Thousand Oaks, CA: Sage Publications.

Meyer, E. (2010). *Gender and sexual diversity in schools: Explorations of educational purpose.* New York: Springer.

Oakes, J., Lipton, M., Anderson, L., & Stillman, J. (2012). *Teaching to change the world* (4th ed.). St. Paul, MN: Paradigm Publishers.

PART 2 *The Leadership Aspects of Teaching*

This part of *Learning to Teach* is about the leadership aspects of teaching. Teachers, like leaders in other settings, are expected to provide leadership to students and to coordinate a variety of activities as they and their students work interdependently to accomplish the academic and social goals of schooling. Teacher leadership is critical because if students are not motivated to participate in and persist with academic learning tasks, or if they are not managed effectively, all the rest of teaching can be forgotten. Yet, these complex aspects must be performed in classrooms characterized by fast-moving events and a large degree of unpredictability. Unlike many of the instructional aspects of teaching, many leadership functions cannot be planned ahead of time. They require on-the-spot judgments.

Part 2 focuses on five important aspects of leadership: planning, motivating students, building productive learning communities, managing classroom groups, and assessing and evaluating student progress. Even though each aspect is described and discussed separately, in the real day-to-day life of teaching, the distinctions are not nearly so tidy. When teachers plan, as described in Chapter 3, they are also setting conditions for allocating time, determining motivation, and building productive learning communities, the subjects of Chapter 4. The way students behave and how they are managed on any particular day, the focus of Chapter 5, cycles back to influence future plans and resource allocation decisions, as does assessment and grading, the focus of Chapter 6.

There is a substantial knowledge base on each aspect of teacher leadership that can provide a guide for effective practice. There is also considerable wisdom that has been accumulated by teachers over the years to help beginning teachers get started with learning to plan, to allocate resources, and to deal with students in group settings.

You will discover as you read and reflect on the leadership aspects of teaching that providing leadership in classrooms is no easy matter and, as with other aspects of teaching, cannot be reduced to simple recipes. Instead, leadership is tightly connected to specific classrooms and schools and to your own leadership style. You will find that what works in general may not work in any specific case. Learning to read specific situations and to act on them effectively in real classrooms through reflection and problem solving is one of the most important challenges facing beginning teachers. When mastered, this can be a most rewarding ability.

CHAPTER 3
Teacher Planning

Learning Goals

After studying this chapter you should be able to

Perspective on Planning	Explain why teacher planning is important and describe different perspectives on planning.
Theoretical and Empirical Support	Explain the consequences of planning for student learning and discuss how beginning teachers and experienced teachers approach planning differently.
Planning Domains	Describe the three phases of teacher planning and the types of decisions made during each phase and discuss how planning cycles vary throughout the school year.
The Specifics of Planning	Provide definitions and explanations about how to use the following planning processes and tools: planning what to teach, using and reconstituting standards and curriculum frameworks, using instructional objectives, using taxonomies, and constructing daily and unit instructional plans.
Planning for Time and Space	Describe how to plan for effective use of time and space and how to use curriculum mapping to plan with colleagues.
A Final Thought about Planning	Consider how planning processes may be more student-centered in the future.

 Reflecting on Teacher Planning

Think about personal experiences you have had in your life that required considerable planning. Examples might be planning what college to attend or planning for a wedding or for an extended trip. They might also include experiences for which you did not plan. Divide these experiences into two categories: experiences that were well planned and experiences that were not well planned. Now consider the following questions:

- What did the well-planned experiences have in common?
- What did the poorly planned experiences have in common?
- What were the consequences, if any, of good planning? Of poor planning?

Now think about your own planning skills. Are you the type of person who likes to plan? Do you make to-do lists? Do you think through each step of an activity before you begin? Or are you the type of person who feels more at home with allowing experiences to go unplanned and letting things evolve?

How do you think your own attitudes toward planning might influence your teaching and the planning required of teachers?

 Go to the Online Learning Center at www.mhhe.com/arends10e to respond to these questions.

Even though planning and making decisions about instruction are demanding processes that call for rather sophisticated understanding and skills, as a beginning teacher you do not have to feel overwhelmed. Most of you have planned trips that required complicated travel arrangements. You have planned college schedules, made to-do lists, and survived externally imposed deadlines for term papers and final examinations. Graduation celebrations and weddings are other events most people have experienced that require planning skills of a high caliber. Planning for teaching may be a bit more complex, but the skills you already have can serve as a foundation on which to build.

This chapter describes some of what is known about the processes of teacher planning and decision making. The rationale and knowledge base on planning, particularly the impact of planning on student learning and on the overall flow of classroom life, are described, as are the processes experienced teachers use to plan and make decisions. Also included is a rather detailed explanation of specific planning procedures and a number of aids and techniques used for planning in education and other fields. The discussion that follows strives to capture the complexity of teacher planning and decision making and to show how these functions are performed by teachers under conditions of uncertainty. Although the chapter's emphasis is on the planning tasks carried out by teachers in solitude prior to instruction, attention is also given to the varied "in-flight" planning decisions teachers make in the midst of teaching lessons to students and how joint planning with colleagues can help produce increased student learning. The chapter ends with a brief discussion about the importance of teachers attending to their own personal time management.

Perspective on Planning

Good planning involves allocating the use of time, choosing appropriate content and methods of instruction, creating student interest, and building a productive learning environment.

People today express great confidence in their ability to control events through sophisticated planning. The importance given to planning is illustrated by the many special occupational roles that have been created for just this purpose. For example, a professional cadre of land-use planners, marketing specialists, systems analysts, and strategic planners, to name a few, work full-time putting together detailed, long-range plans to influence and direct the economy and to ensure appropriate military efforts. Family planning, financial planning, and career planning are topics taught to students in high schools and universities and to adults in many settings. Put simply, "planning reduces uncertainty."

Planning is also vital to teaching. One measure of the importance of planning is illustrated when you consider the amount of time teachers spend on this activity.

Studies done over a period of three decades have shown that teachers spend between 10 and 20 percent of their time on planning. The importance of planning is also illustrated when you consider the wide variety of educational activities affected by the plans and decisions made by teachers, as described by Clark and Lampert (1986):

> Teacher planning is a major determinant of what is taught in schools. The curriculum as published is transformed and adapted in the planning process by additions, deletions, interpretations, and by teacher decisions about pace, sequence, and emphasis. And in elementary classrooms, where a teacher is responsible for all subject matter areas, planning decisions about what to teach, how long to devote to each topic, and how much practice to provide take on additional significance and complexity. (p. 28)

Indeed, the process of learning to teach is described by some as learning how to decide what curriculum content is important for students to learn and how it can be enacted in classroom settings through the execution of learning activities and events (Doyle, 1990; Schmoker, 2011; Stronge, 2007).

This chapter will emphasize the importance of planning and highlight that there is much more to planning than good lesson plans. Most important, it will attempt to convey the message that planning is complex and that effective teachers believe "plans are made to be bent."

Planning—The Traditional View

The rational-linear approach to planning focuses on setting goals first and then selecting particular strategies to accomplish these goals.

The planning process in all fields, including education, has been described and studied by many researchers and theorists. The dominant perspective that guides most of the thinking and action on this topic has been referred to as the **rational-linear model**. This perspective puts the focus on goals and objectives as the first step in a sequential process. Modes of action and specific activities are then selected from available alternatives to accomplish prespecified ends. The model assumes a close connection between those who set goals and objectives and those charged with carrying them out. Figure 3.1 illustrates the basic linear planning model.

This model owes its theoretical base to planners and thinkers in many fields. In education, the basic concepts are usually associated with early curriculum planners and theorists, such as Ralph Tyler (1949), and with later instructional designers, Mager (1962, 1997), Gronlund and Brookhart (2009), and Popham (2013). It is also the perspective that guides the ideas behind standards-based education described in Chapter 1.

Planning—An Alternative Perspective

During the last twenty-five years, some observers have questioned whether the rational-linear model accurately describes planning in the real world (Fullan, 2007; McCutcheon & Milner, 2002; Weick, 1979, for example). The view that organizations and classrooms are goal-driven has been challenged, as has the view that actions can be carried out with great precision in a world characterized by complexity, change, and uncertainty.

Careful planning is required for many aspects of modern life.

Figure 3.1 *Rational-Linear Planning Model*

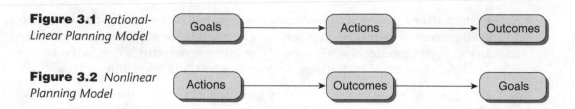

Figure 3.2 *Nonlinear Planning Model*

Nonlinear planning turns this around. Planners start by taking action and attach goals at some later time.

Note that the rational-linear model found in Figure 3.1 is turned upside down in the **nonlinear model,** in which planners start with actions that in turn produce outcomes (some anticipated, some not) and finally summarize and explain their actions by assigning goals to them. Proponents of this model of planning, illustrated in Figure 3.2, argue that plans do not necessarily serve as guides for actions but instead become symbols, advertisements, and justifications for what people have already done. As will be shown later, this model may describe the way many experienced teachers actually approach some aspects of planning. Although they set goals and strive to get a sense of direction for themselves and their students, their planning proceeds in a cyclical, not a straight linear, fashion with a great deal of trial and error built into the process. Indeed, experienced teachers pay attention to features of both the linear and nonlinear aspects of planning and accommodate both. If this view of planning is accurate, it may help explain why many teachers have resisted efforts to standardize the curriculum and to use standardized tests to assess what students have learned.

Mental Planning

Check, Extend, Explore

Check
- Contrast the traditional, rational-linear view of planning with nonlinear perspectives.
- In what ways do planning and decision-making activities impact other aspects of teaching?

Extend
- Which perspective of planning most closely fits the way you approach planning?

Explore
- Using your school's library digital resources, look up and read the McCutcheon and Milner (2002) study on "mental planning."
- Go online and search for the many teacher planning resources.

Most of what is described and prescribed in this chapter pertains to formal planning processes used by teachers as they design units of work and daily lessons. However, there is another side of planning labeled "reflective thought" or "mental" planning (McCutcheon, 1980; McCutcheon & Milner, 2002). One aspect of **mental planning** consists of reflective thought prior to the actual writing of long-term or daily plans. This could be reflecting back about what the teacher did in previous years when teaching a similar unit or thinking about new ideas that he or she has acquired from reading, studying, or attending a recent professional development workshop. Mental planning also consists of "imaging" or engaging in "mental" rehearsals prior to presenting a particular lesson. You likely have engaged in this type of activity in other aspects of your life—for example, when running through what you are going to say in an upcoming speech or rehearsing how you are going to respond when introduced to a person for the first time. Finally, mental planning includes the spontaneous, in-flight plans teachers make during lessons as they respond to particular classroom events and situations. Because mental planning goes on in the mind, it cannot be observed directly as can formal planning. This makes it difficult to describe and to teach others about it. We will come back to the issue of mental planning later in the chapter.

Theoretical and Empirical Support

The research on teacher planning and decision making is substantial and grew significantly in the decades of the 1970s and 1980s but slowed down over the past decade. It has shown that planning has consequences for what students learn, that beginning teachers and experienced teachers plan differently, and that experienced teachers do not always plan as expected. This research also illustrates the complexity of teacher planning and how certain kinds of planning can produce unanticipated and surprising results.

Planning Influences What Students Learn

Both theory and common sense suggest that planning for any kind of activity improves results. Karen Zumwalt (1989) made observations about teacher planning and how it influences student learning:

> Decisions, made explicitly and implicitly during the planning and interactive phases of teaching, influence and are influenced by one's vision [for student learning]. When one makes instructional decisions (e.g., use whole group instruction in math; use reading workbooks for practicing separate component skills; use the tests which accompany the social studies textbook), the nature of the curriculum for students . . . is affected. Choices of "how" are more than instrumental; they influence the curriculum, often in profound ways . . . teachers need to understand this interrelationship if they are to be thoughtful and reflective about their practice. (p. 175)

Research also favors instructional planning over undirected events and activities, but, as you will see, some types of planning may lead to unexpected results.

Planning processes initiated by teachers can give both students and teachers a sense of direction and can help students become aware of the goals implicit in the learning tasks they are asked to perform. Studies done in the 1970s were among the first to highlight the effects of planning on teacher behavior and subsequent student learning. For example, Duchastel and Brown (1974) were interested in the effects of instructional objectives on student learning. They randomly assigned college students taking a course in communications at Florida State University into two groups. Subjects were asked to study several units on the topic of mushrooms. Twenty-four objectives had been written for each unit, and a specific test item had been written to correspond to each objective. Students in group 1 were given twelve of the twenty-four objectives to use as a study guide. Students in group 2 were not given any of the objectives, but they were told to learn as much as they could from the mushroom materials.

When the subjects were tested later, the researchers found that both groups scored the same on the total test. What is interesting and important, however, is the fact that the students who were given twelve of the twenty-four objectives to focus their learning outscored other students on test items associated with these twelve objectives. Of equal interest is that students without any objectives as study aids outscored their counterparts on the items associated with the other twelve objectives. Duchastel and Brown concluded that learning objectives have a *focusing effect* on students, which leads to the recommendation that teachers make students aware of the objectives they have for their lessons.

Working about the same time as Duchastel and Brown, Zahorik (1970) was interested in the effects of planning on *teacher behavior*. He wanted to find out if teachers who planned lessons were less sensitive to pupils in the classroom than teachers who did not plan.

Zahorik studied twelve fourth-grade teachers from four suburban schools. The twelve teachers in the study were randomly divided into two groups designated "teachers who planned" and "teachers who did not plan." Teachers in the planning group were given a lesson plan with objectives and a detailed outline on the topic

Planning and the use of objectives have a focusing effect on students and their learning.

of credit cards. They were asked to use it with their classes. Teachers in the non-planning group were asked to reserve an hour of classroom time to carry out some unknown lesson.

Zahorik found *significant* differences between the teachers who had planned and those who had not planned. Teachers who planned were less sensitive to student ideas and appeared to pursue their own goals regardless of what students were thinking or saying. Conversely, teachers who had not planned displayed a higher number of verbal behaviors that encouraged and developed student ideas.

> **Planning can also have the unintended consequence of causing teachers to be insensitive to student needs and ideas.**

The question that immediately arises from these studies is, if goal-based planning makes teachers less sensitive to students, should teachers eliminate planning? Zahorik concluded that the answer is obviously no. Elimination of planning might bring about completely random and unproductive learning. Studies from the 1970s on teacher planning, plus other studies done or reviewed later (Cotton, 1995; Marzano, 2007; Rosenshine & Stevens, 1986), have consistently demonstrated the importance of goal-based planning, but they have also found that this type of planning can lead to unanticipated consequences. It can cause teachers to be insensitive to students' ideas and can lead to less student learning when planning is too detailed and rigid.

> **Careful planning by teachers can lead to smoothly running classrooms.**

Another consequence of teacher planning is that it produces a smoothly running classroom with fewer discipline problems and fewer interruptions. Chapter 5 is devoted to classroom management, so the research on this topic will not be highlighted here. It is important to note, however, that educational research for the past three decades has consistently found that planning is the key to eliminating most management problems. Teachers who plan well find they do not have to be police officers because their classrooms and lessons are characterized by a smooth flow of ideas, activities, and interactions. Such planning encompasses the rules and goals teachers establish for their classrooms and emphasizes how responsible and businesslike classroom behavior is an integral part of learning. Figure 3.3 summarizes the consequences of careful planning and of having clear instructional goals and objectives.

Planning and the Beginning Teacher

Researchers and educators also have puzzled over why it seems so difficult for some beginning teachers to learn some of the important planning skills. One insight gleaned over the past few years is that it is difficult to learn from experienced teachers, not

Figure 3.3 *Consequences of Clear Instructional Planning*

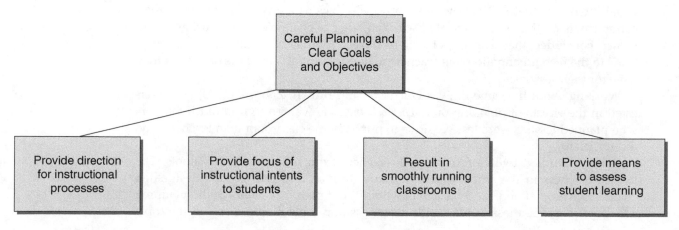

only because they think differently about planning, but also because they approach planning and interactive decision making differently. Two interesting studies highlight these differences.

Gael Leinhardt (1989) conducted a study that compared planning and lesson execution skills of experienced and inexperienced math teachers. Leinhardt found that experienced teachers had more complete "mental notepads" and agendas compared to inexperienced teachers. They also built in and used many more checkpoints to see if students were understanding the lesson than did the inexperienced teachers. The experienced teachers, according to Leinhardt, "weave a series of lessons together to form an instructional topic in a way that consistently builds upon and advances materials introduced in prior lessons":

> Experts also construct lessons that display a highly efficient within-lesson structure, one that is characterized by fluid movement from one type of activity to another. . . . Novice teachers' lessons, on the other hand, are characterized by fragmented lesson structures with long transitions between lesson segments. . . . Their lessons do not fit well together within or across topic boundaries. (p. 73)

In a more recent case study of a high school English teacher, McCutcheon and Milner (2002) found another instance where teacher planning differed significantly from the more traditional views described earlier. We have chosen to highlight their study for this chapter's Research Summary.

Planning skills can sometimes be difficult for beginning teachers to learn because the process itself cannot be directly observed.

Check, Extend, Explore

Check
- What are the benefits and consequences of good planning?
- How did Zahorik's study demonstrate that planning possibly impedes a teacher's level of sensitivity and flexibility? Does his research suggest that planning should be eliminated? Why or why not?
- In what ways do planning approaches of new teachers differ from those used by experienced teachers? How do you explain this, and what can the novice teacher do to improve planning?

Extend
- From your own experiences, what consequences have you observed as a result of planning? Were these positive or negative?
- On a scale of 1 to 10, how detailed do you think a teacher's plans should be? Go to "Extend Question Poll" on the Online Learning Center to respond.

Explore
- Go to the Online Learning Center and listen to Jason O'Brien and Angella Transfeld in the Teachers on Teaching area discuss their approach to planning.

Research Summary

How an Experienced Teacher Approaches Planning

McCutcheon, G., & Milner, H. (2002). A contemporary study of teacher planning in a high school English class. *Teachers and Teaching Theory and Practice, 8*(1), 81–94.

Problem: The researchers were interested in exploring approaches to planning used by experienced teachers.

Sample and Setting: The researchers studied a twenty-five-year veteran teacher (Bill) in his high school English classroom.

Procedures: This is an example of a single case study described in the "Reading and Using Research Handbook" found at the back of *Learning to Teach.* McCutcheon and Milner conducted extended observations of Bill's teaching and interviewed him extensively about his approach to planning.

Results: The researchers found that though "many teachers seem to plan on a day-to-day or weekly basis, Bill planned each course (long) before he teaches it . . . a form [labeled by the researchers] as 'long-range pre-active planning'" (p. 84). For example, in preparation for a new course on major British writers, Bill read through his school's course of study and state standards and researched how other teachers had taught the course. He rejected some of the standards and previous approaches because they depended too much on the textbook. Instead he organized his course thematically and selected literature to study that was available on the Web; he reported with pride that he did not follow "someone else's curriculum" (p. 86). Bill also said that he did not do much short-term planning: "He strives to have an improvisatory nature to discussions in class. . . . [He says] too much

planning restricts the flow of discussion and exploration" (pp. 85–86). For example:

> As we are having a discussion, maybe something in the literature strikes me, but they (students) may not have had the experience to draw on it. So sometimes I have to be able to go out in left field, and I don't always know ahead of time where I'm going to go or exactly where the discussion will take us. That preempts too much short-term planning. (p. 86)

In summary, McCutcheon and Milner found from their study of Bill that he attended to long-range, pre-active planning rather than short-range lesson planning. He did not plan by objectives but through a form of mental imaging and rehearsal that he labeled "backward building," which refers to teachers "envisioning where we want the students to end up and then making plans backwards from there" (pp. 91–92).

Discussion and Implications In their conclusion, McCutcheon and Milner speculated that the reason some teachers were using this approach to planning rather than more traditional approaches was because today's teachers have been influenced by new knowledge and constructivist theories about how students learn. However, this speculation brings up two questions about Bill's approach: (1) Does his more informal approach actually lead to more student learning? (2) If it does, how will standards-based educational environments and Common Core Standards described in Chapter 1 and in this chapter impact the more interactive planning of teachers like Bill?

Teachers plan for different time spans ranging from a few minutes to a full year.

The fact that experienced teachers attend to different planning tasks and cues from those attended to by inexperienced teachers presents some challenging problems for a beginning teacher. Unlike other acts of teaching, most teacher planning occurs in private places, such as the teacher's home, office, or the morning shower. Also, by their very nature, planning and decision making are mental, nonobservable activities. Only the resulting actions are observable by others. Even when written plans are produced, they represent only a small portion of the actual planning that has gone on in the teacher's head. The private nature of planning thus makes it difficult for beginning teachers to learn from experienced teachers. Beginning teachers may ask to look at lesson plans, or they may talk to experienced teachers about planning and decision-making processes. However, many experienced teachers cannot describe in words the novice can understand the thinking that went into specific plans and decisions. This is particularly true of moment-to-moment planning decisions that characterize the rapid flow of classroom life, such as those described by Leinhardt, McCutcheon and Milner. Teacher planning and decision making may be one of the teaching skills for which research can be of most assistance in helping beginning teachers learn about the hidden mental processes of the experienced expert.

Planning Domains

Teacher planning interacts with all other aspects of teaching and is influenced by many factors. Understanding the planning process and mastering the specifics of planning are important skills for beginning teachers.

Planning and the Instructional Cycle

Teacher planning is a multifaceted and ongoing process that covers almost everything teachers do. It is also part of an overall instructional cycle. It is not just the lesson plans that the teachers create for the next day, but also the in-flight adjustments they make as they teach as well as the planning done after instruction as a result of assessment. Figure 3.4 illustrates the overall flow of planning as it is connected to the instructional cycle.

Notice in Figure 3.4 how some aspects of planning precede instruction and, in turn, precede assessment of student learning. The whole planning process, however, is cyclical. Assessment information influences the teacher's next set of plans, the instruction that follows, and so on. Further, the mental processes of planning vary from one phase of the cycle to the next. For example, choosing content can only be done after careful analysis and inquiry into instructional standards and frameworks, students' prior knowledge, the teacher's understanding of the subject matter, and the nature of the subject itself. Most postinstructional decisions, such as the type of assessments to use or how to assign grades, can also be made as a result of consideration. Planning and decision making during instruction itself, on the other hand, most often must be

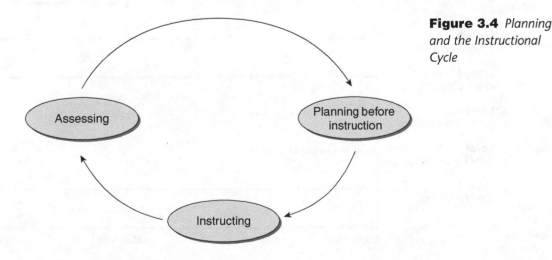

Figure 3.4 *Planning and the Instructional Cycle*

Check, Extend, Explore

Check
- What are the three primary phases of the overall instructional cycle? What types of plans and decisions do teachers make at each phase?
- For what time spans must teachers establish plans?

Extend
- Why do you think it is important to develop unique plans for different time spans? How might these plans interrelate with each other, requiring modification as lessons evolve?

Explore
- There are numerous Web sites on the "instructional cycle." Search this topic on the Internet.

Table 3.1 *Three Phases of Teacher Planning and Decision Making*

Before Instruction	During Instruction	After Instruction
Choosing content	Presenting	Checking for understanding
Choosing approach	Questioning	Providing feedback
Allocating time and space	Assisting	Praising and criticizing
Determining structures	Providing for practice	Testing
Considering motivation	Making transitions	Grading
	Managing and disciplining	Reporting

done spontaneously, on the spur of the moment. Examples of decisions made at each phase of the cycle are listed in Table 3.1.

The Time Spans of Planning

Teachers plan for different time spans, ranging from the next minute or hour to the next week, month, or year. If schoolwide planning or one's own career planning is involved, time spans may even cover several years. Obviously, planning what to do tomorrow is much different from planning for a whole year. However, both are important. Also, plans carried out on a particular day are influenced by what has happened before and will in turn influence plans for the days and weeks ahead.

The most definitive study of the time spans of planning was done a number of years ago by Robert Yinger (1980), when he studied one first- and second-grade elementary school teacher in Michigan. Using participant-observation methods, he spent forty full days over a five-month period observing and recording the teacher's planning activities. As can be observed in Figure 3.5, Yinger was able to identify five time spans that characterized teacher planning: daily planning, weekly planning, unit planning, term planning, and yearly planning. Note also in Figure 3.5 how different planning tasks are emphasized and occur at different times across the school year.

Figure 3.5 *Five Planning Time Spans*

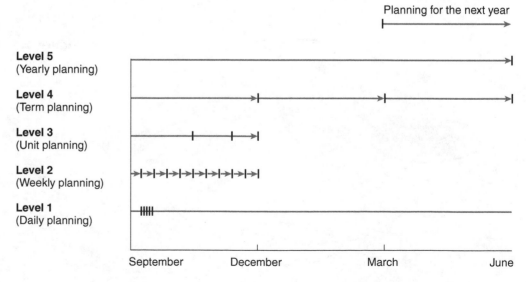

The Specifics of Planning

By now it must be obvious that planning is important and that teachers must consider a broad range of planning tasks. In this section, the primary tasks associated with teacher planning are described in some detail, starting with choosing *what to teach* and the use of *instructional objectives,* followed by the use of *long-range and short-range* plans and the tools available to teachers to accomplish planning tasks.

Planning What to Teach

Deciding what to teach is among one of the most fundamental decisions of teaching. It helps define the overall purposes of education and, as just described, has major influences on what students learn. Making curricula decisions, however, is no easy task. Every year knowledge and access to knowledge increases immensely while instructional time remains scarce. Educators, citizens, and students hold different opinions about what is important to learn. Although guided by standards and curriculum frameworks, at the "end of the day" it is the classroom teachers who must decide what is worthy of teaching in the context of their own perspectives and assessments of their students' needs. This section discusses several important factors that exist today that impact these decisions.

Deciding what to teach is among the most difficult aspects of teacher planning because there is so much to learn and so little time.

Many Voices. Many groups and factors influence what is taught to students in schools situated in a democracy in the twenty-first century. The influences of several groups are illustrated in Figure 3.6.

As indicated in Figure 3.6, professional subject matter associations play a huge role in defining what should be taught. Frameworks and standards, such as the current Common Core Standards, have been developed by such groups as the National Council of Teachers of Mathematics (NCTM), the National Council for the Social Studies (NCSS), the National Council of Teachers of English (NCTE), and the International Reading Association (IRA). The curriculum and **performance standards** adopted by professional associations, in turn, influence the curriculum frameworks, performance content standards, and the assessments developed by national, state, and local curriculum committees. All of this, however, is most often the result of community values and societal viewpoints, particularly for subjects that contain topics that are controversial.

Figure 3.6 *Factors Influencing What Is Taught in Schools*

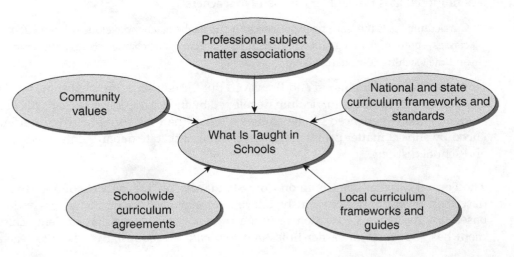

Common Core refers to a recently developed set of state standards in mathematics and the language arts and literacy that have been adopted by most states.

Indeed, the whole process of developing curriculum standards is messy and controversial. For example, several areas of controversy have been reported. Recently, a set of standards called the **Common Core Standards** has been developed in the language arts and literacy and mathematics. These have been adopted by forty-six states. These standards, explained later, have opened up a perennial debate between those who believe in having one set of nationwide common standards to "fit all" versus those who favor more local control of curriculum and/or one that is tailored to the diverse needs of students in particular local schools and communities (Ravitch, 2010, 2013; Wolk, 2011, 2012). Controversies exist at the state level with regard to various proposed history and social studies standards. Views differ about which topics are most important to teach and how much emphasis should be given to prominent historical figures such as Thomas Jefferson or Joe McCarthy. The role religion played in the writing of the U.S. Constitution, the meaning of nineteenth-century expansion, modern-day descriptions of such concepts as free markets and socialism, and the proper place of prayer in the schools are also contentious. Similarly, actions in several states have had the effect of reducing the amount of attention paid to evolution in the science curriculum, an issue that has been controversial for most of the past century.

Local community values also impact local curriculum frameworks and standards. Movements in many communities to get schools "back to the basics" or to use a "phonetic approach" to teaching reading are two examples of how beliefs get translated into curriculum decisions at the local level. The proper approach to teach mathematics has caused considerable debate in the community where the author lives. On one side of the issue are parents and educators who want to adopt a textbook that emphasizes what is often referred to as a more "traditional approach" to teaching mathematics, whereas others prefer a textbook that incorporates "inquiry-oriented and problem-solving" approaches. The topic of sex education always remains controversial, as is the amount of curriculum time that should be spent on the visual and performing arts.

But What Is Curriculum? At this point you may be asking an important question: "What exactly is this curriculum thing?" Many definitions have been given over the years. Some (Tyler, 1949) viewed the curriculum as a set of purposes and important bodies of knowledge that students should learn or at least be exposed to. Others (Apple, 1990; Chomsky, 2002) have argued that the curriculum is an attempt by political and economic interest groups to make what goes on in schools consistent with their views of the world. More recently, Darling-Hammond and Bransford (2005) provided a definition that is probably most useful to teachers:

> Curriculum . . . is the learning experiences and goals the teacher develops for particular classes—both in planning and while teaching—in light of the characteristics of the students and the teaching context. (p. 170)

Note that Darling-Hammond and Bransford put the emphasis on what some label the **enacted curriculum,** the curriculum developed by the teacher (and perhaps his or her students) and experienced by the students, rather than the **formal curriculum** influenced by subject matter professional associations and state departments of education and school districts.

The Formal Curriculum: Common Core Standards, Testing, and Accountability. As described several times previously, education today is characterized by a standards-based environment, a condition resulting from societal beliefs that student achievement has slipped from earlier times and that *only* by requiring teachers to teach to a required common set of performance standards will the situation improve. The achievement gap and beliefs that teachers hold low expectations for particular low-income and minority students also have encouraged standards setting in the hopes that the result will be high expectations for all students (Haycock, 2006; Landsman, 2004; Schmidt & Burroughs, 2013). Remember that the key features of a standards-based system are (1) agreeing on a set of standards to guide teaching and learning, (2) having expectations that every child can meet these standards, and (3) holding schools and teachers accountable for student learning assessed by standardized achievement tests. Here is how this approach works and how it affects the formal curriculum now found in schools.

It begins by setting standards—statements about what students should know and/or be able to do. Over the past two decades an array of standards have been written and adopted by subject matter associations such as the National Council of Teachers of Mathematics, by state departments of education, and by many local education agencies. You are already aware of several sets of standards: those used in your school when you were a student if you are younger than age 30 and the standards developed by the Interstate New Teacher Assessment and Support Consortium (InTASC, 2011), which sets forth what teachers should know and be able to do. As described earlier, standards are influenced by many sources and consist of three important components: (1) the adoption of **standards** organized by grade level around specified content areas and skills; (2) **benchmarks** (check points) on where students should be at a particular point in time; and (3) **performance indicators** or **assessments** used to measure student mastery of particular standards and benchmarks. The relationship among standards, benchmarks, and example performance indicators is illustrated in Figure 3.7.

Today the latest initiative in developing and implementing standards is the Common Core State Standards. The Common Core State Standards have resulted from collaborative efforts among the various states begun 2009. By 2010, standards had been developed and released in two important curricula areas: (1) language arts and literacy and (2) mathematics. As this textbook is being written in 2013, forty-six states have

Academic Content Standards

What students should know and be able to do.

Academic Content Areas

Reading
Mathematics
English
Social studies
Art, music, PE, etc.

Benchmarks

Checkpoints used to monitor progress to achieving standard organized by grade-level clusters.

K–3 4–6 7–9 10–12

Grade-Level Performance Indicators

What students should know and be able to do at each grade level. Helps monitor progress toward each benchmark.

K/1	2	3	4
5	6	7	8
9	10	11	12

Figure 3.7

Relationship among Content Standards, Benchmarks, and Performance Indicators

Table 3.2 *Sample Performance-Based Common Core State Standards*

Language Arts and Literacy

Fifth Grade

- CCSS.ELA-Literacy.L.5.1 Demonstrate command of the conventions of standard English grammar and usage when writing or speaking.
  - CCSS.ELA-Literacy.L.5.1a Explain the function of conjunctions, prepositions, and interjections in general and their function in particular sentences.
  - CCSS.ELA-Literacy.L.5.1b Form and use the perfect (e.g., *I had walked; I have walked; I will have walked*) verb tenses.

Grades 9/10

- CCSS.ELA-Literacy.L.9-10.1 Demonstrate command of the conventions of standard English grammar and usage when writing or speaking.
  - CCSS.ELA-Literacy.L.9-10.1a Use parallel structure.*
  - CCSS.ELA-Literacy.L.9-10.1b Use various types of phrases (noun, verb, adjectival, adverbial, participial, prepositional, absolute) and clauses (independent, dependent; noun, relative, adverbial) to convey specific meanings and add variety and interest to writing or presentations.

Mathematics

Fifth Grade

- CCSS.Math.Content.5.NBT.A.3 Read, write, and compare decimals to thousandths.
  - CCSS.Math.Content.5.NBT.A.3a Read and write decimals to thousandths using base-ten numerals, number names, and expanded form, e.g., $347.392 = 3 \times 100 + 4 \times 10 + 7 \times 1 + 3 \times (1/10) + 9 \times (1/100) + 2 \times (1/1000)$.
  - CCSS.Math.Content.5.NBT.A.3b Compare two decimals to thousandths based on meanings of the digits in each place, using $>$, $=$, and $<$ symbols to record the results of comparisons.

High School Algebra

- CCSS.Math.Content.HSA-REI.B.4 Solve quadratic equations in one variable.
  - CCSS.Math.Content.HSA-REI.B.4a Use the method of completing the square to transform any quadratic equation in x into an equation of the form $(x - p)^2 = q$ that has the same solutions. Derive the quadratic formula from this form.
  - CCSS.Math.Content.HSA-REI.B.4b Solve quadratic equations by inspection (e.g., for $x^2 = 49$), taking square roots, completing the square, the quadratic formula and factoring, as appropriate to the initial form of the equation. Recognize when the quadratic formula gives complex solutions and write them as $a \pm bi$ for real numbers a and b.

Source: Common Core Web site: http://corestandards.org.

adopted the standards and are in process of implementing them. Table 3.2 provides some example of standards from the Common Core language arts and literacy and the mathematics standards.

Note in Figure 3.7 how performance indicators are organized by grade level and in Table 3.2 how overall standards are first written at a more general level and then broken down into more specific performance indicators.

Curriculum standards have had and will continue to have an important influence on what is taught in schools because state achievement or mastery tests are designed around the performances identified in the standards. These tests are administered to students on a regular basis. The No Child Left Behind (NCLB) legislation required states to measure student learning yearly in grades 1–8 and at least once in high school. Student scores are summarized by school, racial groups, and learning disabilities. Results are often published in local newspapers and reported to parents and citizens so they know how students in their schools compare to students elsewhere. More recent proposals by the Obama administration's Race to the Top initiative use student achievement data to evaluate teacher performance. Similar requirements and procedures are associated with the Common Core Standards. Obviously, these actions heighten the influence of state standards and curriculum frameworks and the use of standardized tests.

As described in Chapter 1, some educators and policymakers are critical of this standards-based approach to education, including the Common Core. They argue that it has tended to narrow the curriculum and put too much emphasis on teaching only what can be tested. The debate evolves around the issue discussed earlier of whether common standards are required to ensure that all students have access to the same knowledge and skills or whether it is best to have local control over what students should know and be able to do and to grant teachers considerable decision-making authority based on the needs of their students.

Other, more specific criticisms have been made about the Common Core Standards and the testing associated with them. Some report (Gewertz, 2013a) that the test associated with the Common Core Standards may take up to ten hours at each grade level to administer. At the time of this writing, one state, Alabama, has withdrawn from the consortium that is designing assessments for the Common Core Standards. Many teachers report that they are unprepared for the Common Core Standards (Gewertz, 2013b). Still others have issued complaints about the actual content of the standards, such as too much or too little emphasis on fiction in the language arts and literacy standards. Recently, Diane Ravitch, a prominent educator who has been an advocate of common standards, has indicated that she could no longer support the Common Core Standards (see her Web site at dianeravitch.com and Ravitch, 2013). She has also helped to form a new advocacy organization, the Network for Public Education, that opposes high-stakes testing and the privatization of public schools.

Regardless of its critics, its flaws, and the current debate, the standards-based movement has become an important part of the educational policy environment and curriculum development. It is *not* likely to go away in the near future.

Tools and Strategies for Curriculum Enactment

Even though standards such as those developed in the Common Core and in other subject areas are important, *they are not the only curriculum.* They are a set of expectations about the knowledge and skills that students should learn to be successful. Implementation, however, requires teachers to devise unit and lesson plans (an enacted curriculum) tailored to the particular needs of the students in their classrooms. Fortunately, several ideas and tools exist to help accomplish this important job.

Setting Curriculum Priorities. It has been observed that as teachers, most of us try to teach too much information and too much information that is irrelevant. Students are hampered in learning key ideas because of verbal clutter. Bruner (1962) a long time ago argued that teachers should strive for **economy** in their teaching. Using economy means being very careful about the amount of information and the number of concepts presented in a single lesson or unit of work. The economy principle argues for taking a difficult concept and making it clear and simple for students, not taking an easy concept and making it difficult. It means helping students examine a few critical ideas in depth rather than bombarding them with unrelated facts that have little chance of making an impact on learning.

Bruner also described how the principle of **power** should be applied when selecting content. A powerful lesson or unit is one in which basic concepts from the subject area

> Teaching a few ideas well is more important than covering everything lightly.

Figure 3.8 *Establishing Curricular Priorities*

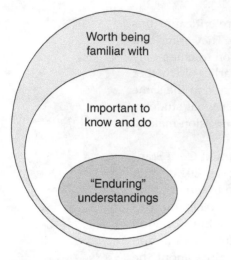

Source: Adapted from Wiggins and McTighe (2005).

Essential questions are questions that reflect the big ideas in any subject and the heart of the curriculum.

are presented in straightforward and logical ways. It is through logical organization that students come to see relationships between specific facts and among the important concepts of a topic. Both of these principles admonish us to "make less more."

Another way to think about setting curriculum priorities is to consider the **enduring understandings** that constitute an area of study. Grant Wiggins and Jay McTighe (1998, 2005) have provided a simple but very useful framework for putting into operation the economy, power, and enduring understandings principles, as illustrated in the nested rings shown in Figure 3.8. The background of the illustration represents the whole field of possible contents, which obviously can't be covered. The largest of the rings represents knowledge and skills that a teacher might determine that students should be familiar with, whereas the middle ring would be that knowledge that is determined to be very important. The students' education would be incomplete if they do not master these **essential questions.** The third ring in the framework represents the "enduring" understandings, the big ideas that should remain with students after they have forgotten most of the details. Wiggins and McTighe offer four questions for teachers to ask as they select what to teach.

Question 1: To what extent does the idea, topic, or process represent a big idea having enduring value beyond the classroom?

Question 2: To what extent does the idea, topic, or process reside at the heart of the discipline?

Question 3: To what extent do students have misconceptions about the idea, topic, or process and find it difficult to grasp?

Question 4: To what extent does the idea, topic, or process offer potential for engaging students?

Working with and Deconstructing Standards. As described previously, standards developed by state departments of education or local agencies play a major role in classrooms across the United States, and they provide an overall sense of direction for what should be taught in particular fields of study. However, it is up to local educators, particularly teachers (and students in learner-centered planning), to implement these standards. The major job for classroom teachers in many instances is to winnow down the overall number of standards and to translate them into specific objectives and learning targets suitable for students in their classroom. Many observers (Marzano & Haystead, 2008; Nichols & Berliner, 2007; Wolk, 2012) have reported that currently the number of standards is exhaustive and that their sheer number detracts from effective teaching. Marzano and Haystead (2008), for instance, reported that in one of their analyses they found that one state's framework had over 200 standards and more than 3,000 benchmarks across 14 subject areas. When this information was presented to a group of teachers, the teachers reported that to have students meet all of the identified standards would require instructional time to be increased by 71 percent, a situation that would extend schooling to grade 22. They also found that many standards had more than one dimension. Some of these flaws have been corrected with the Common Core Standards, but the overall number of standards is still quite exhaustive.

Several steps described below can be taken to *work with and simplify* standards:*

Step 1: Identify and Understand Essential Standards. This step consists of identifying those standards deemed essential. A particular standard is essential if it addresses an important question or enduring idea and/or if it is included prominently on mastery tests students are required to pass.

Step 2: Analyze Standards for Declarative and Procedural Knowledge. Later, in Chapters 7 and 8, distinctions will be made between declarative knowledge and procedural knowledge. Most standards communicate two important outcomes: what students should know (declarative knowledge) and what they should be able to do (procedural knowledge). Both kinds of knowledge are obviously important, and a critical aspect of working with standards is to separate the two kinds of knowledge. A simple process of reading through a standard and underlining key ideas or concepts (declarative knowledge) and circling skills (procedural knowledge) is a way to do this. Most often, key concepts will be nouns; skills will be verbs. For example:

Declarative knowledge to be underlined: Student can list the major elements of a contour map.
Procedural knowledge to be circled: The student will be able to read a contour map.

Step 3: Identify Precursory Subskills and/or Bodies of Enabling Knowledge. Some standards contain numerous subskills and/or understandings tucked into the overall standard. This situation makes it difficult to communicate an outcome clearly to students and to assess whether it has been achieved. Popham (2008) has provided us with a tool he labeled the **learning progression** that defines learning outcomes more precisely. Popham defined a learning progression as a *"sequenced set of subskills* and *bodies of enabling knowledge* that . . . students must master enroute to mastering a more remote curriculum aim [standard]" (p. 24).

One way to think about learning progressions is to view them as "building blocks" that need to be set in place in order to get to the overall standard. Here are some examples of familiar learning progressions. In mathematics, before students can calculate the area of a rectangle, they must be able to measure the rectangle and know how to multiply. Subskills and enabling knowledge for writing a good essay are numerous: knowing the structure of an essay, being able to write a capturing introduction, mastering accepted practices of sentence and paragraph construction, and the like.

Figure 3.9 provides a visual representation of a learning progression adapted from Popham (2008). Note that the hypothetical standard targeted in Figure 3.9 has two enabling knowledge objectives and two subskill objectives, and that teaching these enabling and precursory objectives will require a total of six lessons.

Step 4: Determine Assessments. This step consists of determining the assessments needed for each enabling knowledge and subskill and for the overall standard or instructional outcome. This is an important step, because if there are no ways to measure, formally or informally, then there is no way to collect evidence of whether students have reached the desired learning outcomes associated with the standard.

---

*The five-step process is based on the work of Marzano and Haystead (2008) and Popham (2008) and adapted from descriptions by Arends and Kilcher (2010).

Figure 3.9 *Example of a Learning Progression*

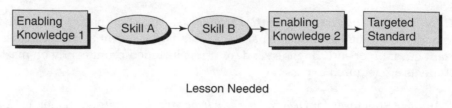

Lesson Needed

2............................1......................2......................1................(6 lesson total)

Source: Based on information from Popham (2008).

Step 5: Build an Instructional Sequence. A final step in the process of working with standards is to design an instructional sequence to teach in some logical order the enabling knowledge and precursory skills. In most instances, the teacher's understanding of the standard will influence this sequence, as will the building blocks required for getting there, and students' prior knowledge and understanding.

The five-step process described here has been shown to be a good way to identify standards deemed essential and to analyze each for multidimensionality.

Instructional Objectives

> **Instructional objectives describe a teacher's intent for student learning.**

By definition, teaching is a process of promoting growth in students. The intended growth may be far-reaching, such as developing a whole new conceptual framework for thinking about science or acquiring a new appreciation for literature. It may be as precise and simple as learning how to tie a shoestring. Teachers' intentions for student learning are called a variety of names. In the past, they have been referred to as *aims, purposes, goals,* or *outcomes* (Bobbitt, 1918; Rugg, 1926; Tyler, 1949). Today, they are often referred to as standards or learning targets (Moss & Brookhart, 2012). In *Learning to Teach,* the term **instructional objective** is used to describe teachers' own intentions for students' growth and change. You will find that instructional objectives are like road maps: They help you and your students know where they are going and when they have arrived at their destination. Like different kinds of road maps, some instructional objectives are and are easy to make and to read. Others are more complex. For this reason, there are several different approaches to guide the writing of instructional objectives and a variety of formats to use. A major issue (sometimes controversial) has been differences among theorists and teachers about how specific or general instructional objectives should be. Regardless of the approach, having clear learning objectives is always at the top of everyone's list of effective teaching.

The Mager Format of Behavioral Objectives. In 1962, Robert Mager wrote a little book titled *Preparing Instructional Objectives* that set off a debate over the most desirable "form of a usefully stated objective" (p. i). The general message of Mager's work was the argument that for instructional objectives to be meaningful, they must clearly communicate a teacher's instructional intent and should be very specific. Objectives written in the Mager format became known as **behavioral objectives** and required three parts:

- *Student behavior.* What the student will be doing or the kinds of behavior the teacher will accept as evidence that the objective has been achieved.
- *Testing situation.* The condition under which the behavior will be observed or expected to occur.
- *Performance criteria.* The standard or performance level defined as acceptable.

Table 3.3 *Sample Behavioral Objectives Using Mager's Format*

Parts of the Objective	Examples
Student behavior	Identify nouns
Testing situation	Given a list of nouns and verbs
Performance criteria	Mark at least 85 percent correct
Student behavior	List five causes of the Civil War
Testing situation	Essay test without use of notes
Performance criteria	Discuss four of five reasons

A simple mnemonic for remembering the three parts of a behavioral objective is to think of it as the STP approach: student behavior (S), testing situation (T), and performance criteria (P). Table 3.3 illustrates how Mager's three-part approach works and provides examples of each.

When teachers write behavioral objectives using the Mager format, the recommendation is to use precise words that are *not* open to many interpretations. Examples of precise words include *write, list, identify, compare.* Examples of less precise words are *know, understand, appreciate.* There are also recommendations about how to link the three parts of the instructional objective together using the following steps: Begin by noting the testing situation, follow this by stating the student behavior, and then write the performance criteria. Table 3.4 illustrates how behavioral objectives written in this format might look.

Over the years Mager's behavioral approach has been widely accepted among teachers and others in the educational community. Well-written behavioral objectives give students a very clear statement about what is expected of them, and they help teachers when it comes time to measure student progress, as you will see in Chapter 6. The behavioral approach, however, is not free from criticism.

Well-written behavioral objectives give students a clear statement of what is expected of them.

Critics have argued that Mager's format leads to reductionism and, when used exclusively, it leads to neglect of many of the most important goals of education. Putting an emphasis on precision and observable student behaviors forces teachers to be specific in their objectives. To accomplish this specificity, they must break larger, more global educational goals into very small pieces. The number of objectives, as in the case with standards, for almost any subject or topic could run well into the thousands,

Some critics believe that relying on specific student behaviors as the sole measure of learning does not provide evidence of larger learning goals that may not be observable.

Table 3.4 *Three Parts of Behavioral Objectives Applied*

Testing Situation	Student Behavior	Performance Criteria
Given a map . . .	The student will be able to:	At least 85 percent
Without notes . . .	Identify	Four of five reasons
With the text . . .	Solve	Correct to nearest percentages
	Compare	
	Contrast	
	Recite	

an unmanageable list for most teachers. The teacher also runs the risk of paying attention only to specific objectives, which are of minor importance in themselves, while neglecting the sum total, which is more important than all the parts.

Critics have also pointed out, and rightfully so, that many of the more complex cognitive processes are not readily observable. It is easy, for instance, to observe a student add two columns of numbers and determine if the answer is correct. It is not easy to observe the thought processes or the mathematical problem solving that goes into this act. Along the same line, it is rather easy to observe students recall the major characters in a Tolstoy novel. It is not so easy to observe and measure their appreciation of Russian literature or the novel as a form of creative expression. Critics worry that the emphasis on behavioral objectives may lead to the neglect of the more important aspects of education merely because the latter are not readily observed and measured.

More General Approaches. Several curriculum theorists, as well as measurement specialists, have developed alternative approaches to the behavior objective. Gronlund (2005), Gronlund and Brookhart (2009), and Moss and Brookhart (2012), for example, illustrated how objectives can be written first in more general terms, with appropriate specifics added later for clarification. Gronlund, unlike the strict behaviorists, is more willing to use words such as *appreciate, understand, value,* or *enjoy* with his approach. He believes that although these words are open to a wide range of interpretations, they nonetheless communicate more clearly the educational intents of many teachers. Table 3.5 illustrates how an objective might look using the Gronlund format.

Notice that the initial objective is not very specific and perhaps not very meaningful or helpful in guiding lesson preparation or measuring student change. It does, however, communicate the overall intent the teacher wants to achieve. The subobjectives help clarify what should be taught and what students are expected to learn. They provide more precision, yet are not as precise as the three-part behavior objective. Popham's (2008) idea of the learning progression decribed earlier can also be a useful tool for providing more precision for this type of instructional objective.

A third approach for writing objectives has been developed by scholars who recently revised Bloom's *Taxonomy of Educational Objectives,* a topic of the next section. The Bloom revisionists (Anderson et al., 2001) argue that objectives that use more traditional frameworks have focused only on content and skills of instruction and have ignored the cognitive—the "way-students-think" dimension of teaching and learning. They have identified a standard format for stating objectives that requires only a *verb*

Table 3.5 *More General Approach to Writing Objectives*

Format	Example
Overall objective	Understands and appreciates the diversity of the people who make up American society.
Subobjective 1	Can define diversity in the words of others and in his or her own words.
Subobjective 2	Can give instances of how diverse persons or groups have enriched the cultural life of Americans.
Subobjective 3	Can analyze in writing how maintaining appreciation for diversity is a fragile and difficult goal to achieve.

and a *noun.* The verb generally describes the intended *cognitive process* and the noun describes the *knowledge* students are expected to acquire. Take the following as examples of what an objective would look like using the taxonomy framework:

- The student will *learn to distinguish* (verb for cognitive process) among *federal and unitary systems of government* (noun for knowledge).
- The student will *learn to classify* (verb for cognitive process) different types of *objectives* (noun for knowledge).
- The student will *be able to analyze* (verb for cognitive process) various types of *social data* (noun for knowledge).

This approach will become clearer to you after reading the next section on Bloom's taxonomy.

Which Approach to Use? The form and use of instructional objectives, as with many other aspects of teaching, are likely to remain subject to controversy and inquiry for a long time. The approach teachers use will be influenced somewhat by schoolwide policies, but in most instances, considerable latitude exists for individual preference and decisions. It is important to remember that the purposes behind instructional objectives are to communicate clearly to students a teacher's intents and to aid in assessing student growth. Common sense, as well as the research summarized earlier, suggests adopting a middle ground between objectives stated at such a high level of abstraction that they are meaningless and a strict adherence to the behavioral approach. Gronlund's approach of writing a more global objective first and then clarifying it and getting as specific as the subject matter allows is probably the best advice at this time. Similarly, after reading the next section, you will see the importance of identifying not only the content to be learned but also the cognitive process associated with the learning.

> Some educators advocate first writing global objectives and then writing specific objectives that are consistent with the larger (usually unobservable) ones.

Taxonomies for Selecting Instructional Objectives

Taxonomies are devices that classify and show relationships among things. You already know about a variety of taxonomies; for instance, those that classify plants and animals in science and those that classify food groups, the colors, and the periodic table of the elements. One taxonomy that has been a very useful tool for making decisions about instructional objectives and for assessing learning outcomes has been Bloom's *taxonomy for educational objectives.* This taxonomy was initially developed by Bloom and his colleagues in the 1950s (Bloom, 1956). Recently, it was revised by a group of Bloom's students (Anderson et al., 2001) and renamed *taxonomy for learning, teaching, and assessing.* As the name implies, the revised taxonomy provides a framework for classifying learning objectives and a way for assessing them.

Bloom's revised taxonomy is two-dimensional. One dimension, the **knowledge dimension,** describes different types of knowledge and organizes knowledge into four categories: factual knowledge, conceptual knowledge, procedural knowledge, and metacognitive knowledge. These categories lie along a continuum from very concrete knowledge (factual) to the more abstract (metacognitive). The second dimension, the **cognitive process** (ways of thinking) **dimension,** contains six categories: remember, understand, apply, analyze, evaluate, and create. The categories of the cognitive process dimension are assumed to lie along a continuum of cognitive complexity. For example, understanding something is more complex than simply remembering it; applying and analyzing an idea is more complex than understanding the idea.

> Cognitive processes are the ways of thinking engaged in by students.

Table 3.6 *Two Dimensions of Bloom's Revised Taxonomy*

The Knowledge Dimension	The Cognitive Process Dimension
Factual knowledge	Remembering
Conceptual knowledge	Understanding
Procedural knowledge	Applying
Metacognitive knowledge	Analyzing
	Evaluating
	Creating

Source: Adapted from Anderson et al. (2001).

Table 3.6 shows the two dimensions of the taxonomy and the relationship between the knowledge and cognitive process dimensions.

Categories of the Knowledge Dimension. The revised taxonomy divides knowledge into four categories: **Factual knowledge** includes the basic elements that students need to know to be acquainted with a topic. **Conceptual knowledge** is knowledge about the interrelationships among basic elements. **Procedural knowledge** is knowing how to do "something." **Metacognitive knowledge** is knowledge about one's own cognition as well as knowing when to use particular conceptual or procedural knowledge. Table 3.7 explains the four major types of knowledge and provides examples of each type.

Categories of the Cognitive Process Dimension. The cognitive dimension provides a classification scheme of various **cognitive processes** that might be included in an instructional objective. These processes lie along a continuum that ranges from the rather simple (remembering) to the more complex (creating). As shown in Table 3.8, **remember**, according to the taxonomy's creators, means to retrieve relevant information from long-term memory, whereas **understand** means to construct meaning from instructional messages. **Apply** means to carry out or use a procedure; **analyze** means to break material into its constituent parts and determine how the parts relate to one another. **Evaluate** and **create,** the two categories situated at the more complex end of the continuum, mean to make judgments based on criteria, and to put elements together to form a new pattern or structure, respectively. Notice also in Table 3.8 that each process category is associated with two or more specific cognitive processes. "Remember," for example, includes the cognitive processes of recognizing and recalling. "Evaluate" includes the cognitive processes of checking and critiquing.

Bloom's revised taxonomy helps us to understand and classify objectives and, also, as described later in Chapter 6, how to assess them. Figure 3.10 shows how a particular objective can be classified. Note that the objective "the student will be able to apply the supply and demand principle" is classified as conceptual knowledge (knowledge of principles) and requires the cognitive process of apply (carry out or use a principle).

The ability to classify objectives with this tool allows teachers to consider their objectives from the wide range of available possibilities and provides a way of remembering the "integral relationship between knowledge and cognitive processes inherent in any objective" (Anderson et al., 2001, p. 35). Also, categorization of objectives helps

Table 3.7 *Major Types of Knowledge in the Knowledge Dimension*

Major Types and Subtypes	Examples
A. Factual Knowledge—The basic elements students must know to be acquainted with a discipline or solve problems in it	
Aᴀ. Knowledge of terminology	Technical vocabulary, music symbols
Aʙ. Knowledge of specific details and elements	Major natural resources, reliable sources of information
B. Conceptual Knowledge—The interrelationships among the basic elements within a larger structure that enable them to function together	
Bᴀ. Knowledge of classifications and categories	Periods of geological time, forms of business ownership
Bʙ. Knowledge of principles and generalizations	Pythagorean theorem, law of supply and demand
Bᴄ. Knowledge of theories, models, and structures	Theory of evolution, structure of Congress
C. Procedural Knowledge—How to do something, methods of inquiry, and criteria for using skills, algorithms, techniques, and methods	
Cᴀ. Knowledge of subject-specific skills and algorithms	Skills used in painting with watercolors, whole-number division algorithm
Cʙ. Knowledge of subject-specific techniques and methods	Interviewing techniques, scientific method
Cᴄ. Knowledge of criteria for determining when to use appropriate procedures	Criteria used to determine when to apply a procedure involving Newton's second law, criteria used to judge the feasibility of using a particular method to estimate business costs
D. Metacognitive Knowledge—Knowledge of cognition in general as well as awareness and knowledge of one's own cognition	
Dᴀ. Strategic knowledge	Knowledge of outlining as a means of capturing the structure of a unit of subject matter in a text book, knowledge of the use of heuristics
Dʙ. Knowledge about cognitive tasks, including appropriate contextual and conditional knowledge	Knowledge of the types of tests particular teachers administer, knowledge of the cognitive demands of different tasks
Dᴄ. Self-knowledge	Knowledge that critiquing essays is a personal strength, whereas writing essays is a personal weakness; awareness of one's own knowledge level

Source: Anderson et al. (2001), p. 29.

point out consistencies or inconsistencies among an array of objectives for a given unit of study and, as will be described later, helps teachers deal more effectively with assessment of their instructional objectives.

Bloom's initial taxonomy was not free from criticism. Some misinterpreted it to say that certain, less complex types of knowledge are not as important as those that are

Table 3.8 *The Cognitive Process Dimension and Related Cognitive Processes*

Process Categories	Cognitive Processes and Examples
1. Remember—Retrieve relevant knowledge from long-term memory	
1.1 Recognizing	(e.g., Recognize the dates of important events in U.S. history)
1.2 Recalling	(e.g., Recall the dates of important events in U.S. history)
2. Understand—Construct meaning from instructional messages, including oral, written, and graphic communication	
2.1 Interpreting	(e.g., Paraphrase important speeches and documents)
2.2 Exemplifying	(e.g., Give examples of various artistic painting styles)
2.3 Classifying	(e.g., Classify observed or described cases of mental disorders)
2.4 Summarizing	(e.g., Write a short summary of the events portrayed on videotapes)
2.5 Inferring	(e.g., In learning a foreign language, infer grammatical principles from examples)
2.6 Comparing	(e.g., Compare historical events to contemporary situations)
2.7 Explaining	(e.g., Explain the causes of important eighteenth-century events in France)
3. Apply—Carry out or use a procedure in a given situation	
3.1 Executing	(e.g., Divide one whole number by another whole number, both with multiple digits)
3.2 Implementing	(e.g., Determine in which situations Newton's second law is appropriate)
4. Analyze—Break material into constituent parts and determine how parts relate to one another and to an overall structure or purpose	
4.1 Differentiating	(e.g., Distinguish between relevant and irrelevant numbers in a mathematical word problem)
4.2 Organizing	(e.g., Structure evidence in a historical description into evidence for and against a particular historical explanation)
4.3 Attributing	(e.g., Determine the point of view of the author of an essay in terms of his or her political perspective)
5. Evaluate—Make judgments based on criteria and standards	
5.1 Checking	(e.g., Determine whether a scientist's conclusions follow from observed data)
5.2 Critiquing	(e.g., Judge which of two methods is the best way to solve a given problem)
6. Create—Put elements together to form a coherent or functional whole; reorganize elements into a new pattern or structure	
6.1 Generating	(e.g., Generate hypotheses to account for an observed phenomenon)
6.2 Planning	(e.g., Plan a research paper on a given historical topic)
6.3 Producing	(e.g., Build habitats for certain species for certain purposes)

Source: Anderson et al. (2001), p. 31.

Figure 3.10 *Classifying an Objective in the Taxonomy Table*

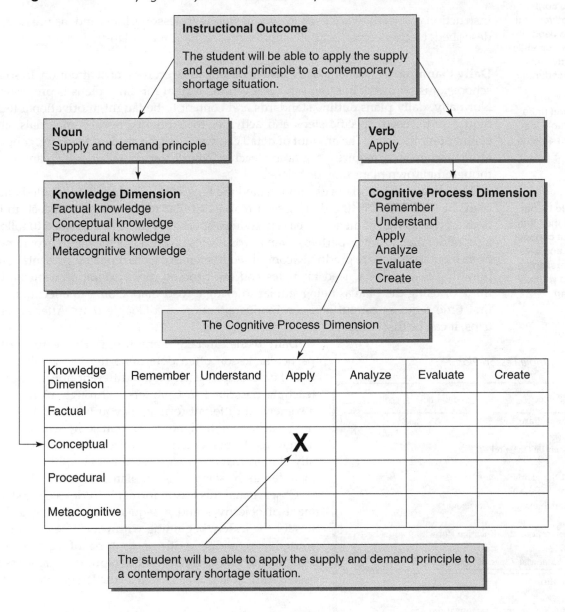

more complex. This was not Bloom's intent. Others challenged the hierarchical ordering of the instructional objectives. The same criticisms have been made of the revised taxonomy, particularly in regard to the new complexity continuum. Finally, critics have argued, and rightfully so, that the taxonomy and the ordering of categories do not fit all fields of knowledge equally well.

Regardless of the criticism and identified weaknesses in the taxonomy, it remains popular with teachers. It provides a valuable way of thinking about instructional intents and assessment and a good reminder that we want students to learn a variety of knowledge and skills and be able to think and act in a variety of straightforward as well as complex ways.

Daily lesson plans normally outline the content to be taught, motivational techniques to be used, materials needed, specific steps and activities, and assessment procedures.

Most teachers organize instruction around units that require multiple lessons spread over several days.

Unit plans should be put in writing, since they function as maps that connect several lessons and give teachers, students, and others an idea of where lessons are going.

Lesson Plans and Unit Plans

Instructional objectives are used in conjunction with **lesson plans,** and, as previously described, teachers construct both short-term and long-term plans.

Daily Planning. A teacher's daily plan is the one that receives most attention. In some schools, it is required. In other schools, even the format for daily plans is prescribed. Normally, daily plans outline standards and content to be taught, motivational techniques to be used, specific steps and activities for students, needed materials, and evaluation processes. The amount of detail can vary. During student teaching, cooperating teachers may require a beginning teacher to write very detailed daily plans, even though their own plans may be briefer.

Most beginning teachers can understand the logic of requiring rather detailed daily plans at first. Think of the daily lesson plan as similar to the text of a speech to be delivered to a large audience. Speakers giving a speech for the first time need to follow a set of detailed notes or perhaps even a word-for-word text. As they gain experience, or as their speeches are gradually committed to memory from repeated presentations, they find less and less need for notes and can proceed more extemporaneously. Or think of using the plan as being similar to using a road map. Going to a location the first time requires careful and continuous attention to a Google map. After several trips, it can be discarded.

Daily plans can take many forms. The features of a particular lesson often determine the lesson plan format. For example, each of the different approaches to teaching described in Chapters 7 through 13 requires a somewhat different format, as you will see. A beginning teacher will find, however, that some schools have a preferred format that they require of all teachers. Usually, that format contains most, if not all, of the features included in the sample lesson plan in Figure 3.11.

Observe that this lesson format includes a clear statement of objectives and a sequence of learning activities for the lesson, beginning with ways to get students started and ending with some type of closure and assignment. The lesson format also provides a means to assess student learning as well as the lesson itself.

Weekly and Unit Planning. Most schools and teachers organize instruction around weeks and units. A unit is essentially a chunk of content and associated skills that are perceived as fitting together in a logical way. The objectives of an instructional unit are tied to curricula standards and more than one lesson is required to accomplish the unit's purposes. The content of the unit may come from either state or local frameworks and in some instances from the teacher's own long-range plans. Textbooks also influence the content of an instructional unit.

Unit planning is, in many ways, more critical than daily planning. The **unit plan** links together a variety of goals, content, and activities the teacher has in mind. It

Figure 3.11 *Sample Lesson Plan*

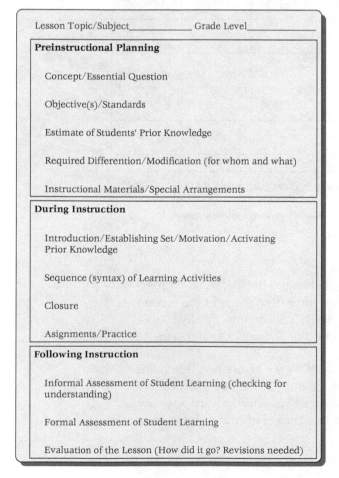

Lesson Topic/Subject_____ Grade Level_____

Preinstructional Planning

Concept/Essential Question

Objective(s)/Standards

Estimate of Students' Prior Knowledge

Required Differention/Modification (for whom and what)

Instructional Materials/Special Arrangements

During Instruction

Introduction/Establishing Set/Motivation/Activating Prior Knowledge

Sequence (syntax) of Learning Activities

Closure

Asignments/Practice

Following Instruction

Informal Assessment of Student Learning (checking for understanding)

Formal Assessment of Student Learning

Evaluation of the Lesson (How did it go? Revisions needed)

determines the overall flow for a series of lessons over several days, weeks, or perhaps even months. Often it reflects the teacher's understanding of both the content and processes of instruction and, perhaps most important, *it provides an opportunity to connect learning objectives to previous and future learning.*

Most people can memorize plans for an hour or a day, but they cannot remember the logistics and sequencing of activities for several days or weeks. For this reason, teachers' unit plans are generally written in a fair amount of detail. When unit plans are put into writing, they also serve as a reminder later that some lessons require supporting materials, equipment, motivational devices, or assessment tools that cannot be obtained on a moment's notice. If teachers are working together in teams, unit planning and assignment of responsibilities for various unit activities are most important. The content usually contained in a unit of instruction can be found in the sample unit plan illustrated in Figure 3.12.

It is important to share unit plans with students because they provide the overall road map that explains where the teacher or a particular lesson is going. Through the communication of unit goals and activities, students can recognize what they are expected to learn. Knowledge of unit plans can help older students allocate their study time and monitor their own progress.

Beginning teachers often rely on plans and materials developed by state and local curriculum committees or those found on the Internet, and there is nothing wrong with this. However, a note of caution is worth mentioning. Some teachers, even after several years of experience, still rely on textbooks for planning and sequencing their instruction. Teaching and learning are creative, evolutionary processes that should be keyed to curriculum standards and to a particular group of students at a particular point in time. Only when this is done can lessons rise above the humdrum and provide students with intellectual excitement.

Figure 3.12 *Sample Unit Plan*

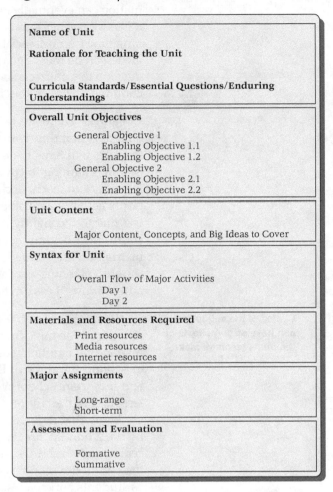

Yearly Planning. Yearly plans are also critical but, because of the uncertainty and complexity in most schools, cannot be done with as much precision as daily or unit plans. The effectiveness of yearly plans generally revolves around how well they deal with the following three features:

Overall Themes and Attitudes. Most teachers have some global attitudes, standards, and themes they like to leave with their students. Perhaps a teacher in a mixed-race elementary classroom would like his or her students to end the term with a bit less bias or misunderstanding and a bit more tolerance of people who are racially different. No specific lesson or unit can teach this attitude, but many carefully planned and coordinated experiences throughout the year can. Or perhaps a high school biology teacher would like students to understand and embrace a set of attitudes associated with scientific methods. A single lesson on the scientific method will not accomplish this goal. However, personal modeling and formal demonstrations showing respect for data, the

> Most teachers have a few long-term global goals that can be achieved only by infusing them into many lessons and units during the year.

relationships between theory and reality, or the process of making inferences from information can eventually influence students to think more scientifically. As a last example, a history teacher may want students to leave her class with an appreciation of the very long time frame associated with the development of democratic traditions. Again, a single lesson on the Magna Carta, the Constitution, or the Fourteenth Amendment will not develop this appreciation. However, building a succession of lessons that come back to a common theme on the "cornerstones of democracy" can achieve this end.

Coverage. There are few teachers who run out of things to do. Instead, the common lament is that time runs out with many important lessons still to be taught. Beginning teachers will have to develop yearlong plans if they want to get past the Civil War by March. Planning to cover desired standards and topics requires asking what is really important to teach, deciding on priorities, and attending carefully to the instructional hours actually available over a year's time. In most instances, teachers strive to teach too much, too lightly. Students are better served if a reduced menu is planned. In short, most beginning teachers overestimate how much time is actually available for instruction and underestimate the amount of time it takes to teach something well. Careful planning can help minimize this error in judgment. Remember the earlier admonition: "Less can be more."

Cycles of the school year can have strong effects on the plans teachers make.

Cycles of the School Year. Experienced teachers know that the school year is cyclical and that some topics are better taught at one time than another. School cycles and corresponding emotional or psychological states revolve around the opening and closing of school, the days of the week, vacation periods, the changes of season, holidays, and important school events. Some of these can be anticipated; some cannot. Nonetheless, it is important to plan for school cycles as much as possible. Experienced teachers know that new units or important topics are not introduced on Friday or the day before a holiday break. They know that the opening of school should emphasize processes and structures to facilitate student learning later in the year. They know that the end of the school year will be filled with interruptions and decreasing motivation as students anticipate summer vacation. They also know that it is unwise to plan for a unit examination the night after a big game or the hour following the Halloween party.

As beginning teachers, you will know something about these cycles and corresponding psychological states from your own student days. You can use this information, along with information provided by experienced teachers in a school, as you proceed with making long-range, yearly plans.

Time tables are chronological maps showing how a series of instructional activities are carried out over time.

Time-Tabling Techniques to Assist Unit and Yearly Planning. There are several techniques to assist teachers in making clear and doable instructional plans that extend over several days or weeks or that include many specific, independent tasks to be completed before moving on. One such technique is **time-tabling.** A time table is a chronological map of a series of instructional activities or some special project the teacher may want to carry out. It describes the overall direction of activities and any special products that may be produced within a time frame. The most straightforward time-tabling technique consists of constructing a special chart called a Gantt chart. A **Gantt chart** allows you to see the work pieces in relation to each other—when each starts and finishes. Gantt charts can be used similarly to previously described curriculum maps to show how particular content is to be covered over a period of time, such as a semester. They can also be used to plan logistics for instructional activities, such as the one illustrated in Figure 3.13 used by a teacher to plan a field trip to a local museum.

There are many formats for making time tables, and several different software packages are available today to assist with time-tabling tasks. Some teachers believe

Figure 3.13 *Gantt Chart, Museum Trip*

TASK	TIME			
	Mar 10–15	Mar 18–23	Mar 26–31	April 3–7
Call museum director	xx			
Talk to principal	xx			
Request bus for field trip	xx			
Introduce unit on art history	xxxxxxxx			
Prepare field trip permission slips	xx			
Send home permission slips		xx		
Require slips to be returned			xx	
Teach unit on art history		xxxxxxxxxxxxxxxxxxxxxxxxx		
Go over logistics of field trip				xxxxxxxx
Discuss what to look for on trip				xxxx
Take trip				X
Follow up trip in class				xxxx
Write thank-you letters				xxx

It is often important for teachers to communicate their plans to parents.

in evolving processes and prefer a more open and nonspecific approach. Others prefer just the opposite and write everything down in great detail. One's own personal
philosophy and work style influence the exact approach and level of detail required.

The Enhancing Teaching and Learning with Technology box for this chapter
describes several tools that can assist teachers with planning and time-tabling.

Enhancing Teaching and Learning with Technology
Planning Tools and Software Evaluation

Technology is related to teacher planning in two important ways: (1) It can be a powerful tool for organizing learning activities, keeping attendance records, and creating lesson plans and learning materials. (2) It presents an important planning task for teachers in deciding how to integrate technology into particular lessons and how to evaluate particular technologies such as computer software, CDs, and Web-based materials.

Planning Tools

A variety of tools are available to assist teachers with planning tasks. Because specific electronic tools are constantly changing, the list below consists of more general categories that can be used to search for specific up-to-date tools.

- *Lesson planning software*—Software designed to organize lesson plans and to tie particular plans to learning targets.
- *Worksheet and puzzle tools*—Software designed to create worksheets and puzzles and link these to learning targets.
- *Concept and mind mapping tools*—Software for organizing ideas into conceptual maps or webs and showing relationships among various ideas.
- *Certificate production software*—Software for creating certificates that can be given to students to reward achievement and special effort.
- *Poster and bulletin board production tools*—Software that enables teachers to create and print posters and other devices to post on bulletin boards and classroom walls.
- *Time and meeting management tools*—Software and handheld computers that allow teachers to plan, keep track of, and organize meetings, schedules, things to do, telephone numbers, and so on. Examples include:
  - Calendars, such as Google Calendar or Microsoft Outlook.
  - Thought catchers and note takers, such as Microsoft Notes and Tasks, OneNote, or Google Tasks.
  - To-do lists, such as Microsoft and Apple Sticky Notes.

More general tools such as database software and spreadsheets included in software suites such as Apple's iWorks and Microsoft Office can also be helpful to teachers for keeping records, summarizing information, and performing a variety of other planning and organizing activities. Examples of planning tools and Web sites and where they can be accessed can be found in the *Learning to Teach* Online Learning Center (OLC).

Selecting Software

Today's teachers will definitely make technology part of their classroom and their teaching. Here are some general guidelines for choosing and using technology:

1. Choose technology with a goal of how it can help students explore and construct information.
2. Choose technology that can promote cooperative learning and problem solving.
3. Choose technology that is accurate, reliable, and free from bias.

Software Review

As with any educational material or resource, teachers must review and evaluate technological tools such as computer software, CDs, and Web sites for their quality and their appropriateness for particular groups of students. Numerous criteria have been developed to evaluate technology-based teaching resources. Following are some questions that can be used to evaluate software and Web sites:

Quality Questions and Technical Questions

- Is the particular software/Web site the best medium to use to accomplish your goals?
- Is the software/Web site content aligned with your curriculum or learning standards?
- Is the content accurate?
- Is the content free of bias, stereotypes, and violence?
- Is the level of difficulty appropriate for your students?
- Is the software or Web site student and teacher friendly? Easy to access? Easy to navigate?
- Is the software/Web site designed for individuals or groups of students?
- If designed for individuals, can students use it independently?
- If designed for groups of students, does it support cooperative learning?
- Does the software/Web site provide useful feedback to students?
- Does the software/Web site have sufficient motivational appeal?
- Can your school's computers access the Web site and/or do they have sufficient memory to use the software?

So many software programs, CDs, and Web sites exist today that it is impossible for teachers to review each and every piece or site. Fortunately, special groups have been formed for the purpose of reviewing software and Web sites. You might think about and use these groups the same way you do *Consumer Reports*—these groups test a wide variety of technology products and provide evaluation information for teachers. One that the author has found useful is SuperKids: Educational Software Review (www.superkids.com).

Other Planning Decisions. Most of this discussion has been devoted to how teachers choose curriculum content, instructional objectives, and learning activities. There are, however, other decisions teachers make about their classroom that require advanced planning. For example, classroom teachers and students are expected to perform certain housekeeping activities such as taking attendance, keeping the classroom space safe and livable, making assignments, collecting papers, and distributing and storing materials. These tasks, like instructional tasks, require careful planning. Experienced teachers plan housekeeping tasks so thoroughly and efficiently that the naïve observer may not even notice they are occurring. A beginning teacher who has not planned efficient ways to accomplish housekeeping routines will suffer from ongoing confusion and wasted instructional time. The following planning guidelines for routines derive from effective teachers' practice and from experience.

Guideline 1. Make sure detailed plans exist for taking roll, giving assignments, collecting and distributing papers, and storing books and equipment.

Guideline 2. Distribute these plans and procedures to students the first time a housekeeping activity occurs in a particular year or with a particular class.

Guideline 3. Provide students with time to practice routines and procedures, and give them feedback on how well they are doing.

Guideline 4. Post copies of the housekeeping plans on the bulletin board or on chart paper to serve as public reminders about how particular activities are to be carried out.

Guideline 5. Train student helpers immediately to provide leadership and assistance in carrying out routines. Students at all ages can and like to be in charge of taking roll, picking up books, getting and setting up the movie projector, and the like.

Guideline 6. Follow the plan that has been developed consistently, and make sure that plenty of time exists to carry out each activity, particularly early in the year.

Guideline 7. Be alert to ways to make housekeeping activities more efficient and seek feedback about how students think the housekeeping activities are going.

Diversity and Differentiation

Differentiation through Planning

This is the first chapter where you find the feature Diversity and Differentiation, a topic so important that it is given special consideration. This feature, found here and in subsequent chapters, will highlight how teachers can adapt and differentiate instructional practices to the wide range of abilities, diverse cultural backgrounds, and various special needs of their students.

Effective teachers use their planning activities to differentiate instruction and to meet the needs of every student. By planning carefully teachers can provide more time for some students to complete assignments, adjust the level of difficulty of instructional materials, and provide varied learning activities for others. In some instances, what students are expected to learn can also vary. Below are several specific ways teachers can individualize instruction through planning. This topic will be elaborated on later when instructional differentiation is discussed in Chapter 13.

Keep Learning Objectives the Same for All Students. Sometimes content taught to students is so important that teachers do not have the luxury of tailoring their objectives

Check, Extend, Explore

Check
- What are the major factors that influence teachers' decisions about what to teach?
- What is curriculum? How do formal and enacted curricula differ?
- What are standards? Benchmarks? Performance indicators?
- What methods do teachers use to set curriculum priorities?
- What is meant by deconstructing standards? How can this process be used to enhance student learning?
- What is a learning progression? How can it be used to help define standards more precisely?
- How do the various approaches to writing objectives differ? What have been the major criticisms of the behavioral approach to writing objectives?
- What are taxonomies? What are the category schemes in Bloom's revised taxonomy?
- What are the differences between unit plans and daily plans?
- How can teachers adapt instruction to meet the individual needs of their students?

Extend
- Do you think teachers should be required to hand in their lesson plans to the principal? Go to "Extend Question Poll" on the Online Learning Center to respond.

Explore
- There are literally thousands of Web sites on how to write objectives and prepare lesson plans. Search these topics on the Internet and find the variety of approaches that exist.
- Go to the Common Core Web site and read about these standards. Consider how these will influence the way you plan for instruction.

to meet the needs of particular students. For example, all students are expected to know the answers to specific questions that appear on required mastery tests. These questions normally cover the basics in core curriculum areas: mathematics, reading and writing, the sciences, and history. Because students do not come to class with the same backgrounds and abilities in these subjects, the teacher's plan must reflect ways to help them make progress according to their abilities. Normally, teachers do this by varying one of three aspects of instruction: time, materials, or learning activities.

Vary Time. Every experienced teacher knows that it takes some students longer than others to master particular content. To accommodate these differences, teachers devise plans with a common assignment but provide more time for students who need it to complete the assignment. To make this work, however, teachers must plan for the students who are likely to complete their work ahead of others. Generally, this means providing enrichment activities for students who complete the assignment quickly or making technology centers and other resources available to these students so they can pursue advanced topics of their choosing.

Adapt Materials. Teachers can also tailor their instruction through planning by varying the level of difficulty of the instructional materials. Some schools provide a variety of books and learning materials that are written at different levels. In other schools, teachers will have to make their own adjustments. Materials can be adapted by rewriting, although this can be very time-consuming. Other ways to adapt materials include providing students with specially designed study guides or notes that make the materials easier to understand or making flashcards and other practice devices available.

Use Different Learning Activities. As described in Chapter 2, students vary in the way they prefer to learn. Some students can glean a great amount of information from text, while others are more adept at listening to the teacher explain things. Some students like to deal with abstract ideas, whereas others are more successful when they are working with hands-on materials and projects. Still others learn as they talk about their ideas with each other. Effective teachers vary the teaching strategies they use and provide students with options for the learning activities they can use in pursuit of common learning goals.

Vary the Learning Objectives. In some instances, teachers can vary the learning objectives they hold for students. For instance, students can be allowed to select topics that interest them within a unit of study or they can choose projects that are consistent with their own abilities. The risk of this approach, like the risk of grouping students by ability, is that students in the slower groups or those who pursue less difficult or less complex projects may fall further and further behind in the essential core content of the curriculum and never accomplish the objectives of their peers. These are decisions that each teacher will have to make for particular students and situations.

Planning for Time and Space

A final aspect of teacher planning has to do with the use of time and space, resources over which teachers have considerable control. This includes how much time to spend on academic tasks in general, how much time to allocate to particular subjects, and where to place students, materials, and desks. Because there is much useful research on the relationship between teachers' use of classroom time and student achievement, we now look more carefully at this topic. Following that, we briefly consider the topic of classroom space. A more thorough discussion about the use of space can be found in Chapters 7 through 12, where particular approaches to teaching are examined.

Time Is of the Essence

The management of classroom time is a complex and difficult task for teachers, although on the surface it may appear to be a rather simple and straightforward matter. Fortunately, there is a well-developed knowledge base on the use of classroom time that can guide teacher planning in this area. Essentially, the research validates what experienced teachers have always known: The time available for instruction that appears to be so plentiful when the year begins soon becomes a scarce resource. Too often, inexperienced teachers find themselves racing through topics in as little time as possible in order to cover targeted content. Unfortunately, what appears to them as efficient use of time often produces little, if any, student learning. This suggests that the effective use of time is just as important as the amount of time spent on a topic. Current interest in the use of classroom time stems mainly from thought and research done in the 1970s and 1980s. A number of studies during that era produced three important findings (Brophy & Good, 1986; Fisher et al., 1980; Rosenshine, 1980). More recent work has confirmed these results (Gewerts, 2008; Houston & Miller, 2011; Viadero, 2008).

> **Research has validated that time available for instruction is far less than one might believe, even though it may seem plentiful at the beginning of the year.**

1. Time allocated and used for specific tasks is strongly related to academic achievement. What the researchers have found is that regardless of the specific methods used by teachers in particular programs, classrooms in which students spend the most time *engaged in academic work* are those in which students make the highest achievement gains in reading and mathematics.

> **A direct relationship exists between time engaged in academic tasks and high achievement gains in reading and math.**

2. Teachers vary considerably in the amount of time they allocate to particular studies. For instance, in one study, researchers found some fifth-grade classrooms allocated sixty minutes each day to reading and language arts whereas others spent almost two and a half hours on these subjects. These findings have led many schools to require a minimum amount of instructional time to be allocated to core subjects such as reading, writing, and mathematics.
3. Regardless of the amount of time teachers allocate to a particular topic, the amount of time students actually engage in learning activities varies considerably. A large proportion of time is devoted to nonacademic, noninstructional, and various housekeeping activities.

These time studies led Weinstein, Romano, and Mignano (2010) to divide instructional time into seven categories:

1. *Total time.* This is the total amount of time students spend in school. In most states, the mandated time consists of 180 days of school per year and from six to seven hours of school each day.
2. *Attended time.* This is the amount of time that students actually attend school. Sickness, broken heating systems, and snow days reduce the amount of attendance time from the total time required by law.
3. *Available time.* Some of the school day is spent on lunch, recess, pep rallies, and other extracurricular activities and, consequently, is not available for academic purposes.

4. *Planned academic time.* When teachers fill in plan books, they set aside a certain amount of time for different subjects and activities, called *planned academic time.*

5. *Actual academic time.* The amount of time the teacher actually spends on academic tasks or activities is called *allocated time.* This is also called **opportunity to learn** and is measured in terms of the amount of time teachers have their students spend on a given academic task.

6. *Engaged time.* The amount of time students actually spend on a learning activity or task is called **engaged time,** or **time on task.** This type of time is measured in terms of on-task and off-task behavior. If a teacher has allocated time to seatwork on math problems and the student is working on these problems, the student's behavior is on task. Conversely, if the student is doodling or talking about football with another student, the behavior is counted as off task.

7. *Academic learning time (ALT).* The amount of time a student spends engaged in an academic task at which he or she is successful is **academic learning time.** It is the aspect of time most closely related to student learning.

The graph illustrated in Figure 3.14, developed by Carol Weinstein and her colleagues, shows how much time is available in each of the seven categories. Based on the time studies described previously, this figure shows how the almost eleven hundred hours of mandated time for schooling is reduced to slightly over three hundred hours when it comes to actual academic learning time, because there is slippage each step of the way. Thus, although there is great variation in the way school and classroom time is managed, the lesson from the research on how time is used clearly shows that far less academic learning time is available to teachers and students than initially meets the eye.

Time studies done by prominent educational researchers gained worldwide attention from both practitioners and researchers alike. If strong relationships existed between time on task and academic achievement, the obvious follow-up research would be to discover what some teachers do to produce classrooms with high on-task ratios and what can be done to help other teachers improve in this direction. Two domains of immediate concern were the ways teachers organized and managed their classrooms and the particular teaching methods they employed. More is said about these two topics in Chapters 4–5 and 7–12.

Finally, all teachers, but particularly beginning teachers, are required to juggle the many demands on their time, and they need to learn how to prioritize their use of

Figure 3.14 *How Much Time Is There, Anyway?*

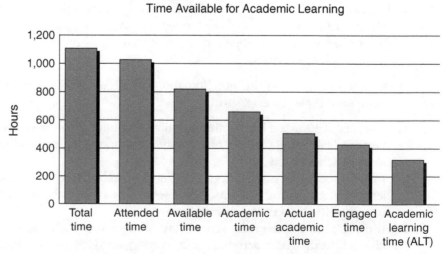

Time Available for Academic Learning

Source: After Weinstein, Romano, and Mignano (2010).

professional and personal time. Heyck-Merlin (2012) has written a timely little book, *The Together Teacher: Plan Ahead, Get Organized, and Save Time.* Referenced in the Books for the Professional section at the end of this chapter, Heyck-Merlin identifies five essential time management skills:

- Prioritization: Getting the right things first
- Planning: Looking ahead
- Organization: Getting clear on processes and systems
- Execution: Getting things done as planned
- Efficiency: Maximizing every little bit of time

We will return to this topic in more detail in Chapter 14.

Space, a Critical Element

The arrangement of classroom space is critical and does not have simple solutions. Most important, the way that space is used influences how classroom participants relate to one another and what students learn. Consider, for example, how a teacher might conduct a discussion with students. The teacher and students could be arranged in a circle that permits equal communication among all parties or, as is more usual, the students could be arranged in straight rows with all information directed to and from a central figure (the teacher). In the latter arrangement, the discussion does not occur among students but between the students and the teacher. As this example shows, the way space is designed influences not only communication patterns but also power relationships among teachers and students. These relationships are important because they may affect the degree to which students take ownership of the lesson and become independent learners.

Arrangements of students, desks, and chairs not only help determine classroom communication patterns and interpersonal relationships, but also influence a variety of daily decisions teachers must make concerning the management and use of scarce resources. The choices involved are not clear-cut. Fortunately, a substantial body of research provides guidelines for teachers as they think about these decisions. Space arrangements to facilitate particular teaching models are described in some detail in Chapters 7–12.

Planning with Colleagues

As described previously, much of teacher planning occurs alone. Of late, however, many have pointed out the advantages gained from joint planning, because even though teachers work together in the same school or school district, they often have only a sketchy knowledge about what others are teaching. Even teachers teaching next door to one another often do not know what the other is teaching.

Hale (2009), Hale and Fisher (2013), and Jacobs (2004) have offered the idea of "curriculum maps" as a way for teachers in particular buildings or school districts to chart what they are doing and to help make sure neither gaps in important skills and understanding nor too much overlap and repetition occur. **Curriculum mapping** begins with each teacher describing the processes and skills he or she emphasizes, the essential concept and topics he or she teaches, and the kind of learner outcomes expected. Then, depending on the situation, these descriptions are shared with other teachers across grade levels or across the school, and curriculum maps are constructed showing the school's curriculum, including gaps that may exist and topics that are unnecessarily taught more than once. Although beginning teachers will not be asked to be in charge of this process, understanding that it exists will help them enter into curriculum mapping and gain a clearer understanding of what is really going on in other teachers' classrooms and how what they are teaching fits in. Figure 3.15 illustrates two curriculum maps: one shows a generic template for curriculum mapping; the other is an example of a language arts curriculum map. Both illustrate how curriculum mappers are integrating Common Core Standards into their work.

Figure 3.15 *Two Examples of Curriculum Maps*

Unit Curriculum Map

Theme, Enduring Understandings, & Essential Questions for This Unit	How Students Will Demonstrate Their Understanding	Standards-Based Essential Skills & Concepts to Be Targeted throughout the Unit	Strategies/Best Practices Used to Explicitly Teach the Skills & Concepts	Resources for This Unit
Theme/Unit: Enduring Understandings: Essential Questions:	Summative Assessment (at the end of the unit): Formative Assessments (throughout the unit):	**PROCESS STANDARDS** Problem Solving: Communication: Reasoning: Connections: Representation: **CONTENT STANDARDS**		Textbook Lessons: Manipulatives: Technology: Support Materials: Personally Designed Materials: Other Resources:

Language Arts
Curriculum Map by Quarter

	Themes & Essential Questions	Standards-Based Essential Skills & Concepts to Be Targeted & Instructional Strategies	Formative/Summative Assessments (writing assignments, projects, performances)	Multigenre Thematic Texts (novel, drama, short fiction, poetry, nonfiction)
1st Quarter				
2nd Quarter				
3rd Quarter				
4th Quarter				

Source: Curriculum Mapping. Retrieved October 13, 2013, from http://ok.gov/sde/curriculum-mapping.

For more information on curriculum mapping, see "Heidi Hayes Jacobs—What Is Curriculum Mapping" and "Janet Hale—Different Types of Curriculum Maps" on YouTube. The Common Core Web site is another good source of information on curriculum mapping (www.commoncore.org/maps/).

A Final Thought about Planning

Today, many aspects of teaching are in a state of change. Planning may be one of these. In *Learning to Teach,* as well as in many other books, perspectives on and procedures for planning stem mainly from the traditional view that puts the teacher at the center of the planning process. However, over the past two decades, perspectives have emerged that move the focus of planning from the teacher to the student. Interest in **learner-centered planning** stems from work done by a task force of the American Psychological Association (see Learner-Centered Work Group, 1997), planning studies done by researchers such as McCombs (2001; McCombs & Miller, 2007), and a wide range of books that have been published over the past decade, such as Maryellen Weimer's *Learner-Centered Teaching: Five Key Changes to Practice* (2002).

The work by the American Psychological Association's Task Force developed several learner-centered principles that are described in more detail in Part 2 of *Learning to Teach.* The emphasis of these principles, however, pertains to recent developments in our understanding of the learner and of the learning process. Mainly, they endorse constructivist principles such as these:

- Successful learners over time and with support create their own meaningful representation of knowledge.
- Successful learners link new information to existing knowledge in meaningful ways.
- Successful learners think strategically and think about their own learning.
- Learning is influenced significantly by environmental factors such as culture and instructional practices.

Weimer (2002), in contrast, puts the emphasis on classroom practices. She argues that student learning, *not* teaching, should be the focus of classrooms. According to Weimer, for learner-centeredness to dominate, five important teaching practices must change: (1) balance of power must be shifted from teachers to students, (2) content must change from something only to be mastered to a tool for developing learning skills, (3) paradigm must change from one where teachers do all the planning and perform good pedagogy to one where teachers are guides and facilitators, (4) responsibility for learning must shift from the teacher to the student with the aim of helping students become autonomous learners, and (5) evaluation must be used to provide feedback and to generate learning with strong emphasis on student participation in self-evaluation.

More about learner-centered classrooms will be found throughout the remaining chapters. For now and as it informs planning, it is important to remain aware of the learner-centered principles and to explore ways that students can become involved in the planning process. However, the push for adopting a common set of standards and creating tighter alignment between what is taught and what is assessed narrows the choices teachers can make and may work against student-centered planning and learning. Hopefully, the next generation of teachers and policymakers can devise systems that are concerned about holding students to high standards while at the same time affording teachers and students opportunities to develop learning experiences that are tied to students' interests and their learning needs.

Check, Extend, Explore

Check

- What does research show about how teachers vary as to the amount of time they spend on similar subjects and work activities?
- What are the seven categories of instructional time as defined by Weinstein and Mignano?
- How might different types of lessons affect the way a teacher arranges classroom space?
- What is the primary purpose of curriculum mapping?

Extend

- Some educators argue that we pay too much attention to the way time is spent and that we have gone overboard in insisting on a set amount of ALT, even to the point of doing away with recess. Do you agree or disagree that we should eliminate recess? Go to the "Extend Question Poll" on the Online Learning Center to respond.

Explore

- Go to the Online Learning Center at www.mhhe.com/arends10e for links to Web sites related to planning for classroom space and time.
- Use Google to search the topic "lesson plans" and look at a few of the over 7 million (at the time of this writing) Web sites listed. Which ones appear to be useful? Not very useful?
- Go to your university's digital resources and look up the full text of the article by McCutcheon and Milner described in the Research Summary for this chapter. (Hint: Use the database Academic Search Premier by EBSCOhost.) Did you learn anything new that was not included in the summarized version?

Reflections from the *Classroom*

To Plan or Not to Plan

Considerable debate has existed over the years about best practice in regard to teacher planning. On one side of the debate are those who hold more behaviorist views about teaching and learning and who see planning as a rational-linear process. This view would argue for detailed delineation of content and skills to be taught and careful use of behavioral objectives. On the other side of the debate are those who hold a more constructivist view of teaching. This view holds that planning is not always linear and should take into account the complexity and serendipity of teaching and learning.

Write a reflective essay that gives your views on teacher planning in a way that would provide a principal who is considering hiring you insight into the type of planner you will be. Approach this situation from the perspective of the grade level or subject area you are preparing to teach. Compare your views with those of the following two teachers. You may want to include your essay in your professional portfolio.

Donald Early
5th Grade

In my teacher education program, my professors emphasized the importance of tying all instructional activities to student learning outcomes. In an ideal world, I agree with this approach. However, in the real world, it just doesn't seem to work that way. As I plan, I normally start with big ideas I want students to understand. Sometimes I write these out; sometimes I don't. Also, over the years, I have developed many lessons that I know will interest the students and keep them engaged. I try to incorporate these highly motivational lessons into my teaching on a regular basis. Finally, I believe that students are mainly responsible for their own learning. My job is not to cram information and ideas into their brains. Instead, my job is to create learning experiences that will allow them to discover things on their own and to build knowledge out of experience. This calls for a different kind of planning that I find difficult to explain to others.

Angela Adams
Jacksonville Middle School, 7th and 8th Grade, Jacksonville, TX

During my first year of teaching, lesson planning was the most overwhelming aspect of my job. Several things have to be considered when planning lessons such as individual education plans, school curriculum requirements, national and state standards, and available resources. Many mornings I woke up with my first thought, "What are we going to do today?" Never a good way to start the day. Gradually I learned to develop integrated units that lasted a long period of time and also allowed for flexibility when standardized test days, pep rallies, or assemblies were scheduled.

A goal I set for my second year was to plan for the entire year in the summer to alleviate stress once the school year started. Once again, I began to feel overwhelmed and did not know where to begin. So, I divided the year into teaching units and planned objectives for each unit. This helped me design a flexible scope and sequence in my head that could be developed more fully later in the school year.

Lesson planning is a source of stress for even the best, most experienced teachers. Every teacher has to develop a system of lesson planning that fits his or her needs and resources.

Summary

Explain why teacher planning is important, and describe different perspectives on planning.

- Planning and making decisions about instruction are among the most important aspects of teaching because they are major determinants of what is taught in schools and how it is taught.
- The traditional perspective of planning is based on rational-linear models characterized by setting goals and taking specific actions to accomplish desired outcomes.
- The knowledge base suggests that teacher planning and decision making do not always conform to rational-linear planning models. Newer perspectives on planning put more emphasis on planners' nonlinear actions and reflections.
- A third form of teacher planning, called mental planning, is based on reflective thinking prior to the construction of more formal plans and imaging and mental rehearsal prior to presenting particular lessons.

Explain the consequences of planning for student learning and discuss how beginning teachers and experienced teachers approach planning differently.

- Studies have shown that planning has consequences for both student learning and classroom behavior. It can enhance student motivation, help focus student learning, and decrease classroom management problems.
- Planning can have unanticipated negative effects as well; for example, it can limit self-initiated learning on the part of students and make teachers insensitive to student ideas.
- Experienced teachers and beginning teachers have different planning approaches and needs. Experienced teachers are more concerned with establishing structures ahead of time to guide classroom activities and plan ahead for the adaptations needed as lessons get under way. In general, beginning teachers need more detailed plans than experienced teachers do. They devote more of their planning to verbal instructions and respond more often to student interests.
- It is sometimes difficult to learn planning skills from experienced teachers because mental planning activities are hidden from public view.

Describe the three phases of teacher planning and the types of decisions made during each phase and discuss how planning cycles vary throughout the school year.

- Teacher planning is multifaceted but relates to three phases of teaching: prior to instruction, when decisions are made about what will be taught and for how long; during instruction, when decisions are made about questions to ask, wait time, and specific orientations; and after instruction, when decisions are made about how to assess student progress and what type of feedback to provide.
- Planning cycles include not only daily plans but also plans for each week, month, and year. The details of these various plans differ, however. Plans carried out on a particular day are influenced by what has happened before and will in turn influence future plans.

Provide definitions and explanations about how to use the following planning processes and tools: planning what to teach, using and reconstituting standards and curriculum frameworks, using instructional objectives, using taxonomies, and constructing daily and unit instructional plans.

- One of the most complex planning tasks is choosing curriculum content. Standards and frameworks developed by professional societies and by state and local curriculum committees assist in making these decisions. A number of planning tools also can help teachers, including curriculum mapping.

- The use of learning progression helps specify a set of subskills and enabling knowledge that must be learned prior to mastering a more complex curriculum standard or learning outcome.
- Instructional objectives are statements that describe student learning that should result from instruction. Behavioral objectives include statements about expected student behavior, the testing situation in which the behavior will be observed, and performance criteria. An objective written in a more general format communicates the teacher's overall intent but lacks the precision of a behavioral objective.
- Taxonomies are devices that help classify and show relationships among things. Bloom's taxonomy has been widely used in education to classify objectives. The original taxonomy for the cognitive domain, developed in the 1950s, has recently been revised to reflect new perspectives and research about the relationships between types of knowledge and the cognitive processes.
- Formats for lesson plans can vary, but in general a good plan includes a clear statement of objectives, a sequence of learning activities, and a means of assessing student learning.
- Unit plans cover chunks of instruction that can span several days or weeks. Like lesson plans, the format can vary, but a good unit plan includes overall objectives for the unit, major content to be covered, syntax or phases of the unit, major assignments, and assessment procedures.
- Time-tabling techniques, such as making a chronological map of a series of instructional activities, can assist with long-range planning tasks.
- Through the planning process, teachers can vary time, materials, and learning activities to meet the needs of every student in the class.

Describe how to plan for effective use of time and space and how to use curriculum mapping to plan with colleagues.

- Time and space are scarce commodities in teaching, and their use should be planned with care and foresight.
- Research on time shows considerable variation from teacher to teacher on the amount of time allocated to different subject areas.
- The amount of time students spend on a task is related to how much they learn. Students in classrooms in which allocated time is high and a large proportion of students are engaged learn more than in classrooms where allocated time is low and students are found off task.
- Space—the arrangement of materials, desks, and students—is another important resource that is planned and managed by teachers. The way space is used affects the learning atmosphere of classrooms, influences classroom dialogue and communication, and has important cognitive and emotional effects on students.
- The use of time and space is influenced by the demands of the learning tasks. Effective teachers develop an attitude of flexibility and experimentation about these features of classroom life.
- Curriculum mapping is a planning tool that allows groups of teachers to chart what they are teaching across grade levels and content fields. This type of planning identifies gaps and overlaps.

Consider how planning processes may be more student-centered in the future.

- Recent knowledge about learners and learning, such as constructivist perspectives and the importance of prior knowledge, argue for planning processes that put the student instead of the teacher at the center of the planning process.

Key Terms

academic learning time 128	enduring understandings 110	nonlinear model 98
analyze 116	engaged time 128	opportunity to learn 128
apply 116	essential questions 110	performance indicators 107
assessments 107	evaluate 116	performance standards 105
behavioral objectives 112	factual knowledge 116	power 109
benchmarks 107	formal curriculum 106	procedural knowledge 116
cognitive process dimension 115	Gantt chart 122	rational-linear model 97
cognitive processes 116	instructional objective 112	remember 116
conceptual knowledge 116	knowledge dimension 115	standards 107
Common Core Standards 106	learner-centered planning 131	taxonomies 115
create 116	learning progressions 111	time on task 128
curriculum mapping 129	lesson plans 120	time-tabling 122
economy 109	mental planning 98	understand 116
enacted curriculum 106	metacognitive knowledge 116	unit plan 120

Interactive and Applied Learning

Study and Explore

- Access your Study Guide, which includes practice quizzes, from the Online Learning Center.

Observe and Practice

- Listen to audio clips on the Online Learning Center of Jason O'Brien (fifth grade) and Angella Transfeld (tenth-grade English) talking about teacher planning in the *Teachers on Teaching* area.

Complete the following **Practice Exercises** that accompany Chapter 3:

- Practice Exercise 3.1: What Makes a Good Lesson Plan?
- Practice Exercise 3.2: Writing Objectives
- Practice Exercise 3.3: Using a Taxonomy Table to Analyze Objectives
- Practice Exercise 3.4: Developing a Lesson Plan

Portfolio and Field Experience Activities

Expand your understanding of the content and processes of this chapter through the following field experiences and portfolio activities. Support materials to complete the activities are in the *Portfolio and Field Experience Activities* area on the Online Learning Center.

1. Complete the Reflections from the Classroom exercise for this chapter. The recommended reflective essay will provide insight into your views and approach to teacher planning. **(InTASC Standard 7: Planning for Instruction)**

2. **Activity 3.1: Assessing My Planning Skills.** Check the level of your planning skills. **(InTASC Standard 7: Planning for Instruction)**

3. **Activity 3.2: Writing Objectives.** Write instructional objectives and evaluate them. **(InTASC Standard 7: Planning for Instruction)**

4. **Activity 3.3: Observing Lesson Activities and Segments.** This activity provides guidelines for discovering the internal structure of an experienced teacher's lesson. **(InTASC Standard 7: Planning for Instruction)**

5. **Activity 3.4: Portfolio: Demonstrating My Planning Skills.** This activity will provide you with an artifact for your portfolio that demonstrates your understanding and skill for planning lessons and units for diverse student populations. **(InTASC Standard 2: Learning Differences; InTASC Standard 7: Planning for Instruction)**

Books for the Professional

Diller, D. (2008). *Space and places: Designing classrooms for literacy*. Portland, ME: Stenhouse Publishers.

Gronlund, N., & Brookhart, S. (2009). *Gronlund's writing instructional objectives* (8th ed.). Columbus, OH: Pearson.

Heyck-Merlin, M., & Atkins, N. (2012). *The together teacher: Plan ahead, get organized, and save time*. San Francisco: Jossey-Bass.

Jacobs, H. H. (2004). *Getting results with curriculum mapping*. Alexandria, VA: Association for Supervision and Curriculum Development.

Johnson, S. (2011). *Digital tools for teaching: 30 E-tools for collaborating, creating, and publishing across the curriculum*. Gainesville, FL: Maupin House Publishing.

McCombs, G., & Miller, L. (2007). *Learner-centered classroom practices and assessments*. Thousand Oaks, CA: Corwin Press.

Moss, C., & Brookhart, S. (2012). *Learning targets: Helping students aim for understanding in today's lesson*. Alexandria, VA: Association for Supervision and Curriculum Development.

Reeves, A. (2011). *Where great teaching begins: Planning for student thinking and learning*. Alexandria, VA: Association for Supervision and Curriculum Development.

Wiggins, G., & McTighe, J. (2005). *Understanding by design* (2nd ed.). Alexandria, VA: Association for Supervision and Curriculum Development.

CHAPTER 4
Learning Communities and Student Motivation

Learning Goals

After studying this chapter you should be able to

Perspectives on Classrooms as Learning Communities

Describe why motivating students and developing learning communities are important and describe the different perspectives on these topics.

Theoretical and Empirical Support

Define human motivation and describe the major theories of motivation relevant to education.

Define a productive learning community and describe the features of classrooms shown by research to impact student motivation and learning.

Strategies for Motivating Students and Building Protective Learning Communities

Describe and discuss major strategies teachers can use to motivate students and to build productive learning communities.

Some Final Thoughts

Speculate about the reasons students find schoolwork to be less than meaningful and the need for new school structures and curricula.

Reflecting on Classrooms as Learning Communities

Before you read this chapter, think for a moment about some of the classrooms you were in when you were in elementary or high school or, for that matter, classrooms you have been in as a college student. Some of these classrooms were definitely teacher-centered places where teaching practices were characterized by transmitting knowledge to students. Some were efficient, and students were well behaved. Others may have been out of control. Still others were places where students were friends with one another and where everyone worked hard to learn things that had meaning for them.

Make two lists, one describing the attributes of classrooms that you thought led to positive learning communities and the other detailing attributes that were negative and prevented the development of a positive learning community.

Positive Attributes   Negative Attributes

_____   _____

_____   _____

_____   _____

Now analyze your lists and reflect on what you think teachers did to make those classrooms the way they were. Consider other factors that may have influenced the situation such as the type of student, physical conditions, and so on.

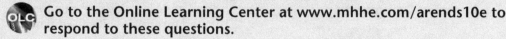 **Go to the Online Learning Center at www.mhhe.com/arends10e to respond to these questions.**

Making one's classroom a productive learning community is one of the most important things a teacher can do, even more important perhaps than the practices used in the more formal aspects of instruction. The classroom learning community influences student engagement and achievement, and it determines how a teacher's class will evolve from a collection of individuals into a cohesive group characterized by high expectations and achievement, caring relationships, and productive inquiry. Creating positive learning communities, however, is no simple task, nor are there easy recipes that will ensure success. Instead, it is a process of doing many things well and of having the courage to create classrooms that are different from some now found in schools. Let's begin this process by looking at two teachers who do this aspect of their work very well:

Carolyn Barnes has come to love her fifth-grade class. She is now in her third year of teaching at Kennedy Elementary School in a medium-size city. Her class is organized as a learning community, and she is pleased to be able to focus on the real learning needs of her students rather than being preoccupied with classroom management problems. She believes that her class is a democratic society in which she and the students are devoted to learning about themselves and the world around them. She sees herself as playing two roles— instructional leader and participant—in the community of scholarship they are building together. Barnes believes that what is learned must be socially constructed and that what is constructed affects what it is possible to learn. She finds herself reflecting frequently on the balance between initiating actions and responding to student initiatives within the class.

One of Barnes's students, Steve, is a good example of the payoff of her approach to teaching. Steve had a low opinion of himself and of schooling in general before he started in Carolyn's fifth-grade class. He didn't seem to care about anything. In fact, his favorite response to most everything was, "Who cares?" However, in Carolyn's learning community, students learn to trust their ability to think through problems in many areas of the curriculum. Steve first became excited when he discovered that he could solve simple algebraic problems. Later on, he found that he could apply his problem-solving skills in the social arena. The leadership Steve developed within his study team in dealing with mathematical problems helped him when he was faced with social problems within the team. Success in one area spread to other areas.

How did Carolyn Barnes get Steve to change so radically from a bored and indifferent nonparticipant to an enthusiastic learner? "It wasn't what I did so much," Carolyn says, "as what Steve's done for himself." Steve, however, thinks differently. He says, "Ms. Barnes's class is like a continuous debate. It's nothing like any class I've ever known." Steve is referring to the continuing discussions that characterize Barnes's class. No matter what the subject, students are involved in defining concerns, focusing on issues, gathering information, suggesting hypotheses, and defending their theories. Instead of focusing on facts and rote learning, students in Barnes's class strive to make sense of what they experience and to communicate that sense to others.

Mark Hicks now teaches social studies in the Walden Middle School in his midwestern home state. He found out about this job when he visited his parents during summer vacation several years after he started teaching. Walden is a professional development school associated with a nearby midwestern research university and located in an urban setting in a medium-size city. Hicks is a team leader in a . . . learning community that consists of sixty students. His team includes two interns from the university; an aide who is a specialist in reading; . . . a university professor who teaches language arts; and a graduate student who works as a researcher and documenter. The students are organized into study groups, and the whole group is organized into a cooperative learning community. The students leave their groups when it is time for them to take their mathematics, science, art, and physical education classes in different rooms and different groups. However, for half the day, the students are all together in one area of the school. Hicks is the instructional leader for social studies (including civics, history, geography, and economics), and the professor is the instructional leader for the language arts (literature, writing, speech, and drama). Mark also teaches one history class in the afternoon, for another learning-community group.

The whole group is also considered the home room for all sixty students. Insofar as possible, Hicks and his teaching colleagues organize their instruction themes around interdisciplinary issues. The students keep journals in which they write their thoughts and feelings about what they are studying and what is happening in the class. Their entries give Hicks insights into their fears and other emotions, as well as their cognitive development. Hicks is particularly interested in what the students understand and can use conceptually to build new ideas about the world they live in. The students are challenged to connect what they are studying in school with the outside world. For example, during the last national election campaign students organized into research groups and followed particular candidates, read their speeches, watched them on television, checked on their positions, and compared their voting records. The study groups prepared presentations for the whole group and made predictions about the election outcome.

After the elections, the students studied the results and compared them with their predictions. Where they missed the mark, the groups tried to find reasons for the difference between the outcomes and their predictions. This project combined many areas of knowledge and gave the students a feeling that what they were doing was relevant to the world around them. (after descriptions found in Putnam & Burke, 2005)

Classrooms like Carolyn's and Mark's do not happen by chance. Instead, they are the result of skillful planning and execution by their teachers. The intent of this chapter is to give you the understandings and skills to develop classrooms like Carolyn's and Mark's. The first section of the chapter, Perspectives on Classrooms as Learning Communities, provides an overview of motivation and the concept of learning communities. This overview is followed by a discussion of the theoretical and empirical support for these topics. The focus of the chapter then shifts to a discussion of specific actions teachers can take to motivate their students and to build productive learning

Productive learning communities do not happen automatically. They require a lot of insight and hard work on the part of teachers.

communities. Several of these ideas were introduced in Chapter 2, where the focus was on the nature of classrooms with students from diverse backgrounds, and will be revisited in Chapter 5, Classroom Management.

You will discover as you study these three chapters that concepts that lead to productive learning communities are strongly connected to those that describe how teachers think about their students and about the diversity that characterizes today's classrooms. They also relate to how teachers go about creating approaches to classroom management that are caring and democratic.

Perspective on Classrooms as Learning Communities

The process of developing classrooms as learning communities necessitates that teachers attend to many features of their students and their classrooms. Some of the ideas that inform this work date back many years. Other ideas are of more recent origin. This section discusses three topics. First, a rather old perspective is presented, one that conceives of classrooms as places where individual and group needs are played out and where daily activity mirrors life outside of school. Second, a brief description is offered of human motivation and how teachers' choices of motivational strategies influence the development of learning communities as well as how much students remain engaged in learning. Finally, the concept of learning community itself and attributes that contribute to positive learning communities are described.

There are always built-in dilemmas in our society and in our classrooms between the needs of the group and the rights of individuals.

Fusion of the Individual and the Group

The relationship between individuals and the group is complex in any setting and often fraught with dilemmas. In some ways, it mirrors the dilemma we have built into our larger system of government and economics in the United States. For instance, Americans value collective action, and we have built an elaborate system around democratic principles aimed at ensuring that the voices of citizens are heard and that actions are based on the will of the majority. We have many traditions such as singing the "Star-Spangled Banner" and saying the Pledge of Allegiance that define and promote our *groupness*. At the same time, we value liberty and freedom and have ensured through the Constitution and the Bill of Rights that individuals can say what they want, believe what they want, bear arms, and pursue their lives independently and without interference of others. This is the *individual* aspect of our lives.

The same dilemma exists in classrooms. We find a situation where, on the one hand, we want to establish communities that provide encouragement, safety, and support for individual learners. John Dewey (1916) observed a long time ago that children learn as they participate in social settings. More recently, scholars, such as Jerome Bruner (1996), Doyle (1986), and Vygotsy (1978, 1994), have argued that people create meaning out of relationships and membership in particular social settings and cultures. So groups and learning communities become an important aspect of learning. On the other hand, group life can limit an individual's initiative and promote norms opposed to creativity and academic learning. Let's look more closely at the relationships between these two features of classroom life.

Thinking about the individual–group connection stems from the work of early social psychologists, led by Kurt Lewin (Lewin, Lippitt, & White, 1951), Getzel and Thelen (1960), and their colleagues, who were interested in how a combination of individual needs and environmental conditions explain human behavior. More recently, Rothstein-Fisch and Trumbull (2008) have explored the individual–group connection as it relates to the diversity found in today's classrooms. When their work has been applied to education, as Rothstein-Fisch and Trumbull (2008) did, it has produced a two-dimensional model for considering the relationship between the needs of individual students and the conditions of classroom life. The first dimension of the model describes how, within a classroom, there are individuals with certain motives and needs. This perspective can be labeled the *individual dimension* of classroom life. From this perspective, particular classroom behavior results from the personalities and attitudes of students and their actions to satisfy their individual needs and motives.

The second dimension of the model describes how classrooms exist within a social context and how certain roles and expectations develop within that setting to fulfill goals of the system. This dimension can be labeled the *group dimension* of the classroom. From this perspective, classroom behavior is determined by the shared expectations (norms) of the school and the classroom. Classroom life, thus, results from individually motivated students and teachers responding to each other in a social setting. It is out of this sustained development and interaction that learning communities evolve and produce desired social and academic learning.

For teachers, the most important factor on the individual side of the model is *motivation*. This is true because, unlike a student's personality and other individual features that are rather stable and enduring, many features of motivation are alterable, as will be described later in the chapter.

The concept of *learning community* is the most important factor on the social dimension of classroom life. A learning community, as contrasted to a collection of individuals, is a setting in which individuals within the community have mutual goals, have common relationships, and show concern for one another. It is a place in which people share tendencies and norms to feel and act in certain ways. These features are

Classroom life consists mainly of individually motivated students and teachers responding to each other in a social setting.

Check, Extend, Explore

Check

- What are the two major aspects of classroom life?
- What is the most important factor related to the individual aspect of classroom life? The group aspect? Why?
- What is the main feature of a classroom learning community?

Extend

- In your own life, how do you resolve the tension between individual and group needs?

Explore

- There are many, many Web sites on learning communities and motivation. Search these topics on the Internet and compare ideas you find with those expressed in *Learning to Teach*.

Intrinsic motivation causes people to act in a certain way because it brings personal satisfaction or enjoyment.

Extrinsic motivation is characterized by individuals working for rewards that are external to the activity.

Table 4.1 *Individual and Group Features of Productive Learning Communities*

Individual	Group
• Students and teachers share common goals.	• Norms exist for expecting everyone to do their best.
• Students see themselves as feeling competent and self-determining.	• Norms exist for getting academic work done.
• Students see themselves as colleagues with high levels of attraction for one another.	• Norms exist for helping and being helped.
• Students and teachers reflect on past experiences and celebrate accomplishments.	• Norms support open communication and dialogue.

summarized in Table 4.1. Developing productive learning communities with these features is no easy task. However, for teachers who meet this challenge, no aspect of the job is more rewarding.

Theoretical and Empirical Support

Perspectives about Human Motivation

Motivation is usually defined as the processes that stimulate our behavior or arouse us to take action. It is what makes us do what we do. Pintrich (2003) has observed that *motivation* comes from the Latin verb *movere* and refers to "what gets individuals moving" toward particular activities and tasks. Think about this definition for a minute, and consider what arouses you to take action. What prompted you to get up this morning? Why did you choose to eat or ignore breakfast? Why are you reading this book now rather than earlier or later? Is it because you find it interesting? Are you preparing for a classroom discussion on the topic? Or perhaps for a test? All these factors and more have the potential to arouse us to act.

Psychologists make the distinction between two major types of motivation—intrinsic and extrinsic—as illustrated in Figure 4.1. When behavior is sparked internally by one's own interest or curiosity or just for the pure enjoyment of an experience, this is called **intrinsic motivation.** Lingering to watch the sun go behind the horizon on a beautiful evening is an example of intrinsic motivation as is doing one's homework because it is fun or running daily for the enjoyment this kind of physical activity brings. In contrast, **extrinsic motivation** kicks in when individuals are influenced to action from external or environmental factors, such as rewards, punishments, or social pressures Well-known extrinsic motivators include working to get a good grade, putting in overtime for extra money on one's paycheck, and studying hard to get a high score on Praxis II. Intrinsic and extrinsic motivation are both important in classrooms. How teachers can use both to accomplish desirable behavior and learning is discussed more thoroughly later in the chapter.

Many theories have been proposed over the years that help explain human motivation. Some of these date back to the early part of the twentieth century, whereas others are of more recent origin. Here, our discussion of motivation is selective and follows the work of Graham and Weiner (1996), Pintrich and Schunk (2002), Spaulding (1992), Stipek (1996, 2001), and Tollefson (2002). In general, the discussion is limited to those aspects of motivation that help explain behavior within academic or achievement

Figure 4.1 *Intrinsic and Extrinsic Motivation*

situations rather than behavior within a full range of situations. The discussion concentrates on five theories or perspectives: behavioral theory, needs theory, cognitive theory, social cognitive theory, and sociocultural theory.

Behavioral Theory. In the early twentieth century **behavioral theory** dominated thinking about both human learning and motivation. This approach to motivation emphasized the centrality of external events in directing behavior and in the importance of reinforcers (Skinner, 1956). Reinforcers, whether positive or negative, are stimulus events that occur contingent with a behavior and increase the likelihood of particular behaviors. Reinforcers can be either positive or negative. **Positive reinforcers,** following desired behaviors, enhance the probability that the behavior will be repeated. **Negative reinforcers,** in contrast, are stimulus events removed after particular behaviors. These stimuli also increase the likelihood of the behavior being repeated. In other words, people or animals repeat behavior to keep the negative reinforcer away—rats push a bar to avoid electric shock or kids do homework to avoid nagging by their parents or teachers. In teaching, it is important to make distinctions between negative reinforcers and **punishments.** Punishments decrease the likelihood of a behavior being repeated, or at least are intended to do so. For instance, if a rat removes the shock by pushing the bar, it will continue to push the bar, and that is negative reinforcement; if the rat gets a shock when it pushes the bar, it will stop pushing the bar, and that is punishment. If a student misbehaves and gets to leave class as a result, that is negative reinforcement; the student will continue to misbehave, assuming the class is more annoying than going to the principal's office. If a student misbehaves and gets detention after school, that is punishment, and it is intended to stop the misbehavior.

Educators have embraced behavioral theory for a long time, and many of the practices found in contemporary classrooms stem from this perspective. The use of good grades, praise, and privileges are examples of incentives and rewards teachers have at their disposal to get students to develop desirable habits and to behave in certain ways. Negative reinforcers, such as bad grades, punishments, and loss of privileges, are used to discourage undesirable tendencies or actions. Behavior modification programs, the use of token economies, and assertive discipline (Canter, 2009; Canter & Canter, 1976, 2002) are formal programs that have developed based on behavioral theory and have

A positive reinforcer is a stimulus such as a reward intended to get individuals to repeat desirable behavior.

A negative reinforcer is a stimulus that is removed, and also intends to get individuals to repeat desired behaviors.

been used widely in classrooms during the past thirty years. Over the past several years experiments have been pursued that have provided "cash" to get students to work harder, to read at higher levels, and to stay in school (Ash, 2008; Ripley, 2010).

Although ideas stemming from behavioral theory still dominate many practices found in classrooms, they are increasingly in disrepute among reformers such as Kohn (1995, 2006), Noddings (1992, 2001), and Oakes and Lipton (2006; Oakes, Lipton, Anderson, & Stillman, 2012), who believe these practices contribute to many of the problems schools face today because they tend to keep students in passive roles and ignore intrinsic motivation. Efforts to use money as a motivator have achieved mixed results.

Needs disposition theory posits that people are motivated to take action to satisfy basic and higher-level needs.

Needs Theory. Developed in the middle part of the twentieth century in part as a reaction to behavioral theory, **needs theory** emphasizes that individuals are aroused to action by innate needs and intrinsic pressures, rather than by extrinsic rewards or punishments. There are several major variations within this overall theory, but three are of the most importance to classroom teachers.

Abraham Maslow, one of America's foremost mid-twentieth-century psychologists, posited that human beings have a hierarchy of needs that they strive to satisfy. This is a perspective that many of you already know about. These needs were categorized by Maslow (1970) into seven levels. At the lower levels, needs exist to satisfy basic physiological requirements, such as food and shelter, to be safe, and to belong and be loved. The needs at the higher level of Maslow's hierarchy are more complex and refer to human growth needs, such as self-understanding, living up to one's potential, and self-actualization. Maslow's hierarchy of needs is illustrated in Figure 4.2.

According to Maslow, it is only when basic physical needs and the needs for love and self-esteem are met that individuals strive to meet higher-order needs. Critics of Maslow's theory argue that people do not always act in the ways he describes. However, the implications of his theory are helpful for thinking about children in the classroom. Children who come to school without lower-level needs for food and security

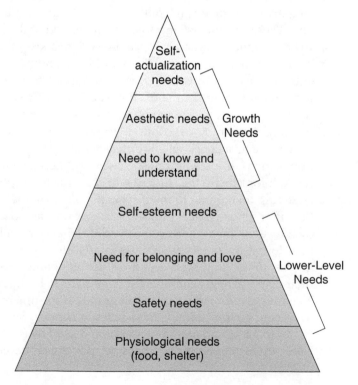

Figure 4.2 *Maslow's Needs Hierarchy*

satisfied are unlikely to spend much energy in satisfying their higher-level needs for knowing and understanding. Students who lack a sense of belonging, either at home or at school, are less likely to seek knowledge of mathematics or history than they are to search for friends and colleagues.

David McClelland (1958), Atkinson and Feather (1966), and Alschuler, Tabor, and McIntyre (1970) took Maslow's more general needs theory and applied it to the specific needs relevant to teaching and classrooms. Sometimes called *needs disposition theory,* this theory of motivation suggests that individuals are motivated to take action and to invest energy in pursuit of three outcomes: achievement, affiliation, and influence.

Individuals are motivated to take action to satisfy needs for achievement, influence, and affiliation.

The **achievement motive** is evident when students try hard to learn a particular subject or when they strive to reach the objectives of particular tasks. **Affiliative motives** become important when students and teachers come to value the support and friendship of their peers. The motivation toward **influence** can be seen in students who strive to have more control over their own learning. Students' feelings of self-esteem are related to feelings they have about their competence, affiliation, and influence. When these emotional states are frustrated by the activities in a classroom or a school, students become less involved in the school. Achievement motivation, or a student's "intent to learn," is the most important aspect of this theory of motivation for classroom teaching (see Wigfield & Eccles, 2002) and one for which many strategies exist.

The desire to take action and to excel for the purpose of experiencing success and feeling competent is called achievement motivation.

A third cluster of ideas about the relationship between human needs and motivation is associated with the work of deCharms (1976), Deci and Ryan (1985), Ryan and Deci (2000), and Csikszentmihalyi (1990, 1996). Although the ideas of these theorists differ in significant ways, they have in common the idea that people strive to satisfy needs for choice and self-determination in what they do and that actions taken as a result of internal pressures are more satisfying than those resulting from external influences.

DeCharms used the concepts of *origin* and *pawn* in his analysis. Pawns are persons who have no control over what happens to them. They are aroused to action not from intrinsic values but from a sense of obligation or from external rewards. They always feel they are doing what others want them to do. Origins, in contrast, are in charge of their own behavior. They behave in particular ways because of themselves, not because of others. As origins, they resist external pressures such as orders and rules. DeCharms believed that tasks imposed externally, such as by a teacher, make people feel like pawns and dampen the internal motivation they may have to perform the task on their own. The implication of this point of view for classroom practices is considered in more detail later.

University of Chicago psychologist and educator Mihaly Csikszentmihalyi (1990, 1996) views the importance of self-determination in regard to motivation differently. For over two decades, Csikszentmihalyi studied what he labeled "states of optimal experience," defined as times in people's lives when they experience total involvement and concentration as well as strong feelings of enjoyment. These types of experiences are called **flow experiences,** because the respondents Csikszentmihalyi studied often reported that what they were doing during the experience was so enjoyable "it felt like being carried away by a current, like being in a flow" (p. 127).

Perhaps you can think about a time in your life when you were doing something you became totally involved in. It could have been climbing a mountain, reading a novel, working on an old car, playing chess, engaging in a challenging run, or writing a poem. If you experienced flow, you were totally absorbed and concentrating on the activity alone, even to the point of losing track of time. In Csikszentmihalyi's (1990) words, "actor and action become one," and participation is sustained because of intrinsic rather than extrinsic motivation (p. 127).

Obviously, the concept of flow has implications for education and for teaching. In fact, Csikszentmihalyi concluded that the main obstacles to student learning do not stem from

During flow experiences, individuals experience pure enjoyment and total involvement.

the cognitive abilities of students but instead from the way we structure classrooms and schools and from learning experiences that inhibit intrinsic motivation and corresponding flow experiences. Emphasis on external rules and evaluation and on rewards such as grades deters flow experiences for students. Similarly, standardized curricula and lessons that keep students in passive roles may also be likely to inhibit involvement and enjoyment.

Cognitive Theory. Cognitive theories provide a third perspective about human motivation. Like cognitive learning theorists, described elsewhere, cognitive motivation theorists believe that individuals are aroused to action by their thinking. It is not external events or whether individuals are rewarded or punished that is important in explaining behavior, but instead it is the beliefs and attributions they hold about the event.

Attribution theories emphasize the way individuals come to perceive and Interpret the causes of their successes and failures.

Bernard Weiner is a major cognitivist theorist, and his **attribution theory** is of particular importance to teachers. Attribution theory is based on the proposition that the ways individuals come to perceive and to interpret the causes of their successes or failures are the major determinants of their motivation, rather than innate needs or fixed earlier experiences. According to Weiner (1986, 1992), Pintrick (2003), and Pintrick and Schunk (2002), students attribute their successes or failures in terms of four causes: ability, effort, luck, and the difficulty of the learning task. These attributions can be classified as *internal* or *external.* Internal attribution occurs when individuals explain success or failure in terms of themselves; external attribution occurs when they give external causes as reasons for failure. Attributing success to ability and effort are examples of internal attributions; luck and circumstances are external examples.

Attribution theory has several important implications for teachers. Students with high achievement motivation tend to associate their successes with their abilities and their failures with lack of effort. Conversely, students with low achievement motivation tend to attribute their successes to luck and their failures to lack of ability. There are ways in which teachers can change students' perceptions of themselves and the things around them, as will be described later in the chapter.

Cognitive theorists have also studied the views that students have about their goals and their goal orientations (Maehr & Zusho, 2009). Some students have **performance goal orientations.** They either strive to reach particular performance standards, often set externally, or they try to better their own performance as compared to the performance of others. These students are often overly competitive and rely on positive evaluations by others—praise from peers or grades from teachers—for their motivation. Other students have **learning goal orientations.** These students compete mainly with themselves and are motivated by internal factors such as the satisfaction of learning something new. According to Tollefson (2000), goal orientation interacts with students' attributions of success and failure. She writes, "Students with performance goals are most likely to interpret failure as a sign of low ability and (in turn) withdraw effort. Students with learning goals see failure as a cue to change their strategy for completing a task and increase their effort" (p. 70).

The time frame for accomplishing goals is also an important feature. Students are likely to persist in the pursuit of a goal if it can be accomplished in the near future as compared to goals that will be realized only in the far distant future. This often requires breaking long-term goals into proximal goals that can be accomplished in the short term. A complex writing assignment, such as a term paper, is an example of a goal that can take a long time to complete. Writers often give up before the task is finished. Motivation and persistence can be enhanced if the writing task is divided into several smaller tasks such as making an outline, collecting background information, and writing a two- or three-page section at a time.

Social Cognitive Theory. A fourth perspective about motivation that has importance for teachers is Bandura's (1977, 1986) social learning theory, or **social cognitive theory.** In some ways, social cognitive theory has similarities to attribution theories. However, the important idea for teachers stems from Bandura's assertion that motivation is the product of two things: an individual's expectations about his or her chances of reaching a particular goal and the degree of value or satisfaction that will accrue if the individual achieves the goal. For instance, if a student who is working on a project for the local science fair believes that the project will win an award (high expectation) and if that reward is something he or she badly wants (high value), then motivation to work and persist until the project is done will be high. Conversely, if either the expectation for success or the value of the reward is low, then perseverance will be low. The implications of this theory to teaching are clear. It is important to provide learning tasks that students value and have a high chance of completing successfully.

Sociocultural Theory. The final theory about motivation that we will discuss in this section is **sociocultural theory,** which stems from the work of Russian psychologist Lev Vygotsky (1986), who theorized that human activity takes place in cultural settings and that these settings influence greatly what we do and think. With regard to teachers and students in classrooms this means that the classroom group and learning community described previously has much influence on what students learn and

Enhancing Teaching and Learning with Technology

Is Technology an Effective Tool for Student Motivation?

As you have read, motivation is not a simple topic, and there is no single approach for teachers to take to ensure student engagement and learning. However, most teachers who use computers and new media technologies in their classrooms report their strong motivational aspects. The effects of educational technology on student engagement and learning, however, are not completely consistent. Several important studies done in the 1990s seemed to confirm the motivational elements of teaching practices that make use of technology. For example, an essential element for improving basic skills such as spelling and math operations is keeping students interested and engaged. Several studies have demonstrated that computers can motivate students to stay engaged in learning tasks. Hatfield (1996) found that the use of computer stations in classrooms increased student computer use and overall motivation. Terrell and Rendulic (1996) found that feedback via the computer had a positive effect on student motivation. In a rather large-scale study of the Apple Classrooms of Tomorrow (ACOT), Ringstaff, Sandholtz, and Dwyer (1995) found that students in technology-rich classrooms worked together more often and, in turn, were more interested in school. Students in these classrooms went beyond expectations of particular assignments and often chose to explore topics and projects during their free time. More recently, Collins and Halverson (2009), Rosen (2010), and West (2012) report similar positive results in increased motivation and engagement when computers and media technologies are used appropriately in the classroom.

Other researchers, however, have pointed out that the evidence about the motivational aspects of technology and whether computers advance learning is mixed, and some evidence has revealed negative effects on young children's motivation and learning (Alliance for Children, 2004; Wenglinsky, 2006). Larry Cuban (2001) reported that he believed the positive claims had been overstated. Viadero (2007) wrote that the best evidence from research reviews and from meta-analyses suggests that across the board educational technology has yielded "small but significant gains in learning and in student engagement" (p. 30).

The theories of motivation described in this chapter help to explain why computers and related technologies have at least the "potential" to motivate learning. For example:

- Many software programs and computer tutors, such as Math Blaster, are developed based on *behavioral theory*, and they are highly interactive. This kind of learning environment provides learners with instant feedback and reinforces desirable behavior. It appears that these are much more engaging than more traditional learning activities and worksheet-type assignments.

- Other software programs are developed to satisfy an individual's *achievement motivation* and aim at being both entertaining and educational. These software programs with game-like and competitive features are motivational to most students and not only can be used in schools but also can be purchased by parents for use at home.

One major reason why social networking is so popular is because it helps students satisfy their need for *affiliation*. West (2012) makes a strong case that blogs, wikis, and social media are strongly motivational because they provide ways for students "to share information, convey material, and express their views" (p. 34) while also engaging in peer-to-peer activity.

Motivation to achieve meaningful learning and higher-level goals is also important. Achieving higher-level goals requires students to do hard mental work and bear most of the responsibility for their own learning. This type of motivation is often highly personal and stems from needs and *cognitive theories* of motivation. Working through tutorials, interacting with computer simulations, or creating Web sites provides interesting challenges to students and helps them sustain the required mental activity to process and learn meaningful information and ideas.

Many teachers use educational software with game-like qualities or allow time on the Internet to reward students who have worked hard or have completed their work early. The fact that students perceive "working on the computer," "surfing the Internet," or "posting to Facebook" as rewarding is perhaps the best evidence of the motivational qualities of computers and media technologies. Teachers, however, must always remain cautious and not allow educational technology to become a "high-tech" toy or babysitter.

Table 4.2 *Five Perspectives of Motivation*

Theory	Theorists	Main Idea
Behavioral	Skinner	Individuals respond to environmental events and *extrinsic* reinforcement.
Needs	Maslow, Deci, McClelland, Csikszentmihalyi	Individuals strive to *satisfy* needs such as self-fulfillment, self-determination, achievement, affiliation, and influence.
Cognitive	Stipek, Weiner	Individuals' actions are influenced by their *beliefs and attributions*, particularly attributions about success and failure situations.
Social Cognitive	Bandura	Individuals' actions are influenced by the value particular *goals* hold for them and their *expectations* for success.
Sociocultural	Vygotsky	Actions are influenced by a variety of groups that help *socialize* and provide for individual identity.

their willingness to engage in academic tasks. It also highlights the importance of the cultures of other groups, such as families, peers, the school, and communities, that students identify with and that help socialize them (Lee & Shute, 2010). Motivation comes not only from factors within the individual, such as needs, goal orientations, and expectancies, but also from the expectations and behaviors of family members (Grolnick, Friendly, & Bellas, 2009), from peers (Ladd, Herald-Brown, & Kochel, 2009), and from the school itself (Roeser, Urdan, & Stephens, 2009).

The five perspectives about motivation are summarized in Table 4.2. Lessons for teachers and strategies that stem from these theories are described later.

In sum, motivation is a complex concept and numerous theories contribute to its understanding. Motivation often involves affective variables but also variables that are cognitive and metacognitive in nature. In the final section of this chapter, we will strive to show how complex theories can be applied by teachers to motivate students to engage in classroom life and academic learning. This chapter's Enhancing Teaching and Learning with Technology box, found on the previous page, looked at using technology as a motivational tool.

Perspectives and Features of Learning Communities

Now let's turn to the social dimension of classrooms and explore theories that explain the community aspect of classroom life. Let's do this by first looking into the classroom of Marie Cuevas, a sixth-grade teacher at Martin Luther King Middle School. She meets daily with her students in an integrated science and language arts class. The students in her class have been heterogeneously grouped so that all ability levels are represented. If we were to visit Ms. Cuevas's classroom on a typical day, we would likely see the following things going on.

Ms. Cuevas sits with a cluster of students in one corner of the room discussing a story they have just read on the life cycle of the Pacific Coast salmon, while several other students are working alone at their desks. They are writing their own stories about how salmon are threatened with extinction because hydroelectric activities have disturbed their breeding grounds. In another corner, a special education teacher is working with Brenda, a young girl who still reads at a second-grade level. Elsewhere, Ms. Cuevas's aide is administering a test to three children who were absent the previous Friday. At a far science table, a pair of students who are supposed to be practicing with a microscope are really discussing yesterday's football game. Overhearing their discussion, Ms. Cuevas stops to get them back on task. At the same moment, a squabble erupts between two students who are returning from the library. Ms. Cuevas asks the teacher's aide to resolve the conflict, then returns to the life-cycle discussion, in which irrelevant comments from Joey about last week's fishing trip with his father has caused it to drift.

As the class period draws to a close, the principal slips in to remind Ms. Cuevas that they have a short meeting scheduled during the lunch break and also to ask if she objects to having a small group of parents visit her next period. All this occurs as learning materials are being returned and readied for the next class, as today's homework assignments are collected, and as the squabble between the two students continues.

This scenario is not an atypical situation. Classrooms everywhere are extremely busy places, characterized by a variety of simultaneous activities: individual and group instruction, socializing, conflict management, evaluation activities, and in-flight adjustments for unanticipated events. In addition to being a specially designed learning community, classrooms are social settings where friendships form and conflicts occur. They are settings for parties, visits, and myriad other activities. Three basic ideas can help us understand the complexity of the classroom and will provide guidance on how to build a more productive learning community. These three dimensions are highlighted in Figure 4.3 and described in the following text.

> An ecological perspective views classrooms as places where teachers, students, and others interact within a highly interdependent environment.

Classroom Properties. One way to think about classrooms is to view them as **ecological systems** in which the inhabitants (teachers and students) interact within a specific environment (the classroom) for the purpose of completing valued activities and tasks. Using this perspective to study classrooms, Walter Doyle (1986, 2006) has written widely about the ecological perspective of classroom life, and he has pointed out that six **classroom properties** make classrooms complex and demanding systems.

Multidimensionality. This refers to the fact that classrooms are crowded places in which many people with different backgrounds, interests, and abilities compete for scarce resources. Unlike a dentist's or an optician's office where a narrow range of predictable events occur, a multitude of diverse events are planned and orchestrated in classrooms. Teachers explain things, give directions, manage conflict, collect milk money, make assignments, and keep records. Students listen, read, write, engage each other in discussion and conversation, form friendships, and experience conflict. Teachers must learn to take these multidimensional activities into account and accommodate them in an effective way.

Figure 4.3 *Three Dimensions of Classrooms*

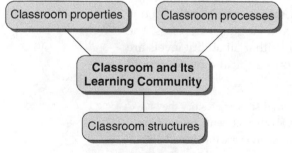

Simultaneity. While helping an individual student during seatwork, a teacher must monitor the rest of the class, handle interruptions, and keep track of time. During a presentation, a teacher must explain ideas clearly while watching for signs of inattention, noncomprehension, and misbehavior. During a discussion, a teacher must listen to a student's answer, watch other students for signs of comprehension, and think about the next question to ask. Each of these situations illustrates a basic feature of classroom life—the simultaneous occurrence of difficult events that effective teachers must be able to recognize and manage.

Immediacy. A third important property of classroom life is the rapid pace of classroom events and their immediate impact on the lives of teachers and students. Teachers have hundreds of daily exchanges with their students. They are continuously praising, reprimanding, explaining, scolding, and challenging. Students also have hundreds of interactions with their teachers and with each other. Pencils are dropped, irrelevant comments are made, squabbles surface, and conflicts are resolved. Many of these events are unplanned, and their immediacy gives teachers little time to reflect before acting.

Unpredictability. Classroom events not only demand immediate attention but also may take unexpected, unpredictable turns. Distractions and interruptions are frequent. Sudden illnesses, announcements over the intercom, and unscheduled visitors are common. Consequently, it is difficult to anticipate how a particular lesson or activity will go on a particular day with a particular group of students. What worked so well last year may be a complete flop this year. Even a lesson that produced enthusiasm and full participation first period may be greeted with stony silence during sixth period.

Publicness. In many work settings, people work mostly in private or in view of only a few others. Doctors' diagnoses of patients' illnesses happen in the privacy of their offices; clerks and waitresses attend to their customers without much attention from others; technicians and accountants do their work unobstructed by an observing public. The classroom, however, is a very public place, and almost all events are witnessed by others. Teachers describe their existence as "living in a fishbowl." This feature of publicness or lack of privacy is just as acute for students. Student behavior is constantly being scrutinized by teachers, many of whom seem (from the students' perspective) to have eyes in the back of their heads. Students also watch each other with considerable interest. It is very difficult, therefore, for any aspect of one's classroom life, whether it is the score on the latest test or a whisper to a neighbor, to go unnoticed.

History. Classrooms and their participants gradually become a community that shares a common history. Classes meet five days a week for several months and thereby accumulate a common set of experiences, norms, and routines. Early meetings shape events for the remainder of the year. Each classroom develops its own social system with particular structures, organization, and norms. Though classrooms may look *alike* from a distance or on paper, each class is actually as unique as a fingerprint. Each class develops its own internal procedures, patterns of interaction, and limits. It is as if imaginary lines guide and control behavior within the group. In spite of day-to-day variation, there is a certain constancy in each class that emerges from its individual history.

Classroom properties directly affect the overall classroom environment and shape the behavior of participants. They have profound effects on teaching. As you will learn, some of these features can be altered by teachers; others cannot.

Classroom Processes. Richard Schmuck and Patricia Schmuck (2001) developed a slightly different framework for viewing classrooms. They highlight the importance of interpersonal and group processes in the classrooms.

The Schmucks believe that positive learning communities are created by teachers when they teach students important interpersonal and group process skills and when

Distinctive features of classrooms—such as multidimensionality, simultaneity, immediacy, unpredictability, publicness, and history—are called classroom properties.

Interpersonal and group processes that help classroom participants deal with issues of expectations, leadership, attraction, norms, communication, and cohesiveness are important ingredients in developing productive learning communities.

they help the classroom develop as a group. The Schmucks identify five group processes that, when working in relation to one another, produce a positive classroom community.

Communication. Most classroom interaction is characterized by verbal and nonverbal communication and is a reciprocal process. The Schmucks argue for communication processes that are open and lively and have a high degree of participant involvement.

Friendship and Cohesiveness. This process involves the degree to which people in a classroom have respect for and value one another and to how friendship patterns within classrooms affect climate and learning. This process takes on increasing importance, as researchers such as Wentzel, Barry, and Caldwell (2004) showed in a recent study in which middle school students without a friend showed lower levels of prosocial behavior, academic achievement, and emotional distress. The Schmucks encourage teachers to help create classroom environments characterized by peer groups free from cliques, and with no student left out of the friendship structure.

Norms. Norms are the shared expectations students and teachers have for classroom behavior. The Schmucks value classrooms with norms that support high student involvement in academic work but at the same time encourage positive interpersonal relationships and shared goals.

Leadership. This process refers to how power and influence are exerted in classrooms and their impact on group interaction and cohesiveness. The Schmucks view leadership as an interpersonal process rather than as a characteristic of a person, and they encourage leadership to be shared in classroom groups.

Conflict. Conflict exists in any human setting, and classrooms are not exceptions. Teachers are encouraged to develop classrooms in which conflict is recognized and processes exist for conflict to be dealt with and resolved in productive ways.

Unlike the *properties* described by Doyle, **classroom *processes*** are highly influenced by the teacher's actions and can be altered to build productive classroom communities, as you will see later in this chapter.

Classroom Structures. The structures that shape classrooms and the demands particular lessons place on students offer a third perspective on classroom learning communities. Researchers such as Gump (1967), Kounin (1970), and more recently Doyle (1986, 1990, 2006), Doyle and Carter (1984), and Kaplan, Gheen, and Midgley (2002) believe that behavior in classrooms is partially a response to the structures and demands of the classroom. This view of classrooms attends closely to the kinds of structures that exist within classrooms and to the activities and tasks students are asked to perform during particular lessons. Figure 4.4 shows how the lesson and its activities can vary in three important ways: structures of the learning task, structures for participation, and goals and reward structures.

Unlike the classroom properties described earlier, which are mostly fixed, or classroom processes, which

Figure 4.4 *Three Types of Classroom Structures and Their Relationship to Classroom Lessons and Activities*

are highly alterable, the three **classroom structures** highlighted in Figure 4.4 are sometimes fixed by tradition, but they can also be altered if a teacher or school choose to do so. In fact, one might compare classroom structures to the design of a house. The way space in a house is designed and partitioned can be thought of as the house's structure. This structure influences how people in the house normally interact with one another. For example, if all the rooms are small and closed off, it is difficult to have a party where lots of people can move around and interact easily. Conversely, if the house is wide open, it is difficult for individuals to find privacy. These structures influence certain types of behavior, but they do not guarantee or prevent specific behaviors. For example, you know of instances in which good parties have occurred in small spaces; you also know of instances in which ideal structural conditions have not produced positive interactions. Structures, however, can be changed. Using the house analogy again, walls can be removed to encourage wider interaction, or screens can be stationed to provide privacy. Classroom structures can also be changed. The following sections describe the three classroom structures in more detail.

Task Structures. The academic and social tasks and activities planned by teachers determine the kinds of work students carry out in classrooms. In this instance, *classroom tasks* refers to what is expected of students and the cognitive and social demands placed upon them to accomplish the task. **Classroom activities,** in contrast, are the things students can be observed doing: participating in a discussion, working with other students in small groups, doing seatwork, listening to a lecture, and so forth. Classroom tasks and activities not only help shape the way teachers and students behave but also help determine what students learn.

Task structures differ according to the various activities required of particular teaching strategies or models used by teachers. As described in later chapters, lessons organized around lectures place far different demands on students than do lessons organized around small-group discussions. Similarly, the demands of students during discussion periods differ from those associated with seatwork.

Whereas some learning tasks and the demands they place on teachers and students stem from the nature of the learning activities themselves, others are embedded in the subjects being taught. Sometimes the academic disciplines (their concepts, organizing frameworks, and methods of revealing new knowledge) provide the basis for these differences. To understand this idea, think about the college classes you have taken in various disciplines and the demands placed on you as a learner in various situations. For instance, the task demands and your behavior when you were doing an experiment in the chemistry lab were different from the demands placed on you as you provided thoughtful analysis of a Shakespearean tragedy. Similarly, the task demands placed on you in anthropology to understand preliterate cultures were different from those required of you to understand the industrial revolution in European history.

Sometimes different task demands exist within particular academic subjects. A lesson aimed at teaching multiplication tables in arithmetic, for instance, makes a different set of demands on learners than does a lesson aimed at increasing skill in mathematical problem solving. Learning the names and locations of the major cities of the world requires different behaviors and actions for learners and teachers than does a geography inquiry lesson exploring the importance of location in determining standard of living. A literature lesson on character development makes different demands than does a spelling lesson.

Classroom structures are the ways classrooms are organized around learning tasks and participation and the ways goals and rewards are defined.

The work students are expected to do in classrooms and the cognitive and social demands placed on them as they perform particular lessons are called task structures.

The important thing to remember is that classroom task structures influence the thoughts and actions of classroom participants and help determine the degree of student cooperation and involvement. As later chapters emphasize, students need to be taught specific and appropriate learning strategies to help them satisfy the task demands being placed on them in classrooms.

Goal and Reward Structures. A second type of classroom structure is the way goals and rewards are structured. Chapter 3 introduced the concept of instructional goals, which, as you remember, were desired outcomes teachers hold for their students, such as being able to spell a list of words, explain natural selection, or solve a mathematics problem. The concept of goal structure is different from that of instructional goals. **Goal structures** specify the *type of interdependence* required of students as they strive to complete learning tasks—the relationships among students and between an individual and the group. Johnson and Johnson (2013) and Slavin (1995) identified three different goal structures.

Cooperative goal structures exist when students perceive that they can achieve their goal if, and only if, the other students with whom they are working can also reach the goal.

Competitive goal structures exist when students perceive they can reach their goal only if other students do not reach the goal.

Individualistic goal structures exist when students perceive that their achievement of a goal is unrelated to achievement of the goal by other students.

The three types of goal structures are illustrated in Figure 4.5.

Classroom rewards can be categorized in the same manner as goals. **Reward structures** can be competitive, cooperative, or individualistic. Grading on a curve is an example of a competitive reward structure, in that students' efforts are rewarded in comparison with other students. Winners in most field and track events are similarly competitive. In contrast, cooperative reward structures are in place when individual effort helps a whole group succeed. The reward system for a football team's effort (winning) is an example of a cooperative reward structure, even though the team as a whole is in competition with other teams.

Classroom goal and reward structures are at the core of life in classrooms and influence greatly both the behavior and learning of students. Regardless of a teacher's personal philosophy on the use of rewards, the current reality is that student motivation often centers on the dispensation of grades. In fact, Doyle (1979) argued that the primary features of classroom life are the way students engage in academic work and how they "exchange [their] performance for grades." The way teachers organize goal and reward structures determines which types of goals are accomplished and how the exchange occurs. They also influence classroom management and student disruptive behavior (see Kaplan, Gheen, & Midgley, 2002).

Classroom Participation Structures. Additionally, teaching and learning are influenced by classroom **participation structures**. Participation structures, according to Cazden (1986) and Burbules and Bruce (2001), determine who can say what, when, and to whom.

Sidenotes (left margin):

Goal structures determine the degree of interdependence sought among students. There are three different types of goal structures: cooperative, competitive, and individualistic.

Reward structures determine the ways in which rewards can be distributed within a classroom. There are three types: competitive, cooperative, and individualistic.

Participation structures help determine who can say what, when, and to whom during classroom discourse.

Figure 4.5 *Three Different Goal Structures*

Cooperative   Competitive   Individualistic

These structures include the way students take turns during group lessons and the way they ask questions and respond to teacher queries. These structures also vary from one type of lesson to another. During a lecture, for example, student participation is limited to listening to the teacher and perhaps individually taking notes. A discussion or recitation connected to a lecture, in contrast, requires students to answer questions and to give their ideas. Listening to one another is another expectation for students during a discussion or a recitation, as is raising one's hand to take a turn. When the teacher plans seatwork for students, the prescribed participation is normally to work alone and to interact one-on-one with the teacher when help is required. Small-group and cooperative learning activities obviously require a different kind of participation on the part of students. Small-group activities require that students talk to each other, and cooperative learning activities require joint production of academic tasks. Chapters 10, 11, and 12 provide additional information about participation structures and describe steps teachers can take to increase the amount of student participation in their classrooms.

Sociocultural Perspective. A final perspective and the most contemporary one about classrooms as learning communities stems from sociocultural theorists and school reformers who have been heavily influenced by the work of Dewey, Piaget, and Vygotsky. This perspective views the traditional classroom as a place designed to promote certain types of formal learning and envisions classroom settings in the future that will be modeled after more informal settings in which individuals learn naturally. Often these settings are described as those that enhance authentic learning, where students are involved in inquiry that helps them construct their own meaning and where talk and action by teachers and students strive for social justice. Authentic learning is defined as students' accomplishments that have significance and meaning in the real world and in their own lives outside the classroom, not just in the classroom. Constructing one's own knowledge means being actively involved in inquiry that builds on what one already knows, rather than being treated to fixed knowledge defined and transmitted by the teachers.

Oakes and Lipton (2006) have summarized the sociocultural perspective. They argue that the pedagogy associated with this perspective cannot be translated into a "proven set of best practices" but instead evolves from "qualities of the learning relationships among teachers and students" and that "practices cannot be judged independently of the cultural knowledge students bring with them to school" (p. 215).

They do, however, posit a set of guidelines, not too much different from those described by the Schmucks, that teachers can use to construct learning communities that are authentic and socially just:

- Teachers and students are confident that everyone learns well.
- Lessons are active, multidimensional, and social.
- Relationships are caring and interdependent.
- Talk and action are socially just.
- Authentic assessment enhances learning.

Research on Motivation and Learning Communities

The research literature on classrooms and motivation is extensive and represents scholarship from many fields: psychology, social psychology, group dynamics, and social context of teaching. This section provides interesting studies selected to give you insights into the way some of this research is carried out and to provide examples of some important findings. The studies cover a span of a half century and focus on the effects of classroom environments on motivation, how teacher behaviors influence motivation and group life, and how students themselves can influence each other and their teachers.

Relationship between Classroom Environments and Motivation. One of the most difficult aspects of teaching is to get students to persist at learning tasks. Some students persist longer than others, and some tasks appear to be more interesting than other tasks to some students. Researchers have been interested for a long time in how classroom environments influence student motivation. The general finding is that environments characterized by mutual respect, high standards, and a caring attitude are more conducive to student persistence than other environments.

> **Students persist longer in their studies and learning tasks if the learning environment is happy and positive.**

In an interesting and unique study conducted in the 1970s, Santrock (1976) studied the relationships between some of the dimensions of the classroom environment—happy and sad moods—and students' motivation to persist on learning tasks. Santrock randomly assigned first- and second-grade children into different treatment groups. On the way to a classroom, students were told a happy story and a sad story. The experimenter acted happy in relating a happy story and sad in relating the sad story. The various classrooms involved were decorated in one of two ways: with happy pictures or with sad pictures. In the room, the children were asked to work at a task at which they were interrupted from time to time and asked to think either happy or sad thoughts. Students could stop working on the task whenever they liked.

Students thinking happy thoughts who experienced a happy experimenter in a happy room persisted much longer at the learning task than did students thinking sad thoughts with a sad experimenter in a sad room. This type of result has been replicated many times, and it is important because it indicates that persistence at a task for students is not simply a function of the their self-control or interest but also can be influenced by the environment and by aspects of the environment under the teacher's control—room decor and happy moods.

Relationship between Leadership and Group Life. For many years, teachers have known that what they do influences the behavior of their students. Furthermore, many educators believe that a teacher's behavior should be "democratic" in character, thus reflecting the larger societal values about the way people should interact with one another. Take, for example, the following comments written by John Dewey (1916) almost 100 years ago.

> **Researchers have known for a very long time that students respond more favorably to teachers who are democratic than to teachers who are authoritarian.**

> We can and do supply ready-made "ideas" by the thousand; we do not usually take pains to see that the one learning engages in significant situations where his own activities generate, support, and clinch ideas—that is, perceived meanings or connections. This does not mean that the teacher is to stand off and look on; the alternative to furnishing ready-made subject matter and listening to the accuracy with which it is reproduced is not quiescence, but participation, sharing, in an activity. In such shared activity the teacher is a learner, and the learner is, without knowing it, a teacher—and upon the whole, the less consciousness there is, on either side, of either giving or receiving instruction, the better. (p. 176)

But what effects do democratic behaviors and procedures have on students and group life? This question was first explored well over a half century ago in a set of classic studies conducted by Kurt Lewin, Ron Lippitt, and Richard White (1939; Lippitt & White, 1963). The researchers studied 11-year-old boys who volunteered to form clubs and to participate in a series of club projects. Clubs such as the Sherlock Holmes Club, Dick Tracy Club, and Secret Agents Club (names that were popular at the time that may seem quaint today) were formed, and club leaders (teachers) were taught to exhibit three different forms of leadership: authoritarian leadership, democratic leadership, and laissez-faire (passive) leadership. The boys were observed as they participated in club activities, including a time when the leader purposively left the boys on their own.

The researchers found that the boys reacted to authoritarian leadership by becoming rebellious and that they were much less involved than the boys under democratic leadership. What was most telling, however, was the boys' behavior when the leaders were out of the room. Boys under authoritarian and laissez-faire leadership stopped working as soon as the leader was absent. Boys in the democratic group, on the other hand, kept working, and certain boys even stepped in and provided leadership to the group.

Many educators have concluded from this and many similar studies over the past fifty years that teacher behavior has important influences on students' willingness to cooperate and stick to learning tasks (see, for example, Dolezal, Welsh, Pressley, & Vincent, 2003; Jussim, Robustelli, & Cain, 2009; and Pintrich & Schunk, 2002). Teachers who are too strict and directive may get a lot of work from their students if they are physically present, but that involvement will drop off once close supervision is removed.

Certain motivational strategies used by teachers have also been the focus of considerable research, particularly over the past two decades. Of particular interest have been those strategies used by teachers that support student motivation to learn. An example of this research is highlighted in a very interesting study summarized in the Research Summary for this chapter.

Effects of Students' Behavior on Each Other and on Their Teachers. Studies such as the one described in the Research Summary focus on the influence that teacher behavior has on students. Influence in the classroom group, however, does not always flow just from the teacher. Students also influence each other and can even influence their teachers. One particularly interesting line of inquiry over the years has been research that investigates how the student peer group, through both formal and informal interactions, affects attitudes and achievement. Peer group influences have been documented in studies of college dormitories and living houses (Newcomb, 1961, for example) and in many different public and private school settings. Much of the research shows that many students conform to peer group norms and that all too often these norms are in contradiction to those held by educators and teachers. James Coleman (1961) studied ten American high schools in the 1950s. He found many instances wherein the adolescent peer group supported norms for being popular and being athletic over the school's norms in support of academic achievement. This finding has been replicated in American high schools in every decade since Coleman's original work (see for example, Ellis, Dumas, Mandy, & Wolfe, 2012; Honig, Kahne, & McLaughlin, 2001; Ogbu, 1995, 1997; and Wolk, 2007). Today, peer group pressure is used often to explain high dropout rates and low achievement of many youth.

The peer group has important influences on students' behavior and their motivation to engage in learning activities.

Check, Extend, Explore

Check
- Contrast behavioral, needs, cognitive, social cognitive, and sociocultural theories of motivation.
- What are the differences between extrinsic and intrinsic motivation?
- Contrast the classroom properties defined by Doyle with the classroom processes described by the Schmucks.
- How can classroom task-and-reward structures vary?
- Contrast the sociocultural perspective of learning communities with more traditional views.

Extend
- In your own experiences, what are the most important factors that motivate you to persevere in academic tasks?
- Some educators believe that too much emphasis is put on the use of extrinsic motivation. Do you agree or disagree with this view? Go to the "Extend Question Poll" on the Online Learning Center to respond.

Explore
- Do an Internet search on the topic of motivational aspects of computers. Is what you find consistent with the discussion in the chapter's Enhancing Teaching and Learning with Technology box?

Research Summary
Can Particular Strategies Influence Students' Motivation to Learn?

Dolezal, S. E., Welsh, L. M., Pressley, M., & Vincent, M. M. (2003). How nine third-grade teachers motivate student academic engagement. *Elementary School Journal, 103*(3), 239–269.

An enduring concern among teachers is how to motivate students to persist in their academic work. Keen observers of classrooms, as well as experienced teachers, have long recognized subtle differences among classrooms and among the practices used by particular teachers.

Problem and Approach: University of Notre Dame researchers were interested in what teachers do to motivate students' academic engagement and endeavored to compare teaching practices that support or undermine motivation. This study is interesting for two reasons. One, the results provide keen insights into practices that support engagement, and two, the study is a good illustration of ethnographic research described in the Resource Handbook at the end of *Learning to Teach*. This type of research relies on collecting empirical information through extended observation and interviews. This has been done well in this study.

Methods: Nine third-grade teachers in eight Catholic elementary schools in Indiana participated in the study. The teachers had taught between five and twenty-three years in schools comprising students from all socioeconomic levels.

Primary data for the study came from field notes of classroom observations. Two researchers at a time observed each class approximately three times per month starting in October for an average total of ten to fifteen hours over the course of the school year. Every ten to fifteen minutes observers noted what students were doing and what percentage were engaged in academic work. During the visits to the classrooms, researchers also collected samples of student work, teacher notes, assignments, and worksheets. An in-depth ethnographic interview was conducted with each teacher at the end of the school year. Results were coded and checked using methods recommended for this type of data collection and analysis.

Results: Researchers found clear differences among the teachers with respect to student academic engagement. Four teachers were found to have a high level of engagement, over 80 percent on-task behavior most of the time. Two teachers, on the other hand, displayed a low level of engagement; their students were off task most of the time. The other three teachers had engagement rates somewhere in the middle. High-engagement teachers also had students working on tasks that were appropriately challenging, whereas the low-engagement teachers assigned a high proportion of easy tasks (such as games and worksheets) that could be completed in a fraction of the time allotted.

Table 4.3 *Examples of Practices That Support or Undermine Motivation*

Practices That Support Motivation	Practices That Undermine Motivation
Holding students accountable	Attributing ability
Providing appropriate homework	Fostering competitiveness
Checking for understanding	Providing ineffective scaffolding
Providing a positive classroom environment	Lack of monitoring of student work
Having clear goals and expectations	Assigning tasks of low difficulty
Using cooperative learning	Having poor/incomplete planning
Having difficult tasks that students can do	Having pacing that is too slow
Monitoring student work	Having negative classroom environment
Providing positive encouragement	Using uninspired instructional practices
Providing strategies instruction	Using negative classroom management
Valuing students	Failing to make connections
Stimulating cognitive thought	Using public notice and punishment

Source: Dolezal et al. (2003), p. 246.

The researchers coded teaching practice into two categories: (1) those that *support* motivation and (2) those that *undermine* motivation. Examples of each are provided in Table 4.3. The complete list of these behaviors can be seen by reading the full study, which is available online and listed under the Interactive and Applied Learning feature at the end of this chapter.

Researchers next calculated the ratio of supportive practices used by the nine teachers to the undermining practices used by each teacher. These data are shown in Table 4.4.

As can be observed, some classrooms had very high ratios whereas others had low ratios. Note that in Irving's classroom (the name is fictitious), no undermining practices were observed, while forty-five supporting practices were observed. Compare that to Aden's classroom, where only four supportive practices were observed compared to eleven undermining practices.

Finally, researchers provided examples of what they observed in classrooms of low-engaging teachers, moderately engaging teachers, and highly engaging teachers. Their descriptions are summarized here:

Low-engaging teachers. Students typically showed passive attention, and a majority were not participating in work. Teachers used few supportive motivating practices, seldom praised students, had sparse classroom environments and little display of student work or colorful decoration. These teachers had frequent management problems, conducted poorly planned lessons, and relied heavily on recitation teaching.

Moderately engaging teachers. The moderately engaging teachers had classrooms more positive in tone, and students were engaged quite a bit of the time. Supportive practices and effective classroom management were more common than with the low-engaging teachers. According to the researchers, "despite these teachers' ability to capture student attention, they were not able to maintain engagement, probably because the tasks assigned were too easy." (p. 251)

Highly engaging teachers. The highly engaging teachers had created warm and caring classroom communities, used many supportive motivation practices, and always showed good planning. They displayed enthusiasm, assigned cognitively demanding work, and were careful to monitor and check students for understanding. Samples of student work showed high levels of accomplishment.

Discussion and Implications The researchers discussed their finding by pointing out that highly engaging teachers "do much" to motivate their students and do not rely on any single mechanism or theory of motivation, whereas the low-engaging teachers relied on teaching practices that undermine motivation. Researchers concluded their study by posing an interesting question: "Why are some teachers completely motivating in their teaching, whereas others fill their instruction with teaching behaviors that . . . undermine achievement?" (p. 256). How would you answer this question?

Table 4.4 *Ratio of Teaching Practices Supporting Motivation to Practices Undermining Motivation*

Teacher	No. of Supporting Motivational Practices	No. of Undermining Motivational Practices	Ratio
Aden	4	11	0.36
Bonstead	12	12	1.00
Christopher	16	12	1.33
Davis	17	10	1.70
Edwards	14	6	2.33
Fitzpatrick	18	5	3.20
Grant	18	4	4.50
Hackett	26	5	5.20
Irving	45	0	infinity

Source: Dolezal et al. (2003), p. 248.

Strategies for Motivating Students and Building Productive Learning Communities

Building productive learning communities and motivating students to engage in meaningful learning activities are major goals of teaching. Yet, as you have read, many ingredients make up a student's motivation to learn. Success depends on using motivational strategies stemming from each of the perspectives described previously as well as on employing strategies that help a group of individuals develop into a productive learning community. Motivational and learning community development strategies, however, cannot be reduced to a few simple guidelines. No single dramatic event will produce motivation and a productive learning community. Instead, effective teachers employ strategies interdependently until motivation is a permanent aspect of their classrooms, where students' psychological needs are met, where they find learning activities that are interesting, challenging, and meaningful, and where they will know they can be successful.

Believe in Students' Capabilities and Attend to Alterable Factors

There are many parts of their lives that students bring with them to school that teachers can do little about. For example, teachers have little influence over students' basic personalities, their home lives, or their early childhood experiences. Unfortunately, some teachers attend only to these aspects of their students, and such attention is mostly unproductive. It is true that social factors, such as students' backgrounds or their parents' expectations, influence how hard they work in school. Similarly, their psychological well-being, anxieties, and dependencies also affect effort and learning. However, there is not much teachers can do to alter or influence these social and psychological factors. Instead, teachers are more effective in enhancing student motivation if they concentrate their efforts on factors that are within their abilities to control and influence.

One important thing that teachers can control is their own attitudes and beliefs about children, particularly those they may have about students who come from different backgrounds than they do. Believing that every child can learn and that every child sees the world through his or her own cultural lens can shift the burden of low engagement and low achievement from the child's background to where it often belongs—a nonunderstanding classroom and school.

A second important action teachers can take is to teach to student strengths and recognize strengths that have gone unrecognized or been neglected. For example, Sternberg and his colleagues (Grigoroenko et al., 2004; Sternberg et al., 2001) reported on studies they did with Native Alaskan children and children from Kenya. They found that children from these non-mainstream cultures had an abundance of practical knowledge and skills valued in their culture but neglected by traditional schooling. Pawak (2008) and Armstrong (2012) have made similar observations about the importance of recognizing students' strengths. Teachers who are aware of this kind of practical knowledge can use it as scaffolding to help students be successful in the demands of formal education.

Avoid Overemphasizing Extrinsic Motivation

Most of us know a great deal about extrinsic motivation because many commonsense ideas about human behavior rest on reinforcement principles, particularly on the principles of providing extrinsic rewards (positive reinforcers) to get desired behavior and

Teachers are more effective if they concentrate their efforts on things they can do something about.

using punishment to stop undesirable behavior. This theory of motivation is pervasive in our society. Parents get their children to behave in particular ways by giving them weekly allowances. They withhold these allowances or use "grounding" when their children behave inappropriately. People who work hard at their jobs are given merit raises; those who don't are fired. We give individuals medals for acts of bravery and put them in jail for acts of crime. Good grades, certificates of merit, praise, and athletic letters are extrinsic rewards used by teachers to get students to study and to behave in desirable ways. Poor grades, demerits, and detention are employed to punish undesirable behaviors.

On the surface, behavioral theory makes good common sense, and certainly there may be instances in all aspects of life in which extrinsic rewards are necessary. At the same time, extrinsic rewards do not always produce the intended results. For instance, providing extrinsic rewards for learning tasks that are already intrinsically interesting can actually decrease student motivation, as will be described in Chapter 6. Further, for any reward or punishment to serve as a motivator, it must be valued or feared. Many students in today's schools don't care about good grades. If that is so, then grades will *not* cause students to study. Similarly, if getting demerits or being assigned to detention are considered "badges of honor," as they are to some students, then they will not deter undesirable behavior. Effective teachers use extrinsic rewards cautiously and learn to rely on other means to motivate their students. Ways this is accomplished include:

Although behavioral theory is pervasive in our culture, effective teachers find ways to minimize its potentially harmful effects.

- Use extrinsic rewards only when other intrinsic motivation is missing.
- Use extrinsic rewards in ways that do not undermine students' self-determination or self-control.
- Use extrinsic rewards in ways that students can view them as opportunities to make choices.

Create Learning Situations with Positive Feeling Tones

Needs and attributional theories of motivation discussed previously stress the importance of building learning environments that are pleasant, safe, and secure and in which students have a degree of self-determination and assume responsibility for their own learning.

The overall learning orientation and tone of the classroom are critical. As observed in studies summarized in the previous section, teachers' attitudes and orientations toward particular learning situations have considerable influence on how students respond to learning situations. Jane Roberts and Madeline Hunter (Hunter 1982, 1995) have used the term **feeling tone** to describe this aspect of the learning environment and provide the following examples of simple things teachers can say to establish a positive, neutral, or negative feeling tone:

Positive: "You write such interesting stories, I'm eager to read this one."
Negative: "That story must be finished before you're excused for lunch."
Neutral: "If you aren't finished, don't worry; there'll be plenty of time later."

Students put forth more effort in environments with positive feeling tones and less in environments that are negative. An important point for teachers to consider, if they choose to use unpleasant feeling tones to motivate students to complete a difficult learning task, is to return as soon as possible to a positive one: "I really put a lot of pressure on you, and you've responded magnificently," or "I know you were angry

Students put forth more effort in environments where particular learning tasks are perceived as pleasant.

about the demands being made, but you should be proud of the improvement in your performance." Feeling tones in the classroom are not only the result of specific things teachers say at a particular moment but are also the result of many other structures and processes created by teachers to produce productive learning communities, as later sections of this chapter describe.

Build on Students' Interests and Intrinsic Values

Needs and attributional theories of motivation also stress the importance of using intrinsic motivation and building on the students' own interests and curiosity. A teacher can do a number of things to relate learning materials and activities to students' interests. Here are some examples:

- *Relate lessons to students' lives.* Find things that students are interested in or curious about, such as popular music, and relate these interests to topics under study (Mozart, for instance).
- *Use students' names.* Using students' names helps personalize learning and captures students' attention. For example: "Suppose Maria, here, were presenting an argument for electing her friend, and Charles wished to challenge her position . . . ," or "John, here, has the pigmentation most commonly associated with Nordic races, whereas Roseanne's is more typical of Latinos."
- *Make materials vivid and novel.* A teacher can say things that make the ordinary vivid and novel for students. For example: "When you order your favorite McDonald's milkshake, it won't melt even if you heat it in the oven. That's the result of an emulsifier made from the algae we're studying," or "Suppose you believed in reincarnation. In your next life, what would you need to accomplish that you didn't accomplish satisfactorily in this life?"

Using games, puzzles, and a variety of digital tools that are inviting and carry their own intrinsic motivation is another way teachers make lessons interesting for students. Similarly, using a *variety* of activities (field trips, simulations, music, guest speakers) and instructional methods (lecture, seatwork, discussion, small-group) keeps students interested in school and their schoolwork.

It is important to highlight two cautions about using student interests for motivational purposes. Stressing the novel or vivid can sometimes turn into mere entertainment and can distract student learning. Similarly, new interests are formed through learning about a new topic. Teachers who expose their students only to materials in which they are already interested prevent them from developing new interests.

Structure Learning to Accomplish Flow

Schools and teachers can structure learning activities to emphasize their intrinsic value so students become totally involved and experience the type of flow described earlier. However, such total involvement, according to Csikszentmihalyi, is possible only with learning experiences that have certain characteristics.

First, flow experiences require that the challenge of a particular learning activity corresponds to the learner's level of skill. All of the learner's skill is required, yet the activity cannot be so difficult that the participant becomes frustrated. Perhaps rock climbing can provide a good example of the need to match the degree of challenge and skill. If you are an advanced beginning rock climber, you will be bored if you are asked to climb the slightly sloping, 15-foot-high rock in your backyard. This would not

Vivid and novel materials and examples can serve as powerful motivators for student learning.

Highly motivational flow experiences require an appropriate level of challenge.

require use of your skills or provide you with challenging practice. On the other hand, as an advanced beginner, you will become very frustrated and stressed if you are asked to climb El Capitan, one of the most challenging climbs in North America. You will read later how experienced teachers plan lessons that balance the level of difficulty and the amount of challenge.

The definition of clear and unambiguous goals is another characteristic of learning experiences likely to produce flow. As you read in Chapter 3, lessons that make clear to students what is expected of them and what they are supposed to accomplish are more likely to produce extended engagement and learning than are lessons with unclear goals and expectations. Finally, people who report having had flow experiences say they gained relevant and meaningful feedback about their activity as they were doing it, a feature of motivation discussed next.

Establishing "flow" may not be as easy as it may seem, particularly in classrooms that are culturally and linguistically diverse. For instance, learning activities that may appear to be interesting and challenging to middle-class teachers may have little meaning to students with different cultural heritages or who are English language learners. Failing to make meaningful connections with students can leave teachers frustrated with the lack of engagement on the part of students and students feeling that their voices are not being heard.

Feedback is important to eliminate incorrect performance—and to enhance student learning.

Use Knowledge of Results and Don't Excuse Failure

Feedback (also called *knowledge of results*) on good performance provides intrinsic motivation. Feedback on poor performance gives learners needed information to improve. Both types of feedback are important motivational factors. To be effective, feedback must be more specific and more immediate than a grade a teacher puts on a report card every six to nine weeks. In Chapter 8, Direct Instruction, specific guidelines for giving feedback are provided. This topic is also covered in Chapter 6, Assessment and Evaluation. It is enough to say here that feedback should be as immediate as possible (handing back corrected tests the day after an exam), as specific as possible (comments in addition to an overall grade on a paper), and nonjudgmental ("Your use of the word *effect* is incorrect—you should have used *affect* instead" rather than "What's wrong with you? We have gone over the difference between *effect* and *affect* a dozen times."). Additionally, feedback should focus on and encourage internal attributions—such as effort or lack of effort—rather than external attributions—such as luck or special circumstance like "my printer wouldn't work." Feedback should help students see what they *did not* do rather than what they *cannot* do.

Feedback or knowledge of results is information given to students about their performance.

Sometimes teachers, particularly inexperienced teachers, do not want to embarrass students by drawing attention to incorrect performance. Also, it is sometimes easier to accept students' excuses for failure than to confront them with the fact of their failure. These kinds of teacher actions are most often counterproductive. Teachers should not impose severe punishments for failures or use feedback that is belittling. At the same time, effective teachers know that it is important to hold high expectations for all students and that if things are being done incorrectly, this incorrect performance will continue and become permanent unless it is brought to the students' attention and instruction is provided for doing it right.

Attend to Student Needs, Including the Need for Self-Determination

You read in the discussion of needs theory that individuals invest energy in pursuit of achievement, affiliation, and influence as well as to satisfy needs for choice and self-determination. Most motivational research has focused on achievement motivation, and less is known about influence, affiliation, and the role of choice. All of these motives, however, play a role in determining the type of effort students will expend on learning tasks and how long they will persist. In general, students' influence and self-determination needs are satisfied when they feel they have some power or say over their classroom environment and their learning tasks. Some years ago Cheryl Spaulding (1992) related an interesting story about how important choice and self-determination are to most people. Imagine the following scenario:

> You are a person who loves to travel, and your favorite form of traveling is by car. Each summer you take off on a vacation, driving to and through some of the interesting places in this country. You prefer this sort of vacation because you enjoy discovering for yourself country inns and bed-and-breakfast homes run by unusual people in out-of-the-way places. This year an anonymous benefactor has awarded you with an all-expenses-paid, two-month driving tour through parts of the northeastern United States and Canada, a trip you have long wanted to take. To assist you, this benefactor has gone ahead and planned your itinerary, down to the minutest detail. Your travel route, including the specific roads on which you will travel, has been thoroughly mapped out so that you will never get off course. All your room and dinner reservations have already been made. Even your meals have been preordered for you. All you have to do to take advantage of this wonderful offer is agree to follow the planned itinerary down to the last detail. Would you accept this offer? Would this vacation be as enjoyable as your usual tours through the states? (p. 22)

Spaulding writes that the answers to these questions are likely to be no, because much of the pleasure derived from a driving tour comes from the freedom of being able to make choices on a moment-to-moment basis rather than having these decisions made by someone else.

Here are a few specific examples of how teachers can provide students choice and a sense of self-determination:

- Hold regular (daily or weekly) meetings with students, assessing how well previous lessons have gone and what they would like to see included in lessons that follow. Some experienced teachers use a technique called "pluses and wishes." On large newsprint charts, the teacher makes two columns and labels them as shown in Table 4.5. Together, students and teachers list their suggestions for all to consider. The teacher can use information from this list in his or her own planning and can

Table 4.5 *Pluses and Wishes Chart*

Pluses	Wishes
The presentation on cells was clear.	We wish we had more time on the experiment.
The group work was interesting.	We wish more students would cooperate.
We enjoyed the principal's visit.	We wish the test had been fairer.

come back to it to show students that particular lessons and activities were influenced by their input. More on classroom meetings will be described in Chapter 5.

- Assign students to perform important tasks, such as distributing and collecting books and papers, taking care of the aquarium, taking roll, acting as tutors to other students, taking messages to the principal's office, and the like.
- Use cooperative learning and problem-based instructional strategies described in Chapters 10 and 11, because these approaches can allow students considerable choice in the subject they study and the methods they use.

Satisfying affiliative needs is also important. In most schools, it is the peer group that students look to for satisfying their affiliation needs. Unfortunately, norms for peer group affiliation often conflict with the strong achievement norms teachers would like to see. In some instances, very competitive cliques that exclude many students from both the academic and social life of the school are found. In other instances, peer group norms exist that apply negative sanctions to those students who try to do well in school. Teachers can make needs for affiliation work in a positive way by following some of these procedures.

Students look mainly to each other to satisfy their affiliation needs.

- Make sure that all the students in the class (even in high school) know one another's names and some personal information about each other.
- Initiate cooperative goal and reward structures, as described previously and in Chapter 10.
- Take time to help the students in the classroom develop as a group, using procedures described in the following section.

Attend to the Nature of Learning Goals and Difficulty of Instructional Tasks

Social cognitive theory reminds us of the importance of the ways learning goals and tasks are structured and carried out. Three aspects of learning goals and tasks should be considered here: goal structures, goal orientation, and task difficulty.

You read earlier about three types of classroom goal structures: competitive, cooperative, and individualistic. Competitive goal structures lead to comparisons and win-lose relationships among students and make a student's ability, rather than effort, the primary factor for success. Cooperative goal structures, in contrast, lead to social interdependence, and shared activity makes student effort the primary factor for success. Chapter 10 goes into greater detail about how to set up cooperative goal structures.

You also read earlier about two different types of goal orientations: learning goal orientation, in which students strive to compete with themselves and to learn something new, and performance goal orientation, in which students strive to reach standards often imposed by others. Teachers can help students develop more productive learning goal orientations by teaching them the differences between performance goals and learning goals and by encouraging them to set learning goals in which they compete with themselves rather than others. Teachers can also focus assessment and evaluation on "improvement" rather than only on "performance."

Closely connected to the ways goals are structured is the level of difficulty of goals students choose for themselves. Students who set very high goals that are unachievable can be encouraged to rethink what might be more realistic goals. Similarly, students who always set low goals can be encouraged to raise their sights. The important thing for teachers to remember is that students are motivated to persevere longer in pursuing goals that are challenging but realistic and achievable. Remember the findings of the study by Dolezal et al. (2003) highlighted as this chapter's Research Summary.

Learning tasks that are too easy require too little effort and produce little feeling of success.

An additional factor that can influence a student's motivation is associated with the actual degree of difficulty of the learning task and the amount of effort required to complete it. As described previously, tasks that are too easy require too little effort and produce no feelings of success and, consequently, are unmotivational. At the same time, tasks that are too difficult for students, regardless of the effort they expend, will also be unmotivational. Effective teachers learn how to adjust the level of difficulty of learning tasks for particular students. Sometimes this means providing special challenges for the brightest in the class and providing more support and assistance for those who find a particular task too difficult. Effective teachers also help students see the connections between the amount of effort they put into a learning task and their successes and accomplishments. This is done by discussing with students why particular efforts led to success and, conversely, why in other instances they led to failure.

Diversity and Differentiation

Using Multidimensional Tasks

As emphasized throughout *Learning to Teach*, classrooms today are characterized by great diversity. One way for teachers to tailor their instruction for a diverse group of students is to make opportunities available so students can work together on community activities and to pursue tasks that are motivational and challenging. Elizabeth Cohen (1994) and Oakes, Anderson, Lipton, and Stillman (2012) have called this type of learning situation *using multidimensional tasks*. This approach emphasizes students working together on interesting tasks and problems and students making contributions according to their own backgrounds, interests, and abilities. According to Cohen, multidimensional tasks:

- Are intrinsically interesting, rewarding, and challenging
- Include more than one answer or more than one way to solve the problem
- Allow different students to make different contributions
- Involve various mediums to engage the senses of sight, hearing, and touch
- Require a variety of skills and behaviors
- Require reading and writing

Following is an example of how Kim Man Thi Pham uses multidimensional tasks in her eleventh-grade history classroom:

> The room is alive with activity. Desks are pushed to the edge of the classroom, accommodating various groups. Some students discuss how to share their recent experience of working with migrant farm workers in the fields. One student patiently charts a graph showing the economic breakdown of maintaining a large farm. Two students and I plan the presentation order. Other students complete a poster on the United Farm Workers, focusing on the leadership of Cesar Chavez and Philip Vera Cruz. Their photographs, news clippings, and markers are sprawled across the floor. Laughter erupts from the back of the room where four students debate the idea of dressing up as fruit while presenting information on the movement of farm workers across the state following the peak harvest times of the fruit and vegetable season. Someone asks me if she can give her classmates a test after the presentation. "Certainly," I reply, "but consider—'What do you want them to know?' " The student thinks about the question while slowly returning to the group. Activity continues unabated until the final minutes. I remind students to document progress with a short journal entry highlighting individual concerns and feelings. Students write until the end of class. (Oakes & Lipton, 2006, pp. 230–231)

Facilitate Group Development and Cohesion

Developing a positive classroom environment will lead to enhanced motivation and heightened achievement. This requires attending to the social and emotional needs of students as well as their academic needs. Also, it requires helping students grow as a group. Sometimes people may not notice, but groups, like individuals, develop and pass through discernible stages in the process. Several social psychologists have studied classrooms and found that classroom groups develop in similar patterns (Schmuck & Schmuck, 2001). The following stages of **group development** represent a synthesis of their ideas.

Classroom groups go through stages in the process of developing into cohesive and effective groups.

Stage 1: Facilitating Group Inclusion and Psychological Membership. Everyone wants to feel that they belong, that they are accepted by significant others. This is especially important in a classroom setting because being a learner is a risky business. In order to have the courage to make the mistakes that are a natural part of learning, students need to feel they are in a safe environment. This feeling of safety comes only when students feel accepted and liked by those in their class. Therefore, early in classroom life, students will seek a niche for themselves in the classroom group. They will likely be on their good behavior and present a positive image. Teachers have considerable influence during this period because of their assigned authority. During this period, teachers should spend considerable time forging personal connections with students, helping them learn each others' names, and assisting them in building relationships with each other. When new students enter the group, special efforts must again be made to ensure their acceptance. What teachers do during the initial period of group development represents key first steps in creating a positive learning environment for students.

Stage 2: Establishing Shared Influence and Cooperation. It does not take very long, even with very young children, to facilitate psychological membership. However, inevitably, there will be problems. Members of the class soon enter into two types of power struggles. One struggle tests the authority of the teacher; the other establishes the peer group pecking order. These are signals that the classroom has entered stage 2, in which individuals begin struggling to establish their influence within the group.

Well-developed groups are ready to work productively on academic goals.

At this stage, it is important for teachers to show students that they have a voice in classroom decision making and that classroom life will be more satisfying if tensions among students can be resolved. Several techniques for dealing with tensions and conflict in the classroom are described in Chapter 5 and include classroom meetings, conflict resolution, active listening, and dealing with misbehavior. At this point, it is enough to know that such unpleasant experiences as challenges to the teacher's authority, fights between students, and off-task behavior are all normal occurrences on the road to establishing a positive classroom environment. A caution, however, is in order. If these tensions cannot be resolved and power relationships balanced, the group will not be able to move toward collaboration or into the next stage.

Stage 3: Pursuing Academic Goals. At this stage, the classroom group is functioning smoothly and productively. Students feel comfortable in the class and are confident that difficulties can be worked out. The frequency of conflicts and off-task behavior decreases, and when they do happen, they are dealt with quickly and effectively. At this time, the classroom enters a stage of development for working productively on academic goals. Students during this stage are very good at setting goals and accomplishing work. They "know the ropes," and little time is lost in miscommunication, conflict, or confusion. Teachers recognize this stage of their group's development and know that this is the time that the best teaching takes place. It is a time to communicate high expectations for students and to encourage them to aspire to high individual and group achievement. Good teachers are also aware that the group can be pulled back into earlier stages during this period. If that happens, academic work will slow down as membership and power issues are again resolved.

Stage 4: Accomplishing Self-Renewal. As the school year proceeds, teachers should help class members think about their continuous growth and about how to take on new and more challenging tasks. As the semester or year comes to an end, so too does the classroom group. Having worked side by side for several months, students develop close ties with each other, and teachers must address the heartache involved in the breaking of those ties. Similar moments of emotional strain can happen during the year as students move to new schools or as long vacations cause separations. The teacher's job in stage 4 is to watch for these emotional changes, to be ready to assist the group in revisiting and reworking previous stages as needed, and to aid students in synthesizing and bringing to closure the bonds they have formed. Additionally, teachers must help prepare students for what is to come next—the next grade, teacher, or school.

Those who study classroom groups are quick to point out, and rightfully so, that the stages of classroom development are not always sequential. Instead, they are often cyclical in nature, with many of the stages repeating themselves several times during the school year. When new students are placed in classrooms, membership issues again become important. Student growth in interpersonal skills keeps influence issues unstable and in constant flux. Larger societal issues cause change and a need to renegotiate norms associated with academic goals and performances.

The stages of classroom group development also have no *definite* time frames associated with them. The time it takes each group to work out issues associated with membership, influence, and task accomplishment depends on the skill of individual members within the class and the type of leadership the teacher provides. *General* time frames, however, can be inferred from the statements of experienced teachers. They report that membership issues consume students during the first month of school and that the most productive period for student learning and attention to academic tasks is between November and early May.

Teachers assist the development of the classroom group at each stage in the ways described and also by helping students understand that groups grow and learn in the same ways that individuals do. It is critical that teachers recognize that positive communication and discourse patterns are perhaps the single most important variable for building groups and productive learning environments. It is through classroom discourse that norms are established and classroom life defined. It is through discourse that the cognitive and social aspects of learning unite. Much more about this important topic is included in Chapter 12.

Some Final Thoughts

Many teachers and schools have developed positive school and classroom learning communities where students are interested in school, display strong engagement, and are motivated to learn. However, this is not the situation everywhere. Polls of twelfth-grade students over a twenty-five-year period in the 1980s and 1990s revealed that only slightly more than 25 percent of those surveyed found schoolwork "meaningful," only 20 percent found courses "interesting," and only 39 percent perceived school learning to be "important" in later life (*The Condition of Education,* 2009). Further, it appears that the percentages of students who report positive attitudes toward school declined during that period of time. Studies conducted over the past decade have produced similar results—that is, a large number of students find their work in school to be meaningless and irrelevant. For instance, Collins and Halverson (2009) reported on research about student disengagement done by Yazzie-Mintz (2006) and Hart (2006). One study found that over 50 percent of high school students reported that they were bored "every day" in their classes; another found that in California 82 percent of ninth- and tenth-graders believed that their school was "boring and irrelevant."

How do we explain these negative attitudes students have toward formal schooling, particularly when so much effort over the last twenty-five to thirty years has gone into making education more challenging and meaningful?

Some observers argue that outdated school organizational structures and curricula are mainly to blame for students' lack of interest in schools. They believe we have focused too much on the "individualistic" and "academic achievement" aspects of education and have ignored the emotional and social aspects of learning. They would agree with Csikszentmihalyi, who, as you read earlier, believes that structuring middle and high schools around many subjects taught for short periods of time inhibits intrinsic motivation and that reliance on external rewards and grades deters "flow experiences" and the intrinsic value of learning. Using standardized curricula and external testing and keeping students in passive roles also may inhibit enjoyment, interest, and commitment. Still other observers, such as Collins and Halverson (2009) and Rosen (2010), believe that if student engagement is going to be enhanced, then learners must be given more control over their learning. They argue that the Internet and new media technologies may be venues that allow more control and choice and that new findings from the cognitive and learning sciences will show how teachers can align their instruction to how their students' minds work (Willingham, 2010).

Perhaps your generation of teachers will find ways to figure out why students "don't like school" and provide opportunities for all students to be educated in learning communities that are challenging, meaningful, and engaging. Do you think this is possible?

Check, Extend, Explore

Check

- Contrast the major strategies for accomplishing motivation and a productive learning community.
- Why should teachers focus on controllable factors when attempting to heighten student motivation?
- When and how should extrinsic motivation be used? What cautions should be used?
- What is meant by *flow*? Why are flow experiences often missing in formal education?
- How does a teacher's role as facilitator evolve through each stage of the classroom group's development?

Extend

- Some teachers believe they are responsible for only their students' academic learning and not for students' personal or social development. Do you agree or disagree? Go to "Extend Question Poll" on the OLC to respond.

Explore

- Use your university's digital library resources and look up the full text of the article described in the Research Summary for this chapter. (Hint: Use the database Academic Search by EBSCOhost.) Did you learn anything useful that was not included in the summarized version?

 Reflections from the *Classroom*

The Lonely Student

It's mid-November, and Patti is sitting by herself again at lunch. Patti came to your school last year after her parents moved to the community from Florida. You have Patti in your homeroom and also for language arts. She is a pretty good student and moderately attractive, but she just hasn't been able to connect with other students or make any friends. You have noticed on several occasions when friendships seem to be forming between someone and Patti, that she goes overboard and gets too demanding. Soon the emerging friendship disappears. At other times, she seems overly shy. Of late, she seems to be distant in class, and her work is starting to fall off.

Think for a minute about this situation, then sketch out a reflective essay with the following questions in mind: Do you think teachers should have concerns for this kind of situation? What concerns would you have for Patti? Why do you think Patti is unable to make friends? What would you do, if anything, to help Patti establish a good friendship?

Approach this situation from the perspective closest to the grade level or subject area you are preparing to teach. Compare your ideas with those of the following teachers and determine how you can make your answer to this situation an exhibit for your portfolio.

Sandy Frederick

Apple Springs Elementary School, 3rd–5th-Grade Reading Specialist
Apple Springs ISD, TX

School is often the only place where children develop social skills. Those who do not have many friends feel left out and usually have low self-esteem. Low self-esteem can be disastrous for any child. Teachers must put forth every effort to build a community within the classroom so each child can find his or her niche, feel supported, and learn important social skills.

Patti seems to overreact to new friendships because she's not secure about making and maintaining friends. Friendships don't always come about easily, and Patti needs to be given the opportunity to socialize with her classmates without the pressure of trying to make a friend.

Cooperative learning activities, paired activities, or small group games would benefit a student like Patti. She would benefit by working in a situation where each student has a specific job, leaving no opportunity for one student to dominate the group nor for any student to be left out. This will give Patti a role to play in the learning community and give her a sense of belonging. Other students will learn to work with Patti as well, and hopefully will begin to enjoy her company.

I often have students create friendly cards for each other. The children draw names from a bowl that tells them who their secret buddy will be for the activity. The card should be friendly and include at least five nice things about the student it's for and a sentence thanking that student for something he/she has done for the child who created it. It's always nice to open a card with nothing but positive things about you on it.

By keeping a class working as a team and demonstrating appreciation of one another, students learn to work together and build lasting relationships.

Jason Shotels

8th Grade

Although I feel sorry for this student and would worry that she might move into groups that don't care much about school, I don't think there is much I could do as a teacher. I am not trained to work with these kinds of problems. However, our school has an array of special programs and services to help students form friendships and get involved in extracurricular activities. One way I could help Patti would be to refer her to the counselor and have the counselor talk to her. Another way would be to recommend to Patti that she become involved in after-school activities and introduce her to the After-School Activities Coordinator. This would provide her with situations and settings in which she would meet other students. If I thought Patti's shyness was very serious, I might also treat it as a disability and consult with the special education faculty to see if Patti qualifies for special education assistance.

Summary

Describe why motivating students and developing learning communities are important and describe the different perspectives on these topics.

- Motivating students and providing leadership for learning communities are critical leadership functions of teaching.

- A classroom community is a place in which individually motivated students and teachers respond to each other within a social setting.

- Classroom communities are social and ecological systems that include and influence the needs and motives of individuals, institutional roles, and the interaction between member needs and group norms.

Define human motivation and describe the major theories of motivation relevant to education.

- The concept of human motivation is defined as the processes within individuals that arouse them to action. It is what gets individuals "moving" toward specified activities and tasks.

- Psychologists make distinctions between two types of motivation: intrinsic motivation, which is sparked internally, and extrinsic motivation, which results from external or environmental factors.

- Many theories of motivation exist. Five that are particularly relevant to education include behavioral theory, needs theory, cognitive theory, social cognitive theory, and sociocultural theory.

- Behavioral theory emphasizes the importance of individuals responding to environmental events and extrinsic reinforcements.

- There are several different needs theories. In general, these theories hold that individuals strive to satisfy internal needs such as self-fulfillment, achievement, affiliation, influence, and self-determination.

- Cognitive theories of motivation stress the importance of the way people think and the beliefs and attributions they have about life's situations.

- Social cognitive theory posits that individuals' actions are influenced by the value particular goals hold for them and their expectations for success.

- Sociocultural theory holds that motivation is influenced not only from factors within the individual, such as needs, goal orientations, and expectancies, but also from the expectations and behaviors of groups with whom individuals identify with.

Define a productive learning community and describe the features of classrooms shown by research to impact student motivation and learning.

- A productive learning community is characterized by an overall climate in which students feel positive about themselves and their peers, individual needs are satisfied so students persist in academic tasks and work cooperatively with the teacher, and students have the requisite interpersonal and group skills to meet the demands of classroom life.

- Three important features that help us understand classroom communities include classroom properties, classroom processes, and classroom structures.

- Classroom properties are distinctive features of classrooms that help shape behavior. Six important properties include multidimensionality, simultaneity, immediacy, unpredictability, publicness, and history.

- Classroom processes define interpersonal and group features of classrooms and include communication, friendship and cohesiveness, norms, leadership, and conflict.

- Classroom structures are the foundations that shape particular lessons and behaviors during those lessons. Three important structures include task, goal, and participation structures.

- Some classroom features can be altered by the teacher; others cannot. Some classroom properties, such as multidimensionality and immediacy, cannot be influenced readily by the teacher. Group processes and the classroom goal, task, reward, and participation structures are more directly under the teacher's control.

- Studies on classrooms and teaching show that student motivation and learning are influenced by the types of processes and structures teachers create in particular classrooms.

- Studies have uncovered important relationships among teacher practices, student engagement, and academic achievement. In general, students react more positively and persist in academic tasks in classrooms characterized by democratic as opposed to authoritarian processes, in classrooms characterized by positive feeling tones and learning orientations, and in classrooms where learning activities are interesting and challenging.

- Influence in classrooms does not flow just from the teacher. Studies show that students also influence each other and the behavior of their teachers.

Describe and discuss the major strategies teachers can use to motivate students and to build productive learning communities.

- Effective teachers create productive learning communities by focusing on things that can be altered, such as increasing student motivation and encouraging group development.

- Factors associated with motivation that teachers can modify and control include the overall feeling tone of the classroom, task difficulty, students' interests, knowledge of results, classroom goal and reward structures, and students' needs for achievement, influence, affiliation, and self-determination.

- Although the use of extrinsic rewards makes good common sense, teachers should avoid overemphasizing this type of motivation.

- Teachers assist the development of their classrooms as a group by teaching students how groups grow and by describing the stages they go through as well as by helping students learn how to work in groups.
- Allocating time to building productive learning environments will reduce many of the frustrations experienced by beginning teachers and will extend teachers' abilities

to win student cooperation and involvement in academic tasks.

Speculate about the reasons students find schoolwork to be less than meaningful and the need for new school structures and curricula.

Key Terms

achievement motives 145	extrinsic motivation 142	needs theory 144
affiliative motives 145	feedback 163	negative reinforcers 143
attribution theory 146	feeling tone 161	participation structures 154
behavioral theory 143	flow experiences 145	performance goal orientations 147
classroom activities 153	goal structures 154	positive reinforcers 143
classroom processes 152	group development 167	punishments 143
classroom properties 150	individualistic goal structures 154	reward structures 154
classroom structures 153	influence 145	social cognitive theory 147
competitive goal structures 154	intrinsic motivation 142	sociocultural theory 147
cooperative goal structures 154	learning goal orientations 147	task structures 153
ecological systems 150	motivation 142	

Interactive and Applied Learning

🔵 Study and Explore

- Access your Study Guide, which includes practice quizzes, from the Online Learning Center.

🔵 Observe and Practice

- Listen to audio clips on the Online Learning Center of Diane Caruso (fourth/fifth grade) and Angela Adams (seventh/eighth grade) talking about learning communities in the *Teachers on Teaching* area.

Complete the following **Practice Exercises** that accompany Chapter 4:
- Practice Exercise 4.1: Practices That Support or Undermine Motivation
- Practice Exercise 4.2: Motivating Individual Students
- Practice Exercise 4.3: Developing a Positive Learning Community
- Practice Exercise 4.4: Facilitating Group Development at the Beginning of the School Year

🔳 Portfolio and Field Experience Activities

Expand your understanding of the content and processes in this chapter through the following field experience and portfolio activities. Support materials to complete the activities are in the *Portfolio and Field Experience Activities* area on the Online Learning Center.

1. Complete the Reflections from the Classroom exercise for this chapter. The recommended reflective essay will

provide insights into your view about a teacher's responsibilities for the emotional and social well-being of students. (**InTASC Standard 3: Learning Environments**)

2. **Activity 4.1: Assessing My Ability to Build Productive Learning Communities.** Check your understanding of and your level of skill for building productive learning communities. (**InTASC Standard 3: Learning Environments**)

3. **Activity 4.2: Surveying or Interviewing Students about Classroom Life.** Use your field experience to capture students' perceptions about classroom life. **(InTASC Standard 3: Learning Environments)**

4. **Activity 4.3: Interviewing Teachers about Classroom Goal and Reward Structures.** Find out how experienced classroom teachers employ the concepts of goal and reward structures in their classrooms. **(InTASC Standard 3: Learning Environments)**

5. **Activity 4.4: Portfolio: My Ideas about Motivation and Positive Classroom Learning Communities.** Create what you believe to be an ideal classroom learning community and place your creation in your portfolio. **(InTASC Standard 3: Learning Environments; InTASC Standard 9: Professional Learning and Ethical Practice)**

Books for the Professional

Anderman, E., & Anderman, L. (2009). *Classroom motivation.* New York: Prentice Hall.

Feriazzo, L. (2011). *Helping students motivate themselves: Practical answers to classroom challenges.* Fitchburg, MA: Eye on Education.

Johnson, D. W., & Johnson, F. (2013). *Joining together. Group theory and groups skills* (10th ed.). Boston: Allyn & Bacon.

Lippman, P. (2010). *Evidence-based design of elementary and secondary schools: learning environments: A responsive approach to creating learning environments.* Hoboken, NJ: John Wiley & Sons.

McDonald, E., & Hershman, D. (2010). *Classrooms that spark!: Recharge and revive your teaching.* San Francisco: Jossey-Bass.

Ritchhart, R., Church, M., & Morrison, K. (2011). *Making thinking visible: How to promote engagement, understanding, and independence of all learners.* San Francisco: Jossey-Bass.

Spady, W., & Schwahn, C. (2010). *Learning communities 2.0: Educating in the age of empowerment.* Lanham, MD: Rowman & Littlefield Education.

Willingham, D. (2010). *Why don't students like school: A cognitive scientists answers questions about how the mind works and what it means.* San Francisco: Jossey-Bass.

CHAPTER 5
Classroom Management

Learning Goals

After studying this chapter you should be able to

Perspective on Classroom Management	Explain why classroom management is such an important topic to beginning teachers and describe various perspectives on this topic.
Theoretical and Empirical Support	Describe the well-developed knowledge base on classroom management and important guidelines that grew out of this research.
Strategies for Effective Classroom Management	Describe and discuss the strategies and procedures teachers can employ to ensure effective classroom management.
Dealing with More Challenging Discipline Problems	Describe and explain how to use particular strategies and approaches that have been developed for working with secondary students and students with special needs and for dealing constructively with bullying.
Classroom Management Programs	Describe the various classroom management programs that have been developed and discuss the strengths and weaknesses of each.
A Final Thought and Look to the Future	Describe how your generation of teachers may challenge traditional view of classroom management.

Reflecting on Classroom Management

Beginning teachers report that the most difficult aspect of their first years of teaching is classroom management. They worry about it; they even have recurring nightmares about this issue. Before you read this chapter, reflect a bit about your own student experiences with this topic. What stands out in your mind about the ways your teachers managed their classrooms?

- Think about teachers who were strong disciplinarians and very strict. What did they do in regard to classroom management? How did you respond to this type of teacher and classroom? How did other students respond? What were the advantages of this type of management? Disadvantages?

- Now think about teachers who were very lax. What did they do in regard to classroom management? How did you respond to this type of teacher and classroom? How did other students respond? What were the advantages of this type of management? Disadvantages?

- Finally, write down the kind of classroom manager you want to be. Will you be strict? Lax? Friendly? What about your students? Do you want them to behave because you say they should? Or have you thought about helping your students develop self-discipline?

OLC **Go to the Online Learning Center at www.mhhe.com/arends10e to respond to these questions.**

When teachers talk about the most difficult problems they experienced in their first years of teaching, they mention **classroom management** and discipline most often. Although a rich knowledge base on classroom management has been developed, beginning and student teachers continue to feel insecure about managing their first classrooms, and many spend sleepless nights worrying about this issue.

Many of these anxieties are, in fact, similar to the anxieties experienced by people in any field when they are asked to assume positions of leadership and to exert influence for the first time. Nonetheless, gaining a repertoire of basic classroom management understandings and skills will do much to reduce the anxiety that naturally accompanies one's first classroom assignment. Describing the important concepts and skills associated with classroom management is the aim of this chapter. The first section of the chapter builds on the conceptual frameworks introduced in Chapters 3 and 4 and then presents a sampling of key research studies from the classroom management literature. The final section of the chapter describes specific strategies beginning teachers can use as they prepare for effective classroom management within the context of a democratic learning community.

Perspective on Classroom Management

Effective teachers have a repertoire of management strategies to be used as situations dictate.

Although this chapter has a point of view, as you will discover, it also is eclectic in regard to specific classroom management procedures. For example, you will find procedures that have grown out of the research that shows how effective management is connected to teachers' abilities to be "with it," to use effective instructional strategies, and to make lessons interesting for their students. At the same time, the shortcomings of this perspective are described, and approaches stemming from child-centered theorists are also presented for consideration, as are perspectives and strategies for working with students who present special challenges to teachers. Multiple perspectives and approaches are provided because they exist in today's schools, and, as beginning teachers, you will not always be free to choose the approach you think best. Some schools, for instance, will have a very definite behavioral approach to classroom management; all teachers are expected to develop rules and procedures in their classrooms consistent with this approach. Other schools will foster more child-centered approaches to classroom management. Finally, as is the case with most aspects of teaching, the most effective classroom managers are those with a repertoire of strategies and approaches that can be used with students as particular situations dictate.

Many of the ideas for understanding classroom management were presented in previous chapters and need only brief mention here. For example, the idea that the

Classroom management is one of the most important challenges beginning teachers face.

teacher's biggest job is to develop a positive learning community where all students are valued, respect one another, and are motivated to work together remains central for thinking about classroom management. The same is true for the idea that good classroom management requires teachers who can create authentic relationships with their students and develop an "ethic of care." There are, however, two more ideas that can provide additional perspective on effective classroom management.

First, *classroom management is possibly the most important challenge facing beginning teachers.* A new teacher's reputation among colleagues, school authorities, and students will be strongly influenced by his or her ability to perform the managerial functions of teaching, particularly creating an orderly learning environment and dealing with student behavior. Sometimes, beginning teachers think this is unfair and argue that schools and principals put too much emphasis on order as contrasted to learning. Perhaps it is unfair. Nonetheless, a teacher's leadership ability is tested in the arena of management and discipline, and when something goes wrong, it is known more quickly than other aspects of teaching. More important, without adequate management, little else can occur or, to put it another way, if classroom management problems are not solved the rest of teaching can be given away.

Second, *classroom management and instruction are highly interrelated.* An important perspective stressed in the first part of this chapter is what Brophy and Putnam (1979) and Evertson and Emmer (2012) have labeled **preventative management.** This perspective has dominated views about classroom management for quite some time. Classroom management is not an end in itself; it is merely one part of a teacher's overall leadership role. In this regard, classroom management cannot be separated from the other aspects of teaching. For example, when teachers plan carefully for lessons, as described in Chapter 3, they are doing much to ensure good classroom management. When teachers plan ways to allocate time to various learning activities or consider how space should be used in classrooms, they are again making important decisions that will affect classroom management. Similarly, all the strategies for building productive learning communities described in Chapter 4, such as helping the classroom develop as a group, attending to student motivation, and facilitating honest and open discourse, are also important components of classroom management.

Further, each teaching approach or strategy a teacher chooses to use places its own demands on the management system and influences the behaviors of both teachers and learners. The instructional tasks associated with giving a lecture, for example, call

Preventative management is the perspective that many classroom problems can be solved through good planning, interesting and relevant lessons, and effective teaching.

for behaviors on the part of students that are different from those needed for tasks associated with learning a new skill. Similarly, behavioral demands for students working together in small groups are different from those required for working alone on a seatwork assignment. Instructional tasks are integrally related not only to the problem of instruction but also to the problems of management.

Finally, alternative perspectives to the preventative approach exist and stem mainly from the work of child-centered theorists such as John Dewey and the Swiss educator Johann Pestalozzi, as well as an array of twentieth-century humanistic reformers such as Abraham Maslow and Carl Rogers. This perspective is critical of processes aimed at controlling students and instead focuses on the basic goodness of children and youth. Educators holding this perspective argue for treating children in schools humanely and respectfully and for creating learning communities (Kohn, 2006) characterized by what Nel Noddings (2001, 2005) and Wilde (2012) have called an "ethic of care" (see also Lake & Berliner, 2013). These settings assist student development not only academically but also socially and emotionally.

Theoretical and Empirical Support

Three traditions have guided the theory and research on classroom management: behavioral theory, the ecological and group processes perspectives, and child-centered views. This section is organized around these perspectives.

Behavioral Theory

You read in Chapter 4 how behavioral and reinforcement theory dominated thinking about motivation for most of the twentieth century. This perspective has also had a strong influence on classroom management. Remember that behavioral theory emphasizes the centrality of external events in directing behavior and the importance of positive and negative reinforcers. Teachers who apply behavioral principles to classroom management use rewards in the form of grades, praise, and privileges to reinforce desired behavior and punishments, such as bad grades, reprimands, and loss of privileges, to discourage undesirable tendencies or actions.

Many times this approach has focused on the individual student and has sought to understand the causes of a particular student's classroom behavior rather than causes that may stem from the features of the classroom group or the teaching situation.

Behavioral approaches often emphasize how to control the behavior of individual students as compared to considering the classroom group and overall learning situation.

This tradition has been led mainly by clinical and counseling psychologists, such as Dreikurs (1968) and Dreikurs and Grey (1968), and by behavioral psychologists and those who apply behavioral theory, such as Canter (2009), Canter and Canter (2001), and Sprick (2008). Their practice has focused on such psychological causes as insecurity, need for attention, anxiety, and lack of self-discipline as well as on sociological causes such as parent overprotection, bad peer relationships, or disadvantaged backgrounds. Recommendations to teachers stemming from this tradition normally emphasize ways to help individual students through counseling or behavior modification and show less concern for managing the classroom group. Behavior modification programs, the use of token economies, and assertive discipline (Canter, 2009; Canter & Canter, 2002; Walker, Shea, & Bauer, 2003) are formal programs that have been developed based on behavioral theory and have been used widely in classrooms during the past forty years. Although many of the behavioral-oriented programs have shortcomings, they nonetheless are found in many schools today, and beginning teachers should be knowledgeable about them. These will be described later in the chapter in the Classroom Management Programs section.

Classroom Ecology and Group Processes

Chapter 4 described several ideas that help explain classroom life from ecological and group processes perspectives, and the work of such researchers as Barker (1968), Doyle (1986, 2006), Gump (1967), Kounin (1970), and Schmuck and Schmuck (2001) were cited. The ecological perspective addresses directly the problem of classroom control and group management procedures.

Classroom management researchers in this tradition study the way student cooperation and involvement are achieved so that important learning activities can be accomplished. The major function of the teacher from this point of view is to plan and orchestrate well-conceived group activities that flow smoothly. Misbehavior of students is conceived as actions that disrupt this activity flow. Examples of disruptions include students talking when quiet is desired, students not working on a seatwork assignment the teacher has given, or students getting out of their seats at inappropriate times. Teacher interventions in regard to student misbehavior, as will be described later, should be quick, often minor, and aimed at keeping the flow of learning activities and tasks on the right track.

Kounin's Research. The classic piece of research in the **classroom ecology** tradition was done in the late 1960s by Jacob Kounin and his colleagues. After several years of trying to understand classroom discipline, Kounin started to consider that maybe it was not the way teachers disciplined their students that was important but instead the way the classroom as a group was coordinated and managed that made a difference. Kounin's work has greatly influenced the way we think about classroom management. His study is described in the Research Summary for this chapter. Even though this study was conducted forty years ago, it is included here because it is considered a classic and many of Kounin's research findings have heavily influenced contemporary perspectives on classroom management.

Doyle and Carter's Research. Other researchers of particular interest who have used the ecological framework to guide their research are Doyle and Carter (1984) and Doyle (1986, 2006). They have been interested in how specific academic tasks are connected to student involvement and classroom management. To explore this topic, they observed one junior high school English teacher and the students in three of her classes in a middle-class suburban school for a period of almost three months. The teacher, Mrs. Dee, was selected for study because she was an experienced teacher and she was considered to have considerable expertise in teaching writing to students.

This work is informative to the topic of classroom management because the researchers found that students had considerable influence over the task demands of the classroom. For instance, over a period of time, Mrs. Dee assigned students a variety of major and minor writing tasks. Examples include writing an essay comparing Christmas in Truman Capote's story "A Christmas Memory" with Christmas today, writing a short story report, and writing descriptive paragraphs with illustrations. In some of the writing tasks, Mrs. Dee tried to encourage student creativity and self-direction, and to do that, she left the assignments somewhat open-ended. From detailed observations of Mrs. Dee's classroom, Doyle and Carter found, however, that students pressed to reduce the amount of self-direction and independent judgment in some of the writing

Check, Extend, Explore

Check
- Why do most people consider classroom management the most important challenge for beginning teachers?
- How is classroom management linked to other aspects of instruction?
- What examples can you give to demonstrate that order in the classroom is considered extremely important by most educators?

Extend
- Reflect on the kinds of worries and anxieties you experience in regard to classroom management.
- Do you agree or disagree with child-centered theorists that too much emphasis is put on controlling students? Go to the "Extend Question Poll" on the Online Learning Center to respond.

Explore
- Classroom management is a very popular Web topic. Search "Classroom Management" on the Internet to consider the many, many different views on this topic and the variety of resources that are available to teachers.

Researchers in the ecology and group process tradition are interested in how student cooperation and involvement are achieved in group settings.

Classic

Research Summary

What Do Teachers Do to Create Well-Managed Classrooms?

Kounin, J. S. (1970). Discipline and group management in class-rooms. New York: Holt, Rinehart & Winston.

The most challenging aspect of teachers' work is developing and maintaining a well-managed classroom. This challenge has led many researchers to examine how effective teachers manage their classrooms. The interesting result that stems from all this research is that good classroom managers actually prevent problems from occurring through the way they plan for and pace their lessons and the means they use to nip misbehavior in the bud. The classic study on this topic was done by Jacob Kounin in the 1960s.

Problem and Approach: After several years of trying to understand discipline in classrooms, Jacob Kounin started to consider that perhaps the key was not so much the way teachers disciplined individual students but, instead, the way they managed the whole classroom group. So, he decided to study group management. This is an interesting and important study because Kounin was one of the first researchers to go directly into classrooms and observe exactly what was going on. His study was also one of the first to use a video camera as an observation tool.

Sample: The sample of Kounin's study reported here consisted of forty-nine teachers and their students in upper elementary classrooms.

Procedures: Kounin developed elaborate procedures for observing classrooms, including videotaping teacher and student interaction and transcript analysis. Many variables were measured in the complete study. Here, only a few of the more important variables are described.

Dependent Variables: For Kounin, managerial success was demonstrated by classrooms in which work involvement was high and student deviancy was low.

1. Work involvement fell into three categories: (a) definitely doing the assigned work, (b) probably doing the assigned work, and (c) definitely not doing the assigned work.
2. Deviancy consisted of a three-category scheme: (a) student not misbehaving, (b) student mildly misbehaving, and (c) student engaging in serious misbehavior.

Contextual Variables: Kounin observed two types of learning activities: recitations and seatwork.

Independent Variables: Kounin conceptualized eight different variables for describing the group management behavior of teachers.

1. *"With-itness."* The ability to accurately spot deviant behavior, almost before it starts.
2. *"Overlappingness."* The ability to spot and deal with deviant behavior while going right on with the lesson.
3. *Smoothness.* Absence of behaviors that interupt the flow of activities.
4. *Momentum.* Absence of behaviors that slow down lesson pacing.
5. *Group alerting.* Techniques used by teachers to keep non-involved students attending and forewarned of forthcoming events.
6. *Accountability.* Techniques used by teachers to keep students accountable for their performance.
7. *Challenge arousal.* Techniques used by teachers to keep students involved and enthusiastic.
8. *Variety.* The degree to which various aspects of lessons differed.

Pointers for Reading Research: In the Research Summaries described so far, researchers summarized results with mean scores and qualitatively with words. If comparisons were made, they used *t* tests or analysis of variance. In the study summarized for this chapter, a different statistic is introduced—the *correlation coefficient.* This statistic is described in the Resource Handbook. In brief, correlation refers to the extent of a relationship that exists between pairs of measures. The coefficient can range from +1.00 through .00 to −1.00. The sign does not have the traditional mathematical meaning. Instead, a plus sign represents a positive relationship, a minus sign a negative relationship. A .00 means no relationship exists, +1.00 means a perfect relationship exists, and −1.00 means a reverse relationship exists. Correlations can be tested for significance just as mean scores can.

Results: Table 5.1 shows the correlations Kounin found between various aspects of teacher management behavior and children's behavior during recitation and seatwork.

Discussion and Implications Kounin's research provides a rich source of ideas for how teachers can approach the problem of classroom management. Table 5.1 shows that with-itness, momentum, overlappingness, smoothness, and

Table 5.1 *Correlation of Selected Teacher Management Behaviors and Children's Behavior in Recitation and Seatwork Settings**

	Recitation		Seatwork	
Dependent Variable	**Work Involvement**	**Freedom from Deviancy**	**Work Involvement**	**Freedom from Deviancy**
Momentum	.656	.641	.198	.490
With-itness	.615	.531	.307	.509
Smoothness	.601	.489	.382	.421
Group alerting	.603	.442	.234	.290
Accountability	.494	.385	.002	−.035
Overlappingness	.460	.362	.259	.379
Challenge arousal	.372	.325	.308	.371
Overall variety and challenge	.217	.099	.449	.194
Class size (Range = 21–39)	−.279	−.258	−.152	−.249

*N = 49 classrooms (correlation of .276 is significant at .05 level).

Source: After Kounin (1970), p. 169.

group alerting all appear to increase student work involvement, particularly during recitation lessons. Similarly, with-itness and momentum decrease student deviancy. With-itness also decreases student deviancy in seatwork lessons, whereas variety appears to be the major behavior that helps promote work involvement in seatwork.

Note that all the relationships in the table, although not significant, are positive, except for the negative correlation coefficients for the relationships between accountability and freedom from deviancy during seatwork and those associated with class size. These negative correlations are small and what they mean essentially is that no relationships were found between those variables.

The implications for teacher behavior from Kounin's work are great and are described in more detail in later sections of this chapter.

assignments. Students, even those considered very bright, used tactics such as asking questions or feigning confusion to force Mrs. Dee to become more and more concise and explicit. In other words, the students influenced the teacher to do more and more of their thinking.

Doyle and Carter also found that by asking questions about content and procedures, students, in addition to changing the assignment, also slowed down the pace of classroom activities. This was done to get an assignment postponed or just to use up class time. When Mrs. Dee refused to answer some of the students' delaying questions, things seemed only to get worse. Here is a direct quotation from a report of what the researchers observed:

> Some students became quite adamant in their demands. . . . On such occasions, order began to break down and the normal smoothness and momentum of the classes were reinstated only when the teacher provided the prompts and resources the students were requesting. The teacher was pushed, in other words, to choose between conditions for students' self-direction and preserving order in the classroom. (p. 146)

Mrs. Dee was an experienced enough teacher to know that *order had to come first* or everything else was lost.

Effective Teaching Research

Some classroom management researchers have been influenced by both behavioral theory and the ecological orientation. These researchers worked for over four decades to identify the behaviors of effective teachers, meaning teachers who could consistently produce high student engagement with academic activities. They pursued this approach because, as you read in Chapter 3, strong relationships had been found between student engagement and student achievement.

This research, which has spread over forty years, has been led by Edmund Emmers, Carolyn Evertson, and several of their colleagues (see the Books for the Professional section at the end of this chapter). Like Kounin before them, teacher-effectiveness researchers found strong relationships between student on-task behavior and a number of teacher behaviors. Specifically, when effective classroom managers were compared to ineffective classroom managers, the following teacher behaviors were observed:

1. Effective managers gave *clear presentations and explanations,* and their directions about note taking were explicit.
2. The more effective classroom managers had *procedures* that governed student talk, participation, and movement; turning in work; and what to do during downtime.
3. Laboratory and group activities in the effective managers' classrooms ran smoothly and efficiently. *Instructions were clear,* and student *misbehavior was handled quickly.*
4. Effective managers had very *clear work requirements* for students and monitored student progress carefully.

The implications of this research, along with recommendations for teachers, will be discussed in more detail in the next section, Strategies for Effective Classroom Management.

Child-Centered Traditions

The child-centered perspective on classroom management views the chief source of the problem as irrelevant curricula and overemphasis on quietude and uniformity.

There is also a theoretical and research tradition that provides an alternative to behavioral and preventative perspectives. Relying on theories of John Dewey and humanistic psychologists Abraham Maslow, Carl Rogers, and William Glasser, current researchers and reformers such as Nel Noddings, Jeannie Oakes, Alfie Kohn, and George Noblit argue that behavioral-minded researchers have it all wrong. Developing smooth-running classrooms or making lessons interesting, they argue, are simplistic solutions to much more complex problems. They agree with the observation made by John Dewey many years ago:

> The chief source of the "problem of discipline" in schools is that . . . a premium is put
> on physical quietude, on silence, on rigid uniformity of posture and movement; upon a
> machine-like simulation of the attitudes of intelligent interest. The teachers' business is to
> hold the pupils up to these requirements and to punish the inevitable deviations which
> occur. (Dewey, cited in Kohn, 1996, p. 7)

This perspective embraces child-centered rather than subject-centered classrooms. Misbehavior, according to Oakes and Lipton (2003), "follows from instruction that attempts to coerce students, even if it is for their own and society's good" (p. 278), or, according to Kohn (1996), from situations "where we 'manage' behavior and try to make students do what we want . . . [rather than] . . . help them become morally sophisticated people who think for themselves and care about others" (p. 62). Curriculum should *not* be prescribed by teachers but instead should aim at promoting students' development and at meeting students' social and emotional as well as academic needs.

Child-centered educators do not have a set of specific guidelines for achieving effective classroom management, nor do they offer artificial recipes for teachers to follow. Instead, as Nel Noddings (1992) has written, "schools should be committed to a great moral purpose: to care for children so that they too will be prepared to care" (p. 65). Caring and developing democratic classrooms become the alternative to preventative management and behavioral control.

Research in this tradition is often qualitative and ethnographic. A study done by George Noblit (1995) characterizes this approach. Noblit and his colleagues studied how two experienced inner-city teachers (one white, the other African American) developed caring relationships with their students. Noblit and his colleagues spent one full day every week for over a year in these teachers' classrooms and conducted interviews with teachers and children in the school. The vignettes displayed in Figure 5.1 illustrate how these teachers dealt with problem students and what it meant to develop "caring relationships."

Strategies for Effective Classroom Management

This section focuses directly on strategies beginning teachers can use to ensure effective classroom management. It is organized around three major topics: preventative classroom management, managing inappropriate and disruptive behavior, and working toward caring communities and self-discipline.

Preventative Classroom Management

Many of the problems associated with student misbehavior are dealt with by effective teachers through preventative approaches. Much of this section is based on over fifty years of research emanating from Kounin's work and the research on effective teaching. The ideas and procedures are introduced here and revisited in later chapters in regard to management demands of particular approaches to teaching.

Establishing Rules and Procedures. In classrooms, as in most other settings where groups of people interact, a large percentage of potential problems and disruptions can be prevented by having effective rules and procedures. To understand the truth of this statement, think for a moment about the varied experiences you have had in nonschool settings where fairly large numbers of people come together. Examples most people think about include driving a car during rush hour in a large city, attending a football game, going to Disneyland, or buying tickets for a movie or play. In all of these instances, established rules and procedures indicated by traffic lights and queuing stalls help people who do not even know each other to interact in regular, predictable ways. Rules such as "the right of way" and "no cutting in line" help people negotiate rather complex processes safely and efficiently.

Think again about what happens when procedures or rules suddenly break down or disappear. You can probably recall instances when a power outage caused traffic lights to stop working or when a large crowd arrived to buy tickets for an important game before the ticket sellers set up their queuing stalls. Recently, a teacher friend was in Detroit for a conference, and her return flight was booked on an airline that had merged with another airline on that particular day. When the two airlines combined

Check, Extend, Explore

Check
- What are the major theories that have guided classroom management research practices? What are the advantages and disadvantages of each?
- How did research conducted by Kounin and Doyle and Carter demonstrate that optimal learning is most likely achieved in an orderly classroom?
- What specific teacher behaviors lead to the most effective classroom management, according to teacher-effectiveness researchers?
- What are the major features of classroom management from the perspective of child-centered theorists?
- Contrast child-centered views with those of behaviorists.

Extend
- Do you think you will incorporate mostly behavioral or child-centered classroom management practices in your classroom? Go to the "Extend Question Poll" on the Online Learning Center to respond.

Explore
- On the Web search for "child-centered education" and "caring approaches to classroom management" and compare what you find with what has been written here.

Figure 5.1 *Vignettes from Noblit's Study of Caring Teachers*

Robert's Story

Robert was a challenge from his first day in Martha's classroom. He was a pudgy boy who had spent the previous school year at a special school for youths with severe behavioral problems. During the two years prior to that he had continually been removed from classrooms for exhibiting "inappropriate and aggressive" behavior.

Martha invested herself in helping him. She waited daily at the classroom door to greet Robert, and she always told him goodbye in the afternoon. She spent a few moments every day talking with him about anything and everything, from TV shows to his mother. And she firmly insisted that he participate in classroom activities—especially cooperative learning groups with the other children.

Because of the attention she paid to him, Robert slowly began to realize that Martha was committed to him. By November Robert had become a marginally accepted and fairly productive member of this class. He was still ornery and still had small outbursts in class, but he responded to Martha and to the other students in much more positive ways. Not once was Robert sent to the principal or suspended, a dramatic reversal for him. Martha was able to help Robert become a more academically and socially competent person despite the stigma of being labeled behaviorally disordered.

What was significant about Martha's influence on Robert was her dogged determination that he be given the opportunities to succeed in school and to attain social competence. There were no magic tricks, no technical fixes—just consistent, day-in and day-out, hour-to-hour, even minute-to-minute reminders to Robert to complete his work and respect others. She simply refused to give up on him. Martha explained, "I have a tendency not to give up on anybody. It is my responsibility."

Martha encouraged and enhanced Robert's social and academic growth despite the system. He usually participated in classroom discussions and activities, seemed to enjoy coming to school (in fact, never missed a day!), and appeared to have made a few friends in the class, all of whom showed up for his birthday party. Martha and Robert's caring relationship set a new context for Robert as a student. And within that context he was able to improve both his behavior and his academic achievement.

John's Story

John had been mainstreamed into Pam's class. He had the unique ability of disappearing during any classroom event. He was painfully shy and would physically hide from interaction with Pam by lining up behind other students, dropping his head and shoulders below desk level, and so on. During group work, John would not talk or participate in any way beyond sitting with the other students. Pam decided it was her responsibility to help John become more a part of the class. She demanded that he take part by sitting up, attending to assigned tasks, and working with other students.

In addition to being stern with him, Pam moved his desk close to hers and kept him near her during small-group activities. She found that touching him was a key to his attending, and over time his response to her touching changed from alarm to acceptance and finally to a perception of support. Her hand on his shoulder would allow him to speak and to participate—and, by the end of the year, eye contact with Pam was sufficient assurance for him. Pam was tough but supportive in her caring for John, and he reciprocated.

Like Martha with Robert, Pam recognized John's need to become part of the class and disregarded the implicit belief that special children really do not belong in a regular classroom. Her concern for him, her fidelity to him rather than to a mandated curricular objective, guided her search for appropriate strategies to ensure his participation and inclusion in the class. Their relationship made the classroom a safe and nurturing environment for John and led him to take part in classroom activities and to complete academic work.

Source: Adapted from Noblit (1995).

their information systems, something went wrong with their electronic booking system. This malfunction made it impossible for the ticket agents to know who was on a particular flight and prevented them from issuing seat assignments. The result was bedlam, full of disruptive behavior. People were shoving each other as individuals tried to ensure a seat for themselves; passengers were yelling at each other and at the cabin crew. At one point, members of a normally well-disciplined crew were even speaking sharply to each other. The incident turned out okay because a seat was found for everyone. The boarding process, however, did not proceed in the usual orderly, calm manner because some well-known procedures were suddenly unavailable.

Classrooms, in some ways, are similar to busy airports or busy intersections. They, too, require rules and procedures to govern important activities. As used here, **rules** are statements that specify the things students are expected to do and not do. Normally, rules are written down, made clear to students, and kept to a minimum. Before establishing classroom rules, teachers should ask themselves whether the rules are necessary and can be justified to students. For example, if the teacher decides that "showing respect for others" is to be a classroom rule, then it is important to justify the need for this rule in specific language. In addition, all rules should be clear, understandable, reasonable, and age appropriate, and they need to be consistent with the school's rules and the teacher's instructional program.

Procedures, in contrast, are the ways of getting work and other activity accomplished. These are seldom written down, but effective classroom managers spend considerable time teaching procedures to students in the same way they teach academic matter. Student movement, student talk, and what to do with downtime are among the most important activities that require rules to govern behavior and procedures to make work flow efficiently.

> **Classroom rules specify what students are expected to do and what they are *not* to do.**

Student Movement. In many secondary classrooms, such as a science laboratory, the art room, or the physical education facility, and in all elementary classrooms, students must move around to accomplish important learning activities. They need to obtain or put away materials, sharpen pencils, form small groups, and so on.

Effective classroom managers devise ways to make needed movements by students flow smoothly. They organize queuing and distribution procedures that are efficient; they establish rules that minimize disruptions and ensure safety. Examples of rules include limiting the number of students moving at any one time and specifying when to be seated. How to line up, move in the halls, and go unattended to the library are procedures that assist with student movement.

> **Classroom procedures are established for dealing with routine tasks and coordinating student talk and movement.**

Student Talk. Students talking at inappropriate times or asking questions to slow down the pace of a lesson pose a classroom management problem that is among the most troublesome to teachers. This problem can vary in severity from a loud, generalized classroom clamor that disturbs the teacher next door to a single student talking to a neighbor when the teacher is explaining an important idea.

Effective classroom managers have a clear set of rules governing student talk. Most teachers prescribe when no talking is allowed (when the teacher is lecturing or explaining), when low talk is allowed and encouraged (during small-group work or seatwork), and when anything goes (during recess and parties). Effective classroom managers also have procedures that make classroom discourse more satisfying and productive, such as talking one at a time during a discussion, listening to other people's ideas, raising hands, and taking turns. These procedures are important in both elementary and secondary classrooms.

Downtime occurs when lessons are completed early or when students are waiting for upcoming events, such as moving to another class, going to an assembly, or going home.

As with any other subject, rules and procedures must be taught to students.

Downtime. A third aspect of classroom life for which rules and procedures are required is during **downtime.** Sometimes, lessons are completed before a period is over, and it is inappropriate to start something new. Similarly, when students are doing seatwork, some finish before others. Waiting for equipment to arrive for a scheduled activity is another example of downtime.

Effective classroom managers devise rules and procedures to govern student talk and movement during these times. Examples include: "If you finish your work, you can get a book and engage in silent reading until the others have finished." "While we wait for the video to start, you can talk quietly to your neighbors." "If your work is complete, please see if your neighbor needs your help." Table 5.2 shows sets of rules developed by two different teachers: one set is for an elementary classroom, the other is for a secondary classroom. Notice that both lists are fairly brief. Also note the differences and similarities between the two sets.

Teaching Rules and Procedures. Rules and procedures are of little value unless participants learn and accept them. This requires active teaching. Effective classroom managers generally establish only a few rules and procedures, then teach them carefully to students and make them routine through their consistent use. In most classrooms, only a few rules are needed, but it is important for the teacher to make sure students understand the purpose of each rule and its moral or practical underpinnings. Concepts and ideas associated with rules have to be taught just the same as any other set of concepts and ideas. For instance, very young children can see the necessity for keeping talk low during downtime when the teacher explains that loud talk disturbs students in neighboring classrooms who are still working. Taking turns strikes a chord with older students who have heightened concerns with issues of fairness and justice. Potential injury to self and others can be given as the reason why movement in a science laboratory has to be done a certain way. One point of caution about teaching rules should be noted, however. When teachers are explaining rules, they must walk a rather thin line between providing explanations that are helpful to students and sounding patronizing or overly moralistic.

Table 5.2 *Sample Rules for Elementary and Secondary Classrooms*

Elementary Classroom Rules	Secondary Classroom Rules
Be the best student I can be.	Be the best student I can be by completing all assignments on time and as accurately as I can make them.
Treat others with respect.	Treat all members of our class with respect by being helpful and courteous.
Be helpful and polite to others.	Bring all required materials such as pencils and reading or electronic materials to class every day.
Be respectful of the property of others.	
Listen to others and wait your turn to speak.	Listen and pay attention to others when they are speaking; wait your turn to speak.
Follow directions the first time I hear them.	Be seated when the class is ready to start.
When you have finished with a seatwork assignment, see if your neighbor needs help.	When you have finished with a seatwork assignment, see if your neighbor needs help.

Most movement and discourse procedures have not only a practical dimension but also a skill dimension that must be taught, like academic skills. In Chapter 12, several strategies will be described for teaching students how to listen to other people's ideas and how to participate in discussions. Student movement skills also need to be taught. Even with college-age students, it takes instruction and two or three practices to make getting into a circle, a fishbowl formation, or small groups move smoothly. Effective classroom managers devote time in the first week or so of the school year to teaching rules and procedures and then provide periodic review as needed.

Maintaining Consistency. Effective classroom managers are consistent in their enforcement of rules and their application of procedures. If they are not, any set of rules and procedures soon dissolves. For example, a teacher may have a rule for student movement that says, "When you are doing seatwork and I'm at my desk, only one student at a time can come for help." If a student is allowed to wait at the desk while a first student is being helped, soon several others will be there too. If this is an important procedure for the teacher, then whenever more than one student appears, he or she must be firmly reminded of the rule and asked to sit down. If it is not important to the teacher, it should not be set forth as a rule. Another example is if a teacher has a rule that no talking is allowed when he or she is explaining important ideas or procedures. If two students are then allowed to whisper in the back of the room, even if they are not disturbing others, soon many students will follow suit. Similarly, if the teacher wants students to raise their hands before talking during a discussion and then allows a few students to blurt out whenever they please, the hand-raising rule is soon rendered ineffective.

It is sometimes difficult for beginning teachers to establish consistency for at least two reasons. One, rule breaking normally occurs when more than one event is going on simultaneously. A novice teacher cannot always maintain total awareness of the complex classroom environment and thus does not always see what is occurring. Two, it takes considerable energy and even personal courage to enforce rules consistently. Beginning teachers may find it easier and less threatening to ignore certain student behavior rather than to confront and deal with it. Experienced teachers know that avoiding a difficult situation only leads to more problems later.

Preventing Interruptive Behaviors with Smoothness and Momentum. Another dimension of preventative classroom management involves pacing instructional events and maintaining appropriate **momentum.** The research by Doyle (2006) and Doyle and Carter (1984) described how students can delay academic tasks, and Kounin's research (1970) pointed out the importance of keeping lessons going in a smooth fashion. Kounin also described how teachers themselves sometimes do things that interfere with the flow of activities. For example, a teacher might start an activity and then leave it in midair. Kounin labeled this type of behavior a **dangle.** A dangle occurs, for example, when a teacher asks students to hand in their notes at the end of a lecture and then suddenly decides that he or she needs to explain one more point. Teachers also slow down lessons by doing what Kounin labeled **flip-flops.** A flip-flop occurs when an activity is started and then stopped while another is begun and then the original started again. A flip-flop occurs, for example, when a teacher tells students to get out their books and start reading silently, then interrupts the reading to explain a point, and then resumes the silent reading. Dangles and flip-flops interfere with the **smoothness** of classroom activities, cause confusion on the part of some students, and, most important, present opportunities for noninvolved students to be disruptive.

Maintaining consistency in applying rules and procedures is an aspect of classroom management that is often troublesome for beginning teachers.

A dangle is when a teacher starts an activity and then leaves it in midair.

Table 5.3 *Common Problems in Maintaining Smoothness and Momentum*

Problem	Definition
Dangle	Leaving a topic dangling to do something else.
Flip-flop	Starting and stopping an activity and then going back to it.
Fragmentation	Breaking instruction or activity into overly small segments.
Overdwelling	Going over and over something even after students understand it.

Fragmentation occurs when a teacher breaks a learning activity into overly small units.

Kounin described two other frequent types of lesson slow-down behaviors— **fragmentation** and **"overdwelling."** A teacher who goes on and on after instructions are clear to students is overdwelling. A teacher who breaks activities into overly small units, such as "sit up straight, get your papers out, pass them to the person in front, now pass them to the next person," and so on is fragmenting instructions. Slowing down momentum disrupts smoothness and gives uninvolved students opportunities to interrupt classroom activities. Table 5.3 summarizes and illustrates the common problems found to disrupt smoothness and momentum in lessons.

"Overdwelling" occurs when a teacher goes on and on after a subject or a set of instructions is clear to students.

Minimizing disruptive and slow-down behaviors is difficult for beginning teachers to learn, as are many other effective management skills, because so many aspects of management are situational. Smoothness and momentum definitely vary with the nature of individual classes—what may be a dangle in one classroom may not be so in another, or what may be overdwelling with one group of students may be appropriate for another group.

Orchestrating Classroom Activities during Unstable Periods. Preventative classroom management also involves planning and orchestrating student behavior during unstable periods of the school day—periods of time when order is most difficult to achieve and maintain.

Opening Class. The beginning of class, whether it is the first few minutes of the morning in an elementary classroom or the beginning of a period in secondary schools, is an unstable time. Students are coming from other settings (their homes, the playground, another class) where a different set of behavioral norms apply. The new setting has different rules and procedures as well as friends who have not been seen since the previous day. The beginning of class is also a time in most schools in which several administrative tasks are required of teachers, such as taking roll and making announcements.

Effective classroom managers plan and execute procedures that help get things started quickly and surely. For example:

- They greet their students at the door, extending welcomes to build positive feeling tones and to keep potential trouble outside the door.
- They train student helpers to take the roll, read announcements, and perform other administrative tasks, so they can be free to start lessons.
- They write instructions on the board or on newsprint charts so students can get started on lessons as soon as they come into the room.
- They establish routine and ceremonial events that communicate to students that serious work is about to begin.

Transitions. Numerous research studies (Doyle, 1986, 2006; Rosenshine, 1980) have identified that many **transitions** occur every day in both elementary and secondary classrooms. As many as thirty transitions occur every day in elementary classrooms, and although there are fewer transitions in secondary classrooms they still are numerous and take considerable time. It is during transition periods (moving from whole group to small groups, changing from listening to seatwork, getting needed materials to do an assignment, getting ready to go to recess) when many disruptions occur. Prior planning and the use of cuing devices are two techniques that can help teachers handle transitions.

> **Transitions are the times during a lesson when the teacher is moving from one type of learning activity to another.**

Planning is crucial when it comes to managing transitions. Chapter 3 described how transitions must be planned just as carefully as any other instructional activity. At first, beginning teachers should conceive of each transition as a series of steps they want students to follow. These steps should be written down in note form and, in some instances, given to the students on the chalkboard or on newsprint charts. For example, making the transition from a whole-class lecture to seatwork might include the following steps:

Step 1: Put away your lecture notes and clear your desk.
Step 2: Make sure you have pencils and a copy of the worksheet being distributed by the row monitor.
Step 3: Begin your work.
Step 4: Raise your hand if you want me to help you.

As beginning teachers become more experienced with managing transitions, they will no longer need to list the steps for minor transitions and may instead rely on clear mental images of what is required.

Cuing and signaling systems are used by effective teachers to manage difficult transition periods. The best way to understand cuing is to think of it as an alerting device similar to the yellow light on a traffic signal or the "slow" sign on a curving road. Cues are used by teachers to alert students that they are about to change activities or tasks and to start getting ready. Here are some examples of cues:

- During a small-group activity, a teacher goes around to each group and announces, "You have five minutes before returning to the whole group."
- During a discussion activity, a teacher tells students, "We must end the discussion in a few minutes, but there will be time for three more comments."
- During a laboratory experiment, the teacher says, "We have been working for twenty minutes now, and you should be at least halfway done."
- In getting ready for a guest speaker, the teacher tells the class, "Our speaker will arrive in a few minutes; let's straighten up the chairs and get ready to greet her."

Many teachers also develop a signal system for alerting students to a forthcoming transition or for helping them move through the steps of a transition smoothly. Signal systems are particularly effective with younger children and in classrooms where the activities are such that it is difficult to hear the teacher. The band instructor raising his or her baton is an example of a signal for students to get quiet and ready their instruments to play the first note. Figure 5.2 shows a set of hand signals developed by one experienced teacher to alert and assist his students with difficult transitions and to check their understanding of what is being taught. The teacher who developed these cuing signals taught in an elementary school; however, many of these signals have also been found to be useful in secondary and some college classrooms. Other response signals are described in Chapter 6.

Figure 5.2 *Examples of Signals for Communicating with Students*

Rhythm or echo clapping can be used to get attention of the students in the classroom. When the teacher claps four beats, the students respond with a two-clap echo, and this signals that all activity stops.

Bell signaling can be used to gain the attention of the students. Just a short ring will cue the students to stop all activities and listen (small handbell).

Light signaling is often used by teachers to capture attention and can be effective. The light switch is flicked once, quickly. This signal should not be overused.

Arm signals can be used at times to gain the attention of students without having to use an audible signal. When children are in the hallway, lining up, or on the playground, the teacher raises an arm; this will cue the students to do the same and become quiet.

Finger signals can be used effectively in managing small groups, dismissing students, or conducting other tasks. When dismissing groups of students by areas, code the groups numerically and dismiss by signals.

Looks are often effective in gaining a student's attention. A quizzical or firm look may be all that is needed.

Charts can signal directions and important messages. Use a smiley face or sad face suspended from the ceiling. Flip to the sad face when students' behavior is unacceptable; return to a smiley face when acceptable behavior occurs.

Charts that tell students what to do when they finish work are also very useful and assist students in becoming more independent and involved in purposeful activities. The ideas on these charts should be varied and changed frequently.

Source: After Bozeman (1995).

Closing Class. The closing of class is also an unstable time in most classrooms. Sometimes the teacher is rushed to complete a lesson that has run over its allocated time; sometimes materials such as tests or papers must be collected; almost always students need to get their own personal belongings ready to move to another class, the lunchroom, or the bus. Effective teachers anticipate the potential management problems associated with closing class by incorporating the following procedures into their classroom organizational patterns:

- Leaving sufficient time to complete important closing activities, such as collecting books, papers, and the like.
- Assigning homework early enough so that possible confusion can be cleared up before the last minute of class.
- Establishing routine procedures for collecting student work (such as placing a box by the door) so class time does not have to be used for this activity.
- Using alerting and cuing procedures to give students warning that the end of the class is approaching and that certain tasks need to be completed before they leave.
- Teaching older students that class will be dismissed by the teacher, not by the school bell or buzzer.

Developing Student Accountability. Every day teachers give their students assignments. Sometimes assignments are brief in duration and can be completed as seatwork. Others are more long term and require work at home. Most often, assignments provide students opportunities for practice, and this is an important aspect of the learning process, as later chapters will discuss. However, unless student work is handled consistently and unless students are held accountable for its completion, little learning will be accomplished. Therefore, an additional dimension of classroom management involves rules and procedures for managing and holding students accountable for their work. The following guidelines, which were adapted from the recommendations of Emmer and Evertson (2012), Evertson and Emmer (2012), and Weinstein and Novodvorsky (2010), should be incorporated into the teachers' overall preventative management plan:

1. *Communicate assignments clearly and specify work requirements.* All assignments should be communicated clearly so all students have a full understanding about what they are supposed to do. Specific requirements must be clearly described, including such things as length, due date, neatness, spelling, grading procedures, and how missed work can be made up. Verbal explanations alone usually are not sufficient for students of any age. Teachers assist clarity when they describe assignments on worksheets or post them on a chalkboard, a newsprint chart, or Web site.

2. *Have procedures for monitoring student work.* It is very important for teachers to be aware of student progress once assignments have been made. For seatwork, teachers can circulate around the room to check how things are going. For longer-term assignments, breaking down the assignment into smaller parts and requiring students to file progress reports every few days helps monitor their progress. Examples of forms to assist with the monitoring of long-term projects are provided Chapter 11. Recitations and discussions are other means for checking if students understand their assignments and if they are making satisfactory progress.

3. *Be consistent in checking students' completed work.* In most classrooms the amount of student work is enormous. Teachers need procedures for collecting assignments, such as placing baskets or trays in front of the room, and for returning corrected work in a timely fashion. Teachers also need a system for checking all work. Sometimes this can be accomplished by getting students to check each other's work. This is particularly appropriate for assignments with specific answers. Some assignments require careful reading by the teacher. All checking should be accomplished within a day or two after completion.

4. *Provide appropriate feedback on assignments.* As will be described in detail in Chapter 6, learning occurs when students receive feedback on their performance. All student work should be corrected and feedback should be given that is appropriate to the age of the students. This should occur as soon as possible after the assignment has been handed in. Often it is a good idea to spend class time going over assignments and discussing common errors or problems. Detailed guidelines for effective feedback are provided in Chapter 8.

Managing Everyday Misbehavior

Preventative planning and skilled orchestration of classroom activities can prevent many of the management problems faced by teachers, but not all. As in other social settings, every classroom will have a few students who will choose not to involve themselves in classroom activities and, instead, be disruptive forces. Everyday disruptions can range from students talking when they are supposed to be listening to the teacher or refusing to go along with a small-group activity to yelling at the teacher.

Considering the Causes of Misbehavior. Because beginning teachers have observed disruptive behavior in classrooms for many years as students, most can readily list the major causes of student misbehavior. These are the causes that appear on most lists: (1) students find schoolwork boring and irrelevant and try to escape it; (2) students' out-of-school lives (family or community) produce psychological and emotional problems that they play out in school; (3) students are imprisoned within schools that have authoritarian dispositions, which causes them to rebel; (4) student rebelliousness and attention seeking are a part of the growing-up process; and (5) students have learning challenges such as learning disabilities, hyperactivity and attention disorders, and behavioral difficulties.

Beginning teachers will want to think about the causes of inappropriate behavior, but they should beware that knowing the cause of student misbehavior, although helpful in analyzing the problem, does not necessarily lead to any change in that behavior.

Dealing with Misbehavior. The general approach recommended to beginning teachers for dealing with everyday disruptive behavior is to focus on the misbehavior itself and to find ways to change it, at least during the period of time the student is in the classroom. This approach emphasizes the importance of teachers accurately spotting misbehavior and making quick, precise interventions.

Being With It and Overlapping. You can all remember a teacher from your own school days who seemed to have "eyes in the back of her head." Kounin calls this skill **"with-itness."** Teachers who are with it spot deviant behavior right away and are almost always accurate in identifying the student who is responsible. Teachers who lack this skill normally do not spot misbehavior early, and they often make mistakes when assigning blame.

"Overlappingness" is a second skill teachers use to spot and deal with deviant behavior. Overlapping means being able to spot a student acting inappropriately and inconspicuously deal with it so the lesson is not interrupted. Moving close to an offender is one overlapping tactic effective classroom managers use. Putting a hand on the shoulder of a student who is talking to his neighbor while continuing with instructions about how to do a project is another. Integrating a question intended to delay instruction or a "smart" remark right into an explanation about Edgar Allan Poe's syntax is a third example of overlappingness.

Home and School

Understanding Families and Gaining Cooperation

Families can be very effective partners in dealing with classroom management problems, particularly in regard to inappropriate or disruptive behavior. In racially and culturally diverse classrooms, this requires teachers to understand that the idea of *appropriate behavior* is often relative to one's culture. It also means that *inappropriate behavior* should *not* necessarily be attributed to cultural deficits in a student's family or their child-rearing practices. It is important to work with families in sensitive ways and to communicate classroom and school expectations.

This can be accomplished using both informal and formal strategies. Informal contacts and communications are often the most effective in building relationships with families. For example, in elementary schools teachers can be present to greet family members as they drop off their children in the morning or when they pick them up after school. In secondary schools, special activities or athletic events can provide opportunities to talk informally with parents.

On a more formal level, teachers can use letters home, discussions during family conferences, home visits, or special presentations on rules and procedures during back-to-school nights. In all these communications, it is important to remain sensitive to cross-cultural differences and to tailor messages so family members can understand them. This is particularly important if students' parents use English as a second language. E-mail and cell phones can also be used, and these technologies make communication with parents or other family members about student behavior much easier to accomplish. E-mail, for example, makes it possible to inform many parents on a moment's notice about behaviors that have been disruptive. It is equally important to send messages and make phone calls about positive behaviors. This type of communication and involvement of family members, as well as other examples provided in later chapters, can improve student behavior, increase student achievement, and improve the overall quality of the relationships between the school and the home.

With-it and overlapping skills are difficult to learn because they call for quick, accurate reading of classroom situations and the ability to perform several different teaching behaviors simultaneously. Once learned, however, they ensure more smoothly running lessons and classrooms.

Responding Quickly to Desist Incidences. In classrooms, just as in any social setting, there are some participants who commit deviant acts. An example of deviant behavior on the freeway is driving ten or fifteen miles an hour above the speed limit; in church, it might be falling asleep during the sermon; in a library, it is talking loudly while others are trying to study. Those charged with the responsibility of enforcing rules and procedures may or may not choose to respond to each occurrence of deviancy. For example, most highway patrol officers will not stop a motorist for going seventy miles an hour on the freeway where the speed limit is sixty-five; most ministers don't confront a single parishioner who falls asleep; and those who talk very softly in libraries will probably not be reprimanded by the librarian. There are times, however, when those in charge will choose to respond to deviant behaviors. This is called a **desist incident,** which is an incident serious enough that, if not dealt with, will lead to further and widening management problems.

Teachers respond to desist incidents in a variety of ways. Several teacher **desist behaviors** have been identified. Three of these behaviors are illustrated in Table 5.4. Several different groups of procedures have been developed to deal with student misbehavior and to bring student attention back to a lesson once it has strayed. These include the Jones model (Jones & Jones, 2009), Evertson and Emmer's model (2012),

A desist incident is a classroom occurrence serious enough that, if not dealt with, will lead to widening management problems.

Teachers who can spot disruptive student behavior quickly and accurately are called "with-it."

Table 5.4 *Examples of Teacher Desist Behaviors*

Clarity—The degree to which a teacher specifies what is wrong.

Unclear desist:	"Stop that!"
Clear desist:	"Do not sharpen your pencil while I am talking."

Firmness—The degree to which a teacher communicates "I mean it."

Unfirm desist:	"Please don't do that."
Firm desist:	"I absolutely will not tolerate that from you!"

Roughness—The degree to which a teacher expresses anger.

Unrough desist:	"You shouldn't do that anymore."
Rough desist:	"When you do that, I get angry and I intend to punish you."

and the LEAST model. The procedures for each model are summarized in Table 5.5. As you can see, the Jones model is primarily nonverbal and is useful for minor misbehavior. Procedures recommended by Evertson and Emmer concentrate on stopping inappropriate behaviors swiftly and making sure students understand what they are doing wrong. The LEAST model (an acronym for the steps teachers follow) includes procedures for minor misbehaviors as well as more serious problems that need to be handled over a period of time. Effective teachers create procedures that work for them, and these likely will include aspects of each of the models.

Using Rewards. A rather well-established principle in psychology is that when certain behaviors are *reinforced*, they tend to be repeated; conversely, behaviors that are

Table 5.5 *Three Models for Dealing with Mild Student Misbehavior*

Jones	Evertson and Emmer	LEAST
1. Move close to where student is sitting.	1. Ask the student to stop the inappropriate behavior. Teacher maintains contact with child until appropriate behavior is correctly performed.	1. Leave it alone. Is the behavior going to become troublesome? If not, ignore it.
2. Make eye contact.	2. Make eye contact with student until appropriate behavior returns. This is suitable when the teacher is certain the student knows what the correct response is.	2. End the action indirectly. Distract the student from the misbehavior by giving him or her something to do, preferably in a different area.
3. Provide gentle pat on the shoulder, if needed.	3. Restate or remind the student of the correct rule or procedure.	3. Attend more fully. Get to know the student better before you decide on a course of action. Is there something disturbing happening at home? Is there some kind of learning problem?
4. Keep pace and momentum of lesson going.	4. Ask the student to identify the correct procedure. Give feedback if the student does not understand it.	4. Spell out directions. Remind the student of what he or she should be doing. If necessary, also remind him or her about the consequences for failing to comply.
	5. Impose the consequence or penalty of rule or procedure violation. Usually, the consequence for violating a procedure is simply to perform the procedure until it is correctly done.	5. Track the behavior. If this is a continuing problem, keep systematic records of the behavior and your actions to correct it. This can evolve into a contract with the student.
	6. Change the activity. Frequently, off-task behavior occurs when students are engaged too long in repetitive, boring tasks or in aimless recitations. Injecting variety is appropriate when off-task behavior spreads throughout a class.	

not reinforced tend to decrease or disappear. This principle holds true for classrooms and provides teachers with one means for managing student behavior. The key to using **reinforcement principles** to influence student behavior obviously rests on the teacher's ability to (1) identify desirable behaviors, (2) identify appropriate reinforcers, and (3) skillfully use these reinforcers to strengthen and encourage desired behaviors.

Using Praise. The reinforcer most readily available to the classroom teacher is **praise.** However, there are important guidelines for the effective use of praise. For example, general praise, such as "great job," "oh, that's wonderful," or "excellent" is not very effective. Nor is insincere praise apt to have the desired effect. Jere Brophy reviewed a massive amount of research on the subject of praise and came up with the guidelines

Praise is the reward most readily available for teachers. However, praise must be used appropriately to be effective.

Table 5.6 *Guidelines for Effective Praise*

Effective Praise	Ineffective Praise
Is specific	Is global and general
Attends to students' accomplishments	Rewards mere participation
Helps students appreciate their accomplishments	Compares students with others
Attributes success to effort and ability	Attributes success to luck
Focuses attention on task-relevant behavior	Focuses attention on external authority

for teachers (Brophy, 1981, 2004; Brophy & Good, 1986). More recently, Marzano (2007) has summarized the research on teacher praise. Guidelines that grow out of the work by Brophy and by Marzano are summarized in Table 5.6.

Granting Rewards and Privileges. Teachers can also encourage desirable behaviors through granting *rewards* and *privileges* to students. Rewards teachers have at their disposal include

- Points of value to students for certain types of work or behavior
- Symbols such as gold stars, happy faces, or certificates of accomplishment
- Special honor rolls for academic work and social conduct

Privileges that are at the command of most teachers to bestow include

- Serving as a class leader or helper who takes notes to the office, collects or passes out papers, grades papers, runs the movie projector, and the like
- Extra time for recess or other valued activity
- Special time to work on a special individual project
- Free reading time

An overemphasis on external rewards can hinder student growth in self-management.

A carefully designed system of rewards and privileges can help immensely in encouraging some types of behavior and reducing others. However, rewards and privileges will not solve all classroom management problems, and beginning teachers should be given two warnings: First, what is a reward or a privilege for some students will not be perceived as such by others. The age of students obviously is a factor; family, ethnic, and geographical background are others. Effective teachers generally involve their students in identifying rewards and privileges in order to ensure their effectiveness. Second, as described in Chapter 4, an overemphasis on extrinsic rewards can interfere with the teacher's efforts to promote academic work for its own sake and to help students practice and grow in self-discipline and management.

Using Coercive Punishment and Penalties. Rewards and privileges are used to reinforce and strengthen desirable behaviors. *Punishments* and *penalties* are used to discourage infractions of important rules and procedures. Socially acceptable punishments and penalties available to teachers are, in fact, rather limited and include

- Taking away points for misbehavior that, in turn, affects students' grades
- Making the student stay in from recess or after school for detention
- Removing privileges
- Expelling from class or sending a student to a counselor or administrator

1. Use reductions in grade or score for assignment- or work-related behaviors such as missing or incomplete work.
2. Use a fine or demerit system to handle repeated violations of rules and procedures, particularly those involving willful refusal to comply with reasonable requests. Give them one warning, and if the behavior persists, assess a fine or demerit.
3. If you have a student who frequently receives penalties, try to set a more positive tone. Help the student formulate a plan to stop the inappropriate behavior.
4. Limit the use of penalties such as fines or checks to easily observable behaviors that represent major or chronic infractions of rules and procedures. The reason for this limitation is that penalty systems work only when they are used consistently. In order for this to take place, you must be able to detect the misbehavior when it occurs. If you cannot, you will find yourself constantly trying to catch students who misbehave.
5. Keep your classroom positive and supportive. Penalties should serve mainly as deterrents and should be used sparingly. Try to rely on rewards and personal encouragement to maintain good behavior.

Source: After Emmer and Evertson (2012).

Figure 5.3 *Guidelines for the Use of Penalties*

Check, Extend, Explore

Check
- What are the major steps teachers can take to prevent classroom management problems?
- What specific classroom times seem to lead to discipline problems? Why?
- What are some actions teachers commonly practice that can disrupt the momentum of lessons?
- What is the general approach for dealing with students who are disruptive? Do you agree? Why or why not?
- What factors should a teacher consider to effectively use a reward system?

Extend
- Do you agree or disagree with the proposition that students are inherently good and that misbehavior stems from the way classrooms are structured and managed? Go to the "Extend Question Poll" on the Online Learning Center to respond.

Explore
- Go to the Online Learning Center at www.mhhe.com/arends10e and listen to the audio clips of Vickie Williams and Richard Beyard in the *Teachers on Teaching* area as they discuss their approaches to classroom management.

Beginning teachers should be careful about the types of punishments and penalties they establish. Emmer and his colleagues (2012) offer the guidelines found in Figure 5.3. Today, many believe that giving points that affect grades for good behavior or taking them away for misbehavior is not a very good idea, for reasons that will be discussed in Chapter 6.

Dealing with More Challenging Discipline Problems

Negative Antisocial Behaviors

In addition to the everyday, milder forms of misbehavior, teachers must sometimes confront more serious and chronic problems, such as tattling, cheating, stealing, profanity, defiance, and sexually related behaviors. Space does not allow in-depth discussions of each of these topics, but Table 5.7 lists several of these problems and summarizes actions Weinstein, Romano, and Mignano (2010) recommend for teachers to take.

Special Challenges Presented by Secondary Students

In many ways managing elementary and secondary classrooms are similar, particularly for procedures aimed at preventive classroom management. However, middle and high school teachers face several special challenges. For instance, absenteeism, not completing homework on time, and failing to bring necessary materials to class are

Table 5.7 *Dealing with Serious and Chronic Problems*

Discipline Problem	Recommended Teacher Actions
Cheating	• Reduce temptation to cheat. • Minimize opportunity to cheat. • Talk privately to student. • Express concern about cheating. • Explain consequence of cheating, such as having student redo the assignment and/or reporting the cheating to school authorities and parents.
Stealing	• Help student operationalize the rule "respect other people's property." • Recognize that there may be cultural differences about "what is mine and what is yours." • Have private conversation with the culprit of stealing and encourage stolen property to be returned. • If stealing continues, refer problem to principal and contact parents.
Excessive profanity	• Explain which words cannot be used in school. • For younger students, ask if they know what the word means. • Contact parents and ask them to speak to their son or daughter.
Defiance	• Try to figure out what is behind the defiant behavior. • Stay in control of yourself during defiant situations. • Move student away from rest of class and have class work on something else. • Don't get in student's face. Stand a few feet away. • Avoid a power struggle.
Sexually related behavior	• In lower grades, students often rub their genitals. Divert the student's attention to something else. If masturbation continues, have private conversation with student. • By grades 4 to 6, students need to be aware of what constitutes sexual harassment and know that these behaviors will not be tolerated. • For continuous masturbation and/or sexual harassment, contact parents and, in some cases, child welfare and/or psychological support authorities.

Source: Weinstein, Romano, and Mignano (2010).

consistent problems that are more prevalent in secondary classrooms as compared to elementary classrooms. These problems exist partly because many students become less enamored with school as they get older and because parents become less involved in monitoring homework and attendance, and obviously once students reach "driving age" they have considerably more freedom to move around as they please. These problems also exist because secondary teachers, who face many more students every day, cannot monitor their students as closely as can their elementary colleagues.

Absenteeism and not completing homework, as with most disruptive behaviors, must be confronted quickly at their outset. Teachers need to find out what is causing the student to be absent from school or to not complete work on time. If there are special factors leading to this behavior, then appropriate responses are required. In most instances, teachers should seek out the expertise and support of the school's counseling and student services personnel and work with them to develop appropriate intervention strategies. In general, however, actions taken should be to inform students and their parents about the consequences of continued absenteeism and lack of work completion. Although rules and consequences should remain somewhat flexible, students should *not* be passed if they miss class continually and/or if they do not do their work, regardless of how bright they may be.

Teachers can facilitate work completion by teaching students how to monitor their own behavior and by showing them how to use various planning devices to keep track of required materials and assignments. Several of these devices are described in the later chapters. Teachers can also craft assignments so that they are clearly aligned to purposes of learning and not perceived as "just busy work" to be completed. Finally, a teacher's classroom assessment and grading system, described in the next chapter, must factor in credit for being present, for having work done accurately, and for turning in work on time. See also Casoli-Reardon, Rappaport, Kulick, and Reinfeld (2012) for reasons for school avoidance and steps teachers can take.

Another major difference between managing secondary and elementary classrooms is that older students are more likely to be defiant and hostile, and they can quickly turn desist situations into events that have the potential of becoming destructive and dangerous. The guidelines for de-escalating potentially explosive situations in Table 5.8 have been adapted from Weinstein (2003), Weinstein and Novodvosky (2010), and from the work of Walker, Colvin, and Ramsey (1995).

Working with Students who have Special Needs

Chapter 2 described the large number of found in today's classrooms. These may be students who suffer from neglect and abuse or they may have a variety of special needs, including behavior and emotional challenges. These challenges can range from attention deficit hyperactivity disorder (ADHD) and autism to milder forms of anxiety and depression. All these students bring their challenges and needs to school with them, and they require special attention, not only in regard to instructional strategies but also to the management and discipline strategies used by teachers. Space does not allow an in-depth discussion of these strategies; however, a brief discussion is provided here with references to good books on this topic referenced in Books for the

---

Table 5.8 *Managing Potentially Explosive Situations in Secondary Classrooms*

- Move *slowly and deliberatively* toward the problem situation.
  When possible speak *privately and calmly*. Avoid power struggles.
- Show *respect*, do not threaten, and use the student's name.
- Be *brief*, stay as still as possible, and keep with the agenda. Do not get in the "student's face."
- *Inform* the student of expected behavior and the negative consequences as a choice for the student to make. Then withdraw and allow time for the student to decide on next steps.

Sources: Adapted from Weinstein (2003), Weinstein and Novodvosky (2010), and Walker et. al (1995).

Professional section at the end of this chapter. The discussion is also extended briefly in a later section of this chapter where the FAIR approach is described.

Students with emotional and behavioral disorders or difficulties often display inappropriate classroom behavior toward themselves or others. These can range from a very high and sometimes inappropriate level of activity to defiance toward the teacher and other students, including fighting, displaying cruelty, and bullying. Many students who display emotional and behavioral difficulties are students who have been identified as students with special needs and, as described in Chapter 2, they have individualized education plans (IEPs) with extensive "due process" rights. Managing and disciplining these students most often will require a team effort. Beginning teachers need to seek assistance from the school and district's special education personnel. However, there are several general guidelines that can be followed by teachers independently. The following guidelines are summarized from the work of Weinstein (2007) and Woolfolk (2013):

- Communicate expectations about behavior clearly and in writing. Make sure students with special needs and their parents are aware of these expectations.
- Be aware of the student's IEP and due process rights in regard to discipline, particularly actions associated with removal from the classroom.
- Maintain a learning environment that is safe and orderly, fairly structured, and consistent from day to day.
- Keep good records of all problem situations and keep everyone involved (students, parents, special education personnel) informed.
- If punishments or corrections are used, make sure they have a clear educational purpose, that they are reasonable, and that they are age appropriate.
- Recognize accomplishments and use positive consequences whenever appropriate behavior is demonstrated.

The Challenges of Bullying

Bullying of students in and out of school is a worldwide phenomenon that, unfortunately, has been around for a very long time. Over the past decade, however, several bullying situations in the United States have made headlines and have been widely covered on television and in social media. This has caused alarm among the public at large, policymakers, and educators. Several state legislatures have passed laws that define bullying, establish consequences for bullying behavior, and outline steps teachers and others are required to take when they become aware of bullying acts.

Bullying* has been defined as persistent physical and/or verbal abuse (including teasing and goading) by one person toward a less powerful person aimed at causing physical or emotional harm. Bullies are individuals who, for a variety of reasons, are in situations where they have some degree of power and control over their victims. They have often experienced abuse in their own lives. The victims of bullying are most often individuals who are lonely, have low-self esteem, and/or display behaviors that are viewed as different. For example, a large proportion of LGBTQ students report that they have been bullied. The victims of bullying often feel embarrassed and do not defend themselves against their tormentors.

---

*Recently, Emily Bazelon (2013), writing for the *New York Times*, has pointed out that the term "bullying" may be overused and too often includes "garden-variety teasing" or natural "two-person conflict." She argues that "crying wolf" about bullying has led to unfair accusations and unrealistic demands on schools.

Action from several individuals and groups is required to stop bullying and to help bullying victims. Jacobs (2011) has described what the law and justice system can do as well as its limitations. He writes that over forty states have passed laws that require bullying prevention programs. Many school districts have also developed these types of prevention programs. Programs aimed at developing positive school culture variables are particularly important, because according to Weissbourd and Jones (2012) bullying:

> is far less likely to take root in school cultures where caring and responsibility for others are the norm, where students see the entire community as within their circle of concern and influence, and where a large number of students model positive behavior for other students. (p. 27)

This observation leads Weissbourd and Jones to recommend that the best strategies to combat bullying are those that are schoolwide and community-wide and that aim at engaging students, parents, and teachers in the whole school to promote a positive school climate, ethical standards, and moral development. These programs also strive to find ways for students themselves to play larger roles through student governance and by leading student efforts to establish positive school norms in support of caring and respect. Rappaport (2013), a respected child psychiatrist at Harvard Medical School, has written about the need for this broad-based whole-school approach:

> it [is] critical that schools provide a sanctuary for all children—those who may act out, those who may suffer in silence—and their classmates. Schools can offer a place for children to communicate their distress without either being victimized further or victimizing others. (Rappaport Blog, retrieved March 14, 2013)

Individual teachers in their classrooms also have an important role to play in bullying prevention and in helping students who are the victims of bullying. Teachers need to see their responsibilities not only for their own classrooms but also beyond the classroom walls. They need to intervene when they observe teasing, taunting, abusive language, or more severe acts of aggression. The guidelines described below are summarized from Collins (2009), Hirsch, Lowen, and Santorelli (2012), Weissbourd and Jones (2012), and Weinstein and Novodvorsky (2010):

- *Recognize* students who are being bullied. These students often display a decreased interest in school, sudden absenteeism, and a decrease in the quality of their work. They may have unexplained bruises, scratches, or other marks.
- Be prepared to *report* situations of bullying to appropriate school and/or criminal justice personnel and to help investigate by finding out what happened and by keeping an ongoing log.
- *Talk* to the victims of bullying in sensitive and nonjudgmental ways. Remember that they may be embarrassed and ashamed.
- Help keep a *watchful eye* and monitor areas in the school that are not always tightly supervised and where bullying can take place unobserved, such as hallways, bathrooms, the cafeteria, and playgrounds.

Further, considerable research has shown that teachers can help prevent bullying at school by developing classrooms such as those described in Chapter 4. These are classrooms with a sense of community, where students treat each other with trust and respect, and where norms exist for taking care of one another in and out of the classroom. Teaching students anger management, conflict resolution skills, and attitudes of tolerance can also lead to less bullying and violence. This chapter's Enhancing Teaching and Learning with Technolgy describes another type of bullying known as cyberbullying.

Check, Extend, Explore

Check
- How best can teachers deal with secondary students who have a pattern of absenteeism and/or who seldom turn in their homework?
- What are the recommended guidelines for teachers to follow for de-escalating explosive situations?
- What are the recommended guidelines for teachers to follow when considering disciplining students with special needs?
- What actions can schools take to help prevent bullying? What actions can teachers take?

Extend
- What are your opinions about how teachers and schools should treat students who remain disruptive regardless of "best efforts"?
- Do you think students who are chronic disrupters should be permanently suspended from school? Go to the "Extend Question Poll" in the Online Learning Center to respond.

Explore
- Interview a principal or teacher and ask how serious a problem bullying is at his or her school. How does the school prevent bullying? Also probe about how successful or unsuccessful the school's efforts have been and why.

Enhancing Teaching and Learning with Technology
Threats of Cyberbullying

Today, with widespread access to the Internet and social media by children and youth, bullies have found new ways to tease, harass, and goad their victims. Called **cyberbullying,** bullies make use of e-mail, Facebook, Twitter, YouTube, and an array of negative blogs with the aim of causing harm. Likely you have read or observed several well-known examples of cyberbullying that have made recent headlines:

* A young man committed suicide by jumping off a bridge because someone had streamed a video of him kissing anther man in his room.
* A student placed in a "psychiatric" hospital because he created a "Satan's web page" was subsequently ridiculed on social media for his behavior.
* A 13-year-old girl committed suicide following an Internet hoax by the mother of a fellow student.

Preventing cyberbullying and helping victims present special challenges to educators and to parents because bullies can hide under anonymity and victims are extremely embarrassed for their sometimes innocent involvement. Many schools today have explicit policies that define cyberbullying and rules about in-school use of the Internet. Schools have also worked to inform parents about cyberbullying, steps parents can take to monitor Internet use at home, and how to make use of "parental control" features.

Teachers can also perform an important role to prevent cyberbullying by providing important instructions about how to use the Internet effectively and behaviors that should be avoided. As described in other technology sections of *Learning to Teach,* teachers should not assume that students, even those who are active Internet and social media users, have an in-depth understanding about how the Internet and social media sites work. Teachers can:

* Provide instruction about how the Internet works and the ethics that govern its use.
* Show students what they can do to block e-mail, chat, and Facebook.
* Explain to students how to notify authorities, such as the police, if they discover messages that contain physical threats.

Similarly, students need to learn about behaviors to avoid, such as:

* Deleting threatening messages before showing them to an adult.
* Replying to threatening messages.
* Opening messages from an unknown e-mail address.

Finally, teachers have the responsibility to report instances of cyberbullying to appropriate authorities and to inform parents or family members about what is going on.

Classroom Management Programs

A number of classroom management programs have been developed by psychologists, researchers, and educational practitioners. Many of these programs stem from a specific theory or perspective and require schoolwide participation. Program creators develop materials to help teachers understand the program, and they provide training on how to use it. Though the effectiveness of particular programs has not always been studied, these programs nonetheless have been adopted and used widely. Four programs are described here to give beginning teachers a cursory understanding of what they may be confronted with in student teaching or their first teaching position.

Traditional Programs Based on Behavioral Theory

Assertive Discipline. Some classroom management and discipline programs have been built around the central concepts of the teacher acting in confident and assertive ways toward student misbehavior and administering predetermined penalties for infractions of classroom rules. During the past thirty years, one of the more popular programs based on these ideas has been developed by Lee Canter and Marlene Canter (2002; Canter, 2009). Called **assertive discipline,** the Canters' program maintains that teachers can gain control of their classrooms by insisting on appropriate student behavior and by responding assertively to student infractions.

Teachers (and sometimes whole schools) trained in assertive discipline start by developing a set of classroom and school rules deemed necessary for learning to occur. Consequences for disobedience are also clearly specified in advance. Students and their parents are then given clear explanations of these rules, and the consequences for infractions are explained. The Canters stress the importance of teachers following through with their rules, being consistent with administering consequences, and expecting support from parents.

> **Assertive discipline is an approach to classroom management that emphasizes teachers insisting on appropriate student behavior and responding assertively to student infractions.**

The Assertive Response Style. At the center of the Canters' approach is their belief that teachers should respond to student misbehavior with an assertive style instead of responding passively or in hostile ways. Responding to student misbehavior with a rhetorical question such as, "Why are you doing that?" is an example of a passive style. A passive teacher, according to the Canters, is not using interpersonal influence effectively and appears wishy-washy to students. A hostile teacher, in contrast, often responds angrily to student misbehavior and makes threats such as, "You'll be sorry you did that," or tries to produce guilt such as, "You should be ashamed of yourself." Passive and hostile styles are not effective, according to the Canters. Teachers who use a passive style are not communicating clearly to students what they expect, and the hostile style often produces meaningless threats that are difficult to enforce.

The assertive style calls for teachers to be very clear about their expectations and to respond to student misbehavior firmly and confidently. Teachers are counseled to specify the misbehaving student by name and to keep eye contact with the student. The Canters maintain that teachers should not accept excuses from misbehaving students. They argue that even though students may have inadequate parenting, special health problems, or great stress in their lives, these unfortunate circumstances should not excuse students from acting appropriately in the classroom or taking responsibility for their own behavior.

Consequences. Under the Canter approach, consequences are kept simple and are designed so their implementation will not cause severe disruption to ongoing instructional activities. Cangelosi (2007) reported one example of an assertive discipline program in a particular junior high school:

1. Each classroom teacher specifies for students the rules for classroom conduct.
2. The first time each day a student violates a rule during a particular class session, the teacher writes the student's name on a designated area of a chalkboard. The number of the rule that was violated is put next to the name. The teacher does not say anything.
3. The second time a student violates a rule (not necessarily the same rule), the number of that rule is added to the student's name on the board. Again, the teacher makes no other response to the off-task behavior.
4. Upon the third violation of the rules in the same class period, the student must leave the class and report to a detention room.
5. There are no penalties or requirements for students who have no more than one violation during any one class period.

6. Students with two violations are required to meet with the teacher after school to discuss the misbehavior and map out a plan for preventing recurrences.

7. A parent of students with three violations must appear at school to discuss the misbehavior and make plans for preventing recurrences. (pp. 32–33)

Though the Canters' approach has been very popular, it also has its critics. Some teachers find it difficult to administer consequences without significantly disrupting their instructional programs. It takes time and energy, for instance, to write names on the chalkboard and to keep track of rule infractions. Also, some believe that the behavioristic approach behind assertive discipline puts too much emphasis on penalties and teacher-made rules and not enough emphasis on involving students in establishing their own classroom rules and learning how to be responsible for self-discipline. Finally, assertive discipline remains to be evaluated thoroughly, and its effectiveness remains unclear.

Logical Consequences. Chapter 4 provided a description about how people's behavior can be attributed to goal-directed activity aimed at satisfying human motives and needs. Dreikurs and his colleagues (1968, 1988, 1998), and more recently Elias and Schwab (2006), have developed approaches to classroom discipline based on the idea that most student behavior, acceptable and unacceptable, stems from the fundamental need to belong and to feel worthwhile. According to Dreikurs, when the need to belong or feel worthwhile is frustrated through socially acceptable channels, students misbehave. Dreikurs categorized this misbehavior into four types: (1) attention getting, (2) power seeking, (3) revenge seeking, and (4) displays of inadequacy. Each instance requires a different response from the teacher. If a student is trying to get attention, the best thing to do, according to Dreikurs, is to ignore the behavior. If the student is trying to upstage or gain power over the teacher, the teacher should decline to get involved in the power struggle and try instead to find a way to give the student more influence and responsibility.

> Logical consequences are punishments administered for misbehavior that are directly related to the infraction.

The logical consequences approach is still used in some schools, although not as much as it once was. Teachers trained in the approach learn how to identify the type of student misbehavior partly by getting in touch with their own emotional response. If the teacher feels "bugged," it is likely the student is seeking attention; if the teacher is getting angry, perhaps it is because the student is seeking power. Trained teachers also learn how to administer **logical consequences** according to the type of misguided goal behind the student's behavior. Logical consequences are punishments related directly to a misbehavior rather than the more general penalties of detention or reprimands used in many classrooms. Making a student who wrote on the bathroom wall repaint the wall is a classic example of a logical consequence.

The logical consequences approach emphasizes the importance of democratic classrooms in which students have a say in making the rules. Dreikurs views the logical consequence of misbehavior as more than just arbitrary punishment. He encourages teachers to administer logical consequences in a friendly and matter-of-fact manner, without elements of moral judgment. The long-range goal of this approach to discipline is to have students understand the reasons for their misbehavior and find ways to satisfy their self-worth and affiliation needs in socially acceptable ways.

The difficulties teachers have with the logical consequences approach are twofold. Without extensive training, some find it difficult to develop the skill in identifying the specific motive that is causing the student to misbehave. Others find it difficult to identify logical consequences for many misbehaviors that occur in classrooms. For instance, what is the logical consequence for speaking out of turn? For sassing the teacher? For smoking in the bathrooms or carrying a weapon to school? Nonetheless, some teachers who possess the necessary counseling skills have found the logical consequences approach a powerful tool for dealing with disruptive students and helping them develop self-management skills.

The FAIR Approach

Nancy Rappaport and Jessica Minahan (2012) have accurately observed that "despite their best efforts, teachers [often] feel defeated by . . . disruptive students and it [feels] like they are fighting a losing battle" (p. 18). These two behavioral specialists, a child psychiatrist at Harvard Medical School and a behavioral analyst for the Newton, Massachusetts, public schools, have teamed up to develop a programmatic set of strategies for working with challenging students (see Minahan & Rappaport, 2012; Rappaport & Minahan, 2012). They call their program **FAIR,** an acronym to highlight steps teachers are encouraged to take when dealing with troubled students to them get on a path to success. Teachers are encouraged to take the following actions when dealing with behavioral situations caused by troubled students:

- Understand the *function* (F) and cause of the student's behavior.
- Make *accommodations* (A) to help the student succeed.
- Develop *interactive strategies* (I) to show students they are valued.
- Find ways to *respond* (R) to students that de-escalate explosive situations.

Space does not allow a complete set of recommended teacher behaviors, but Table 5.9 provides examples adapted from Minahan and Rappaport's work. As you can see, the actions recommended for teachers to take are similar to some of those listed in the guidelines developed by Woolfolk and by Weinstein for working with challenging students in explosive situations. Critical elements of this approach include showing respect for students regardless of their disruptive or explosive acts, making accommodations that can help minimize disruptive behaviors, using interactive strategies that recognize students' strengths and that avoid power struggles, and responding to students by setting limits that are reasonable and clear.

Programs That Aim toward Self-Management and Community

There are also classroom management programs that have been built on premises stemming from humanistic psychology and child-centered, constructivist principles of teaching and learning.

Classroom Meetings. Trained first as an engineer and later as a physician and clinical psychologist, William Glasser (1969, 1986, 1998, 1999) devoted much of his professional life to finding ways to make schools more satisfying and productive for students. Glasser believed that most classroom problems stem from a failure to satisfy the basic needs of students. In his early work, Glasser emphasized students' need for love and feelings of self-worth; in his later work, he expanded his list of basic needs to include survival and reproduction, belonging and love, power and influence, freedom and fun. Glasser believed that school structures need to be modified. He proposed the **classroom meeting,** a regular thirty-minute nonacademic period in which teachers and students discuss and find cooperative solutions to personal and behavior problems and in which students learn how to take responsibility for their own behavior

Classroom meetings are an approach to classroom management in which the teacher holds regular meetings for the purpose of helping students identify and resolve problem situations.

Table 5.9 *FAIR Strategies for Working with Three Categories of Students who are Difficult and Troubled*

Strategies	Students who are Oppositional	Students who are Withdrawn	Students who are Anxious
	(Characterized by frequent tantrums; excessive arguing and questioning rules; blames others for mistakes)	(Characterized by lack of energy and motivation; may be depressed and experiencing headaches or stomachaches)	(Characterized by being easily frustrated or upset; exhibiting fear, irritability, or anger; expressing worry)
Sample accommodations	• Modify schedule to alternate classes liked and disliked. • Provide choice in assignments, places to work. • Offer hands-on lessons. • Provide self-calming practice.	• Initiate buddy system during recess. • Use student's interest in the curriculum. • Teach positive-thinking skills. • Teach multisensory lessons.	• Provide safe spaces in and out of the classroom. • Schedule regular breaks. • Arrange alternate lunch with two peers. • Encourage daily calming practice.
Sample interaction strategies	• Recognize student's strengths and use language to describe. • Avoid power struggles. • After demand, move away; avoid making eye contact.	• Be cautious in using humor. • Give positive feedback in a low-key way. • Reframe student's negative perceptions.	• Use precise language. • Use self-esteem building activities. • Work on explicit relationship building activities.
Sample response strategies	• Use natural consequences as a motivator. • Set limits that are enforceable, reasonable, and clear. • Use incremental rewards and consequences (e.g., offering two free breaks a day).	• Avoid one-on-one talks. • Avoid overhelping or overprompting a student. • Help student understand misconceived social situations.	• Avoid responses that reinforce escape-motivated behavior. • Teach and reward self-regulation skills. • Clearly state student's level of anxiety.

Sources: Adapted from Minahan, J., & Rappaport, N. (2012). *The behavior code: A practical guide to understanding and teaching the most challenging students.* Cambridge, MA: Harvard Education Press; and Rappaport, N., & Minahan, J. (2012). Cracking the behavior code. *Educational Leadership, 70*(2), 18–25.

and their personal and social development. Subsequent to Glasser's initial work, others, such as Rothstein-Fisch and Trumbull (2008) and Weinstein and Novodvorsky (2010), have also suggested the "classroom meeting" as a way to help manage classrooms and to teach students self-management.

Facilitating Classroom Meetings and Student-Centered Discussions. Although several variations have been proposed, in general, the classroom meeting requires several critical elements and steps to be successful. When the classroom meeting is first being introduced and taught to students, the teacher keeps the learning environment tightly structured. More and more freedom can be given to students as they become successful in meetings. The teacher must maintain responsibility for ensuring participation, keeping student problem solving focused, and providing overall leadership. Usually, the teacher acts as discussion leader and asks students to sit in a circle during the classroom meetings. However, with younger students, participants sometimes sit on the floor, and with older students, the role of discussion leader is sometimes assumed by a student in the class.

In preparation for classroom meetings, teachers need to think through what they want the meeting to accomplish and have some problems ready for discussion in case none come from students. Most important, overall planning must allow time for classroom meetings on a regular basis. In elementary schools, many teachers who use classroom meetings start each day with this activity; others schedule it as a way to close each day; still others schedule classroom meetings on a weekly basis. In most middle and high schools, teachers schedule meetings less frequently, perhaps thirty minutes every other Friday, with special meetings if serious problems arise. The frequency of meetings is *not* as important as their regularity.

Conducting a classroom meeting calls for considerable skill on the part of teachers. The rewards of this approach, however, are worth the effort.

The Caring Classroom

Finally, programs have been developed on constructivist, child-centered principles that aim at building threat-free learning communities and helping students make their own choices and develop self-management. These programs, advocated by reformers such as Charney (1992, 2002), Kohn (1996, 2006), Lundy and Swartz (2011), Noddings (2001, 2005), and Wilde (2012), are more difficult to describe in a textbook than traditional classroom management programs. This is true because their developers emphasize no single alternative to more traditional approaches but instead argue that the alternatives are endless. Consistent with their perspective, constructivist, child-centered educators do not believe that their approach can be anchored in a set of simple recipes. However, they have enunciated principles for teachers to follow, such as those outlined by Kohn (2006):

- Act in ways that are socially just.
- Develop authentic relationships free of power and control.
- Allow students to construct moral meaning.
- Limit structures and procedures.
- Give students a say and have them solve problems together.

The meaning of teaching in socially just ways has been described by Oakes and Lipton (2003, 2006) as creating classrooms where teachers stand up for social justice and work to change the inequities that exist in the educational system. All talk and action in the classroom is aimed at understanding and working toward social justice. Here is what two teachers had to say about this perspective and its meaning for their approach to classroom management:

> I intend to break the cycle of an educational system that treats my current and future students as children who need to be controlled and "schooled." I intend to take advantage of my students' open-mindedness and susceptibility to instill in them a strong sense of social responsibility. My teaching means nothing if I am not leaving my students with unforgettable experiences and transformative dialogues through which they view themselves as conscious, competent participants in some larger reality—a community, which has the potential of being transformed only through their collaborative efforts. (Oakes & Lipton, 2003, p. 32)
>
> As a first-year teacher, I also cannot get discouraged if I am not able to create a socially just and democratic classroom in two weeks, or two months. The fact that the journey is a difficult one signifies its existence. I should keep this in mind and not get discouraged or overwhelmed. If you are passionately acting towards a just and transformative ideal, then you are a social justice advocate. (Oakes & Lipton, 2003, p. 33)

Developing authentic, caring relationships free of power and control is another principle that guides teachers in caring, child-centered classrooms. This means creating the type of learning community described in Chapter 4 in which teachers care for students and students care for each other in an atmosphere of participation and trust. These conditions can best be achieved if teachers limit the structure and procedures imposed on students. Kohn (1996, 2006), for example, says structures and restrictions should meet certain criteria. They are okay if they protect students, provide for flexibility, are developmentally appropriate, and lead to student involvement. They are inappropriate if they are simply to impose order or quiet voices, for adults only, or are developmentally inappropriate.

Finally, educators who believe in caring, child-centered classrooms have recommendations for dealing with disruptive and misbehaving students. Note the differences between Kohn's suggestions found in Table 5.10 and those described early in

Table 5.10 *Kohn's Ten Suggestions for Dealing with Misbehaving Students in Caring Classrooms*

Relationship	It is not possible to work with students who have done something wrong unless a trusting relationship has been developed.
Skills	Teachers need to help students develop the skills to solve problems and resolve conflicts. These would include listening skills and the ability to calm themselves and take another's point of view.
Diagnose	Teachers need to make sure they are accurately interpreting what is going on and are able to help students do their own analysis.
Question practices	Teachers need to look at their own practices and ask themselves if they are the cause of the misbehavior.
Maximize student involvement	Teachers need to be constantly on the lookout for ways to expand the role students play in making decisions.
Construct authentic solutions	Teachers and students need to develop real solutions to complex problems and not just a solution that can be done quickly.
Make restitution	Teachers should help students think about how they can make restitution and reparations for truly destructive actions.
Check back later	Teachers should encourage students to check back later to see if the solution and agreements are working.
Flexibility	Good problem solving for difficult situations requires flexibility about logistics and substance.
Minimize punitive impact	On those rare occasions when teachers see no alternative to an intervention that a student may experience as controlling, every effort should be made—by adopting a warm and regretful tone and expressing confidence that the problem can be solved together—to minimize the chance that the intervention will be seen as punitive.

Source: Kohn (1996), p. 47.

this chapter. Kohn's suggestions emphasize the importance of building a relationship, joining in mutual problem solving, and keeping punishments to a minimum.

Many believe that the ideas and approaches associated with the child-centered, caring classroom represent the best hope for creating socially just classrooms, where students and teachers can develop authentic relationships free of power and control. These ideas, however, are not free from critics, who argue that child-centered principles are too idealistic, too difficult for many teachers to implement, and not embraced by many parents, who prefer more traditional approaches for managing classrooms.

A Final Thought and Look to the Future

As with so many other aspects of teaching, approaches to classroom management are in a state of transition in the twenty-first century. What this means for a beginning teacher is that you will likely get your first job in a school where very traditional views of learning and classroom management may still prevail. Perhaps students will be treated as passive receptacles for teacher-transmitted knowledge, and they will be expected to do what the adults in the school tell them to do. At the same time, many of you and others like you will have been influenced by a constructivist view of teaching and learning that holds that teachers should help students take active roles in constructing their own intellectual and moral meaning. This approach to teaching requires a different kind of classroom management system. It requires developing caring, learning communities in which students have a say in what they do and how they behave. It requires spending less time controlling students and more time helping them think for themselves and care for others. This will be the challenge of teaching and providing leadership for twenty-first-century classrooms.

Check, Extend, Explore

Check
- What are the advantages and disadvantages of the assertive discipline approach in the classroom?
- How does Dreikurs explain misbehavior? In what ways do logical consequences teach a student to behave appropriately?
- What teacher activities are required to make classroom meeting successful?
- According to the FAIR approach, what are the critical actions teachers should take when dealing with difficult student situations?
- What principles guide classroom management from a child-centered perspective?
- Contrast Kohn's suggestions for dealing with disruptive behavior with the Canters' recommendations.

Extend
- What are your opinions on behavioral approaches such as assertive discipline?
- Do you think child-centered approaches to classroom management will work for you? Go to the "Extend Question Poll" on the Online Learning Center to respond.

Explore
- Do a Google search for "classroom management" and look at a couple of the Web sites on this topic in the OLC Weblinks. What kinds of resources for teachers did you find?

Reflections from the Classroom

The Out-of-Control Classroom

A teacher in the school where you have just finished your student teaching has resigned at mid-year for personal reasons. The principal has asked if you would be willing to take her place until the end of the academic year. You are pleased to have been asked, but you also know that the class has been completely out of control. You have observed students in the class fighting with one another. Other teachers have told you that the resigning teacher found the class impossible to manage: Students talk when they should be listening; they get up and move around the classroom regardless of what is going on; they are unruly and disrespectful. It is even rumored that this out-of-control situation is the reason behind the teacher's sudden departure. You know that if you take the position and are unsuccessful, your reputation and chances for future jobs will be ruined. Nonetheless, you decide that you can do it. But now you have to decide where to start and what to do.

Write a reflective essay about this situation that can be used in your portfolio to let others know your overall views and approach to classroom management. Approach this situation from the perspective closest to the grade level or subject area you are preparing to teach. Consider the following questions as you think through this problem: What are your long-range goals for this group of students? What specific problems would you tackle first? Would you lean toward dealing with this situation using behavioral approaches? Or would you strive toward working toward self-management? When you have finished your portfolio entry, compare your views with the following ideas expressed by two experienced teachers.

Amy Callen
Lyndon Pilot School, 4th and 5th Grade, Boston, MA

Dealing with an out-of-control classroom can be extremely taxing for any teacher, but especially so for new teachers. In accepting this position, you have not only taken on the responsibility of teaching these students what is required of them but also teaching them how to become respectful members of the school and classroom community. It is important to walk into this situation with realistic expectations. Do not expect to work miracles overnight. Create small, achievable goals for yourself and for them.

Begin by doing your research. A good place to start is Ruth Charney's *Teaching Children to Care: Management in the Responsive Classroom*. This is an excellent social curriculum that clearly outlines effective management practices. Talk to

the teachers who have had these students in the past and find out what has worked for them. Finally, plan your days carefully. Avoid finding yourself at 2:00 with nothing to do. It is better to have too much planned than not enough.

Your first few days should be spent creating a tone in the classroom. Do not let yourself be thrown by inappropriate and disrespectful behavior. Deal with it calmly and consistently. In some instances, you may want to ignore it. It is important to choose your battles. Academics will happen, but they should not be the focus at first. Tasks that are teacher directed are best. Whole class activities or individual seatwork (reading, writing, math, etc.) have worked really well for me in the past. Before you begin each of these activities, explicit instructions regarding what is expected will be necessary. At the end of each working session be sure to compliment those students who worked effectively.

By the end of the first week you should hope to have created a list of "rules" with the class. These rules or expectations should be displayed prominently in the classroom and always stated in the positive. Consequences for behaving outside of the expectations should be logical, fair, meaningful, and consistent to the students.

Over the course of the year, keep your assignments concise, make your expectations clear, and recognize positive behaviors. In time, the children will see that you are fair, consistent, and trustworthy and will strive to emulate the positive behavior that you are modeling.

Peter Fernandez
9th Grade

I do not know all of the reasons that this class has gotten out of control. However, I suspect three culprits—a curriculum not matched to the needs of the students, a lack of any kind of management system, and perhaps a teacher who didn't care for the students all that much. Here is what I would do. . . .

Before I accept the job, I would have a long meeting with the principal, explain my classroom management philosophy, and ask for her support. I would describe changes that would have to be made in the curriculum and in the overall structure of the classroom. If her support was not forthcoming, I would not accept the position.

If she agreed to my approach, I would do three things. First, I would tell the students that I expected to win their respect and that I think they would be happier and learn more if we all got along with each other. I would spend at least one hour every morning for as long as it takes, teaching students how to talk to one another and how to resolve conflicts. I would start formal "problem-solving groups" for the purpose of giving students a say in classroom rules and in what they are expected to learn. I would spend a lot of time getting students to talk about what they think is wrong and what they think we should do about it.

Second, I would spend time talking to students, trying to discover their interests and prior knowledge. The day-to-day curriculum would then be built around their interests and knowledge.

Finally, I would ask all of the parents to come to school to discuss the class. They likely know that things have been out of control. I would explain my approach, ask for their suggestions, and then close with some concrete steps they can take at home to help their sons or daughters become more cooperative students.

Summary

Explain why classroom management is such an important topic to beginning teachers and describe various perspectives on this topic.

- Unless classroom management issues can be solved, the best teaching is wasted, thus making it possibly the most important challenge facing beginning teachers.
- Classroom management is not an end in itself but a part of a teacher's overall leadership role.
- Managerial and instructional aspects of teaching are highly interrelated and cannot be clearly separated in real-life teaching.

Describe the well-developed knowledge base on classroom management and important guidelines that grew out of this research.

- A well-developed knowledge base on classroom management provides guidelines for successful group management as well as ways of dealing with disruptive students.
- A large portion of disruptive student behavior can be eliminated by using preventative classroom management measures, such as clear rules and procedures and carefully orchestrated learning activities.
- "With-itness," momentum, "overlappingness," smoothness, and group alerting all increase student work involvement and decrease off-task behavior and management problems.
- Effective managers have well-defined procedures that govern student talk and movement, make work requirements clear to students, and emphasize clear explanations.
- Researchers in the child-centered tradition study how teachers develop threat-free learning communities that allow students to make choices and develop self-management.

Describe and discuss the strategies and procedures teachers can employ to ensure effective classroom management.

- Effective managers establish clear rules and procedures, teach these rules and procedures to students, and carefully orchestrate classroom activities during such unstable periods as the beginning and end of class and transitions.
- Effective managers develop systems for holding students accountable for their academic work and classroom behavior.
- Regardless of planning and orchestration skills, teachers are still often faced with difficult or unmotivated students who choose to be disruptive forces rather than involve themselves in academic activity.
- Effective managers have intervention skills for dealing quickly with disruptive students in direct but fair ways.
- Teachers can encourage desirable behaviors by giving praise and granting rewards and punishments.
- Specific approaches to classroom management, such as assertive discipline, emphasize the importance of being clear about expectations and consistent in administering consequences.

Describe and explain how to use particular strategies and approaches that have been developed for working with secondary students and students with special needs and for dealing constructively with bullying.

- Absenteeism and not turning in homework should be confronted quickly, and students and their parents need to be informed of consequences.
- Moving slowly and deliberatively, speaking calmly, showing respect, and informing students of expected behavior are actions to de-escalate potentially explosive situations.

- When disciplining students with special needs, teachers should be aware of the student's individualized education plan (IEP), particularly those aspects of the plan that address removal from the classroom.
- Bullying prevention requires schoolwide efforts, particularly in developing cultures of care and respect. Teachers, however, play an important role by identifying and reporting bullying situations, talking to victims in sensitive ways, and by developing classrooms characterized by care and support.

Describe the various classroom management programs that have been developed and discuss the strengths and weaknesses of each.

- In the long run, effective teachers find ways to reduce management and discipline problems by helping students learn self-management skills.
- As with other teaching functions, effective teachers develop an attitude of flexibility about classroom management

because they know that every class is different and plans, rules, and procedures must often be adjusted to particular circumstances.
- Although many aspects of thinking about classroom management can be learned from research, some of the complex skills of classroom orchestration will come only with extended practice and serious reflection.
- Approaches to classroom management may be in a state of transition. Perhaps in the future we will find teachers spending less time controlling students and more time helping them think for themselves and care for others.

Describe how your generation of teachers may challenge traditional views of classroom management.

- Classroom management in the future may be guided by more caring perspectives about classrooms and students.

Key Terms

assertive discipline 205
bullying 202
classroom ecology 181
classroom management 178
classroom meeting 207
cuing 191
cyberbullying 204
dangle 189
desist behaviors 195

desist incident 195
downtime 188
FAIR approach 207
flip-flops 189
fragmentation 190
logical consequences 206
momentum 189
overdwelling 190
overlappingness 194

praise 197
preventative management 179
procedures 187
reinforcement principles 197
rules 187
smoothness 189
transitions 191
with-itness 194

Interactive and Applied Learning

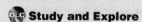 Study and Explore

- Access your Study Guide, which includes practice quizzes, from the Online Learning Center.

Observe and Practice

- Listen to audio clips on the Online Learning Center of Vickie Williams (K–8 reading specialist) and Richard Beyard (9th-grade biology) talking about their overall

approaches to classroom management in the *Teachers on Teaching* area.

Complete the following **Practice Exercises** that accompany Chapter 5:

- Practice Exercise 5.1: Developing Classroom Rules
- Practice Exercise 5.2: Developing Management Plan for an Individual Student
- Practice Exercise 5.3: Developing a Classroom Management Plan

✹*Portfolio and Field Experience Activities*

Expand your understanding of the content and processes of this chapter through the following field experience and portfolio activities. Support materials to complete the activities are in the *Portfolio and Field Experience Activities* on the Online Learning Center.

1. Complete the **Reflections from the Classroom** exercise at the end of this chapter. The recommended reflective essay will provide insights into your overall views and approach to classroom management.

2. **Activity 5.1: Assessing My Classroom Management Skills.** Check your level of understanding and effectiveness with classroom management. **(InTASC Standard 3: Learning Environments)**

3. **Activity 5.2 Observing Teachers' Management Behavior.** Observe and note what experienced teachers do to keep students engaged and how they deal with disorderly behavior. **(InTASC Standard 3: Learning Environments)**

4. **Activity 5.3: Observing Management Practices during Unstable Periods.** Observe the actions taken by experienced teachers to manage their classrooms during the opening and closing of class and during transitions. **(InTASC Standard 3: Learning Environments)**

5. **Activity 5.4: Observing Teacher Responses to Student Misbehavior.** Observe a classroom to see how a teacher responds to students when they misbehave. **(InTASC Standard 3: Learning Environments)**

6. **Activity 5.5: Portfolio: My Classroom Management Platform.** Create an artifact for your portfolio that communicates your current thinking about classroom management. **(InTASC Standard 3: Learning Environments)**

Books for the Professional

Bazelon, E. (2013). *Defeating the culture of bullying and rediscovering the power of character and empathy.* New York: Random House.

Emmer, E., & Evertson, C. (2012). *Classroom management for middle and high school teachers* (9th ed.). Boston: Allyn & Bacon.

Evertson, C., & Emmer, E. (2012). *Classroom management for elementary teachers* (9th ed.). Boston: Allyn & Bacon.

Kohn, A. (2006). *Beyond discipline: From compliance to community* (10th annual ed.). Alexandria, VA: Association for Supervision and Curriculum Development.

Lundy, K., & Swartz, L. (2011). *Creating caring classrooms: How to encourage students to communicate, create, and be compassionate to others.* Markham, Ontario: Pembrooke Publishers.

Minahan, J., & Rappaport, N. (2012). *The behavior code: A practical guide to understanding and teaching the most challenging students.* Cambridge, MA: Harvard Education Press.

Nodding, N. (2005). *The challenge to care in schools: An alternative approach to education* (2nd ed.). New York: Teachers College Press.

Rothstein-Fisch, C., & Trumbull, E. (2008). *Managing diverse classrooms: How to build on cultural strengths.* Alexandria, VA: Association for Supervision and Curriculum Development.

Weinstein, C., & Novodvorsky, I. (2010). *Secondary classroom management: Lessons from research and practice* (5th ed.). New York: McGraw-Hill.

Wilde, S. (2012). *Care in education: Teaching with understanding and compassion.* New York: Routledge.

CHAPTER 6
Assessment and Evaluation

Learning Goals

After studying this chapter you should be able to

Perspective on Assessment and Evaluation	Define assessment and evaluation, discuss why these functions are important, and provide definitions of key assessment concepts.
Theoretical and Empirical Support	Describe the knowledge base on assessment that speaks to the effects of assessment on student motivation and learning and on teacher bias.
Standardized Tests	Describe the nature of standardized tests and the teacher's role in standardized testing.
A Teacher's Classroom Assessment Program	Describe the key features of a teacher's classroom assessment program and the three major purposes and uses of assessment information.
Formative Assessment for Student Learning	Describe the importance of formative assessment and the most effective ways of providing students with feedback.
Self and Peer Assessment as Learning	Describe ways of involving students in their own and peer assessment as means for them to monitor their own learning.
Summative Assessment of Student Learning Using Traditional Measures	Describe the general principles of designing and implementing traditional assessments and teacher-made tests.
Summative Assessment of Student Learning Using Performance Measures	Describe, design, and score performance and authentic assessments.
Evaluation and Grading	Describe why grading is important and provide guidelines for making grading more effective and fairer.
A Final Thought and Look to the Future	Describe how newer approaches may represent ways to work toward more transparent and fairer assessment practices in the years ahead.

Reflecting on Assessment and Evaluation

The best way to approach this chapter is to reflect back on your own experiences as a student. You have been tested hundreds of times during your years in elementary and high school and college. These tests have ranged from simple pop quizzes to the high-stakes state mastery tests, SATs, and ACTs. Also you have received grades many times. Sometimes you have received grades that you deserved; other grades have been unfair and reflected a bias against you. What are the experiences with tests and grades that stand out in your mind?

- How did you react to testing situations and grades? Are you the kind of student who relishes a good, hard test and who feels a real sense of accomplishment when you do well? Or are you the kind of student who tenses up in testing situations and always comes away from the experience with negative feelings?

- What do you think about standardized tests, such as IQ tests, state mastery tests, the SATs, or Praxis I and II for teachers? Do these tests ensure that students and teacher candidates learn what they are supposed to learn? Or do they simply get in the way of real learning and establish unfair barriers?

- Have you thought about what kind of assessment system you are going to establish in your classroom? Do you look forward to being the type of teacher who is considered to have tough standards and grading policies? Are you going to use these to make students work hard? Or do you dread the whole idea of making judgments about students' work and plan to do everything you can to play down competition and make sure everyone passes your classes?

Go to the Online Learning Center at www.mhhe.com/arends10e to respond to these questions.

Assessing and evaluating students is one of the things teachers do that has important and lasting consequences for students.

eaders in almost all situations are responsible for assessing and evaluating the people who work for them. So, too, are teachers responsible for the assessment and evaluation of students in their classrooms—an aspect of their work that some find difficult. Nonetheless, assessment, evaluation, and grading are of utmost importance to students and parents, and the way these processes are performed has long-term consequences. Assessment and evaluation processes also consume a fairly large portion of teachers' time. For instance, a review by Schafer and Lissitz (1987; Schafer, 1991) reported that teachers spend as much as 10 percent of their time on matters related to assessment and evaluation. More recently Stiggins (2007) found that teachers could spend as much as one-third of their time on "assessment-related" activities. For these reasons, it is critical that beginning teachers build a repertoire of effective strategies for assessing and evaluating their students and for understanding standardized testing.

Although certain measurement techniques associated with assessment and evaluation are beyond the scope of this book, basic concepts and procedures are well within the grasp of the beginning teacher. The first section of this chapter provides a perspective about why assessment and evaluation are important and defines several key concepts. This is followed by sections that sample the knowledge base on this topic and describe the nature and use of standardized tests in today's schools. The purposes and key features of a teacher's classroom assessment system are described next, along with methods and procedures for assessing student learning using both traditional and more recent performance assessment measures. The chapter concludes with a discussion of traditional and alternative methods for grading student performance.

Perspective on Assessment and Evaluation

If you think back to your own school days, you will recall the excitement (and the anxiety) of getting back the results of a test or of receiving your report card. When these events occurred, they were almost always accompanied by a friend's question, "Wadja get?" You also remember (in fact, you still hear) another favorite student question, "Is it going to be on the test?" These questions and the emotion behind them highlight the importance of assessment and evaluation in the lives of students. With the widespread use of high-stakes standardized testing over the past two decades, this importance has increased exponentially for both students and their teachers.

Importance of Assessment and Evaluation

Probably since the time the first test or the first grade was given, controversy has surrounded their use. For instance, some have argued that grades dehumanize education and establish distrust between teachers and students. Others have said that grading and comparing students lead to harmful anxiety and to low self-esteem for those who receive poor grades. Even those who acknowledge the importance of assessment and evaluation have often condemned current practices for the emphasis on testing basic skills out of context and the excessive competition that results. They say that we are *overvaluing testing and undervaluing learning.* Still others have commented that grades are really a "rubber yardstick," measuring the whims of particular teachers or policymakers rather than mastery of important educational goals. With all of this said, today's teachers must assess and evaluate, and they must respond to the use of standardized tests on their students and on themselves. This chapter strives to describe important contemporary features of assessment, testing, and evaluation. It also, as you will read, strives to encourage teachers to be informed questioners of the current situation and to consider alternative approaches of assessment that may be more personalized and authentic, and fairer.

Era of Accountability. As described previously, we live in an era when citizens and policymakers believe that schooling should be conducted in a standards-based environment and that teachers should be accountable for student learning. State legislatures and state departments of education have mandated standards and benchmarks for student learning and have established testing programs to ensure that these standards are met. The federal government, until recently a relatively minor voice in educational matters, has become a major influence in how schools are run, how teachers teach, and how they assess students as a result of the No Child Left Behind (NCLB) and the more recent Race to the Top initiatives. The Common Core Standards described in some detail in Chapters 1 and 3 also contain several elements of accountability. These trends, although at times controversial, are important and have resulted in yearly and sometimes more often assessment of student learning, imposed sanctions for failing schools, and, in some instances, teacher evaluations tied to student progress (Darling-Hammond, Amrein-Beardsley, Haertel, & Rothstein, 2012).

Several other important conditions of schooling and teaching also help explain the current emphasis on assessment and evaluation.

Schools today help sort students for future opportunities.

Sorting Function of Schools. Sociologists have observed that schools in large, complex societies are expected to help prepare and sort people for societal roles and occupational positions. Although some may wish for the day when better and fairer means are found for making these judgments, at present, the larger society assigns the job of assessing and evaluating student growth and potential in large part to schools and teachers. How well students perform on tests, the grades they receive, and the judgments their teachers make about their potential have important, long-term consequences for students. These judgments determine who goes to college, the type of college they attend, the careers open to them, and their first jobs, as well as the lifestyles they will maintain. Enduring perceptions about self-worth and self-esteem can also result from the way students are assessed and evaluated in school. For these reasons, of all the leadership aspects of teaching, assessing and evaluating student growth and potential may be the most far-reaching.

Grade-for-Work Exchange. Chapter 4 pointed out how classroom reward structures can influence the overall learning community and how much of what students choose to do, or not do, is determined by what Walter Doyle (1986, 2006) labeled the "grade-for-work exchange." This idea described how students, like the rest of us, can be motivated to do certain things for extrinsic rewards. We may work hard and do what employers want so we will receive a merit raise; we may volunteer for community service hoping to receive public recognition for our work. This does not mean that our work has no intrinsic value or that altruistic reasons do not prompt us to help others. It simply means that for many people in our society, extrinsic rewards are valued and provide a strong incentive to act in particular ways.

Some say students work for grades just as adults work for money.

Academic tasks such as completing assignments, studying for tests, writing papers, and carrying on classroom discourse comprise the work of students. Many teachers want their students to perform this academic work for the intrinsic value of learning itself. Although this is an admirable and, in many instances, attainable goal, grades remain important and should not be overlooked. It is important to remember that just as adults work for a salary, students work for grades. These exchanges are critically important and help explain some of classroom life.

Importance of Grades to Parents. Finally, parents are very concerned about their children's grades. Most parents can recall critical judgments made about their work and the consequences of these judgments. Similarly, they are keenly aware of the judgments being made when their child is placed in a lower-level reading group or a general math class instead of algebra.

Teachers have been known to complain about this type of parental concern, and sometimes these complaints are justified. For instance, some parents let unrealistic expectations for their children interfere with the teacher's professional judgment about the most appropriate level of work for their child. Conversely, other parents seem indifferent to their children's academic evaluation and offer little encouragement at home for doing good work or getting good grades.

Most parental concern, however, is natural and can be potentially beneficial. A growing literature (Epstein, 2001, 2009; Feriazzo & Hammond, 2009; Russell & Airasian, 2011) shows that parental concern about grades and performance can be tapped and used by teachers for the purpose of enhancing student learning. For example, involving parents in appropriate ways through homework is an excellent means of extending the teacher's instructional time. Several studies (Cooper, 2006; Cooper et al., 2001; Corno, 1996, 2001) have also shown that when teachers show regard for parental concerns by using more frequent reporting procedures and by getting parents to support the school's reward systems at home, these actions can result in more homework completed, better attendance, more academic engagement, and generally increased student output.

Key Assessment and Evaluation Concepts

Assessment and evaluation are functions to gather accurate information needed to make wise instructional decisions and to reach fair judgments about student learning. Several key concepts can help you understand this topic more fully.

Assessment. The term **assessment** usually refers to the full range of information gathered and synthesized by teachers about their students and their classrooms. Information can be gathered on students in *informal* ways such as through observation and verbal exchange. It can also be gathered through *formal* means such as homework, tests, and written reports. Information about classrooms and the teacher's instruction can also be part of assessment. The range of information here can also vary from informal feedback provided by students about a particular lesson to more formal reports resulting from course evaluations and standardized tests. As you will see later, assessment is a continuous process and, when effective, is tightly tied to instruction and results in enhanced student learning.

> **Assessment is the process of collecting information about students and classrooms for the purpose of making instructional decisions.**

Evaluation. Whereas assessment focuses on gathering and synthesizing information, the term **evaluation** usually refers to the process of making judgments, assigning value, or deciding on worth. A test, for example, is an assessment technique to collect information about how much students know on a particular topic. Assigning a grade, however, is an evaluative act, because the teacher is placing a value on the information gathered on the test.

> **Evaluation is the process of making judgments or deciding on the worth of a particular approach or of a student's work.**

Formative and Summative Assessment. Assessment and evaluation specialists make distinctions between formative and summative assessment depending on when the information is collected and how it is used. **Formative assessments** are collected before or during instruction and are intended to inform teachers about their students' prior and current knowledge and skills, to assist with planning, and to help students guide their own learning. Information from formative assessments is not used for evaluative purposes to make judgments about a student's work; it is used to make judgments about such matters as providing feedback to students about how they are doing, student grouping, unit and lesson plans, and instructional strategies. **Summative assessments,** in contrast, are efforts to use information about students or programs after a set of instructional segments has occurred. Their purpose is to summarize how well a particular student, group of students, or teacher performed on a set of learning standards or objectives. Information obtained from summative assessments is used by teachers to determine grades and to explain reports sent to students and their parents. Table 6.1 compares key aspects of formative and summative assessments.

Table 6.1 *Formative and Summative Assessments*

Type of Assessment	When Collected	Type of Information Collected	How Information Is Used
Formative	Before or during instruction	Information about student prior and current knowledge and/or instructional processes	To assist teacher planning and decision making and to assist students in their own learning
Summative	After instruction	Information about student and/or teacher performance achievement or accomplishments	To assist making judgments about student or teacher accomplishments

Quality of Assessments. If teachers and others are to make important decisions about students, it is only common sense that the information they use to make these decisions should be of high quality. Measurement and evaluation specialists use three technical terms to describe the quality of assessment information: reliability, validity, and fairness.

A test is said to be **reliable** when it produces dependable results consistently. Measurement experts measure reliability in several ways. **Test-retest reliability** is a measure showing whether a test produces consistent results for persons who take it more than once over a period of time. For instance, if a student took a test on Friday and then the same student took the test again the next Friday and received the same score, it is likely the test is reliable. If a group of students took the test one week and repeated the same test the following week and the rankings of the various students stayed about the same, it is even more likely that the test is reliable.

Alternate-form reliability indicates that two different forms of a test produce consistent results for the same group of students. This type of reliability is particularly important for teachers who develop two tests with similar but different test items, one test to be given to students who are absent on the day that the primary test was administered.

A third form of reliability is **split-half reliability.** Test items on a test are divided into two halves, and student performance is compared for each half. When the comparisons are similar, the test is said to have good internal consistency. This type of reliability is more likely to be used by those who develop standardized tests than by teachers who are designing tests for classroom assessment.

A reliable test, thus, is one that measures a student's ability on some topic or trait consistently over time. A reliable test gives teachers accurate and dependable assessment information; however, it is important to remember that no single test can be expected to be perfect. Factors such as student guessing, mistakes made by teachers in scoring, as well as the students' feeling of well-being on the testing day all introduce error, inconsistency, and unreliability. Later, we will describe procedures that can cut down on the amount of error in tests.

A test, and the inferences we draw from it, is said to be **valid** when it measures what it claims to measure. For example, a test that claims to measure students' attitudes toward mathematics is invalid if it really measures their attitude toward their mathematics teacher. Or, a test is invalid if its goal is to measure students' skills in higher-level thinking and instead it measures the basic skill to recall factual information.

A test has reliability if it produces consistent results over several administrations or across several forms.

A test is valid if it measures what it claims to measure.

Figure 6.1 *Reliability, Validity, and Fairness of a Measurement*

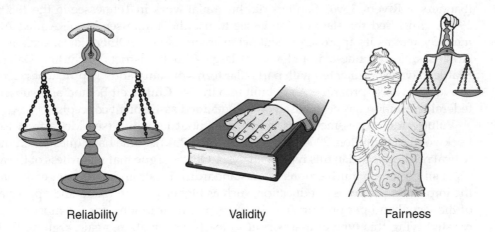

Reliability   Validity   Fairness

Obviously, if a test is not measuring what it is intended to measure, the information it produces is of no value for teacher decision making. As you will see later, it is possible to increase the validity of tests and other assessment devices.

Finally, a test is **fair** if it offers all students the same chance of doing well and if it does not discriminate against a particular group of students because of their race, ethnicity, or gender. A test may be unfair if individuals from one race or gender consistently score lower than individuals from other races or gender, as is sometimes the case with some standardized tests. However, other factors, such as poor schools or unqualified teachers, may cause the differences in performance. Figure 6.1 illustrates the concepts of validity, reliability, and fairness.

Rich Stiggins and his colleagues (2010, 2013) have provided another way of looking at the quality of classroom assessments. They view a quality assessment as having five elements:

- It collects *accurate information* to meet the needs of intended users.
- It measures *clear and appropriate* achievement targets.
- It accurately *reflects student achievement.*
- It produces results that can be *effectively communicated* to intended users, such as students, parents, or policymakers.
- It involves students.

Value-Added Assessment. **Value-added assessment** is a final concept that needs to be highlighted. This type of assessment is actually a way of analyzing test data so that the contributions of particular teachers or schools can be measured. It works this way: Students are tested initially in several subjects, normally reading and language arts, mathematics, and science. Each student's achievement is tracked from grade to grade. The gains made by a particular student or class of students are then compared to gains expected from a normative sample for the same subjects and/or the same grades. As a result of this type of analysis, a gain for a particular student or group of students can be identified as an average amount of gain or above or below expectations. The more traditional analysis of achievement test data shows a student score at a particular point in time. Value-added analysis shows the amount of student growth or gain as compared to a normative group and helps answer the question about how much "value" a particular teacher or school added to students' growth.

Check, Extend, Explore

Check

- Why is assessment and evaluation of students such an important aspect of a teacher's work?
- What is meant by the "grade-for-work" exchange?
- Contrast the terms *assessment* and *evaluation* as they pertain to classroom teaching.
- What are the meanings of the terms *reliability, validity,* and *fairness?*
- What are the differences between formative and summative assessments?
- What is meant by value-added assessment?

Extend

- Do you agree or disagree that schools should be used as a "sorting mechanism" for students? Go to the "Extend Question Poll" on the Online Learning Center to respond.

Explore

- Search "formative and summative evaluation" on the Internet. Are the definitions you find there the same as those provided here?

Value-added assessment and analysis are normally attributed to William Sanders (Sanders & Rivers, 1996). Sanders did his initial work in Tennessee in the 1980s and 1990s, which led the state of Tennessee to use the Tennessee Value-Added Assessment System as its approach to statewide accountability. Other states, such as Ohio, Arkansas, and Minnesota, and several large schools districts, including Dallas and Seattle, have experimented with particular forms of value-added approaches. The idea of average yearly progress (AYP) built into the No Child Left Behind and subsequent federal legislation has been based on value-added assessment concepts.

Value-added assessment has *not* been without its critics (see McCaffrey, Koretz, Lockwood & Hamilton, 2004; and Ravitch, 2010, 2013). Some have questioned the statistical methods used in this type of analysis. Others argue that regardless of the analysis, it still puts too much emphasis on standardized tests and does not get at many of the important purposes of education, such as higher-level thinking and appreciations of the visual and performing arts. Teachers and their unions, for the most part, have resisted tying this type of assessment to teacher evaluation, again arguing that it is too narrow. In general, however, many teachers and educators, as well as citizens and policymakers, believe that the approach, used appropriately, makes some sense and when used in conjunction with other measures of student learning can help highlight the importance of teaching and classroom instruction for influencing student learning.

Theoretical and Empirical Support

The knowledge base for assessment and evaluation is immense. The underlying concepts used for measuring all kinds of traits and attributes, such as academic achievement, personality, and performance, have long intellectual traditions. Similarly, technical topics associated with test construction, grading, and the use of assessment information have been studied thoroughly for most of the twentieth century and continue to receive attention. Two lines of inquiry important to beginning teachers are sampled in this section: the effects of assessment on student motivation and learning and bias in teachers' assessments.

Effects of Assessments and Grades on Student Motivation and Learning

For obvious reasons, one of the most important and frequently asked questions by beginning teachers is, Do tests, feedback, grades, and grading procedures influence student learning? Fortunately, this question has also been of interest to educational researchers. Much is known about the effects of various aspects of assessment on students' motivation and learning. In general, researchers have concluded that the way assessment is carried out in a teacher's classroom has a direct effect on how students study and what they learn (Brookhart & Durkin, 2003; Russell & Airasian, 2011). However, a note of caution is in order about this research because, as Marzano (2007) has pointed out, the issues involved are complex and intricate. As you will see, simple recipes do not exist.

Effects of Grades. One line of research stemmed from natural experiments that occurred in the late 1960s and the 1970s. During this period, several colleges and universities began the practice of giving students the choice of taking classes on a graded or a pass-fail basis. Several studies (for example, Gold et al., 1971) compared the students' performance, and the findings were pretty consistent: Students performed better in graded situations than they did in pass-fail situations.

However, studies of the effects of grades on getting students to do their homework have not been quite as clear-cut and leave teachers confronted with a dilemma. On one hand, most teachers prefer that students complete assignments because of the work's intrinsic value. On the other hand, many experienced teachers declare, "If I don't grade it, they won't do it." Francis Cullen and her colleagues (1975) conducted an interesting piece of research that shed some light on this problem.

The researchers experimentally manipulated two types of incentives (positive and negative) to see what effects they would have on getting students to complete a simple library assignment. They studied 233 students in fourteen high school classes across three suburban schools. Students in the study were asked to complete a one-page library assignment. Although the assignment varied according to the subject of the class, it was the same for all classes in terms of length and difficulty. The fourteen classes were randomly assigned to three different categories: (1) the positive-incentive group, where students were told that if they handed in the assignment, they would receive x number of points on their final grade, but if they did not complete the assignment, no points would be taken away; (2) the negative-incentive group, where students were told that if they did not hand in the assignment, they would lose x number of points on their final grade; and (3) the control group, where students were told that completing or not completing the assignment would not affect their grade.

Sixty-four percent of the students in the negative-incentive group completed the assignment compared to 42 percent in the positive-incentive group and only 14 percent in the control group. These data confirmed the researchers' hypothesis that grades used as negative incentives would be more powerful than grades used as positive incentives.

More recent studies (Milton et al., 1986; Paullio, 1985, 1992; Tuckman, 1992) have examined the relationships among tests, grades, and student learning. In general, these studies confirm earlier research that the use of grades can increase student achievement, but the influences remain complex. Kohn (2002), for example, reported studies that demonstrated that "tougher grading was initially correlated with higher test scores . . . but the long term effects were negligible" (p. B9). As you read in Chapter 4, how intrinsically interesting the learning task is impacts motivation, as does the value particular students place on grades themselves. Obviously, the status parents and close friends attach to grades also influences students' attitudes.

Effects of Formative Assessment on Student Motivation and Learning. Perhaps the most conclusive evidence about the effects of assessment are the findings that formative assessment used often and linked to day-to-day instruction produces substantial gains in student learning. Beaulieu and Utecht (1987) concluded that student achievement on final exams improves in classes in which teachers give weekly quizzes. Other studies (Bangert-Drowns, Kulik, & Kulik, 1991; Dempster, 1991) have shown the same thing, that student learning is enhanced when assessments are brief and more frequent as opposed to more spread out.

Landmark studies about the effects of formative assessment include the interesting study by Brookhart and Durkin (2003), which we have chosen to highlight in this chapter's Research Summary; a meta-analysis done by Black and Wiliam (1998a, 1998b); and a follow-up study a few years later by Black, Harrison, Lee, Marshal, and Wiliam (2004). As you will read, Brookhart and Durkin found that effective teachers use multiple assessments to measure student learning and that they assess frequently. In the

Black and Wiliam study, the researchers provided meta-analyses of 280 studies. They found that the effect sizes (see Resource Handbook, Reading and Using Research) were much larger for formative assessment than other types of educational interventions. They concluded that formative assessment, used appropriately, can lead to significant learning gains and is particularly effective in helping low-achieving students. All of this led Wiliam (2007, 2011, 2012) to conclude that when implemented appropriately and effectively formative assessment can *double the speed of learning*. The topic of what constitutes appropriate and effective formative assessment will be described in more detail in a later section.

Finally, formative assessment can help students become clear about the goals of instruction (as described in Chapter 3), and providing feedback from either formal or informal assessments increases student motivation and learning (Brookhart, 1997, 2008; Brookhart & Durkin, 2003; Brookhart & Nitko, 2007). As will be described in some detail later in this chapter and in Chapter 8, to be most effective, feedback must be clear and direct rather than general and ambiguous. The research study selected for this chapter shows the effects of various forms of assessment on student motivation and achievement.

Effects of Standardized Testing. As you have read, the use of standardized tests in schools is widespread today, and people in general think that if test scores are high, the school and its teachers are effective. Many instances have been reported where this is at least partially true (Cavanagh, 2008; *The Condition of Education*, 2012; Education Trust, 1998; Sanders & Rivers, 1996). However, for a variety of reasons, the effects of standardized tests may not always be as positive as some would believe. Shepard and her colleagues (2005) reported that the results are mixed. On one hand, some studies (Grissmer et al., 2000) have shown that high-stakes standardized testing leads to greater achievement gains. On the other hand, other studies (Nichols & Berliner, 2007; Pedulla et al., 2003; Ravitch, 2010) suggest that use of standardized tests tends to narrow the curriculum because teachers focus instruction only on topics covered by the test. Another mixed result is the finding that larger gains in achievement on some state standardized tests are not confirmed by smaller gains found on the National Assessment of Educational Progress (Shepard et al., 2005). Finally, many teachers complain about the overall effects of standardized tests on their students. Read below how one teacher expressed his frustration about what "testing" is doing to his teaching.

John Spencer is a sixth-grade teacher in Phoenix, Arizona. He writes that his students, all of whom struggle with English, gain the most when they "discover their own voice," when they get the nerve to speak up in class, and when they learn to solve problems by making mistakes (Spencer, 2013). Yet, he says "mandated assessments" cripple his ability to teach for "learning" rather than just "performance." He goes on:

> I teach math and reading cautiously, trying to convert what I believe is best for students into what will allow them to score high on the test. I respond to failure with impatience, rather than empathy or support. I promote basic skills over critical thinking. I start to believe that what is measurable matters more than the immeasurable. I begin to view students not as individuals thinking well about life, but as data points and colored dots and means to a positive evaluation. . . . I can blame the testing system, but the truth is it's me. Somehow, the fear of being labeled as needing "corrective action" doesn't work for me. . . . When I know a subject will be tested, I'm more likely to teach in a way that *isn't best* for students. Instead of pushing for discourse, critical thinking, creativity, and constructivist pedagogy, I go for certain middle ground that will allow students to succeed on tests. (p. 73)

Research Summary

Classroom Assessment, Student Motivation, and Achievement in High School Social Studies Classes

Brookhart, S.M., & Durkin, D.T. (2003). Classroom assessment, student motivation, and achievement in high school social studies classes. *Applied Measurement in Education, 16*(1), 27–54.

Problem and Approach: Important questions asked by classroom teachers often include, How can I motivate my students to extend effort and achieve? and Do you suppose the way I assess students makes a difference? Susan Brookhart and Daniel Durkin conducted an interesting study exploring relationships among a teacher's classroom assessments and student motivation and achievement. They wanted to find answers to two important questions: (1) How do students perceive particular assigned learning and assessment tasks, their ability to be successful with these tasks (self-efficacy), and the amount of effort they will expend on particular tasks? (2) Do these perceptions differ depending on the type of assessments: Paper-and-pencil test versus performance assessment? Individual versus group assignments? Teacher-written rubrics versus student-written rubrics?

Pointers for Reading Research: This is an example of a case study. This type of study allows the researcher to study a particular teacher (and his assessment events) in some depth, and it provides rich detail from observation and interviews. It does not, however, allow wide generalizable conclusions about the effects of assessment environments (only one environment was studied) to be drawn.

Sample: The overall design of this research represents a single-case descriptive study. In collaboration with a social studies teacher, the researchers sampled, observed, and studied a variety of what they labeled *classroom assessment events.* The teacher taught in a large urban high school where 42 percent of the students were classified as low income. Five classrooms were observed: two regular sections of tenth-grade world cultures, two honors sections of eleventh-grade U.S. history, and one section of a philosophy elective. A total of twelve assessment events were studied. These are displayed in Table 6.2. Note that the assessment types included

Table 6.2 *Description of Classroom Assessment Events*

Event	Type of Assessment
U.S. History Assessment Events	
Test on American Revolution	Paper-and-pencil individual exam
Civil War comic book	Performance assessment; Group project
History board game	Performance assessment; Student-written rubric
Evaluating JFK project	Performance assessment; Student-written rubric
Philosophy Assessment Events	
Test on early philosophers	Paper-and-pencil individual exam
Philosopher presentation	Performance assessment; Group project
Hinduism presentation	Performance assessment; Student-written rubric
Current issues presentation	Performance assessment; Student-written rubric
World Cultures Assessment Events	
Renaissance quiz	Paper-and-pencil individual quiz
Hobbes/Locke conversation	Written individual performance
Industrial Age game	Performance assessment; Student-written rubric
World War II time line	Performance assessment; Student-written rubric

Source: Adapted from Brookhart and Durkin (2003), p. 33.

paper-and-pencil tests, performance assessments with both student- and teacher-written rubrics, and group and individual assignments.

Methods and Procedures: The researchers administered two questionnaires to students before and after each of the twelve classroom assessments: Several different constructs were measured. Four were of interest for this Research Summary:

1. *Perceived task characteristics* (importance and nature of the assessment); for example, "It is important for me to learn about (The assessment topic)."
2. *Perceived self-efficacy* (student's perceived ability to step up to the challenge of the learning or assessment task); for example, "How difficult do you think the (assessment) will be for you?"
3. *Goal orientation;* for example, "I wanted to learn as much as possible."
4. *Invested mental effort;* for example, "How hard did you try on the (assessment)?"

In addition, each classroom was observed by the researchers, and two students in each class were interviewed.

Results: The overall analyses from the data collected through questionnaires, interviews, and observation were lengthy and complex. Provided here are only partial results from the total study.

From these data, the researchers reported that the students' perceptions of assessment tasks were characterized by two themes: (1) the assessment belonged to the teacher, and the primary task was to "internalize" information provided by the teachers or the textbook, and (2) hard work in regard to the task was work that would take a large amount of time, not "necessarily conceptually difficult." In regard to "self-efficacy," students in general expressed more confidence in group work. These tasks were described as more fun and easier to accomplish. However, other students expressed difficulty working in groups. In regard to motivation, students expressed three reasons to study beyond getting a good grade: (1) wanting to learn for its own sake, (2) wanting to show what I learned, and (3) wanting to help others to learn (for group tasks).

Next the researcher took a closer look at four specific assessment tasks:

1. The traditional test over the American Revolution

2. The group project on the Civil War. Students wrote and illustrated a comic book on events leading up to the Civil War
3. The group project where students constructed a board game about an event in American history from 1977 to 1990
4. The project where students wrote a report card or another evaluation of John F. Kennedy's presidency

From their analyses the researchers were able to discover which types of assessments are associated with which kinds of motivation and effort. Here is a summary of their conclusions:

Performance Assessment versus Paper-and-Pencil Tests: Students appeared to be more motivated by performance assessments than by paper-and-pencil tests. They reported expending more *mental effort*—"trying harder" and wanting to "learn for learning's own sake." Performance assessments were also associated with student *self-efficacy.* Students who perceived themselves the most able scored higher on paper-and-pencil tests, but this was not necessarily the case with performance assessments.

Group versus Individual Performance Assessment: For the most part, "no discernable patterns" between group and individual performance assessments were observed. Some students preferred group work and were more confident when working with others; other students reported difficulty working in groups and preferred working alone.

Teacher versus Student-Written Rubrics: Again, the researchers could find no concrete discernable patterns. However, they speculated that if "grading is based on rubrics, who writes them is less important than whether they are followed and used to guide performance." (p. 51)

Discussion and Implications There are several intriguing results from this study. First, it shows the variety of assessments used by a single teacher over the course of a school year and also shows that he followed the admonition often offered to teachers, "test frequently and use multiple methods." Second, the finding that performance assessments may be connected to student motivation and effort is important and timely. Finally, the researchers emphasized that it is important for teachers to design interesting assessments that allow students to feel ownership and to design assessments students clearly "see they can accomplish with reasonable effort."

One reason for mixed results is that most standardized tests measure only a small range of abilities, mainly those that focus on quantitative and verbal tasks. And, as you read in Chapter 2, leading educators today believe that there are various forms of intelligence, including the eight types identified by Gardner (1994, 2011). Students who possess artistic, interpersonal, or intrapersonal abilities, for example, are at a disadvantage because these abilities are not measured on the standardized tests used today.

Teacher Bias in Assessment and Grading

From your own student experiences, you undoubtedly know how important it is for teachers to be perceived as fair and impartial in their judgments of young people. Being free from bias is particularly important when teachers judge student work and assign grades. Teacher bias is also a topic that has been extensively researched. Some of the most interesting studies were done almost a century ago by Starch and Elliot (1912, 1913), who showed the subjectivity of teachers in assessing and assigning grades to essay exams. In their first study, the researchers asked teachers in a number of different schools to grade student-produced essay exams in English. Later the researchers asked history and mathematics teachers to perform the same task. Starch and Elliot found that teachers used many different criteria when assessing essays and, consequently, the scores or grades they gave to the same paper varied widely. On one English essay, for instance, the percentage of points awarded varied from 50 to 97.

Similar studies conducted over the years continue to show that teachers hold different criteria for judging student work and that they are influenced by numerous subjective factors, such as the student's handwriting, whether or not the opinions expressed agree with those of the teacher, and the expectations teachers have for a particular student's work. (Remember the concept of self-fulfilling prophecy described in Chapter 2.) Fortunately, a number of strategies have been devised, such as the use of rubrics, to reduce bias and subjectivity in assessment and grading. These procedures and techniques will be described more fully later in this chapter.

Standardized Tests

The concept of **standardized tests** was developed in the early part of the twentieth century; and though they were administered to students throughout the country, the results did not take on importance until the advent of the standards-based and accountability movements of more recent years. Today, it has become common practice for state departments of education, with the authority of state and federal legislation, to use standardized tests to assess students' academic achievement on a yearly basis. As described in Chapter 3, these tests vary from state to state, but in the main they assess students' abilities in math, reading, and writing in the elementary grades. High school tests sometimes branch out into science, history, and geography.

The results of these tests are given to teachers, who can use them for diagnostic purposes. They are also given to students and their parents. Test scores are summarized by the school and by subgroups within schools. Each school is compared to other schools in the state. These comparisons are often published in local newspapers. Figure 6.2 is an example of a particular standardized test report. The trend is to

Check, Extend, Explore

Check
- In what ways have grades been shown to increase student performance? Why is an overemphasis on the extrinsic grade reward system possibly a disadvantage?
- In what ways do standardized tests affect student motivation and performance?
- What subjective criteria have been shown to influence teachers when they judge student work?

Extend
- Do you agree or disagree with the current movement to test students frequently with standardized tests? Go to the "Extend Question Poll" on the Online Learning Center to respond.

Explore
- There are several Web sites on test fairness. Search this topic on the Internet and on the Weblinks in the OLC.

Tests have become more and more important in the lives of students and of teachers.

Figure 6.2 *Sample Standardized Test Report*

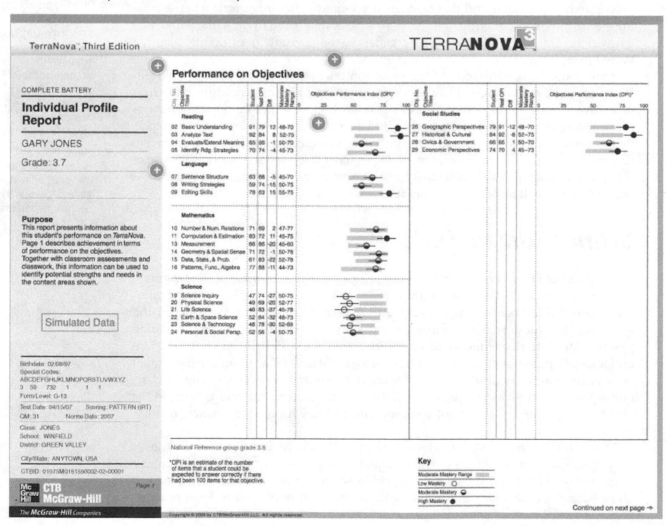

make these tests more and more important in the lives of teachers and students and to use them to make **high-stakes** decisions. For example, schools in some communities have been taken over by the state government because their students have consistently done poorly on these tests.

Many school districts also have their own standardized testing programs. In larger school systems, whole units of specially trained personnel exist to coordinate and manage this important educational activity. It is a rare school in which students are not tested at least yearly on such topics as study skills, reading, language acquisition, mathematical operations, verbal reasoning, and concept development. Sometimes schools use tests developed and distributed by national test publishers. Others use tests developed and distributed by state or district testing authorities. The results of tests are used to make judgments about the effectiveness of schools and teachers and, most important, to decide the future educational and job opportunities available to students.

Beginning teachers will *not* be required to select the standardized tests to be used on a statewide or schoolwide basis, nor will they be held responsible for the scoring or initial interpretations of these tests. They will, however, be expected to understand the nontechnical aspects of the testing program, and they will be expected to use test results and to communicate these clearly to students and their parents. In many school districts, teachers are also held accountable for their students' success on these tests and, as previously described, several states are beginning to use these test scores as one part of teachers' performance evaluations.

Nature of Standardized Tests

Standardized tests, as contrasted to tests made by teachers, are those that have been designed and validated by professional test makers for specific purposes such as measuring academic achievement or literacy levels. They can usually be administered in many different settings and still produce somewhat valid and reliable information. In some instances, standardized tests also provide information about how some nationwide "norm group" performed on the test, thus providing a basis of comparison for students subsequently taking the test. Examples of standardized tests include the Stanford Achievement Test, the California Achievement Test, the Measure of Academic Progress, or the well-known SATs and ACTs used by many colleges and universities in making entrance selections. Many of you took the SAT or ACT and soon will be taking Praxis II, a standardized test on teaching developed and administered by the Education Testing Service (ETS).

Norm-Referenced and Criterion-Referenced Tests

Today, two major types of standardized tests are used to measure student abilities and achievement. These are called norm-referenced and criterion-referenced tests. It is important to understand the differences between these two approaches to testing and to be able to communicate to others the assumptions, the advantages, and the disadvantages of each approach.

Norm-referenced tests attempt to evaluate a particular student's performance by comparing it to the performance of some other well-defined group of students on the same test. Many of the achievement tests you have taken as a student were norm-referenced. Your score told you how you performed on some specific topic or skill in comparison with students from a national population who served as the "norming" group for the test. Most norm-referenced tests produce two types of scores—a raw score and a percentile rank. The *raw score* is the number of items on the test a student answers correctly. The *percentile-rank score* is a statistical device that shows how a student compares with others, specifically the proportion of individuals who had the same or lower raw scores for a particular section of the test. Table 6.3 shows how raw scores are converted to percentile ranks on standardized, norm-referenced tests. Look at the row representing a student who answered thirty-eight out of the forty-eight test items correctly. You can see this score placed the student in the 71st percentile, meaning that 71 percent of the students in the norm group scored 38 or lower on the test. If you look at the row representing a student who had a raw score of 30 on the test, you can see this converts to a percentile score of 22, meaning that only 22 percent of the students in the norm group scored 30 or below.

Whereas norm-referenced tests measure student performance against that of other students, **criterion-referenced tests** measure it against some agreed-upon level of performance or criterion. To show the major difference between a norm-referenced and criterion-referenced test, let us use as our example a runner's speed on the 100-yard dash. If a runner were compared to a larger group of runners using concepts from norm-referenced testing, the tester would report that a student who ran the 100-yard dash in thirteen seconds was in the 65th percentile for all other students in his or her age group. Using concepts from criterion-referenced testing, the tester would report that the established criterion for running a 100-yard dash was twelve seconds and that the student can now run it in thirteen seconds, one second short of criterion.

Generally, the content and skills measured on criterion-referenced tests are much more specific than those on norm-referenced tests. Obviously, each provides different types of information for teachers to use. You will read later in this chapter how those who advocate assessment procedures that are more performance-based and

Criterion-referenced tests are those that evaluate a particular student's performance against a preestablished standard or criterion.

Table 6.3 *Conversion of Raw Scores to Percentile Ranks*

Raw Score	Percentile Rank	Raw Score	Percentile Rank
48		34	44
47		33	40
46		32	36
45	99	31	30
44	96	30	22
43	93	29	18
42	90	28	15
40	81	27	11
39	76	26	7
38	71	25	4
37	65	24	3
36	56	23	1
35	49	22	1—

authentic challenge the processes associated with both norm-referenced and criterion-referenced testing. But for now, let's consider the advantages and disadvantages of the two approaches.

Advantages and Disadvantages of Different Approaches

If a teacher is interested in how his or her students compare to students elsewhere, results from norm-referenced tests are obviously called for. Norm-referenced tests allow comparisons within a particular school, district, or state. For example, achievement levels in all third grades in a particular district might be compared with those from other districts. Norm-referenced tests, however, will not tell very much about how well a specified set of school or district standards and objectives are being accomplished, nor will they tell how students are currently doing in comparison to past performance on locally derived objectives.

Criterion-referenced tests, in contrast, can provide information about a student's level of performance in relation to some specified body of knowledge or list of agreed-upon standards. This is important information to have when making judgments about the effectiveness of particular instructional programs and activities. The results of criterion-referenced tests, however, do not allow for comparing the performance of students in a particular locale with national norms. More and more schools and teachers are using criterion-referenced tests because their information is better for diagnosing student difficulties, for providing students with information to guide their own learning, and for assessing the degree to which schoolwide or systemwide purposes are being achieved.

The Teacher's Role in Standardized Testing

Teachers play several important roles in regard to standardized testing. These include preparing students for the test, administering the test, communicating test results to students and parents, and using test results for diagnosis and feedback to students.

Preparing Students. Most test experts (McMillan, 2010; Russell & Airasian, 2011) agree that students who have good test-taking skills do better on standardized tests than do those with poor skills. Teachers can improve their students' test-taking skills in two important ways. First, they can familiarize students with a test's formats and provide practice opportunities for them to use these formats. Beginning teachers will find that many school districts have designed programs specifically to improve test-taking skills.

Second, teachers can communicate a positive attitude toward standardized tests and explain to students how important it is for them to try their best. They can strive to get students to see the test as an opportunity to discover how much they have learned rather than as a burden. As Brookhart and Durkin (2003) have observed, a test "presented after appropriate instruction in a supportive environment may be perceived differently and have different student response than the same test presented after ambiguous lessons and in a judgmental environment" (p. 29).

"Teaching to the test" is always an issue that comes up among teachers and test administrators. In general, teachers are admonished not to teach directly to the test, while at the same time taking steps to ensure that the school's curriculum is aligned, to the extent appropriate, to topics and skills covered by the test. For older students, it is generally accepted that preparing for the SAT or ACT by taking special classes or

Home and School

Keeping Parents and Community Informed

Parents are very concerned about their child's test results. It is important for teachers to be able to explain the results of standardized tests in honest and straightforward ways. They may be asked to go over test scores with students, to explain test results to parents, and to interpret test scores that are published in the newspaper. Students and their parents need to know that a single score on a test does not pretend to measure all aspects of an individual's abilities. At the same time, they need to know how standardized test scores are used to make decisions that can affect students' lives.

Community members often need to be reminded of the strengths and limitations of particular testing programs and of the assumptions underlying all standardized tests. Some believe that as educators we have not done a very good job of explaining, in nontechnical terms, the assumptions behind norm-referenced testing and their limitations for judging the effectiveness of a particular school's educational program, nor have we explained the severe limitations of most paper-and-pencil standardized tests for making judgments about the multiple intelligences and skills of human beings. Knowledgeable teachers find ways to communicate to parents and others that norm-referenced tests only compare students against a norm group and do not necessarily provide a good measure for how well a particular teacher, school, or system is achieving particular objectives. Teachers can also communicate to parents and the community that students' abilities and dispositions toward learning help determine how well they do on standardized tests and that a school with a predominance of less-motivated students will never perform as well as schools with a predominance of highly motivated students. Finally, teachers can caution parents and others about possible test bias as well as the narrow range of objectives that are actually measured on any standardized test.

being coached can help somewhat. Last-minute preparation, however, will not make up for lack of important coursework and studying hard. The National Council of Measurement Task Force (Canner et al., 1991; Russell & Airasian, 2011) has provided the following guidelines for practices teachers should avoid:

• Focusing instruction only on the task or item format used on the test
• Using examples during instruction that are identical to test items or tasks
• Giving pupils practice taking actual test items

Administering the Test. Sometimes teachers are required to administer standardized test. In most instances, these tests describe in some detail how the test should be administered. Directions about how to set up the room and the time allowed for each section should be followed closely. If a script is provided, it should be read word for word. Later in this chapter guidelines are provided for reducing the test anxiety often experienced by students.

Using Test Results. Standardized tests also provide information that is helpful in diagnosis and curriculum planning. For example, if a few students have low scores on the test, teachers may wish to explore why and to consider instructional or curriculum adaptations for particular students. On the other hand, if a large proportion of students consistently scores poorly on a section of the test, it is likely that this content is not being taught thoroughly or is sequenced inappropriately. This can prompt teachers to look at their curriculum design and make appropriate changes. It may be that important topics have been left out of the curriculum entirely; perhaps topics covered on the fourth-grade version of the test are not taught until the fifth grade. However, as you will read in the next section, information from standardized tests cannot substitute for the information generated by teachers' day-to-day formative assessments when it comes to spotting students' difficulties.

A Teacher's Classroom Assessment Program

Large-scale assessments and standardized testing are much better funded than classroom assessments, and their high-stakes nature demands attention. However, the assessments that students experience most often and that impact their learning the most are those designed and implemented by classroom teachers on a day-to-day basis.

Primary Purposes of Assessment

Most educators and assessment specialists conceptualize a teacher's assessment program as serving three important purposes: (1) assessment *for* learning, (2) assessment *as* learning, and (3) assessment *of* learning. **Assessments for learning** (also called formative assessment) collect information to diagnose students' prior knowledge, misconceptions, and interests. This information provides feedback and helps monitor student learning. It is ongoing and assists with teacher planning and with students' efforts to improve their own learning. **Assessment as learning** (Earl, 2003) involves information collected by students themselves and/or their peers about their own learning. **Assessments of learning** (also called summative assessment) collects information about what students have learned and the growth they have accomplished as a result of instruction. This information is normally collected at the end of an instructional segment and is used to determine grades, promotions, and placements. All three types of assessments are not something done once in a while but instead are ongoing and an integral part of instruction. These three purposes of assessment are summarized in Table 6.4.

Formative Assessment for Student Learning

Often much more attention is paid to summative assessments such as standardized tests used to measure student achievement and teacher-made tests given to make decisions about students' grades than to assessments designed to help students learn. Today, however, there is a growing body of evidence (Hattie, 2008; Hattie & Timperley, 2007; Timperley, 2013; Wiliam 1998, 2011) that assessments used primarily for the purpose of improving student learning, or formative assessments, have a much larger influence on what students learn than do the use of summative assessments. As you have read in the previous section, these assessments are used to diagnose students' prior knowledge and interests, to monitor their learning, and to provide corrective feedback.

Diagnosing Prior Knowledge

To differentiate instruction for specific students or to tailor instruction for a particular classroom group requires reliable information about students' capabilities, interests, and prior knowledge. Both norm- and criterion-referenced standardized tests provide

Check, Extend, Explore

Check
- How have state testing programs impacted the curriculum and the way teachers teach?
- What is meant by "high-stakes" testing?
- What different roles are teachers asked to play in regard to standardized testing?
- How do norm-referenced tests and criterion-referenced tests differ? What are the advantages and disadvantages of each approach?
- Why is it important that teachers have a thorough understanding of standardized testing methods?

Extend
- Do you think there are instances when parents and the community should not be apprised of test results?
- Do you agree or disagree that teachers should be evaluated based on the students' standardized test scores? Go to the "Extend Question Poll" on the Online Learning Center to respond.

Explore
- Go to the NCLB Web site and explore what is posted by the Department of Education. Also go to the CCSSO Web site and find out this organization's perspective about the Common Core Standards and standardized testing.

Table 6.4 *Three Major Purposes of a Teacher's Classroom Assessment Program*

Purpose of Assessment	Use of Assessment Information	When Used	Examples
Assessment **for** Learning (Formative Assessment)	Diagnose students' prior knowledge, misconceptions, and interests. Monitor learning and provide feedback. Guide teacher planning.	Prior to and during instruction Ongoing	Diagnostic instruments Student interviews Knowledge surveys Formal and informal observations
Assessment **as** Learning	Student self-assessment used for self-monitoring and self-direction. Peer assessment to facilitate learning together.	Prior to and during instruction Normally ongoing	Self-assessment instruments Peer-interview schedules
Assessment **of** Learning (Summative Assessment)	Assessments to measure student growth and to make evaluative judgments.	At the end of an instructional segment, unit of work, or grading period	Teacher-made unit exams End-of-grading-period exams Performance assessments Standardized tests

some of this information, but they have limited value. Reliable measures are available only in a limited number of subjects, such as reading, language development, mathematics, and science, and often are not made available to teachers in a timely manner. This means that formative assessment falls mainly on the classroom teacher.

In larger school systems, beginning teachers will be assisted by test and measurement personnel or by counseling and special education staff who have been specifically trained to help diagnose student capabilities and achievement. In other school systems, this type of assistance may be unavailable. If formal diagnostic information is not available, beginning teachers will have to rely on more informal techniques for assessing **prior knowledge.** For example, teachers can observe students closely as they approach a particular task and get some sense about how difficult or easy it is for them. Similarly, by listening carefully to students and by asking probing questions, teachers can get additional cues about students' prior knowledge on almost any topic. In fact, teacher and student questions are a major means of ascertaining student understanding. Verbal responses help teachers decide whether to move forward with the lesson or to back up and review. Nonverbal responses such as frowns, head nodding, puzzled looks, and the like also provide hints about how well students understand a topic. Be aware, however, that sometimes these nonverbal behaviors can be misinterpreted.

Because many students will not admit their lack of knowledge or understanding in large groups, some teachers have found that interviewing students in small groups can be a good way to gather the diagnostic information they need. This technique is particularly useful for getting information from students who do not participate regularly in classroom discussions or who give off few nonverbal signals. Student portfolios, described later, can also be used for diagnosing prior knowledge.

Prior knowledge refers to knowledge and skills held by students before they receive instruction.

Monitoring Learning

Finally, teachers have invented a variety of informal **response techniques** to collect information from students as the lesson is progressing. Two inexpensive and simple techniques taken from Leahy, Lyon, Thompson, and Wiliam (2005) are described next.

Whiteboards. To use this response technique, the teacher provides each student with a small (8" × 12") whiteboard or chalkboard. During the lesson, the teacher can stop and ask students a question that can be answered in a phrase or a few words. The teacher can then scan students' responses to see if students understand the main ideas of the lesson or if they are confused. Obviously, if students are confused further instruction is required.

Traffic Lights. This response technique is another way to collect informal information to monitor students' level of understanding of ideas being taught. The teacher gives each student three cones or cups (one green, one yellow, one red) and has them stack them on their desks, with the green cup on top. At a particular point in the lesson, the teacher can stop and check for levels of students' understanding. If students have a good understanding, they display their green cones or cups. Partial understanding requires showing a yellow cone or cup. Red indicates confusion. Some teachers teach their students to display an appropriate cone independently as the lesson proceeds. In either instance, once the teacher starts seeing lots of yellow or red cones, he or she knows that students are not getting what is going on and that further or different instruction is required.

Providing Corrective Feedback

There is almost universal agreement based on research and on the practice of experienced teachers that providing effective feedback to students is one of the most powerful influences on student achievement (Black et al., 2004; Brookhart, 2008; Hattie, 2008; Tobey & Goldsmith, 2013).

As with diagnosing students' prior knowledge, this is easier to do for some topics and skills than others. Test makers have developed rather sophisticated and reliable procedures for measuring discrete skills such as word recognition or simple mathematical operations. It is also quite easy to collect information on how fast a student can run the 100-yard dash or how long it takes to climb a 30-foot rope. Biofeedback techniques are also available to help students monitor their own physical reactions to stress and certain types of exertion. However, as instruction moves from a focus on such basic skills and abilities to a focus on more complex thinking and problem-solving skills, the problem of providing **corrective feedback** becomes more difficult because there are fewer reliable measures and acceptable procedures for these more complex processes.

Many teachers misunderstand feedback and the role it plays in student learning. Often confusion also exists about differences among evaluative statements, advice, and corrective feedback. Table 6.5 illustrates these differences following examples taken from Wiggins (2012).

Note that evaluative statements are value judgments and advice statements provide guidance. Corrective feedback, in contrast, provides information that is descriptive and nonevaluative and allows the recipients to respond and change behavior if they so desire.

> **Corrective feedback provides students with information about how well they are doing.**

Table 6.5 *Examples Showing Differences among Evaluative Statements, Advice Statements, and Corrective Feedback*

Evaluative Statements	Advice Statements	Corrective Feedback
This paper was poorly written.	You should have used more examples in your paper.	Your lack of examples left me confused.
Excellent shot.	Always shoot that way.	The way you held the basketball on your fingertips made that a successful shot.
Your story was boring and didn't keep my attention.	You should make your story more interesting.	Your story would have been more interesting if you had used examples from your own life.

Hattie (2012) has observed that there is as much ineffective feedback as there is effective feedback. Thus, you might be wondering, "What makes feedback effective?" Actually, much is known that will help answer that question. Table 6.6 lists guidelines for effective feedback provided by three assessment specialists.

Although there are some differences among the three lists in Table 6.6, they also have much in common. Effective feedback focuses on the learning task, is timely and ongoing, is clear and specific, is positive and nonjudgmental, and is consistent and trustworthy.

Assessing Frequently

Often assessments are too far apart. They fall at the end of an instructional segment, a unit of study, or at the end of a marking period. Several studies and meta-analyses (Bangert et al., 1991; Black et al., 2004) have demonstrated the effects of frequent assessment. These researchers recommend that five to ten assessments should be given over a unit of study and at least two or three weekly for each particular subject. You might want to go back and review the Research Summary for this chapter.

Table 6.6 *Guidelines for Effective Feedback According to Three Assessment Specialists*

Grant Wiggins	Susan Brookhart	Jan Chappuis
Effective feedback is:	Effective feedback is:	Effective feedback:
Goal referenced	Connected to learning targets	Is directed at learning outcomes
Timely	Timely	Occurs during learning
Tangible and transparent	Descriptive	Addresses partial understanding
Actionable	Positive	Does not do the thinking for the students
User-friendly	Clear and specific	Limits corrective information to an amount the student can act on
Ongoing		
Consistent	Differentiated (individualized)	

Sources: Lists taken from Wiggins (2012), Brookhart (2012), and Chappuis (2012).

Self and Peer Assessment as Learning

Space does not allow a thorough explanation of how assessment can be used as part of the learning process. However, a brief discussion is provided about how students can be involved in their own assessment and how peer assessment can be integrated into a teacher's overall assessment program.

Self-Assessment

Chapter 1 described how helping students become independent and self-regulated learners is one of the most important goals of teaching. Self-assessment processes help accomplish this goal by encouraging students to be involved in identifying and clarifying their own learning goals, monitoring their progress toward achieving those goals, and making adjustments, if needed, in the learning strategies they are using. Experienced teachers have developed numerous self-assessment strategies, and these have been reported elsewhere (Arends & Kilcher, 2010; Earl, 2003; Himmele & Himmele, 2011, 2012). Three strategies are described here.

Learning Logs. The learning log is a strategy to help students consider their learning goals and monitor their progress. Teachers have students keep a log and make entries on a regular basis. Sometimes teachers ask students to divide the learning log into two columns. In one column, students describe the learning task or activity they are involved in and the goals for the lesson. In the other column, they record what they have learned, the problems they have had, and reflections on their learning. Teachers might use the following questions to help students with their learning logs:

- How can you best describe the learning activity you just completed and what do you think was the purpose of the activity?
- What were your most successful responses or actions in regard to the activity and what made them successful?
- What errors did you make or do incorrectly as you completed the activity and why do you think this happened?
- What would you do differently when doing a similar kind of learning activity in the future?

KWL. Ogle (1986) and researchers from the *Visible Thinking Program* (Ritchhart & Perkins, 2008) have developed and used the KWL as a means to help students assess their prior knowledge before an instructional activity and to reflect about what they have learned after the activity. Three questions guide the KWL strategy:

1. What do I think I know?
2. What do I want to know?
3. What have I learned?

Teachers can use a handout similar to the one in Figure 6.3 to assist students when using KWL. Teachers can also use KWL as a whole-class assessment strategy by using the KWL chart and having a group discussion.

Check, Extend, Explore

Check
- Why has formative assessment taken on greater importance over the past decade?
- What methods can teachers use to diagnose students' prior knowledge?
- How does corrective feedback differ from evaluative statements and advice?
- What are the guidelines for making feedback effective?

Extend
- Think about teachers you have had and how they provided feedback to you. What did they do that was effective? Ineffective?

Explore
- Go to the Online Learning Center at www.mhhe.com/arends10e and listen to the audio clips of Dennis Holt and Sandy Frederick as they discuss their approaches to classroom assessment.

Figure 6.3 *KWL Self-Assessment Learning Aid*

KWL Thinking Sheet   Name _____

What do I think I know?	What do I want to know?	What have I learned?

Use at beginning of lesson   Use toward end of lesson

Total Participation and Learning Logs. Himmele and Himmele (2011) have developed a number of techniques to get feedback about what students know and to help students assess their own learning. These involve students participating in group activities such as all coming to the chalkboard at the same time to respond to a prompt such as: "What have you learned about Hiroshima from reading . . . ?" Called "chalkboard splash" by the Himmeles, these kinds of strategies can help students monitor their own learning and set new learning goals.

Marzano (2012) has described "exit slips," which is another technique for obtaining information about students' levels of understanding. Teachers have students respond on index cards to a prompt such as:

> How would you rate your level of understanding of today's lessons on a scale of 1–3: (1) means you understand very little; (2) means you understand parts of the lesson; (3) means you understand everything.

Teachers can tally students' responses and use them in two ways. Responses can serve as diagnostic information that can be used to plan the next day's lesson. Or, the responses can be used to help students reflect on what they know and don't know and to develop steps they might take to clear up areas of confusion.

Peer Assessment

You may remember times when you were in school and the teacher had you exchange a test with a neighbor for the purpose of checking correct answers. Today, this type of activity is likely to be used not for the purpose of saving the teacher time, but as a self-assessment strategy for helping students obtain information about their learning. As with self-assessment strategies, many peer-assessment strategies exist; however, space allows for only a brief description of two.

Preflight Checklist. Experienced teachers often admonish their students about the importance of checking their work before handing it in. The preflight checklist technique described by Wiliam (2004) is a way to get students to do this checking with a partner. Teachers provide students with a checklist that shows required components and criteria for a particular assignment. Students then exchange papers (products) with a peer and compare the peer's work against the required components. If a component is missing, it is returned for revision. Peers must sign off on the checklist before the paper or product can be handed in to the teacher.

Two Stars and a Wish. This is another strategy where students exchange their work and provide feedback. After the exchange, each student reviews his or her partner's work and identifies two strengths (stars) and one area that needs improvement (wish). They then discuss the stars and wishes with each other and sometimes with another pair.

Summative Assessment of Student Learning Using Traditional Measures

Regardless of the very positive effects of formative assessment on student learning, teachers must also devote considerable time and energy to assessing student achievement, determining grades, and reporting progress. Although some teachers do not like this aspect of their work and find it too time-consuming, it must be done and done well for reasons enumerated earlier and reiterated here. First, many students perform academic work for grades, and they expect their work to be evaluated fairly. Teachers who take this work-for-grade exchange lightly or who do it poorly normally face serious classroom problems. Second, the larger society has assigned the job of making judgments about student achievement and capabilities to teachers. It is unjust if this aspect of the job is not done well. Ways to assess student learning using both traditional and alternative assessment measures are discussed in the next sections.

One very important aspect of assessment of student learning in most classrooms involves the tests teachers make and give to students. Good test construction requires both skill and a commitment to this aspect of teaching. The general principles that follow offer beginning teachers some much-needed guidelines for constructing traditional paper-and-pencil tests. Methods that explain how to construct more complex performance tests are discussed in a later section.

General Principles

Gronlund (2005) and Waugh and Gronlund (2012) provided several principles that should guide teachers as they design an assessment system and create their own tests.

Assess All Instructional Objectives. An often-heard student complaint is that the test did not "cover what we covered in class." For whatever reasons, students who say this believe that they have been unfairly judged. Thus, one general principle is that teachers should construct their test so it measures clearly the learning objectives they have communicated to students and the materials they have covered. In short, the test should be goal referenced and in harmony and aligned with the teacher's instructional objectives.

Cover All Cognitive Domains. Most lessons and units of instruction contain a variety of learning objectives ranging from the recall of factual information to the understanding, analysis, and creative application of specific principles. A good test does not focus entirely on one type of objective such as factual recall; rather, it measures a representative sample of the teacher's learning objectives. Measuring more complex skills such as higher-level reasoning is more difficult and time-consuming.

Check, Extend, Explore

Check
- What are the ways teachers can use self-assessments to help students assess their own learning?
- How can peer-assessment be used to help students assess their own learning?

Extend
- What are your views about self-assessments and peer assessments and the roles they should play in a teacher's assessment system? Are they important? Not important?

Explore
- Go to the Online Learning Center at www.mhhe.com/arends10e and listen to the audio clips of Dennis Holt and Sandy Frederick as they discuss their approaches to classroom assessment.

Gronlund's general principles provide important guidance for teachers as they develop their assessment system.

Use Appropriate Test Items. There are, as you know from your own experiences, many different kinds of test items and testing formats available to teachers. Some types of test items, such as matching or fill-in-the-blanks, are better for measuring recall of specific information; others, such as essay items, are better for tapping higher-level thinking processes and skills. A good test includes items that are most appropriate for a particular objective. More about this aspect of constructing tests is provided later.

Use Tests to Improve Learning. This final principle is meant to remind teachers that although a particular test may be used primarily to assess student achievement, it can also be, as explained in the previous section, a learning experience for students. Going over test results, for instance, provides teachers with opportunities to reteach important information that students may have missed. Debate and discussion over "right" answers can stimulate further study about a topic. Effective teachers integrate their summative testing processes into their total instructional programs for the purpose of guiding and enhancing student learning.

Test Construction

Planning the Test. In every class, teachers teach many different things. Some of what they teach is influenced by curriculum frameworks and standards and by the textbooks made available to them. Some elements that are taught stem from a teacher's own interest and judgment about what is important; still others are influenced by what students are interested in and what they choose to study. Also, the instructional objectives of a particular course can cover a range of behaviors, including important facts about a topic, major concepts and principles, simple and complex skills, appreciations, and the ability to think critically and analytically. Obviously, every piece of knowledge, skill, or cognitive process cannot be included on a particular test. Thus, teachers must make decisions about what to include and what to leave out. The **test blueprint** is a device invented by assessment specialists to help make these decisions and to determine how much space to allocate to certain kinds of knowledge and to the different levels of student cognitive processes. Table 6.7 shows a sample test blueprint using the dimensions of Bloom's Revised Taxonomy, which was described in Chapter 3. This table was created with the assumption that the teacher taught a unit titled "Colonial Life in America" with the following six instructional objectives:

Although tests are used to grade students, they can also be used to improve student learning.

Objective 1: Acquire knowledge about the workings of a New England town and a southern plantation during the sixteenth century.

Objective 2: Remember the names of four colonial figures: Cotton Mather, Anne Hutchison, Lord Calvert, and Thomas Hooker.

Objective 3: Apply knowledge by comparing life in colonial times with life in the same locale today.

Objective 4: Evaluate the actions of people in Massachusetts who were involved with the Salem witchcraft trials.

Objective 5: Create a written advertisement encouraging people in Europe to move to New England or to the South.

Objective 6: Check how the understanding of life in the colonies influences a student's own thinking about contemporary life.

"I'm forced to teach to the test. Let's hope you can all look forward to careers as test-takers!"

Table 6.7 *Blueprint for Assessments of Unit on Life in Colonial America Using Categories of Bloom's Revised Taxonomy*

Knowledge Dimension	Remember	Understand	Apply	Analyze	Evaluate	Create
Factual	**Objective 2 Test item(s):** Four items asking students to match names with accomplishments					
Conceptual	**Objective 1 Test item(s):** Twelve true-and-false items on towns and plantations	**Objective 1 Test item(s):** Twenty multiple-choice items on towns and plantations	**Objective 3 Test item(s):** One essay question applying knowledge about colonial life to life today		**Objective 4 Test item(s):** One essay question asking for reasoned judgment about witchcraft trials	
Procedural						**Objective 5 Test item(s):** A performance measure requiring production of an advertisement
Metacognitive				**Objective 6 Test item(s):** Essay question requiring reflection of student's own thinking processes		

Key to Objectives:

Objective 1: Acquire knowledge about the workings of a New England town and a southern plantation during the sixteenth century.

Objective 2: Remember the names of four colonial figures: Cotton Mather, Anne Hutchison, Lord Calvert, and Thomas Hooker.

Objective 3: Apply knowledge by comparing life in colonial times with life in the same locale today.

Objective 4: Evaluate the actions of people in Massachusetts who were involved with the Salem witchcraft trials.

Objective 5: Create a written advertisement encouraging people in Europe to move to New England or to the South.

Objective 6: Check how the understanding of life in the colonies influences a student's own thinking about contemporary life.

At the top of the blueprint in Table 6.7, the teacher listed the six cognitive processes in Bloom's Revised Taxonomy. The four types of knowledge in the taxonomy are listed in the rows along the side of the blueprint. In the corresponding cells of the blueprint, the teacher categorized the six objectives. Notice that there is not an objective for every cell, which would be typical of most units. Finally, within the table the teacher has also estimated the type and number of test items required to assess student learning for each type of knowledge and each of the cognitive processes.

Making the Test. Once the teacher has decided which types of knowledge and cognitive processes to cover on a particular test, the next step is to decide on the test's format and the type of test items to use. Traditional test items can be divided into two main types: (1) selected-response items and (2) constructed-response items. As the names imply, **selected-response items,** such as multiple-choice and true-false allow students to select their response from alternatives provided. **Constructed-response items,** on the other hand, such as essays or short answers, require students to construct their own responses. Sometimes selected-response items are also called *objective,* which in this instance means that answers to the items can be scored relatively free of bias.

> A test blueprint is a tool for constructing a test so it will have a balance of questions representing an array of instructional objectives organized around type of knowledge and cognitive processes.

In the example provided in Table 6.7, the teacher has decided to use three types of selected-response items: matching, true-false, and multiple-choice. The teacher has also decided to use three essay questions and a performance measure. The next section describes how to construct and score selected-response and constructed-response test items. A discussion of performance measures will follow later in the chapter.

Constructing and Scoring Selected-Response Test Items. True-false, matching, and multiple-choice are examples of test items that are called selected-response items, which means students respond from a limited number of selections. The advantages of these types of test items are obvious. They allow greater coverage of the various topics a teacher has taught, and they can be easily and objectively scored. One disadvantage of these types of test items is that it is difficult to write items that measure higher-level cognitive skills and processes. Another disadvantage is that good test items take a long time to construct. They simply cannot be put together in a few minutes the night before. Also, teachers always worry about the "guessing factor" associated with selected-response items. This is particularly true when matching or true-false items are used.

True-False Items. When the content of instruction or a learning objective calls for students to compare alternatives, true-false items can be a useful means to measure their understanding. True-false items are also useful as an alternative to a multiple-choice item if the teacher is having trouble coming up with

Good test items can be time-consuming to prepare.

several distracters. A good true-false item should be written so the choice is clear and the answer unambiguous. Look, for instance, at these examples of good and poor true-false items:

Good: An island is a land mass that is smaller than a continent and is surrounded by water.

Poor: Islands have been more important in the economic history of the world than have peninsulas.

The first example requires students to know the definition of the concept *island* as compared to other land forms. The answer is unambiguous. The second example, however, is very ambiguous. The word *important* would likely be interpreted in many different ways by students.

An obvious shortcoming with true-false test items is that students, whether they know the material or not, have a 50 percent chance of getting the correct answer.

Matching. When a teacher wants to measure student recall of a fairly large amount of factual information, matching items can be useful. Students are presented with two lists of items (concepts, dates, principles, names) and asked to select an item from one list that most closely matches an item from the other list. Most evaluation specialists caution against making either list too long—perhaps no more than six to eight items—or having more than one match for each set of items. As with true-false items, there is an element of guessing that the teacher needs to consider when choosing to use matching items. Following is an example of a matching question used by an English teacher who wanted to see if students knew the authors of the various literary works they studied.

Directions: Match the author listed in column B with the work he or she wrote, listed in column A.

Column A	**Column B**
1 _____ *Leaves of Grass*	A. Melville
2 _____ *Walden*	B. Baldwin
3 _____ *A Thousand Acres*	C. Smiley
4 _____ *Moby Dick*	D. Bronte
5 _____ *The Fire Next Time*	E. Whitman
6 _____ *Jane Eyre*	F. Thoreau

Multiple-Choice. Multiple-choice items are considered by most evaluation specialists to be the best kind of selected-response test item. Multiple-choice items are rather robust in their use, and, if carefully constructed, they minimize guessing. Also, if appropriately written, multiple-choice items can tap some types of higher-level thinking and analytical skills.

Multiple-choice items consist of providing students with three types of statements: a *stem*, which poses a problem or asks a question; the *right answer*, which solves the problem or answers the question correctly; and *distracters*, statements that are plausible but wrong. Although the number of distracters can vary, normally three or four are recommended.

Good multiple-choice items are somewhat difficult to write. The stem must provide enough contextual information so students thoroughly understand the problem

Good multiple-choice questions are considered by most as the best type of selected-response test item.

or question being posed. At the same time, it must be written so that the correct answer is not easily revealed. Distracters must be such that they provide plausible solutions to students who have a vague or incomplete understanding of the problem, yet they must be clearly recognized as the wrong answer by students who have command of a topic. General guidelines for writing multiple-choice items include recommendations to

- Make the stem specific but with sufficient contextual information
- Make all the distracters plausible and grammatically consistent with the stem
- Make all aspects of the item clear so that students will not read more than was intended into the answer

Stems should be straightforward and specific but provide sufficient context. Here is an example of a good stem:

Historians attached historical significance to the Battle of Antietam because

A. So many people were killed in the bloodiest battle of the Civil War.
B. It gave Lincoln the victory he needed to issue the Emancipation Proclamation.
C. Strategically, it was the strongest victory to that point by the Confederate Army.
D. It showed how vulnerable the North was to invasion by forces from the South.

And here is an example of a poor stem:

Antietam was

A. The bloodiest battle of the Civil War.
B. The battle that gave Lincoln the victory he needed to issue the Emancipation Proclamation.
C. The strongest victory to that point by the Confederate Army.
D. The battle that showed how vulnerable the North was to invasion by forces from the South.

Most Civil War historians point out that the Battle of Antietam was tactically a draw. Strategically, however, it was a Confederate defeat, and it did give Lincoln a victory he thought he needed before formally issuing the Emancipation Proclamation. The stem in the good example alerts students that it is the "historical significance" of the battle that they should consider. Those who had a good understanding of this specific era of the Civil War would know the link between Antietam and the Emancipation Proclamation. Without that context, however, distracter A might also be a very plausible answer because the Battle of Antietam was the most costly in human life for a single day's engagement during the Civil War.

Just as the stem for a multiple-choice question needs to be carefully constructed, so too do the distracters. Teachers may make two common errors when they write distracters: lack of grammatical consistency and implausibility. Look at the following example:

Historians attached historical significance to the Battle of Antietam because

A. So many people were killed.
B. It gave Lincoln the victory he needed to issue the Emancipation Proclamation.
C. The Confederate Army.
D. Most Americans love bloody battles.

As you can see, several things are wrong with the distracters in this example. Distracters A, C, and D are much shorter than B. This may cue students to the right answer. Distracter C does not complete the sentence started in the stem; thus, it is grammatically different from B, the right answer, and distracters A and D. Finally, for the serious student, distracter D could likely be eliminated almost immediately.

Constructing and Scoring Written-Response Test Items. Another form of test item is written-response. This type of item requires students to provide the response without the help of any selections. Teachers use two major types of constructed-response test items: (1) fill-in-the-blanks/short answer and (2) essay.

Fill-in-the-Blanks. A popular test format is fill-in-the-blank. This kind of test is rather easy to write and it does a good job of measuring students' abilities to recall factual information. The element of guessing is virtually eliminated because choices of possible correct answers are not provided. The tricks of writing good fill-in-the-blank items are to avoid ambiguity and to make sure questions have no more than one correct response. To show how two correct answers are possible, read the following example:

> The Civil War battle of Antietam was fought in _____.

Some students might write in "Maryland" (the place); others might write in "1862" (the date). Some subjects and instructional objectives lend themselves to clarity and this type of test item better than others.

Essay and Short Answer Tests. Many teachers and test experts agree that **essay tests** and short answer tests do the best job of tapping students' higher-level thought processes and creativity. Obviously, this is a decided advantage of an essay test over an objective test. Another advantage is that it usually takes less time to construct. A note of caution, however. Good, clear essay questions don't just happen. And bear in mind the time it takes to construct sample answers and read and grade essay questions.

Essay tests have been criticized because they cover fewer topics than objective tests, that they are difficult to grade objectively, and that they may be heavily influenced by writing skills rather than knowledge of the subject. The first criticism can be resolved partially by using a combination of items—objective items to measure student understanding of basic knowledge and essay items to measure higher-level objectives as was shown in Table 6.7.

As for grading bias, several guidelines have been developed by experienced teachers and evaluation specialists that help reduce the influence of writing prowess and grading bias.

> **Essay tests, in which students express their thoughts in writing, can tap complex ideas and concepts.**

> **Writing sample answers and using holistic scoring are two techniques teachers can use to reduce bias in grading essay tests.**

1. *Write the essay question so it is clear and explains to students what should be covered in the answer.* For example, if the teacher wants students to apply information, the questions should say that; if the teacher wants students to compare two different ideas or principles, the question should state that clearly. For instance, "Discuss the Civil War" is too broad and does not tell students what to do. Consequently, answers will vary greatly and will be difficult for the teacher to score. On the other hand, "Describe and compare economic conditions in the North and the South during the 1840s and 1850s, and explain how these conditions influenced decisions by both sides to engage in civil war" describes more clearly the topics to be covered in the essay and the type of thinking about the topic the teacher wants.
2. *Write a sample answer to the question ahead of time and assign points to various parts of the answer.* Writing a sample answer can become a criterion on which to judge each of the essays. Assigning points to various aspects of the answer (for instance, 5 points for organization, 5 points for coverage, and perhaps 5 points overall) helps deal with the problem of uneven quality that may exist within a given answer. Students should be made aware of the point distribution if this technique is used.

3. *Use scoring rubrics.* Teachers can reduce grading bias by using a scoring rubric. This device provides a rather detailed description of how a particular piece of writing or performance should look and the criteria used to judge various levels of performance. Scoring rubrics are described more fully and examples are provided in a later section.

4. *Use techniques to reduce expectancy effects.* Chapter 2 introduced the concept of expectancy effects—a phenomenon whereby teachers expect some students to do well and others to do poorly. Having students write their names on the back of their essays is one technique that prevents this type of bias.

5. *Consider using holistic scoring.* Some evaluation specialists have argued that the best procedure for scoring essay questions and other types of student writing (reports, essays, etc.) is one they have labeled **holistic scoring.** The logic behind this procedure is that the total essay written by a student is more than the sum of its parts and should be judged accordingly. Teachers who use this approach normally skim through all the essays and select samples that could be judged as very poor, average, and outstanding. These samples then become the models for judging the other papers. Note the difference in opinion between those who advocate the use of rubrics as compared to those who prefer holistic scoring.

> The technique for grading essay questions or other written work that emphasizes looking at the work as a whole rather than at its individual parts is called holistic scoring.

Giving the Traditional Test

The format of the test and the kind of coverage it provides are important ingredients. However, the conditions under which students take the test are equally important. As with many other aspects of teaching, having appropriate procedures and routines can help make test taking a less stressful and more productive activity for students. Several guidelines stemming from the practices of effective teachers should be considered:

> Conditions of the testing situation are very important and can significantly influence how well students do.

1. *Find ways to deal with test anxiety.* When confronted with a test, it is normal, and even beneficial, for students to be a little bit anxious. However, some students (often more than teachers suspect) experience a degree of **test anxiety** that prevents them from doing as well as they could. Effective teachers learn to recognize such students and help reduce anxiety in a number of ways. One way is to simply help students relax before a testing situation. Some teachers use humor and the release

More and more teachers require their students to demonstrate that they can perform important skills.

from tension it provides. Other teachers use simple relaxation methods, such as a few moments for reflection or deep breathing. Sometimes anxious students lack the requisite test-taking skills. Setting aside periods of instruction to help students learn how to pace themselves, how to allocate time during a test, how to make an outline for an essay question before writing, or how to skip over the questions for which they do not know the answers, has been shown to reduce *test anxiety* and to improve test performance.

2. *Organize the learning environment for conducive test taking.* In Chapter 3, you read how critical the use of space is for instruction. In Chapter 4, other aspects of the overall learning community were discussed. The physical environment for test taking should allow students ample room to do their work; this in turn helps minimize cheating. Obviously, the test environment should be quiet and free from distractions.

3. *Make routines and instructions for the test clear.* Common errors made by beginning teachers include lack of carefully developed test-taking routines and unclear instructions. Most experienced teachers routinize the process of getting started on a test. They pass out the tests face down and ask students not to start until told to do so. This procedure is important for two reasons. One, it gives each student the same amount of time to complete the test. Two, it allows the teacher a chance to go over the instructions with the whole group. In giving instructions for the test, experienced teachers know that it is important to go over each section of the test and to provide students with guidelines for how long to spend on each part. If a new format or type of question is being introduced, procedures and expectations need to be explained. Checking to make sure students understand the tasks they are to perform is another critical feature of getting students ready to take the test.

4. *Avoid undue competition and time pressures.* Even if teachers are using the cooperative learning strategies described in Chapter 10, it is still likely that there is going to be some competition among students. Competition comes into focus most clearly during testing situations. Experienced teachers use a variety of means to reduce the effects of harmful competition such as grading to a criterion instead of on a curve (explained later); making the final grade for the course dependent on many samples of work, not just one or two tests; and having open discussions with students about competition and its effects on learning.

5. *Provide students with sufficient time.* Insufficient time is another factor that produces poor test performance. In fact, teachers often hear students complain, "I knew the material, but I didn't have enough time." Except in instances in which time is the criterion (for example, running the 100-yard dash), tests should be constructed so that students will have ample time to complete all aspects of the test. Beginning teachers often have trouble predicting the amount of time required for a particular test. Until these predictions become more accurate, a safe rule of thumb is to err on the side of having too much time. Making some of the tests "take-homes" is another way to avoid the pressures of time associated with test taking.

6. *Provide appropriate support for students with special needs.* Students with special needs, such as those who are blind or physically challenged in some other way, require special support when they are taking tests. Similarly, some otherwise capable students may have trouble reading quickly enough to complete a test in the time required. It is important for teachers to provide the special support (readers, more time, special tables) that students with special needs require.

Providing students with sufficient time to take a test is very important if teachers want students to perform well on their tests.

Check, Extend, Explore

Check
- What are the major guidelines that teachers should follow when they construct tests?
- What purposes are served by a "test blueprint"?
- What are the advantages and disadvantages of selected-response tests? Of essay tests?
- What can teachers do to create an encouraging and stress-free test-taking environment?

Extend
- Do you think that all objective, pencil-and-paper tests should be abolished? Go to the "Extend Question Poll" on the Online Learning Center to respond.

Explore
- Go to the Online Learning Center at www.mhhe.com/arends10e for links to Web sites with information about testing and test construction.

Summative Assessment of Student Learning Using Performance Measures

Up to this point in the chapter, you have read about assessment mainly from the perspective of traditional testing practices. The discussion has explored the effects of traditional testing and grading on student learning, as well as the importance these processes hold for parents and the long-run consequences they have for students. You have also read that many aspects of traditional testing and grading are controversial. Some reformers believe that the emphasis over the past two decades on literacy and numeracy standards measured with standardized tests has raised the basic skill level of students slightly but has failed to promote and measure higher-level thinking, problem-solving skills, and important dispositions toward learning and citizenship. Some educators, parents, and test and measurement experts (Brookhart, 2010; Stiggins & Chappuis, 2012; Wiggins, 1998; Wiggins & McTighe, 2005) believe that this situation can be partially corrected by introducing new approaches to student assessment such as the use of performance assessments, student portfolios, and grading in new and improved ways. The innovative processes and procedures that have been proposed are described in this section. They may provide foundations for you to think about the future of assessment, evaluation, and grading.

Performance Assessment

Instead of having students respond to selected-response items on paper-and-pencil tests, advocates of **performance assessments** want students to demonstrate that they can *perform* particular tasks, such as writing an essay, doing an experiment, interpreting the solution to a problem, playing a song, or painting a picture.

Figure 6.4 compares a standardized test question and a multiday performance assessment on the concept of *volume.* Note how thoroughly the task is described and how clearly the test developers present how to score the test.

This particular performance test has several features that are important. It is an attempt to integrate several topics (science, writing, group work) into the assessment process rather than assessing specific skills. It requires students to perform a variety of tasks carried over several days rather than tasks that can be assessed in a few minutes. Additionally, it is an effort to measure complex intellectual skills and processes.

Performance assessment specialists (Stiggins, Arter, Chappuis, & Chappuis, 2009, 2012) specify that the two important parts of a performance assessment are the performance task and the performance criteria. **Performance tasks** are the activities or undertakings that students are asked to engage in, such as conducting a science experiment, solving a math problem, or writing a sentence or essay. The **performance criteria** are the standards for judging the quality of the student's performance, such as the degree to which reasoning was used in the science experiment or correct sentence structure was used in an essay. Table 6.8 provides examples of performance tasks and performance criteria in five school subjects.

Performance tasks are activities students are asked to undertake so a performance can be judged.

Performance criteria are standards used to judge the quality of a student's performance.

What about Authentic Assessments?

Performance assessments ask students to demonstrate certain behaviors or abilities in testing situations. **Authentic assessment** takes these demonstrations a step further and stresses the importance of the application of the skill or ability within the context of a real-life situation. Reformers of assessment procedures such as Stiggins and Chappuis

Figure 6.4 *Two Approaches to Testing Volume*

Selected-Response Test Questions on Volume

1. What is the volume of a cone that has a base area of 78 square centimeters and a height of 12 centimeters?
   a. 30 cm^3
   b. 312 cm^3
   c. 936 cm^3
   d. 2808 cm^3

2. A round and a square cylinder share the same height. Which has the greater volume?
   a. Round
   b. Square

A Multiday Performance Assessment on Volume

Background: Manufacturers naturally want to spend as little as possible not only on the product but on packing and shipping it to stores. They want to *minimize* the cost of production of their packaging, and they want to *maximize* the amount of what is packaged inside (to keep handling and postage costs down: the more individual packages you ship, the more it costs).

Setting: Imagine that your group of two or three people is one of many in the packing department responsible for m&m's candies. The manager of the shipping department has found that the cheapest material for shipping comes as a flat piece of rectangular paperboard (the piece of posterboard you will be given). She is asking each work group in the packing department to help solve this problem: *What completely closed container, built out of the given piece of paperboard, will hold the* largest volume *of m&m's for safe shipping?*

1. Prove, in a *convincing* written report to company executives, that both the *shape* and the *dimensions* of your group's container maximize the volume. In making your case, supply all important data and formulas. Your group will also be asked to make a 3-minute oral report at the next staff meeting. Both reports will be judged for *accuracy, thoroughness,* and *persuasiveness.*

2. Build a model (or multiple models) out of the posterboard of the container shape and size that you think solves the problem. The models are *not* proof; they will *illustrate* the claims you offer in your report.

Source: Adapted from Wiggins (1998).

(2012) and Wiggins and McTighe (2005) point out that "meaningful performances in real-world" settings can more closely capture the richness of what students understand about how they can apply this knowledge than can testing for "bits and pieces" with conventional assessment procedures. Examples of authentic assessments include demonstrating work in exhibitions such as a science fair or art show, showing skill in a portfolio

Table 6.8 *Examples of Performance Tasks and Performance Criteria*

Example	Tasks	Performance Criteria
Science	Design and conduct an experiment to test a hypothesis that answers a question and create a visual presentation for an audience that includes the experiment and its conclusion(s).	Use a 4-point rubric (advance to beginner) where 4 means that all elements of the scientific process were listed and presented and where 1 means all elements were missing or incomplete.
Writing	Submit three writing samples demonstrating understanding and use of six-trait writing.	Use a 6-point rubric (exceptional to insufficent) where 6 means exceptional demonstration of each of the six traits and where 1 means all traits were missing or incomplete.
Reading	Read an editorial from the *New York Times* about climate change and evaluate the degree to which it is accurate.	Use a 6-point rubric (exemplary to insufficient) where 6 shows that all facts and assertions were made and accurate and where 1 shows little or no facts or assertions were accurately identified.
Mathematics	Using information on a graph draw a conclusion and provide two reasons to support the conclusion.	Use a 4-point rubric where 4 on the scale means two accurate reasons were given, 2 or 3 means one reason was given, and where 1 means no reasons were given.
Social Studies	Analyze an original historical document, such as a cartoon, law, or letter, and provide two possible interpretations that a historian might make from this source.	Use a 4-point rubric with 4 on the scale means that two interpretations were provided and that both were plausible and explained to 1 where no interpretations were given.

collection, performing in dance or music recitals, participating in debates, and presenting original papers to peers or parents. Obviously, many desired and important skills and understandings taught in school cannot always be assessed in real-life situations.

Designing and Scoring Performance and Authentic Assessments

You may be asking, "if performance and authentic assessments have so many advantages over more traditional approaches, why aren't these approaches used more often and why did it take us so long to invent them?" Most measurement experts agree (as do teachers who have tried to devise and use performance assessments) that performance tests take a great deal of time to construct and administer and that often they are more expensive. Think, for instance, how long it would take and the cost that would be involved to administer performance assessments to cover all the traditional topics currently found on the SAT or state standardized mastery tests.

For teachers who choose to begin constructing their own assessments to measure student performance, Brookhart (2013), Stiggins and Chappuis (2012), and Wiggins (1998) provided the following guidelines to improve the quality of these efforts:

1. Focus on learning outcomes that require complex cognitive skills and student performance.
2. Select or develop tasks that represent both the content and the skills that are central to important learning outcomes.

3. Minimize the dependence of task performance on skills that are irrelevant to the intended purpose of the assessment task.

4. Provide the necessary scaffolding for students to be able to understand the task and what is expected.

5. Construct task directions so that the students' task is clearly indicated.

6. Clearly communicate performance expectations in terms of the criteria by which the performance will be judged.

Most performance assessment specialists argue that for performance and authentic assessments to be effective, the criteria and standards for student work must be clear, known, and nonarbitrary. Students doing academic tasks need to know how their work will be judged in the same ways that divers and gymnasts competing in the Olympics know how their performances will be judged. Scoring rubrics is one technique assessment experts have derived to make criteria clear and nonarbitrary.

Scoring Rubrics. Like performance tasks, **scoring rubrics** have two parts: (1) the criteria associated with the learning students are asked to demonstrate and (2) descriptions of a continuum of performance quality, normally on a scale of 1–6 or 1–4 points (Brookhart, 2013). To put it another way, scoring rubrics make explicit the performance task and criteria that will be used to judge the performance. In most instances rubrics are communicated to students ahead of time. In the performing arts and sports (as well as in teaching), rubrics are often based on how an expert would perform. Students might be supplied with videotapes or other examples showing superior performance.

> **A scoring rubric is a detailed description of some type of performance and the criteria that will be used to judge it.**

Designing good scoring rubrics is an important aspect of performance assessment. Fortunately, good advice exists from measurement experts. Following are guidelines and steps summarized from Brookhart (2013), Mertler (2001), and Stevens and Walvoord (2012) for use in categorizing and designing scoring rubrics.

Types of Rubrics. In general, there are two types of scoring rubrics: holistic rubrics and analytic rubrics. A holistic rubric allows the scorer to make judgments about the performance (product or process) as a whole, independent of component parts.

Authentic assessments have students demonstrate their abilities to perform particular tasks in real-life settings.

An analytic rubric, in contrast, requires the scorer to judge separate components or individual tasks associated with the performance. Mertler (2001) says that a "holistic rubric is probably more appropriate when performance tasks require students to create some sort of response and where there is no definitive correct answer. Analytic rubrics are usually preferred when a fairly focused type of response is required" (p. 2). Table 6.9 provides a template for holistic rubrics and Table 6.10 for analytic rubrics. It is generally accepted that teachers need to decide whether a performance will be scored holistically or analytically before beginning to design a rubric.

Steps in Designing Rubrics. Based on Brookhart (2013), Russell and Airasian (2011), and Mertler (2001), the following step-by-step process is recommended for designing scoring rubrics:

Step 1: Examine the learning objectives or standards to be demonstrated by the performance task. Decide how you are going to use the rubric for formative and/or summative assessment. There should be a match between your objectives, your actual instruction, and the scoring rubric.

Step 2: Identify specific observable attributes (skills, procedures, processes) that you want to see and those you don't want to see students demonstrate in their performance.

Step 3: Brainstorm characteristics that describe each attribute. This is the step where you should describe the qualities of a performance along a continuum—what you expect in an "above average" or "exemplary" performance, an "average" performance, and a performance that is "below average."

Step 4a: For holistic rubrics, write thorough descriptions for excellent work and poor work, incorporating each attribute into the description. Describe the highest and lowest level of performance combining the descriptors for all attributes.

Step 4b: For analytic rubrics, write thorough narrative descriptions for excellent work and poor work for each individual attribute. Describe the highest and lowest levels of performance using the descriptors of each attribute separately.

Step 5a: For holistic rubrics, complete the rubrics by describing other levels on the continuum that ranges from excellent to poor work for the collective attributes. Write descriptions for all intermediate levels of performance.

Step 5b: For analytic rubrics, complete the rubrics by describing other levels on the continuum that ranges from excellent to poor work for each attribute. Write descriptions for intermediate levels of performance for each attribute separately.

Table 6.9 *Example of a Holistic Rubric for a Cooperative Group Presentation*

Score	Description
4	Demonstrates all group members participating as a team in process, presentation, and understanding.
3	Demonstrates most group members participating in process, presentation, and understanding.
2	Demonstrates only one leader doing the work of the group.
1	Demonstrates a lack of cooperation and lack of understanding.

Source: Mertler (2001), p. 2.

Table 6.10 *Example of an Analytic Rubric for a Six-Trait Writing Task*

	Beginning	Developing	Effective	Skilled
Ideas and content	Topic or theme is unclear and details are not evident.	Topic or theme is present but not supported or developed.	Topic or theme is clear with some supporting details and specificity.	Topic or theme is clear and well developed with supporting details focused on exploration and expansion of the topic.
Organization	An opening or closing is not present. Paragraphs are missing or unrelated.	An opening and closing are only loosely related or connected.	An opening and closing are logically supported by main ideas.	A well-thought-out order of ideas is apparent. There is a clear opening and closing, each paragraph deals with a main idea, and transitions tie the paragraphs together to a central idea.
Sentence fluency	Sentences are incomplete, distracting, or clumsy.	Sentences are short, predictable, and without rhythm.	Sentences are complete, are somewhat varied, but few complex sentences are attempted.	Sentence structure is strong, contains relevant vocabulary, and is varied in length. Sentences create a rhythm that invites reading aloud.
Voice	The writing is "flat," without interest.	The writer's voice does not fit the topic or there is limited connection with the reader.	The writer's voice is present, but uneven and not consistent throughout.	A strong sense of the writer is present through point of view, personality, or interest in the subject. Strong emotions are evoked in the reader.
Word choice	Vocabulary is limited, sometimes inappropriate, or jargon is overused.	Vocabulary is appropriate, but lacking interest.	Vocabulary is lively, but sometimes redundant or lacking power.	Vocabulary is interesting, powerful, and conveys strong meaning. The reader "sees" mental pictures.
Conventions	Correct spelling, capitalization, punctuation, paragraphs, and format are missing or have serious errors.	Spelling, capitalization, punctuation, paragraphs, and format are inconsistent and have many errors.	Spelling, capitalization, punctuation, paragraphs, and format are mostly correct.	Spelling, capitalization, punctuation, paragraphs, and format are appropriate with minor errors.

Step 6: Collect samples of student work that exemplify each level. These will serve as benchmarks for future scoring.

Step 7: Revise the rubric, as necessary. Consider how effective it was in helping score the performance and how it might be changed before it is used again.

Before moving on, a note of caution about the use of rubrics is necessary. For the most part, discussions about using rubrics, including the one included here, describe how rubrics will make assessments more reliable, efficient, and precise. To some extent this is true. However, some observers have argued (Kohn, 2006, for example) that rubrics do not provide the precision promised, and, regardless of how much detail is provided, assessment will still require teacher judgment and discretion, both of which are always somewhat subjective. Critics such as Kohn also believe that rubrics, like standardized testing, will tend to narrow the curriculum and jeopardize student independent thinking and creativity. And, as described previously, devices such as rubrics can lead students to concentrate too much attention on the details of their performances at the expense of focusing on the processes required to obtain an exemplary performance.

Student Portfolios

Portfolio assessment is a form of assessment that evaluates a sample of students' work and other accomplishments over time.

Closely related to performance assessments is the use of **student portfolios.** Many of you are already aware of the portfolio process in that it has been used in various fields of the visual arts for a long time. It is common practice for painters, graphic designers, and cartoonists, for example, to select illustrative pieces of their work and organize them into a portfolio that can be used to demonstrate their abilities to potential clients or employers. Often actors, musicians, and models use the same process. You have been provided with instructions about how to create portfolio products associated with your work as you read *Learning to Teach* and participate with a variety of field experiences.

Portfolios are a collection of a student's work that requires performance in context. What goes into a student portfolio varies according to the purposes of the portfolio. These can vary. Some portfolios serve primarily instructional purposes; others serve assessment purposes and, in many instances, serve both purposes. If the purpose of the portfolio is primarily instructional and formative, evaluation portfolio entries are often chosen by the student and become a showcase for exemplary work and work that shows growth over time. However, if the portfolio is used mainly for summative and high-stakes assessment, the entries most often are required by the teacher and chosen to allow students to demonstrate mastery of particular objectives or standards.

Below are some examples of what might be included in a student's portfolio:

1. *Test and quizzes.* This could include self-assessments or tests and quizzes taken in class.
2. *Prompts:* Evaluated work for required class assignments.
3. *Performance Tasks:* Scored work from elective and/or on-demand performance tasks.
4. *Projects/Products/Artifacts:* Projects (papers, plans, videos) completed by students either as part of an assignment or on their own.

Portfolios are scored using rubrics in the same manner as performance tasks. The same rules apply for deciding whether to use holistic or analytic scoring rubrics. The idea here is to have students prepare their portfolios so that they reflect on their own learning. As described in the Enhancing Teaching and Learning with Technology feature found later in this chapter, students today often create electronic portfolios to display artifacts of their work on CDs or Web sites.

Assessing Group Effort and Individually Contracted Work

In Chapter 10, you will read about cooperative learning procedures through which students are awarded points and grades for their work in teams and for their individual work. These procedures hold good potential for reducing the destructive process of comparing students with their peers as well as excessive competition.

Interest is also growing among educators today in using criterion-referenced evaluations of individual work or projects. Learning materials for some subjects can be broken down into smaller units of study and students can be given the opportunity to work toward a specified objective (criterion) until they have mastered it. Grades under these systems are determined *not* by comparing students with their peers but by the number of standards they have met. Systems in which teachers make contracts with individual students allow each student to compete with himself or herself on mutually agreed-upon criteria rather than to compete with others. Grading for team effort and for individually contracted work, however, are difficult processes for teachers to implement by themselves. These experiments sometimes run strongly against current norms and traditions, and they require schoolwide policies and collegial support to be successful. Also, putting too much emphasis on assessing group work may put some students at a disadvantage. For example, Beals (2013) has written that children on the autism spectrum are often unfairly challenged when forced to fulfill group assignments.

When to Use Different Kinds of Assessments

Which type of assessments to use is yet another issue facing teachers in regard to their assessment programs. As with many other aspects of teaching, there are no absolute solutions or recipes, nor is one type of assessment superior to others in every assessment situation. In general, the best advice is to choose a type of assessment that best measures the type of objectives a teacher has for particular units or lessons and the type of knowledge students are expected to master. Table 6.11 illustrates this idea. The rows of the table are labeled with the different types of knowledge (described in Chapter 3). The columns represent the various types of assessments described in the previous sections of this text. Note that in general selected-response items are best to measure factual knowledge, whereas written-response items such as an essay exam do a better job of assessing conceptual knowledge. Procedural knowledge (remember this

Table 6.11 *Choosing the Right Kind of Assessment*

Type of Learning	Selected-Response Items (e.g., Multiple-Choice)	Written-Response Items (e.g., Essays)	Performance Assessments	Reflective Essays or Communications through Questioning or Think Alouds
Factual knowledge	Good and efficient way of assessing factual knowledge.			
Conceptual and higher-level thinking		Best for assessing complex knowledge and higher-level thinking.		
Procedural knowledge/skills			Best for assessing skills. Skills can be observed while being performed.	
Metacognitive knowledge				Good way to get learners to "think about their own thinking."

Check, Extend, Explore

Check

- What are some of the controversies in regard to traditional testing practices? What solutions have been considered to remedy these problems?
- How do performance assessments and authentic assessments differ? How do they differ from traditional testing methods?
- Describe the steps involved in designing performance assessments and scoring rubrics.
- What is a student portfolio? How can it be used in a teacher's assessment program?
- What factors should teachers consider when choosing the types of assessments to use?

Extend

- Do you agree or disagree with the proposition that your generation of teachers will change the traditional ways for assessing and grading students? Go to the "Extend Question Poll" on the Online Learning Center to respond.

Explore

- Visit Grant Wiggins's Web site for his latest ideas about performance assessment.

Grading on the curve is the practice of assigning grades so they will follow a normal curve.

Grading to criterion is the practice of assigning grades according to how well students do on a predefined set of objectives or standards.

is knowledge about how to do something) is best assessed with performance measures, and metacognitive knowledge (knowledge about one's own thinking) lends itself to assessment with reflective essays and other kinds of learner-directed communications.

Evaluation and Grading

As with the debates about student assessment practices, so, too, have there been debates about how best to evaluate and grade students. Currently, many assessment specialists believe that our traditional grading practices do not lead to student learning and that they inhibit motivation (Brookhart, 2013; Marzano, 2006; Stiggins & Chappuis, 2012; Winger, 2009). At the same time, many experienced teachers have found that attempts to change traditional grading practices often result in stiff opposition from peers and parents who prefer the grading system they experienced as students.

One reason that grading controversies and dilemmas exist stems from the fact that people (teachers and parents) hold different views about the purpose of grading. On the one hand, there are those who believe that the primary purpose of grading is to compare and sort students. They believe that grades, as traditionally conceived, provide an objective means for determining class rankings, promotions, graduations, and college admissions. On the other hand are those who believe that the primary purpose of grading is to provide a quantifiable mark that summarizes a student's achievement of specified curricula aims and standards. One's belief about the purpose of grading obviously influences the approach to grading that parents may prefer and that teachers are likely to adopt.

Two basic approaches currently exist: norm-referenced grading and criterion-referenced grading. Norm-referenced grading (often referred to as **grading on a curve**) is a commonly used procedure in secondary schools and colleges, where students compete with each other for positions along a predetermined grading curve. A teacher following a strict interpretation of the grading-on-a-curve concept would perhaps give 10 percent of the students A's, 20 percent B's, 40 percent C's, 20 percent D's, and 10 percent F's. Under this grading scheme, even students with a high degree of mastery of the testing material sometimes fall into one of the lower grading areas and vice versa.

An alternate approach to grading on a curve is **grading to criterion** or mastery. Teachers using this approach define rather precisely the content and skills objectives and standards for their class and then measure student performance against those criteria. For example, in spelling, the teacher might decide that the correct spelling of 100 specified words constitutes mastery. Student grades are then determined and performance reported in terms of the percentage of the 100 words a student can spell correctly. A teacher using this approach might specify the following grading scale: A = 100 to 93 words spelled correctly; B = 92 to 85 words spelled correctly; C = 84 to 75 words spelled correctly; D = 74 to 65 words spelled correctly, and F = 64 or fewer words spelled correctly.

Table 6.12 illustrates the differences between these two approaches for a particular group of students. As you can see, the two approaches produce different grades for individuals within the same class of students. Both grading on a curve and grading on mastery present some dilemmas for teachers. When grading on a curve, the teacher is confronted with questions about the relationship of grades to native ability. For example, should 10 percent of a class of very able students be given F's? Should 10 percent of a class of students with learning disabilities be given A's?

Criterion testing and grading also present troublesome issues for teachers. If criterion levels are set in relation to what is realistic for a particular group of students, then able students should be expected to perform more work and at higher levels than their

Enhancing Teaching and Learning with Technology

Assessment and Evaluation Tools

Most teachers today use a wide array of software programs designed to help generate and score tests, assist with authentic and performance assessments, record student performance and grades, and report results to students and their parents. Most important, digital technologies provide opportunities, previously impossible, to measure all kinds of student performance and provide feedback to students in what West (2012) has labeled "real time." Following are brief descriptions of how technology can assist teachers and student in assessment and evaluation.

Test Generators

Test generators allow teachers to create a bank of test questions that can be organized for a particular test. This makes it easy to add and delete questions from year to year, as well as to create more than one version of the same test to give to students who may be absent on the day the test is given. Some test-generator programs also provide printed answer keys for the test. The test questions come from those the teacher creates, either following the guidelines provided in this chapter or from those provided by the textbook's publisher on CD-ROM or online. Some test-generator programs provide authoring software that helps teachers write and organize questions in a variety of formats, including multiple-choice, true-false, matching, and completion. Software and Web sites are also available to help teachers develop rubrics for scoring essay questions and performance tasks. All of these technologies allow teachers to format questions in a variety of ways and to design different tests for different classes or levels of students over the same content. Examples of test-generator software, such as Class Manager, Easy Grade Pro, and others, can be accessed from the *Learning to Teach* Online Learning Center.

Rubric Generators

Software and Web sites are also available to assist in the generation of scoring rubrics on a variety of topics. Most of these, such as Rubricator, help teachers align their objectives and standards to performance tasks and criteria. The Web sites annotated in the Online Learning Center provide examples and templates for developing rubrics on a variety of topics.

Electronic Portfolios

Students can use computer and Web-based software to create what has been referred to as "electronic" or "digital" portfolios (Costantino & DeLorenzo, 2009; Milman & Kilbane, 2008). In fact, you may be using such software to keep the professional portfolio required for your teacher education program. Electronic portfolios display products and artifacts of a student's work and store them on CD-ROM or on a Web site.

Electronic Grade Books

Keeping student attendance records and test scores is very time-consuming for teachers. It also requires great accuracy. Electronic grade books are similar to spreadsheet and database software programs. They record scores, grades, and other statistical information in a database; calculations are then performed using the spreadsheet function of the grade book. Grade-book software allows teachers to give weight to different assignments, handle missing assignments, and perform grade calculations. This software also allows teachers to create reports with charts that map a student's performance over time. This is an excellent way of generating reports for students and their parents and saves teachers many hours of work.

Real-Time Student Assessment

As described in some detail earlier in this chapter, wise and appropriate use of formative assessment can have significant impact on student learning. Numerous online devices make it possible today to expand significantly the range of student knowledge and skills assessed as well as tracking student learning in real time. Data generated in these real-time assessments can be used to provide important information to students about the progress they are making and serve as a valuable tool for diagnosis and planning.

Making Grades and Homework a Click Away

One way that schools, as a whole, have made use of technology is through the development of Web sites that provide a variety of information to students and their parents. One of the most interesting applications is a school-based Web site that posts daily grades, attendance records, summaries of lesson plans, and homework assignments. This is made possible with software programs that link a teacher's electronic grade book to the school's Web site. Students and parents access the site from home with a password.

These Web sites provide advantages for teachers, students, and parents. They allow teachers to keep everyone informed about what is going on in their classrooms by posting comments on students' work for students and their parents to see. Students no longer have excuses for not knowing when an assignment is due. Even if they have forgotten or were absent, they can find the assignment and due date on the Web site. Similarly, they can keep track of their grades and know where they stand in the class at all times. Parents can monitor their children's work in a much more positive atmosphere. They can follow how their child is doing in school on a regular basis, thus preventing surprises associated with the quarterly report card.

Check, Extend, Explore

Check
- Contrast grading on a curve and grading to criterion.
- Explain the advantages and disadvantages of grading on a curve and grading to criterion.
- Describe how test generators and electronic grade books can be used by teachers.

Extend
- Do you agree or disagree with the practice of grading on a curve? Go to the "Extend Question Poll" on the Online Learning Center to respond.

Explore
- Go to the Online Learning Center at www.mhhe.com/arends10e for links to Web sites with information about approaches to grading.

less-talented peers. However, when grades are assigned, the question arises: should students who complete all work accurately, even though it is at a lower level, be given the same grade as students who complete all work accurately at a higher level?

Learners with special needs present teachers with another set of troublesome decisions in regard to grading. For example, it doesn't seem fair to most teachers to give students with learning challenges or who are English language learners a failing grade because they have not met grade-level standards after they have worked hard and done everything the teacher asked them to do. At the same time, it seems equally unfair to assign a passing grade to a student who did not meet the specified performance criteria. Jung and Guskey (2010) say that given the right kind of grading system teachers do not have to choose between "fairness and accuracy."

Table 6.12 *Assigning Spelling Grades from Test Scores Using Two Approaches*

	Grading on a Curve		Grading to Criterion	
Eric	98	A	98	A
Maria	97		97	
Ruth	96	B	96	
John	96		96	
Tanisha	96		96	
Sam	95		95	
Denise	92	C	92	B
Mohammed	90		90	
Louise	90		90	
Elizabeth	90		90	
Betty	87		87	
Marcos	87		87	
Martha	86		86	
Tom	83		83	C
Chang	80	D	80	
Dick	78		78	
Beth	73		73	D
Lane	69		69	
Mark	50	F	50	F
Jordan	50		50	

The following guidelines from Jung and Gusky (2010) and Marzano (2006) are aimed at making grading more effective in support of student learning and at dealing with exceptional learners fairly and accurately:

- *Ensure clarity about learning outcomes.* Communicate aims and standards clearly to students (and their parents) and then have part of the grade represent the degree to which students have mastered particular aims and standards.
- *Grade academic and nonacademic work separately.* A common practice among teachers, and one supported by many parents, is to factor nonacademic criteria, such as class-room behavior, participation, and turning in assignments, into a student's grade. Assessment specialists Marzano (2006), however, recommends the development of a system that gives two types of grades—one that reflects achievement and another that reflects effort and work habits.* Jung and Guskey (2010) recommend the use of three criteria when determining grades: (1) *product criteria* (what students know and can do), (2) *process criteria* (how students behave and amount of effort they display), and (3) *progress criteria* (how much learning and growth has occurred).
- *Include marks given on homework only if they represent achievement of specified aims or standards.* Often homework is given, as will be described in later chapters, to pro-vide students with practice or to prepare them for the next day's lesson. These are important features of a teacher's formative assessment program. They should not, however, be factored into a student's final grade that represents achievement.
- *Avoid the use of zero.* Traditionally, teachers give students a "zero" if they fail to com-plete an assigned piece of work. This practice may be important in producing high completion rates; however, when the zero is averaged into a total body of work it does not accurately reflect a student's overall academic achievement.
- *Base final (report card) grades on a student's best performance rather than the average of many performances.* This is a difficult one to implement and often provides a dilemma for teachers. For instance, what does a teacher do when a student does average C work all semester but then obtains a perfect mark on the final assessment? McTighe and O'Conner (2007) have provided advice to help solve this dilemma. They believe that an effective grading system should provide students with a second chance and that it should allow for "new evidence to replace old evidence," particularly if the new evidence is a better representation of what the student actually knows and can do.
- *Remember the emotional aspect of grades and the importance grades have for many student and their parents.* Develop processes to help reduce anxiety around testing and grading.

A Final Thought and Look to the Future

By now, you understand that assessment and grading of student learning is no simple task and that it is likely that we will never develop a system that is completely noncon-troversial and just. Nonetheless, new approaches, such as standards-based practices and alternative and performance assessments, represent ways to work toward a more transparent and fairer system. Most important, beginning teachers need to heed the admonishment made at the beginning of this chapter: *Assessment and evaluation of stu-dent work is among the most important aspects of a teacher's job and carries heavy responsibili-ties. It is an integral feature for accomplishing student learning.* As teachers, we must not only do this job well, but also make sure that no harm comes to our students as a result of our assessment and grading practices.

*It is interesting to note that several decades ago many report cards had two marks: achievement and deportment.

Reflections **from the** *Classroom*

My A, B, C's

You have just met with the principal at the school where you have been hired for your first teaching position. You asked him about the school's grading and reporting policies. He said that teachers have considerable freedom. They are required to give A's, B's, C's, D's, and F's, and they must conform to the district's grading periods. Outside of these requirements, they can design their own system for how much weight to give to tests, quizzes, homework, participation, and the like. They can also decide whether to grade on a curve or base grades on particular standards. He told you that most students are very concerned about their grades and most already have plans to attend college. They and their parents are not afraid to complain if they believe a teacher has evaluated their work unfairly.

The principal encouraged you to talk to other teachers in the school, come up with your own approach for assessment and grading, and then discuss your plan with other teachers at your grade level or in your department. You have always believed that a teacher should have a grading system that is fair and acceptable to students. You also believe that a teacher's grading system should be one that will promote learning for all the students in a classroom.

Develop an assessment plan consistent with your teaching situation and your beliefs. Approach this situation from the perspective closest to the grade level or subject area you are preparing to teach. Address the following questions in your plan: What will be your overall approach? What weight will you give to tests, assignments, and projects? Will you give credit for participation? For effort? Will you hold all students to the same standards, or will you establish different standards for gifted students and those who have learning disabilities? How will you justify your system to your students? Their parents? Before you begin, consider how your assessment plan can become an important artifact in your professional portfolio. After you finish, compare your plan to the following ideas expressed by experienced teachers.

Vickie Williams

Arthur Slade Regional Catholic School, K through 8th Grades
Glen Burnie, MD

My assessment system involves evaluating authentic performances, student participation in class, special projects or products (10 percent of grade, respectively), quizzes (20 percent), and major tests (30 percent). I believe my assessment system is fair, well communicated to the students and parents, and addresses multiple intelligences. I do not feel the need to grade

on a curve; however, I do include one measure of growth, a reading and writing portfolio (20 percent), which is evaluated each quarter according to the progress the student has made. This provides a mechanism for those with learning disabilities, as well as gifted students, to experience success based on their own baseline achievement level rather than a mastery criterion. I have received favorable reactions to my growth portfolio from my students, as well as their parents.

I have found that the majority of students in my classes can be academically successful if I provide scoring rubrics, rating scales, and information about the quizzes and tests in advance. I make the criteria for academic success explicit and obtainable. Consistently, I make individual and aggregated assessment data available to both students and parents. I look for trends in my assessment data that might point to unfair tests, test items, or scoring criteria. If I discover items or criteria that are unfair or confusing, I change them accordingly. I do not attempt to "trick" the students or "catch them by surprise." Rather, I set reasonable expectations in advance and make adjustments when necessary to maintain an assessment system that promotes the learning success of all students.

Ellen Thomas-Covell

Timberlane Middle School, 8th Grade
Hopewell Valley School District, NJ

I teach an eighth-grade Introductory Physical Science class, which is mostly laboratory-based. Students are required to write up lab reports for each experiment, and I give periodic quizzes and chapter tests. When I first began teaching, I graded each assignment on a percentage basis. At the end of the marking period, I then calculated the weighted average—making lab reports 50 percent, quizzes 10 percent, and tests 30 percent. For the final 10 percent, I gave a grade for overall participation/preparedness/and homework completion. However, there were two problems with my system. First, grading the lab reports was difficult because some reports were very short and to the point, while others were more lengthy and in-depth. I found myself constantly reevaluating the overall rubric so that the longer labs were not being graded lower simply because there was more information to grade and more room for error. The second problem was that when I had special projects or any other assignments, I had to rethink the original weighting. Should I make something worth less than planned, or lump the special project in with one of the existing categories? Naturally, reassessing is part of teaching, whether you're looking at your methods, your content, your goals, or your grading. However, in this case I felt that I was unnecessarily burdening myself with the decision-making process for every new assignment collected.

I resolved this problem by going to a point system. It works very simply. Each assignment is worth a certain number of points, based on particular criteria: amount of data required, time allotted, and importance. For instance, labs are now worth from 20 points (for a one day, quick exploration) up to 100 points (for culminating, two-week activities requiring a detailed progress log, procedural flow chart, and in-depth conclusion). The "weighting" is therefore built into each assignment! Quizzes are typically 20 to 30 points, and tests are 60 to 80 points. Special projects and graded homework are also given appropriate point values. Extra credit points for

exceptional effort, marked improvement, and/or participation can be added easily to the "numerator." Penalties for missed assignments or incomplete homework can be subtracted. At any given time, students may add up their earned points and divide it by the total possible points to find their current average. I tell students that I only calculate averages for mid-term progress reports and report cards, so they need to keep a running record of their grades if they think they may want to know their average at any other time. I generated a "Marking Period Grade Sheet," which they may use for this purpose.

There are many grading plans that work. I think it is best to find a plan that works for you, but stay flexible and open-minded, and know that grading, as in all areas of teaching, is an ever-evolving skill!

Summary

Define assessment and evaluation, discuss why these functions are important, and provide definitions of key assessment concepts.

- Assessment and evaluation can be defined as functions performed by teachers to make wise decisions about their instruction and about their students. A fairly large portion of a teacher's time is consumed by assessment and evaluation processes.
- The consequences of testing and grading students are immense. They can determine the colleges students attend, the careers open to them, and the lifestyles they ultimately maintain.
- Evaluation specialists make key distinctions between formative and summative evaluation. Formative evaluation information is collected before or during instruction and is used to inform teachers about their students' prior knowledge and to make judgments about lesson effectiveness. Summative evaluation information is collected after instruction and is used to summarize how students have performed and to determine grades.
- Because the decisions made are so important, it is essential that the information used by teachers to make judgments be of high quality. Measurement specialists use three technical terms to describe the quality of assessment and evaluation information: reliability, validity, and fairness.
- Reliability refers to the internal consistency of a test, its ability to produce consistent scores over time for individuals or groups who take the test more than once, and its ability to produce the same results if two different forms of the test are used.

- Validity refers to the ability of a test or other device to measure what it claims to measure.
- Test fairness refers to the degree that it does not discriminate against a particular group of students because of their race, ethnicity, or gender.

Describe the knowledge base on assessment that speaks to the effects of assessment on student motivation and learning and on teacher bias.

- There is an extensive knowledge base about the technical aspects of assessment and evaluation.
- Studies show that external rewards, such as grades, can provide a strong incentive for students to perform work and can affect student learning.
- Studies also show that external rewards can sometimes have negative effects, particularly with tasks students find intrinsically interesting anyway.
- It has been known for a long time that teacher bias can influence the evaluation of students and their work.

Describe the nature of standardized tests and the teacher's role in standardized testing.

- Most states today have testing programs that measure student achievement in grades 3–8 and at the high school level. Information from statewide tests is often used to compare how well schools are doing. In some instances, scores on statewide tests determine a student's promotion to the next grade or graduation from high school. They also can be used to sanction schools that have too many nonachieving students.

- Standards-based education and frequent testing are believed by many to have positive effects on student learning. Some leading educators and teachers, however, believe that frequent testing may impede learning.
- Assessment programs include the use of norm- and criterion-referenced tests usually chosen and administered by school district specialists.
- Norm-referenced tests evaluate a particular student's performance by comparing it to the performance of some other well-defined group of students.
- Criterion-referenced tests measure student performance against some agreed-upon criterion.
- It is important that teachers understand the advantages and disadvantages of various types of standardized assessment procedures, be able to prepare students for standardized tests, and be able to communicate the advantages and disadvantages to students and their parents.

Describe the key features of a teacher's classroom assessment program and the three major purposes and uses of assessment information.

- The teacher's classroom assessment program has three purposes: assessment for student learning, assessment as student learning, and assessment of student learning.
- Assessment for student learning includes collecting information to diagnose prior knowledge, monitor student learning, and provide corrective feedback.
- Assessment as student learning aims at helping students assess their own learning and that of their peers.
- Assessment of student learning consists of collecting information that can be used to make accurate judgments about student achievement and for assigning grades, determining placements, and facilitating admission to post-secondary education.
- Formal tests to diagnose students' prior knowledge are more fully developed in fields such as mathematics and language arts. Asking questions, interviewing, and listening to students' responses as well as using portfolios are informal means of ascertaining what students know about a subject.

Describe the importance of formative assessment and the most effective ways of providing students with feedback

- Although sometimes more attention is paid to summative assessment as compared to formative assessment, a growing body of evidence suggests that the latter actually has much greater influence on what students learn.

- Effective feedback has several characteristics. Among the most important are that it focuses on the learning task, is timely and ongoing, is clear and specific, is positive and nonjudgmental, and is consistent and trustworthy.

Describe ways of involving students in their own and peer assessment as means for them to monitor their own learning.

- Involving students and peers in the assessment of their learning is an important part of a teacher's assessment system.
- "Learning logs" and "KWL" are examples of tools that can be used for self-assessment.
- "Preflight Checklist" and "Two Stars and a Wish" are tools used by teachers to facilitate peer assessment.

Describe the general principles of designing and implementing traditional assessments and teacher-made tests.

- A variety of guidelines exist for teachers to follow as they construct tests to measure student learning and make judgments and assign grades for student work.
- General principles for test construction consist of making test items in alignment with instructional objectives; covering all learning tasks; making tests valid, reliable, and fair; interpreting test results with care; and using the appropriate test items.
- A test blueprint is a device to help teachers determine how much space to allocate to various topics covered and to measure various levels of student cognitive processes.
- Teacher-made tests can consist of true-false, matching, fill-in-the-blank, multiple-choice, and essay items. Each type has its own advantages and disadvantages.
- Teacher bias in judging student work from essay questions is an important issue. To reduce bias, teachers should make their expectations for essay answers clear to students, write sample answers ahead of time, and use techniques to reduce expectancy effects.
- When giving tests, effective teachers find ways to reduce students' test anxiety, organize their learning environments to be conducive to test taking, make instructions clear, and avoid undue competition.

Describe, design, and score performance and authentic assessments.

- Currently, there appears to be a nationwide call for more accountability by schools and better and fairer ways to test and evaluate students.

- Performance and authentic assessments, as well as the use of portfolios, are likely to partially replace the more traditional paper-and-pencil tests in the near future.
- Performance and authentic assessments ask students to demonstrate that they can perform particular real-life tasks, such as writing an essay, doing an experiment, or playing a song.
- Developing performance and authentic assessment devices is a difficult and complex task, as is making sure these newer forms of assessment are valid, reliable, and fair.

Describe why grading is important and provide guidelines for making grading more effective and fairer.

- Testing students' progress and determining grades is an important aspect of teachers' work, and society expects it to be done well.

- Grading on a curve is when teachers determine a particular student's grade based on comparing one student's work with that of other students. Grading to criterion is when teachers determine students' grades based on the proportion of predetermined criterion or goals they have mastered.
- Each grading approach has its advantages and its shortcomings.

Describe how newer approaches may represent ways to work toward more transparent and fairer assessment practices in the years ahead.

- Remember the importance of assessment and evaluation and take responsibility for doing it well.

Key Terms

Interactive and Applied Learning

🌐 Study and Explore

- Access your Study Guide, which includes practice quizzes, from the Online Learning Center.

🌐 Observe and Practice

- Listen to audio clips on the Online Learning Center of Sandy Frederick (elementary reading specialist) and Dennis Holt (high school American history and

economics) talking about assessment in the *Teachers on Teaching* area.

Complete the following **Practice Exercises** that accompany Chapter 6:
- Practice Exercise 6.1: Creating a Testing and Assessment Blueprint
- Practice Exercise 6.2: Selected Response versus Performance Assessment
- Practice Exercise 6.3: Creating Scoring Rubrics
- Practice Exercise 6.4: Making Assessment Decisions

Portfolio and Field Experience Activities

Expand your understanding of the content and processes of this chapter through the following field experiences and portfolio activities. Support materials to complete the activities are in the *Portfolio and Field Experience Activities* area on the Online Learning Center.

1. Complete the **Reflections from the Classroom** exercise at the end of this chapter. The recommended assessment plan will provide evidence of your understanding and proficiency in assessment and evaluation. (**InTASC Standard 6: Assessment**)

2. **Activity 6.1: Assessing My Assessment and Evaluation Skills.** Check your level of understanding and skill in regard to assessment and evaluation. (**InTASC Standard 6: Assessment**)

3. **Activity 6.2: Interviewing Teachers about Their Evaluation and Grading Procedures.** Gain practical knowledge about how experienced teachers approach testing and grading in their classrooms. (**InTASC Standard 6: Assessment**)

4. **Activity 6.3: Analyzing Teacher-Made Tests.** Learn about test construction by analyzing a test designed by an experienced teacher. (**InTASC Standard 6: Assessment**)

5. **Activity 6.4: Portfolio: Demonstrating My Skill for Performance Assessment.** Design an artifact for your portfolio that will serve as a way to communicate your ability to develop and use various kinds of assessment devices. (**InTASC Standard 6: Assessment**)

Books for the Professional

Brookhart, S. (2008). *How to give effective feedback to your students.* Alexandria, VA: Association for Supervision and Curriculum Development.

Brookhart, S. (2013). *How to create and use rubrics for formative assessment and grading.* Alexandria, VA: Association for Supervision and Curriculum Development.

Fisher, D., & Frey, N. (2007). *Checking for understanding: Formative assessment techniques for your classroom.* Alexandria, VA: Association for Supervision and Curriculum Development.

Popham, W. J. (2008). *Transformative assessment.* Alexandria, VA: Association for Supervision and Curriculum Development.

Russell, M., & Airasian, P. (2011). *Classroom assessment: Concepts and applications.* (7th ed.). New York: McGraw-Hill.

Stiggins, R., & Chappuis, J. (2012). *An introduction to student-involved assessment for learning* (6th ed.). Boston: Pearson.

Tovani, C. (2011). *So what do they really know? Assessment that informs teaching and learning.* Portland, ME: Stenhouse.

Wiliam, D. (2011). *Embedded formative assessment.* Bloomington, IN: Solution Tree.

Wormeli, R. (2006). *Fair isn't always equal: Assessing and grading in the differentiated classroom.* Portland, ME: Stenhouse.

PART 3 Overview of More Teacher-Centered Transmission Approaches to Teaching

Parts 3 and 4 of *Learning to Teach* focus directly on what most people think of as teaching—the actual face-to-face interaction between teachers and their students. The first six chapters in Parts 3 and 4 will describe one of the basic instructional approaches: (1) presenting and explaining, (2) direct instruction, (3) concept and inquiry-based teaching, (4) cooperative learning, (5) problem-based learning, and (6) classroom discussion. Presenting and explaining and direct instruction will be described in Part 3; the other four in Part 4. Chapter 13 describes how to connect the different approaches and how to differentiate instruction for students with various interests and abilities.

As you study these approaches to teaching, you will learn that each has been designed to achieve certain learning outcomes at the expense of others; and as a result, each approach has advantages and disadvantages. No one approach is necessarily better than another. Appropriate use of each depends on the nature of the students in a teacher's classroom and the type of learning outcomes the teacher wants to achieve. All require adaptation to meet the needs of particular setting and conditions.

The various approaches described in Parts 3 and 4 of *Learning to Teach* could have been labeled with other terms, such as *teaching strategies, teaching methods,* or *teaching models.* Conceptually, all of these terms share similar characteristics. They imply something larger than a particular teaching technique or tactic, and they rest on coherent theoretical perspectives about how students learn. Each approach also requires specified teacher and student behaviors built into the syntax or overall flow of a lesson. Each also requires a certain type of learning environment for motivating and managing students. There is nothing magical about the classification system used here. It simply provides us with a language for communicating about various kinds of teaching activities, when they should occur, and why.

The theoretical perspectives for the six approaches described in Parts 3 and 4 rest on theories of human development and how people learn. You read in Chapter 1 how teachers develop or progress systematically through stages. They begin with novice-like and survival perspectives and later develop more complex views characterized by expertise and concern about student learning. This idea of teacher development is actually a subset of a larger perspective about human development in general, defined as changes that take place over time in the physical, social, emotional, and cognitive aspects of our lives.

Some aspects of development are a result of natural maturation. Reaching puberty, losing "baby fat," and growing taller are examples of natural physical developments. How we relate to our peers or use our emotions, however, are examples of social development, which occurs mainly due to interactions with our environment. Cognitive development, our primary concern in regard to student learning, results from both maturation and environmental factors. In several chapters in Parts 3 and 4, you will find more detailed explanations of human development and its importance to teaching and learning.

The instructional approaches described in *Learning to Teach* stem primarily from four theories of learning, all of which strive to explain how changes in cognitive processes and knowledge and in social/emotional and physical skills are the result of learning. The theories include behaviorism, social cognitive theory, cognitive and information processing theories, and sociocultural and constructivist theories. Each is described briefly below as an introduction to more detailed information that will be provided later:

> *Behaviorism.* Focuses on observable behaviors and how learning is the consequence of external events, such as reinforcement, conditioning, rewards, and punishments.
> *Social cognitive theory.* Posits that most human learning is the result of observing others and is influenced by the expectations and beliefs of the learner.
> *Cognitive and information processing theories.* Concerned with how the mind works and how the memory system affects knowledge acquisition, transfer, and retention for later retrieval.
> *Sociocultural and constructivist theories.* Hold that knowledge, rather than being fixed, is flexible and is constructed by learners as a result of interaction with the environment They are also concerned with social and cultural aspects of learning.

The accompanying table compares the four theories of learning, their implications for teaching, and shows the chapters where each will be considered.

The descriptions of the approaches to teaching in the chapters that follow may appear to suggest that there is only one correct way to use a particular approach. In some respects, this is true. If teachers deviate too far from the syntax or environmental demands, they are not using the approach correctly. However, once teachers have mastered a particular approach, they often adapt it to their own particular teaching style and to the particular group of students with whom they are working. As with most other aspects of teaching, the particular approaches are guides for thinking and talking about teaching. They should not be viewed as strict recipes to follow in every instance.

The two approaches described in Part 3 include presentation and direct instruction. The theoretical foundations for both of these approaches rest mainly on behavioral, information processing, and social cognitive theories of learning. They are more or less teacher-centered and are similar in several ways. They aim at helping students accomplish prespecified goals for knowledge and skill acquisition. Use of presentation and direct instruction requires a fairly structured learning environment. However,

Theories of Learning and Implications for Approaches to Teaching

Learning Theories	Major Theorists	Main Idea and Sample Concepts	Primary Implications for Teaching	Where Considered
Behaviorism	Skinner	Knowledge is fixed, and learning is affected mainly by external events.	Teaching is mainly transmission. Have clear learning outcomes and create precise, structured learning environments.	**Chapters 8 and 9:** Practice aspects of direct instruction and direct concept teaching.
Social Cognitive Theory	Bandura	Learning results from observation and is influenced by environment, beliefs, and expectations.	Teaching is modeling procedural knowledge. Present and demonstrate desired behaviors precisely and accurately and provide for practice.	**Chapter 8:** Demonstration and practice aspects of direct instruction.
Cognitive and Information Processing Theories	Bruner, Gagne, Anderson, neuroscientists	Knowledge is mainly fixed. Learning consists of acquisitions and retention of accurate information through the use of cognitive and mental processes.	Teaching is mainly transmission. Help students acquire and retain accurate declarative knowledge and strive to develop their cognitive processes.	**Chapters 7 and 9:** Guidelines for presenting and acquiring information and foundation for inquiry processes.
Sociocultural and Constructivist Theories	Dewey, Piaget, Vygotsky	Knowledge is flexible. Cognitive and social learning consist of active construction of knowledge through interactions with others.	Teachers facilitate and guide student interaction and help them construct their own understanding and ideas.	**Chapters 9–12:** Social interaction aspects of inquiry-based teaching, cooperative learning, problem-based instruction, and discussion.

this structured environment does not need to be unfriendly or authoritarian. The two approaches also differ. Presentation teaching, for example, is more suited for helping students acquire declarative knowledge, whereas direct instruction is best for acquiring procedural knowledge or skills. As with most attempts to classify and form categories, often there are instances when something fits into more than one category.

There is a substantial knowledge base for the interactive aspects of teaching as well as wisdom that has been accumulated by experienced teachers over the years. Part of the excitement and challenge in learning to teach is in figuring out the complexities of teaching, which the organizational pattern of a book can never portray with complete accuracy.

CHAPTER 7
Presenting and Explaining

Reflecting on Presenting and Explaining

Think of all the lectures you have heard in your lifetime or the many instances when a teacher or coach tried to explain something to you. You can conjure up some that were stimulating, leaving you eager to learn more about the topic; others may have been boring, causing you to struggle to stay awake; still others may have been humorous and entertaining, but you didn't learn very much. You may remember some explanations that were very concise and clear, whereas others were ambiguous and confusing.

Before reading this chapter, take a few minutes to think about and do the following:

- Make a list of the essential characteristics of the best lectures you have ever heard.
- Make a similar list of the characteristics of the worst lectures you have ever heard.
- Make a third list of the characteristics of clear and unclear explanations.

Now, study your lists and consider what you think your teachers did to develop the best lectures or explanations and what they did or didn't do that produced poor lectures and unclear explanations. How did different types of lectures and explanations influence what you learned? Did you learn anything from the bad lecture or the unclear explanations? Why? Why not?

 Go to the Online Learning Center at www.mhhe.com/arends10e to respond to these questions.

Presentations (lectures) and explanations by teachers comprise one-sixth to one-fourth of all classroom time. The amount of time devoted to presenting and explaining new knowledge increases at the higher grade levels of elementary school, in middle schools, and in high schools (Dunkin & Biddle, 1974; Rosenshine & Stevens, 1986; Stronge, 2002). Some educators have argued that teachers devote too much time to talking, and over the years considerable effort has gone into creating approaches to teaching aimed at decreasing the amount of teacher talk and making instruction more student-centered. Nonetheless, presentation of information remains a popular model of teaching, and the amount of time devoted to it has remained relatively stable over time (Cuban, 1993, 2003; Lobato, Clarke, & Burns, 2005).

Despite criticism, presentation or lecture maintains its popularity among teachers.

The popularity of presenting and explaining is not surprising, because the most widely held objectives for education at the present time are those associated with the acquisition and retention of information. Curricula in schools are structured around bodies of knowledge organized as science, mathematics, English, and the social sciences. Consequently, curriculum standards, textbooks, and tests are similarly organized. Further, many exams that students are required to take test primarily knowledge acquisition. Experienced teachers know that exposition is an effective way of helping students acquire the array of information society believes it is important for them to know.

The appropriate use of the presentation teaching varies, depending on a teacher's objective and the particular students in the class.

The purpose of this chapter is to introduce **presentation teaching** and to describe how to use it effectively. We cannot judge the ideal amount of time a teacher should devote to presenting and explaining. Instead, these activities are described as valuable teaching approaches that can be used in all subject areas and at all grade levels. The appropriate use of presentation teaching is situational; that is, its use depends on the objective the teacher is striving to achieve and the students in a particular class.

Fortunately, the knowledge base on teacher presentations and explanations is fairly well developed. Beginning teachers can learn this approach quite easily. As you read this chapter, you will find much that is familiar. You already know some of the material from speech classes in high school or college. You know some of the difficulties of presenting from informal talks or speeches you have made. Although the goals of public speaking and classroom presentations are quite different, many of the basic communication skills are the same.

We first provide a general overview of presentation teaching using an analytical scheme that consists of three elements: (1) the type of learner outcomes it produces, (2) its syntax or overall flow of instructional activities, and (3) its learning environment. Following the overview, we take a brief look at the theoretical and empirical support for presentation teaching and provide rather detailed descriptions about how to plan and conduct presentation lessons.

Overview of Presentation Teaching and Explanations

Figure 7.1 *Presentation Teaching Aims at Accomplishing Three Learner Outcomes*

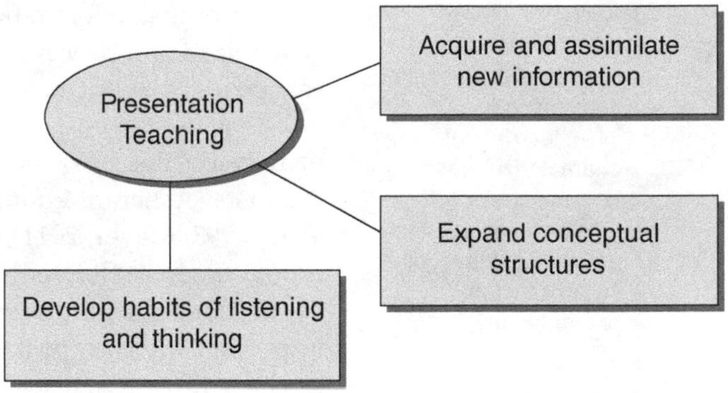

The particular view about presentation teaching highlighted here includes not only more formal presentation commonly referred to as *lectures*, but also the more informal *explanations* used by teachers in a variety of instructional settings, such as stopping during group discussion to explain a difficult concept or bending down to a student during seatwork to explain an idea that seems to be confusing.

The learner outcomes of presentation teaching shown in Figure 7.1 are rather clear and straightforward: namely, to help students acquire, organize, and retain new knowledge; expand conceptual structures; and develop important habits of listening and thinking. You will discover that although presentation teaching is effective for some purposes, it is not very effective for others. For instance, it does not do a very good job of helping students acquire particular skills, nor does it encourage higher-level thinking. Other approaches described in subsequent chapters are better suited to achieve these types of learner outcomes.

Presentation is mainly teacher-centered and consists of four major phases. The flow proceeds (1) from the teacher's initial attempt to clarify the aims of the lesson and to get students' attention through (2) presentation of an advance organizer and (3) presentation of the new factual and conceptual knowledge to (4) interactions aimed at checking student understanding of the new information and extending and strengthening their thinking skills. When using presentation teaching, teachers strive to structure the learning environment tightly. Except in the final phase, the teacher is an active presenter and expects students to be active listeners. Presentation teaching requires a physical learning environment that is conducive to presenting and listening, including appropriate facilities for use of multimedia technology. More detail about the syntax of presentation teaching will be provided later in the chapter in the section Planning and Conducting Presentation Lessons.

> **Presentation teaching requires a highly structured environment characterized by a teacher who is an active presenter and students who are active listeners and responders.**

Theoretical and Empirical Support

Several theoretical frameworks come together to provide the theoretical and empirical support for presentation teaching. These include (1) cognitive views of learning, including recent knowledge contributed by the neurosciences about how people learn; (2) perspectives about how the human memory system works and how knowledge is organized and represented; and (3) particular practices identified by studies of experienced teachers about the most effective ways of conducting presentations and providing explanations. It is important to understand these ideas because they provide the base upon which teachers choose, organize, and present new knowledge to their students. These frameworks also support several features of direct instruction and concept teaching presented in Chapters 8 and 9, respectively.

Check, Extend, Explore

Check

- What are the four phases of a presentation lesson?
- What learner outcomes characterize presentation lessons?
- What type of learning environment is required for an effective presentation?

Extend

- Many people believe that teachers spend too much time talking to students. Do you agree or disagree with this opinion? Go to the "Extend Question Poll" on the Online Learning Center to respond.

Explore

- Go to the Online Learning Center at www.mhhe.com/ arends10e and listen to Patricia Merkel in the *Teachers on Teaching* area talk about her approach to presentation teaching.

Factual knowledge is knowing about the basic elements of a topic.

Procedural knowledge is knowing how to do something.

Conditional knowledge is knowing about when to use or apply particular declarative or procedural knowledge.

Conceptual knowledge is knowing about the relationships among elements.

Cognitive Views of Learning

The rapidly expanding fields of **cognitive psychology** and neuroscience have provided important insights into how our minds work, how people learn, and how information is acquired and processed in the human memory system. These fields have expanded earlier ideas about learning in significant ways and have had a powerful influence on the way teaching and learning is viewed today. The discussion that follows relies heavily on the work of several cognitive psychologists and information processing theorists (Ashcraft & Radvansky, 2009; Bransford, Brown, & Cocking, 2000; E. Gagné et al., 1993; Mayer, 2011), as well as those in the field of cognitive neuroscience (Willis, 2006; Wilson & Conyers, 2013; Zull, 2002) who have organized the ideas and research in the field that apply directly to teaching. The discussion that follows emphasizes important ideas from the cognitive sciences that are most relevant to teaching, particularly those associated with presenting and explaining new knowledge to students. The discussion begins with descriptions of distinctions made among different types of knowledge and then proceeds to explanations about how knowledge is organized and how the human memory and information processing system works.

Types of Knowledge. Traditionally, learning theorists have distinguished between two major types of knowledge: *declarative knowledge* and *procedural knowledge* (E. Gagné et al., 1993; R. Gagné, 1977; Ryle, 1949). **Declarative knowledge** is knowledge *about something* or knowledge that something is the case. **Procedural knowledge** is knowledge about *how to do something.* More recently a third category has been added, labeled **conditional knowledge.** This type of knowledge is knowledge about *when to apply our declarative or procedural knowledge.* Also, the category of declarative knowledge has been expanded by the scholars who revised *Bloom's Taxonomy of Educational Objectives* (Anderson et al., 2001). The revised scheme (described in some detail in Chapter 3) includes two kinds of declarative knowledge: factual knowledge and conceptual knowledge. **Factual knowledge** is knowing about the basic elements of a topic, whereas **conceptual knowledge** is knowing about the interrelationships among the basic elements.

An example of factual declarative knowledge is knowing that there are three branches of government defined by the Constitution, that the legislative branch has two chambers (the House and the Senate), and that representatives to the House are elected to two-year terms whereas senators are elected to six-year terms. Conceptual knowledge is understanding the relationship among the three branches, both as defined by the Constitution and as a consequence of tradition. Procedural knowledge about this same topic is knowing how to go to the polling place to vote on election day, how to write a letter to a senator, or if one is a senator, how to guide a bill through the Senate until it becomes a law. Conditional knowledge is knowing which of many political actions might be most effective in getting a desired piece of legislation passed, as well as one's own opinions and, perhaps, lack of knowledge on this whole topic. Table 7.1 summarizes the types of knowledge and provides examples of each.

In addition, as you read in Chapter 3, knowledge can be classified according to the cognitive processes required to use the knowledge in particular ways. At the lowest level is straightforward recall of factual knowledge that one acquires and may or may not use. Recalling the rules of poetry written in iambic pentameter is an example of recalling factual knowledge. In contrast, the higher levels of cognitive processing generally involve using knowledge in some way, such as critiquing one of Robert Browning's poems or comparing and contrasting it with the work of Keats. Often, procedural knowledge

Table 7.1 *Kinds of Knowledge and Examples of Each*

Kind of Knowledge	Definition	Examples
Declarative	Knowing about something	
Factual	Knowing basic elements about a topic	Rules of a game; definition of triangle; definitions of the economic terms *supply* and *demand*
Conceptual	Knowing the relationship among basic elements	Relationship between supply and demand in the law of supply and demand
Procedural	Knowing how to do something	Playing basketball; using word processing; writing a letter; voting
Conditional	Knowing when to use particular declarative or procedural knowledge	Knowing when to skim a passage; when to pass instead of run; when to invest based on supply and demand

requires the previous acquisition of factual or conceptual knowledge—in this case, basic concepts of poetry. Teachers want their students to possess all four kinds of knowledge. They want them to acquire large bodies of basic factual knowledge; they also want them to acquire important conceptual, procedural, and conditional knowledge so they can take action and do things effectively.

Finally, cognitive psychologists (Brown, 1987; Flavel, 1985; E. Gagné et al., 1993; Pressley et al., 2003) describe what is referred to as a special dimension of knowledge, **metacognitive knowledge.** This dimension is "knowing about knowing" or one's knowledge about cognition in general as well as awareness of one's cognitive processes. As we will describe later, possession of metacognitive knowledge is an important factor in how well students can regulate and monitor their own learning.

Different types of knowledge are acquired in different ways. Presentation teaching is most useful in helping students acquire straightforward, factual knowledge as well as conceptual knowledge. Direct instruction described in Chapter 8, in contrast, has been specifically designed to promote student learning of procedural and some types of conceptual and metacognitive knowledge.

Memory and Information Processing. Ashcraft and Radvansky (2009) have defined memory as the mental processes associated with "acquiring and retaining information for later retrieval and the mental storage system that enables these processes" (p. 9), and they and others refer to this as the **information processing** model. This model conceives of memory as consisting of three components: *sensory memory, short-term working memory, and long-term memory.* Figure 7.2 illustrates these three types of memory. The arrows in the figure are intended to illustrate that the process is not linear or unidirectional but instead multidirectional, and where each component can affect the others. Understanding this model is important because it explains what is at work when teachers present new knowledge to their students.

Figure 7.2 *Information Processing Model*

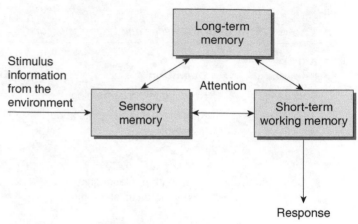

Source: Adapted from Ashcraft and Radvansky (2010), p. 46.

Short-term working memory is the place in the mind where conscious mental work is done.

Sensory memory is the place in the mind where new information coming from the senses is initially processed.

New knowledge enters the brain and memory system as a result of picking up stimuli from the environment through one of the senses: sight, hearing, touch, smell, feel. It is first noted in **sensory memory.** Sensory memory does the initial processing of stimuli and although sensory memory can take in rather large quantities of information it lasts there for only a short time before it is either forgotten or moved to short-term working memory. **Short-term working memory,** sometimes referred to as the "workbench" of the memory system, is the place where conscious mental work is done. For example, if you are solving the problem 26 × 32 mentally, you hold the intermediate products 52 and 78 in short-term working memory and add them together there. Both sensory and working memory can process only small amounts of material at any one time. This is an important idea that leads to advice provided later in the chapter that presenters need to be very selective in regard to how much new material they present to students.

Long-term memory is the place in the mind where information is stored, ready for retrieval when needed.

Information in short-term working memory may soon be forgotten unless stored more deeply in **long-term memory.** Long-term working memory can be likened to a computer. Information must first be coded before it can be stored and, although stored for perhaps a lifetime, cannot be retrieved unless first given appropriate cues. Information or ideas stored in long-term memory must also be retrieved to working memory before they can be used.

Figure 7.3 provides an example showing how short-term working and long-term memory interact in instructional settings.

Knowledge Organization and Representation. Today, it is generally accepted that knowledge is stored, organized, and represented in long-term memory as either visual images or verbal units. This concept highlights the importance of describing ideas not only in words but also visually, a topic to which we will return later. Also, individuals are conscious of some things stored in long-term memory (explicit memory) and remain unconscious of others (implicit memory).

An individual's schema reflects the way information has been organized and stored in memory in networks.

Prior knowledge refers to the information an individual has prior to instruction.

Cognitive psychologists use the label **schema** to define the way people organize information about particular subjects and how this organization influences their processing of new information and ideas. Individuals' schema differ in important ways, and schemata (pl.) held about various topics prepare the learner to process new information and to see relationships. The more complete a person's **prior knowledge** and schema are for a particular topic, the easier it becomes to process new information and to see more abstract relationships. Although cognitive psychologists do not always agree about the exact way knowledge is represented in the memory system, they do

Figure 7.3 *An Example of Short-Term Working and Long-Term Memory*

Suppose that a second-grade teacher wants Joe to learn the fact that the capital of Texas is Austin. The teacher asks Joe, "What is the capital of Texas?" and Joe says, "I don't know." At the same time Joe may set up an expectancy that he is about to learn the capital of Texas, which will cause him to pay attention. The teacher then says, "The capital of Texas is Austin." Joe's ears receive this message along with other sounds such as the other pupils' speech and traffic outside the school.

All of the sounds that Joe hears are translated into electrochemical impulses and sent to the sensory register. The pattern that the capital of Texas is Austin is selected for entry into short-term working memory, but other sound patterns are not entered.

Joe may then code the fact that the capital of Texas is Austin by associating it with other facts that he already knows about Austin (e.g., that it is a big city and that he once visited it). This coding process causes the new fact to be entered into long-term memory. If Joe has already developed special memory strategies (which is somewhat unlikely for a second grader), his executive control process would direct the coding process to use these special strategies.

The next day Joe's teacher might ask him, "What is the capital of Texas?" This question would be received and selected for entry into short-term working memory. There it would provide cues for retrieving the answer from long-term memory. A copy of the answer would be used by the response generator to organize the speech acts that produce the sounds, "Austin is the capital of Texas." At this point Joe's expectancy that he would learn the capital of Texas has been confirmed.

Source: After E. Gagné et al. (1993), p. 78.

agree that it is organized in knowledge networks and that prior knowledge definitely filters new information and thereby determines how well new information presented by a teacher will be integrated and retained by a learner (Macbeth, 2000).

Contributions from the Neurosciences. During the past three decades a rather extensive literature has emerged from the neurosciences about the human mind and how learning occurs. Some of this research has been applied to education for the purpose of gaining insight and its implication for teaching. It is beyond the scope of *Learning to Teach* to provide a full discussion about how the brain is studied and the results that have accrued from brain research. Instead, a very brief summary is provided here. Hopefully, this is a topic of which you already have some knowledge from your study of biology and/or courses in educational psychology.

- *Neurons and synapses.* The brain is made up of nerve cells called neurons, perhaps as many as 100 billion. These minuscule cells receive information from our sensory organs as well as other neurons through neurotransmitters and across synapses. Learning results in physical changes in the neurons, their networks, and synapse production. *Rich learning environments and active learner involvement help spur these changes.*
- *Brain regions and functions.* Different regions of the brain perform different functions; for instance, problem solving and planning occur mainly in the frontal lobe, whereas visual processing occurs in the occipital lobe. Different parts of the brain are ready to learn at different times, thus *requiring developmentally appropriate learning activities* (Ashcraft & Radvansky, 2009; Bransford et al., 2000).
- *Brain growth.* Every time a learner participates in a learning activity neurons are activated and the physical structure of the brain is altered. Learning causes brain

growth and alters the structure of the brain. Implications for teaching according to Willis (2006) and Mayer (2011) are (1) *to enrich all lessons with multisensory input to help connect to various parts of the brain* (for example, use both words and visuals in presentations) and (2) to create and *maintain rich learning environments.*

- *Brain filtering.* The brain is very effective in filtering information. It decides what to attend to and what to ignore, which leads to the importance of *gaining students' attention, using cues and advance organizers, and attending to teachable moments.*
- *Prior knowledge.* As described previously, knowledge is stored in the brain in long-term memory and enters the brain through the senses. New knowledge that can be connected to prior knowledge and that has personal meaning moves more efficiently into working and long-term memory. Implications for teaching are clear. Lessons and presentations need to *make connections to what students already know and must help students personalize the new materials.*

Teaching implications about presenting or explaining new knowledge growing out of ideas from cognitive psychology and the neurosciences are important for teachers and are summarized in Table 7.2.

Table 7.2 *Key Ideas from Cognitive Psychology and the Neurosciences and Their Implications for Presentation Teaching*

Key Idea	Implications for Presentation Teaching
The type of knowledge to be conveyed in a lesson determines which teaching approach should be used.	Presentation and explanation work best for teaching declarative knowledge; direct instruction works best for teaching procedural knowledge.
New knowledge enters into short-term working memory through the senses (sensory memory). Sensory and short-term working memory have only limited capacity and can process only small amounts of new information at one time.	Show restraint in the amount of new knowledge presented to students at any one time. Teach in small chunks.
The brain filters information as it decides what to pay attention to and what to ignore.	Gain student attention so new knowledge can be initially processed into sensory memory.
New knowledge is transferred to long-term memory where it is organized and made ready for later retrieval.	Provide "assists" to help transfer new information from short-term working memory to long-term memory.
Knowledge is organized and structured around basic propositions and unifying ideas. Students' abilities to learn new ideas depend on their prior knowledge and existing cognitive structures that help or hinder learning.	Provide students with advance organizers and cues that will activate prior knowledge from long-term memory and connect it to new knowledge being presented.
Brain growth is enhanced when stimulated by multiple modalities and rich learning environments.	Use multiple modalities in presentations to stimulate multiple senses. Create and maintain rich learning presentation platforms and environments.

Empirical Support

The knowledge base on presenting and explaining information to learners has been developed by researchers working in several different fields, especially in the cognitive and neurosciences, as described in the previous section. Other aspects of the knowledge base come from the study of teaching and have focused on such topics as set induction, use of prior knowledge, and advance organizers. Still other work has studied teacher clarity and enthusiasm and how these attributes of effective presentations affect student learning. Because it is impossible to provide full coverage of this extensive research base, only selected works have been highlighted in this section.

Prior Knowledge, Establishing Set, and Providing Cues. Research has been conducted during the past half century on the influence of prior knowledge for learning to read, learning to use new information, and learning to write. In general, this research points toward the importance of prior knowledge for learning new information and new skills.

> Establishing set is an important procedure teachers use at the beginning of a lesson for getting students ready to learn.

One important teaching procedure for helping students use their prior knowledge is *induction,* or **establishing set,** as it will be called here. Establishing set is a technique used by teachers at the beginning of a presentation to prepare students to learn and to establish a communicative link between the learners' prior knowledge and the information about to be presented. Several informative studies have been conducted on this topic. One of the most interesting was conducted in Australia by R. F. Schuck in the early 1980s. In a rather sophisticated experimental study, Schuck (1981) randomly assigned 120 ninth-grade biology students to two groups. Teachers for the experimental group were given four hours of training on techniques for establishing set. When the experimental students' achievement was compared to that of the control students, Schuck found that the use of establishing set had a clear impact on student achievement. This impact existed not only immediately following instruction but also when students were tested twenty-four to twenty-six weeks later.

As you will see later, establishing set is not the same as an advance organizer, although both serve the similar purpose of using students' prior knowledge. By establishing set, teachers help students retrieve appropriate information and intellectual skills from long-term memory and get it ready for use as new information and skills are introduced. More information about and examples of establishing set are provided later.

Teachers also help students activate prior knowledge by providing cues. Cues provide hints about what the students are about to experience or what they are expected to learn. Sometimes teachers cue students by telling them what they are about to see or hear. At other times, teachers cue by asking questions that evoke students' prior knowledge. There is a substantial research base about the effects of cuing spanning a twenty-year period (Dean, Hubbel, Pitler, & Stone, 2012; Guzzetti, Snyder, & Glass, 1993; Marzano, 2007; Ross, 1988). More information about establishing set and using cues will be provided in the next section.

The Research Summary for this chapter addresses the problem of how teachers can help student acquire and retain new knowledge presented in a lesson.

Making Learning Meaningful and Using Advance Organizers. David Ausubel (1963), an American educational psychologist, did some interesting and groundbreaking work in the 1960s. He was one of the first to emphasize the importance of prior knowledge. Ausubel believed that **cognitive structures** determined a learner's ability to deal with new ideas and relationships and that *meaning* can emerge from new materials only if they are connected to prior knowledge. Ausubel (1961) conducted an experiment with two groups of students who were assigned a "learning passage." One group was

> Teachers use advance organizers to help make information more meaningful to students by relating prior knowledge to the new lesson.

Research Summary

Enhance Your Presentations with Interactive Strategies

Bulgren, J., Marquis, J., Lenz, B., & Deshler, D. (2011). The effectiveness of a Question-Exploration Routine for enhancing the content learning of secondary students. *Journal of Educational Psychology, 130(3), 578–593.*

A common problem faced by teachers is how to help students retain new knowledge gained in presentations and to enhance their abilities to think about and consider complex questions about the information.

Problem and Purpose: The researchers of this study experimented with a particular instructional technique called "Question-Exploration Routine" (QER) that was designed to accompany teacher presentations to see if its use would enhance students' ability to think about and answer complex questions.

Sample and Setting: The research was conducted in two middle schools in a midwestern suburban school district. A total of 116 students participated it the study. Ninety-six of the students were enrolled in seven seventh-grade science classrooms in one school; twenty students were enrolled in two seventh-grade social studies classroom in another school in the same district. Using achievement data from previous standardized tests, researchers determined that the students from all classes had academic skills that were relatively the same.

Procedures: The researchers used what they called a counterbalanced design. The seven science classrooms were randomly assigned to one of two groups (three classes in one group; four in the other group). Students in the two social studies classrooms were also randomly assigned: one class in one group, one class in the other group.

The Intervention: Classes of students were assigned to two groups; each group received a different type of instruction on two different topics:

- *Presentation topics:* Two topics were the focus of the presentations: "Chemical Weapons" and "Biological Weapons." The same instructor taught both topics to all classes, science and social studies.
- *Group 1:* Students in group 1 received instruction using what was labeled regular *lecture-discussion* format on the

two topics. Each topic was presented in a twenty-five minute scripted lesson within the school's fifty-minute period. Overhead transparencies were used, and students were asked to take notes.

- *Group 2:* Students in group 2 received the same instruction taught by the same instructor but in a more interactive format. Information presented to this group used what the researchers labeled the *QER format.* Instruction in this format consisted of three phases:

1. A "cue" phase where teachers (a) presented an advance organizer at the beginning of the lesson, (b) emphasized to students the importance of the information, and (c) provided students with a graphic organizer called "Question-Exploration Guide" on which to take notes.
2. A "do" phase where information was presented to students along with the development of and analysis of critical questions to promote transfer and generalization of knowledge.
3. A review phase where teacher and students reviewed the information covered and the processes used to answer critical questions.

Measurement of Student Achievement: A variety of test items were constructed to test student understanding of the information presented for the two topics. Questions were constructed in four formats: matching, multiple choice, main ideas multiple choice, and main ideas short answer.

Pointers for Reading Research: Explanations about the meaning and use of mean scores and standard deviation were provided in previous research summaries.

Results: Mean scores and standard deviations for each subtest and overall are displayed in Table 7.3.

As can be observed, students who experienced the presentation using advance organizers, graphic organizers for note taking, and the QER earned significantly higher scores on all question types and overall than did students who were instructed using the traditional lecture-discussion format. These differences were not only substantial but also, according to the researchers, significant and with large effect sizes.

Table 7.3 *Total Test and Subtest Scores for Two Groups*

	% Correct Answers on Chemical Weapons Test Chemical Weapons Test Scores						% Correct Answers on Biological Weapons Test Biological Weapons Test Scores					
	Traditional Lecture			**QER***			**Traditional Lecture**			**QER***		
Question Type	**M**	**N**	**SD**	**M**	**N**	**SD**	**M**	**N**	**SD**	**M**	**N**	**SD**
Matching	50.57	66	21.64	75.00	50	22.59	53.00	50	23.22	70.08	66	23.91
Multiple Choice	51.36	66	21.90	77.60	50	22.00	51.60	50	21.51	71.36	66	21.04
Main Ideas (MC)**	62.88	66	38.54	85.00	50	29.01	52.00	50	39.07	77.27	66	29.33
Main Ideas (SA)**	0.76	66	6.15	29.00	50	36.55	13.00	50	24.35	62.12	66	36.23
Total	**45.98**	66	16.92	71.70	50	18.67	**48.30**	50	17.54	**69.92**	66	19.91

*Question-Exploration Routine

**Multiple Choice

**Short Answer

Discussion and Implications The very large differences between the two groups provide pretty compelling evidence that presentation of conceptual information using features such as advance and graphic organizers and critical questions can enhance students' understanding and retention of important new knowledge. It underscores the important role these features play in promoting the type of understanding and thinking we want our students to display.

provided historical relevant materials about the passage. The other group was provided an "**advance organizer**," or scaffold to connect the new materials in the passage to what students' already knew. Students who were given the advance organizer retained substantially more information three days later as compared to the other group.

From these results, Ausubel (1963) argued that the teacher's job was to make presentation of new knowledge "meaningfully and effectively—so that clear, stable and unambiguous meanings emerge and . . . [are] retained over a long period of time as an organized body of knowledge" (p. 81). For this learning to occur, according to Ausubel, the teacher should create two conditions: (1) present learning materials in a potentially meaningful form, with major and unifying ideas and principles, consistent with contemporary scholarship, highlighted rather than merely listed as facts; and (2) find ways to anchor the new learning materials to the learners' prior knowledge. The major pedagogical strategy proposed by Ausubel (1960) to make new knowledge meaningful to students was the use of advance organizers. He wrote that it is the job of an advance organizer to "delineate clearly, precisely, and explicitly the principal similarities and differences between the ideas in a new learning passage, on the one hand, and existing related concepts in cognitive structure on the other" (p. 83). For Ausubel, an advance organizer consists of statements made by teachers just before actual presentation of the learning materials. These statements are at a higher level of abstraction than the subsequent information. Later in this chapter, advance organizers are defined more precisely; however, here it is important to say that advance organizers help students use prior knowledge just as establishing set does. They differ, however, in that they are tied more tightly to the subsequent information and provide an anchor for later learning.

Since David Ausubel (1960) first published research that demonstrated the effectiveness of advance organizers, other psychologists and educational researchers have been actively testing his hypothesis. Walberg (1986, 1999) reported that from 1969 to 1979, advance organizers were the subject of thirty-two studies. Walberg also described a synthesis of research done by Luiten, Ames, and Aerson (1980) that identified over 135 studies on the effects of advance organizers. Similarly, Mayer (1979, 2003) has spent many years defining advance organizers and showing their effects, particularly for increasing comprehension and enhancing transfer. Finally, reviews by Marzano (2007) and Dean and colleagues (2012) again showed the mainly positive results of using advance organizers. Although not all studies have shown the effectiveness of advance organizers, the findings seem to be consistent enough over time to recommend that teachers use advance organizers when presenting information to students.

> **The clarity of a presentation is a very important factor in determining how much students will learn.**

Teacher Clarity. Using advance organizers, establishing set, and attending to prior learning all affect student learning. Another variable associated with the presentation of information that has been shown to influence student learning is **teacher clarity.** An important early study on teacher clarity was conducted by Hiller, Gisher, and Kaess (1969). They asked teachers to deliver two different fifteen-minute presentations to their students—one on Yugoslavia and the other on Thailand. Teachers were encouraged to make the presentations in their normal fashion. They studied five teacher presentation variables: verbal fluency, amount of information, knowledge structure cues, interest, and vagueness. The researchers found significant relationships on two factors: verbal fluency (clarity) and vagueness. The researchers suggested that lack of clarity in a presentation most often indicates that the speaker does not know the information well or cannot remember the key points. This, of course, suggests several steps for teachers who are about to present information to their students: (1) make sure the content is thoroughly understood, (2) practice and commit the key ideas to memory prior to presentation, or (3) follow written notes very carefully.

Teacher clarity has been the subject of many studies and many reviews over the past four decades (Bransford, Brown, & Cocking, 2000; Marzano, 2007; Rosenshine & Furst, 1973; Rosenshine & Stevens, 1986). In each instance "clarity" of presentation and explanation has been shown to have a positive impact on student learning.

Teachers show enthusiasm for their subjects by using uplifting language and dramatic body movement.

Teacher Enthusiasm. A final variable shown to impact student learning in teacher presentations is **enthusiasm.** This is an interesting concept for two reasons. First, enthusiasm is often confused with theatrics and its associated distractions. Second, the research on the relationship between teacher enthusiasm and student learning is mixed.

In the 1970s, Rosenshine reviewed the research on teacher enthusiasm and reported that it showed fairly consistent relationships between teacher enthusiasm and student learning. Since that time, researchers have tried to study teacher enthusiasm and have developed training programs to help teachers become more enthusiastic in their presentations. For example, Collins (1978) developed and tested a training program that looked at a specific set of enthusiastic behaviors: rapid, uplifting, varied local delivery; dancing, wide-open eyes; frequent, demonstrative questions; varied, dramatic body movements; varied emotive facial expressions; selection of varied words, especially adjectives; ready, animated acceptance of ideas and feelings; and exuberant overall energy. Collins found that students in classes of enthusiasm-trained teachers did better than those in classes of untrained teachers.

However, a study conducted by Bettencourt (see Borg & Gall, 1993) could find no difference between enthusiasm-trained and untrained teachers. More recently, however, Patrick, Hisley, and Kempler (2000) demonstrated greater intrinsic motivation among students who heard enthusiastically delivered lectures as compared to those who did not, and Keller, Neuman, and Fischer (2013), after reviewing more recent literature, concluded that overall the evidence supports the importance of enthusiasm for "fostering meaningful learning" (p. 248).

Planning and Conducting Presentation Lessons

Understanding the theoretical and research bases underlying presentation teaching is not sufficient for its effective use. That requires expert execution of particular decisions and behaviors during the preinstructional, interactive, and postinstructional phases of teaching. This section describes guidelines for planning and conducting effective presentations and explanations.

Planning for Presentations

Except for people who are really shy, it is quite easy for someone to get up in front of a class of students and talk for twenty to thirty minutes. *Talking, however, is not teaching.* Making decisions about what content to include in a presentation and how to organize content so it is logical and meaningful to students takes extensive preparation by the teacher. Four planning tasks are most important: (1) choosing objectives and content for the presentation, (2) diagnosing students' prior knowledge, (3) selecting appropriate and powerful advance organizers, and (4) planning for use of time and space.

Choosing Objectives and Content. The objectives for presentation lessons consist mainly of those aimed at the acquisition of declarative knowledge. Figure 7.4 provides examples of typical objectives teachers might choose. In addition to helping students acquire new knowledge, a teacher may choose to use presentations for other reasons. For example, a presentation delivered with excitement and enthusiasm can spark students' interest in a topic and motivate them to learn. Sometimes teachers use presentation to summarize a topic, synthesizing and tying everything together for students.

Check, Extend, Explore

Check
- What does Ausubel mean by "meaningful verbal learning"?
- What are the different types of knowledge and why are they important to teaching?
- What is the difference between short-term working and long-term memory?
- How can the research on prior knowledge, establishing set, using cues, and teacher clarity be used in planning a classroom presentation?

Extend
- As you read, the research on the effects of enthusiasm on student learning appear to produce mixed results. What are your own personal views about the use of enthusiasm? Of theatrics?

Explore
- There are many Web sites and articles about advance organizers. Search this term on the Internet or in your library's digital resources to see how many you turn up. Compare what you find with the treatment here.

Teaching is more than just talking. Successful presentation lessons require extensive preparation.

Figure 7.4 *Sample Instructional Objectives for a Presentation Lesson*

- Student will be able to describe the significance of the Fourteenth Amendment.
- Student will be able to identify the women authors of three nineteenth-century American novels.
- Student will be able to list the basic rules of ice hockey.
- Student will be able to define the meaning of photosynthesis.
- Student will be able to describe the contributions of three African Americans to United States history.

Another example of appropriate use of lecture is to go over materials already made available to students but with which they seem to be experiencing difficulty. Finally, presentations are an effective means to provide an "alternative point of view" if the teacher deems that one is required to provide balance for one-sided or biased materials presented in the text or elsewhere. However, the amount of declarative knowledge in any field is endless, and several principles can assist beginning teachers as they plan particular presentations or series of presentations.

Power, Economy, and Essential Questions. In Chapter 3, the concepts of power, economy, and essential questions were introduced as tools for curriculum selection. These concepts can also be used by teachers as they select content to include in a presentation. Remember, the concept of power holds that only the most important and powerful concepts should be taught, rather than those of interest but not central to understanding the subject at hand. The economy concept recommends that teachers stay away from verbal clutter and limit their presentations to a minimum amount of information. Essential questions are those understandings without which, if not mastered, a student's education would be incomplete. Achieving economy and power in a presentation depends not so much on a teacher's delivery style as it does

Students' prior knowledge and interests are important when planning presentations.

on planning. In fact, a carefully organized presentation read in a monotone might be more effective in producing student learning than a dynamic presentation void of powerful ideas, even though students may enjoy the latter more.

Conceptual Mapping. One particular tool that is useful in deciding what to teach is that of **conceptual mapping.** Conceptual maps show relationships among ideas, and like road maps, they help users get their bearings. They also help clarify for the teacher the kinds of ideas to teach, and they provide students with a picture for understanding relationships among ideas. To make a conceptual map, you identify the key ideas associated with a topic and arrange these ideas in some logical pattern. Chapter 9 provides more detailed instructions on how to make a conceptual map, gives examples, and provides valuable resources.

Diagnosing Students' Prior Knowledge. Information given in a presentation is based on teachers' estimates of their students' existing cognitive structures and their prior knowledge of a subject. As with many other aspects of teaching, there are no clear-cut rules or easy formulas for teachers to follow. There are, however, some ideas that can serve as guides for practice as well as some informal procedures to be learned from experienced teachers.

Cognitive Structures. As has been stated repeatedly, for new material to be meaningful to students, teachers must find ways to connect it to what they already know. Students' existing ideas on a particular topic determine which new concepts are potentially meaningful. Figure 7.5 illustrates how a student's cognitive structure might look in relation to certain concepts about government. Note that Figure 7.5 illustrates that some concepts have been learned and others have not. Note also the illustrator's judgment (shaded areas) about which concepts will be relevant because of the student's prior knowledge. Discussion on how to adapt presentations for students of differing conceptual and ability levels is discussed later in the chapter.

Intellectual Development. Cognitive structures are influenced by students' prior knowledge. They are also influenced by maturation and development. Several theorists have put forth developmental theories, including Hunt (1974), Piaget (1954, 1963), Perry (1969), and Santrock (2012). Space does not allow a full discussion of the

Figure 7.5 *An Individual's Cognitive Structure with Respect to Representative Government*

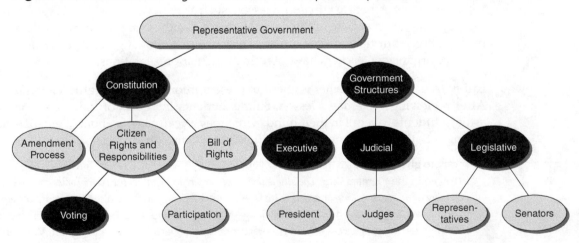

similarities and differences among developmental theorists, but they agree that learners go through developmental stages ranging from very simple and concrete structures at early ages to more abstract and complicated structures later on. It is important that teachers tailor information they present to the level of development of the learners.

Ideas about how students develop intellectually can assist teachers as they plan for a particular presentation; however, they cannot provide concrete solutions for several reasons. As experienced teachers know, development is uneven and does not occur precisely at any given age. Within any classroom, a teacher is likely to find students at extremely varied stages of development. The teacher will also find some students who have developed to a high level of abstraction in some subjects, say history, and still be at a very concrete level in another subject, such as mathematics.

Another problem facing the teacher striving to apply developmental theories to planning for a particular presentation is the problem of measuring the developmental levels of students. Most teachers must rely on informal assessments like some of the ones described in Chapter 6. For example, teachers can watch students as they approach specific problem-solving tasks and make a rough assessment of the degree to which they use concrete or abstract operations. By listening carefully to students and asking probing questions, teachers can determine whether or not the information they are presenting is meaningful. Watching for nonverbal cues during a presentation, such as silence, frowns, or expressions of interest, can provide insights into what students are picking up from the presentation. Silence, for example, can mean that students are bored; most often it means they do not understand what the teacher is saying. It may be that part of the "art of teaching" and a major difference between expert and novice teachers is expert teachers' abilities to read subtle communication cues from students and then adapt their lessons so that new learning materials become meaningful.

Selecting Advance Organizers. The third planning task associated with presentation teaching is choosing appropriate advance organizers. Remember, advance organizers become the hooks, the anchors, the "intellectual scaffolding" for subsequent learning materials. They help students see the "big picture" of things to come in the presentation. Ausubel suggested that advance organizers should be slightly more abstract than the content to be presented. Others have suggested that concrete examples from the forthcoming lesson might work better than more abstract advance organizers. Regardless of the degree of abstraction, a good advance organizer contains materials familiar to students and is designed to relate to students' prior knowledge.

We should repeat one point here: The advance organizer *is not* the same as *other techniques* used by teachers *to introduce* a lesson, such as reviewing past work, establishing set, or giving an overview of the day's lesson. All of these are important for effective presentations, but they are not advance organizers. Following are three examples of advance organizers teachers have used in particular presentations:

Example 1. A history teacher is about to present information about the Vietnam War. After reviewing yesterday's lesson, telling students the goals of today's lesson, and asking students to recall in their minds what they already know about Vietnam (establishing set), the teacher presents the following advance organizer:

> I want to give you an idea that will help you understand why the United States became involved in the Vietnam War. *The idea is that most wars reflect conflict between peoples over one of the following: ideology, territory, or access to trade.* As I describe for you the United States' involvement in Southeast Asia between 1945 and 1965, I want you to look for examples of how conflict over ideology, territory, or access to trade may have influenced later decisions to fight in Vietnam.

Students' intellectual development is an important factor to consider when planning a presentation.

Teachers can successfully ascertain student understanding by asking questions and watching for nonverbal cues.

Advance organizers are scaffolds for new information. They are not merely a means of introducing a lesson.

Example 2. A science teacher is about to present information about foods the body needs to function well. After going over the objectives for the lesson, the teacher asks students to list all the foods they ate yesterday (establishing set) and then presents the following advance organizer:

> In a minute, I am going to give you some information about the kinds of foods the body needs to function well. Before I do that, however, *I want to give you an idea that will help you understand the different kinds of food you eat by saying they can be classified into five major food groups: fats, vitamins, minerals, proteins, and carbohydrates.* Each food group contains certain elements, such as carbon or nitrogen. Also, certain things we eat (potatoes, meat) are the sources for each of the elements in the various food groups. Now as I talk about the balanced diet the body needs, I want you to pay attention to the food group to which each thing we eat belongs.

Example 3. An art teacher is going to show and explain to students a number of paintings from different historical eras. After giving an overview of the lesson and asking students to think for a minute about changes they have observed between paintings done during different historical eras, the teacher presents the following advance organizer:

> In a minute, I am going to show and talk about several paintings—some painted in France during the early nineteenth century, others during the late nineteenth and early twentieth centuries. Before I do that I am going to give you an idea to help you understand the differences you are going to see. *That idea is that a painting reflects not only the individual artist's talent but also the times in which it is created. The "times" or "periods" influence the type of techniques an artist uses as well as what he or she paints about and the type of colors used.* As I show you the various paintings, I want you to look for differences in color, subject of the painting, and specific brush techniques used by the artists and see how they reflect the artist's time.

Planning for Use of Time and Space. Planning and managing time and space are a final important task to ensure effective presentations. Two concerns should be foremost in teachers' minds: ensuring that allocated time matches the aptitudes and abilities of the students in the class, and motivating students so that they remain attentive and engaged throughout the lesson. Many teachers, particularly beginning teachers, underestimate the amount of time it takes to teach something well and are not always adept at checking how things are going as a lesson unfolds. Later in this chapter, assessment strategies that help teachers check for understanding are presented. Teachers use this assessment information to determine whether they have allocated sufficient time to a particular topic. Making sure that students understand the purposes of a presentation and tying lessons into their prior knowledge and interests are ways of increasing student attention and engagement. Guidelines for doing this also are provided in the next section.

Planning and managing space is equally important for a presentation lesson. In most situations, teachers prefer the *row-and-column formation* of desks, as illustrated in Figure 7.6. This is the most traditional way of arranging classroom space, and it was so prevalent during earlier times that desks in rows were attached to the floor so they couldn't be moved. This formation is best suited to situations in which students need to focus attention on the teacher or on information displayed on the chalkboard, or electronic projection devices.

Effective presentations rely on the effective management of time and space.

Figure 7.6 *Row-and-Column Desk Formation*

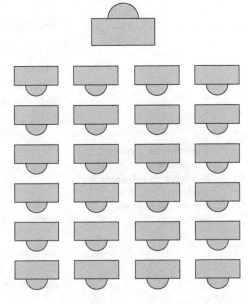

♟ *Diversity and Differentiation*

Adapting Presentations for Differing Student Abilities

Except in rare instances, no presentation will be equally suitable for all students in a class, because students have different prior knowledge and different levels of intellectual development. Therefore, it is very important for teachers to tailor their presentations and explanations to meet the varying needs and backgrounds of the students in their class. Teachers can adapt a presentation in a variety of ways to make it relevant and meaningful to as many students as possible.

Make Ready Use of Pictures and Illustrations. There is much truth to the saying, "A picture is worth a thousand words." Pictures and illustrations can illuminate ideas and concepts in a way that words cannot, particularly for younger children and students who do not deal well with abstractions. To test this recommendation, try to explain the color green to a 3-year-old using only words. Now do it again using pictures of the color green.

Use Varying Cues and Examples. This chapter has emphasized the importance of prior knowledge and the way it serves as a filter through which new information must pass. Information provided to students for which they have no prior knowledge will not be meaningful, and it will not be learned. The use of cues and examples is one way that teachers help students to connect new information to what they already know. Because prior knowledge differs widely in most classrooms, teachers who use varying cues and examples can help make information meaningful to all students.

Be More or Less Concrete. Older and higher-achieving students can think more abstractly than can younger and most low-achieving students. When both are in the same classroom, it is important for teachers to explain ideas both concretely and abstractly to meet the needs of students of differing levels of intellectual development.

Conducting Presentation Lessons

The syntax or flow of a presentation lesson consists of four basic phases: (1) clarifying the aims of the lesson and getting students attention to learn, (2) presenting the advance organizer, (3) presenting the new information, and (4) monitoring and checking students' understanding and extending and strengthening their thinking skills. Each phase and required teacher behaviors are illustrated in Table 7.4.

It is important to begin a lesson with an introduction that will capture students' attention and motivate them to participate.

Gaining Attention, Explaining Goals, and Establishing Set. Effective instruction using any instructional model requires teachers to take an initial step aimed at getting students' attention and motivating them to participate in the lesson. Behaviors consistently found effective for this purpose are using a variety of attention-getting devices, sharing the goals of the lesson with students, and establishing a set for learning.

Gaining Attention. Gaining and maintaining students' attention is critical if they are to successfully take in, process, and store new information. Making sure the aims of the lesson are clear and establishing set, as described next, are two ways teachers can

Table 7.4 *Syntax of a Presentation Lesson*

Phase	Teacher Behavior
Phase 1: Gain attention, explain goals, and establish set.	Teacher gets students' attention, goes over the aims of the lesson, and gets them ready to learn.
Phase 2: Present advance organizer.	Teacher presents advance organizer, making sure that it provides a framework for later learning materials and is connected to students' prior knowledge.
Phase 3: Present learning materials.	Teacher presents learning materials, paying special attention to clarity, logical ordering, and meaningfulness.
Phase 4: Monitor and check for understanding and strengthen student thinking.	Teacher asks questions and elicits student responses to the presentation to see if they understand and to extend their thinking and to encourage critical thinking.

gain attention. They also use other attention-getting strategies, such as creating surprise or arousing curiosity. Surprises such as staging a special incident not normally part of the classroom routine, moving to the back of the room, or jumping up on the desk, generally will capture everyone's attention. Curiosity can be aroused by "what if" types of questions (described in Chapter 12), or by introducing something that stimulates senses not usually associated with a presentation lesson, such as a surprise, music, or unique smells.

Explaining Goals. In the discussion on motivation, you learned that students need a reason to participate in particular lessons and they need to know what is expected of them. Effective teachers telegraph their goals and expectations by providing abbreviated versions of their lesson plans on the chalkboard, on newsprint charts, or on electronic projection devices. Effective teachers also outline the steps or phases of a particular lesson and the time required for each step. This allows the students to see the overall flow of a lesson and how the various parts fit together. Sharing the time parameters for the lesson also encourages students to help keep the lesson on schedule. Figure 7.7 shows how a social studies teacher shared her goals and the phases of her presentation with a group of eleventh-grade students who were studying World War II.

Making students aware of what they are going to learn will help them make connections between a particular lesson and its relevance to their own lives. This motivates students to exert more effort. It also helps them to draw prior learning from long-term memory to short-term working memory, where it can be used to integrate new information provided in a presentation.

Establishing Set and Providing Cues. To get runners ready and off to an even start in a foot race, the command from the starter is "Get ready. . . . *Get set.* . . . Go!" The *get set* alerts runners to settle into their blocks, focus their attention on the track ahead, and anticipate a smooth and fast start.

Figure 7.7 *Aims and Overview of Lesson on World War II*

Today's Objective: The objective of today's lesson is to help you understand how events and circumstances bring about change in the way people think about things.

Agenda

5 minutes	Introduction, review, and getting ready
5 minutes	Advance organizer for today's lesson
20 minutes	Presentation on the demise of the battleship and the concept of decisive engagement
15 minutes	Discussion for critical thinking
5 minutes	Wrap-up and preview of tomorrow's lesson

Brief reviews that prompt students to reflect on a prior lesson or knowledge have been found to be an effective way to start a new lesson.

Figure 7.8 *Establishing Set through Review*

"Yesterday we learned how at the beginning of the WWII in the Pacific that the American navy was not well prepared and operated on old and dated naval strategies. Today, we want to explore this topic more thoroughly and look at how a new strategy, using aircraft carriers instead of battleships, evolved."

Navy in World War II

Advance organizers should be set off from introductory activities and the subsequent presentation of learning materials.

Establishing set for a lesson in school is very much the same. Effective teachers have found that a brief review that gets students to recall yesterday's lesson or perhaps a question or anecdote that ties into students' prior knowledge is a good way to get started. Note the words used by the teacher in Figure 7.8 as he establishes set and provides cues for his students.

Set activities also help students get their minds off other things they have been doing (changing classes in secondary schools; changing subjects in elementary schools; lunch and recess) and begin the process of focusing on the subject of the forthcoming lesson. These activities can also serve as motivators for lesson participation. Each teacher develops his or her own style for establishing set, but no effective teacher eliminates this important element from any lesson.

Presenting the Advance Organizer. A previous section explained the planning tasks associated with choosing an appropriate advance organizer. Now consider how an advance organizer should be presented.

Effective teachers make sure the advance organizer is set off sufficiently from the introductory activities of the lesson and from the presentation of learning materials. As with the lesson goals, it is effective to present the advance organizer to students using some type of visual format such as a chalkboard, a newsprint chart, an overhead projector, or PowerPoint image. The key, of course, is that students must understand the advance organizer. It must be taught just as the subsequent information itself must be taught. This requires the teacher to be precise and clear.

Presenting the Learning Materials. The third phase of presentation teaching is the presentation of the learning materials. Remember how important it is for a teacher to organize learning materials in their simplest and clearest form using the principles of power and economy. The key now is to present previously organized materials in an effective manner, giving attention to such matters as clarity, examples and explaining links, the use of metaphors and analogies, the rule-example-rule technique, the use of transitions, and finally, enthusiasm. You will read in this chapter's Enhancing Teaching and Learning with Technology box that some teachers are doing what has been labeled **flipped classrooms**. This means they tape their presentations and assign them as homework. Matters of clarity and features of explanation are equally important is flipped classrooms as they are in traditional classrooms.

Clarity. As described previously, a teaching behavior that has consistently been shown to affect student learning is the teacher's ability to be clear and specific. Common sense tells us that students will learn more when teachers are clear and specific rather than vague. Nonetheless, researchers and observers of both beginning and experienced teachers find many instances of presentations that are vague and confusing. Vagueness occurs when teachers do not sufficiently understand the subjects they are teaching or when they lack sufficient examples to illuminate the subject.

Clarity of presentation is achieved through planning, organization, and lots of practice. Figure 7.9 provides suggestions to follow based on reviews of research by Cruickshank and Metcalf (1994), Marzano (2007), and Rosenshine and Stephens (1986).

Teach in Small Chunks. One way to achieve clarity is to reduce the size of a topic and practice what Rosenshine (2002) has referred to as *teaching in small chunks.* He reported that effective teachers present small parts of new materials at a single time. This practice is consistent with our knowledge of short-term working memory, which has a limited capacity and can handle only small amounts of information at a time.

Explaining Links and Examples. Effective presentations contain precise and accurate explaining links and examples. **Explaining links** are prepositions and conjunctions that indicate the cause, result, means, or purpose of an event or idea. Examples of such links include *because, since, in order to, if . . . then, therefore,* and *consequently.* Explaining links help students see the logic and relationships in a teacher's presentation and increase the likelihood of understanding.

Explaining links used in presentations helps learners understand cause and effect and other kinds of relationships.

Figure 7.9 *Aspects of Clear Presentations*

1. Be clear about aims and main points.
   - State the goals of the presentation.
   - Focus on one main point at a time.
   - Avoid digressions.
   - Avoid ambiguous phrases.

2. Go through your presentation step by step.
   - Present materials in small steps.
   - Present students with an outline when material is complex.

3. Be specific and provide several examples.
   - Give detailed explanations for difficult points.
   - Provide students with concrete and varied examples.
   - Model or illustrate the idea whenever possible and remember, a picture is worth a thousand words.

4. Check for student understanding.
   - Make sure students understand one point before moving on to the next.
   - Ask questions to monitor student comprehension.
   - Ask students to summarize or paraphrase main points in their own words.
   - Reteach whenever students appear confused.

Examples are another means used by successful presenters to make material meaningful to students. Good examples, however, are difficult for beginning teachers to think up and use. Following are guidelines that experienced teachers find useful in selecting examples:

- Identify the critical attribute(s) of the concept or idea.
- Select from students' own lives some previous knowledge or experience that exemplifies the same critical attribute.
- Check your example for distracters.
- Present the example.
- Label the critical attributes or elements in the example.
- Present exceptions.

Here is an example of an example. Say the teacher has been explaining the differences between mammals and reptiles to a group of young learners. She might proceed as follows:

- State an important generalization, such as "All mammals have warm blood."
- Then move to an example and say, "Examples of mammals you know about in your everyday lives include human beings, dogs, and cats. All of these animals are mammals with warm blood."
- Finally, conclude with, "Reptiles, on the other hand, are cold-blooded and are not mammals. One of the best-known reptiles is the snake. Can you think of others?"

Another example of a teacher using an example follows:

> There are important differences in the meanings of *climate* and *weather*. *Climate* means the overall pattern of weather a region experiences over many months and years. *Weather* is the day-to-day temperature and precipitation of a place.
>
> Here is an example that will show you the difference between weather and climate. When Kevin and Krista visited Boston last summer, the weather was very hot, in the high 90s. We would not, however, say that Boston has a hot climate, because the weather in the winter can be very cold.

Understanding the subject being taught helps the presenter be more concise and complete.

Presenting material clearly and using precise and accurate explaining links and examples require that teachers thoroughly understand both the materials being presented and the structure of the subject area being taught. For beginning teachers having trouble, no solution exists except studying the content and the subject until they achieve mastery.

Rule-Example-Rule Technique. A third technique used by effective presenters is the **rule-example-rule technique.** To apply this technique, perform the following steps:

Step 1: State the rule, such as, "Prices in a free market are influenced by supply and demand."

Step 2: When hybrid cars started to be widely used (decrease in demand) and fracking provided new sources of fuel (increase in supply), the price of gasoline went down. Or, when there was a shortage of gasoline because refineries could not refine fast enough (decrease in supply), prices of gasoline at the pumps went up.

Step 3: Summarize and restate the original rule, such as, "So, as you can see, the fluctuation of supply, along with people's desire for a product, influences what the price of a product will be."

Signposts and transitions help learners move from one topic to another and alert them to what is important.

Signposts and Transitions. Particularly in longer presentations that contain several key ideas, effective presenters help learners capture main ideas and move from one

Enhancing Teaching and Learning with Technology
Can You Flip Your Students' Learning?

Traditionally, the general sequence of instruction has been first to provide new knowledge through presentation or demonstration, followed by checking for students' understanding, and concluding with guided practice and homework. With the help of video and the Internet, some teachers have turned this sequence on its head. They create videos and PowerPoints of their presentations and shift them from their classrooms to Web sites and YouTube. Thus, what happens with face-to-face time with students is significantly changed, as are the homework tasks students are asked to perform. Instead of watching and listening during class, students watch or listen as part of their homework assignment. Class time is thus freed up for teachers to provide guided practice, individual help, and discussion.

Teachers who have flipped their classrooms in this manner report several important advantages. Here are some advantages provided by Kathleen Fulton (2012):

- Students can pace their own learning. Unlike listening in class to a presentation, when they watch and listen alone they can pause and come back to portions they don't understand and watch confusing segments again.
- Students report that they find this kind of homework more meaningful and effective as compared to the ineffectiveness reported with traditional homework.
- Teachers in flipped classrooms can interact with students during class time, gain insight into difficulties they are having with the lesson, and provide timely assistance and feedback.
- Flipping has the potential of increasing engagement because it reflects today's students' preferences for seeking information on the Web.

The flipped classroom seems to be a growing practice. Instructional theory, as well as common sense, would argue that "flipping," because it allows increased interaction and

opportunities for feedback, would have positive effects on student learning.

However, as Goodwin and Miller (2013) have observed, this practice, though growing in popularity among teachers, has *not* been carefully evaluated; the evidence they say is "still coming in." There are also some logistical problems that must be overcome. Many teachers may find it daunting to create an instructional video. Take, for example, the time it took Julie Schell, a teacher in Cambridge, Massachusetts, to produce a three-minute video for YouTube (www.flippedclassroom.org). It took her approximately three hours to complete the following tasks:

- Writing a script of 254 words
- Preparing the slide deck
- Editing the video (she made twenty-three cuts of mistakes, breaths, etc.)
- Exporting to YouTube (took two tries)

To do it well also requires a laptop with decent video or a webcam, a video camera, and recording and screencasting software.

Other questions might also be raised by flipping. For instance:

- Will videos that lack professional quality or the attributes of effective face-to-face presentations capture the students' interest and promote engagement?
- Will some students rush quickly through the prepared visual material just to get it done, similar to the way some treat more traditional homework?
- Will watching a presentation or demonstration independent of the teacher prevent teachers from picking up on informal cues that student are confused?

Finally, even though flipping may make better use of face-to-face class time, doesn't it still rely on the traditional approaches to instruction?

---

part of the lesson to another by using **verbal signposts** and transitional statements. A signpost tells the learner what is important. Examples include statements such as, "This is the main point I have been trying to make," "Please remember this point," and "The most important point to remember is . . .".

Sometimes a transitional statement can be used to alert listeners to important points just made, such as, "Now let me summarize the important points for you before I move on." In other instances, a transitional statement telegraphs what is to follow; for example, "We have just covered the important eras in Hemingway's life. Let's now turn to how his involvement in the Spanish Civil War influenced his writings." Or, "Now that we know the purposes of a conjunction, let's see how they work in some sample sentences." Transitional statements are important because they highlight the relationships among various ideas in a presentation and they help display the internal organization of the information to learners.

Analogies and Metaphors. Often the best way to explain something is to compare it to something else. In teaching, this often means comparing a new idea and connecting it to ideas that student already have. Analogies and metaphors are explanatory devices to help make these connections. **Analogies** highlight similarities between two ideas. Some of you will be familiar with Miller's analogy test items or analogy questions found on some intelligence or aptitude tests. These pose situations such as BEEF : BOVINES :: PORK :_____. The answer of course is beef is to bovines as pork is to pigs. Here are two other examples provided by Grothe (2008):

- Reading is to the mind, as exercise is to the body.
- As soap is to the body, tears are to the soul (Yiddish proverb).

Teachers can use analogies to explain numerous ideas, for example:

- Explaining cricket by comparing it to baseball
- Explaining how humans process information by making a comparison to computers.

The **metaphor** is another device that allows comparison. There are many types of metaphors, but normally they compare two unlike things that actually have something in common. Metaphors that most of us are familiar with include:

"Today, students think the future looks like the Gulf oil spill."
"All the world's a stage, and all the men and women merely players" (Shakespeare).
"The moon was as ripe as a tropical fruit."

Using analogies and metaphors in a presentation can help students better understand important new ideas to which they are being applied. Their use also makes presentations more interesting and engaging.

Enthusiasm. As discussed in the section on empirical support, some evidence points to the importance of enthusiasm as an influence on student learning. However, results are somewhat contradictory.

Many teachers, particularly those in secondary schools and colleges, argue that the key to effective presentation is for the presenter to use techniques and strategies borrowed from the performing arts. In fact, books have been written describing this approach, such as Timpson and Tobin's *Teaching as Performing* (1982) and Felman's *Never a Dull Moment* (2001). Emphasis is given to wit, energy, and charisma. Presentation is full of drama, anecdotes, and humor. However, this type of presentation can produce a positive evaluation from student audiences without regard for learning outcomes.

Although making presentations interesting and energizing for learners is desirable, it is also important to consider a note of caution. Too many theatrics may, in fact, detract from the key ideas a teacher is trying to convey and focus students' attention on the entertaining aspects of the presentation. This does *not* mean that teachers should not display enthusiasm for their subjects or a particular lesson. There is a fine line between the teacher who uses humor, storytelling, and involvement to get major ideas across to students and the teacher who uses the same techniques for their entertainment value alone.

It is important to make presentations interesting and energizing.

Monitoring and Checking for Understanding and Extending Student Thinking. The final phase of a presentation lesson is to check to see if students understand the new materials and to extend their thinking about these new ideas.

Checking for Understanding. It is obvious that if teachers do a lot of teaching but students are not learning, nothing has been accomplished. Periodically (weekly, unit-by-unit, quarterly), effective teachers use homework, tests, and other formal devices to find out what students understand and what they don't understand. Teachers should also use informal methods to monitor student understanding during a presentation. Watching for verbal and nonverbal cues, described earlier, is one method teachers can use. When students ask questions that don't seem to connect to the topic, they are sending a verbal signal that they are confused. Puzzled looks, silence, and frowns are nonverbal signs that students are not "getting it." Eyes wide open in amazement, smiles, and positive head nodding all signal that understanding is occurring.

Experienced teachers become very effective in monitoring verbal and nonverbal cues; however, a surer means of **checking for understanding** is to ask students to make direct responses to statements or questions. Several easy-to-use techniques can become valuable pieces of the beginning teacher's repertoire. One is the technique of posing a question about the materials just presented and having students as a group signal their responses. Here are examples of how this works with younger students, as adapted from the work of the late Madeline Hunter.

> Thumbs up if the statement I make is true, down if false, to the side if you're not sure.
> Make a plus with your fingers if you agree with this statement, a minus if you don't, and a zero if you have no strong feelings.
> Show me with your fingers if sentence 1 or sentence 2 has a dependent clause.
> Raise your hand each time you hear (or see) an example of. . . .

Note in the examples that students are encouraged to use the signal system to report confusion or things they are not quite sure of. These are areas, obviously, where

Checking for understanding during presentations lets teachers know if their students are grasping the new ideas.

Check, Extend, Explore

Check
- Why is prior knowledge such a critical factor in what students learn from a presentation?
- What are the four phases of a presentation lesson? What kinds of teaching behaviors are associated with each phase?
- What are the four key features of a clear presentation?
- What role does explaining links and examples play in a presentation?
- Summarize why checking for student understanding is an important phase of a presentation lesson.

Extend
- At this point in your education, do you agree or disagree that you have enough understanding of your subject area(s) to explain it (them) extemporaneously to others? Go to the "Extend Question Poll" on the Online Learning Center to respond.

Explore
- Go to the Online Learning Center at www.mhhe.com/arends10e and view the video clip that shows how one teacher used student PowerPoint presentations in her middle school science class. Visit www.flippedclassroom.org, a flipped learning network where teachers discuss how to flip classrooms.

teachers need to provide additional explanation. The signal system is even used at the college level, where students are appreciative of having their misconceptions cleared up immediately rather than having them revealed later on an important test. Choral responses (having students answer in unison) is another means to check for understanding, as is sampling several individuals in the class. Informal response techniques such as traffic lights, which were described in Chapter 6, are additional simple, but effective, ways to check for student understanding.

There are also several methods used by experienced teachers that are *not* very effective. For instance, sometimes a teacher will conclude a presentation and ask, "Now, you all understand, don't you?" Students normally perceive this as a rhetorical question and consequently do not respond. Asking more directly, "Now, does anyone have any questions?" is an equally ineffective way to check for student understanding. Most students are unwilling to admit publicly to confusion, particularly if they think they are the only ones who didn't understand what the teacher said or if they are afraid of being accused of not listening.

Extending Student Thinking. Although an effective presentation should transmit new information to students, that is not the only goal for presenting and explaining information to students. More importantly, teachers want students to use and to strengthen their existing cognitive structures and to increase their ability to monitor their own thinking. The best means for extending student thinking following a presentation of new information is through classroom discourse, primarily by asking questions and having students discuss the information. It is through this process that students integrate new knowledge with prior knowledge, build more complete knowledge structures, and come to understand more complex relationships. The techniques of asking appropriate questions and conducting effective discussions are among the most difficult for teachers to master and thus become the subject matter for Chapter 12.

Managing the Learning Environment

As described in Chapter 5, research has produced some general classroom management guidelines that apply to virtually all classrooms and all instructional models. These approaches address the way teachers strive to gain student cooperation, the means they use to motivate students, the way they establish and teach clear rules and procedures, and the actions they take to keep lessons moving smoothly and at a brisk pace. Although these general aspects of classroom management are extremely important, it is equally important for teachers to recognize that management behavior varies depending on the instructional approach a teacher is using and the type of learning tasks that derive from that approach. What might be considered "out of control" in one instance might be "in order" in another. For instance, when the teacher is presenting to the whole class, it is not appropriate for students to be talking to each other. Talk, however, is appropriate, even required, during a lesson using small-group discussion. In this section, we describe the unique management requirements for an effective presentation.

In a presentation lesson, a teacher generally structures the learning environment quite tightly. In the early stages of the lesson, the teacher is an active presenter and expects students to be active listeners. A successful presentation requires good conditions for presenting and listening—a quiet area with good visibility, including appropriate facilities for using multimedia. Success also depends on students being sufficiently motivated to watch what the teacher is doing and to listen to what the teacher is saying. It is not a time for students to be sharpening pencils, talking to neighbors, or working on other tasks. Later, when students are asked to discuss or to expand on what was presented, different management concerns will surface. In essence, presentation requires rules governing *student talk*, procedures to ensure good *pacing*, and methods for *dealing with misbehavior*.

Students talking at inappropriate times or asking questions that slow down the pace of a lesson are among the most troublesome management concerns during a teacher presentation. This problem can vary in severity from a loud, generalized classroom clamor that disturbs the teacher next door to a single student talking to a neighbor when the teacher is explaining or demonstrating an important idea. As described in Chapter 5, teachers are well advised to have a rule that prescribes no talking when they are explaining things, and this rule must be consistently reinforced. During the recitation or discussion phase of the lesson, students must be taught to listen to other students' ideas and to take turns when participating in the recitation or the discussion.

Presentation lessons break down when the instructional events become sluggish and appropriate momentum is not maintained. In Chapter 5, you read about how students in Mrs. Dee's classroom sometimes tried deliberately to break up the pace of instruction by asking questions and feigning confusion. This resulted in the teacher reducing the amount of content being taught and doing more and more of the students' thinking for them. Effective teachers spot this type of student behavior, nip it in the bud, and move on with a well-paced and smooth-flowing presentation.

Effective presentation and explanation depends on an environment characterized by active student listening and also by interaction when required.

Presentations break down if appropriate momentum is not maintained or if students behave in inappropriate ways.

Assessment and Evaluation

Assessment of student learning is an important postinstructional task for presentation lessons. Presentation teaching is particularly adept at transmitting new information to students and at helping them retain that information. Therefore, the testing of students' knowledge acquisition and retention is the appropriate evaluation strategy for the model. This type of testing situation lends itself nicely to the paper-and-pencil tests and selected-response test items with which you are familiar. In testing for student knowledge, however, several factors should be considered. Teachers should test at all levels of knowledge and not for simple recall of factual information. Furthermore, teachers should communicate clearly to students what they will be tested on. Finally, it is better to test frequently than to wait for midterm or final testing periods.

Check, Extend, Explore

Check
- Describe the characteristics of the learning environment during a presentation lesson.
- What are the means teachers use to assess what students have learned from presentations or explanations?

Extend
- Think about the learning environments in classrooms where you have experienced effective presentation. What characterized these environments?

Explore
- Go to the Online Learning Center at www.mhhe.com/arends10e for links to Web sites related to classroom learning environments and assessment.
- Use Google to search the topic "use of the lecture method." You will find thousands of Web sites devoted to this topic, many from university centers on effective teaching. View two or three of these sites and compare the suggestions found in them with those in *Learning to Teach*.

Reflections from the *Classroom*

Pleasing the Principal

You are in your first year of teaching. The principal at your school believes that teachers spend too much time talking to kids. If she walks by your room and sees you lecturing, she frowns and expresses her disapproval. At staff meetings, the principal often voices the opinion that teachers should be "facilitators of learning" and not "fountains of information." You agree that teachers should do more than just talk to students and that they should provide students with many active learning experiences. However, you also believe that you need to use presentations on a regular basis if you are going to cover all the material in the curriculum guide and if your students are going to perform well on the required standardized tests.

This situation seems to present you with a dilemma. On one hand, you want the principal to think you are a good teacher. On the other, you feel strongly that presenting new information and ideas is central to the job of teaching.

Reflect on ways to deal with this situation. Approach it from the perspective closest to the grade level or subject area you are preparing to teach. When you have finished, write up your ideas for an exhibit in your professional portfolio and compare them with the following ideas expressed by experienced teachers who have faced the same or similar situations. You might want to consider the appropriate uses for presentation and explanation. When is this model misused?

Jason O'Brien

Sacred Heart Academy, 3rd through 5th Grade
Diocese of St. Petersburg, FL

It is important for the administration to have confidence in the abilities of first-year teachers. That said, teachers are professionals, not technicians. Consider yourself fortunate if you have a principal that does not want you doing all the talking, or expect you to give lectures every period. If your principal is the opposite, I would explain to her that I agree that facilitation of learning is of utmost importance in teaching social studies. I would ask the principal to observe a particular lesson where I demonstrate lecturing but also where I incorporate many questions and provide for cooperative learning. Very few students are motivated enough to gain important knowledge completely on their own. Thus, it is important for the teacher to present important information followed by asking both lower- and higher-order questions. This enables students to become active participants in the presentation. As you gain teaching experience, you will know when you "have" your students and when you don't. Learn from your mistakes and always try to improve the ways in which you present information. Use [hands-on material], music, and primary documents to support and make your presentations interesting and motivating. By virtue of your status as a teacher you have the responsibility to discover the most effective ways to teach your content.

Sometimes you'll succeed, sometimes you'll fail, but don't be afraid to try new and creative ways of teaching.

Michael T. Girard

Bristol High School, 9th and 10th Grade, Bristol, PA

Of course, the best strategy for any teacher, novice or veteran, is to establish an open, professional relationship before she offers that frown of disapproval. Having said that, I would actively respond to the principal's reactions as soon as possible. I would set up a meeting to reassure the principal that spewing out information is not the core of my classroom

instruction and that our views on how to deliver effective education actually are in harmony.

In the meeting, I would explain fully why it was necessary within the context of the lesson to present information to the class. I would bring my lesson plans so that the objectives, standards, activities, and assessments can be clearly seen and understood. I would emphasize how lecturing she observed fits within my lesson.

Next, I would invite her to my classroom to observe the follow-up activities or assessments that show the students actively learning as I help them achieve the goals of the lesson.

Summary

Provide an overview of presentation teaching and explain its appropriate use.

- Presentations, explanations, and lectures by teachers comprise a large portion of classroom time primarily because curricula in schools have been structured around bodies of information that students are expected to learn.
- The instructional goals of presentation teaching are mainly to help students acquire, assimilate, and retain information.
- The general flow or syntax for a presentation lesson consists of four main phases: presenting objectives and establishing set, presenting an advance organizer, presenting the learning materials, and using processes to monitor student understanding and to help extend and strengthen student thinking.
- Successful presentations require a fairly tightly structured learning environment that allows a teacher to effectively present and explain new information and allows the students to see and hear.

Describe the theoretical foundations of presentation teaching and summarize research that supports its use.

- Presentation teaching draws support primarily from three streams of theory and research: ideas associated with the cognitive views of learning and the neurosciences, perspectives about how the human memory works, and effective practice identified from teacher effectiveness research.

- Bodies of knowledge have logical structures from which key concepts and ideas are drawn for teacher presentations.
- Knowledge can be divided into four main categories: declarative knowledge, procedural knowledge, conceptual knowledge, and metacognitive knowledge. Declarative knowledge is knowing about something or knowledge that something is the case. Procedural knowledge is knowing how to do something. Conceptual knowledge is knowing the relationships among basic elements. Metacognitive knowledge is awareness of one's own knowledge and thinking processes and knowing when to use particular knowledge.
- People take in information and knowledge through their senses and transform it into sensory memory, short-term working memory, and long-term memory. Meaningful verbal learning occurs when teachers present major unifying ideas in ways that connect these ideas to students' prior knowledge.
- The empirical support for presentation teaching is well developed. Studies have shown the positive effects of using advance organizers, connecting new information to students' prior knowledge, and presenting the information with clarity, enthusiasm, economy, and power.

Explain how to plan and use presentation teaching, including how to design advance organizers and how to make effective presentations.

- The planning tasks for presentation teaching include carefully selecting content, creating advance organizers, and matching both to students' prior knowledge.

- Presenting information to students requires preparing students to learn from presentation as well as delivering learning materials.
- Clarity of a presentation depends on both the teacher's delivery and the teacher's general mastery of the subject matter being presented.
- Advance organizers serve as intellectual scaffolding on which new knowledge is built.
- Specific techniques used in presenting new material include explaining links, rule-example-rule, and verbal transitions.
- Teachers can help students extend and strengthen their thinking about new materials through discussion, questioning, and dialogue.

Describe how to implement a learning environment conducive to presentation teaching.

- In a presentation lesson, a teacher structures the learning environment fairly tightly and makes sure students are attending to the lesson.

- Most important, presentation lessons require clear rules that govern student talk; procedures to ensure a brisk, smooth pace; and effective methods for dealing with student off-task behavior or misbehavior.

Describe the appropriate ways to assess student learning consistent with the learning outcomes of presentation teaching.

- Because the primary goal of most presentations is knowledge acquisition, it is important to assess major ideas at various levels of knowledge. If testing is limited to the recall of specific facts or information, that is what students will learn. If teachers require higher-level cognitive processing on their tests, students will also learn to do that.
- Goals of presentation teaching lend themselves to being assessed with selected-response test items, but other assessment methods should be considered.

Key Terms

advance organizers 281	enthusiasm 282	presentation teaching 272
analogies 294	establishing set 279	prior knowledge 276
checking for understanding 295	explaining links 291	procedural knowledge 274
cognitive psychology 274	factual knowledge 274	rule-example-rule technique 292
cognitive structure 279	flipped classroom 291	schema 276
conceptual knowledge 274	information processing 275	sensory memory 276
conceptual mapping 285	long-term memory 276	short-term working memory 276
conditional knowledge 274	metacognitive knowledge 275	teacher clarity 282
declarative knowledge 274	metaphors 294	verbal signposts 293

Interactive and Applied Learning

Study and Explore

- Access your Study Guide, which includes practice quizzes, from the Online Learning Center.

Observe and Practice

- Listen to audio clips on the Online Learning Center of Patricia Merkel and Dennis Holt (high school American history and economics) talking about presentation in the *Teachers on Teaching* area.

Complete the **Practice Exercise 7.1,** Planning a Presentation Lesson, including

- Write Objectives
- Establish Set
- Present an Advanced Organizer
- Present Learning Materials

- Check for Understanding and Strengthen Student Thinking
- Reflect on Planning for Presentation

Complete the following additional **Practice Exercises** that accompany Chapter 7:

- Practice Exercise 7.2: Teaching Dilemma: Holding Student Interest
- Practice Exercise 7.3: Differentiating a Presentation for a Range of Abilities
- Practice Exercise 7.4: Reflecting on the Use of Presentation

Portfolio and Field Experience Activities

Expand your understanding of the content and processes of this chapter through the following field experience and portfolio activities. Support materials to complete the activities are in the *Portfolio and Field Experience Activities* area on your Online Learning Center.

1. Complete the **Reflections from the Classroom** exercise at the end of this chapter and use the recommended reflective essay as an exhibit of your views about the use or misuse of presentation teaching. **(InTASC Standard 8: Instructional Strategies)**

2. **Activity 7.1: Assessing My Presentation Skills.** Assess your level of understanding and skill to plan and implement a presentation teaching lesson. **(InTASC Standard 8: Instructional Strategies)**

3. **Activity 7.2: Observing a Presentation in Microteaching or Classrooms.** Observe a peer or classroom teacher giving a presentation lesson and note how different aspects of the method are performed. **(InTASC Standard 8: Instructional Strategies)**

4. **Activity 7.3: Observing Teacher Clarity.** Observe an experienced teacher and keep track of the degree to which he or she speaks with clarity or with vagueness. **(InTASC Standard 8: Instructional Strategies)**

5. Activity 7.4: **Portfolio: Creating a Presentation Lesson Using an Advance Organizer.** Use the lesson planning exercises or Portfolio and Field Experience Activity 7.4 at the Online Learning Center to plan your own presentation lesson using an advance organizer. Place the product(s) of your work in your professional portfolio to demonstrate your understanding and skill to plan and conduct presentation lessons. **(InTASC Standard 8: Instructional Strategies; InTASC Standard 7: Planning for Instruction)**

Books for the Professional

Dean, C., Hubbell, E., Pitler, H., & Stone, B. (2012). *Classroom instruction that works: Research-based strategies for increasing student achievement* (2nd ed.). Alexandria, VA: Association for Supervision and Curriculum Development.

Klingberg, T. (2012). *The learning brain: Memory and brain development in children.* New York: Oxford University Press USA.

Riddle, J. (2009). *Engaging the eye generation: Visual literacy strategies for the K-5 classroom.* Portland, ME: Stenhouse.

Silver, H., & Perini, M. (2010). *The interactive lecture: How to engage students, build memory, and deepen comprehension.* Alexandria, VA: Association for Supervision and Curriculum Development.

Willis, J. (2006). *Research-based strategies that ignite student learning.* Alexandria, VA: Association for Supervision and Curriculum Development.

Wilson, D., & Conyers, M. (2013) *Five big ideas for effective teaching: Connecting mind, brain, and education research to classroom practice.* New York: Teachers College Press.

Zoller, K., & Landry, C. (2010). *The choreography of presenting: The seven essential abilities of effective presenters.* Thousand Oaks, CA: Corwin Press.

CHAPTER 8
Direct Instruction

Learning Goals

After studying this chapter you should be able to

Overview of Direct Instruction	Provide an overview of direct instruction and explain its appropriate use.
Theoretical and Empirical Support	Describe the theoretical foundations of direct instruction and summarize research that supports its use.
Planning and Conducting Direct Instruction Lessons	Explain how to plan and use direct instruction, including how to adapt its use for students of differing abilities and backgrounds.
Managing the Learning Environment	Describe how to implement a learning environment conducive to using direct instruction.
Assessment and Evaluation	Describe appropriate ways to assess student learning consistent with the goals of direct instruction lessons.
A Final Thought: Considering the Use of Direct Instruction	Discuss why direct instruction has remained popular and list some of the shortcomings of this approach to teaching.

 Reflecting on Direct Instruction

Take a minute to list the things you remember your parents or teachers doing that helped you learn the following:

- The first ten amendments to the Constitution
- How to ride a bicycle
- How to tie your shoelaces
- The fifty state capitals
- The multiplication tables

Were there particular steps or activities they used regardless of the subject? Were some things particularly helpful to your learning? What did these have in common? Were there things they did that hindered your learning?

 Go to the Online Learning Center at www.mhhe.com/arends10e to respond to these questions.

Skills—cognitive and physical—are the foundations upon which more advanced learning (including learning to learn) are built. Not always, but often before students can discover powerful concepts, solve problems, or write creatively, they must first acquire basic skills and information. For example, before students can acquire and process large amounts of information, they must be able to decode and encode spoken and written messages, take notes, and summarize. Before students can think critically, they must have basic skills associated with logic, such as drawing inferences from data and recognizing bias in presentation. Before students can write an eloquent paragraph, they must master basic sentence construction, and correct word usage, and acquire the self-discipline required to complete a writing task. In essence, in most instances we must *learn the mechanics before the magic.*

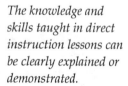

A major difference between novices and experts in any field is the degree to which they have mastered the basic skills of their trade.

In fact, a major difference between novices and experts in almost any field is that experts have mastered certain basic skills to the point where they can perform them unconsciously and with precision, even in new or stressful situations. For example, expert teachers seldom worry about classroom management, because after years of experience, they have mastered and are confident of their group control skills. Similarly, top NFL quarterbacks read every move of a defense without thinking and automatically respond with skillful actions to a safety blitz or double coverage of prize receivers, something novice quarterbacks cannot do as well.

This chapter focuses on an approach to teaching that is aimed at helping students learn basic skills and knowledge that can be taught in a step-by-step fashion. For our purposes here, this approach is labeled **direct instruction.** This approach does not always have the same name. Sometimes it has been referred to as *active teaching* (Good, Grouws, & Ebmeier, 1983). Hunter (1982, 1995) labeled her approach *mastery teaching.* Rosenshine and Stevens (1986) called this approach *explicit instruction.* The label *direct instruction* also has been used to describe a particular approach to teaching reading, and although the reading approach has many similarities to the type of direct instruction

The knowledge and skills taught in direct instruction lessons can be clearly explained or demonstrated.

described here, the model described in this chapter is more generic and appropriate for instruction in any subject from art to zoology.

This chapter begins with an overview of direct instruction, which is followed by a discussion of its theoretical and empirical support. The chapter then gives concrete details about how to plan, conduct, and evaluate direct instruction lessons. Reflection and exercise materials on the Online Learning Center are provided to help you practice and reflect on your own approach to teaching using direct instruction.

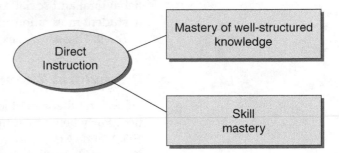

Figure 8.1 *Direct Instruction Aims at Accomplishing Two Learner Outcomes*

Overview of Direct Instruction

Even though you may never have thought about direct instruction in any systematic way, you are undoubtedly familiar with certain aspects of it. The rationale and procedures underlying this approach to teaching were probably used to teach you to drive a car, brush your teeth, hit a solid backhand, write a research paper, or solve algebraic equations. Behavioral principles on which this model rests may have been used to correct your phobia about flying or wean you from cigarettes. Direct instruction is rather straightforward and can be mastered in a relatively short time. It is a "must" in all teachers' repertoire.

As with other approaches to teaching, direct instruction can be described in terms of three features: (1) the type of learner outcomes it produces, (2) its syntax or overall flow of instructional activities, and (3) its learning environment.

Briefly, direct instruction was designed to promote mastery of skills (procedural knowledge) and declarative knowledge that can be taught in a step-by-step fashion. These learner outcomes are shown in Figure 8.1. Direct instruction is not intended to accomplish social learning outcomes or higher-level thinking, nor is it effective for these uses. Direct instruction is mainly teacher-centered and proceeds in five steps: establishing set, explanation and/or demonstration, guided practice, feedback, and extended practice. A direct instruction lesson requires careful orchestration by the teacher and a learning environment that is businesslike and task-oriented. The direct instruction learning environment focuses mainly on academic learning tasks and aims at keeping students actively engaged.

After taking a brief look at the theoretical and empirical support for direct instruction, we will provide a more detailed discussion on how to plan for, conduct, manage, and evaluate direct instruction lessons.

Theoretical and Empirical Support

A number of historical and theoretical roots come together to provide the rationale and support for direct instruction. Some aspects of the model derive from training procedures developed in industrial and military settings. Barak Rosenshine and Robert Stevens (1986), for example, reported that they found a book published in 1945 titled *How to Instruct* that included many of the ideas associated with direct instruction. For our purposes here, however, we will describe three theoretical and empirical

Check, Extend, Explore

Check
- What are the five phases of a direct instruction lesson?
- What are the learner outcomes of a direct instruction lesson?
- What type of learning environment is best for a direct instruction lesson?

Extend
- Think about a basic skill that you have mastered to the point where you can perform it more or less automatically. How long did it take? What were the defining moments when you accomplished mastery? Were you aware this was happening?

Explore
- Go to the Online Learning Center at www.mhhe.com/arends10e for links to Web sites related to direct instruction.

traditions that provide the rationale and guidelines for contemporary use of direct instruction: behaviorism, social cognitive theory, and teacher effectiveness research. Behavioral and social cognitive theories were introduced in Chapter 4 as they pertain to student motivation and again briefly in the introductory pages for Part 3 of *Learning to Teach*. These initial explanations are expanded in the following sections.

Behavioral Theory

Behavioral theories of learning have made significant contributions to direct instruction. Early behavioral theorists included the Russian physiologist Ivan Pavlov (1849–1936) and American psychologists John Watson (1878–1958), Edward Thorndike (1874–1949), and, more recently, B. F. Skinner (1904–1990). Recall that the theory is called **behaviorism** because theorists and researchers in this tradition are interested in studying observable human behavior rather than things that cannot be observed, such as human thought and cognition. Of particular importance to teachers is B. F. Skinner's work on operant conditioning and his ideas that humans learn and act in specific ways as a result of how particular behaviors are encouraged through reinforcement. You remember from Chapter 5 that the concept of reinforcement has a special meaning in behavioral theory: Consequences strengthen particular behaviors either positively by providing some type of reward or negatively by removing some irritating stimulus.

> Behavioral theories maintain that humans learn to act in certain ways in response to positive and negative consequences.

As you will read later in this chapter, when using behavioral principles teachers devise objectives that describe with precision the behaviors they want their students to learn; provide learning experiences, such as practice, in which student learning can be monitored and feedback provided; and pay particular attention to how behaviors in the classroom are rewarded.

Social Cognitive Theory

More recently, theorists such as Albert Bandura have argued that classical behaviorism provided too limited a view of learning, and they have used social cognitive theory (initially called social learning theory) to help study the unobservable aspects of human learning, such as thinking and cognition. **Social cognitive theory** makes distinctions between learning (the way knowledge is acquired) and performance (the behavior that can be observed). This theory also posits that much of what humans learn comes mainly through the observation of others. According to Bandura, most human learning is done by selectively observing and placing into memory the behavior of others. Bandura (1977) wrote:

> Social cognitive theory posits that much of what humans learn comes through the observation of others.

> Learning would be exceedingly laborious, not to mention hazardous, if people had to rely solely on the effects of their own actions to inform them of what to do. Fortunately, most human behavior is learned *observationally* through modeling: from observing others one forms an idea of how new behaviors are performed, and on later occasions this coded information serves as a guide for action. Because people can learn from example what to do, at least in approximate form, before performing any behavior, they are spared needless errors. (p. 22)

Unlike earlier behaviorists, social cognitive theorists believe that something is learned when an observer consciously attends to some behavior (e.g., striking a match) and then places that observation into long-term memory. The observer hasn't yet *performed* the observed behavior, so there have been no behavioral consequences (reinforcements), which behaviorists maintain are necessary for learning to occur. Nevertheless, as long as the memory is retained, the observer knows how to strike a match, whether or not he or she ever chooses to do so. The same claim can be said for thousands of simple behaviors such as braking a car, eating with a spoon, and opening a bottle.

According to Bandura (1986), **observational learning** is a three-step process: (1) the learner has to pay attention to critical aspects of what is to be learned, (2) the learner has to retain or remember the behavior, and (3) the learner must be able to reproduce or perform the behavior. Practice and mental rehearsals used in direct instruction are processes that help learners retain and produce observed behaviors. The principles of social cognitive theory translate into the following teaching behaviors:

- Use strategies to gain students' attention.
- Ensure that the observation is not too complex.
- Link new skills to students' prior knowledge and abilities to perform the skill.
- Use practice to ensure long-term retention.
- Ensure a positive attitude toward the new skill so students will be motivated to reproduce or use the new behavior.

More detail on how to apply the principles stemming from social cognitive theory will be provided in the next section.

Teacher Effectiveness Research

The clearest empirical support for direct instruction comes from the **teacher effectiveness research** conducted mainly in the 1970s and 1980s, a type of research that studied the relationships between teacher behaviors and student learning defined mainly as achievement on standardized achievement tests.

Early studies (Stallings and Kaskowith, 1974, for instance) investigated classrooms where teachers were using quite different approaches to instruction. Some teachers used highly structured and formal methods, whereas others used more informal teaching methods associated with the open classroom movement of the time. Stallings and her colleagues wanted to find out which of the various approaches were working best in raising student achievement. The behaviors of teachers in 166 classrooms were observed, and their students were tested for achievement gains in mathematics and reading. Although many findings emerged from this large and complex study, two of the most pronounced and long-lasting were the findings that time allocated and used for specific academic tasks was strongly related to academic achievement and that teachers who were businesslike and used teacher-directed (direct instruction) strategies were more successful in obtaining high engagement rates than those who used more informal and student-centered teaching methods.

Following this early work, literally hundreds of studies conducted between 1975 and 1990 produced somewhat the same results; namely, that teachers who had well-organized classrooms in which structured learning experiences prevailed produced higher student time-on-task ratios and higher student achievement in basic skills than teachers who used more informal and less teacher-directed approaches. This research has been summarized on numerous occasions (see Brophy & Good, 1986; Marzano, 2007; Rosenshine & Stevens, 1986; Schmoker, 2011; Stronge, 2002). The Research Summary for this chapter describes briefly the nature of the research that produced these findings and provides an illustration of a group of studies conducted by Tom Good and his colleagues. Though this study was conducted over thirty five years ago, it is included here for two reasons. One, it is now considered a classic; two, it is an exemplary example of the genre of teacher effectiveness research.

Learning through observation involves three steps: attention, retention, and production.

Teacher effectiveness research is an approach to studying teaching that looks at the relationship between teachers' observable behaviors and student achievement.

Check, Extend, Explore

Check
- What are the primary features of behaviorism?
- What is the critical feature of social cognitive theory?
- What characterizes the methods of process-product research?
- How do most process-product researchers define achievement?

Extend
- Some people are critical of process-product research mainly because it ignores the cognitive dimension of learning. Do you agree or disagree with this perspective? Go to the "Extend Question Poll" on the Online Learning Center to respond.

Explore
- Go to the Online Learning Center at www.mhhe.com/arends10e for links to Web sites containing information on direct instruction.

Research Summary

How Do We Study Relationships between Teacher Behavior and Student Achievement?

Good, T. L., & Grouws, D. A. (1977). Teaching effect: A process-product study in fourth-grade mathematics classrooms. *Journal of Teacher Education, 28,* 49–54.

Good, T. L., & Grouws, D. A. (1979). The Missouri mathematics effectiveness project: An experimental study in fourth-grade classrooms. *Journal of Educational Psychology, 71,* 355–362.

This Research Summary highlights, instead of a single study, a series of studies conducted by Good and his colleagues during the 1970s. Good's work is important for two reasons. One, it is a fine illustration of the process-product research, a unique approach to studying relationships between teacher behavior and student achievement. And two, it shows how knowledge is produced and refined over a number of years and through a number of studies.

Problem: Before the 1970s, many educational researchers focused mainly on teachers' personal characteristics and how they related to student learning. Researchers became disillusioned with this line of inquiry, and in the early 1970s, a new paradigm for research on teaching and learning emerged. Called **process-product research,** this approach to research had profound effects on our views of effective teaching. Process-product research was characterized both by the type of questions asked and by the methods of inquiry used by the researcher. The overriding question guiding process-product research was, "What do individual teachers do that makes a difference in their students' academic achievement?"

There are two key words in this question. One, the word *do,* suggests the importance of teachers' actions or behaviors, in contrast to earlier concerns about their personal attributes or characteristics. These teacher behaviors were labeled *process* by the researchers. The second key word is *achievement.* For the process-product researchers, achievement was the *product* of instruction. In most instances, achievement was defined as the acquisition of those skills and that knowledge that could be measured on standardized tests. Teachers were judged effective if they acted in ways that produced average to above-average achievement for students in their class. Process-product research, thus, can be summarized as the search for those teacher behaviors (process) that led to above-average student achievement scores (product).

Process-product research was also characterized by particular methods of inquiry. Typically, process-product researchers went directly into classrooms and observed teachers in natural (regular) classroom settings. Teacher behaviors were recorded using a variety of low-inference observation devices, and student achievement was measured over several time periods, often at the beginning and end of a school year. Particular teacher behaviors were then correlated with student achievement scores, and successful and unsuccessful teacher behaviors were identified.

Procedures: Let's now look at what process-product research has contributed to our understanding of teacher effectiveness in general and to direct instruction specifically. Although hundreds of such studies were completed in the 1970s and 1980s, the work of Good and Grouws between 1972 and 1976 is illustrative of process-product research at its best, and it is illustrative of the type of evidence that supports the effectiveness of direct instruction.

The Initial Study: Between 1972 and 1973, Good, Grouws, and their colleagues studied over one hundred third- and fourth-grade mathematics teachers in a school district that skirted the core of a large urban school district in the Midwest. The Iowa Test of Basic Skills was administered to students in their classrooms in the fall and spring for two consecutive years. From analyses of achievement gains made by students, the researchers were able to identify nine teachers who were relatively effective in obtaining student achievement in mathematics and nine teachers who had relatively low effectiveness. This led the researchers to plan and carry out an observational study to find out how the effective and ineffective teachers differed.

The Observational Study: To protect the identity of the "effective" and "ineffective" teachers, the researchers collected observational data from forty-one classrooms, including those in which the nine effective and nine ineffective teachers taught. Trained observers visited each classroom six or seven times during October, November, and December of 1974. *Process* data were collected on many variables, including how instructional time was used, teacher-student interaction patterns, classroom management, types of materials used, and frequency of homework assignments. Student achievement was measured with the Iowa Test of Basic

Skills in October 1974 and in April 1975. The classroom process data were analyzed to see if there were variables on which the nine high-effective and nine low-effective teachers differed.

Results: From the comparisons, Good and Grouws concluded that teacher effectiveness was strongly associated with the following clusters of behaviors:

- *Whole-class instruction.* In general, whole-class (as contrasted to small-group) instruction was supported by this study, particularly if the teacher possessed certain capabilities such as an ability to keep things moving along.
- *Clarity of instructions and presentations.* Effective teachers introduced lessons more purposively and explained materials more clearly than ineffective teachers did.
- *High performance expectations.* Effective teachers communicated higher performance expectations to students, assigned more work, and moved through the curriculum at a brisker pace than ineffective teachers did.
- *Task-focused but productive learning environment.* Effective teachers had fewer managerial problems than ineffective teachers. Their classrooms were task-focused and characterized by smoothly paced instruction that was relatively free of disruptions.

- *Student-initiated behavior.* Students in effective teachers' classrooms initiated more interactions with teachers than students in the classrooms of ineffective teachers did. The researchers interpreted this as students' perceiving the effective teachers as being more approachable than the ineffective teachers.
- *Process feedback (knowledge of results).* Effective teachers let their students know how they were doing. They provided students with process or developmental feedback, especially during seatwork, and this feedback was immediate and nonevaluative.
- *Praise.* Effective teachers consistently provided less praise than ineffective teachers. This reflected the nonevaluative stance of the effective teachers. This finding flew in the face of the common wisdom at that time that praise was to be used by teachers very liberally. The result of process-product research showed that praise was effective only when used under certain conditions and in particular ways and that too much praise, or praise used inappropriately, did not promote student learning.

In sum, process-product researchers found that teachers who had well-organized classrooms in which structured learning experiences prevailed produced certain kinds of student achievement better than teachers who did not use these practices.

Planning and Conducting Direct Instruction Lessons

As with any approach to teaching, expert execution of a direct instruction lesson requires specific decisions and behaviors by teachers during planning and while conducting the lesson. Some of these teacher actions are similar to those found in other instructional models. Other behaviors, however, are unique to direct instruction. The unique features of conducting a direct instruction lesson are emphasized here.

Planning for Direct Instruction

Chapters 3 and 7 described different kinds of knowledge. Factual declarative knowledge, you remember, was knowing the *basic element of something;* conceptual knowledge was knowing about the *relationships* among various elements; procedural knowledge was knowing *how to do something.* Direct instruction was specifically designed to promote student learning of well-structured, factual knowledge that can be taught more or less in a step-by-step fashion and to help students master the procedural knowledge required to perform simple and complex skills.

Table 8.1 contrasts the instructional objectives aimed at promoting knowledge acquisition with those aimed at skill development. Differences can easily be observed

Table 8.1 *Contrasting Objectives for Knowledge Acquisition and Skill Development*

Knowledge Acquisition	Skill Development
1. The student will be able to list the basic rules of ice hockey.	1. The student will be able to pass while moving.
2. The student will be able to identify the subjects in the following sentences: a. Whose brother are you? b. Ralph always walked to school. c. Josie loves to read mysteries.	2. The student will supply an appropriate verb in the following sentences: a. Where _____ you? b. Ralph always _____ to school. c. _____ the apples to your sister.
3. Given the equation $y = 2.6x + 0.8$, the student will correctly select the number corresponding to the y intercept.	3. The student will be able to solve for x in the equation $9 = 2.6x + 0.8$.
4. The student can list the major characteristics of a contour map.	4. The student will be able to read a contour map.

in the two sets of objectives listed in Table 8.1. For instance, in the first set of objectives, the student is expected to know ice hockey rules. This is important factual knowledge for students in a physical education class. However, being able to identify the rules does not necessarily mean that the student can perform any skills associated with ice hockey, such as passing while on the move, the content of the procedural knowledge objective found in column 2. Another example illustrating the differences in the two types of objectives is from the field of music. Many people can identify a French horn; some are even familiar with the history of the instrument. Few, however, have sufficient procedural knowledge to play a French horn well.

Direct instruction is applicable to any subject, but it is most appropriate for performance-oriented subjects such as reading, writing, mathematics, music, and physical education. It is also appropriate for the skill components of the more information-oriented subjects such as history or science. For example, direct instruction would be used to help students learn how to make or read a map, use a time line, or adjust a microscope to focus on a slide.

Prepare Objectives. When preparing objectives for a direct instruction lesson, the more specific behavioral format described in Chapter 3 is usually the preferred approach. Remember the STP guidelines specifying that a good objective should be *student*-based and specific, specify the *testing* (assessment) situation, and identify the level of expected *performance*. The major difference between writing objectives for a skill-oriented lesson and writing lessons with more complex content is that skill-oriented objectives usually represent easily observed behaviors that can be stated precisely and measured accurately. For example, if the objective is to have students climb a 15-foot rope in seven seconds, that behavior can be observed and timed. If the objective is to have students go to the world globe and point out Iraq, that behavior can also be observed.

Learning Progressions and Task Analysis. Learning progressions and task analysis are tools teachers use to define learning outcomes associated with a particular chunk of knowledge or skill and to determine how best to sequence the instruction. The learning progression process was described in Chapter 3. This device, sometimes attributed to Popham (2008), is used to identify a set of subskills or enabling knowledge (building blocks) that students must master en route to a more global or overall goal or standard.

Task analysis is a similar tool. The central idea behind task analysis is that complex understandings and skills cannot be learned at one time or in their entirety. Instead, for ease of understanding and mastery, complex skills and understandings must first be divided into significant component parts.

Task analysis involves dividing a complex skill into its component parts so it can be taught in a step-by-step fashion.

Task analysis helps a teacher define precisely what it is the learner needs to do to perform a desired skill. It can be accomplished through the following steps:

Step 1: Find out what a knowledgeable person does when the skill is performed.
Step 2: Divide the overall skill into subskills.
Step 3: Put subskills in some logical order, showing those that might be prerequisites to others.
Step 4: Design strategies to teach each of the subskills and how they are combined.

Sometimes a task analysis can take the form of a flow chart. This allows the skill and the relationships among subskills to be visualized. It also can show the various steps that a learner must go through in acquiring the skill. A complex skill required of students taking science classes is how to use a microscope. There are several steps and subskills students must master before they can focus and use a microscope effectively and safely. Figure 8.2 illustrates a task analysis done by a high school biology teacher illustrating the steps and subskills for using a microscope properly.

Figure 8.2 *Viewing a Specimen in an Electric Microscope*

Subskill 1, *Getting Started:* Plug in the microscope and make sure it is on low power.

Subskill 2, *Positioning the Slide:* Place the slide with the specimen directly over the center of the glass circle on the microscope's stage. If you see your eyelashes, move closer. Be sure to close one eye.

Subskill 3, *Focusing:* Only if you are on low power, lower the objective lens to the lowest point, then focus using first the course knob, then the fine focus knob.

Subskill 4, *Finding Detail:* Adjust the diaphragm as you look through the eyepiece; you will see more detail when you allow less light.

Subskill 5, *Using High Power:* Once you have found the specimen in low power, switch to high power without changing the focus knobs. If you don't have the specimen centered, you will lose it, as illustrated in the diagram below.

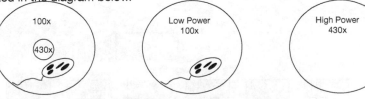

Subskill 6, *Using Fine Focus Knob:* Once you have your specimen on high power you can use the fine focus knob. Caution: Do not remove the slide when on high power and do not use the course focus knob. This will scratch or crack the lens.

Source: Adapted from instructions found on http://shs.westport.k12.ct.us/mjvl/biology/microscope/microscope.htm. Retrieved April 12, 2005.

It would be a mistake to believe that teachers do detailed learning progression or task analysis for every skill they teach. Effective teachers, however, rely on the main concept associated with these tools; that is, that most skills have several subskills and that learners cannot learn to perform the whole skill well unless they have mastered the parts. However, teachers should remain cognizant that knowing how to do all the parts may not automatically result in putting all the parts together so the larger, more complex skill can be performed appropriately.

Plan for Time and Space. Planning and managing time is very important for a direct instruction lesson. The teacher must ensure that time is sufficient, that it matches the aptitudes and abilities of the students in the class, and that students are motivated to stay engaged throughout the lesson. Making sure that students understand the purposes of direct instruction lessons and tying lessons into their prior knowledge and interests are ways of increasing student attention and engagement.

Planning and managing space is also very important for a direct instruction lesson. Many teachers prefer to use the more traditional row-and-column desk formation that was illustrated in Chapter 7. This formation, you remember, is best suited to situations in which attention needs to be focused on the teacher or on information being displayed in the front of the room. A variant on the traditional row-and-column arrangement is the horizontal row desk arrangement illustrated in Figure 8.3. Students sit quite close to each other in a fewer number of rows. This arrangement is often useful for direct instruction demonstrations in which it is important that students see what is going on or for them to be quite close to the teacher. Neither the row-and-column nor the horizontal arrangement is conducive to student-centered teaching approaches that depend on student-to-student interaction.

Conducting Direct Instruction Lessons

Experienced teachers learn to adjust their use of direct instruction to fit various situations; nonetheless, most direct instruction lessons have five essential phases or steps. The lesson begins with the teacher providing a rationale for the lesson, establishing set, and getting students ready to learn. This preparational and motivational phase is then followed by presentation of the subject matter being taught or demonstration of a particular skill. The lesson then provides opportunities for guided student practice and teacher feedback on student progress. In the practice-feedback phase, teachers try to provide opportunities for students to transfer the knowledge or skill being taught to real-life situations. Direct instruction lessons conclude with extended practice and the transfer of skills. The five phases of a direct instruction lesson are summarized in Table 8.2.

Figure 8.3 *Horizontal Desk Formation*

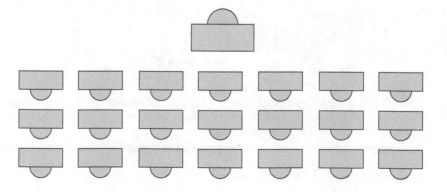

Table 8.2 *Syntax of a Direct Instruction Lesson*

Phase	Teacher Behavior
Phase 1: Gain attention, clarify goals, and establish set.	Teacher gains students' attention and ensures they are ready to learn by going over goals for the lesson, giving background information, and explaining why the lesson is important.
Phase 2: Demonstrate knowledge or skill.	Teacher demonstrates the skill correctly or presents step-by-step information.
Phase 3: Provide guided practice.	Teacher structures initial practice.
Phase 4: Check for understanding and provide feedback.	Teacher checks to see if students are performing correctly and provides feedback.
Phase 5: Provide extended practice and transfer.	Teacher sets conditions for extended practice with attention to transfer of the skill to more complex situations.

Provide Objectives and Establish Set. Regardless of the situation, good teachers begin their lessons by explaining their objectives, establishing a learning set, and getting their students' attention. As previously described, an abbreviated version of the objectives can be written on the chalkboard, displayed on an electronic device, or printed and distributed to students. This provides students with cues about what is going to happen. In addition, students should be told how a particular day's objective ties into previous ones and, in most instances, how it is a part of longer-range objectives or themes. They should also be informed about the flow of a particular lesson and about how much time the lesson is expected to take. Figure 8.4 shows what a science teacher provided for his students before a lesson on microscopes.

Giving the rationale and overviews for any lesson is important, but it is particularly so for skill-oriented lessons. Such lessons typically focus on discrete skills that students may not perceive as important but that require substantial motivation and commitment to remain engaged. Knowing the rationale for learning a particular skill helps

Today's objective: The objective of today's lesson is to learn how to bring into focus the lens on a compound light microscope so you can make an accurate observation of a specimen.

Agenda

5 minutes	Introduction, review, and objectives.
5 minutes	Rationale.
10 minutes	How to use and focus an electric microscope. Demonstrate each subskill.
20 minutes	Practice with your microscope (I'll come around and help).
10 minutes	Wrap-up and assignment for tomorrow.

Figure 8.4 *Aims and Overview of Today's Lesson on Microscopes*

"And then, of course, there's the possibility of being just the slightest bit too organized."

Reprinted by permission of Glen Dines/KAPPAN.

Effective demonstration requires a thorough mastery of what is being taught and careful rehearsal before the classroom event.

to motivate and bring the desired commitment, unlike such general statements as, "It's good for you," "You'll need it to find a job," or "It is required in the curriculum standard."

Conduct Demonstrations. Direct instruction relies heavily on the proposition that much of what is learned and much of the learner's behavioral repertoire comes from *observing* others. Remember, social cognitive theory holds that it is from watching particular behaviors that students learn to perform them and to anticipate their consequences. The behaviors of others, both good and bad, thus become guides for the learner's own behavior. This form of learning by imitation saves students much needless trial and error. It can also cause them to learn inappropriate or incorrect behaviors. To effectively demonstrate a particular concept or skill requires teachers to *acquire mastery*, or a thorough understanding, of the concept or skills before the demonstration and to carefully *rehearse* all aspects of the demonstration before the actual classroom event. The Enhancing Teaching and Learning with Technology box for this chapter describes how interactive whiteboards and responders can be used to make demonstrations more effective.

Acquiring Mastery and Understanding. To ensure that students will observe correct rather than incorrect behaviors, teachers must attend to exactly what goes into their demonstrations. The old adage often recited to children by parents, "Do as I say, not as I do," is not sufficient for teachers trying to teach precise basic information or skills. Examples abound in every aspect of human endeavor where people unknowingly perform a skill incorrectly because they observed and learned the skill from someone who was doing it wrong. The important point here is that if teachers want students to do something right, they must ensure that it is demonstrated correctly.

Attend to Rehearsal. It is exceedingly difficult to demonstrate anything with complete accuracy. The more complex the information or skill, the more difficult it is to be precise in classroom demonstrations. Ensuring correct demonstration and modeling requires practice ahead of time. It also requires that the critical attributes of the skill or concept be thought through clearly and distinctly. For example, suppose you want to teach your students how to use a computerized system for locating information in the library and you are going to demonstrate how call numbers correspond to a book's location. It is important to prepare and rehearse so the numbering system demonstrated is consistent with what students will find in their particular library. If the demonstration consists of such steps as turning on the computer, punching in identifying information on the book, writing down the call number, and then proceeding to the stacks, it is important that these steps be rehearsed to the point that none (such as writing down the call number) is forgotten during the actual demonstration.

Provide Guided Practice. Practice is at the heart of direct instruction, and common sense says that practice makes perfect. In reality, this principle does not always hold up. Everyone knows people who drive their cars every day but who are still poor drivers or people who have many children but who are poor parents. All too often, the assignments teachers give students do not really provide for the type of practice that is needed. Writing out answers to questions at the end of a chapter, doing twenty mathematics problems, or writing an essay does not always help students master important skills.

Enhancing Teaching and Learning with Technology

Consider Using Interactive Whiteboards and Responders

Teachers can make their presentations and demonstrations more interesting and thoughtful with the use of computers and interactive multimedia devices such as interactive whiteboards. Unlike presentations and demonstrations that use the chalkboard or the overhead projector, multimedia presentations on interactive whiteboards can incorporate text, sound, pictures, graphics, and video. When used in conjunction with student responders, these interactive demonstrations and presentations can also facilitate student involvement. Both interactive whiteboards and responders are technological tools that most (if not all) of you have likely experienced in some of your K–12 or college classrooms. The explanation provided here is to provide information about how these devices can facilitate student learning from the perspective of a teacher as contrasted to the one you may hold from your use as a student.

Multimedia Presentations

Multimedia refers to integrating more than one medium, such as text, graphics, audio, and video, into a presentation. As you have learned, sending instructional messages with both words *and* pictures is much more effective than using a single modality (Meyer, 2011a, 2011b). Today, teachers can enhance their presentations and demonstrations in any subject with the use of multimedia software. On one end of the difficulty spectrum would be presentations designed to illustrate new information or ideas simply with text and pictures, perhaps by using PowerPoint software. At the other end would be the use of interactive whiteboards and student responders.

Interactive Whiteboards

It is likely that most of you have observed some of your teachers and professors using interactive whiteboards, which are essentially large display screens mounted in front of the classroom and connected to a computer that has Internet access and that can display video and audio.

An interactive whiteboard presentation, like any presentation, requires teachers to make clear decisions about content, the sequencing of information and ideas, the correct use of advance organizers, and the proper use of demonstration techniques. However, unlike traditional presentations or demonstrations that use only words, the use of multimedia requires planning for the visual and audio aspects of the presentation or demonstration. Many teachers accomplish this by using storyboards, a device for showing what information (text, image, audio) goes on each slide or flipchart. Putting information about each slide on a 5 × 8 card allows easy arrangement until the "story" is presented in the manner that makes the most sense.

Once the content of a demonstration or presentation has been determined, other design issues need to be considered. Following are several, drawn mainly from Bitter and Pierson (2002) and Marzano (2009):

- Limit the amount of text on any single slide or flipchart.
- Group information into small, meaningful segments; teach and demonstrate in small chunks.
- Use graphics or other types of visuals to break up large amounts of text.
- Choose a font that is legible. Those between 19 and 24 points with no decorative features work best.
- Use phrases or key words.
- Don't use all capital letters; they are difficult to read. The "wizard" in PowerPoint helps make suggestions on the use of capital letters.
- Use appropriate color. Contrast text and background (for example, a dark background with light text).
- Use graphics or sound for a real purpose, not as mere decoration.

Many teachers have embraced interactive whiteboards and see their potential to enhance student learning. However, others have written that they are nothing more than glorified chalkboards and that less-expensive alternatives will do the same thing. An exercise at the end of the chapter encourages you to practice using interactive whiteboards and then make your own assessment about their value.

Teachers have found the usefulness of having students create their own multimedia presentations that incorporate text, sound, video, and graphics. This type of learning activity can help students achieve multiple learning objectives. Students are highly motivated and learn the content more thoroughly as a result of having to design a presentation and present it to others. In addition, students learn how to use technology and software widely used in the adult world. Teachers have helped students of all ages develop multi-media presentations. Obviously, younger students will require more assistance than older students, and the projects they create will not be as complex as those done by older students. Some research evidence suggests that using multimedia can be constructivist in nature and improve the self-directedness of learners.

Student Responders

Responders are handheld devices that you have likely used in your college classes. Today, many school districts have purchased these devices, which allow students to respond to questions posed by teachers during a presentation or demonstration. Responders are a form of formative assessment that allow teachers to collect information about what students understand several times during a presentation lesson. They are an electronic version of the "help cards" and "traffic lights" described in Chapters 5 and 6. Although responders have positive benefits, they also have their critics. Some

worry that their use may push out other and more meaningful and complete forms of formative assessment. Marzano (2009) has observed how they are often misused. He provides the following pitfalls to avoid:

- Using responders, but doing little or nothing with the results (for example, moving forward with a presentation or demonstration even though most of the students report a lack of understanding)
- Failing to discuss correct and incorrect answers after getting student responses
- Failing to get students to focus on "why" an answer is correct or incorrect

Regardless of how well interactive whiteboards and responders are used in presentation and demonstration lessons, we all need to remember that they are still basically a transmission approach to instruction limited to achievement of certain instructional outcomes at the expense of others.

Guided practice increases retention, makes skills more automatic, and promotes transfer to new situations.

A critical step in direct instruction is the way the teacher approaches **guided practice.** Fortunately for teachers, a considerable amount of research evidence now exists that can guide efforts to provide practice (Kumar, 1991; Marzano, 2007; Rosenshine, 2002, 2012). For example, we know that active practice can increase retention, make learning more automatic, and enable the learner to transfer learning to new or stressful situations. The following principles can guide the ways teachers provide for practice.

Assign Short, Meaningful Amounts of Practice. In most instances, particularly with a new skill, it is important to ask students to perform the desired skill for short periods of time and, if the skill is complex, to simplify the task at the beginning. Brevity and simplification, however, should not distort the pattern of the whole skill.

Assign Practice to Increase Overlearning. For skills that are critical to later performance, practice must continue well beyond the stage of initial mastery. Many skills associated with the performing arts, athletics, reading, and typing have to be over-learned so they become automatic. It is only through **overlearning** and complete mastery that a skill can be used effectively in new situations or under stress. This ability to automatically perform a skill or combination of skills is what separates a novice from an expert in all fields. Particular skills or understandings that are not sufficiently mastered through careful rehearsal will not be transferred and stored into long-term memory. Teachers must be careful, however, because efforts to produce overlearning can become monotonous and may decrease students' motivation to learn.

Overlearning a skill produces the automaticity needed to use it in various combinations and in both novel and stressful situations.

In general, massed practice is recommended when students learn new skills. Distributed practice is recommended when they refine existing skills.

Be Aware of the Advantages and Disadvantages of Massed and Distributed Practice. Psychologists have typically defined this issue as **massed** (continuous) **practice** versus **distributed** (divided into segments) **practice.** Although the research literature does not give direct principles that can be followed in every instance, massed practice is usually recommended for learning new skills, with the caution that long periods of practice can lead to boredom and fatigue. Distributed practice is most effective

Some skills can be practiced with computers.

for refining already familiar skills, again with the caution that the interval of time between practice segments should not be so long that students forget or regress and have to start over again.

Attend to the Initial Stages of Practice. The initial stages of practice are particularly critical, because it is during this period that the learner can unknowingly start using incorrect techniques that later must be unlearned. It is also during the initial stages of practice that the learner will want to measure success in terms of his or her performance as contrasted to technique. This issue is described more completely in the following section.

Check Understanding and Provide Feedback. This is the phase of a direct instruction lesson that most closely resembles what is sometimes called *recitation*. It is often characterized by the teacher asking students questions and students providing answers they deem to be correct, or the teacher calling on students and asking them to demonstrate a particular skill or subskill. This is a very important aspect of a direct instruction lesson because without knowledge of results, practice is of little value to students. In fact, the most important task of teachers using direct instruction is providing students with meaningful feedback and **knowledge of results.** Teachers can give feedback in many ways, such as verbally, by video- or audiotaping performance, by testing, or through written comments. Without specific feedback, however, students will not learn to write well by writing, read well by reading, or run well by running. The critical question for teachers is how to provide effective feedback for large classes of students. Guidelines considered most important, some of which were described in Chapter 6, include the following.

Without knowledge of results (feedback), practice is of little value to students.

Guideline 1: Provide Feedback as Soon as Possible after the Practice. It is not necessary that feedback be provided instantaneously, but it should be close enough to the actual practice that students can remember clearly their own performance. This means that teachers who provide written comments on essays should be prompt in returning corrected papers. It means they should immediately correct tests gauged to measure performance and go over them with students. It also means that arrangements for verbal, video, or audio feedback should be such that delay is kept to a minimum.

For best results, feedback should be as specific as possible, be provided immediately following practice, and fit the developmental level of the learner.

Guideline 2: Make Feedback Specific. In general, feedback should be as specific as possible to be most helpful to students. For example:

"Your use of the word *domicile* is pretentious; *house* would do nicely."
Instead of:
"You are using too many big words."
Or:
"Your hand was placed exactly right for an effective backhand."
Instead of:
"Good backhand."
Or:
"Three words were spelled incorrectly on your paper: *Pleistocene, penal,* and recommendation."
Instead of:
"Too many misspelled words."

Guideline 3: Concentrate on Behaviors and Not Intent. Feedback is most helpful and raises less defensiveness with students if it is aimed directly at some behavior rather than at one's interpretation of the intent behind the behavior. For example:

"I cannot read your handwriting. You do not provide enough blank space between words, and you make your O's and A's identical."
Instead of:
"You do not work on making your handwriting neat."
Or:
"When you faced the class in your last speech, you spoke so softly that most students could not hear what you were saying,"
Instead of:
"You should try to overcome your shyness."

Guideline 4: Keep Feedback Appropriate to the Developmental Stage of the Learner. As important as knowledge of results is, feedback must be administered carefully to be helpful. Sometimes, students can be given too much feedback or feedback that is too sophisticated for them to handle. For example, a person trying to drive a car for the first time can appreciate hearing that he or she "let the clutch" out too quickly, causing the car to jerk. A beginning driver, however, is not ready for explanations about how to drop the brake and use the clutch to keep the car from rolling on a steep hill.

A young student being taught the "i before e" rule in spelling probably will respond favorably to being told that he or she spelled *brief* correctly but may not be ready to consider why *recieve* was incorrect.

Guideline 5: Emphasize Praise and Feedback on Correct Performance. Everyone prefers to receive positive rather than negative feedback. In general, praise will be accepted whereas negative feedback may be denied. Teachers, therefore, should try to provide praise and positive feedback, particularly when students are learning new concepts and skills. However, when incorrect performance is observed, it must be corrected. Here is a sensible way to approach the problem of dealing with incorrect responses and performance:

> **Although incorrect performance must be corrected, teachers should try to provide positive feedback when students are learning new skills.**

1. Dignify the student's incorrect response or performance by giving a question for which the response would have been correct. For example, "George Washington would have been the right answer if I had asked you who was the first president of the United States."
2. Provide the student with an assist, hint, or prompt. For example, "Remember the president in 1828 had also been a hero in the War of 1812."
3. Hold the student accountable. For example, "You didn't know President Jackson today, but I bet you will tomorrow when I ask you again."

A combination of positive and negative feedback is best in most instances. For example, "You did a perfect job of matching subjects and verbs in this paragraph, except in the instance in which you used a collective subject." Or, "You were holding the racket correctly as you approached the ball, but you had too much of your weight on your left foot." Or, "I like the way you speak up in class, but during our last class discussion, you interrupted Ron three different times when he was trying to give us his point of view."

> **Negative feedback should be accompanied by demonstrations of how to correctly perform the skill.**

Guideline 6: When Giving Negative Feedback, Show How to Perform Correctly. Knowing that something has been done incorrectly does not help students do it correctly. Negative feedback should always be accompanied by teacher actions that demonstrate the correct performance. If a student is shooting a basketball with the palm of the hand, the teacher should point that out and demonstrate how to place the ball on the fingertips. If a writing sample is splattered with incorrectly used words, the teacher should pencil in words that are more appropriate. If students are holding their hands incorrectly on the computer keyboard, the teacher should model the correct placement.

Guideline 7: Help Students to Focus on Process, Not Just Outcomes. Many times beginners want to focus their attention on measurable performance. "I just typed thirty-five words per minute without any errors." "I wrote my essay in an hour." "I drove the golf ball 175 yards." "I cleared the bar at 4 feet, 6 inches." It is the teacher's responsibility to get students to look at the *process,* or technique, behind their performance and to help students understand that incorrect techniques may achieve immediate objectives but will probably prohibit later growth. For example, a student may type thirty-five words per minute using only two fingers but will probably never reach one hundred words per minute using this technique. Starting the approach on the wrong foot may be fine for clearing the high jump bar at 4 feet, 6 inches, but will prevent the athlete from ever reaching 5 feet, 6 inches.

Guideline 8: Teach Students How to Provide Feedback to Themselves and How to Judge Their Own Performance. It is important for students to learn how to assess and judge their own performance. Teachers can help students judge their own performance in many ways. They can explain the criteria used by experts in judging performance; they can give students opportunities to judge peers and to assess their own progress in relation to others; and they can emphasize the importance of self-monitoring, goal setting, and not being satisfied with only "extrinsic" feedback from the teacher.

The process of assigning practice and giving students feedback is a very important job teachers have, and it requires learning a complex set of behaviors. A learning activity in the *Portfolio and Field Experience Activities* is designed to help you observe how experienced teachers use practice and provide feedback.

Provide Independent Practice. In most instances guided practice is typically followed by **independent practice**. This provides students with opportunities to perform newly acquired skills on their own. Additional rehearsal is also important because it helps secure mastery or fluency with a particular understanding or skill. There are two important guidelines for providing independent practice. First, independent practice should be over the same skill or material as the guided practice. It should not be over new skills or material. Second, students need to be fully prepared to accomplish the tasks associated with the independent practice. Independent practice can be accomplished in class as **seatwork** or after class as **homework**.

> Homework is most often a continuation of practice and should involve activities that students can perform successfully.

Seatwork. Seatwork refers to work and practice assigned to be completed in the classroom; its use is very common, particularly among teachers in the elementary grades. The following guidelines are suggested for seatwork:

> Seatwork is independent practice or work performed in the classroom.

1. Assign seatwork that students will find interesting and enjoyable. Restrict the use of standard worksheets.
2. Make sure students understand what the seatwork assignment requires.
3. In general, make seatwork following a direct instruction lesson a continuation of the guided practice, not a continuation or extension of the actual instruction.
4. Have clear procedures about what students should do if they get stuck, and have recommendations for students who finish before others as well as those who lag behind.

> Homework is independent practice or work performed by students outside of the classroom.

Homework. For a long time, the value of homework has been debated and the effects of homework are not as positive and clear-cut as some teachers, parents, and policymakers believe. Further, the popularity of homework has changed over time.

In the nineteenth century it was believed that homework was "good discipline" for the mind. During the early twentieth century progressive educators believed homework was too structured and argued that it intruded on students' family lives. Strauss (2006) reported that in the 1930s the American Health Association declared child labor and homework as leading killers of children with tuberculosis and heart disease. Today, you can find strong advocates for the use of homework (Cooper, Robinson, & Patall, 2006; Marzano & Pickering, 2007) as well as those who view homework as a waste of time and a useless practice (Bennett & Kalish, 2006; Kohn, 2006, 2007, 2012). The exact nature of homework and the amount to assign remains somewhat controversial. Both sides are summarized briefly below.

Harris Cooper and his colleagues have studied the nature and effects of homework for quite some time, including summarizing other research on this topic (Cooper, 1989; Cooper, Jackson, Nye, & Lindsey, 2001; Cooper, Robinson, & Patall, 2006;

Home and School

Gaining Appropriate Participation from Home

It is important for parents to be involved in appropriate ways in their children's homework. However, many parents report that they feel inadequate and that homework often leads to family stress (Corno, 1996, 2001). Epstein (2001, 2010) and Marzano (2007) have helped define ways to encourage effective parent involvement.

- Provide parents with clear guidelines about assignments and how they should help. These guidelines may be defined in overall school policies or they may be instructions from a particular teacher. For example, teachers might attach a note to a particular assignment,

  "The homework tonight is to teach . . ."

  "You can help by . . ."

- Communicate to parents that they are not expected to be experts but can play other important roles such as simply having their child show and explain his or her homework products.

- Encourage parents to be accessible so they can become engaged in conversation about the homework and ask questions that help their child clarify or summarize what he or she has learned.

Some parents and caregivers will be skillful in following teachers' directions about how to provide appropriate participation in homework. Others will not have these skills. Many teachers find that having special sessions or workshops about homework on "family nights" can produce greater and more appropriate family participation and result in higher student motivation and achievement.

Cooper & Valentine, 2001). Over time, Cooper and his colleagues, as well as others (Maltese, Tai, & Fan, 2012), have uncovered the following about the effects of homework:

- *Homework seems to have very little effect on learning in the elementary grades.* However, Cooper and his colleagues (1989, 2006) recommend that elementary students be given some homework because it helps develop good study habits and attitudes toward school.
- *Homework does lead to more learning in grade 6 and higher.* Cooper and his colleagues as well as others (Good & Brophy, 2003) recommend that to be effective homework has to be meaningful and confined to an appropriate amount of time. It also has to be well articulated to students and designed to have a high completion rate. Doing homework just for the sake of "doing homework" is likely a waste of time.
- *Homework has effects beyond just academic learning.* Lyn Corno (2001) observed that "homework involves important social, cultural, and educative issues . . . it is not just an academic task. It is one that infiltrates family and peer dynamics and the nature of teaching in community organizations as well as the school" (p. 529). Homework provides a means for social communication among students and a source of interaction between students and their parents. This issue is explored further in the Home and School feature for this chapter.
- *Student learning is affected by the amount of homework assigned.* Cooper, Robinson, and Patall (2006) report that 7 to 12 hours a week for older students produces the largest effects. Good and Brophy (2003) and Bennett, Finn, and Cribb (1999) recommend that about 5 to 10 minutes per night, per grade level is a good rule of thumb to follow. This translates into 10 to 20 minutes a night for students in the lower grades and up to 30 to 60 minutes for high school students.

On the other side, there are serious critics of homework, such as Kohn (2006, 2007, 2012) and Bennett and Kalish (2006). They challenge the effects of homework and point out several unintended negative consequences. Alfie Kohn, for example, has argued that the correlation between homework and test scores is actually quite small and that non-academic benefits such as good work habits and positive character traits could best be described as "urban myths." He has also questioned relationships between the amount of time spent on homework and the grades students achieve. Critics have also argued that homework is overused and that it leads to "stress, frustration, family conflict, loss of time for other activities, and a possible diminution of interest in learning" (Kohn, 2006b, p. 2). Homework persists, according to critics, because of tradition and because of misconceptions held by parents and by educators about the way people learn.

Regardless of debates over the effects of seatwork and homework, it is likely both will remain institutionalized in American education for some time to come. Thus it behooves teachers to proceed with caution and follow guidelines supported somewhat by research but also to remain aware of possible negative and unintended consequences. Several recommendations seem appropriate. These are summarized next.

1. As with seatwork, assign work that is *interesting* and *potentially enjoyable* and make sure students understand the task.

2. *Give students homework that is appropriately challenging and that they can perform successfully.* Homework, like seatwork, should not involve the *continuation of instruction* but rather it should be the *continuation of practice* or preparation for the next day's instruction.

3. *Use frequent and smaller homework assignments rather than less frequent and large assignments.* Of course, this guideline is influenced by the nature of the subject and the age of the student. For example, larger project-based assignments as described in Chapter 11 are highly desirable, particularly for older students. Practicing specific skills, however, is generally better in smaller rather than larger doses.

4. *Make homework rules clear.* Students should clearly understand whether they can share work with peers, whether parents can help, whether they can use their calculators, the degree to which they can consult the Internet, and consequences of not having homework completed on time.

5. *Inform parents about the level of involvement expected of them.* Are they expected to help their sons or daughters with answers to difficult questions or simply to provide a quiet atmosphere in which to study? Are they encouraged to check homework after it is completed? Do they know the approximate frequency and duration of homework assignments?

6. *Provide feedback and grades on the homework promptly.* Many teachers simply check to determine whether homework was performed. What this says to students is that it doesn't matter how it is done, as long as it is done. Students soon figure out that the task is to get something—anything—on paper. This sets a bad precedent. One method of providing feedback relatively easily is to involve students in correcting one another's homework. Similarly, homework must be returned in a prompt fashion if students are to benefit from the assignment.

7. Consider the *use of flipping* described in this chapter's Enhancing Teaching and Learning with Technology feature

Diversity and Differentiation

Varying Direct Instruction Lessons to Meet Diverse Needs

Chapter 2 described many ways that children and youth can differ. These differences can include many things such as socioeconomic status, race or ethnicity, gender, ability level, prior knowledge, cognitive style, and a variety of special needs. Chapter 3 described how students differ in terms of their motivational needs. Because of these differences, it is safe to conclude that no single lesson will ever be equally effective with all students. This is also true with direct instruction lessons. Whereas we can provide information about how direct instruction is supposed to work in general, it does not always work as planned in. Effective teachers learn how to adapt their instruction to take into account student diversity. Following are some ways that teachers can tailor direct instruction lessons:

Vary the Structure of the Lesson
- Keep lessons for younger and low-achieving students very structured; keep objectives specific; use a moderately brisk pace.
- Promote extension of basic skill instruction and provide opportunities for exploration for older and higher-achieving students.

Vary the Nature of Presentations and Demonstrations
- Highlight main ideas or procedures on the chalkboard, overhead projector, or other projection devices for younger and low-achieving students. Confine presentations and demonstrations to only a few points or ideas; make them short.
- Extend beyond basic ideas or skills for older and higher-achieving students.

Vary the Nature of Interaction
- Base instruction on students' prior knowledge for all students. Teaching what is already known will bore students; teaching ideas or skills for which insufficient knowledge exists is meaningless.
- Pay attention to cultural differences among racial or ethnic groups in terms of willingness to interact in front of others; do the same for gender.

Vary the Nature of Encouragement and Support
- Provide continuous encouragement and support for low-achieving and more dependent students. The less students know, the more instructional support they need.
- Allow higher-achieving and more independent students to figure things out on their own. Too much teacher encouragement can be perceived as interference. Many approaches can be successful when students know quite a bit about a subject.

Vary the Use of Practice, Seatwork, and Homework
- Make sure practice exercises are well understood and keep seatwork and homework assignments brief for lower-achieving students.
- Limit seatwork and keep homework challenging for higher-achieving, more independent students. Less review and independent practice are required.

Check, Extend, Explore

Check
- What are the major planning tasks associated with a direct instruction lesson?
- Why are learning progressions and task analysis important planning tools for some types of direct instruction lessons?
- What are the five phases of a direct instruction lesson? What kinds of teaching behaviors are associated with each phase?
- What are the major factors teachers should consider when they assign guided practice? Independent practice?
- Summarize the guidelines for effective feedback for homework.

Extend
- There has been considerable debate about homework. How valuable do you think homework is for increasing student learning? Go to the "Extend Question Poll" on the Online Learning Center to respond.

Explore
- Go to the Online Learning Center at www.mhhe.com/arends10e for links to Web sites related to using direct instruction, practice, and homework. Visit Alfie Kohn's Web site at www.alfiekohn.org and browse the various articles he has written that question the value of homework.

Managing the Learning Environment

The tasks associated with managing the learning environment during a direct instruction lesson are almost identical to those used by teachers when employing the presentation approach to instruction. In direct instruction, the teacher structures the learning environment quite tightly, keeps an academic focus, and expects students to be keen observers, listeners, and participants. Effective teachers use the methods described in Chapter 5 to govern student talk and to ensure that lesson pace is maintained. Misbehavior that occurs during a direct instruction lesson must be dealt with accurately and quickly. However, maintenance of a structured environment with an academic focus should not rule out an environment also characterized by democratic processes and positive feeling tones.

Assessment and Evaluation

Chapter 6 emphasized the importance of matching testing and evaluation strategies to the goals and objectives for particular lessons and the inherent purposes of a particular model. Because direct instruction is used most appropriately for teaching skills and knowledge that can be taught in a step-by-step fashion, evaluation should focus on performance tests measuring skill development rather than on paper-and-pencil tests of declarative knowledge. For example, being able to identify the characters on the computer's keyboard obviously does not tell us much about a person's keyboarding skills; however, a timed keyboarding test does. Being able to identify verbs in a column of nouns does not mean that a student can write a sentence; it takes an assessment that requires the student to write a sentence to enable a teacher to evaluate that student's skill. Reciting the correct steps in any of the approaches to teaching described in this book does not tell us whether a teacher can design and execute effective lessons for a class of twenty-five students. Only a classroom demonstration can exhibit the teacher's mastery of that skill.

Many times, performance tests are difficult for teachers to devise and to score with precision, and they can also be very time-consuming. However, if you want your students to master the skills you teach, nothing will substitute for performance-based evaluation procedures. Table 8.3 lists examples of the type of test items that would be included on a performance test and contrasts those with items on the same topic that one would find on a test to assess declarative knowledge. Note that the test items correspond to the sample objectives provided in Table 8.1.

A Final Thought: Considering the Use of Direct Instruction

Teacher use of direct instruction comprises a large proportion of classroom time in American classrooms. The amount of time devoted to explaining information, and demonstrating, increases at the higher grade levels of elementary school, in middle schools, and in high schools. It is prevalent everywhere and remains a popular and effective approach to teaching. However, direct instruction is not without its critics, and it will be important for you to be aware of the complaints that have been lodged against direct instruction and to explore your own views and values about its use in your classroom.

Observing actual performance is the best way to assess skill development.

Table 8.3 *Items for Knowledge Test and Skill Test*

Declarative Knowledge Test	**Skill Performance Test**
1. How many players are there on an ice hockey team?	**1.** Demonstrate a pass while moving.
a. 6	
b. 8	
c. 10	
d. none of the above	
2. What is the subject of the following sentence? *"Mary's mother is an artist."*	**2.** Correct the verbs, as needed, in the following sentences:
a. Mary	**a.** Kim ran slowly to the store.
b. mother	**b.** Tommy said it was time to go.
c. an	**c.** Levon sat joyfully to greet her day.
d. artist	**d.** "Please be noisier," said the teacher.
3. At what point is the intercept located?	**3.** Solve for x in the following equations:
a. 1	**a.** $2 = x + 4$
b. 2	**b.** $5x = 1 + (x/2)$
c. 3	**c.** $14 = 2x + 9x$
d. 4	**d.** $x/3 = 9$

Because direct instruction is a popular teaching method, teachers should be aware of problems cited by critics.

The primary criticism of direct instruction is that it is teacher-centered and puts too much emphasis on teacher talk. Most observers claim that teacher talk accounts for between one-half and three-fourths of every class period, and according to Cuban (1982, 1993), and Lobato, Clarke, and Burns (2005), this phenomenon has remained constant during most of the past one hundred years. Some educators argue that too much time is devoted to direct instruction. Others argue that direct instruction is limited to teaching basic skills and low-level information and that it is not useful for accomplishing higher-level objectives. Still others criticize the approach because of the behavioral theory underlying it. They argue that it unavoidably supports the view that students are empty vessels to be filled with carefully segmented information and behaviors rather than active learners with an innate need to acquire information and construct their own knowledge. Finally, there are those, including some of direct instruction's early creators, who criticize direct instruction because of abuses in the way in which the approach has been implemented in many classrooms. For example, in one large public school system on the East Coast, every teacher was expected to give a direct instruction lesson every day. If a teacher used other approaches while being observed by a supervisor, the teacher received a negative evaluation. In another instance, teachers were required to write their objectives in behavioral format on the chalkboard every day, something never envisioned by the developers of direct instruction.

The continued popularity of explaining and demonstrating is not surprising because the most widely held educational objectives are those associated with the acquisition of important skills and the retention of basic information. Consequently, curriculum frameworks and standards, textbooks, and tests are similarly organized and are routinely used by teachers. Experienced teachers know that direct instruction is an effective way to help students acquire the array of basic information and skills believed by society to be important for students to know. Educational researcher Schmoker (2012) agrees, and he reports that traditional direct instruction lessons have maintained their "staying power" over a very long period of time.

This book takes a balanced view toward direct instruction and argues that teachers do not have to choose. As repeatedly stressed, direct instruction is just one of several approaches used by effective teachers. The real key to effective instruction is a teacher's ability to call on a varied repertoire of instructional approaches that permit a teacher to match instructional approaches to particular learning outcomes and to the needs of particular students.

Check, Extend, Explore

Check
- If you observed a direct instruction lesson, what kind of learning environment would you likely find?
- What kinds of assessments are best to measure mastery of direct instruction objectives?

Extend
- Do you agree or disagree that teachers can have a task-oriented, academic-focused learning environment, yet be positive and democratic? Go to the "Extend Question Poll" on the Online Learning Center to respond.

Explore
- Do a Google search on "direct instruction." Over 80,000 Web sites will appear, many related to education. The Association for Direct Instruction sponsors one of particular interest to beginning teachers. Browse through this site to learn more about direct instruction.
- Go to the Online Learning Center at www.mhhe.com/arends10e for links to Web sites related to assessment and managing the learning environment.

Reflections from the *Classroom*

Just the Basics

In your first teaching position, you find yourself in a school where the teachers were trained over ten years ago in a particular approach to direct instruction. Although there has been considerable teacher turnover in the school, the direct instruction approach seems to dominate all others and is used by *all* teachers in the school. Teachers are expected to develop lesson plans using behavioral objectives and to follow the steps of the direct instruction approach. The overall ethos of the school reflects an emphasis on teaching basic skills with heavy emphasis on drill and practice.

You believe in teaching basic skills to students. However, you also believe that curriculum should be individualized for your students and that students should be allowed considerable autonomy in identifying their own goals, asking their own questions, and pursuing some of their own interests.

As you reflect on this situation and your approach to teaching, consider the following:

- Think about a unit you might teach at your grade level or teaching field. What do you want your students to get out of it? Write these goals down. Ask yourself which goals are dictated by your school's curriculum and which are dictated by the faculty's overall approach to teaching? By your own beliefs? By those of your students? You might consider ranking these goals numerically.
- If you are in a field placement, share your goals with a fellow student or a teacher in the school. You might also discuss the goals with some students in the school. Get their opinion about which of the goals are the most important.

Now write down how you are going to approach your unit and which goals and approaches you will emphasize, remembering, of course, that your own personal views of teaching are at odds with those of the majority of teachers in your school. Approach the situation from the perspective closest to the grade level or subject area you are preparing to teach. When you have finished, include your work as an exhibit in your professional portfolio. Compare your thoughts with the following comments from teachers who have faced the same or a similar situation.

Kendra Ganzer

Adams Elementary School, 5th Grade, Des Moines, IA

My best advice to a new teacher is to use your professional judgment to determine what is the most appropriate course of action. As a new teacher, you know that basic skills are important, but you also know there is more than one way to help students learn. The classroom will be a new place for you so other teachers' experiences definitely warrant your attention and respect. Direct instruction does have a place in the classroom. It is an effective method when it fits the desired goals and outcomes of your lesson, but certainly you do not want to be forced to use it as your only method just because the rest of the staff prefers it.

I would plan my lessons using the instructional methods I deem most appropriate, and I would include direct instruction as one. If teachers see me using other methods, such as cooperative learning, I would tell them how I have found it to be successful when used in other classrooms. I would share with them how teacher education and instructional methods are changing. I would also share information from a research article or a textbook that supports the use of cooperative learning or other methods. However, I would not discredit my colleagues' use of direct instruction. If you ask for their advice, you could get great ideas for your lessons. You can then modify them to fit your own teaching situation. After some time, you can show examples of students' work or projects to other teachers and demonstrate how your students are learning the basic skills in the process.

Faye Airey

Thomas R. Grover Middle School, 6th through 8th Grade, West Windsor-Plainsboro, NJ

In my years of teaching, I have witnessed significant shifts of opinion about the teaching of basic skills. Should student learning focus primarily on the fundamentals or are performance-based, real-world, problem-solving tasks more important? This debate has been ongoing for both inexperienced and veteran teachers alike. I support lesson design based on teaching basic skills within a practical, student-centered context, one where students become active participants engaged in tasks directly related to their everyday experiences. These settings present optimal instructional opportunities, where teaching has meaning and learning has purpose.

A practical example might be to design a simulated stock market activity in which students or small student groups invest play money and monitor daily gains/losses based on real-world company performances. What better context for teacher-directed basic-skills lessons on addition and subtraction of fractions or graphing to show stock company trends!

When students are faced with a real need for a particular skill, they become active participants in the learning process. Retention is increased and the ability to make important learning connections is put into practice. Drill and practice without a purposeful context leads to student boredom and frustration; practice within real-life situations is often motivational.

Lesson design that begins by focusing on instructional goals rather than specific teaching objectives places an emphasis on individual student achievement while creating learning opportunities that cultivate natural curiosity. "How are daily stock price changes calculated?" "How can individual stock companies best share performance trends?" Few can question the enthusiasm generated in classrooms where student learning is productive and meaningful. Effective teaching requires a *balance* in which discovery, critical thinking, and questioning lead to a real understanding and mastery of essential basic skills.

Summary

Provide an overview of direct instruction and explain its appropriate use.

- Acquiring basic information and skills is an important goal for students in every subject taught in schools. In almost any field, students must learn the basics before they can go on to more advanced learning.
- The instructional effects of direct instruction are to promote mastery of simple and complex skills and declarative knowledge that can be carefully defined and taught in a step-by-step fashion.
- The general flow or syntax of a direct instruction lesson consists usually of five phases.
- Direct instruction requires a highly structured learning environment and careful orchestration by the teacher. This tight structure does not mean it has to be authoritarian or uncaring.

Describe the theoretical foundations of direct instruction and summarize research that supports its use.

- Direct instruction draws its theoretical support from behavioral theory, social cognitive theory, and teacher effectiveness research.
- Direct instruction has been widely used and tested in school and nonschool settings. The model has strong empirical evidence to support its use for accomplishing certain types of student learning.

Explain how to plan and use direct instruction, including how to adapt its use for students of differing abilities and backgrounds.

- Preinstructional planning tasks associated with the model put emphasis on careful preparation of objectives and performing task analysis.
- The five phases of a direct instruction lesson are (1) providing objectives and establishing set, (2) demonstrating or explaining the materials to be learned, (3) providing guided practice, (4) checking for student understanding and providing feedback, and (5) providing for extended practice and transfer.
- Conducting a direct instruction lesson requires teachers to explain things clearly; to demonstrate and model precise behaviors; and to provide for practice, monitoring of performance, and feedback.
- The use of practice should be guided by several principles: assigning short, meaningful amounts of practice; assigning practice to increase overlearning; and making appropriate use of massed and distributed practice.
- The use of homework has been controversial for a long time, and research about its effects on student achievement has been mixed. It is important to be very clear about the purpose of any homework assignment. Parents should be informed of these purposes and their role.

Describe how to implement a learning environment conducive to using direct instruction.

- Direct instruction lessons require the unique classroom management skill of gaining students' attention in a whole-group setting and sustaining this attention for extended periods of time.
- Particular classroom management concerns include organizing the classroom setting for maximum effect; maintaining appropriate pace, flow, and momentum; sustaining engagement, involvement, and participation; and dealing with student misbehavior quickly and firmly.

Describe appropriate ways to assess student learning consistent with the goals of direct instruction lessons.

- Assessment tasks associated with the model put emphasis on practice and on developing and using appropriate basic knowledge and performance tasks that can accurately measure simple and complex skills and provide feedback to students.

Discuss why direct instruction has remained a popular teaching model, and list some of the model's shortcomings.

- Despite the variety of complaints that have been launched against direct instruction (too teacher-centered, keeps students in passive roles), it remains a very popular teaching model because it allows a teacher to accomplish major goals of education as expressed by the larger society.

Key Terms

behaviorism 306
direct instruction 304
distributed practice 316
guided practice 316
homework 320

independent practice 320
knowledge of results 317
massed practice 316
observational learning 307
overlearning 316

process-product research 308
seatwork 320
social cognitive theory 306
task analysis 311
teacher effectiveness research 307

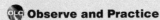

Interactive and Applied Learning

 Study and Explore
- Access your Study Guide, which includes practice quizzes, from the Online Learning Center.

Observe and Practice
- Listen to audio clips on the Online Learning Center of Dennis Walker and Angela Adams (7th and 8th grade special education) talking about direct instruction in the *Teachers on Teaching* area.

Complete **Practice Exercise 8.1,** Planning a Direct Instruction Lesson, including
- Write Objectives
- Plan for Demonstration and Guided Practice
- Differentiate Guided Practice

- Check for Understanding and Provide Feedback
- Plan for Independent Practice
- Assess Student Learning
- Reflect on Planning for Direct Instruction

Complete the following additional **Practice Exercises** that accompany Chapter 8:
- Practice Exercise 8.2: Task Analysis
- Practice Exercise 8.3: Assessing Performance
- Practice Exercise 8.4: Teaching Dilemma: Use of Direct Instruction
- Practice Exercise 8.5: Reflecting on the Use of Direct Instruction
- Practice Exercise 8.6: Using Interactive Whiteboads.

Portfolio and Field Experience Activities

Expand your understanding of the content and processes of this chapter through the following field experience and portfolio activities. Support materials to complete the activities are in the *Portfolio and Field Experience Activities* area located on the Online Learning Center.

1. Complete the **Reflections from the Classroom** exercise at the end of this chapter and use the reflective essay as an exhibit in your portfolio about your views on direct instruction. (**InTASC Standard 8: Instructional Strategies**)

2. Activity 8.1: Assessing My Skills for Using Direct Instruction. Assess your level of understanding and skill to plan and implement a lesson using direct instruction. (**InTASC Standard 8: Instructional Strategies**)

3. **Activity 8.2: Observing Direct Instruction in Micro-teaching or Classrooms.** Observe an experienced teacher during a direct instruction lesson and see how closely he or she follows the syntax described in this chapter. (**InTASC Standard 8: Instructional Strategies**)

4. **Activity 8.3: Observing Teacher Use of Practice.** Observe an experienced teacher assign seatwork or homework to refine your understanding and skill in the use of guided and independent practice. (**InTASC Standard 8: Instructional Strategies**)

5. **Activity 8.4: Portfolio: Demonstrating My Use of Task Analysis.** Complete Activity 8.4 on task analysis and use the product of your work as an artifact in your portfolio. (**InTASC Standard 8: Instructional Strategies**)

Books for the Professional

Fisher, D., & Frey, N. (2010). *Guided instruction: How to develop confident and successful learners.* Alexandria, VA: Association for Supervision and Curriculum Development.

Goeke, J. (2008). *Explicit instruction: Strategies for meaningful direct teaching.* Boston: Allyn & Bacon.

Johnson, S. (2011). *Digital tools for teaching: 30 e-tools for collaborating, creating, and publishing across the curriculum.* Gainesville, FL: Maupin House.

Kohn, A. (2007). *The homework myth: Why our kids get too much of a bad thing.* Cambridge, MA: Capo Lifelong Books.

Kohn, A. (2011). *Feel-bad education: And other contrarian essays on children.* Boston: Beacon Press.

Schmoker, M. (2011). *FOCUS: Elevating the essential to radically improve student performance.* Alexandria, VA: Association for Supervision and Curriculum Development.

PART 4 Overview of Student-Centered Constructivist Approaches to Teaching

The two approaches to teaching described in Part 3 of *Learning to Teach* had their roots in perspectives that grew out of behavioral, cognitive, and information processing theories of learning. These approaches are aimed at helping students learn important, but prescribed, declarative and procedural knowledge and skills. In general, these perspectives lead to teacher-centered instruction, where the teacher specifies the goals of instruction and keeps the classroom learning environment directed and moderately structured.

The approaches described in Part 4 of *Learning to Teach* are mainly student-centered. They rest on a different set of assumptions about teaching and learning. Student-centered instruction rests on the philosophical perspective of John Dewey and other twentieth-century progressive educators as well as on the theoretical perspectives proposed by contemporary developmental and social constructivist theorists. These views hold that knowledge, instead of being objective and fixed, is somewhat personal, social, and cultural. Meaning is constructed by the learner through experience.

This view, often referred to as a *constructivist perspective* on teaching and learning, requires a significantly different set of behaviors for teachers and their students. It also requires different approaches to classroom management and assessment. The accompanying table shows the important differences between teacher-centered and student-centered instruction.

Part 4 of *Learning to Teach* will describe four learner-centered constructivist approaches to instruction: concept and inquiry-based teaching, cooperative learning, problem-based learning, and classroom discussion. You will find that many features of the four approaches are the same. Each encourages student interaction between the teacher and among other students. Each encourages student inquiry and the exploration of ideas. Each requires a learning environment free of threat and characterized by autonomy and support. However, you will also discover some important differences among the four approaches. Some can be used to teach important social skills. Others are more suited for certain kinds of academic learning and inquiry, whereas still other approaches put the emphasis on learning through interaction in small or cooperative learning groups.

Just as with teacher-centered transmission approaches to instruction, there is a substantial knowledge base to support the use of the student-centered constructivist approaches. Wisdom accumulated by experienced teachers over the years also exists. Both of these can guide beginning teachers in their quest to understand and execute these constructivist approaches to teaching.

Comparison of Teacher-Centered Transmission and Student-Centered Constructivist Approaches to Instruction

Feature	Teacher-Centered Transmission Approaches	Student-Centered Constructivist Approaches
Theoretical foundations	Social cognitive, behavioral, and information processing theories	Cognitive and social constructivist theories
Teachers' roles	Teachers design lessons aimed at accomplishing predetermined standards and outcomes; use procedures that support acquisition of specified knowledge and skills.	Teachers establish conditions for student inquiry; involve students in planning; encourage and accept student ideas; and provide them with autonomy and choice.
Students' roles	Students most often in passive roles listening to teachers or reading; practicing teacher-specified skills; some interaction occurs.	Students most often in active roles; interacting with others and participating in investigative and problem-solving activities.
Planning tasks	Mainly teacher dominated; tightly connected to predetermined curriculum standards and goals.	Balance of teacher and student input; flexibly tied to curriculum standards and goals.
Learning environments	For the most part, fairly tightly structured. This does not mean authoritarian or lack of a warm and caring climate.	Loosely structured; characterized by democratic processes, choice, and autonomy to think and inquire.
Assessment procedures	Lends itself to more traditional paper-and-pencil and selected-response procedures and processes.	Lends itself to more authentic and performance assessment procedures and processes.

CHAPTER 9
Concept and Inquiry-Based Teaching

Learning Goals

After studying this chapter you should be able to

Overview of Teaching Students How to Think	Provide an overview of the importance of teaching students how to think and the approaches used to accomplish this goal.
Theoretical Perspectives about Teaching Thinking	Describe the theoretical and empirical support behind teaching students how to think and the use of concept and inquiry-based teaching.
Concept Teaching	Explain how to plan and conduct a concept teaching lesson.
Inquiry-Based Teaching	Explain how to plan and conduct an inquiry-based lesson.
Making Thinking Visible	Explain how to plan and use routines and processes aimed at making thinking visible to students.
Developing Learning Environments That Promote Thinking	Describe how to create a learning environment that will support and promote student thinking.
Assessing Thinking Processes and Skills	Describe appropriate ways to assess student thinking processes and skills.

Reflecting on Concept Teaching

Pick a concept from your teaching field for which you have good knowledge. Examples might include triangle (math); scarcity (economics); movement (PE); love (literature). Write the concept on a piece of paper and make a web that shows other concepts that are related to the one you chose. The figure below shows how a partial web for the concept of *scarcity* might look.

Next, consider how you might teach a young child about the concept of *scarcity*. Using a young child rather than an older one is good for this exercise because you will have to consider using means other than words to teach the concept. Think of the steps you might follow to teach the concept. In doing this, what did you learn about teaching a concept? Was it easier or more difficult than you thought it would be? What would you do differently next time?

 Go to the Online Learning Center at www.mhhe.com/arends10e to respond to these questions.

Overview of Teaching Students How to Think

Educators and parents alike believe that teaching students how to think is among the most important purposes of education. Thousands of books and literally millions of Web sites are devoted to topics about "thinking" and how to help students become self-regulated and autonomous learners. The focus of this chapter is on concept and inquiry-based teaching, two approaches to teaching that have been developed specifically to enhance student thinking. It will also describe a thinking program developed for the same purpose. The first section will address the larger issues of why it is important to teach students how to think, provide a perspective of how best to teach thinking, and outline theoretical bases for this topic. This will be followed by descriptions of how to plan and deliver three types of lessons for enhancing student thinking: concept teaching, inquiry-based teaching, and the use of thinking routines. The final sections consider the best ways to create classroom environments that focus on thinking and how to assess thinking processes and skills.

Theoretical Perspectives about Teaching Thinking

Thinking and its relation to how the mind works have held the interest of theorists, philosophers, and researchers for many years. Thus, the theoretical and empirical support for teaching thinking is extensive and covers a wide range of topics. Recently, this work has centered mainly in cognitive views of learning and includes the contributions of John Dewey, Jean Piaget, Jerome Bruner, David Ausubel, and Howard Gardner, among others. Their work has demonstrated how thinking processes and skills develop in children and youth and how certain approaches can affect these processes.

Universality of Thinking

Important questions you may be asking are: Do we need to teach thinking? Don't humans think automatically? Most observers, such as Nickerson (1987) and Sternberg and Williams (2009), say yes, that humans' capacity to think is somewhat automatic, the same way that breathing and blinking are automatic. It does not require instruction. However, not everyone is an effective thinker. For example, a perusal of the letters-to-the-editor section in your local newspaper will quickly reveal arguments based on bias and fallacious reasoning. Similarly, political debates are often filled with inaccurate information and faulty logic. Thus, important goals of instruction are to teach students how to reason and think more clearly, more critically, and more creatively.

Types of Thinking

Thinking may be universal, but it also has multiple dimensions or types. The major types teachers are interested in are described below.

Higher-Level Thinking. Most contemporary statements about thinking recognize differences between basic and **higher-level thinking** and that teaching higher-level skills requires different approaches as compared to teaching basic thinking skills or routine patterns of behavior. (See, for example, Bonnie & Sternberg, 2011; Palincsar, 1998; Resnick, 1987; Ritchhart, 2002; Ritchhart, Church, & Morrison, 2011; Tishman, Perkins, & Jay, 1995.) You have already read about *Bloom's Revised Taxonomy* in Chapters 3 and 7 about how basic thinking skills are mainly those associated with remembering and recalling, whereas higher-order thinking encompasses such cognitive process as understanding, comparing, evaluating, and creating. Although precise definitions of higher-order thinking cannot always be found, we nonetheless recognize such thinking when we see it in operation. Furthermore, higher-order thinking, unlike more concrete behaviors, is complex and not easily reduced to fixed routines. Consider the following statements of Lauren Resnick (1987) about what she defined as higher-order thinking:

- Higher-order thinking is *nonalgorithmic;* that is, the path of action is not fully specified in advance.
- Higher-order thinking tends to be *complex.* The total path is not "visible" (mentally speaking) from any single vantage point.
- Higher-order thinking often yields *multiple solutions,* each with costs and benefits, rather than unique solutions.
- Higher-order thinking involves *nuanced judgment* and interpretation.
- Higher-order thinking involves the application of *multiple criteria,* which sometimes conflict with one another.
- Higher-order thinking often involves *uncertainty.* Not everything that bears on the task at hand is known.
- Higher-order thinking involves *self-regulation* of the thinking process. We do not recognize higher-order thinking in an individual when someone else "calls the plays" at every step.
- Higher-order thinking involves *imposing meaning,* finding structure in apparent disorder.
- Higher-order thinking is *effortful.* There is considerable mental work involved in the kinds of elaborations and judgments required. (pp. 2–3)

Notice that Resnick used words and phrases such as *nuanced judgment, self-regulation, imposing meaning,* and *uncertainty.* Obviously, thinking processes and the skills people need to activate them are highly complex. Resnick also pointed out the importance of context when *thinking about thinking;* that is, although thinking processes have some similarities across situations, they also vary according to what one is thinking about. For instance, the processes we use to think about mathematics differ from those we

Higher-order thinking skills cannot be taught by using approaches designed for teaching concrete ideas and skills.

use to think about poetry. The processes for thinking about abstract ideas differ from those used to think about real-life situations. Because of the complex and contextual nature of higher-order thinking skills, they cannot be taught using approaches suitable for teaching more concrete ideas and skills. Higher-order thinking skills and processes are, however, clearly teachable, and most programs and curricula developed for this purpose rely heavily on approaches similar to ones described in this chapter.

Critical Thinking. **Critical thinking** is another important type of thinking and dates back to Socrates. In more modern times, according to Bonney and Sternberg (2011), many aspects of critical thinking can be attributed to John Dewey's early work on "reflective thinking" (Dewey, 1909). This form of thinking requires the use of analytical and evaluative cognitive processes and consists mainly of analyzing arguments for logical consistency in order to recognize bias and fallacious reasoning. Bonney and Sternberg (2011) cite Halpern (2007) and define critical thinking as thinking that is "purposeful, reasoned, and goal-directed" (p. 6). Being effective in this type of thinking is particularly important today, because students are exposed continuously to information on television channels, Web sites, and social networks that have *not* been vetted for accuracy. Indeed, many messages found on television and Web sites have been created to confuse and deceive. To be effective at critical thinking requires skills that will help determine the accuracy of information and that will aid in spotting illogical and/or fallacious arguments. It also requires inquiry-oriented attitudes and **dispositions** toward the nature of knowledge and truth.

Scientific Thinking and Reasoning. Most of you are well aware of the processes associated with **scientific thinking:** identifying problem situations, generating and testing hypotheses, collecting data and evidence, and drawing inferences and conclusions. At its core, scientific thinking consists of reasoning and drawing conclusions based on observation and evidence. This type of thinking can be classified into two categories of reasoning: deductive reasoning and inductive reasoning. **Deductive reasoning** is the process of reaching conclusions based on more general premises and goes from the general to the specific. For example, when students are taught the law of supply and demand they can use this law to predict what will happen to prices if supply is increased or if demand goes up or down. **Inductive reasoning,** in contrast, turns this process around, and conclusions are drawn after consideration of specific observation and facts. This type of reasoning goes from the specific to the general. Inductive reasoning is the type of reasoning associated with scientific inquiry and includes the important processes described earlier. You will find that inquiry-based teaching, for the most part, relies on inductive reasoning, whereas concept teaching can employ either deductive or inductive reasoning, depending on the particular approach chosen by the teacher. As you will see, scientific reasoning is the type of thinking that underlies the teaching strategies for *concept and inquiry-based teaching* described in later sections of this chapter.

Metacognitive Thinking. Finally, contemporary theorists are interested in the metacognitive aspect of thinking. Recall from previous discussions in Chapters 3 and 7 that metacognition, or "thinking about thinking," is the knowledge and understanding we have about our own cognitive processes and the capabilities we have to examine our thoughts and to monitor what is going on. Important goals for teaching students how to think are to increase their awareness of their own thinking and to develop metacognitive abilities and capacities to monitor and regulate their own learning. You will see that all of the approaches to teaching thinking described in this chapter aim at accomplishing certain metacognitive goals.

Concept Teaching

"Ball." "Chair." "Box." "Table." "Crayon." Kim is naming things and placing objects into groups or classes. She is developing concepts. Combining something concrete, such as a ball, with an abstract quality, such as roundness, enables Kim to identify classes of objects, events, and ideas that differ from each other. By repeatedly sorting and classifying different balls, she can eventually form an abstract concept for these similar objects that allows her to think about them and, eventually, to communicate with others about them. Experienced teachers know that concepts in any subject are the basic building blocks for thinking, particularly higher-level thinking. Concepts allow individuals to classify objects and ideas and to derive rules and principles; they provide the foundations for the idea networks (schemata) that guide our thinking. The process of learning concepts begins at an early age and continues throughout life as people develop more and more complex concepts, both in school and out. The learning of concepts is crucial in schools and in everyday life because concepts allow mutual understanding among people and provide the basis for verbal interaction.

Concept teaching has been developed primarily to teach key concepts that serve as foundations for student higher-level thinking and to provide a basis for mutual understanding and communication (see Figure 9.1). This approach to teaching is not designed to teach large amounts of information to students. However, by learning and applying key concepts within a given subject, students are able to transfer specific learnings to more general areas. But concept learning, is more than simply classifying objects and forming categories. It is also more than learning new labels or vocabulary to apply to classes of objects and ideas. Instead, concept learning involves the process of constructing knowledge and organizing information into comprehensive and complex cognitive structures. Remember that "conceptual knowledge" was one of the major types of knowledge described in Chapters 3 and 7.

There are numerous approaches to concept teaching, but two basic ones have been selected for this chapter. These are labeled the *direct presentation* approach and the *concept attainment* approach. As will be described in detail later, the syntax for the two approaches varies slightly. Basically, however, a concept lesson consists of four major phases or steps: (1) present goals and establish set, (2) input examples and nonexamples, (3) test for concept attainment, and (4) analyze student thinking processes. The learning environment for concept teaching can described as moderately structured.

Nature of Concepts

When the term *concept* is used in connection with teaching and learning, it has a precise meaning and refers to the way knowledge and experience are categorized. To put it another way, **concepts** are mental abstractions or categories we have for things in the social and physical world.

Figure 9.1 *Learner Outcomes of Concept Teaching*

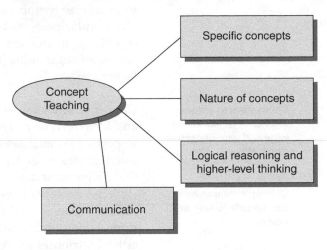

Check, Extend, Explore

Check
- Why is it important to teach students how to think?
- What are the four major types or dimensions of thinking and how do they differ?

Extend
- Think about several lessons aimed at teaching students how to think. What approaches did your teachers use? How did you respond to various approaches?

Explore
- There are thousands of Web sites devoted to teaching thinking. Google "thinking skill" or "teaching thinking" and examine the various perspectives about these topics. Consider how they differ from the perspectives taken here.

Concept learning is essentially "putting things into a class" and then being able to recognize members of that class. This requires that an individual be able to take a particular case, such as his or her pet dog Max, and place it into a general class of objects, in this case a class termed *dog*, that share certain attributes. This process requires making judgments about whether a particular case is an instance of a larger class.

Concepts Themselves Can Be Placed into Categories. Concepts, like other objects and ideas, can be categorized and labeled. Knowing the different types of concepts is important because, as is explained later, different types of concepts require different teaching strategies. One way of classifying concepts is according to the rule structures that define their use.

Some concepts have constant rule structures. The concept of *island,* for example, always involves land surrounded by water. A *triangle* is a plane, closed figure with three sides and three angles. The rule structures for these concepts are constant. Their critical attributes are combined in an additive manner and are always the same. This type of concept is referred to as a **conjunctive concept.**

Other concepts are broader and more flexible and permit alternative sets of attributes. Their rule structures are not constant. For example, the concept of a *strike* in baseball is based on a number of alternative conditions. A strike may occur when a batter swings and misses, when an umpire determines that the pitch was in the strike zone even though the batter did not swing at the ball, or when the batter hits a foul ball. This type of concept is called a **disjunctive concept**—that is, one that contains alternative sets of attributes. The concept *noun* is another example of a disjunctive concept. It may be a person, a place, or a thing, but it cannot be all three at the same time.

A third type of concept is one whose rule structure depends on relationships. The concept *aunt* describes a particular relationship between siblings and their offspring. The concepts *time* and *distance* are also **relational concepts.** To understand either of these concepts, one must know the other, plus the relationship between them. For example, *week* is defined as a succession of days that has as its beginning point day one (usually Sunday) and as its ending point day seven (usually Saturday) and a duration of seven days.

Concepts Are Learned through Examples and Nonexamples. Learning particular concepts involves identifying both *examples* and *nonexamples* of a concept. For instance, a cow is an example of a mammal but is a nonexample of a reptile. Australia is an example of a country in the Southern Hemisphere, but it is a nonexample of a developing country. Cotton and silk are examples of the concept *fabric,* but leather and steel are nonexamples. As we describe later, the way examples and nonexamples are identified and used by teachers is important in a concept lesson.

Concepts Are Influenced by Social Context. The critical attributes of a conjunctive concept, such as *equilateral triangle,* are fixed across social contexts. However, disjunctive or relational concepts, such as *poverty* or *literacy rate,* change from one social context to another. For example, poverty in the United States means something much different than poverty in a developing African country. Concepts with changing critical attributes are often found in the behavioral and social sciences and need an operational definition depending on the social context or cultural environment in which they are used. Consider the concept *aunt.* In some societies, *aunt* or *auntie* refers to any

---

Margin notes:

Concepts are devices used to organize knowledge and experiences into categories.

Concepts themselves can be categorized and labeled.

Teachers should provide clear examples and nonexamples of what is being taught to ensure thorough understanding of the concept.

Social context and culture influence the definition and attributes of some concepts.

adult in the society who has some responsibility for caring for a particular child and has nothing to do with actual blood relationship. Consider also the geographical concepts *north* and *south* as they relate to climate. Children in the Northern Hemisphere are taught that as one goes south, the climate gets warmer. Obviously, this conceptual relationship would not hold true for children in Australia or Argentina. The labeling of concepts is also influenced by context. In England, a car's windshield is called a *windscreen,* and the trunk is called the *boot.* In both instances, the concepts are the same; the label is what is different.

Concepts Have Definitions and Labels. All concepts have names or labels and more or less precise definitions. For example, a relatively small body of land surrounded on all sides by water is labeled an *island.* Labels and definitions permit mutual understanding and communication with others using the concept. They are prerequisites for concept teaching and learning. Labels, however, are human inventions and essentially are arbitrary. Knowing the label does not mean a student understands the concept. This is what makes teaching concepts difficult but also rewarding.

Concepts Have Critical and Noncritical Attributes. As illustrated in Table 9.1, concepts have attributes that describe and help define them. Some attributes are critical and are used to separate one concept from all others. For example, an *equilateral triangle* is a triangle with three equal sides. The **critical attributes** are that it must be a triangle and that each of the sides must be equal. Triangles without three equal sides are not equilateral triangles. In addition, if the concept is a subset of a broader concept, then it must also include the critical attributes of the broader concept. An *equilateral triangle* is a member of the class of concepts called *triangles* and thus must contain all the critical attributes of a triangle.

Concepts also have **noncritical attributes.** For example, size is a noncritical attribute of an equilateral triangle. All concepts have both critical and noncritical attributes, and it is sometimes difficult for students to differentiate between the two. For example, the concept *bird* is typically associated in most people's minds with the noncritical attribute flying. Robins, cardinals, eagles, and most other birds can fly. Flying, however, is not a critical attribute of birds; ostriches and penguins cannot fly, yet they are still classified as birds. Focusing exclusively on critical attributes and typical members of a class can sometimes cause confusion when learning new concepts. Although flying is a noncritical attribute of birds, it is nonetheless typical of most birds and must be accounted for in teaching about them.

Debate exists about how important critical and noncritical attributes are in defining a concept. Some, such as Ashcraft and Radvansky (2009), argue that we carry around from our experiences "prototypes" that best represent particular concepts or categories and that these prototypes are best for defining concepts.

> A concept's critical attributes are what distinguish it from all other concepts.

> Focusing exclusively on the critical attributes of concepts can result in confusion when learning new concepts.

Table 9.1 *Critical and Noncritical Attributes of Birds*

Critical Attributes	Noncritical Attributes
Feathers	Feather color
Warm-blooded	Ability to fly
Feet	Webbed feet

Human Development and Concept Learning

The way concepts are learned is affected significantly by the learner's age and his or her level of intellectual development.

Another important aspect of concept teaching comes from the field of human development. Research in this field, some of which dates back over half a century, has shown how age and intellectual development influence students' readiness and abilities to learn various types of concepts (Barsalou, 2000; Benjafield, 1992; Fischer, 2009; Piaget, 1954, 1963; Starkey, 1980). This research has shown that children begin learning concepts at a very early age through object sorting and classifying activities and that concept learning continues throughout life. The way concepts are learned is affected by the learner's age, language development, and level of intellectual development. Theories of cognitive development of Jean Piaget and Jerome Bruner are important to teachers in regard to concept learning by students.

Piaget's key insight is that learning is a constructive process and that individuals construct knowledge through interaction with their environment.

Swiss psychologist Jean Piaget developed a theory about how humans develop and make sense of their world. From Piaget's perspective, humans are always striving to make sense of their environment, and their biological maturation, their interaction with the environment, and their social experiences combine to influence how they think about things. The primary contribution of Piaget's ideas for teachers is his *stage theory of cognitive development.* According to Piaget, as children grow and mature, they pass through four stages of cognitive development: sensorimotor, preoperational, concrete operational, and formal operational. These stages and the kinds of thinking associated with each are illustrated in Table 9.2. As you can see, the type of learning that a person is capable of is linked to age. Younger children deal with their world in more concrete, hands-on ways, whereas older children and adults can engage in abstract problem solving.

Assimilation occurs when individuals fit new information into existing schemata.

Piaget also provided a theory for understanding how people adapt to their environment through the processes of assimilation and accommodation. When individuals experience a new idea or a new situation, they first try to make sense of the new information by using existing schemata. Remember, *schemata,* described in Chapter 7 refers to the ways individuals store and organize knowledge and experiences in memory. Trying to understand the new information by adapting it to what we already know is called **assimilation.** Take the example of a young child who has a large kitty at home and sees a small puppy for the first time. She may call the puppy "kitty" because she is trying to explain the new animal with her existing schemata for animals, which up to this point only include kitties. If individuals cannot fit the new data or situation into their existing schemata, they must develop new concepts or schemata. This is called **accommodation.** In the kitty-dog example, the child has accommodated when she has added the concept of *dog* and *puppy* to her schemata about animals.

Accommodation occurs when individuals change existing schemata to respond to new ideas or situations.

Table 9.2 *Piaget's Stages of Cognitive Development*

Stage	Age	Kinds of Thinking Abilities
Sensorimotor	Birth–2 years	Begins to recognize objects; can imitate.
Preoperational	2–7 years	Develops use of language; begins ability to think symbolically; can see another person's point of view; lacks logical mental operations at this stage.
Concrete operational	7–11 years	Can solve concrete problems in logical fashion; able to classify.
Formal operational	11–15/adult	Can solve abstract problems in logical fashion; has concern for social issues.

Individuals are always adapting to their environment using prior knowledge and existing schemata. Concept teaching is one way to provide new ideas and expand and change existing schemata. You will read later how the processes of assimilation and accommodation influence the kinds of examples and nonexamples teachers choose to help students understand particular concepts.

An American psychologist, Jerome Bruner, also has provided a conceptualization about how children learn at different stages of maturation. Bruner (1966) identified three distinct modes of learning: (1) learning by doing, called the *enactive mode*; (2) learning by forming mental images, called the *iconic mode*; and (3) learning through a series of abstract symbols or representations, called the *symbolic mode*. As children grow older and progress through the grades, they depend less on the enactive mode and more on mental imagery and symbolic operations. In general, children under age 7 rely mainly on doing, or the enactive mode, for learning concepts. Children between the ages of 7 and 11 still rely on the enactive mode but begin learning concepts by forming mental images. Older children and early adolescents still use the iconic mode but increasingly rely on abstract symbols. Research has shown that children can learn concepts at a fairly early age and that early concept learning facilitates what can be learned later on.

Planning for Concept Teaching

During the planning phase of a concept lesson, teachers must make decisions about what concepts to teach and which approach to use. They must also do a thorough job of defining and analyzing concepts being taught and decide which examples and nonexamples to use and how best to present them to students during the lesson. These tasks are important. They make planning for a concept lesson somewhat difficult, perhaps more so than planning other approaches to teaching.

Selecting Concepts. The curriculum is the primary source for selecting concepts to teach. Concepts may be embedded in textbooks, and the teacher's edition often provides guidance in selecting key concepts to teach. Take, for instance, the following passage on temperature and heat summarized from a typical sixth-grade science textbook:

> Scientists define *work* as a force acting on an object and causing it to move. Such work can be done because moving objects have *energy*. This energy of *motion* is called *kinetic energy*.

In this passage, the concepts of *work, motion,* and *kinetic energy* are described. However, it is likely that most students will not understand these concepts thoroughly unless the concepts become the subjects of particular lessons taught by the teacher.

Curriculum frameworks and content standards are the primary sources for selecting concepts for instruction. In some cases, the key concepts will be listed as vocabulary to be developed in the unit. In other cases, concepts will be found within the main ideas or generalizations for a unit of study. For example, American history courses typically contain a unit on the westward movement. In this unit, students study why people migrated westward during the early eras of the nation's history. In the process, they study such key concepts as *migration, economic gain, religious freedom,* and *political freedom.* They also examine other concepts related to the unit's objectives, such as *expansion, self-sufficiency, heterogeneity, frontier, pioneer, pluralism,* and *terrain.* Obviously, all concepts cannot be taught in a single unit, and teachers must make decisions about which ones to single out for particular lessons.

Teachers also need to make decisions about which of the new vocabulary words need to be directly taught as concepts. They must constantly judge which new terms are essential to students understanding the important ideas of a lesson or a unit. If the students don't know the key concepts within a unit, then a lesson on the unknown concepts should be taught. Concept lessons should always be taught if the materials contain unfamiliar terms, a series of steps not known to students, or the use of some "rule" that is new to students.

In the process of selecting concepts to teach, it is important to remember a point made earlier: Helping students understand a concept involves more than getting them to provide definitions of new vocabulary words.

Deciding on an Approach. A concept teaching lesson has several components. These include the name and definition of the concept, the concept's attributes (some that are critical and some that are not), and examples and nonexamples of the concept. Teachers can choose among several approaches to handle each of these components. As described earlier, this chapter focuses on two approaches: direct presentation and concept attainment.

The **direct presentation** approach employs a deductive *rule-to-example process*. This approach consists of the teacher first naming and defining the concept and then providing students with examples and nonexamples to reinforce their understanding of the concept. The focus is on labeling and defining the concept.

The **concept attainment** approach, in contrast, turns this sequence around and uses an inductive *example-to-rule process* (Bruner, 1996). Teachers give examples and nonexamples of a particular concept first, and students discover or attain the concept themselves through the process of inductive reasoning. Labeling and defining the concept comes at the end rather than at the beginning of the lesson.

The approach a teacher uses depends on the *goals* being sought, the *students* being taught, and the *nature* of the concept. The direct presentation approach usually is best for the development of knowledge about a concept for which students have little or no previous understanding. The concept attainment approach is best when students have some understanding of the concept and the goals of the lesson are to explore the presence or absence of critical attributes of particular concepts and to learn the processes of inductive reasoning. Sometimes both approaches are used when students are learning complicated concepts.

Defining Concepts. Critical or defining attributes, as you read earlier, are those attributes that are present in every example of a concept and distinguish it from all other concepts. For example, the concept *tree* might be defined as a "plant that lives for many years and has a single main stem that is woody." This definition includes the critical attributes *plant, lives for many years, single main stem,* and *woody*. These critical attributes define a concept, and consequently, students must understand them. However, noncritical attributes also enter into the picture. For example, size, shape, and color are noncritical attributes of trees. Blue lagoons, sandy beaches, and palm trees may be desirable on an island, but they are noncritical attributes. When learning concepts, students must not confuse the noncritical attributes, no matter how common, with the critical attributes of the concept.

The source of the definition for a concept and its critical attributes are also important. In some instances, concepts are defined in the glossaries of the students' textbooks, but in other cases they may be defined in the guides published by the local school districts or in content standards or curriculum frameworks. These definitions and critical

Time does not permit teaching every concept that exists in a field. Selecting appropriate concepts to teach is a major planning task for teachers.

The direct presentation approach calls for teacher definition of a concept followed by appropriate provision of examples and nonexamples.

The concept attainment approach entails students deriving a concept themselves using inductive reasoning after being provided with examples and nonexamples.

Complex concepts from academic subjects need to be defined and taught appropriately for the age of the students.

attributes should be examined carefully. When defining concepts, it is important to recognize that some words used in the definition are irrelevant. For example, most dictionaries refer to the domesticated state of dogs. This is an interesting fact, but it is not what identifies a dog or separates dogs from cats. Essentially, there are three steps in defining a concept: (1) identify the concept's name; (2) list the critical and noncritical attributes; and (3) write a concise definition. For the *island* example, this would involve identifying the name as *island,* listing the critical attributes as landmass and water, and providing the following definition: "an island is a landmass that is smaller than a continent and is surrounded by water."

Analyzing Concepts. Once a concept has been selected and defined in terms of its critical attributes, the concept needs to be analyzed for examples and nonexamples. The selection of examples and nonexamples is probably the most difficult aspect of planning for a concept lesson. Examples serve as the connectors between the concept's abstraction and the learner's prior knowledge and experiences. Examples must be meaningful to the learner and must be as concrete as possible.

> Selecting good examples and nonexamples of a concept is one of the most challenging aspects of planning a concept lesson.

Charts, diagrams, and webs as well as pictures should be used as visual examples of abstract concepts. They can also aid the teacher in analyzing the concept for instructional decisions. Table 9.3 contains an analysis of a set of concepts. Numbering the critical attributes and using the word *and* can be a reminder that all the critical attributes must be present to have an example of the concept.

Look at the example "Hawaii" in Table 9.3. It is a landmass not as large as a continent, there is a body of water nearby, and the water completely surrounds it. Each of the three critical conditions of an island is met; therefore, it is an example of the concept. Teachers might also look at Florida as a nonexample of island. Land and water are present, but the land is not completely surrounded by water. All of the criteria are not met; therefore, Florida is a nonexample.

Table 9.3 *Analysis of a Set of Concepts*

Concept	Definition	Example	Nonexample	Critical Attributes
Island	A landmass not as large as a continent, surrounded by water	Hawaii Cuba Greenland	Florida Lake Erie Australia	1. Landmass (not continent), *and* 2. Water, *and* 3. Land surrounded by water
Lake	A large inland body of water surrounded by land	Lake Huron Great Salt Lake Big Lake	Ohio River Hawaii Miller's Pond	1. Large inland body of water, *and* 2. Land, *and* 3. Water surrounded by land
Peninsula	A land area almost entirely surrounded by water but having a land connection to a larger landmass	Florida Italy Delmarva	Cuba Hudson Bay Lake Erie	1. Land connected to larger landmass, *and* 2. Water, *and* 3. Land surrounded almost entirely by water
Bay	A body of water partly surrounded by land but having a wide outlet to the sea	Chesapeake Bay Hudson Bay Green Bay	Florida Lake Louise Gulf of Mexico	1. Body of water connected to the sea by a wide outlet, *and* 2. Land, *and* 3. Water partly surrounded by land

The isolation of the attributes is critical to the analysis and teaching of concepts. The teacher needs to decide if the attributes are critical and should be presented when matching examples and nonexamples, such as Hawaii and Florida, or if the attributes are noncritical and are best used in divergent examples after clear instances of the concept are presented.

Examples that are very different from each other will enable students to focus on common attributes of the concept.

Choosing and Sequencing Examples and Nonexamples. The examples and non-examples selected to illustrate a concept are very important. In general, it is recommended that initial examples should be familiar to the class. Students need to see typical examples clearly before they are ready to consider atypical ones. Similarly, students normally find it easier to identify a concept with its most immediate neighbors before relating it to more distant ones. If a robin is used as the best (most familiar) example of the concept *bird,* it is easier for the learner to distinguish close neighbors to robins, such as cardinals, sparrows, or bluebirds, than to distinguish more distant members, such as ducks, chickens, or penguins.

When selecting a set of examples, teachers will often make the noncritical attributes of the concept as *different* as possible. This helps students focus on the critical attributes common to each of the examples. For instance, if teachers are developing the concept of *island,* they might include Hawaii, a tropical island, and Greenland, which has a cold climate. The obvious differences in climates will help students focus their attention on the common attributes of these two examples. Likewise, when developing a set of examples for the concept *insects,* teachers might include water bugs and ants, which live in different environments but still have the same critical attributes.

When selecting a set of matched examples and nonexamples, teachers generally attempt to make the noncritical attributes of the pairs as similar as possible. This enables students to focus on the differences between the example and the nonexample. In the case of the concept of *island,* for example, the Florida peninsula and the Cuban island could serve as a matched pair because of the similarities in climate. Examples and nonexamples should be sequenced for presentation in a logical fashion, and normally sets should be ordered from the easiest to the more difficult. Teachers may also want to give cues to focus students' thinking before each set of three or four examples.

Visual aids and pictures have been shown to greatly facilitate student understanding of complex concepts.

Use of Visual Images. Using visual images affects the learning of concepts and supports the old adage that "a picture is worth a thousand words" (Mayer, 2011a, 2011b). Anderson and Smith (1987) conducted an interesting study that examined how children come to understand science concepts such as *light* and *color.* They had 113 children in five classrooms study the following passage:

Bouncing Light

    Have you ever thrown a rubber ball at something? If you have, you know that when the ball hits most things, it bounces off them. Like a rubber ball, light bounces off most things it hits.

    When light travels to something opaque, all the light does not stop. Some of this light bounces off. When light travels to something translucent or transparent, all the light does not pass through. Some of this light bounces off. When light bounces off things and travels to your eyes, you are able to see.

They found that only 20 percent of the students could understand that seeing is a process of detecting light that has been reflected off some object. However, in a second experiment, they used a visual aid such as the one illustrated in Figure 9.2. In contrast to the 20 percent who learned the concepts from reading about light, 78 percent of the

Figure 9.2 *Visual Depiction of the Role of Light in Seeing*

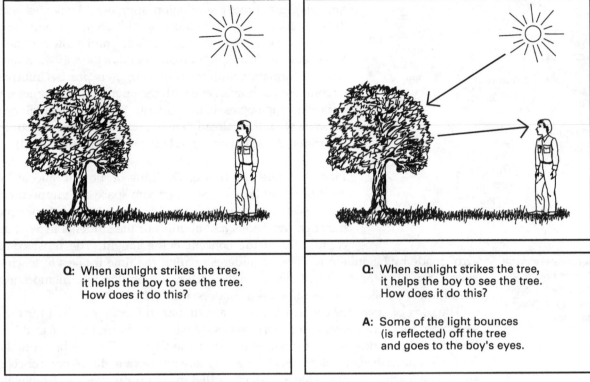

Q: When sunlight strikes the tree,
it helps the boy to see the tree.
How does it do this?

Q: When sunlight strikes the tree,
it helps the boy to see the tree.
How does it do this?

A: Some of the light bounces
(is reflected) off the tree
and goes to the boy's eyes.

Source: After Richardson-Koehler (1987), p. 327.

students understood the concepts the teachers were trying to teach when visual aids were used to illustrate the concepts.

Use of Graphic Organizers and Concept Maps. Graphic organizers and concept maps are other forms of visual representation that can be useful. These devices can help highlight the critical attributes of a concept and make the concept more concrete for students. They can also provide students with an effective means for retrieving information from long-term memory so new concepts can be more easily understood (Novak, 2013).

> Graphic organizers and concept maps provide visual images and are a good way for students to link new information.

There are normally four steps in constructing a concept map for a particular concept:

Step 1: Create the core, which is the focus of the map. This would be the name of the concept.

Step 2: Construct strands branching out from the core. These strands are critical attributes of the concept.

Step 3: Draw strand supports, which connect the critical attributes to the concept.

Step 4: Identify the strand ties, which may show relationships among the various attributes.

Figure 9.3 is a map of the concept *equilateral triangle*. Concepts maps are sometimes called thinking maps. In addition to being used to highlight critical attributes of a particular concept, they can also be used by teachers to show cause-and-effect and part–whole relationships. Many students like to use graphic organizers and concept maps to take notes on reading or viewing assignments.

Figure 9.3 *Web of the Concept Equilateral Triangle*

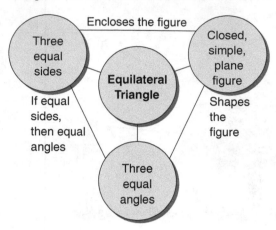

A common mistake made by teachers is underestimating the time it will take to thoroughly teach even simple concepts.

Use of Analogies. Teachers often find that using analogies is effective in teaching particular concepts, especially when they are using the direct presentation approach. Analogies such as, "It's just like . . ." or "It's similar to . . ." point out similarities or like features between two things or ideas and allow comparisons to be made. For example, you can compare the way the brain processes information with the way computers process information or compare the human eye with the operation of a camera. Most important, analogies help students build conceptual bridges between what they already know and the new concept or learning material (see Glynn, 2007; Hofstadter & Sander, 2013).

Plan for Time and Space. Deciding on how to allocate sufficient time and how to use classroom space are important planning tasks for a concept lesson. Time requirements depend on the cognitive levels and abilities of the students as well as the complexity of the concept being taught. The most common error made by beginning teachers is underestimating the time it takes to teach even simple concepts thoroughly. Remember the earlier admonition that memorizing the definition of a concept is not the same as understanding it.

The uses of space for concept teaching are similar to those described for the presentation and direct instruction approaches. Most teachers prefer to use the more traditional row-and-column formation illustrated in Chapter 7 or the horizontal desk formation described in Chapter 8. During the more interactive phases of a concept lesson, some teachers prefer to have students seated in circle or horseshoe arrangements, as described in Chapter 12.

 ## Diversity and Differentiation

Adapting Plans to Meet Diverse Needs

Perhaps more than in any other situation, teachers must remain aware of the great diversity of their students and be ready to tailor their teaching to particular learners when they are teaching concepts. One feature of student diversity is the substantial variation in intellectual development and prior knowledge present in most classrooms. As a result, some concepts will be meaningful and appropriate for some students, whereas they may be too difficult for and not within the experiences of others. One way that teachers can adapt instruction to meet the needs of all learners is to consider the difficulty of the examples and nonexamples used in the concept lesson. Figure 9.4 illustrates easy, medium, and difficult examples and nonexamples for teaching the concept of *adverb*. Remember that an adverb is a word that modifies a verb, an adjective, or another adverb and functions to answer one of these questions: When? How? Where? or To what extent? The critical attributes are *modifies another word* and *function*.

Other features of diversity include the cultural backgrounds of students and the experiences they bring with them to the classroom. For example, conceptual understandings about the relationship between latitude and temperature differ depending on the hemisphere where students live. Students in the Northern Hemisphere learn at a very early age to associate "north" with colder weather. The exact opposite is true for students who grow up in the Southern Hemisphere, where it gets colder as one goes south from the equator. Another example of differences stemming from geography is the concept of *snow*. It is reported that Eskimo languages have many words to define snow, whereas there is only one word for snow in English. As described in some detail in Chapter 2, cultural differences can also influence one's understanding and perception of a particular concept. For example, Native Americans traditionally have a much different concept of time than do Americans of European origins. There are considerable cultural differences and norms around concepts that define social relationships, verbal interaction, and social distance. Lack of experience with a particular concept or situation is one of the largest causes of variation of conceptual understanding. For example, it would be difficult to illustrate or explain the World Wide Web to an individual who has never seen a computer.

To be effective, teachers must remain aware of the vast differences among their students and never assume that any two students' understanding of a concept will be identical.

Figure 9.4 *List of Easy, Medium, and Difficult Examples and Nonexamples of Adverbs*

Easy Examples

1. You are so happy.
2. She has been absent lately.
3. Slowly, she walked home.
4. The train chugged loudly.

Medium Examples

5. Are you fighting mad?
6. Clouds gathered threateningly.
7. It was not difficult to explain.
8. The most dangerous weapon is a gun.

Difficult Examples

9. The small floral print looked pretty.
10. Cats are my number one favorite pet.
11. He wants the dark purple bicycle.
12. The book had three color pictures.

Easy Nonexamples

13. Sewing makes you happy.
14. She has been late.
15. She is slow.
16. The loud train chugged.

Medium Nonexamples

17. Do you fight?
18. The threatening clouds gathered.
19. It is difficult to explain that *not* is a negative word.
20. Most guns are dangerous weapons.

Difficult Nonexamples

21. The small print looked pretty.
22. One special cat is my favorite pet.
23. He wants the dark trim to match.
24. The book had three pictures.

Conducting Concept Lessons

The four phases of a concept teaching lesson are outlined in Table 9.4. The sections that follow describe in some detail teacher and student behavior associated with each phase.

Clarifying Aims and Establishing Set. At the beginning of a concept lesson, just as with all types of lessons, the teacher needs to communicate clearly to students the aims of the lesson and how the lesson will proceed. The teacher might also go over the steps of the lesson and give students reasons why the concepts about to be taught are important to learn. Establishing set for a concept lesson requires procedures no different from those described in Chapters 7 and 8. Teachers get students ready to learn

Establishing set and preparing a class for the lesson to be taught are important parts of concept teaching.

Table 9.4 *Syntax for Concept Teaching*

Phase	Teacher Behavior
Phase 1: Clarify aims and establish set.	Teacher explains the aims and procedures for the lesson and gets students ready to learn.
Phase 2: Input examples and nonexamples.	In the direct presentation approach, teacher names the concepts, identifies the critical attributes, and illustrates with examples and nonexamples.
	In concept attainment, examples and nonexamples are given, and students inductively arrive at the concept and its attributes.
Phase 3: Test for attainment.	Teacher presents additional examples and nonexamples to test students' understanding of the concept. Students are asked to provide their own examples and nonexamples of the concept.
Phase 4: Analyze student thinking processes and integration of learning.	Teacher gets students to think about their own thinking processes. Students are asked to examine their decisions and the consequences of their choices. Teacher helps students integrate new learning by relating the concept to other concepts in a unit of study.

with a brief review, questions about yesterday's lesson, or an interesting anecdote that ties the forthcoming lesson into students' prior knowledge.

Input of Examples and Nonexamples and Testing for Attainment. The exact sequence for defining and labeling a concept or presenting examples and nonexamples varies according to the particular approach being used by the teacher. It is this internal arrangement and flow of activities that give each of the two approaches its unique character and allows each to accomplish the particular learning outcomes for which it was designed.

Direct Presentation. In the direct presentation approach, the internal flow of the lesson includes the following:

1. Naming the concept and providing students with a definition
2. Identifying the critical attributes and giving examples and nonexamples of the concept
3. Testing for concept understanding by getting students to provide additional examples and nonexamples

Taking the concept *island* as analyzed in Table 9.3, a teacher using the direct presentation approach might proceed as follows:

- Tell students that they are going to learn the concept *island* and write the name of the concept on the board so that students can see the word.
- List the critical attributes: (1) landmass (not a continent), (2) water, (3) land surrounded by water.
- Show a simple drawing that contains only the critical attributes and point out each critical attribute. This could be followed by pictures of best examples, such as Hawaii, Greenland, or Cuba. As each picture is presented, point out the critical attributes again.

Lesson flow and sequence of concept teaching will vary depending on the topic and approach selected by the teacher.

Enhancing Teaching and Learning with Technology
Exploring Concepts through Web Sites and Simulations

Good teachers have always known that a picture is worth a thousand words when teaching a difficult concept to students. Yet, it is often difficult to find the right picture, one that will represent an abstract concept in a meaningful way. The Internet and media technology can play a significant role in helping teachers find the right pictures as well as the right motion and sounds. Web sites and simulations provide powerful means for bringing the outside world into the classroom and providing visual and auditory representations of otherwise abstract ideas.

Let's consider an example from history. It is always difficult to get students to visualize different eras in history and concepts that help explain life in other times. Numerous Web sites devoted to the *Silk Road* do an excellent job of bringing history and geography into the classroom. Using still photographs, video clips, other types of moving images, sound, and interesting text, *Silk Road* Web sites show life in thirteenth- and fourteenth-century Asia and describe the economic and social factors that gave rise to the rich trade route between Asia and the Middle East and Europe. Several of these sites do a masterful job of holding the student's interest while illustrating the effects of early trade on the development of the modern world.

Similar sites and/or CDs exist for just about every subject. *The National Gallery of Art CD* and *Windows on Science* use interesting collections of still photographs and video clips to illustrate hard-to-conceptualize concepts and ideas in the visual arts and science.

Simulations can also assist students as they grapple with complex concepts and ideas. Simulations are designed to replicate key elements of a real-life situation—situations that are often dangerous or difficult in real life. The design of simulations allows students to explore and manipulate aspects of the virtual environment. The actions they choose in most instances produce results similar to those that would occur in the real world. Simulations have many other uses:

- They can be used prior to instruction of a concept or idea to enhance student interest.
- They can be used after a topic has been studied to allow students to transfer acquired knowledge to a simulated situation.

Simulations are most effective when used in conjunction with other methods, such as a presentation of factual and conceptual knowledge and inquiry or project-based lessons. Also, teachers need to help students understand that no matter how realistic the simulation, it is still a simulation—it is not real life or entirely accurate.

Finally, Web sites are available that take students on virtual field trips to illustrate concepts that might be difficult to reproduce by other means. For example:

- Students who live in Minnesota can experience deserts.
- Students who live in Nevada can experience tundra.
- Students in Alaska can experience the sandy beaches of Hawaii.

All Web sites must be chosen with care because many have not been vetted for accuracy. More information about evaluating Web sites will be provided in Chapter 11.

- Show students both examples and nonexamples of the concept and ask questions that force judgments about whether a new instance is an example or nonexample of the concept. Have students tell why or why not. Have students come up with their own examples and nonexamples.

Concept Attainment. In concept attainment, students already have some grasp of a concept or set of concepts and are asked to make decisions about whether or not particular examples are instances of a class. Teachers using the concept attainment approach would use the following steps:

1. Provide students with examples, some that represent the concept and some that do not. Best examples are clearly labeled *yes,* and carefully selected nonexamples are clearly labeled *no.*

In the concept attainment approach, a concept is not labeled until students demonstrate understanding and have thought about critical attributes of the concept.

Students learn some concepts through experimentation.

2. Urge students to hypothesize about the attributes of the concept and to record reasons for their speculation. The teacher may ask additional questions to help focus students' thinking and to get them to compare attributes of the examples and nonexamples.

3. When students appear to know the concept, they name (label) the concept and describe the process they used for identifying it. Students may guess the concept early in the lesson, but the teacher needs to continue to present examples and nonexamples until the students attain the critical attributes of the concept as well as the name of the concept.

4. The teacher checks to see if the students have attained the concept by having them identify additional examples as *yes* or *no*, tell why or why they are not examples, and generate examples and nonexamples of their own.

Concept attainment is an inductive process that assists learners in organizing data according to previously learned concepts. Unlike the direct presentation approach, the teacher provides a label and definition only after the students have engaged in the discovery of the critical attributes.

To illustrate the concept attainment approach, consider the following lesson, again using the concept *island:*

- The teacher shows a picture of an island and tells students this is an example of the concept. The teacher then shows a picture of a landform that is not an island and states that this is a nonexample of the concept.
- The teacher continues displaying pictures of islands and other landforms, telling students which are and which are not examples. Students are asked to speculate what they think the concept is. All hypotheses and ideas are listed on the chalkboard. The teacher continues to present examples and nonexamples and asks students to reconsider their original hypotheses.
- Students are asked to state a definition of the concept and, if possible, label it. They also list the critical attributes of the concept.
- The teacher then shows additional pictures of islands and other landforms and asks students to identify each as a *yes* or *no*. The teacher also asks students to provide examples of islands they know about and instances of landforms that are not islands. Students explain why or why not.

The major roles for the teacher during this aspect of a concept attainment lesson are to record student hypotheses and any critical attributes identified, to cue students, and to provide additional data if necessary.

Analyzing Thinking and Integrating Learning. The final phase of both approaches to concept teaching emphasizes teacher-directed activities aimed at helping students to analyze their own thinking processes and to integrate newly acquired conceptual knowledge. To accomplish this, teachers ask students to think back and recount what was going through their minds as they were considering the concepts. What

There are many ways to help students integrate conceptual learning.

Check, Extend, Explore

Check
- What are the major planning tasks associated with concept teaching?
- How do inductive concept lessons differ from those that use a deductive approach?
- What are the four phases of the concept teaching? What types of teacher behaviors are associated with each?
- What steps can teachers take to adapt concept lessons for students of differing abilities and backgrounds?
- How does the use of examples and nonexamples differ in inductive and deductive concept lessons?
- Why is it important to help students analyze their own thinking processes?

Extend
- Some teachers believe that concept teaching takes too much time and is not as efficient as simply presenting conceptual information to students. Do you agree or disagree with this perspective? Go to the "Extend Question Poll" on the Online Learning Center to respond.

Explore
- Go to the Online Learning Center at www. mhhe.com/arends10e for links to Web sites related to how to plan and conduct concept lessons. Go to the Online Learning Center at www.mhhe.com. arends10e and view the video on concept teaching.

criteria did they use for grouping items? When did they first figure out the concept? How? What was confusing in the direct presentation lesson? How does the concept relate to other concepts they know about? Were they focusing on the concept as a whole or on a particular attribute? How did noncritical attributes affect attaining the concept? If they were going to teach the concept to a younger student, what would they do?

The intent of this type of questioning is to get students to think about their own thinking (termed *metacognition* and discussed earlier) and to discover and consider the patterns they use to learn and integrate new concepts into their cognitive frameworks. This phase of a concept lesson relies, obviously, on student discussion and participation. The guidelines for questioning, encouraging, and facilitating student discussion and participation provided in Chapters 4 and 12 can also be used for this final phase of a concept teaching lesson.

Inquiry-Based Teaching

Inquiry-based teaching is another instructional approach that has been developed for the purpose of teaching students how to think. Inquiry-based teaching rests, for the most part, on the same theoretical base as previously described for concept teaching and will not be repeated here. The model was influenced by the early work of John Dewey (1916) and of Jerome Bruner (1960, 1961). Mid-twentieth-century curriculum revisionists in the sciences, history, and the social sciences

Figure 9.5 *Learner Outcomes for Inquiry-Based Teaching*

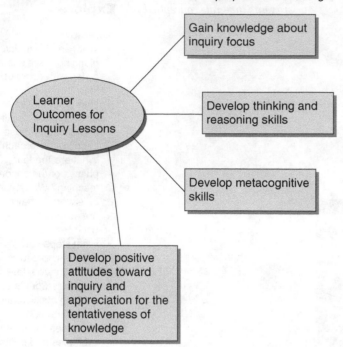

(Fenton, 1966; Schwab, 1966; Suchman, 1962) also helped define how inquiry-based teaching is used in classrooms today. More recently, Lowen and Rikers (2011), Magnusson and Palincsar (1995), Meyer (2004), and individuals associated with the BSCS Science Instructional Model (2009) have extended and refined earlier approaches to inquiry-based teaching. The sections that follow describe procedures and guidelines for planning and conducting effective inquiry-based lessons.

Planning for Inquiry-Based Lessons

Two major planning tasks are required in preparation of an inquiry-based lesson: determining learner outcomes and identifying a suitable problem for inquiry. Like concept teaching, inquiry-based lessons have both content and process goals. Teachers want students to acquire new knowledge associated with the inquiry focus of the lesson. They also want students to learn the processes of inquiry, particularly those associated with scientific inquiry, and to develop positive dispositions toward inquiry and the processes used to investigate the social and physical world.

Specific learner outcomes for inquiry-based lessons are listed in Figure 9.5. It is important for teachers to be clear about both their content and process goals and be able to communicate these to students in straightforward ways.

A second planning task consists of identifying a problem situation or question to spark inquiry. Some (Suchman, 1962) believed that the problem should be launched as a **discrepant event.** Essentially, discrepant events are puzzling situations that surprise students, spark their curiosity, and motivate them to engage in inquiry. Often they are situations that are contrary to what one might normally expect. Consider the following two examples:

> The teacher holds up a pulse glass that has two small globes connected by a glass tube. It is filled partially with a red liquid. When the teacher holds her hand over the left globe, the liquid bubbles and moves to the other side. When the teacher holds her hand on the right globe, red liquid moves to the left side. The teacher asks the students, "Why does the red liquid move?"
>
> The teacher has three glasses. One is filled with plain tap water, another is filled with salt water, the third contains sugar water. The teacher puts a hard-boiled egg in each glass. The eggs sink in the tap water glass and float in salt water and sugar water. The teacher asks the students, "Why do the eggs float in the glasses that contain salt and sugar water and not in the plain water?"

As you will read in the next section, after the inquiry focus is presented teachers encourage students to ask questions about the phenomena they have observed, to generate hypotheses, and to think of ways they might test their hypotheses. (If you search YouTube with the term "discrepant event," you will find dozens of brief videos showing teachers using discrepant events in inquiry-based lessons. Some are very interesting.)

Magnusson and Palincsar (1995) proposed a slightly different approach for defining and identifying an inquiry problem. They believe that it doesn't have to be discrepant, but it does have to be puzzling and meet three criteria:

1. be conceptually rich with regard to opportunities it provides for meaningful inquiry [that will] yield understanding of enduring value.
2. be flexible with regard to developmental issues, and
3. be relevant to the lives of children so that it [is] both accessible and interesting. (p. 45)

Examples of stating a problem situation this way might include the following:

Why do pendulums swing the way they do?
How do whales communicate?
Why did people once believe the world was flat?

Conducting Inquiry-Based Lessons

The teacher's primary role when conducting an inquiry lesson is to facilitate the phases of the inquiry process and to help students be attentive and reflective about their thinking processes. Although there are numerous variations of inquiry-based lessons, the overall flow for most approaches consists of six phases. These six phases are summarized in Table 9.5.

Table 9.5 *Syntax for Inquiry-Based Lessons*

Phase	Teacher Behavior
1. Gain attention and explain the inquiry process.	Teacher gets students ready to learn and describes the process for the lesson.
2. Present the inquiry problem or discrepant event.	Teacher presents the problem situation or discrepant event to students.
3. Have students formulate hypotheses to explain the problem or event.	Teacher encourages students to ask questions about the problem situation and state hypotheses that will explain what is going on.
4. Encourage students to collect data to test the hypothesis.	Teacher asks students how they might collect data to test their hypotheses. In some cases, in-class experiments can be conducted.
5. Formulate explanations and/or conclusions.	Teacher brings inquiry to a close by having students formulate conclusions and generalizations.
6. Reflect on the problem situation and the thinking processes used to inquire into it.	Teachers gets students to think about their own thinking processes and to reflect on the inquiry process.

Gain Attention and Explain the Inquiry Process. As with any lesson, it is important to gain students' attention and motivate them to engage in planned learning activities. In an inquiry lesson, motivation is normally easily secured with a provocative problem situation or discrepant event. When teachers use the inquiry-based teaching model for the first time, they will need to explain to students the goals of the lesson and its overall flow. Of particular importance are explanations that help students understand that the most important goals of this type of lesson are to learn skills and processes associated with the inquiry itself.

Present the Inquiry Problem or Discrepant Event. It is important to present the problem situation or discrepant event clearly and in a manner that arouses student curiosity. Most often teachers use demonstration and presentation to communicate the problem situation to students. Video clips and other media can also be used. The problem situation can be presented for whole-class inquiry. It can also be presented in a way to facilitate small group inquiry.

Here is an example of how one teacher presented the inquiry problem to learning groups in her science classroom.

> Today, we are going to inquire into the nature of pendulums and what influences their "swing." In your learning group, do the following: (1) construct a washer pendulum, (2) hang the pendulum so it swings freely from the desk, and (3) start the pendulum swinging and count and chart the number of swings during a 15-second period of time.

Help Students Formulate Hypotheses to Explain the Problem Situation. During this phase, students are encouraged to ask questions and form hypotheses that help explain what is going on. In the pendulum example, students might say, "it is the length of the string that influences the swing," or, "it is the weight of the pendulum that affects its swing." It is important at this point to accept all ideas.

Encourage Students to Collect Data to Test Hypotheses. Sometimes it is possible to have students conduct experiments and collect data. For example, in the pendulum inquiry the teacher had students conduct several experiments in their learning groups, such as varying the length of the string, the washer's weight, and the starting place. In other instances, students may have to conduct hypothetical experiments or the teacher may choose to provide students with data and ask them how these new data might affect their hypotheses.

Formulate Explanations. This is the phase in the inquiry when the teacher starts to bring closure. Students are asked to state explanations or conclusions that can be drawn based on the experiments and data available. All explanations should be accepted; however, probing questions can be used to get students to consider rival explanations. For example:

- How confident are you in your conclusion?
- What if I said . . . how would that influence your thinking?
- How do you compare your conclusion with Sydney's?
- In what way are they different? Why?

Reflect on the Inquiry Situation and Thinking Processes. This is perhaps the most important phase of an inquiry lesson. During this phase, students are encouraged to

Research Summary

Is There a Case against Concept and Inquiry-Based Teaching?

Meyer, R. (2004). Should there be a three-strike rule against discovery learning? A case for guided methods of instruction. *American Psychologist, 59,* 14–59.

Kirschner, P., Sweller, J., & Clark, R. (2006). Why minimal guidance during instruction does not work: An analysis of failure of constructivist, discovery, problem-based, experiential, and inquiry-based learning. *Educational Psychologist, 41*(2), 75–86.

Even though there are strong theoretical and empirical bases behind concept and inquiry-based teaching, the issue of to what extent students should be free to discover and construct their own knowledge versus how much guidance should be provided remains controversial and unresolved. This Research Summary discusses the work of Richard Meyer (2004) and of Paul Kirschner and his colleagues (2006), both of whom questioned pure discovery approaches and made the case for more guidance.

Kirschner and his colleagues reviewed the arguments both for and against guidance, pointing out that on one side are advocates (Bruner, 1961; Papert, 1980; Steffe & Gale, 1995) who maintain that people learn best in an "unguided or minimally guided environment" where they are afforded opportunities to "discover or construct" information for themselves (p. 82). On the other side are those (Cronback & Snow, 1977; Klahr & Nigam, 2004; Meyer, 2004) who believe that learners, particularly novice learners, should not be left to discover concepts and processes by themselves. They require instructional guidance. The Kirschner group concluded that the evidence overwhelmingly supported guided instruction. Unguided instruction, they wrote, is "much less effective than instructional approaches that place strong emphasis on guidance of the student learning process" (p. 82).

In 2004, Richard Meyer summarized research on discovery learning, problem solving, and discovery associated with computer instruction from the 1950s through the 1990s. Although Meyer said he agreed with constructivist ideas and active teaching and how these ideas have encouraged "new conceptions of teaching and learning," he nonetheless believed that advocates were putting too much emphasis on discovery and "hands-on learning" and on situations where "students are free to work in an environment with little or no guidance" (p. 14). In his review, Meyer focused on studies that compared methods that used what he called "pure discovery" versus those where "guided discovery" was used. From his review, Meyer stated that two consistent findings emerged:

- In inquiry-based or discovery learning, some students do not learn the "rules," "concepts," or "principles" that are the focus of the inquiry very well, and an appropriate amount of guidance seems to be required.
- Students learn better when they are active, but their activity requires guidance.

Meyer made the point that studies do not negate the importance of active learning and the freedom to explore and inquire. He said, however, that with too much freedom students "may fail to come into contact with the to-be-learned material" (p. 17).

Of course, a critical question for teachers is to know when and how much guidance to provide. Meyer's answer to that question was:

Students need enough freedom to become cognitively active in the process of sense making, and students need enough guidance so that their cognitive activity results in the construction of useful knowledge. (p. 16)

It is likely that the truth about how much guidance to use, like many other aspects of teaching, lies somewhere in the middle. The amount of guidance required depends on the prior knowledge and abilities of students and the content and context of specific teaching situations. What do you think?

reflect back over what they have been doing and to analyze their thinking processes as the lesson proceeded. Teachers can use the following kinds of questions to facilitate this aspect of the lesson:

- When did you come up with a hypothesis that made sense to you?
- Did the hypothesis turn out to be accurate?
- Did your thinking change during the inquiry? If so, what prompted the change?
- If I gave you a similar problem situation, how would you tackle it next time?

Check, Extend, Explore

Check

- What are the major planning tasks associated with inquiry-based teaching?
- What are the major phases of an inquiry-based lesson? What type of teacher behaviors are associated with each?
- What purposes do discrepant events serve in an inquiry-based lesson?

Extend

- Some theorists such as Kirschner and Meyer believe that some teachers are putting too much emphasis on discovery and inquiry processes and that students learn more in situations where large measures of guidance are provided. Do you agree or disagree with this perspective? Go to the "Extend Question Poll" on the Online Learning Center to respond.

Explore

- Go to the Online Learning Center at www.mhhe.com/arends10e for Web sites related to how to plan and conduct inquiry-based lessons.

Making Thinking Visible

Concept and inquiry-based teaching are illustrative of approaches that teach thinking by infusing the "teaching of thinking" into regular curricula subjects, mainly science, mathematics, the social sciences, and the humanities. Infusing the teaching of thinking in this way helps students learn important content knowledge while simultaneously learning about the thinking and reasoning processes associated with the content (Stout, 2007; Swartz, 1987). Experienced teachers have found that **infusion strategies** are often effective. At other times they seem not to work all that well. Students (and their teachers) often find it easier to focus on the content goals of the lesson at the expense of "learning to think" objectives. And, even though students are asked to inquire and figure things out on their own, they may not actually be learning important thinking skills. Therefore, some theorists and experienced teachers (Beyer, 2001; Ritchhart, 2002; Ritchhart, Church, & Morrison, 2011) believe that thinking skills and processes of inquiry should be taught separately from subject matter instruction. This separation, they maintain, allows student to focus directly on thinking skills and processes without worrying so much about the subject matter. This is not to say that substantive content is not important as a vehicle within which thinking strategies and skills can be taught.

Numerous programs and approaches have been developed to teach thinking skills and processes this way. Space does not allow a description of all of them. Among the best is Harvard University's *Visible Thinking Project.* This approach will be summarized briefly here as an example of this method of teaching students how to think.

As they studied classrooms, Harvard researchers found that certain teachers cultivated and encouraged "rigorous high-end thinking." Of particular importance is the work of Ron Ritchhart, who studied teachers after they had been nominated as teachers who "really cared about getting their students to think." After many classroom visits, observations, and interviews, Ritchhart and his colleagues came up with several elements of thinking that they argue are essential to understanding. In addition, they found that the teachers in their sample did several things that were often absent from other teachers' classrooms. They developed classrooms characterized by a *culture of thinking,* they made their own and their students' *thinking visible,* and they used specific *thinking routines* to help scaffold student thinking.

Elements of Thinking

Ritchhart and his colleagues report that they identified several elements of thinking processes that aid learners (thinkers) in their quest for deeper understanding. These include:

1. Observing closely and describing what's there
2. Building explanations and interpretations
3. Reasoning with evidence
4. Making connections
5. Considering different viewpoints and perspectives
6. Capturing the heart and forming conclusions
7. Wondering and asking questions
8. Uncovering complexity and going below the surface (from Ritchhart, Church, & Morrison, 2011, pp. 11, 13)

As you will read later, these elements were used in efforts by Ritchhart and his colleagues to develop strategies than can make thinking visible for students.

Developing Classrooms with Cultures of Thinking

Researchers and developers of the *Visible Thinking Program* came to the conclusion that one of the reasons we don't reach the goals most of us hold for teaching thinking is that most classroom learning environments do not have key elements to help students learn how to think. Ritchhart (2002, 2005) concluded that eight elements are required if we want classrooms characterized by a culture of thinking:

- *Expectations and attitudes:* Hold high expectations and have optimistic attitudes for student thinking.
- *Time:* Allocate time for thinking. This means providing both time for exploring topics more in depth as well as time to formulate thoughtful responses to questions. Remember the "wait-time" research described elsewhere.
- *Opportunities:* Provide a rich array of purposeful activities that require students to engage in thinking and in the development of understanding as part of their classroom work.
- *Routines and structures:* Scaffold students' thinking and learning in the moment and provide tools and patterns of thinking that can be used when working independently.
- *Language and conversations:* Use a language of thinking that provides students with the vocabulary for describing and reflecting on thinking.
- *Modeling:* Demonstrate what thinking looks like and show that the teacher is a thoughtful, inquisitive learner.
- *Interactions and relationships:* Show respect for and interest in students' ideas and thinking.
- *Physical environment:* Make thinking and the products of thinking visible in the classroom (summarized from Ritchhart, 2002, pp. 146–147; Ritchhart, 2005).

Making Thinking More Visible

Visible Thinking Program personnel concluded that another reason it has been so difficult to teach students how to think is that the cognitive behaviors associated with thinking are invisible. To address this situation, Ritchhart and Perkins (2008) believe that thinking occurs under the "hoods" of our minds. Success in teaching students how to think, therefore, requires strategies to make thinking more visible. For example, teachers can model thoughtfulness and describe their own thinking processes. They can say:

- "This is what was going on in my mind when I drew that conclusion."
- "What was going on in your mind when you made that statement?"
- "Why is your mind coming up with one conclusion when everyone else has reached a different one?"

Another way to make thinking visible is through the classroom's physical environment. Displaying and labeling the products of student thinking, such as essays, videos, and/or portfolios, throughout the classroom draw attention to students' thinking, as does pictures showing people engaged in thinking activities.

Finally, the way teachers use language can help make thinking and thinking processes visible. For example, processes such as stating a hypothesis, using evidence, or making a generalization can be described and discussed. Using specific terms such as *compare, predict, classify, analyze,* and *apply* helps students see and develop understanding of the cognitive processes associated with thinking.

Using Thinking Routines

At the heart of the *Visible Thinking Program* is what the developers labeled **thinking routines.** These routines are similar in structure to other routines used by teachers, such as classroom management and discourse routines (raising hands, taking turns, lining up) or housekeeping routines (picking up clutter, stacking chairs). Thinking routines are procedures that allow students to explore ideas and to rehearse and reflect on their own thought processes. "See-think-wonder" is an example of one routine that has been developed and consists of three steps, each requiring a different type of cognitive behavior. The steps are described below and the cognitive processes associated with each step are described in Table 9.6:

Step 1. *What do you see?* This step requires students to observe the phenomena under investigation, to identify parts and dimensions, and to look for connections.
Step 2. *What do you think about that?* This step asks students to construct evidence-based interpretations and to synthesize and draw conclusions.
Step 3. *What do you wonder about?* This step requires students to ask questions, reflect on their learning, and perhaps create novel ideas and metaphors.

Many other routines have been developed. Here are two more:

Claim-support-question

1. Make a claim about a topic.
2. Identify support for your claim.
3. Ask a question related to your claim.

Table 9.6 *Examples of Cognitive Behaviors Used in See-Think-Wonder Routine*

Steps in the Routine	Broad Types of Cognitive Behaviors
What do you see?	• Generates lots of ideas.
	• Gives evidence and explanations.
	• Looks for comparisons and connections.
What do you think about that?	• Constructs reason-based syntheses, summaries, and conclusions.
	• Constructs evidence-based interpretations and explanations.
	• Makes discernments and evaluations.
	• Identifies parts, components, and dimensions.
What do you wonder about?	• Asks questions.
	• Identifies and explores multiple perspectives.
	• Creates metaphors.
	• Reflects on and consolidates learning.

Source: Information based on Ritchhart et al. (2006), p. 10.

Claim-extend-challenge

1. How are the ideas and information connected to what you already know?
2. What new ideas did you get that extended your thinking in a new direction?
3. What is still challenging or confusing for you? What questions or puzzles do you now have?

As you can see, thinking routines are rather straightforward and for the most part easy to use. By themselves they do not constitute a complete way to teach students how to think. However, when used effectively they can help students focus directly on their thinking processes and skills.

Developing Learning Environments That Promote Thinking

The tasks associated with managing the learning environment during concept and inquiry-based teaching and those required when using thinking routines are in some ways very similar to those used by teachers when they are using presentation or direct instruction. In other ways they are very different. For instance, when teachers use the direct presentation approach to concept teaching or when they are teaching students a particular thinking routine they normally wish to structure the learning environment fairly tightly. While the lesson is in progress, they expect students to pay close attention to the lesson—to be keen observers and good listeners. Effective teachers use the methods described in Chapter 5 to govern student talk and to ensure that the pace of the lesson is maintained.

However, concept attainment, inquiry-based teaching, and some uses of thinking routines require students to engage in inquiry and discovery, and these inductive processes require discourse and discussion. There are times when the teacher's role is to encourage interaction and to give students opportunities to explore their own thinking processes. Facilitating this kind of student activity requires a less-structured learning environment and norms where students can inquire and express their ideas freely. You read previously how Ritchhart and his colleagues in the *Visible Thinking Program* emphasized the importance of "using a language of thinking," a language that provides students with the vocabulary for describing and reflecting on their own thinking. Inquiry and thinking thrive best in classroom environments characterized by open communication and discourse and where students show respect for one another and feel included. The management system required for more constructivist, student-centered instructional activities will be described in greater detail in Chapters 10, 11, and 12.

Assessing Thinking Processes and Skills

Many of the same ideas and strategies used in defining and analyzing concepts can be employed in evaluating students' understanding of concepts. Similarly, many of the questions posed by teachers in inquiry-based lessons are those that are required to assess student understanding of important thinking processes and skills. However, when evaluating students' understanding of a concept, it is important that teachers ask the students to do more than merely define the concept with words. Similarly,

Check, Extend, Explore

Check
• How does the approach used by Harvard's *Visible Thinking Program* differ from the approaches used for concept and inquiry-based teaching?
• What purposes do "thinking routines" play in teaching students how to think?
• What does "thinking takes place under the hoods of our mind" mean?

Extend
• Some theorists believe that teaching thinking independent of content is the best approach to teaching students how to think. Others believe that infusion strategies work best. At this time, which approach do you prefer? Go to the "Extend Question Poll" on the Online Learning Center to respond.

Explore
• For more information about the *Visible Thinking Program* Google "Visible Thinking Project Zero." This will produce a variety of Web sites associated with this and related programs. Also search YouTube for videos on the *Visible Thinking Program*.

having students define a cognitive process does not mean they understand the process and that they can use it effectively. Asking students to use a concept or thinking skill in a new situation provides teachers with valuable information regarding student understanding.

Teachers can use the more traditional selected-response items described in Chapter 6 to test student knowledge, concept development, and inquiry and thinking processes. However, many of the higher-level cognitive processes and thinking skills can best be assessed using the authentic and performance assessment procedures described in that chapter. Teachers should consider a number of principles when constructing test items to measure students' conceptual development and/or inquiry skills. Test items should include examples that measure students' abilities to generalize to newly encountered examples of a concept. Test items should also assess students' abilities to discriminate among examples and nonexamples and to demonstrate abilities to recognize bias and fallacious reasoning. Tests might also employ different formats, such as true-false, multiple-choice, matching, short answer, or short essay.

Check, Extend, Explore

Check

- How is managing the learning environment for lessons that aim at teaching students how to think similar to managing the learning environments for presentation teaching or direct instruction? How do they differ?
- What are the best ways to assess student thinking processes and skills?

Extend

- Some teachers believe that only brighter students can benefit from concept or inquiry-based teaching. Do you agree or disagree with this perspective? Go to the "Extend Question Poll" on the Online Learning Center to respond.

Explore

- Go to the Online Learning Center at www.mhhe.com/arends10e for Web sites related to approaches for teaching students how to think and how to create learning environments and assessment procedures for these approaches.

Reflections **from the** *Classroom*

Higher-Level Thinking—How Much?

You are in your first year of teaching and you are having a conversation with two of your teacher colleagues. The topic of teaching concepts and higher-level thinking comes up. You say that you have *not* observed many concept lessons in the classrooms the principal has asked you to observe over the past several weeks, and you wonder why. One of your colleagues responds by saying that with so much material to cover, she feels she and other teachers in the school can't justify the time it takes to plan and conduct good concept

lessons. Your other colleague chimes in that many of the students in the school are of low ability and he doesn't believe that they can benefit from lessons on concepts until they have mastered basic skills, mainly through the drill-and-practice of direct instruction. You don't argue with them but their answers don't quite jibe with what you know about concept teaching and about having goals that promote meaningful learning and higher-level thinking for all students, regardless of their abilities.

Reflect on this situation and write a reflective essay about how you will approach the teaching of concepts with your students. Approach the situation from the perspective closest to the grade level or subject area you are preparing to teach. In your reflective essay, consider the following questions: Why is concept teaching important or unimportant? What kinds of students benefit from concept teaching and lessons aimed at higher-level thinking? If concept lessons take more time, how can a teacher justify their use? How central will concept teaching be in your instructional repertoire? At the center? On the fringe? Depending on the students?

Compare your responses to the following provided by two experienced teachers. Include your essay as an exhibit in your professional portfolio.

Diane Caruso

Saltonstall School, 4th and 5th Grade, Salem, MA

The phrase "so much material to cover," particularly considering the constant revision of state educational frameworks, is one that is heard and repeated by thousands of teachers, both novice and experienced. It is extremely important to resist the coverage of material at the expense of concept development and understanding. Covering a topic does not ensure concept mastery for *any* student, regardless of his or her strengths.

As a special needs teacher for many years, I always felt competent in my ability to challenge my students to achieve and to feel positive about themselves. Although this certainly involved the teaching and reinforcement of basic skills, other factors included the development of research techniques (simple and teacher-directed for some students), project work accompanied by clear expectations and rubrics, an exposure to/awareness of world events and hands-on experiences, and encouragement of students to express ideas and opinions through writing and discussion in a safe, accepting environment.

When I transferred to regular education almost ten years ago, one of my main concerns was being able to challenge students at the gifted end of the spectrum. I found that the methods are the same! We must observe, assess, provide activities that allow them to demonstrate success, and then lead them to that next step which will encourage them to achieve even more than they might have believed they could. Yes, concept lessons take more time, and higher-order thinking strategies prolong a lesson, but they also frequently lead to unanticipated teachable moments.

Believing this does not address the real and perceived pressures to cover all of the material. Diversified instructional methods—jigsaw activities, literature circles, other cooperative group practices—help to some degree. Understanding and believing that teaching children to think critically and contribute to higher-order discussions help teachers justify concept teaching. Inviting skeptics into the classroom to observe the process is also extremely helpful. Recently, the children's brainstorming generated a very heavy-duty discussion comparing mistreatment of poor, disenfranchised colonists during the Salem Witch Trials, Native Americans during the 1800s, and African Americans during the past century, along with other groups. An observing teacher in my class stated, "Are you sure these kids are only in fourth and fifth grade?" That's justification. Do not give up that type of educational excitement for coverage!

Ian Call

McKeel Academy, 10th Grade, Polk County, FL

All students, whether they have strong or weak academic abilities, can benefit from concept lessons. One of the main reasons to include concept lessons in the curriculum for low-performing students is to create interest in the content being taught. Too often, drill-and-practice methods are not relevant to the students and school becomes boring and an inefficient use of their time. By utilizing concept lessons, teachers can create curriculum that interests their students in learning the material and makes their classrooms more effective.

In addition, basic skills such as reading and writing do not have to be separate from higher-order thinking. Effective concept lessons can be created to both enhance students' skills as well as promote higher-order thinking. While there is a large amount of material to cover in a school year, effective teachers can create concept lessons that not only cover the material, but also include thinking skills that students will need in the future. Students need more than just basic skills, and it is up to you to provide them with the experiences necessary to build their higher-thinking skills while they are in school.

As a first year teacher, you have a long career ahead of you, but the way you start your career will have a large impact on the many years that will follow. Planning concept lessons may take more time at the beginning, but once you get started you will find that not only do they have benefits for your students, but also yourself. Teachers who use concept lessons in their classrooms are more in tune with their students, are more intellectually challenged by the job, and are less likely to fall into the dreaded world of "Burned Out Land."

Summary

Provide an overview of the importance of teaching students how to think and the approaches used to accomplish this goal.

- Educators and parents alike believe that teaching students how to think is among the most important goals of education.
- Concept learning and logical thinking are critical goals for almost everything taught in schools. These become important scaffoldings for building student understanding of school subjects.
- Concept teaching, inquiry-based teaching, and making thinking visible are approaches for teaching students how to think.

Describe the theoretical and empirical support behind teaching students how to think and the use of concept and inquiry-based teaching.

- The theoretical and empirical support for concept and inquiry-based teaching is very extensive and covers a wide range of topics. It includes the contributions of Jean Piaget, Jerome Bruner, David Ausubel, and Howard Gardner, among others.
- Most theorists believe that thinking is universal and automatic but not necessarily always effective. The goals of instruction are to teach students not how to think but how to think more clearly and critically.
- There are numerous types of thinking. Among the most common include higher-level thinking, critical thinking, scientific thinking and reasoning, and megacognitive thinking.

Explain how to plan and conduct a concept teaching lesson.

- The instructional goals of concept teaching are mainly to help learners acquire conceptual understandings of the subjects they are studying and to provide a foundation for higher-level thinking.
- There are several different approaches to teaching concepts. Two of the most prevalent are direct presentation and concept attainment. In direct presentation, the teacher labels and defines the concept early in the lesson and then presents the best examples through exposition. In concept attainment, the teacher presents examples and nonexamples of a particular concept but does not define or label the concept until the end of the lesson.
- Planning tasks for concept lessons include selecting and analyzing concepts and choosing the most appropriate approach.
- The general flow or syntax of a concept lesson consists of four major phases: present goals and establish set, provide examples and nonexamples, test for concept attainment, and analyze student thinking processes.
- The exact sequencing for defining and labeling a concept and presenting examples and nonexamples varies according to the approach being used by the teacher. In direct presentation, the teacher presents the definition first, whereas in concept attainment, the teacher presents examples and nonexamples first, and students discover and define the concept using an inductive process.
- Through questioning and discussion, teachers help students analyze their thinking processes and integrate new learning with old as the final phase of a concept lesson, regardless of approach.

Explain how to plan and conduct an inquiry-based lesson.

- Two major planning tasks are required for an inquiry-based lesson: determining goals for the lesson and identifying a suitable problem for inquiry.
- Discrepant events or puzzling situations are used at the beginning of an inquiry lesson. The purpose of these events or situations is to spark curiosity at the beginning of the lesson.
- The general flow or syntax of an inquiry-based lesson consists of six phases: explaining the inquiry process, presenting the inquiry problem, having students formulate hypotheses to explain the problem, collecting data to test hypotheses, formulating explanations, and reflecting and analyzing thinking processes.

Explain how to plan and use routines and processes aimed at making thinking visible to students.

- Harvard University's *Visible Thinking Program* is another approach to teaching students how to think. Central to this approach are developing classrooms characterized by cultures of thinking and using specific processes that made thinking visible.

- One reason it is so difficult to teach students how to think is that thinking or cognitive behaviors are invisible.
- Thinking routines have been developed and provide procedures that allow students to explore ideas and to rehearse and reflect on their own thought processes.

Describe how to create a learning environment that will support and promote student thinking.

- During the presentation and attainment phases of a concept lesson, the teacher maintains a structured learning environment. However, the final phases of a concept lesson encourage student interaction and require a more flexible, student-centered learning environment.
- During an inquiry-based lesson, the learning environment is open and flexible and situations are expected to engage in inquiry and discovery.

- The visible thinking classroom environment is one characterized by open communication and discourse and where everyone shows respect for one another and for all ideas.

Describe appropriate ways to assess student thinking processes and skills.

- As with other approaches to teaching, the major post-instructional task for lessons aimed at teaching students how to think is for teachers to make sure assessment procedures are consistent with the goals and outcomes of particular lessons.
- When evaluating students' understanding and skills associated with thinking processes, it is important to ask students to demonstrate what they know and how they think using a variety of performance measures and reflective techniques.

Key Terms

accommodation   342
assimilation   342
concept   339
concept attainment   344
concept teaching   339
conjunctive concept   340
critical attributes   341

critical thinking   338
deductive reasoning   338
direct presentation   344
discrepant event   354
disjunctive concept   340
dispositions   338
graphic organizers   347

higher-level thinking   337
inductive reasoning   338
infusion strategies   358
noncritical attributes   341
relational concepts   340
scientific thinking   338
thinking routines   360

Interactive and Applied Learning

🅞🅛🅒 Study and Explore

- Access your Study Guide, which includes practice quizzes, from the Online Learning Center.

🅞🅛🅒 Observe and Practice

- Listen to audio clips on the Online Learning Center of Kendra Genzer (5th grade) and Felton Wrust (11th grade chemistry) talking about teaching students how to think in the *Teachers on Teaching* area.

Complete Exercise 9.1: Planning a Concept Teaching or Inquiry-Based Lesson including
- Selecting a model and particular approach
- Writing objectives for the lesson

- Differentiating for two students
- Reflecting on the lesson

Complete the following additional **Practice Exercises** that accompany Chapter 9:
- Practice Exercise 9.2: Concept Mapping
- Practice Exercise 9.3: Teaching Dilemma: Comparing Instructional Strategies
- Practice Exercise 9.4: Reflecting on the Benefits of Concept and Inquiry-Based Teaching

Portfolio and Field Experience Activities

Expand your understanding of the content and processes of this chapter through the following field experience and portfolio activities. Support materials to complete the activities are in the *Portfolio and Field Experience Activities* area on the Online Learning Center.

1. Complete the **Reflections from the Classroom** exercise at the end of this chapter, and use the recommended reflective essay as an exhibit in your professional portfolio to show your views about concept teaching. **(InTASC Standard 5: Application of Content; InTASC Standard 8: Instructional Strategies)**

2. **Activity 9.1: Assessing My Skills for Teaching Students How to Think.** Assess your level of understanding and skill for using the concept teaching approach. **(InTASC Standard 5: Application of Content; InTASC Standard 8: Instructional Strategies)**

3. **Activity 9.2: Observing a Concept Attainment or Inquiry-Based Lesson.** Observe an experienced teacher teach a concept attainment or inquiry-based lesson and consider how closely he or she adhered to the syntax as described in this chapter. **(InTASC Standard 5: Application of Content; InTASC Standard 8: Instructional Strategies)**

4. **Activity 9.3: Practice Using a Thinking Routine.** Choose one of the thinking routines described in the text and prepare a lesson and teach it to a small group of students. Student may be at your field-experience site or a small group of friends. **(InTASC Standard 5: Application of Content; InTASC Standard 8: Instructional Strategies)**

5. **Activity 9.4: Portfolio: Demonstrating My Webbing Skills.** Construct a conceptual web on a concept in your subject field or grade level. Use the product of your work as an exhibit in your professional portfolio that demonstrates your webbing skills. **(InTASC Standard 5: Application of Content; InTASC Standard 8: Instructional Strategies)**

Books for the Professional

Bellanca, J. (2007). *A guide to graphic organizers: Helping students organize and process content for deeper learning* (2nd ed.). Thousand Oaks, CA: Corwin Press.

Brookfield, S. (2011). *Teaching for critical thinking: Tools and techniques to help students question their assumptions.* San Francisco: Jossey-Bass.

Brookhart, S. (2010). *How to assess higher-order thinking skills in your classroom.* Alexandria, VA: Association for Supervision and Curriculum Development.

Costa, A. (2011). *Developing minds: A resource book for teaching thinking* (3rd ed.). Alexandria, VA: Association for Supervision and Curriculum Development.

Erickson, H. L. (2007). *Concept-based curriculum and instruction for the thinking classroom.* Thousand Oaks, CA: Corwin Press.

Nosich, G. (2011). *Learning to think things through: A guide to critical thinking across the curriculum* (4th ed.). New York: Prentice Hall.

Ritchhart, R. (2002). *Intellectual character: What it is, why it matters, and how to get it.* San Francisco: Jossey-Bass.

Ritchhart, R., Church, M., & Morrison, K. (2011). *Making thinking visible: How to promote engagement, understanding, and independence for all learners.* San Francisco: Jossey-Bass.

CHAPTER 10
Cooperative Learning

Learning Goals

After studying this chapter you should be able to

Overview of Cooperative Learning	Provide an overview of cooperative learning and explain its appropriate use.
Theoretical and Empirical Support	Describe the theoretical foundations of cooperative learning and summarize the research that supports its use.
Planning and Conducting Cooperative Learning Lessons	Explain how to plan and use cooperative learning, including how to adapt its use to students of differing backgrounds and abilities.
Managing the Learning Environment	Describe how to implement a learning environment conducive to using cooperative learning.
Assessment and Evaluation	Describe appropriate ways to assess student academic and social learning consistent with cooperative learning goals.
Cooperative Learning: A Final Thought	Describe why it has been difficult to implement cooperative learning and why it is important not to hold unrealistically high expectations for this approach to teaching.

 ## Reflecting on Cooperative Learning

Think about learning experiences you have had as a student that required you to work with other students. The experience may have been very brief, such as working on a few math problems with the student next to you, or it might have been extensive, requiring collaboration on a major term project.

Write down your thoughts on and reactions to these experiences by considering the following questions:

- What did you like most about working on learning tasks with others? Least?
- Were the experiences you thought about valuable for you? Why or why not?
- What do you think students learn when they work together?

- Are there some aspects of learning together that are particularly effective? What are these?

- Are there some aspects of learning together that are particularly ineffective? What are these?

Considering your answers, do you think you are a person who is prone to be positive toward cooperative learning? Or do you have some serious reservations?

 Go to the Online Learning Center at www.mhhe.com/arends10e to respond to these questions.

The previous chapters described several approaches to teaching—presentation, direct instruction, and concept and inquiry-based teaching. These approaches are used by teachers primarily to help students acquire new knowledge, master important skills, and think about and process information already acquired from prior learning. In essence, this is academic learning, and although this type of learning is extremely important, it doesn't represent the only goals for students. This chapter describes an approach to instruction called *cooperative learning,* which goes beyond helping students acquire academic knowledge and skills to address important social and human relations goals and objectives.

The chapter begins with an overview of cooperative learning, then presents its theoretical and empirical support. Sections that describe the specific procedures used by teachers as they plan, conduct, and manage the learning environment during cooperative learning lessons follow. The final sections highlight the assessment and evaluation tasks associated with cooperative learning.

Overview of Cooperative Learning

Cooperative learning model requires student cooperation and interdependence in its task, goal, and reward structures.

All instructional lessons can be characterized, in part, by their task structures, their goal structures, and their reward structures. **Task Structures** involve the way lessons are organized and the kind of work students are asked to do. They encompass whether the teacher is working with the whole class or small groups, what students are expected to accomplish, and the cognitive and social demands placed on students as they work to accomplish assigned learning tasks. Task structures differ according to the activities involved in particular lessons. For example, some lessons require students to sit and receive information from a teacher's presentation. Other lessons require that students complete worksheets, and still others require discussion and debate.

A lesson's **goal structure** refers to the amount of interdependence required of students as they perform their work. Three types of goal structures have been identified. Goal structures are **individualistic** if achievement of the instructional goal requires no interaction with others and is unrelated to how well others do. **Competitive** goal structures exist when students compete with others to achieve important goals. **Cooperative** goal structures exist when students can obtain their goal only when other students with whom they are linked can obtain theirs. These three goal structures were illustrated previously in Chapter 4.

The **reward structure** for lessons can also vary. Just as goal structures can be individualist, competitive, or cooperative, so, too, can reward structures. Individualistic reward structures exist when a reward can be achieved independently from what anyone else does. The satisfaction of running a four-minute mile is an example of an individualistic reward structure. Competitive reward structures are those for which rewards are obtained for individual effort in comparison to others. Grading on a curve is an example of a competitive reward structure, as is the way winners are defined in many track and field events. In contrast, situations in which individual effort helps others to be rewarded use cooperative reward structures. Most team sports, such as football, have a cooperative reward structure, even though teams may compete with each other.

> The terms *goal* and *reward structures* both refer to the degree of cooperation or competition required of students to achieve their goals or rewards.

Lessons organized around the more teacher-centered transmission approaches to instruction are generally characterized by task structures by which teachers work mainly with a whole class of students or students work individually to master academic content. Goal and reward structures are most often based on individual competition and effort. In contrast, as its name implies, cooperative learning is characterized by cooperative task, goal, and reward structures. Students in cooperative learning situations are encouraged and/or required to work together on a common task, and they must coordinate their efforts to complete the task. Similarly, in cooperative learning, two or more individuals are interdependent for a reward they will share, if they are successful as a group. Cooperative learning lessons can be characterized by the following features:

- Students work in teams to master learning outcomes.
- Teams are normally made up of students of mixed ability levels.
- Whenever possible, teams include a racial, cultural, and gender mix.
- Reward systems are oriented to the group as well as the individual.

All these features are explained more fully later in the chapter.

As illustrated in Figure 10.1, cooperative learning was developed to achieve at least three important instructional outcomes: academic achievement, tolerance and acceptance of diversity, and development of social skills.

> The three instructional outcomes of cooperative learning are academic achievement, tolerance and acceptance of diversity, and development of social skills.

Although cooperative learning encompasses a variety of social objectives, it also aims at improving student performance on important *academic tasks*. Its supporters believe that using a cooperative reward structure raises the value students place on academic learning and changes the norms associated with achievement. Slavin (1996), one of the founders of cooperative learning, believed that the group focus of cooperative learning changes the norms of youth culture and makes it more acceptable to excel in academic learning tasks. He wrote:

> Students often do not value their peers who do well academically, while they do value their peers who excel in sports. . . . This is so because sports success brings benefits to groups (the team, the school, the town), while academic success benefits only the individual. In fact, in a class using grading on the curve or any competitive grading or incentive system, any individual's success reduces the chances that any other individual will succeed. (p. 54)

In addition to changing norms associated with achievement, cooperative learning can benefit both low- and high-achieving students who work together on academic tasks. Higher achievers tutor lower achievers,

Figure 10.1 *Learner Outcomes for Cooperative Learning*

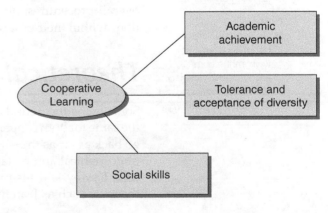

thus providing special help from peers who share youth-oriented interests and language. In the process, higher achievers gain academically because serving as a tutor requires thinking more deeply about the relationships of ideas within a particular subject. This process, however, is sometimes contentious, as will be explained later.

A second important effect of cooperative learning is wider tolerance and acceptance of people who are different by virtue of their race, culture, social class, or ability. Following the premises outlined by Allport (1954) over a half century ago, it is known that mere physical contact among different racial or ethnic groups or children with special needs is insufficient to reduce prejudice and stereotyping. To illustrate this premise, think of instances where whites and African Americans often live in separate neighborhoods and go to separate places of worship. Cooperative learning presents opportunities for students of varying backgrounds and conditions to work interdependently on common tasks and, through the use of cooperative reward structures, to learn to appreciate one another.

A third and important goal for cooperative learning is to teach students skills of cooperation and collaboration. These are critical skills in a world in which much adult work is carried out in large, interdependent organizations and communities are becoming more culturally diverse and global in their orientations. Yet, many youth and adults alike lack effective social skills. This situation is evidenced by how often minor disagreements between individuals can lead to violent acts and by how often people express dissatisfaction when asked to work in cooperative situations. Cooperative learning promotes cooperation because it values and promotes the development of interpersonal intelligence, one of Gardner's eight multiple intelligences described in Chapter 2.

Six major phases or steps are involved in a cooperative learning lesson: (1) A lesson begins with the teacher going over the goals of the lesson and getting students motivated to learn. (2) This phase is followed by the presentation of information, often in the form of text or other media (e.g., video, Internet) rather than lecture. (3) Students are then organized into study teams. (4) Teams of students, assisted by the teacher, work together to accomplish interdependent tasks. Final phases of a cooperative learning lesson include (5) presentation of the group's end product or testing over what students have learned and (6) recognition of group and individual efforts. The six phases of a cooperative lesson are described in more detail later in the chapter.

The learning environment for cooperative learning is characterized by democratic processes and active roles for students in deciding what should be studied and how. The teacher may provide a high degree of structure in forming groups and defining overall procedures, but students are left in control of the minute-to-minute interactions within their groups.

Theoretical and Empirical Support

Some of the theoretical underpinnings and the research and development features are the same for both cooperative and problem-based learning. The roots for each approach go back as far as the early Greeks. Contemporary developments, however, rest on the philosophical and pedagogical ideas of early twentieth-century philosophers such as John Dewey and his progressive colleagues and from cognitive and developmental theorists such as Jean Piaget and Lev Vygotsky. Cooperative learning as practiced in

---

The cooperative learning environment sets the stage for students to learn very valuable collaboration and social skills that they will use throughout their lives.

Check, Extend, Explore

Check
- What are the key characteristics of cooperative learning? How do these differ from other approaches to teaching?
- What are the six phases of a cooperative learning lesson?
- What are the major learner outcomes for cooperative learning?
- What type of learning environment works best for cooperative learning?

Extend
- After reading this short introduction, do you agree or disagree with the basic goals and premises of cooperative learning? Go to the "Extend Question Poll" on the Online Learning Center to respond.

Explore
- Go to the Online Learning Center at www.mhhe.com/arends10e for links to Web sites related to *Cooperative Learning*.

today's classroom has been heavily influenced by many. However, the work of Robert Slavin and David and Roger Johnson, who have spent over three decades developing and studying effective group and classroom practices, stand out.

Theoretical support for both cooperative and problem-based learning rests on ideas associated with *democratic classrooms*, the *constructivist views* of teaching and learning, and theories that help explain *intergroup relations*. These ideas will be described in this chapter and then briefly summarized in Chapter 11 on problem-based learning.

John Dewey and the Democratic Classroom

John Dewey

In 1916, John Dewey wrote a book called *Democracy and Education*. Dewey's concept of education was that the classroom should mirror the larger society and be a laboratory for real-life learning. Dewey's pedagogy required teachers to create a learning environment characterized by democratic procedures and scientific processes. Their primary responsibility was to engage students in inquiry into important social and interpersonal problems. The specific classroom procedures described by Dewey (and his latter-day followers) emphasized small, problem-solving groups of students searching for their own answers and learning democratic principles through day-to-day interaction with one another.

Many years after Dewey's initial work, Herbert Thelen (1954, 1960) developed more precise procedures for helping students work in groups. Like Dewey, Thelen argued that the classroom should be a laboratory or miniature democracy for the purpose of study and inquiry into important social and interpersonal problems. Thelen, with his interest in group dynamics, provided the conceptual basis for contemporary developments in cooperative and problem-based learning.

For Dewey and Thelen, the use of cooperative group work went beyond improving academic learning. Cooperative behavior and processes were considered basic to human endeavor—the foundation on which strong democratic communities could be built and maintained. The logical way to accomplish these important educational objectives, they believed, was to structure the classroom and students' learning activities so that they modeled the desired outcomes.

Intergroup Relations

In 1954, the Supreme Court issued its historic *Brown* v. *Board of Education of Topeka* decision in which the Court ruled that public schools in the United States could no longer operate under a separate-but-equal policy but must become racially integrated. This led to subsequent decisions and actions by judicial and legislative bodies all across the country demanding that public school authorities submit plans for desegregation.

At the time, thoughtful theorists and observers warned that putting people of different ethnic or racial backgrounds in the same location would not, in and of itself, counteract the effects of prejudice or promote integration and better intergroup acceptance. They knew, for example, that the cafeteria in an integrated school might still be characterized by African American students sitting on one side of the room and white students on the other. They also knew that a community might be highly integrated but still have restaurants or churches patronized by only whites or only blacks. Most have concluded that laws alone would not reduce intergroup prejudice and promote better acceptance and understanding.

Dewey and Thelen viewed cooperative behavior as the foundation of democracy and saw schools as laboratories for developing democratic behavior.

Interethnic contacts occurring under conditions of equal status are needed to reduce racial and ethnic prejudice.

Much of the recent interest in cooperative learning has grown out of attempts to structure classrooms and teaching processes to reduce intergroup prejudice and to promote acceptance of diversity. Robert Slavin's work (1996, 2013), which is described later, was conducted in part in the inner cities along the Eastern Seaboard as part of integration efforts. The work of Sharan and his colleagues in Israel (1984, 1999) was prompted by that country's need to find ways to promote better ethnic understanding between Jewish immigrants of European background and those of Middle Eastern background. The work of David and Roger Johnson and their colleagues (Johnson & Johnson, 2013; Johnson, Johnson, & Holubec, 1998) has explored how cooperative classroom environments might lead to better learning by and more positive regard toward students with special needs who were included in regular classrooms as well as toward many others.

Piaget, Vygotsky, and Constructivism

Dewey and his later followers provided the philosophical underpinnings for cooperative learning, but psychology provided much of its theoretical support. The European psychologists Jean Piaget and Lev Vygotsky and America's Jerome Bruner were instrumental in developing ideas that have served as the foundation for **constructivism**, a perspective about learning that pays attention to not only how the brain and memory system works but also to developmental, social, and cultural factors that affect learning. In actuality, there are several different constructivist theories that space will not allow to be described here. Instead the focus will be on two big ideas that have influenced the development and implementation of cooperative and problem-based learning:

- Learners are *active participants* in constructing their own knowledge.
- *Interaction in social settings,* including the classroom, affects greatly the construction process and how people *create meaning* out of experience.

Jean Piaget, a Swiss psychologist, spent over fifty years studying how children think and the processes associated with their intellectual development. In explaining how the intellect develops in young children, Piaget confirmed that children are innately curious, and they are constantly striving to understand the world around them. This curiosity, according to Piaget, motivates them to actively construct representations in their minds about the environment they are experiencing. As they grow older and acquire more language and memory capacity, their mental representations of the world become more elaborate and abstract. At all stages of development, however, children's need to understand their environment motivates them to investigate and to construct theories that help explain it.

The cognitive-constructivist perspective, on which cooperative and problem-based learning rests, borrows heavily from Piaget (1954, 1963). It posits, as did he, that learners of any age are actively involved in the process of acquiring information and constructing their own knowledge. Knowledge does not remain static but instead is constantly evolving and changing as learners confront new experiences that force them to build on and modify prior knowledge. In the words of Piaget:

> good pedagogy: must involve presenting the child with situations in which (he or she) experiments, in the broadest sense of that term—trying things out to see what happens, manipulating things, manipulating symbols, posing questions and seeking (his/her) own answers, reconciling what (he/she) finds one time with what (he/she) finds at another, comparing (his/her) finding with those of other children. (cited in Duckworth, 1991, p. 2)

Lev Vygotsky was a Russian psychologist whose work was not known to most Americans until quite recently. Like Piaget, Vygotsky (1978, 1994) believed that the intellect develops as individuals confront new and puzzling experiences and as they strive to resolve discrepancies posed by these experiences. In the quest for understanding, individuals link new knowledge to prior knowledge and construct new meaning. Vygotsky's beliefs differed from those of Piaget, however, in some important ways. Whereas Piaget focused on the stages of intellectual development that all individuals go through regardless of social or cultural context, Vygotsky placed more importance on the social aspect of learning. Vygotsky believed that social interaction with others spurred the construction of new ideas and enhanced the learner's intellectual development.

The importance to education of Vygotsky's and Piaget's ideas is clear. Learning occurs as learners interact with their environments and through social interaction with others. When provided appropriate challenges, assistance, and learning activities that allow interaction with the teacher and peers, students move forward toward constructing their own knowledge and reality about the world around them.

Research and Development

Cooperative learning has been among one of the most researched approaches to teaching. It is not possible to summarize all the research on cooperative learning here, but the following sections provide brief summaries of the effects of cooperative learning on three types of learner outcomes: cooperative behavior, tolerance of diversity, and academic achievement.

Effects on Cooperative Behavior. Twenty-first-century living is characterized by global, interdependent communities and by complex social institutions that require high degrees of cooperation among members. Consequently, most people prize cooperative behavior and believe it to be an important goal for education. Many of the schools' extracurricular activities, such as team sports and dramatic and musical productions, are justified on this basis. But what about activities within the classroom itself? Do certain types of activities, such as those associated with cooperative learning, have effects on students' cooperative attitudes and behaviors?

Sharan and his colleagues (1984, 1999) sought answers to this question for over two decades. They developed a particular approach to cooperative learning and tested it to see if its use would improve social relations among different Jewish subgroups in Israel. As an example of this research, researchers randomly assigned thirty-three English and literature teachers to three training groups. Teachers in group 1 were taught how to fine-tune their whole-class teaching skills. Those in group 2 were taught how to use Slavin's Student Teams Achievement Divisions (STAD) (explained later), and those in group 3 were taught Sharan's Group Investigation (GI) approach to cooperative learning. The investigators collected massive amounts of information before, during, and after the experiment, including data from achievement tests, classroom observations, and cooperative behavior of students.

For the test of cooperative behavior, students were selected from classrooms using each of the three instructional approaches and were asked to engage in a task called "Lego Man." In six-member teams (each with three European and three Middle Eastern members), students were asked to plan how they would carry out a joint task of constructing a human figure from forty-eight Lego pieces.

Sharan's studies showed clearly that the instructional methods influenced the students' cooperative and competitive behavior. Cooperative learning generated more

> The majority of studies done on the effects of cooperative learning show that it produces both academic and social benefits.

✳ constructivist views

cooperative behavior, both verbal and nonverbal, than did whole-class teaching. Students from both cooperative-learning classrooms displayed less competitive behavior and more cross-ethnic cooperation than those who came from whole-class teaching classrooms.

Effects on Tolerance for Diversity. Two decades after the Supreme Court ended separate-but-equal public schools, Congress passed an equally historic piece of integration legislation in 1975 titled the Education for All Handicapped Children Act and described in Chapter 2. Also known as Public Law 94-142, this legislation required students with special needs to be placed and integrated into regular classrooms rather than placed in special classes. Obviously, this meant that regular classroom teachers now had children with physical, emotional, and mental challenges in their classrooms.

Just as theorists knew that racial integration would not end prejudice, there was considerable evidence in that placing students with special needs (who have traditionally been perceived negatively) in close proximity to others would not end negative attitudes. In fact, some researchers argued that closer contact might even increase prejudice and stereotyping. A critical factor in producing more positive attitudes and behaviors seemed to be the way the interaction between students with and without disabilities was structured. David Johnson, Roger Johnson (1979), and several of their colleagues at the University of Minnesota studied how goal structures influence interaction in a unique and interesting way. Their study, now considered a classic, is summarized in the Research Summary for this chapter.

Studies and reviews similar to the Johnsons' research (Gilles, 2002; Slavin, 2013; Smith, 2006; Vedder & Veendrick, 2003) have shown that not only can cooperative learning influence tolerance and wider acceptance of students with special needs, but it also can promote better relationships among students of varying races and ethnicities.

Cooperative learning helps students become engaged with one another.

Research Summary

What Can Make Us Cheer for Our Peers with Special Needs?*

*Johnson, R., Rynders, J., Johnson, D. W., Schmidt, B., &
Haider, S. (1979).* Interaction between handicapped and
nonhandicapped teenagers as a function of situational goal
structuring: Implications for mainstreaming. *American Educational Research Journal, 16,* 161–167.

Just because people who are different from one another
are placed in close proximity does not mean that they will
interact in positive ways or shed their prejudice and negative
stereotypes. An important question for educators and teachers is, "What can we do to help students be more positive and
more accepting toward peers who represent different racial
backgrounds, come from different social classes, or who are
disabled?" Roger Johnson and David Johnson and their colleagues addressed this question in an important study that
was creative in the way it sought answers to a complex problem in a very simple setting, a bowling alley.

Problem and Approach: The researchers wanted to find
out the effects of various goal structures on the interactions
between nondisabled junior high students and trainable
mentally challenged students in a learning situation, in this
instance, bowling classes.

Sample: Subjects in the study were thirty junior high students (ages 13 to 16, including fifteen boys and fifteen girls)
from three midwestern junior high schools. Nine nondisabled students came from a public junior high school; nine
other nondisabled students came from a private Catholic
school. The twelve disabled students were from a special
school for the mentally challenged. These students were able
to communicate and understand instructions and did not
have any physical disabilities that would prevent them from
bowling.

Procedures: Students were divided randomly into learning
teams of five. Each team contained three nondisabled students
and two students with disabilities. Each of the learning teams
was then assigned to one of three experimental conditions:

- *Cooperative condition.* Team members were instructed to
  "maximize" their team's bowling score at a criterion of
  fifty points improvement over the previous week. They
  were to help each other in any way possible.
- *Individualistic condition.* Students in these teams were
  instructed to "maximize" their individual scores by 10

points over the previous week and to concentrate only on
their own performance.
- *Laissez-faire condition.* Students were given no special
  instructions.

The three bowling instructors in the study were told what to
say and were rotated across groups. All groups received the
same amount of training over a six-week period.

Trained observers, who were kept naive about the purpose of the study, watched the students bowl and recorded
interactions among students in three categories: positive,
neutral, and negative. Observations focused on the period of
time from when a bowler stepped up to bowl until he or she
stepped down from the bowling line.

Pointers for Reading Research: The researchers used the
chi square (χ^2) to test the significance of their results. This
statistic is used by researchers when their data are of a
particular type. It serves the same purpose as other tests
of significance introduced earlier. The results as reported
in this study are straightforward and easy to read and
understand.

Results: Tables 10.1 and 10.2 show the results of the bowling study. Table 10.1 displays the frequency of homogeneous
and heterogeneous interactions among the students in the
three conditions. Table 10.2 displays data on "group cheers"
for disabled students who threw strikes and spares over the
course of the study.

Discussion and Implications The data presented in
Tables 10.1 and 10.2 are clear and straightforward. There
were more interactions among students on the cooperative
bowling team and, more important, more positive interactions that were both heterogeneous and homogeneous.
Further study of the data revealed that "Each student with
a disability on the average participated in 17 positive interactions with nondisabled peers per hour in the cooperative
condition, 5 in the individualistic condition, and 7 in the
laissez-faire condition" (p. 164).

The number of cheers given to disabled students in the
cooperative condition gives additional support to the idea
that a cooperative goal structure is a means for getting
positive response from nondisabled students toward their
disabled peers.

Table 10.1 *Frequency of Homogeneous and Heterogeneous Interactions within Conditions*

	Positive		Neutral		Negative		
	Homo	**Hetero**	**Homo**	**Hetero**	**Homo**	**Hetero**	**Total**
Cooperative	495	336	67	47	4	10	959
Individualistic	243	92	61	17	15	11	439
Laissez-faire	265	136	75	49	9	6	540
Total	1,003	564	203	113	28	27	1,938

$*\chi^2 = 86.87, p < .01.$

Note: Homogeneous interactions took place between nondisabled students and between disabled students; heterogeneous interactions took place between disabled and nondisabled students.

Source: After R. Johnson et al. (1979), p. 165.

Table 10.2 *Frequency of Group Cheers within Conditions*

Condition	**Frequency**
Cooperative	55
Individualistic	6
Laissez-faire	3

Source: After R. Johnson et al. (1979), p. 165.

This study, along with others that have produced similar results, has two important implications for teachers:

1. Individualistic and competitive goal structures associated with so many classroom learning tasks do not encourage positive interactions among people from differing backgrounds and conditions. Redefining the goal structure and making it more cooperative seems to help.

2. Severely disabled students, such as those who are mentally challenged, given the appropriate conditions, can be mainstreamed into learning settings with nondisabled students in ways that can benefit all.

*Even though referring to students with special needs as "disabled" is not the preferred usage today, it was left in this Research Summary. The word was used by the researchers at the time the study was conducted, a time when "disabled" was more acceptable.

Effects on Academic Achievement. One of the important aspects of cooperative learning is that while it is helping promote cooperative behavior and better intergroup relations among students, it simultaneously helps students with their academic learning. Over the past two decades, several researchers have reviewed and summarized the research on cooperative learning (Hmelo-Silver, Chinn, Chan, & O'Donnell, 2013; Johnson, Johnson, & Holubec, 1998; Leinhardt, 1992; Slavin, 1995, 2013; Slavin et al., 1992; Slavin, Hurley, & Chamberlain, 2003; Stronge, 2007). Researchers have reviewed studies at all grade levels and included the following subject areas: language arts, spelling, geography, social studies, science, mathematics, English as a second language, reading, and writing. In most instances, cooperative learning outperformed other types of instruction; none of the studies showed negative effects for cooperative learning.

To summarize, a strong theoretical and empirical framework for cooperative learning reflects the perspective that humans learn from their experiences and that active participation in small groups helps students learn important social skills while simultaneously developing academic skills and democratic attitudes.

Before moving into how to plan and execute cooperative learning lessons, a note of caution may be in order. Most developers of cooperative learning and its use of heterogeneous groups and cooperative reward structures point out the benefits of these practices, mainly that students with lesser abilities learn more by working alongside those who have greater abilities and that the latter benefit from the process of serving as tutors to their less-able peers. Robinson and Clinkenbeard (1998), however, report that intellectually gifted students do not necessarily benefit from working in heterogeneous groups and that using cooperative learning with talented students might be considered a form of exploitation. Mayer (2011) also questions some of the cooperative reward practices. He argues that providing a group reward for a single group product may not always be helpful or effective. Further, he questions the effectiveness of allowing students too much leeway to work on their own, a topic that was explored in the Research Summary in Chapter 9. The lesson for beginning teachers is that although cooperative learning produces important learning outcomes, some practices may also have some unintended and negative consequences.

Planning and Conducting Cooperative Learning Lessons

Planning for Cooperative Learning

Many of the functions of teacher planning described in previous chapters can be applied to cooperative learning. Cooperative learning, however, requires some unique planning tasks as well. For example, time spent organizing or analyzing specific skills required of a direct instruction lesson may instead be spent gathering resource materials or text so small groups of students can work on their own. Instead of planning for the smooth flow and sequencing of major ideas, the teacher can plan how to make smooth transitions from whole-class to small-group instruction. Following are some of the unique planning tasks and decisions required of teachers preparing to teach a cooperative learning lesson.

Choose an Approach. Although the basic principles of cooperative learning do not change, there are several variations that exist today. Four approaches that should be part of the beginning teacher's repertoire are described here.

Student Teams Achievement Divisions. **Student Teams Achievement Divisions (STAD)** was developed by Robert Slavin and his colleagues at Johns Hopkins University and is perhaps the simplest and most straightforward of the cooperative learning approaches (Slavin, 1994, 1995). Teachers using STAD present new academic information to students each week or on a regular basis, either through verbal, visual, or multimedia presentation. Students within a given class are divided into four- or five-member learning teams, with representatives of both sexes, various racial or ethnic groups, and high, average, and low achievers on each team. Team members use a variety of study devices to master the academic materials and then help each other learn the materials through tutoring, quizzing one another, or carrying on team discussions. Individually, students take weekly or biweekly quizzes on the academic materials.

Check, Extend, Explore

Check
- What philosophical and theoretical contributions did John Dewey and Gordon Allport make to the development of cooperative learning?
- Why are constructivist views of teaching and learning important to cooperative learning?
- How strong is the empirical support for cooperative learning?
- On what effects of cooperative learning do researchers seem to agree? Disagree?

Extend
- Do you agree or disagree with Robinson's assertion that the use of cooperative learning is a form of exploitation of talented and gifted students? Go to the "Extend Question Poll" on the Online Learning Center to respond.

Explore
- Go to the Online Learning Center at www.mhhe.com/arends10e for links to Web sites related to *Theoretical and Empirical Support for Cooperative Learning.*

In the STAD model of cooperative learning, students in heterogeneous teams help each other by using a variety of cooperative study methods and quizzing procedures.

Figure 10.2 *Jigsaw Teams*

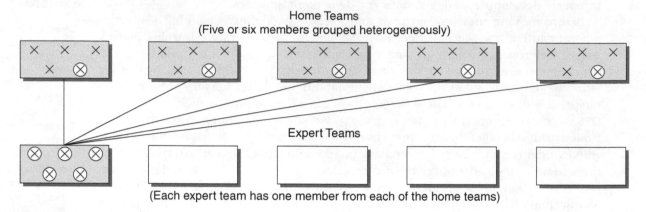

Home Teams
(Five or six members grouped heterogeneously)

Expert Teams

(Each expert team has one member from each of the home teams)

These quizzes are scored and each individual is given an "improvement score." This improvement score (explained later) is based not on a student's absolute score but instead on the degree to which the score exceeds a student's past averages.

In the Jigsaw model, each team member is responsible for mastering part of the learning materials and then teaching that part to the other team members.

Jigsaw. **Jigsaw** was developed and tested by Elliot Aronson and his colleagues (Aronson & Patnoe, 1997, 2011). Using Jigsaw, students are assigned to five- or six-member heterogeneous study teams. Academic materials are presented to the students in audio or visual form, and each student is responsible for learning a portion of the material. For example, if the textual material was on cooperative learning, one student on the team would be responsible for STAD, another for Jigsaw, another for Johnson and Johnson, and perhaps the other two would become experts in the research base and history of cooperative learning. Members from different teams with the same topic (sometimes called the *expert group*) meet to study and help each other learn the topic. Then students return to their home teams and teach other members what they have learned. Figure 10.2 illustrates the relationship between home and expert teams.

Following home team meetings and discussions, students take quizzes individually on the learning materials.

Learning Together. David and Roger Johnson have developed a third approach to cooperative learning that they have labeled **Learning Together** (1998, 2013). The Johnsons' approach is somewhat similar to Slavin's. They have students complete assignments in four- or five-member heterogeneous teams. Rewards are most often based on the product of the team's work. More than other approaches, the Johnsons emphasize the importance of group dynamics, and their approach contains processes for having students debrief and discuss how well they are working together. This emphasis, perhaps more than other approaches, helps students learn important group and social skills.

In the structural approach, teams may have from two to six members, and the task structure may emphasize either social or academic goals.

The Structural Approach. Another approach to cooperative learning has been developed over the past decade mainly by Spencer Kagan (2001, 2013; Kagan & Kagan, 2008). Although it has much in common with other approaches, the **structural approach** emphasizes the use of particular structures designed to influence student

interaction patterns. The structures developed by Kagan are intended to be alternatives to the more traditional classroom structures, such as recitation, in which the teacher poses questions to the whole class and students provide answers after raising their hands and being called on. Kagan's structures call for students to work interdependently in small groups and are characterized by cooperative rather than individual rewards. Some structures have goals for increasing student acquisition of academic content; other structures are designed to teach social or group skills. *Think-pair-share* and *numbered heads together,* described here, are two examples of structures teachers can use to teach academic content or to check on student understanding of particular content. *Active listening* and *time tokens* are examples of structures to teach social skills and are described later in the chapter in the social skills section.

Think-Pair-Share. The **think-pair-share** strategy has grown out of the cooperative learning and wait-time research. The particular approach described here, initially developed by Frank Lyman (1985) and his colleagues at the University of Maryland, is an effective way to change the discourse pattern in a classroom. It challenges the assumption that all recitations or discussions need to be held in whole-group settings, and it has built-in procedures for giving students more time to think and to respond and to help each other. Figure 10.3 illustrates how think-pair-share works. For instance, suppose a teacher has just completed a short presentation or students have read an assignment or a puzzling situation the teacher has described. The teacher now wants students to consider more fully what she has explained. She chooses to use the think-pair-share strategy rather than whole-group question and answer. She employs the following steps:

Step 1—Thinking: The teacher poses a question or an issue associated with the lesson and asks students to spend a minute thinking alone about the answer or the issue. Students need to be taught that talking is not part of thinking time.

Step 2—Pairing: Next, the teacher asks students to pair off and discuss what they have been thinking about. Interaction during this period can be sharing answers if a question has been posed or sharing ideas if a specific issue was identified. Usually, teachers allow no more than four or five minutes for pairing.

Step 3—Sharing: In the final step, the teacher asks the pairs to share what they have been talking about with the whole class. It is effective to simply go around the room from pair to pair and continue until about a fourth or a half of the pairs have had a chance to report.

> The think-pair-share and numbered heads together techniques are alternatives to the more traditional whole-group question-and-answer approach.

Numbered Heads Together. **Numbered heads together** is an approach developed by Spencer Kagan (1998) to involve more students in the review of materials covered in

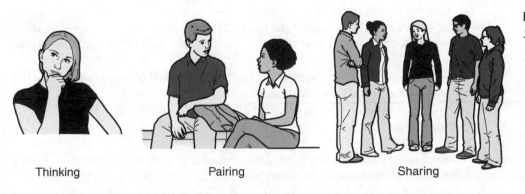

Figure 10.3 *Think-Pair-Share*

Thinking   Pairing   Sharing

a lesson and to check their understanding of a lesson's content. Instead of directing questions to the whole class, teachers use the following four-step structure:

Step 1—Numbering: Teachers divide students into three- to five-member teams and have them number off so each student on the team has a different number between 1 and 5.

Step 2—Questioning: Teachers ask students a question. Questions can vary. They can be very specific and in question form, such as "How many states in the Union?" Or they can be directives, such as "Make sure everyone knows the capitals of the states that border on the Pacific Ocean."

Step 3—Heads Together: Students put their heads together to figure out and make sure everyone knows the answer.

Step 4—Answering: The teacher calls a number and students from each group with that number raise their hands and provide answers to the whole class.

Table 10.3 summarizes and compares the four approaches to cooperative learning.

As with other aspects of teaching, there is no one best approach to cooperative learning. Choice should be guided by the goals teachers have for particular lessons and the nature and composition of the groups of students in their classrooms. Slavin (2013), however, has observed that all too often the use of cooperative learning is "informal and does not incorporate group goals and individual accountability that research has found to be essential to producing positive achievement outcomes" (p. 358). These two features (group goals and individual accountability) need to be incorporated into all cooperative learning lessons.

Choose Appropriate Content. As with any lesson, one of the primary planning tasks for teachers is choosing content that is appropriate for the students given their interests and prior learning. This is particularly true for cooperative learning lessons because this approach requires a substantial amount of student self-direction and initiative. Without interesting and appropriately challenging content, a cooperative lesson can quickly break down.

Veteran teachers know from past experience which topics are best suited for cooperative learning, just as they know the approximate developmental levels and interests of students in their classes. Beginning teachers must depend more on curriculum frameworks and textbooks for appropriate subject matter. However, there are several questions that beginning teachers can use to determine the appropriateness of subject matter:

- Have the students had some previous contact with the subject matter or will it require extended explanation by the teacher?
- Is the content likely to interest the group of students for which it is being planned?
- If the teacher plans to use text, does it provide sufficient information on the topic?
- For STAD or Jigsaw lessons, does the content lend itself to objective quizzes that can be administered and scored quickly?
- For a Jigsaw lesson, does the content allow itself to be divided into several natural subtopics?

Form Student Teams. A third important planning task for cooperative learning is deciding how student learning teams are to be formed. Obviously, this task will vary according to the goals teachers have for a particular lesson, and the racial and ethnic

---

Because cooperative learning requires self-direction and initiative, teachers must be careful to choose content that interests students.

Deciding how student teams are formed is an important planning task for teachers.

Table 10.3 *Comparison of Three Approaches to Cooperative Learning*

	STAD and Learning Together	Jigsaw	Structural Approach
Cognitive goals	Factual and conceptual academic knowledge	Factual and conceptual academic knowledge	Factual and conceptual academic knowledge
Social goals	Group work and cooperation	Group work and cooperation	Group and social skills
Team structure	Four- to five-member heterogeneous learning teams	Five- to six-member heterogeneous learning teams; use of home and expert teams	Varies—pairs, trios, four- to six-member groups
Lesson topic selection	Usually teacher	Usually teacher	Usually teacher
Primary task	Students may use worksheets and help each other master learning materials	Students investigate materials in expert groups; help members of home group learn materials	Students do assigned tasks—social and cognitive
Assessment	Weekly tests	Varies—can be weekly tests	Varies
Recognition	Newsletters and other publicity	Newsletters and other publicity	Varies

mix and the ability levels of students within their classes. Here are some examples of how teachers might decide to form student teams:

- A fifth-grade teacher in a school with a diverse student population might use cooperative learning to help students better understand peers from different ethnic or racial backgrounds. He or she might take great care to have racially or ethnically mixed teams in addition to matching for ability levels.
- A seventh-grade English teacher in a mostly middle-class white school might form student teams according to students' achievement levels in English.
- A fourth-grade teacher with several withdrawn students in her class may decide to form cooperative teams based on ability but also find ways to integrate the isolates with popular and outgoing class members.
- A high school teacher with several students new to the school might form learning teams on a random basis early in the year, thus ensuring opportunities for the new students to meet and work with students they don't yet know. Later, students' abilities could be used to form learning teams.

There has been some research that provides guidance for forming student groups or teams. Much of it points to the advantages of teacher-selected groups to ensure a good gender, ethnic, and ability mix. However, appropriate group composition is not always straightforward. For instance, Leonard (2000) studied how group composition influenced the achievement of sixth-grade math students. She found that although heterogeneous groups produced slightly higher achievement scores in math than homogeneous groups did, the amount of student interaction was influenced more by the group's cohesiveness than by its composition. Sidney and his colleagues (2004) studied teacher-selected as compared to student-selected groupmates in high school science classes. They found that when student-selected procedures were used, students "felt obligated" to choose friends as groupmates, a situation that sometimes led to negative group interaction. They also found that low-achieving students questioned the value of working with other low-achieving students when selected by them.

Obviously, the composition of teams has almost infinite possibilities. During the planning phase, teachers must delineate clearly their academic and social objectives. They also need to collect adequate information about their students' abilities so that if heterogeneous ability teams are desired, they will have the needed information. Finally, teachers should recognize that some features of group composition may have to be sacrificed in order to meet others.

Develop Materials. When teachers prepare for a whole-class presentation, a major task is to gather materials that can be translated into a meaningful presentation or demonstration. Although teachers provide verbal information to students in a cooperative learning lesson, this information is normally accompanied by text, video, study guides, or online sources.

Providing interesting and developmentally appropriate study materials is important if student teams are to work independently.

If teachers give text to students, it is important that it be both interesting and at an appropriate reading level for the particular class of students. If teachers develop study guides, these should be designed to highlight the content deemed most important. If students are expected to collect information from online sources, it is important to teach them how to examine and critically evaluate particular Web sites and Internet information. Evaluating information found on the Internet will be discussed in more detail in Chapter 11.

If students have not had experience with cooperative learning, it is vital that the teacher orient them to its unique task, goal, and reward structures.

Plan for Orienting Students to Tasks and Roles. The way learning tasks and rewards are structured influences the quality of student learning and interaction in cooperative learning groups. Vedder and Veendrick (2003) in an interesting study conducted in the Netherlands showed that for cooperative learning to be effective the task and reward structures must be compatible and must be cooperative rather than competitive in nature. Additionally, it is important that students have a clear understanding about their roles and the teacher's expectations for them as they participate in a cooperative learning lesson. If other teachers in the school are using cooperative learning, this task will be easier because students will already be aware of their role in it. In schools in which few teachers use the cooperative learning approach, beginning teachers will have to spend time describing the cooperative procedures and processes to students and working with them on requisite skills. Chapters 4 and 12 describe procedures to increase communication within classroom groups, along with activities to build group cohesion. These are critical skills for students in classrooms in which teachers plan to use cooperative learning.

An important thing to remember for beginning teachers who have not used cooperative learning before and who are using it with students who are not familiar with the model is that at first, it may appear not to be working. Students may be confused about the cooperative reward structure. Parents may also object. Also, students may initially lack enthusiasm about the possibilities of small-group interactions on academic topics with their peers.

Using the cooperative learning approach can be most difficult for a beginning teacher because it requires the simultaneous coordination of a variety of activities. However, this form of teaching can achieve some important educational goals that

Home and School

Keeping Parents and Caregivers Informed

Often, the success of cooperative learning can rest on parent understanding and acceptance of these practices. Although there are trends toward more collaboration, many aspects of our society, particularly parents' workplaces, are still characterized by competition and hierarchical structures. As a result, parents often lack understanding of the goals and processes teachers are striving to accomplish with cooperative learning. They may be particularly confused about or object outright to cooperative reward structures. Similarly, parents of more advanced and college-bound students often complain about their students acting as tutors, believing that they are being exploited, and carrying the load for their less able peers (Fisher, 2007). Sometimes students feel the same way and attempt to enlist their parents in getting their teachers to change. Finally, remember that seeing the teacher in front of the classroom lecturing was the pedagogy many parents observed in both their K–12 and college education, and other formats may appear inappropriate.

Teachers can take numerous actions to promote understanding and acceptance of cooperative learning. Effective teachers:

- listen to parents' objections and take them seriously.
- are honest with parents about their teaching methods.
- communicate goals and processes verbally and in writing and avoid jargon.
- model cooperative learning activities during open houses and family nights.
- encourage parents to visit the classroom and to observe cooperative learning lessons firsthand.

other approaches cannot, and the rewards of this type of teaching can be enormous for the teacher who plans carefully.

Plan for the Use of Time and Space. A final planning task for cooperative learning is deciding how to use time and space. As described in Chapter 3, time is a scarcer commodity than most teachers realize, and cooperative learning, with its reliance on small-group interaction, makes greater demands on time resources than do some other forms of instruction. Most teachers underestimate the amount of time for cooperative learning lessons. It simply takes longer for students to interact about important ideas than it does for the teacher to present the ideas directly through lecture. Making transitions from whole class to small groups can also take up valuable instructional time. Careful planning can help teachers become more realistic about time requirements, and it can minimize the amount of noninstructional time.

Cooperative learning lessons take more time than most other forms of instruction because they rely on small-group instruction.

Cooperative learning requires special attention to the use of classroom space, along with movable furniture. The **cluster seating** and **swing seating** arrangements are two ways experienced teachers use space during cooperative learning.

Cluster seating and swing seating arrangements lend themselves to cooperative learning because of their flexibility.

Cluster Seating Arrangement. Seating clusters of four or six, such as those illustrated in Figure 10.4, are useful for cooperative learning and other small-group tasks. If the cluster arrangement is used, students may have to move their chairs for lectures and demonstrations so that all students will be facing the teacher.

Swing Seating Arrangement. Lynn Newsome, a reading teacher in Howard County, Maryland, developed a particularly inventive seating approach. For cooperative learning, she uses a flexible seating arrangement that allows her to "swing" from a direct instruction lesson to a cooperative learning lesson. Her desks are arranged in a wing

Figure 10.4 *Four- and Six-Cluster Seating Arrangements*

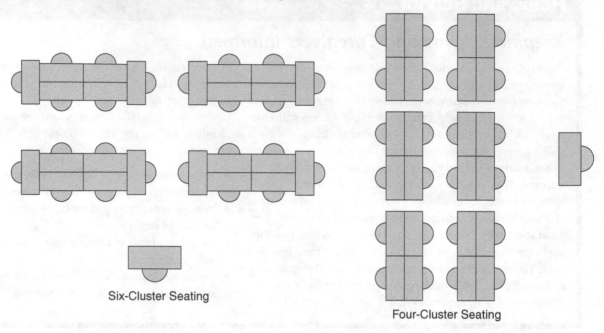

Six-Cluster Seating

Four-Cluster Seating

formation, as shown in the top of Figure 10.5. On cue, students at the shaded wing desks move their desks to the arrangement shown in the bottom of Figure 10.5. Newsome reports that in both formations, she can "maintain eye contact with all students, and the room appears spacious" (Swing from Wings, 1990 p. 5).

Conducting Cooperative Learning Lessons

The six phases of a cooperative learning lesson and associated teacher behaviors for each phase are described in Table 10.4. The first four phases are discussed in this section. Assessment of student learning and recognition are described in the Assessment and Evaluation section later in the chapter.

Clarify Aims and Establish Set. Some aspects of clarifying the aims for the lesson and establishing set are no different for cooperative learning than they were for other instructional approaches. Effective teachers begin all lessons by reviewing, explaining their objectives in understandable language, and showing how the lesson ties into previous learning. Because many cooperative learning lessons extend beyond a particular day or week and because the goals and objectives are multifaceted, the teacher normally puts special emphasis on this phase of instruction. This may also be the time when a teacher talks to students about how they can take responsibility for their own learning and not rely solely on the teacher.

> Clarifying aims for cooperative lessons is important because students must clearly understand the procedures and roles that will be involved in the lesson.

If a teacher is about to introduce Jigsaw, he or she may want to discuss how people are required to work interdependently with others in many aspects of life and how Jigsaw gives students an opportunity to practice cooperative behaviors. Similarly, if the teacher's main objective is to improve relations among students from different ethnic backgrounds or races, he or she may want to explain this idea to students and discuss how working with people who are different from us provides opportunities to know one another better.

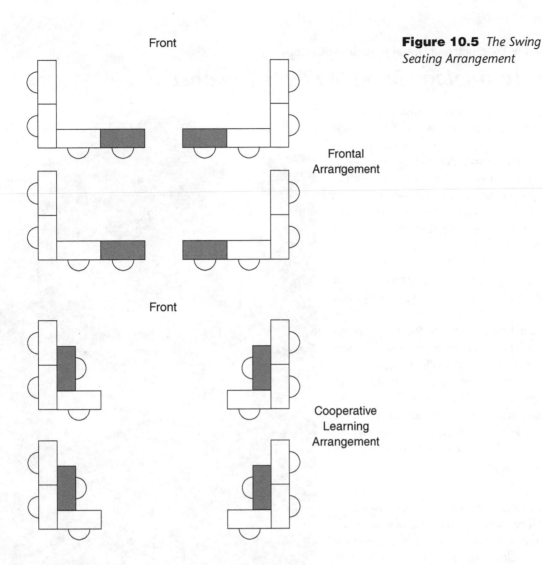

Figure 10.5 *The Swing Seating Arrangement*

Table 10.4 *Syntax for Cooperative Learning Lessons*

Phase	Teacher Behavior
Phase 1: Clarify aims and establish set.	Teacher goes over goals for the lesson and establishes learning set.
Phase 2: Present information.	Teacher presents information to students either verbally, visually, or in print or online text.
Phase 3: Organize students into learning teams.	Teacher explains to students how to form learning teams and helps groups make efficient transition.
Phase 4: Assist teamwork and study.	Teacher assists learning teams as they do their work.
Phase 5: Test on the materials.	Teacher assesses students' knowledge of learning materials or groups present results of their work.
Phase 6: Provide recognition.	Teacher finds ways to recognize both individual and group effort and achievement.

Enhancing Teaching and Learning with Technology
Can Technology Bring Students Together?

Critics of technology often assert that computers and the Internet isolate students from one another and from their teachers. They portray a scenario of students glued alone to a computer in a large room or at home surfing the Internet independent of family and friends. Although these situations are something to be concerned about, isolation does not necessarily have to be the case. Many aspects of the use of technology are under the control of the teacher. If teachers require students to work alone, they will tend to be isolated. However, if teachers require students to work together, technology can indeed enhance interaction and cooperation among students. Let's look at some ways this can happen.

The Internet and social media provide many opportunities for group work and for cooperative learning. Teachers can give students assignments and projects using several of the cooperative learning approaches described in this chapter, such as team learning, learning together, and Jigsaw. Students can be encouraged (required) to use computers and the Internet to carry out tasks or investigations in interdependent ways rather than alone. Following are some examples of cooperative work using technology:

- Conduct Internet searches on particular topics.
- *Create a newspaper.* Using a publication tool, students can work together to write and publish a class newspaper.
- *Create multimedia presentations.* After a group investigation, students can develop a multimedia presentation to display the results of their work and to explain their topic to others.

Technology can also provide opportunities for cognitive apprenticeships. Cognitive apprenticeships and scaffolding, as described earlier, are processes in which less-experienced students acquire knowledge and cognitive capabilities from interacting and modeling the cognitive behaviors of more-experienced adults or students. Working with CD-ROMs, exploring Web-based simulations, or developing and using databases can provide students opportunities for cognitive apprenticeships as they interact and work together. Often, these are experiences that are not available elsewhere.

As with any lesson that provides cooperative learning, those that integrate technology must be structured for task interdependence. Teachers must also help students develop social skills for working together effectively.

Technology provides many opportunities for cooperative learning.

Finally, computers and associated technologies may also prove to be the fuel that drives school reform. Schools have not embraced the use of technology as quickly as have other institutions in our society. Some observers (Collins & Halverson, 2009; Scherer, 2013; Trotter, 2007) have written that traditional classrooms do not accommodate the newer technologies very well and that these technologies will not be widely used until we have major shifts in our views about learning and classrooms. The more traditional views of learning (acquiring information) and classrooms (settings with competitive reward structures) find little advantage in the newer technologies. Instead, the use of computers and the Internet, which are highly interactive and constructivist, work best in cooperative learning settings:

- where students work together in small groups in the classroom and virtually.
- where teachers serve as facilitators of student inquiry.

- where students are allowed to gather information from a variety of sources and not limited to information delivered by the teacher.

Perhaps as cooperative learning gains more acceptance in American classrooms, it will serve as a catalyst for wider use of computers and telecommunication technologies, and, in turn, these new technologies will foster new kinds of classrooms and new forms of learning.

The important point with all these examples is that students are more likely to work toward important goals and objectives if the aims for the lesson have been explicitly discussed.

Present Information Verbally, in Text, or Online. Procedures and guidelines for presenting information to students will not be repeated here because that subject was covered extensively in Chapter 7. It is important, however, to provide some information about the use of text. Most of what is described here is not unique to cooperative learning and can be used by the beginning teacher in many situations involving text.

Teachers of young children know that relying on text to transmit content involves helping the children learn to read the assigned materials. Teachers in the upper grades and secondary schools (and college, for that matter) often assume their students can read and comprehend the assigned materials. Many times this is an incorrect assumption. If a cooperative learning lesson requires students to read print or online text, then effective teachers, regardless of the age level of their students or the subject taught, will assume responsibility for helping students become better readers. Similarly, if students are required to obtain information from the Internet they must be taught to evaluate the quality and accuracy of Web-based information, a process that will be described in Chapter 11.

Organize Students in Study Teams. The process of getting students into learning teams and getting them started on their work is perhaps one of the most difficult steps for teachers using cooperative learning. This is the phase in a cooperative learning lesson where bedlam can result unless the transition is carefully planned and managed. There is nothing more frustrating to teachers than transitional situations in which thirty students are moving into small groups, not sure of what they are to do and each demanding the teacher's attention and help.

The transition from whole-class instruction to small-group work must be orchestrated carefully.

Another issue teachers need to consider as they organize students into study teams is whether or not to assign roles to particular students. Some teachers prefer to have students work in groups without role assignments, believing that it is best to allow each student to be himself or herself. Other teachers, however, prefer to assign roles to students, believing that it encourages participation and supports learning. Some research (Palincsar & Herrenkohl, 2002) supports role assignment and teaching how to perform various roles required of cooperative learning lessons. Teachers who assign roles may find the following list, useful. Notice that the roles are divided into two categories: roles to help group members accomplish the learning task and roles to help the group members with their process.

Check, Extend, Explore

Check

- What are the major planning tasks associated with cooperative learning lessons?
- How does planning for cooperative learning lessons differ from planning for presentation or direct instruction?
- What factors should teachers consider when they are choosing a particular cooperative learning approach? When choosing how to form learning groups?
- What are the six phases of a cooperative learning lesson? What kinds of teacher behaviors are associated with each phase?
- How does the teacher's role in cooperative learning differ from the teacher's role in direct instruction?

Extend

- Think about the various subjects you will be teaching. Which would lend themselves to cooperative learning lessons?
- Do you agree or disagree that it is a teacher's responsibility to teach social skills to students? Go to the "Extend Question Poll" on the Online Learning Center to respond.

Explore

- Go to the Online Learning Center at www.mhhe.com/arends10e for links to Web sites related to *Planning for and Using Cooperative Learning*.

Diversity and Differentiation

Adapting Cooperative Learning Lessons for Diverse Learners

As with other approaches to teaching, teachers who use cooperative learning must find ways to adapt lessons to meet the needs of a diverse group of students. Many features of adapting for diversity that were described in earlier chapters hold true for cooperative learning. However, this approach presents some unique opportunities and some particular challenges for teachers.

The most important opportunity inherent in cooperative learning is the chance for students with special needs and from diverse backgrounds to work together in cooperative groups and on special projects. Cooperative learning is an important way for students with special needs to participate fully in the life of the classroom, just as it is for students from varying racial and ethnic backgrounds to develop better understanding of each other.

However, teachers must adapt cooperative learning lessons to meet the needs of all students. Some examples of appropriate adaptations include:

- Remember that before students can work effectively in cooperative learning groups, they must learn about each other and respect individual differences. Students in any class will possess varying amounts of understanding and respect, so instruction on these topics will need to vary.
- Make available more visual assists and explanations for students with to help them make transitions from whole-group to small-group work.
- Be prepared to give assistance and supportive feedback to students with special needs who may be having difficulty but who are on the right track.
- Help regular students understand how their peers with special needs differ and what they can expect as they work together in learning groups. Point out the strengths and competencies all students bring to group tasks.
- Help all students understand cultural norms of various ethnic and racial groups and how these might affect group interaction and cooperation.
- Help all students become familiar with aids used by students with particular challenges, such as hearing aids, sign language, and the assistive technologies described in Chapter 2.

Task-oriented roles

- Taskmaster—keeps group members on task
- Material supervisor—picks up and returns materials
- Coach—helps members with content of the lesson
- Recorder—records ideas, plans, etc. Best done on newsprint charts

Process-oriented roles

- Gatekeeper—helps members share air space; equalizes participation
- Encourager—encourages reluctant members to participate; provides praise and appreciation for accomplishments
- Checker—helps members check for understanding
- Reflector/timekeeper—reminds members of progress or lack thereof

Assist Teamwork and Study. Uncomplicated cooperative learning activities allow students to complete their work with minimum interruption or assistance by the teacher. For other activities, the teacher may need to work closely with each of the learning teams, reminding them of the tasks they are to perform and the time allocated for each step. There is a fine line for the teacher to follow during this phase of a cooperative learning lesson. Too much interference and unrequested assistance can annoy students. It can also take away opportunities for student initiative and self-direction. At the same time, if the teacher finds that students are unclear about the directions or that they cannot complete planned tasks, then direct intervention and assistance are required. Remember the caution provided by Mayer (2011) in Chapter 9.

Managing the Learning Environment

Unlike presentation and direct instruction described in the previous chapters, cooperative learning is a student-directed approach to teaching, and a cooperative learning environment requires attention to a unique set of rather difficult management tasks. For example, describing to students how to accomplish a group project is much more difficult than assigning them problems at the end of a textbook chapter. It is more difficult to organize students into study teams and to get them to cooperate than it is to get them to line up for recess or to sit and listen to the teacher. Consider, for example, the problems faced by Tom* when he tried to use cooperative learning as a student teacher:

> I couldn't wait to get my students into small groups. I didn't want to be like my cooperating teacher—she does all the talking and students are never allowed to work together. They seem so passive and so isolated from one another. Although she wasn't particularly enthusiastic about small-group work, she gave me her blessing. I was really excited. I was sure that the kids would respond well if they were given the chance to be active and to interact.
>
> I decided to use small groups in science, since my cooperating teacher has given me the most freedom in this area. (I think she doesn't like science and doesn't think it's all that important, so she lets me do whatever I want.) I told the kids that they could choose their own groups. I figured that being allowed to work with friends would be really motivating.
>
> Well, just getting into groups was chaotic. First, we had to move the desks from rows into clusters. Then there was lots of shouting and arguing about who was going to be in which group. The whole process took about ten minutes and was really noisy. My cooperating teacher was *not* pleased, and I was really upset when I saw what happened. My class is real heterogeneous—I've got blacks, whites, Hispanics, Asian-Americans. Well, the groups turned out really segregated. They also tended to be just about all-boy or all-girl. Even worse—I have one mainstreamed girl in my class (she's learning disabled and really hyperactive), and nobody wanted to work with her at all. I ended up *making* a group take her, and they were pretty nasty about it. And there's another kid who's real shy and quiet; I had to get him into a group, too. It was really embarrassing for both of them.
>
> Finally, I got everyone settled down and they started to work on the assignment. We've been talking about seeds and plants, and each group was supposed to plan an experiment that they would actually carry out to demonstrate what plants needed in order to grow. I emphasized that they were supposed to work together and make sure everyone contributed to the plan.

*Tom's story is a true one. It was told by Tom while he was doing his student teaching and was described by Weinstein, Romano, and Mignano (2010).

Well, it was a real mess. A couple of the groups worked out okay, but one group argued the whole time and never got anything written. In another group—all boys—they decided to just let the kid who was smartest in science plan the experiment. He kept coming up and complaining that no one else would do any work. And it was true. The rest just sat and fooled around the whole time. Another group had three girls and one boy. The boy immediately took charge. He dominated the whole thing; the girls just sat there and let him tell them what to do.

I had pictured everyone cooperating, helping one another, contributing ideas. But it didn't work out that way at all. And the noise—it just kept getting louder and louder. I kept turning off the lights and reminding them to use their "indoor voices." For a few minutes, they'd get quieter, but then it would get loud again. Finally, my cooperating teacher stepped in and yelled at everybody. I was really humiliated. I just couldn't control them. Right now, I'm pretty turned off to using cooperative groups. I think maybe she's right. Maybe these kids just can't handle working together. Maybe I should just go back to having everyone sit and listen to me explain the lesson. (Weinstein, Romano, & Mignano, 2010, pp. 276–277)

Many of the general management guidelines described in Chapter 5 as well as those related to presentation and direct instruction apply to cooperative learning lessons and could have assisted Tom with his management problems. When using any approach to teaching, it is important to have a few rules and routines that govern student talk and movement, keep lessons moving smoothly, maintain a general level of decorum in the classroom, and allow teachers to deal quickly and firmly with student misbehavior when it occurs. Management tasks unique to cooperative learning help students make the transitions from whole-class to cooperative learning groups, assist students as they work in groups, and teach students social skills and cooperative behavior.

Helping with Transitions

Transition into small groups is helped by writing directions on the chalkboard, having students repeat them, and assigning each team a specific space.

The process of getting students into learning groups and getting them started on their work is difficult. As Tom's story shows, this process can cause serious problems if not carefully orchestrated. Several simple but important strategies can be used by teachers to make transitions go smoothly:

1. *Write key steps on the chalkboard or on charts.* Visual cues assist large groups of students as they move from one place in the room to another. Think of these as signs similar to those provided for people lining up to purchase theater tickets to a popular play or queuing procedures used at public events such as football games. Here is an example of such a display:

    Step 1: Move quickly to the location where your team's name has been posted on the wall.
    Step 2: Choose one team member to come up to my desk to gather needed learning materials.
    Step 3: Spend ten minutes reading your particular assignment.
    Step 4: At my signal, begin your discussions.
    Step 5: At my signal, return to your learning team and start presenting your information.

2. *State directions clearly and ask two or three students to paraphrase the directions.* Getting several students to repeat the directions helps everyone to pay attention and also gives the teacher feedback on whether or not the directions are understood.

*Teaching cooperation is
an important aspect of
cooperative learning.*

3. *Identify and clearly mark a location for each learning team.* Left to their own devices, students at any age (even adults) will not evenly distribute themselves around a room. They will tend to cluster in areas of the room that are most easily accessible. For effective small-group work, teachers should clearly designate those parts of the room they want each team to occupy and insist that teams go to that particular location.

These procedures are highly prescriptive and structured. Once teachers and students become accustomed to working in cooperative learning groups, more flexibility can be allowed. However, for beginning teachers, and in the earlier stages of using cooperative learning, tightly structured directions and procedures can make lessons move much more smoothly and prevent the frustrations and discouragement experienced by Tom.

First attempts at group learning will likely go smoothly if the teacher defines and calls for highly structured procedures.

Teaching Cooperation

In some schools, students get few opportunities to work on common tasks, and, subsequently, many students do not know how to work cooperatively. To help students cooperate requires attention to the kinds of tasks assigned to small groups. It also requires teachers to teach important social and group skills, such as the ones that follow.

Task Interdependence. As described earlier, cooperative learning requires that task structures be interdependent rather than independent. An example of an **independent task** is when teachers give students a math worksheet, divide them into groups, tell them they can help each other, but then require each student to complete his or her own worksheet, which will be graded individually. Although students may help one another, they are *not* interdependent to accomplish the task. This same lesson would become an **interdependent task** if the teacher divided the class into groups and

Structure lessons to require interdependence.

required each group to complete one math worksheet with all members' names on it. Many teachers using cooperative learning for the first time fail to structure tasks so that students work interdependently, and they become frustrated when their students do not cooperate or choose to work alone.

Having group members share materials, as in the previous example, is one way to structure task interdependence; having pairs of students work on assignments together is another. A third way to structure interdependence around materials is to give some students the problems and others the answers and ask them to find a match between the two through discussion. The Jigsaw cooperative learning lesson, described earlier, is another way to create interdependence as group members are dependent on each other for information.

Social Skills. Teachers should not assume that students have the requisite social or group skills to work cooperatively. Students may not know how to interact with one another, how to develop cooperative plans of action, how to coordinate the contributions of various group members, or how to assess group progress toward particular goals. To make cooperative learning work, teachers may need to teach a variety of group and social skills.

Social skills are those behaviors that promote successful social relationships and enable individuals to work effectively with others. Children learn social skills from many different individuals: parents, child-care providers, neighbors, and teachers. Ideally, children progress from infants who possess few social skills to adults who have a rich repertoire of skills. However, many children and youth do not learn the requisite social skills to live and work together before they attend school. Skills found lacking in many children and youth include sharing skills, participation skills, and communication skills. It is important that teachers help students master these skills.

Sharing Skills. Many students have difficulty sharing time and materials. This complication can lead to serious management problems during a cooperative learning lesson. Being bossy toward other students, talking incessantly, or doing all the work for the group are examples of students' inabilities to share. Domineering students are often well intentioned and do not understand the effects of their behavior on others or on their group's work. These students need to learn the value of sharing and how to rein in their controlling behaviors. Two examples of lessons teachers can use to teach *sharing skills* are described here.

1. *Round robin.* Round robin is an activity that teaches students how to take turns when working in a group. The process is quite simple. The teacher introduces an idea or asks a question that has many possible answers. The teacher then asks students to make their contributions. One student starts, making his or her contribution, and then passes the turn to the next person, who does the same. Turn-taking continues until every person in the group has had a chance to talk.

2. *Pair checks.* A way to help domineering students learn sharing skills is to have them work in pairs and employ the pair checks structure. The version of pair checks described here includes the eight steps recommended by Kagan (1998):

   Step 1—Pair work: Teams divide into pairs. One student in the pair works on a worksheet or problem while the other student helps and coaches.
   Step 2—Coach checks: The student who was the coach checks the partner's work. If coach and worker disagree on an answer or idea, they may ask the advice of other pairs.

Step 3—Coach praises: If partners agree, coach provides praise.

Steps 4 through 6—Partners switch roles: Repeat steps 1 through 3.

Step 7—Pairs check: All team pairs come back together and compare answers.

Step 8—Teams celebrate: If all agree on answers, team members do team hand-shake or cheer.

Participation Skills. Whereas some students dominate group activity, other students may be unwilling or unable to participate. Sometimes students who avoid group work are shy. Often shy students are very bright, and they may work well alone or with one other person. However, they find it difficult to participate in a group. The rejected student may also have difficulty participating in group activity. Additionally, there is the otherwise normal student who chooses, for whatever reason, to work alone and refuses to participate in cooperative group endeavors.

Making sure that shy or rejected students get into groups with students who have good social skills is one way teachers can involve these students. Structuring task interdependence, described previously, is another means to decrease the probability of students wanting to work alone. Using planning sheets that list various group tasks along with the students responsible for completing each task is a third way to teach and ensure balanced participation among group members. *Time tokens* and *high talker tap out* are special activities that teach participation skills.

1. *Time tokens.* If the teacher has cooperative learning groups in which a few people dominate the conversation and a few are shy and never say anything, time tokens can help distribute participation more equitably. Each student is given several tokens that are worth ten or fifteen seconds of talk time. A student monitors interaction and asks talkers to give up a token whenever they have used up the designated time. When a student uses up all of his or her tokens, then he or she can say nothing more. This, of course, necessitates that those still holding tokens join the discussion.

2. *High talker tap out.* It is not uncommon to find only a small percentage of the students participating in group work or discussions. One way to produce more balanced participation is to assign one student to keep track of each student's participation. If the monitor observes a particular student talking repeatedly, he or she can pass a note asking that student to refrain from further comments until everyone has had a turn. The monitor can also encourage shy students to take a turn in the same manner.

Communication Skills. It is quite common to find both younger and older students (adults also) lacking in important **communication skills.** We all have difficulty describing our own ideas and feelings so they are accurately perceived by listeners, and we have equal difficulty in accurately hearing and interpreting what others say to us. Cooperative learning groups cannot function very effectively if the work of the group is characterized by miscommunication. The communication skills described in Chapter 12 (paraphrasing and I-messages) are important and should be taught to students to ease communication in group settings.

Often during classroom interaction, students are not listening to one another. Instead, they sit in the whole group with their hand in the air, waiting for their turn to speak, or in small groups where they may be talking or interrupting incessantly. One way to promote active listening during some classroom discussions (those in which the main objective is learning to listen) is to insist that before a student can speak, he or she must first paraphrase what was said by the student who just finished speaking. More on teaching active listening and paraphrasing can be found in Chapter 12.

> Teachers should help students polish communication skills to ensure success in group learning environments.

Before students can work effectively in cooperative learning groups, they must learn about each other and respect individual differences.

Group Skills. You have likely had experiences working in groups in which individual members were nice people and had good social skills, yet the group as a whole did not work well. Members may have been pulling in different directions and, consequently, work was not getting done. Just as individuals must learn social skills to interact successfully in group or community settings, groups as an entity must also learn **group skills** and processes if they are to be effective. Before students can work effectively in cooperative learning groups, they must also learn about one another and respect one another's differences.

Team Building. You read earlier how the Johnsons' approach to cooperative learning emphasizes the importance of team building. Helping build team identity and member caring is an important task for teachers using cooperative learning groups. Simple tasks include making sure everyone knows other team members' names and having members decide on a team name. Having teams make a team banner or logo can also build esprit de corp among members. The following three activities can also be used to teach group skills and to build a positive team identity:

1. *Team interviews.* Have students in the cooperative learning teams interview one another. They can find out about other members' names, places they have traveled, special interests, or a favorite sport, holiday, color, book, movie, and so forth. Teachers can ask students to interview every student in the group and then share with the total group what they learned about group members and the group as a whole. A variation on this procedure is to have each student interview one other student in the team (or class) and then prepare an introduction for that person, which the student presents to the whole group or class.
2. *Team murals.* Teachers can ask students to use a variety of materials such as markers, crayons, chalk, paints, and pictures from magazines to make a mural illustrating how they would like their team to work together. Encourage all members to participate in making the mural. After it has been completed, have members discuss what they have done and explain their mural to members of other teams.
3. *Magic number 11.* Spencer Kagan (1998) described a team project in which students sit in a circle and hold out a clenched hand. They shake their hand up and down and say, "One, two, three." On the count of three, each student puts out so many fingers. The goal is to have all the fingers put out to add up to 11. No talking is allowed. After they succeed, the teams cheer.

Check, Extend, Explore

Check
• What are the key features of the cooperative learning environment?
• What steps can teachers take to help students make a smooth transition from large groups to small groups?
• Describe the important social and group skills required of students if they are to work together effectively.

Extend
🌐 Given the demands today to teach academic content, do you agree or disagree that using time to teach social and group skills can be justified? Go to the "Extend Question Poll" on the Online Learning Center to respond.

Explore
🌐 Go to the Online Learning Center at www.mhhe.com/ arends10e for links to Web sites related to *Cooperative Learning Environments and Teaching Social and Group Skills.*

Teaching Social and Group Skills. Teaching specific social and group skills is no different from teaching content-specific skills, such as map reading or how to use a microscope. Chapter 8 described direct instruction which requires teachers to demonstrate and model the skill being taught and to provide time for students to practice the skill and receive feedback on how they are doing. In general, this is the approach often used by teachers when teaching important social and group skills.

Assessment and Evaluation

The approaches to teaching described previously emphasize the importance of using evaluation strategies that are consistent with the objectives and learning outcomes of particular lessons. For example, if the teacher is using presentation and explanation to help students master important ideas and to think critically about these ideas, then test questions asking students for both recall and higher-level responses are required. If the teacher is using direct instruction to teach a specific skill, a performance test is required to measure student mastery of the skill and to provide corrective feedback. All the examples and suggestions given in previous chapters, however, are based on the assumption that the teacher is operating to some extent under a competitive or individualistic reward system. Cooperative learning changes the reward system and, consequently, requires a different approach to evaluation and recognition of achievement.

Testing Academic Learning

For STAD and some versions of Jigsaw, the teacher requires students to take quizzes on the learning materials. Test items on these quizzes must, in most instances, be of an objective type, so they can be scored in class or soon after. Figure 10.6 illustrates how individual scores are determined, and Figure 10.7 gives an example of a quiz scoring sheet. Slavin (1994, 1995a), the developer of this scoring system, described it this way:

> The amount that each student contributes to his or her team is determined by the amount the student's quiz score exceeds the student's own past quiz average. . . . Students with perfect papers always receive the . . . maximum, regardless of their base scores. This individual improvement system gives every student a good chance to contribute maximum points to the team if (and only if) the student does his or her best, and thereby shows substantial improvement or gets a perfect paper. This improvement point system has been shown to increase student academic performance even without teams, but it is especially important as a component of STAD since it avoids the possibility that low performing students will not be fully accepted as group members because they do not contribute many points. (1994, p. 24)

Assessing Cooperation

Remember from earlier discussions that one of the primary goals of cooperative learning is social skill development, especially those skills that facilitate cooperation and collaboration. These skills are not as easy to assess as academic skills are, but students

STAD scoring procedures allow each group member to contribute proportionately based on past performance.

Figure 10.6 *Scoring Procedures for STAD and Jigsaw*

Step 1 Establish base line.	Each student is given a base score based on averages on past quizzes.
Step 2 Find current quiz score.	Students receive points for the quiz associated with the current lesson.
Step 3 Find improvement score.	Students earn improvement points to the degree to which their current quiz score matches or exceeds their base score, using the scale provided below.

More than 10 points below base	0 points
10 points below to 1 point below base	10 points
Base score to 10 points above base	20 points
More than 10 points above base	30 points
Perfect paper (regardless of base)	30 points

Source: After Slavin (1994), p. 19.

Figure 10.7 *Quiz Score Sheet for STAD and Jigsaw*

	Date: May 23			Date:			Date:		
	Quiz: Addition with Regrouping			Quiz:			Quiz:		
Student	Base Score	Quiz Score	Improvement Points	Base Score	Quiz Score	Improvement Points	Base Score	Quiz Score	Improvement Points
Sara A.	90	100	30						
Tom B.	90	100	30						
Ursula C.	90	82	10						
Danielle D.	85	74	0						
Eddie E.	85	98	30						
Natasha F.	85	82	10						
Travis G.	80	67	0						
Tammy H.	80	91	30						
Edgar I.	75	79	20						
Andy J.	75	76	20						
Mary K.	70	91	30						
Stan L.	65	82	30						
Alvin M.	65	70	20						
Carol N.	60	62	20						
Harold S.	55	46	10						
Jack E.	55	40	0						

Source: After Slavin (1994), p. 20.

Check, Extend, Explore

Check

• What factors should teachers consider when they think about how to assess student achievement in cooperative learning?

Extend

Ⓐ Grading for group effort is controversial. Do you agree or disagree with this practice? Go to the "Extend Question Poll" on the Online Learning Center to respond.

Explore

Ⓐ Go to the Online Learning Center at www.mhhe.com/arends10e for links to Web sites related to *Assessment and Cooperative Learning.*

• Go to the official Web site for the Cooperative Learning Center at the University of Minnesota, the home of Roger and David Johnson, where you can read various perspectives of cooperative learning. You may also want to link to the "international network for cooperative learning," a network of individuals and groups interested in cooperative learning.

A special challenge for cooperative learning teachers is how to grade for both team and individual effort.

will not think they are important unless they are a part of the teacher's assessment system. Figure 10.8 identifies important collaborative skills that can be assessed and a rubric for doing so.

Grading Cooperative Learning

In cooperative learning, teachers have to be careful about their reward structure. It is important for teachers to reward the group product—both the end result and the cooperative behavior that produced it. Teachers also want to assess each member's contribution to the final product. Remember Slavin's (2013) admonishment about the importance of accountability. These dual assessment tasks, however, can prove troublesome for teachers when they try to assign individual grades for a group product. For instance, sometimes a few ambitious students may take on a larger portion of the responsibility for completing the group project and then be resentful toward classmates who made only minor contributions yet receive the same grade. Similarly, students who have neglected their responsibilities to the group effort may develop cynicism toward a system that rewards them for work they did not accomplish. Some experienced teachers have found a solution by providing two evaluations for students—one for the group's effort and one for each person's individual contribution.

Recognizing Cooperative Effort

Another important postinstructional task unique to cooperative learning is the emphasis given to providing public recognition of student effort and achievement. Some

Figure 10.8 *Rubric for Cooperation and Collaboration*

A. Works toward the achievement of group goals

4 Actively helps identify group goals and works hard to meet them.
3 Communicates commitment to the group goals and effectively carries out assigned roles.
2 Communicates a commitment to the group goals but does not carry out assigned roles.
1 Does not work toward group goals or actively works against them.

B. Demonstrates effective interpersonal skills

4 Actively promotes effective group interaction and the expression of ideas and opinions in a way that is sensitive to the feelings and knowledge base of others.
3 Participates in group interaction without prompting. Expresses ideas and opinions in a way that is sensitive to the feelings and knowledge base of others.
2 Participates in group interaction with prompting or expresses ideas and opinions without considering the feelings and knowledge base of others.
1 Does not participate in group interaction, even with prompting, or expresses ideas and opinions in a way that is insensitive to the feelings or knowledge base of others.

C. Contributes to group maintenance

4 Actively helps the group identify changes or modifications necessary in the group process and works toward carrying out those changes.
3 Helps identify changes or modifications necessary in the group process and works toward carrying out those changes.
2 When prompted, helps identify changes or modifications necessary in the group process or is only minimally involved in carrying out those changes.
1 Does not attempt to identify changes or modifications necessary in the group process, even when prompted, or refuses to work toward carrying out those changes.

Source: Adapted from Marzano, Pickering, and McTighe (1993), pp. 87–88.

developers of cooperative learning have recommended the use of a weekly newsletters to highlight student achievement. The teacher (sometimes the class itself) reports on and publishes the results of team and individual learning in this newsletter.

Others have suggested the use of class-constructed Web sites as a way to recognize student efforts and achievement.

Cooperative Learning: A Final Thought

Cooperative learning should be a part of every teacher's repertoire. Careful developmental work and empirical research have produced an approach that helps to promote greater tolerance for differences, teach important social and group skills, and increase academic achievement. Inexperienced teachers, however, should be careful and should know about the difficulties involved in implementing cooperative learning in some settings.

In some communities, for instance, teachers may find strong resistance to the idea of cooperative reward structures. As described previously, many parents and community members value independent effort and believe these norms should be emphasized in schools to prepare youth for an adult world characterized by competition.

Many students, particularly those who excel in the more traditional, individualistic reward structures, will likewise object to approaches in which interdependent activities are valued and rewards are shared.

Finally, some educators hold high expectations for cooperative learning as an effective means to increase positive student social behavior and to correct many of the social injustices that exist in our society. Though cooperative learning has demonstrated success in helping to accomplish these types of learning outcomes, educators should be careful not to overstate the benefits of cooperative learning and to educate citizens to recognize that no approach to teaching can solve long-standing social ills overnight.

Reflections from the Classroom

Slow Down for Cooperative Learning?

In your first year of teaching, you find yourself in a school (elementary or middle) where teachers have not paid much attention to cooperative learning in the past. It is not that they are against cooperative learning; they simply have chosen to stick to more traditional, teacher-centered approaches. However, you have had extensive exposure to this model in the school where you did your student teaching, and you believe strongly in the effectiveness of cooperative learning for goals you value as a teacher—teamwork and acceptance of diversity. You can't wait to get your students working in small, cooperative work groups.

During the second week of school, you introduce two cooperative learning projects in your language arts class. You choose to use STAD to teach spelling, and you launch a long-term group investigation project in poetry. For spelling, you assign students to groups to ensure a good mix of abilities and ethnic-racial backgrounds; you allow the poetry groups to form according to students' interests, although you make it clear to students that you don't want any groups with all boys or all girls. You explain to your students that they will be tested in spelling weekly and that improvement and group effort will determine each student's grade. You make it clear that the group's effort in the poetry investigation will receive the highest reward.

During the first couple of weeks, you are *not* particularly happy about how things are going. Students find it difficult to settle down and work together and don't appear to be highly engaged. You have received minor complaints about your grading system; however, you haven't taken these complaints too seriously, believing that things will get better soon.

On Monday of the fourth week of school, you get a note from the principal that she wants to meet with you after school. Of course, you are curious and a little worried about why she would want this meeting. At the meeting, you are astounded—the principal tells you that a group of parents of very talented children visited the school to complain about your use of cooperative learning. They told her that their children were being penalized by having to work with less-talented students and that grading on group efforts was not fair. They expressed their belief that individuals should be rewarded for the work they produce independent of others. The principal strongly recommended that you rethink your approach.

Reflect on this situation and consider what you should do. Approach the situation from the perspective closest to the grade level or subject area you are preparing to teach. Is there a way to continue using cooperative learning without angering students, their parents, and the principal? Can you change your approach and still accomplish the teamwork and diversity goals you cherish? If you are in a field experience, share this situation with fellow students or your cooperating teachers. Then compare your thoughts with the following comments from teachers who have faced or known about similar situations. Write up your reflections on this situation as an exhibit in your professional portfolio.

Patricia A. Merkel
Eleanor Roosevelt School, Kindergarten, Pennsbury, PA

Accepting how much time is needed to establish good class rapport is not an easy task. Bravo to you for your efforts toward the cooperative learning approach. Be patient. The first few weeks of school are needed to establish guidelines for the behaviors needed in cooperative learning. The children need modeling of these behaviors and lots of practice before cooperative groups are introduced. Practice is needed in getting to the group. A timer can be used. Practice might be needed in listening and responding to individuals in the group. I assign one member of the group to be the "task master." This person's sole responsibility is to monitor the on-task behavior of other group members. Self-evaluation scales give the students an opportunity to reflect on his or her level of participation in the group. All of this takes time and practice. Do not be discouraged. Do not give up the effort toward cooperative learning. Be very specific with children regarding your expectations of them. Don't forget to "catch 'em being good."

Personally, I do not like the idea of group grades. Cooperative learning allows many social learners an opportunity to learn the way they learn best. The group product or presentation cannot be the only criterion for the individual's grade. The beauty of group activity is to encourage active learning through questions, discussions, and artistic expression. This taps into the skills held by children who might not be the ones to shine in traditional teaching and testing. Even the most successful student can use practice in the social skills needed to participate in cooperative learning.

The principal's happiness is also very important, and you need him or her in your corner. Model for her what you hope to get from your students: listening, reflection, and willingness to adapt to the needs of others. No need to abandon your original, well-thought-out approach. As the students become successful with this model, their pleasure will be communicated to their parents. Meanwhile, you can be proactively engaged with newsletters to remind them of your efforts.

Amy Shin
8th Grade

I have seen several situations such as this one. Normally, they involve beginning teachers who want to immediately solve all of the problems in education. If I were the teacher in this situation, I would not give up on cooperative learning. Instead, I would slow down. Teachers in this middle school have not used cooperative learning in the past, so group work and grading is new to students and to their parents. Rather than implementing a full-blown STAD approach and an extended group investigation, the teacher should get students comfortable working in pairs in low-stakes situations, perhaps using "think-pair-share" after reading a particular poem. The idea of cooperative grading should also be introduced gradually. This is a topic that should be explained, discussed, and perhaps debated with parents at the school's open house and in other settings. It should also be discussed with other members of the faculty, including the principal. A teacher who wants to introduce cooperative learning in a school where it has not been used before should be prepared for the process to take as long as two or three years.

Summary

Provide an overview of cooperative learning and explain its appropriate use.

- Cooperative learning is unique among the approaches to teaching because it uses different goal, task, and reward structures to promote student learning.
- The cooperative learning task structure requires students to work together on academic tasks in small groups. The goal and reward structures require interdependent learning and recognize group as well as individual effort.
- Cooperative learning aims at instructional goals beyond academic learning, specifically intergroup acceptance, social and group skills, and cooperative behavior.
- The syntax for cooperative learning relies on small-group work rather than whole-class teaching and includes six major phases: present goals and establish set; present information; organize students into learning teams; assist teamwork and study; test on the materials; and provide recognition.
- The learning environment of cooperative learning requires cooperative rather than competitive task and reward structures. The learning environment is characterized by democratic processes in which students assume active roles and take responsibility for their own learning.

Describe the theoretical foundations of cooperative learning and summarize the research that supports its use.

- The intellectual roots for cooperative learning grow out of an educational tradition emphasizing democratic thought and practice, constructivist views of learning, and respect for pluralism in multicultural societies.

- A strong empirical base supports the use of cooperative learning for the following educational objectives: cooperative behavior, academic learning, improved race relationships, and improved attitudes toward children with special needs.

Explain how to plan and use cooperative learning, including how to adapt its use to students of differing backgrounds and abilities.

- Planning tasks associated with cooperative learning put less emphasis on organizing academic content and more emphasis on organizing students for small-group work and collecting a variety of learning materials to be used during group work.
- One of the major planning tasks is deciding which cooperative learning approach to use. Four variations of the basic model can be used: Student Teams Achievement Divisions, Jigsaw, Learning Together, and the structural approach.
- Regardless of the specific approach, a cooperative learning lesson has four essential features that must be planned: how to form heterogeneous teams, how students are to work in their groups, how rewards are to be distributed, and how much time is required.
- Conducting a cooperative learning lesson changes the teacher's role from one of center-stage performer to one of choreographer of small-group activity.

Describe how to implement a learning environment conducive to using cooperative learning.

- Small-group work presents special management challenges to teachers.
- During cooperative learning lessons, teachers must help students make transitions to their small groups, help them manage their group work, and teach important social and group skills.

Describe appropriate ways to assess student academic and social learning consistent with cooperative learning goals.

- Assessment and evaluation tasks, particularly evaluation, replace the traditional competitive approaches described for earlier models with individual and group rewards, along with new forms of recognition.
- Newsletters, Web sites, and public forums are three devices teachers use to recognize the results of student work performed in cooperative learning lessons.

Describe why it has been difficult to implement cooperative learning and why it is important not to hold unrealistically high expectations for this approach to teaching.

- In some communities there has been strong resistance to cooperative learning.
- Some educators have made unreasonably high claims for cooperative learning.

Key Terms

cluster seating 385
communication skills 395
competitive 370
constructivism 374
cooperative 370
goal structure 370
group skills 396
independent task 393

individualistic 370
interaction patterns 381
interdependent task 393
Jigsaw 380
Learning Together 380
numbered heads together 381
reward structure 371
social skills 394

structural approach 380
Student Teams Achievement Divisions
  (STAD) 379
swing seating 385
task structures 370
think-pair-share 381

Interactive and Applied Learning

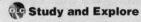 **Study and Explore**

- Access your Study Guide, which includes practice quizzes, from the Online Learning Center.

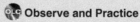 **Observe and Practice**

- Listen to audio clips on the Online Learning Center of Amy Callen (fourth/fifth grade) and Jason O'Brien (fifth grade) talking about cooperative learning in the *Teachers on Teaching* area.

Complete **Practice Exercise 10.1,** Planning a Cooperative Learning Lesson, including
- Plan for Cooperative Learning
- Form Student Learning Teams
- Assist Teams
- Assess Cooperative Learning
- Reflect on Planning for Cooperative Learning

Complete the following additional **Practice Exercises** that accompany Chapter 10:
- Practice Exercise 10.2: Choose a Cooperative Learning Approach

- Practice Exercise 10.3: Providing Assistance to Student Teams
- Practice Exercise 10.4: Designing a Group Participation Rubric
- Practice Exercise 10.5: Teaching Dilemma: Student Participation in Cooperative Learning Groups
- Practice Exercise 10.6: Teaching Dilemma: Student Complaints
- Practice Exercise 10.7: Reflecting on the Importance of Cooperative Learning

 # Portfolio and Field Experience Activities

Expand your understanding of the content and processes of this chapter through the following field experience and portfolio activities. Support materials to complete the activities are in the *Portfolio and Field Experience Activities* area on your Online Learning Center.

1. Complete the **Reflections from the Classroom** exercise at the end of this chapter and use the recommended reflective essay as an exhibit in your portfolio about your views on cooperative learning. **(InTASC Standard 8: Instructional Strategies)**
2. **Activity 10.1: Assessing My Skills for Using Cooperative Learning.** Assess your current understanding and skills to plan and conduct cooperative learning lessons. **(InTASC Standard 8: Instructional Strategies)**

3. **Activity 10.2: Observing Cooperative Learning.** Observe experienced teachers using cooperative learning. **(InTASC Standard 8: Instructional Strategies)**
4. **Activity 10.3: Observing Small-Group Interaction.** Observe a classroom during small-group work. Watch and tally how group members interact. **(InTASC Standard 8: Instructional Strategies)**
5. **Activity 10.4: Portfolio: Creating a Lesson to Teach Social Skills.** Design a lesson to teach social skills to students at the level you are preparing to teach. Arrange the lesson as an artifact in your portfolio. **(InTASC Standard 3: Learning Environments; InTASC Standard 8: Instructional Strategies)**

Books for the Professional

Aronson, E., & Patnoe, S. (2011). *Cooperation in the classroom: The Jigsaw method* (3rd ed.). London: Pinter & Martin Ltd.

Hmelo-Silver, C., Chinn, C., Chan, C., & O'Donnell, A. (2013). *The international handbook of collaborative learning.* New York: Routledge.

Johnson, D., & Johnson, F. (2013). *Joining together: Group theory and skills.* (11th ed.). Boston: Pearson.

Kagan, S., & Kagan, M. (2008). *Kagan cooperative learning.* San Juan Capistrano, CA: Kagan.

Slavin, R., Madden, N., Chambers, M., & Haxby, B. (2008) *Two million children: Success for all* (2nd ed.). Thousand Oaks, CA: Corwin Press.

Williams, R. (2007). *Cooperative learning: A standard for high achievement.* Thousand Oaks, CA: Corwin Press.

CHAPTER 11
Problem-Based Learning

Learning Goals

After studying this chapter you should be able to

Overview of Problem-Based Learning	Provide an overview of problem-based learning and describe the special features that define this approach to teaching.
Theoretical and Empirical Support	Describe the theoretical foundations of problem-based learning and summarize the research that supports its use.
Planning and Conducting Problem-Based Lessons	Explain how to plan and use problem-based learning, including how to adapt its use to students of differing backgrounds and abilities.
Managing the Learning Environment	Describe how to implement a learning environment conducive to using problem-based learning.
Assessment and Evaluation	Describe and discuss appropriate ways to assess student academic and social learning consistent with problem-based learning goals.
Problem-Based Learning: A Final Thought	Speculate about the restraints for using problem-based learning and make predictions about its use in the future.

 ## Reflecting on *Problem-Based Learning*

You have likely had teachers who spent a lot of time getting you to work on special projects and to take responsibility for your own learning. Instead of listening to lectures or participating in classroom discussions as a student in these teachers' classes, you were required to spend a lot of time in the library, on the Web, or out in the community. Instead of taking tests to determine your grade, you wrote reports or created other products that could be assessed. How did you react to these types of learning experiences?

- Did you enjoy them? Or did you find them uninteresting and boring?
- What did you learn from these types of experiences? What didn't you learn that you should have?
- Were there aspects of these teachers' classes that you found particularly effective for you? Ineffective?

Do the answers to these questions say anything about what you might do when you become a teacher? Will you use problem-based learning strategies? Or are you more likely to stick with more teacher-centered approaches to instruction?

 Go to the Online Learning Center at www.mhhe.com/ arends10e to respond to these questions.

A teacher's role in PBL is to pose authentic problems, facilitate student investigation, and support student learning.

This chapter is about problem-based learning and its use in promoting higher-level thinking in problem-oriented situations, including learning how to learn. Problem-based learning is also referred to by other names, such as *project-based instruction, authentic learning,* and *anchored instruction.* Unlike presentation or direct instruction described in Chapters 7 and 8, in which the emphasis was on teachers presenting ideas or demonstrating skills, a teacher's role in problem-based learning is to pose problems, ask questions, and facilitate investigation and dialogue. Most important, the teacher provides scaffolding—a supportive framework—that enhances inquiry and intellectual growth. Problem-based learning cannot occur unless teachers create classroom environments in which an open and honest exchange of ideas can occur. In this respect, you will find many parallels among problem-based learning, cooperative learning, and classroom discussion. You will also note that problem-based learning shares its intellectual roots with concept and inquiry-based teaching, described in Chapter 9. In later sections, common features of all these methods will be explored in more detail.

As with previous chapters, we begin with an overview of problem-based learning and a presentation of its theoretical and empirical underpinnings. A brief discussion of PBL's historical traditions is also provided. This will be followed by sections that describe the specific procedures involved in planning, conducting, and assessing problem-based learning. The chapter concludes with a discussion of how to manage the learning environment during problem-based lessons.

Overview of Problem-Based Learning

The essence of PBL involves the presentation of authentic and meaningful situations that serve as foundations for student investigation and inquiry.

The essence of problem-based learning consists of presenting students with authentic and meaningful problem situations that can serve as springboards for investigations and inquiry. To illustrate this concept, consider the following scenario taking place at the Thurmond County Planning Commission in a large state in the Midwest.

Fourteen-year-old Jeremy rises to speak to the Thurmond County Planning Commission:

"Councilors, we would like to speak to you today about the conditions of the eighteen bridges in our county. You remember we spoke to you earlier about our desire to tackle this problem as part of a project in our combined science and social studies classes. With your encouragement, we proceeded. Today, my classmates and I are ready to share with you the results of our monthlong review and analysis.

"Joanne will begin. She will outline the procedures we used in our 'bridge review and analysis,' providing both procedural and technical details and how we used a variety of consultants (one of our fathers is an engineer) in our work.

"After Joanne's presentation, Marcos will show you a short video we have put together that portrays the seven bridges in the county we determined to have structural defects and are in need of repair.

"After our presentations we will be glad to answer any questions you may have about our study and its recommendations. We will leave a copy of our report with you."

These students are in the final stage of a problem-based learning project where they have learned academic content and problem-solving skills by engaging in a real-life situation. They also have had opportunities to assume adult roles and provide a valuable service to their community.

PBL has certain characteristics that distinguish it from other teaching approaches. These are described below.

Special Features of Problem-Based Learning

Various developers of problem-based learning (Cognition & Technology Group at Vanderbilt, 1990, 1996a, 1996b; Gijbels, Bossche, & Loyens, 2013; Hmelo-Silver, 2004, 2012; Krajcik & Blumenfeld, 2006) have described this approach to instruction as having the following features:

- *Driving question or problem.* Rather than organizing lessons around particular academic principles or skills, problem-based learning organizes instruction around questions and problems that are both socially important and personally meaningful to students. They address real-life situations that evade simple answers and for which competing solutions exist.

  PBL lessons are organized around real-life situations that evade simple answers and invite competing solutions.

- *Interdisciplinary focus.* Although a problem-based lesson may be centered in a particular subject (science, math, history), the actual problem under investigation is normally chosen because its solution requires students to delve into many subjects.
- *Authentic investigation.* Problem-based learning necessitates that students pursue *authentic* investigations that seek real solutions to real problems. They must analyze and define the problem, develop hypotheses and make predictions, collect and analyze information, conduct experiments (if appropriate), make inferences, and draw conclusions. The particular investigative methods used, of course, depend on the nature of the problem being studied.
- *Production of artifacts and exhibits.* Problem-based learning requires students to construct products in the form of *artifacts* and *exhibits* that explain or represent their solutions. It could be a report, a physical model, a video, a computer program, or a student-constructed Web site. Artifacts and exhibits, as will be described later, are planned by students to demonstrate to others what they have learned and to provide a refreshing alternative to the traditional term paper or exam.
- *Collaboration.* As with cooperative learning, problem-based learning is characterized by students working with one another, most often in pairs or small groups. Working together provides motivation for sustained involvement in complex tasks and enhances opportunities for shared inquiry and dialogue, and for the development of social skills.

  Student collaboration in PBL encourages shared inquiry and dialogue and the development of thinking and social skills.

Problem-based learning was not designed to help teachers convey huge quantities of new factual or conceptual knowledge to students. Direct instruction and presentation are better suited to this purpose. Rather, problem-based learning, as illustrated in Figure 11.1, was designed primarily to help students develop their thinking, problem-solving, and intellectual skills; learn adult roles by experiencing them through real or simulated situations; and become independent, autonomous learners. A brief discussion of these three goals follows.

Figure 11.1 *Learner Outcomes for Problem-Based Learning*

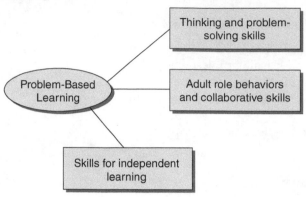

PBL helps students develop their thinking and problem-solving skills, learn authentic adult roles, and become independent learners.

Thinking and Problem-Solving Skills. As you read in Chapter 9, an array of ideas and processes are available for teaching people how to think in different and more effective ways. You learned that most definitions of thinking involve the use of intellectual and cognitive processes, ranging from such basic processes as recalling and remembering to thinking at higher levels, such as analyzing, synthesizing, and evaluating. It is these higher-level abilities—analyzing, criticizing, and reaching conclusions based on sound inference and judgment—that problem-based learning strives to accomplish.

Adult Role Modeling and Collaborative Skills. Problem-based learning also aims at helping students perform in real-life situations and learn important adult roles. Some years ago in her "Learning in School and Out," Resnick (1987a) described how school learning, as traditionally conceived, differs in important ways from mental activity and learning that occurs outside schools. Comparisons of in-school and out-of-school learning differ in the following ways:

1. School learning most often focuses on the individual's performance, whereas out-of-school mental work involves collaboration with others.
2. School learning focuses on unaided thought processes, whereas mental activity outside school usually involves cognitive tools, such as computers, calculators, and other scientific instruments.
3. School learning cultivates symbolic thinking regarding hypothetical situations, whereas mental activity outside school engages individuals directly with concrete and real objects and situations.
4. School learning focuses on general skills (reading, writing, and computing) and general knowledge (world history, chemical elements), whereas situation-specific thinking such as whether to buy or lease a new car dominates out-of-school mental activity.

PBL projects resemble out-of-school learning situations more closely than they do the academic lessons that characterize most school learning.

This perspective provides a strong rationale for problem-based learning because this form of instruction is essential to bridge the gap between formal school learning and the more practical mental activity that occurs outside school. Note how the features of problem-based learning correspond to out-of-school mental activity:

- Problem-based learning encourages collaboration and the joint accomplishment of tasks.
- Problem-based learning has elements of apprenticeship. It encourages observation and dialogue with others so that a student can gradually assume the observed role (scientist, teacher, doctor, artist, historian, etc.).
- Problem-based learning engages students in self-selected investigations that enable them to interpret and explain real-world phenomena and to construct their own understanding about these phenomena.

Independent Learning. Finally, problem-based learning strives to help students become independent and **self-regulated learners.** Guided by teachers who repeatedly encourage and reward them for asking questions and seeking solutions to real problems on their own, students learn to perform these tasks independently later in life.

Problem-based learning usually consists of five major phases that begin with a teacher's orienting students to a problem situation and culminate with the presentation and analysis of student work and artifacts. When the problem is modest in scope, all five phases of the model can be covered in a few class periods. However, more complex problems may take as long as a full school year to accomplish. The five phases of the model are described in more detail later in the chapter.

Unlike the tightly structured learning environment required for direct instruction or the careful use of small groups in cooperative learning, the learning environment and management system for problem-based instruction are characterized by open, democratic processes and by active student roles. In fact, the whole process of helping students become independent, self-regulated learners who are confident of their own intellectual skills necessitates active involvement in an intellectually safe, inquiry-oriented environment. Although the teacher and students proceed through the phases of a problem-based learning lesson in a somewhat structured and predictable fashion, the norms surrounding the lesson are those of open inquiry and freedom of thought. The learning environment emphasizes the central role of the learner, not of the teacher.

Theoretical and Empirical Support

Direct instruction, as you read in Chapter 8, draws its theoretical support from behavioral psychology and social cognitive theory. The teacher's role in a direct instruction lesson consists mainly of modeling particular skills in a clear and efficient manner. Problem-based learning, on the other hand, draws on cognitive and social constructivist theories for its support. The focus is not so much on what students are doing (their behavior), but on what they are thinking (their cognitions) while they are doing it. Although the role of a teacher in problem-based lessons sometimes involves presenting and explaining things to students, it more often involves serving as a guide and facilitator so that students learn to think and to solve problems on their own.

Getting students to think, to solve problems, and to become autonomous learners is not a new goal for education. Teaching strategies, such as *discovery learning and inquiry-based teaching,* described in Chapter 9, have long and prestigious histories. The *Socratic method,* dating back to the early Greeks, emphasized the importance of

The classroom environment of PBL is student-centered and encourages open inquiry and freedom of thought.

Check, Extend, Explore

Check
- What are the key characteristics of problem-based learning? How do these differ from other approaches of teaching?
- What are the major learner outcomes of problem-based learning?
- What type of learning environment works best for problem-based learning?

Extend
- Do you agree or disagree with Resnick's idea that most "in-school" learning is very different from "out-of-school" learning and that teachers should help bridge the gap between the two types of learning? Go to the "Extend Question Poll" on the Online Learning Center to respond.

Explore
- Go to the Online Learning Center at www.mhhe.com/arends10e for links to Web sites related to *Problem-Based Learning.*

PBL draws on cognitive and social constructivist theories for support.

inductive reasoning and of dialogue in the teaching–learning process. John Dewey (1933) described in some detail the importance of what he labeled *reflective thinking* and the processes teachers should use to help students acquire productive thinking skills and processes. Jerome Bruner (1961) emphasized the importance of discovery learning and how teachers should help learners become "constructionists" of their own knowledge. Richard Suchman (1962) developed an approach called *inquiry-based teaching*, also described in Chapter 9, in which teachers within a classroom setting present students with puzzling situations and encourage them to inquire and seek answers. For our purposes, problem-based learning will be traced through three main streams of twentieth-century thought.

Dewey and the Problem-Oriented Classroom

Dewey's view that schools should be laboratories for real-life problem solving provides the philosophical underpinning for PBL.

As with cooperative learning, problem-based learning finds part of its intellectual roots in the work of John Dewey. In *Democracy and Education* (1916), Dewey described a view of education in which schools would mirror the larger society and classrooms would be laboratories for real-life inquiry and problem solving. You remember from Chapter 10 that Dewey's pedagogy encouraged teachers to engage students in problem-oriented projects and help them inquire into important social and intellectual problems. Dewey and his disciples, such as Kilpatrick (1918), argued that learning in school should be purposeful rather than abstract and that purposeful learning could best be accomplished by having children in small groups pursue projects of their own interest and choosing. This vision of purposeful or problem-centered learning fueled by students' innate desire to explore personally meaningful situations clearly links contemporary problem-based learning with the educational philosophy and pedagogy of Dewey.

Constructivist Views of Learning

The constructivist view of teaching and learning was described in the chapter on cooperative learning and will be summarized only briefly here. You will recall that social constructivism holds a set of beliefs about how learning works. Two main ideas were described:

- Learners are *active participants* in constructing their own knowledge.
- *Interaction in social settings*, including the classroom, affects greatly the construction process and how people *create meaning* out of experience.

Constructivist theories of learning, which stress learners' need to investigate their environment and construct personally meaningful knowledge, provide the theoretical basis for PBL.

Among many others, constructivist ideas are often attributed to Jean Piaget and Lev Vygotsky. As you read in Chapter 10, Piaget emphasized the developmental aspect of knowledge construction, mainly as a result of his study of young children.

Vygotsky, in contrast, placed importance on the social interaction aspect of learning and believed that this interaction is what spurred the construction of new knowledge and the enhancement of learners' intellectual development. A key idea stemming from Vygotsky's interest in the social aspect of learning was his concept of the **zone of proximal development.**

The zone of proximal development is the label Vygotsky gave the zone between a learner's actual level of development and his or her level of potential development.

According to Vygotsky, learners have two different levels of development: the level of actual development and the level of potential development. The **level of actual development** defines an individual's current intellectual functioning and the ability to learn particular things on one's own. Individuals also have a **level of potential development,** which Vygotsky defined as the level an individual can function at or achieve with the assistance of other people, such as a teacher, parent, or more advanced peer. The zone between the learner's actual level of development and the level of potential development was labeled by Vygotsky as the *zone of proximal development.* Berger (2004) has illustrated the concept of the zone of proximal development and its implication for teaching in the three circles illustrated in Figure 11.2.

The importance to education and to problem-based learning of Vygotsky's ideas is clear. Learning occurs through social interaction with teachers and peers. With appropriate challenges and assistance from teachers or more capable peers, students are moved forward into their zone of proximal development where new learning occurs.

Bruner and Discovery Learning

The 1950s and 1960s saw significant curriculum reform in the United States that began in mathematics and the sciences but extended to history, the humanities, and the social sciences. Reformers strived to shift elementary and secondary curricula from a near-total focus on the transmission of established academic content to a focus on problem solving and inquiry. Pedagogy of the new curricula included activity-based and hands-on instruction in which students were expected to use their own direct experiences and observations to gain information and to solve scientific problems. Textbooks were often abandoned in favor of lab manuals. Teachers were encouraged to be facilitators and question askers rather than presenters and demonstrators of information.

Jerome Bruner, a Harvard psychologist, was one of the leaders in the curriculum reform of this era. He and his colleagues provided important theoretical support for what became known as **discovery learning,** a model of teaching that emphasized the importance of helping students understand the structure or key ideas of a discipline, the need for active student involvement in the learning process, and a belief that true learning comes through personal discovery. The goal of education was not only to increase the size of a student's knowledge base but also to create possibilities for student invention and discovery.

When discovery learning was applied in the sciences and social sciences, it emphasized the *inductive reasoning* and *inquiry processes* characteristic of the scientific method and problem solving.

Contemporary problem-based learning also relies on another concept from Bruner, his idea of **scaffolding.** Bruner described scaffolding as a process in which a learner is helped to master a particular problem beyond his or her developmental capacity through the assistance (scaffolding) of a teacher or more accomplished person. Note how similar Bruner's scaffolding concept is to Vygotsky's concept of the zone of proximal development.

The role of social dialogue in the learning process was also important to Bruner. He believed that social interactions within and outside the school accounted for much of a child's acquisition of language and problem-solving behaviors. The type of dialogue required, however, was not typically found in most classrooms. Many of the small-group strategies described in this text have grown out of the need to change the discourse structures in classrooms.

Figure 11.2 *Learner Knowledge and Zone of Proximal Development*

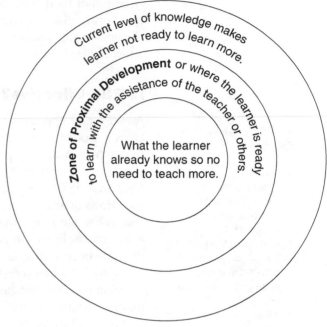

Source: Adapted from Berger (2004).

Discovery learning empha-sizes active, student-centered learning experiences through which students discover their own ideas and derive their own meaning.

In sum, teachers using problem-based learning emphasize active student involvement, an inductive rather than a deductive orientation, and student discovery or construction of their own knowledge. Instead of giving students ideas or theories about the world, which is what teachers do when using presentation or direct instruction, teachers using inquiry or problem-based learning pose questions to students and allow students to arrive at their own ideas and theories.

Is PBL Effective?

Check, Extend, Explore

Check

- What are the major intellectual roots of problem-based learning?
- How does the theoretical perspective of constructivism influence problem-based learning?
- What are the key ideas about problem-based learning that stem from constructivist views of learning?
- What does the concept of *scaffolding* mean? How does it apply to problem-based learning?

Extend

- Some educators believe that too much emphasis is being given to constructivist principles of teaching and learning. Do you agree or disagree with this assertion? Go to the "Extend Question Poll" on the Online Learning Center to respond.

Explore

- Go to the Online Learning Center at www.mhhe.com/arends10e for links to Web sites related to *Information about the Theoretical and Empirical Support for Problem-Based Learning.*

As with any approach to instruction, it is important to ask whether or not it works. Does it motivate students and does it impact learning? Fortunately, there is a growing research literature on problem-based learning, including several meta-analyses. The effects of the model, however, are mixed. Problem-based learning originated in science and medical education. Bredderman (1983) did a meta-analysis of 57 studies on the effects of activity-oriented science programs that had been developed in the 1960s and 1970s. He found that the activity-based curricula had the most effect on student achievement in two important areas: understanding of scientific method and creativity. However, it did not seem to have very much effect on student acquisition of science content when compared to more traditional approaches.

Albanese and Mitchell (1993) did a similar meta-analysis of the use of problem-based learning in medical education between 1972 and 1992. Their results showed that medical students trained with PBL performed better on clinical examinations and engaged in more productive reasoning than students trained with more conventional methods. However, the PBL-trained students scored lower and viewed themselves as less prepared in basic science knowledge.

More recently, studies by Hmelo and colleagues (2000, 2004, 2006, 2012) and meta-analyses by Gijbels, Dochy, Van den Bossche, and Seeger (2005) and by Schmidt and colleagues (2009) have found mainly positive results. Students taught with problem-based learning were highly motivated, reached deeper and more complex understandings, and could apply knowledge to new situations. However, the model, as shown in earlier studies, had weak effects on acquisition of factual knowledge.

Overall, the theoretical foundations for problem-based learning are strong and the evidence on its effects have been compelling and quite positive. Much of the research, however, has been done mainly with students in high school and higher education. One important exception to this is the piece of research described in the Research Summary for this chapter. The study reported demonstrates an interesting and successful application of PBL in an elementary classroom.

Planning and Conducting Problem-Based Lessons

Problem-based learning is quite straightforward, and it is easy to grasp its basic ideas. Effective execution, however, is more difficult. It requires considerable practice and necessitates making specific decisions during its planning and execution. Some of the teaching principles are similar to those already described for presentation, direct instruction, and cooperative learning, but others are unique to problem-based instruction. In the discussion that follows, emphasis is given to the unique features of problem-based instruction.

Planning for PBL Lessons

At its most fundamental level, problem-based learning is characterized by students working in pairs or small groups to investigate puzzling, real-life problems. Because this type of instruction is highly interactive, some believe that detailed planning is not necessary, and perhaps not even possible. This simply is not true. Planning for problem-based learning, as with other interactive, student-centered approaches to teaching, requires as much, if not more, planning effort. It is the teacher's planning that facilitates smooth movement through the various phases of problem-based lessons and the accomplishment of desired instructional goals.

Decide on Goals and Objectives. Deciding on specific goals and objectives for a problem-based lesson is one of three important planning considerations. Previously, we described how problem-based learning was designed to help achieve such goals as enhancing intellectual and investigative skills, understanding adult roles, and helping students to become autonomous learners. Some problem-based learning lessons may be aimed at achieving all these goals simultaneously. It is more likely, however, that teachers will emphasize one or two goals in particular lessons. For instance, a teacher may design a problem-based lesson on environmental issues. But instead of having students simulate adult roles or seek solutions to environmental problems, as was the case in the "study of county bridges" scenario at the beginning of the chapter, the teacher may instead ask students to conduct an online search of the topic in order to develop this type of investigative skill. Regardless of whether a lesson is focused on a single objective or aims to achieve a broad array of outcomes, it is important to decide on goals and objectives ahead of time so they can be communicated clearly to students.

Scaffolding is the process in which a learner is helped by a teacher or more accomplished person to master problems or skills slightly beyond his or her current level of development.

Design Appropriate Problem Situations. Problem-based learning is based on the premise that motivation to learn begins with a problem and that puzzling and ill-defined problem situations will arouse students' curiosity and thus engage them in inquiry. Designing appropriate problem situations or planning ways to facilitate the planning process is a critical planning task for teachers. Some teachers and problem-based specialists believe that students should have a big hand in defining the problem to be studied, because this process will foster ownership of the problem. Others, however, believe teachers should help students refine preselected problems that emanate from the school's curricula and for which the teacher has sufficient materials and equipment.

Some PBL teachers like to give students a strong hand in selecting the problem to be investigated.

A good problem situation must meet at least five important criteria. First, it should be *authentic*. This means that the problem should be anchored in students' real-world experiences rather than in the principles of particular academic disciplines. How to deal with crumbling bridges in Thurmond County is an example of a real-life problem. Learning about the effects of sunlight on nutrients and algae in warm water is an example of an academic (scientific) problem in biology. Second, the problem should be somewhat ill-defined and pose a sense of mystery or puzzlement. Ill-defined problems resist simple answers and require alternative solutions, each of which has strengths and weaknesses. It seems that questions that cause cognitive dissonance on the part of students are powerful motivators to inquire and have greater effects on learning. Puzzling situations also provide fodder for dialogue and debate. Third, the problem should be meaningful to students and appropriate for their level of intellectual development. Fourth, problems should be sufficiently broad to allow teachers to accomplish

Research Summary

Can Problem-Based Learning Work with Elementary Students?

VanSledright, B. A. (2003). Fifth graders investigating history in the classroom: Results from a researcher-practitioner design experiment. *Elementary School Journal, 103*(2), 131–160.

Problem: Bruce VanSledright was interested in investigating how appropriate problem-based learning might be for teaching aspects of United States history to fifth-graders. He sought to explore their readiness to make sense of historical documents and images and to make evidence-based interpretations from their analysis. This study is important and has been included as a research summary for three reasons. One, it challenges an assumption held by some that elementary students are too young to engage in historical investigation and problem-based learning. Two, the qualitative research methods used by the researcher illustrate an important approach for studying complex classroom practices whose goals may not be measurable with more traditional standardized tests. Finally, this is an interesting example where the researcher abandoned his university office, became a teacher of twenty-three fifth-grade students, and with the assistance of his research assistants studied his own teaching practice.

Sample: The researcher studied twenty-three students in a large K–5 elementary school in an urbanized school district in a mid-Atlantic state. The class had a diverse student population: 30 percent African Americans, 30 percent white, 30 percent Hispanic, and 10 percent Asian.

Method: The researcher-teacher taught American history over a four-month period. He made extensive lesson plans, videotaped all his lessons, and had his research assistant visit every eighth session to take detailed "field notes." In addition, the researcher reflected daily in a journal on each lesson and episode.

Information was collected on all twenty-three students, but eight students were selected to be primary informants. More detailed information was collected about and from these students, and they were asked to complete two investigator-designed performance tasks. The first task was administered before the researcher began teaching; the second after the teaching was concluded. The performance tasks were designed to provide insight into students' historical understanding and into their thinking, problem-solving processes.

- Task 1 involved the reading of two documents concerning the "shooting incidence" in Boston in 1770 later called the Boston Massacre. Students were asked individually to read the documents out loud to the researcher and pause at regular intervals to talk about what they were thinking.
- The same procedures were used for Task 2, but this time students were given four texts and two images that dealt with the battle at Lexington Green.

The tasks students were asked to perform were analyzed according to four different levels of strategies that can be used to analyze historical sources:

- *Level 1:* Use comprehension and monitoring, such as checking the details of a source and making initial sense of it.
- *Level 2:* Make judgments and evaluate a source.
- *Level 3:* Identify authors or sources and use multiple sources to make an initial interpretation of a source.
- *Level 4:* Refine evidence-based interpretation of an event based on multiple sources.

Results: The VanSledright study in its original form provided rich information about student growth in historical understanding and analysis of historical documents as well as very detailed descriptions of the eight informants. Space does not allow reproduction here of the ethnographic detail the researcher provided. Instead the results are summarized briefly using the researcher's own words as closely as possible.

- Systematic involvement in "practicing history" moved fifth-grade students from reliance on level 1 and 2 analyses to analyses characterized by levels 3 and 4. Specifically: "opportunities to investigate the past enhanced students' capacity to identify the nature of sources (primary, secondary) and cross-reference them, check and corroborate evidence before drawing conclusions, and read and analyze historical evidence critically" (p. 149).
- Investigative experiences helped students to build sensitivity to reliability issues and problems related to drawing inferences from primary and secondary sources and to appreciate different perspectives.

- The investigative experiences also helped students achieve awareness that some historical events raise questions that the available evidence cannot resolve completely.
- The data indicated that students developed a specialized vocabulary and discourse for talking about historical thinking and analyses.

Finally, the researcher reported that the gains were not the same for all students. Gains for the most part reflected progress from where each student began in regard to their capacities to think, problem-solve, and analyze historical documents and events. According to the researcher, two students did not progress as far as others.

Discussion and Implications This study demonstrated with rather strong evidence that problem-based learning can work with most elementary students. Some students, however, did not respond as well as others, leading to the observation that lessons must be adapted for the special needs of particular students. The researcher also pointed out that the approach he used required considerable time to assemble and arrange resources and required strong subject matter understanding on the part of the teacher. If you want more information about this study, you can read it online using your university library's digital resources.

their instructional goals yet sufficiently confined to make lessons feasible within time, space, and resource limitations. Finally, a good problem should benefit from group effort, not be hindered by it.

Most puzzling situations either explore the cause-and-effect relationships within a particular topic or pose "why" or "what if" questions. The number of puzzling situations in any field is endless. As you approach choosing a particular situation for a lesson, consider these points:

- Think about a situation involving a particular problem or topic that has been puzzling to you. The situation must pose a question or problem that requires explanation through cause-and-effect analyses and/or provides opportunities for students to hypothesize and speculate.
- Decide if a particular situation is naturally interesting to the particular group of students with whom you are working, and decide if it is appropriate for their stage of intellectual development.
- Consider whether or not you can present the problem situation in a fashion that is understandable to your particular group of students and that highlights the "puzzling" aspect of the problem.
- Consider whether working on the problem is feasible. Can students conduct fruitful investigations given the time and resources available to them?

> **A good problem situation should be authentic, puzzling, open to collaboration, and meaningful to the students.**

Obviously, many problem situations can be defined and posed to students. Indeed, the list is almost limitless. Following are several examples that have been reported by teachers. Some of these are tightly focused and can be completed in rather short periods of time. Others are more complex and require a whole course of study to complete.

"Learning Expeditions." Today, many Web sites exist that offer students virtual problem-based learning experiences and organized inquiry activities. One that is very popular among teachers is the Adventure Learning Foundation site that provides curricula materials connected to online "Adventure Learning Expeditions." This Web site and its resources provide virtual cultural and travel experiences for many places in the world, such as Alaska and the Yukon; Baja California; Peru; and Oaxaca, Mexico. As students proceed on their virtual journey, they can communicate and interact with other students from around the world who are also on the expedition.

> **Sometimes simulated problem situations are more useful in the classroom than real-life problems.**

The Web site is packed with information, pictures, maps, and problem-based learning lesson plans for teachers. This site also encourages teachers to design and share their own lessons and expeditions.

As with other problem-based curricula, expeditionary learning strives to spark student interest by addressing authentic problem situations, helping students engage in field-oriented investigations, and helping them arrive at their own solutions.

Rogue Ecosystem Project. Teachers interested in environmental problems have been among the leaders in problem-based instruction. This is illustrated by the problem-based learning approach used by Hans Smith, a biology teacher at Crater High School in Central Point, Oregon.

> Teachers involved in environmental issues have been leaders in the use of problem-based instruction.

Smith designed an interdisciplinary course in which students meet for two hours each day and receive credit for biology, government, and health. The course is centered on two environmental themes—*watersheds* and the *life cycle of the Pacific salmon* (Crater High School Rogue River Project, 1999, 2007). As part of their unit on watersheds, students work on a particular project that requires them to develop a plan for a campground using their scientific knowledge about the Rogue River and the watershed area it serves. Their plan must offer a complete environmental impact study of campground construction and include interaction with the governmental agencies that approve campgrounds in the state of Oregon. Smith reported that these initial projects often prompt further inquiry and even more authentic studies such as

- Studying other rivers in the region by taking stream surveys, testing water, mapping habitats, and determining pool and riffle ratios.
- Designing and building a student-operated fish hatchery in which two thousand coho salmon are raised and released each year.

Smith's use of problem-based instruction asks students to take on very large and complex problems and involves them over a rather long period of time. Smith is an example of a creative teacher willing to give students opportunities to perform numerous out-of-school adult roles such as testing water, constructing buildings, raising fish, writing reports, interacting with government agencies, and giving presentations.

Other PBL Situations. Table 11.1 provides additional examples of PBL situations for different grade levels and subject areas.

Today, the Internet is a valuable planning resource for teachers using problem-based learning. This is the topic of the Enhancing Teaching and Learning with Technology box for this chapter.

Organize Resources and Plan Logistics. Problem-based learning encourages students to work with a variety of materials and tools, some of which are located in the classroom, others in the school library or computer lab, and still others outside the school or on the Internet. Getting resources organized and planning the logistics of student investigations are major planning tasks for PBL teachers.

In almost every instance, PBL teachers will be responsible for an adequate supply of materials and other resources for use by investigative teams. In some instances, these materials may be included in particular curriculum projects, and many science classrooms contain needed supplies and equipment to support student experiments and projects. Access in schools to online and Internet databases also facilitates problem-based learning. When needed materials exist within the school, the primary planning task for teachers is to gather them and make them available to students.

Table 11.1 *Examples of PBL Situations*

Subject	Elementary	Secondary
Science/Environment	How do weather patterns affect how people live? How might a solar-heated home trap and store energy for use at night and on cloudy days? How do laws aimed at protecting endangered species affect other species and the environment in general?	How might efficient and safe wiring be developed for a three-bedroom/two-bath home? (Include ways circuit breakers and outlets should be designed for multiple uses at any given time in the kitchen and bathrooms, plus TV, sound system, and computers.) What potential does climate change have to alter the food supply and impact global economies?
History	How did human movements in earlier times affect the way we live today?	Do things change today faster than in previous times? Is it possible to control change?
Language Arts	Why do people celebrate? What traditions accompany celebrations? What cultural commonalities exist in celebrations around the world?	What does it mean to search for meaning? Use prose, poetry, film, and personal interview to investigate how people find meaning in the midst of great injustice (e.g., the Holocaust, South African apartheid).
Mathematics	How do data and statistics impact a family's economic decisions?	How can we understand really big numbers, like a million or a billion? How can we demonstrate these numbers so they make sense? When are big numbers useful, and how can we use them in ways that are understandable to others?

Sometimes students will need to do their investigative work outside the school. Students involved in the ecosystem project were encouraged to gather water samples, to present plans to local government units, and to release salmon. Sometimes projects require interviewing local business and government leaders. Expecting students to work outside the confines of the school presents special problems for teachers and requires special planning. Teachers must plan in detail how students will be transported to desired locations and how students will be expected to behave while in nonschool settings. It also necessitates teaching students appropriate behavior for observing, interviewing, and perhaps taking photographs of people in the local community.

Projects that require out-of-school investigations or collaboration present special challenges for PBL teachers.

Conducting PBL Lessons

The five phases of problem-based learning and required teacher behaviors for each phase are summarized in Table 11.3. Desired teacher and student behaviors associated with each of these phases are described in more detail in the following sections.

Orient Students to the Problem. At the start of a problem-based learning lesson, just as with all types of lessons, teachers should communicate clearly the aims of the lesson, establish a positive attitude toward the lesson, and describe what students are expected to do. With students who are younger or who have not been involved in

Students need to understand that the purpose of PBL lessons is to learn how to investigate important problems and to become independent learners.

Enhancing Teaching and Learning with Technology
Using the Web with Problem-Based Learning

Until very recently, teachers who used problem-based approaches to teaching were pretty much limited to libraries and their local communities as sources where students could obtain information. All of this has changed dramatically over the past decade. Today, students can access information in libraries and communities all over the world through the Internet. Students involved in problem-based learning projects can use the Internet in a variety of ways, including accessing required information for PBL projects and participating with virtual problem-based learning Web sites. Students in a history class, for example, can visit historical sites such as Gettysburg or museums such as the Smithsonian Institution. Art students can take virtual tours of the Louvre or the East Wing of the National Gallery. Science students can tour and secure data from NASA and scientific institutes around the world.

In addition, there are literally thousands of Web sites that offer students virtual educational experiences, such as Adventure Learning Expeditions described earlier, and thousands of sites that contain informational resources and databases that can be used to assist students with their inquiries and problem-based projects. ThinkQuest, sponsored by the Oracle Foundation, is a large repository of online learning projects and affords teachers and students opportunities to create their own online learning project. Other sites that are currently popular with teachers include SIRS Discoverer, ProQuest Learning, World Data Analyst, and the History Discovery Center. All can be easily located with a Google search.

Teachers need to help students use the Internet effectively. Three concerns need to be addressed.

1. Although many older students can navigate the Internet for their own personal pleasure, they may not be very sophisticated in conducting searches on academic or real-life topics, and many cannot use multiple terms to conduct a Web search. They need to be taught effective search strategies and helped in developing their search skills.

2. As you know not everything found on the Internet is necessarily accurate. Information that appears in most scholarly journals and electronic databases is reviewed by peers and its accuracy is checked before publication. Information that appears in mainline newspapers and magazines is vetted. Journalists are governed by a code of ethics that includes a commitment to report truthfully and accurately. However, anyone can create a Web site, and there are no editors or panels of peers to hold Web providers accountable. It is important that teachers point this out to their students and teach them how to evaluate the accuracy of the information they get from the Web.

3. Many Web sites are meant to deceive, and they promote hate, racism, pornography, and violence. Although there is always concern about First Amendment rights, many parents do not want their children exposed to these kinds of Web sites. Most school districts today employ Internet-filtering software that blocks sites deemed inappropriate or unacceptable to the community. Blocked categories normally include adult content (nudity, sex, lingerie), drugs, gambling, extremist groups, and those that promote illegal activity.

Coiro (2005), Kuiper, Volman, and Terwel (2005), and Johnson (2011) offer the following advice on how to teach

The Internet is an excellent resource for PBL.

students to use the Internet and how to evaluate information acquired there:

- Choose an Internet topic or site that is likely to be motivational to your students—perhaps one that offers animations, graphic illustrations, real-time data, and simulations.
- Explore this site thoroughly for age-appropriate content before using it with students.
- Demonstrate how to access this site and discuss the kind of information found on the site.

- Assign students a topic that requires using this site as well as several others. The assignment should require collection of information and data.
- Have students report their findings and discuss which site had the most accurate and reliable information.

This initial lesson could be followed up with a more thorough analysis using the questions and information found in Table 11.2.

Table 11.2 *Web Site Evaluation Template*

Concern	Questions to Ask	Why
Authorship/Accuracy	What are the Web site author's credentials?	It is important to know something about the Web site's author and to be able to investigate the author's background and credentials.
Sponsorship/Authority	Who is sponsoring the Web site? What domain does the Web site use? (commercial, .com; government, .gov; educational, .edu)? Has the sponsor vetted the information on the Web site?	Knowing about the sponsor or publisher of a Web site helps evaluate the information and whether it has been screened. It helps readers determine the amount of authority to attribute to the Web site.
Currency	Is the information current or is it dated? When was it last updated?	Much information on the Web is outdated. Currency can be somewhat ensured on Web sites that are updated regularly.
Point of View/Objectivity	Why was the Web site created? Does the information reflect a bias? Was the Web site intended to inform, persuade, deceive?	Just as with any information, it is important to know why it was written and for whom.
References/Referral	Where did Web site's author(s) get the information? Is information on the Web site referenced with footnotes or links to other Web sites? Can the links be accessed? Does the Web site include a bibliography?	For information on a Web site to be credible, readers need to know the context in which it is situated. As with print documents, it is important for information to be referenced with footnotes, Web links, and bibliographic information.

Sources: Criteria and implications are adapted from multiple sources: See library Web sites at the Johns Hopkins University and University of California–Berkeley, Online Writing Lab, Purdue University, and Cornell University Library Resources.

Adams' Apples. Copyright 2007, James R. Adams. Reprinted with permission.

problem-based learning before, the teacher must also explain the model's processes and procedures in some detail. Points that need elaborating include the following:

- The primary goals of the lesson are not to learn large amounts of new information but rather to investigate important problems and to become independent learners. For younger students, this concept might be explained as lessons in which they will be asked to "figure things out on their own."
- The problem or question under investigation has no absolute "right" answer, and most complex problems have multiple and sometimes contradictory solutions.

Home and School

Keeping Parents and Caregivers Informed and Involved

Support and involvement from families can be an important ingredient for teachers' use of problem-based learning. As described in Chapter 10, parents often don't understand goals and processes associated with small-group work and cooperative effort. They also worry if students are required to leave the classroom to be involved in the larger community or if they make intensive use of the Internet. Teachers ensure parent understanding by listening if objections are raised, clearly communicating the goals and expectations of PBL lessons, and gaining parents' permission for out-of-school activities.

Engaging family involvement is also important. Family members can become involved through such activities as

- sponsoring a family night where adults can assist students with the PBL projects.
- leading field trips or helping supervise community-based learning activities.

- helping to plan PBL lessons and units.
- serving as liaison between the classroom and the various community organizations to which they belong, such as churches, unions, and service organizations.
- attending events where students report the results of their work.

Increased family involvement will lead to more student learning as well as greater parental understanding and acceptance of PBL activities. A note of caution, however, is in order. Many parents and caregivers work long hours. They have busy schedules and lack time to be engaged. Others may feel uncomfortable being around schools and classrooms. Teachers need to remain sensitive to these conditions and strive to focus on the concerns of family members as well as their own programmatic needs.

Table 11.3 *Syntax for Problem-Based Learning Lessons*

Phase	Teacher Behavior
Phase 1: Orient students to the problem.	Teacher goes over the goals and objectives of the lesson, describes important logistical requirements, and motivates students to engage in problem-solving activity.
Phase 2: Organize students for study.	Teacher helps students define and organize study tasks related to the problem.
Phase 3: Assist independent and group investigation.	Teacher encourages students to gather appropriate information, conduct experiments, and search for explanations and solutions.
Phase 4: Develop and present artifacts and exhibits.	Teacher assists students in planning and preparing appropriate artifacts such as reports, videos, Web sites, and models, and helps them share their work with others.
Phase 5: Analyze and evaluate the problem-solving process.	Teacher helps students to reflect on their investigations and the processes they used.

- During the investigative phase of the lesson, students will be encouraged to ask questions and to seek information. The teacher will provide assistance, but students should strive to work independently or with peers.
- During the analysis and explanation phase of the lesson, students will be encouraged to express their ideas openly and freely. No idea will be ridiculed by the teacher or by classmates. All students will be given an opportunity to contribute to the investigations and to express their ideas.

The teacher needs to present the problem situation with care or have clear procedures for involving students in problem identification. The guidelines provided in Chapter 8 on how to conduct a classroom demonstration can be useful here. The teacher should convey the problem situation to students as interestingly and accurately as possible. Usually being able to see, feel, and touch something generates interest and motivates inquiry. Often the use of discrepant events (a situation, described in Chapter 9, in which the outcome is unexpected and surprising) can prick students' interest. For example, demonstrations in which water runs uphill or ice melts in very cold temperatures can create a sense of mystery and a desire to solve the problem. Short videos of interesting events or situations illustrating real-life problems such as pollution or urban blight are similarly motivational. The important point here is that the orientation to the problem situation sets the stage for the remaining investigation, so its presentation must capture student interest and produce curiosity and excitement.

One way to present problem situations for PBL is to use a discrepant event that creates a sense of mystery.

Organize Students for Study. Problem-based learning requires teachers to develop collaboration skills among students and help them to investigate problems together. It also requires helping them plan their investigative and reporting tasks.

Investigative teams can be formed voluntarily around friendship patterns or according to some social or cognitive arrangements.

Study Teams. Many of the suggestions and issues for organizing students into cooperative learning groups described in Chapter 10 pertain to organizing students into problem-based teams. Obviously, how student teams are formed will vary according to the goals teachers have for particular projects. Sometimes a teacher may decide that it is important for investigative teams to represent various ability levels and racial, ethnic, or gender diversity. If diversity is important, teachers will need to make team assignments. At other times, the teacher may decide to organize students according to mutual interests or to allow groups to form around existing friendship patterns. Investigative teams can thus form voluntarily. During this phase of the lesson, teachers should provide students with a strong rationale for why teams are being organized in a particular way.

Cooperative Planning. After students have been oriented to the problem situation and have formed study teams, teachers and students must spend considerable time defining specific subtopics, investigative tasks, and time lines. For some projects, a primary planning task will be dividing the more general problem situation into appropriate subtopics and then helping students decide which of the subtopics they would like to investigate. For example, a problem-based lesson on the overall topic of weather might be divided into subtopics involving hurricanes, clouds, global warming, and so forth. The challenge for teachers at this stage of the lesson is seeing that all students are actively involved in some investigation and that the sum of all the subtopic investigations will produce workable solutions to the general problem situation.

For projects that are large and complex, an important task during this phase of instruction is to help students link the investigative tasks and activities to time lines. The Gantt chart shown in Figure 11.3 provides an example of how one teacher helped her class plan for a problem-based learning project in history. As described in Chapter 3, Gantt charts allow students to plan particular tasks in relation to when each starts and ends. They are constructed by placing time across the top of the chart and then listing the tasks down the side. X's denote the specific time assigned to accomplish particular tasks.

Most problem-based situations involve data gathering, experimentation, hypothesis development, and solution analysis.

Assist Independent and Group Investigation. Investigation, whether done independently, in pairs, or in small study teams, is the core of problem-based learning. Although every problem situation requires slightly different investigative techniques, most involve the processes of data gathering and experimentation, hypothesizing and explaining, and providing solutions.

Data Gathering and Experimentation. This aspect of the investigation is critical. It is in this step that the teacher encourages students to gather data and conduct mental or actual experiments until they fully understand the dimensions of the problem situation. The aim is for students to gather sufficient information to create and construct their own ideas. This phase of the lesson should be more than simply reading about the problem in books. Teachers should assist students in collecting information from a variety of sources, and they should pose questions to get students to think about the problem and about the kinds of information needed to arrive at defensible solutions. Students will need to be taught how to be active investigators and how to use methods appropriate for the problem they are studying: interviewing, observing, measuring, following leads, or taking notes. They will also need to be taught appropriate investigative etiquette.

Hypothesizing, Explaining, and Providing Solutions. After students have collected sufficient data and conducted experiments on the phenomena they are investigating,

Figure 11.3 *Gantt Chart: Eighth-Grade Monthlong Local History Investigation*

This problem-based lesson has been designed to have students work in four teams for the purpose of investigating local history. The four investigative tasks are interviewing older people about the community; collecting appropriate information from old newspapers in the state's historical society; studying gravestones in the local cemetery; and collecting and reading early histories written about the area.

Task	March 10–15	March 18–23	March 26–31	April 3–7
Orient students to problem situation.	xxx			
Organize study teams.	xxxxxxx			
Discuss with principal when students will be gone from school.	xx			
Gain permission from parents.	xxxxx			
Gain permission for visits from historical society.	xxx			
Have study teams plan their work.		xxxxxxxx		
Go over interviewing protocol.		xx		
Go over logistics for each type of visit.		xx		
Have teams do preliminary visit to make sure logistics are in place.		xx		
Have teams perform their investigative tasks.			xxxxxxxxx	
Have teams prepare required artifacts/exhibits.				xxxx
Share artifacts/exhibits with parents and others.				xxxx

they will want to offer hypotheses, explanations, and solutions. During this phase of the lesson the teacher encourages all ideas and accepts them fully. As with the data-gathering and experimentation phases, teachers continue to pose questions that make students think about the adequacy of their hypotheses and solutions and about the quality of the information they have collected. Teachers should continue to support and model free interchange of ideas and encourage deeper probing of the problem if that is required. Questions at this stage might include, "What would you need to know in order for you to feel certain that your solution is the best?" or, "What could you do to test the feasibility of your solution?" or, "What other solutions can you propose?"

> Teacher support for the free exchange of ideas and the full acceptance of ideas is imperative in the investigative phase of PBL.

Throughout the investigative phase, teachers should provide needed assistance without being intrusive. For some projects and with some students, teachers will need to be close at hand helping students locate materials and reminding them of tasks they are to complete. For other projects and other students, teachers may want to stay out of the way and allow students to follow their own directions and initiatives.

Develop and Present Artifacts and Exhibits. The investigative phase is followed by the creation of artifacts and exhibits. **Artifacts** are more than written reports. They include such things as videos that show the problem situation and proposed solutions,

Check, Extend, Explore

Check

- What are the key planning tasks associated with problem-based learning instruction?
- What are the five phases of a PBL lesson? What kinds of teacher behaviors are associated with each phase?
- Why is orienting students to problem-based learning lessons more complicated than doing so with some other approaches to teaching?
- How do artifacts and exhibits differ from more traditional term papers or exams?

Extend

- Some educators argue that problem-based learning is too time-consuming and that it is unrealistic to expect students to investigate issues and problems on their own. Do you agree or disagree with this assertion? Go to the "Extend Question Poll" on the Online Learning Center to respond.

Explore

- Go to the Online Learning Center at www.mhhe.com/arends10e for links to Web sites related to *Planning and Conducting Problem-Based Learning Lessons* and to *Examples of Students' Work*.

models that comprise a physical representation of the problem situation or its solution, and computer programs and multimedia presentations. Obviously, the sophistication of particular artifacts is tied to the students' ages and abilities. A 10-year-old's poster display of acid rain will differ significantly from a high school student's design for an instrument to measure acid rain. A second-grader's diorama of cloud formations will differ from a middle school student's computerized weather program or a poster display on the causes of global warming.

After artifacts are developed, teachers often organize exhibits to display students' work publicly. These exhibits should take their audiences—students, teachers, parents, and others—into account. **Exhibits** can be traditional science fairs, where each student displays his or her work for the observation and judgment of others, or verbal and/or visual presentations that exchange ideas and provide feedback. Web sites can also be created that allow students to display the results of their work online and to enter into competition with other students if they so desire. As highlighted in the Home and School feature, the exhibition process is heightened in status if parents, students, and community members participate. It is also heightened if the exhibit demonstrates student mastery of particular topics or processes. Newsletters (print or electronic), such as those described in Chapter 10, and Web sites offer other means to exhibit the results of students' work and to bring closure to problem-based projects.

Analyze and Evaluate the Problem-Solving Process. The final phase of problem-based learning involves activities aimed at helping students analyze and evaluate their own thinking processes as well as the investigative and intellectual skills they used. During this phase, teachers ask students to reconstruct their thinking and activity during the various phases of the lesson. When did they first start getting a clear understanding of the problem situation? When did they start feeling confidence in particular solutions? Why did they accept some explanations more readily than others? Why did they reject some explanations? Why did they adopt their final solutions? Did they change their thinking about the situation as the investigation progressed? What caused this change? What would they do differently next time?

Using Learning Centers for Problem-Based Learning*

Learning centers in elementary schools and some secondary schools have long been a vehicle to facilitate problem-based learning and to enable students to work independently or in small groups on problem-based situations. Sometimes learning centers are called *learning stations, inquiry centers,* or *discovery centers*. Regardless of the label, these centers expose students to multiple experiences and hands-on activities and allow students to experience problem-based learning within the confines of the classroom environment. Learning centers are normally stocked with a variety of materials such as books, computers, films, computer software, and audio and video recordings. These rich environments allow students of all ages and abilities to work at their own pace and often on topics of their own choosing.

Teachers can select content for learning centers in several ways. Some teachers organize centers around themes (such as fall); others around content areas (math,

*Thanks goes to Dr. Sharon Castle of George Mason University for her suggestion that the chapter on problem-based learning should include a discussion of learning centers and for providing materials she uses with her class to guide my discussion.

literacy, science, social studies). Centers can also be organized around a particular story or piece of literature, with separate stations to address literacy skills such as listening, reading comprehension, vocabulary, or writing. Other teachers organize their learning centers around Gardner's theory of multiple intelligences (described in Chapter 2). For a particular topic, teachers might have one center emphasizing the visual-spatial aspects of the topic, another focusing on the logical-mathematical, while still another might deal with the interpersonal. An example of a learning center organized around multiple intelligences can be seen on the video on the Online Learning Center.

Teachers also vary in the ways they permit students to work in learning centers. Some teachers provide students with free choice. Most often, however, they provide guidelines and set conditions for students. Regardless of the exact guidelines, it is important that students make choices about their own learning and take some responsibility for managing their time and completing work on their own. Sometimes teachers organize centers to enable students to work together in small groups to develop cooperative problem-solving skills—each small group makes decisions cooperatively about how its members will work.

Successful learning centers require good organization, concise directions, and clear rules and expectations. The most common challenge for teachers in learning centers is helping students manage their time and involvement. Some students wander from center to center without focus; these students require extra guidance from the teacher. Other students rush through the work at a center without really paying much attention. Teachers need to be alert to these problems and check the work of these students very carefully before allowing them to move on to a new learning center.

PBL projects culminate in the creation and display of artifacts such as reports, posters, physical models, and videos.

Diversity and Differentiation

Adapting Problem-Based Lessons for Diverse Students

Sometimes problem-based learning is viewed as more suited for students who are gifted and talented. This is not true. All students, regardless of their abilities, can benefit from PBL In fact, according to Heitin (2012), because students who are at risk and less talented often lack skills to work independently, it makes it all the more important for teachers to use approaches that develop these skills. However, when using PBL with students who lack skills for working independently, teachers should strive to adapt lessons in a variety of ways:

- Provide more direct instruction on particular investigation skills such as locating information, drawing inferences from data, and analyzing rival hypotheses.
- Take more time to explain PBL lessons and expectations for student work.
- Provide more time for students at each phase of their inquiries.
- Establish more precise time lines for checking progress and holding students accountable for work.
- If community activities are required, consider how to facilitate students who are physically challenged or design alternative activities for these students.

Observing students with special needs develop inquiry and problem-solving skills and become autonomous learners can be among a teacher's most rewarding experiences.

Managing the Learning Environment

Many of the general management guidelines described in Chapter 5 apply to the management of problem-based learning. For instance, it is always important for teachers to have a clear set of rules and routines, to keep lessons moving smoothly without

Learning centers allow students to work independently or in small groups.

disruption, and to deal with misbehavior quickly and firmly. Similarly, the guidelines for how to manage group work, provided in Chapter 10 on cooperative learning, also apply to problem-based learning instruction. There are, however, unique management concerns for teachers using problem-based instruction.

Dealing with Multitask Situations

In classrooms where teachers use problem-based learning, multiple learning tasks will be occurring simultaneously. Some student groups may be working on various subtopics in the classroom, while others may be in the library, and still others out in the community or online. Younger students may be using interest centers where students work in pairs and small groups on problems associated with science, math, language arts, and social studies before coming together to discuss their work with the whole class. To make a multitask classroom work, students must be taught to work both independently and together. Effective teachers develop cuing systems to alert students and to assist them with the transition from one type of learning task to another. Clear rules are necessary to tell students when they are expected to talk with one another and when they are expected to listen. Charts and time lines on the chalkboard or SMART board should specify tasks and deadlines associated with various projects. Teachers should establish routines and instruct students how to begin and end project activities each day or period. They should also monitor the progress being made by each student or group of students during multitask situations, a skill that requires a high degree of with-itness, to use Kounin's term.

Special management problems of PBL include adjusting to different finishing rates, monitoring student work, managing materials and equipment, and regulating movement outside the classroom.

Adjusting to Differing Finishing Rates

One of the most complex management problems faced by teachers using problem-based learning is what to do with individuals or groups who finish early or lag behind. Rules, procedures, and downtime activities are needed for students who finish early and have time on their hands. These include high-interest activities such as making available special reading materials or educational games that students can complete on their own or (for older students) procedures for moving to special laboratories to work on other projects. Effective teachers also establish the expectation that those who finish early will assist others.

Late finishers present a different set of problems. In some instances, teachers may give lagging students more time. Of course, this action results in the early finishers having even more downtime. Teachers may alternately decide to get late finishers to put in extra time after school or on the weekend. However, this action is often problematic. If students are working in teams, it could be difficult for them to get together outside school. Furthermore, students who are falling behind often are those who do not work well alone and who need a teacher's assistance to complete important tasks and assignments.

Monitoring and Managing Student Work

Unlike some other types of instruction in which all students complete the same assignment on the same date, problem-based learning generates multiple assignments, multiple artifacts, and often varying completion dates. Consequently, monitoring and managing student work is crucial when using this teaching model. Three important management tasks are critical if student accountability is to be maintained and if teachers are to keep a degree of momentum in the overall instructional

Figure 11.4 *Student Project Form*

Student's Name _____
Study Team's Name_____
Project Name and Scope _____
_____
_____
_____
_____

Particular Assignments and Deadlines
Project 1 _____
Feedback on 1 _____
Project 2 _____
Feedback on 2 _____
Project 3 _____
Feedback on 3 _____
Project 4 _____
Feedback on 4 _____
Final artifact or exhibit_____
_____

process: (1) work requirements for all students must be clearly delineated, (2) student work must be monitored and feedback provided on work in progress, and (3) records must be maintained.

Many teachers manage all three of these tasks through the use of *student project forms*. Maintained on each individual, the student project form (Figure 11.4) is a written record of the work the individual or small group has agreed to complete, agreed-upon time lines for completion, and an ongoing summary of progress.

Managing Materials and Equipment

Almost all teaching situations require some use of materials and equipment, and managing these is often troublesome for teachers. A problem-based situation, however, places greater demands on this aspect of classroom management than other teaching models because it requires the use of a rich array of materials and investigative tools. Effective teachers develop procedures for organizing, storing, and distributing equipment and materials. Many teachers get students to help them with this process. Students can be expected to keep equipment and supplies organized in a science classroom and to distribute books and collect papers in other classrooms. Getting this aspect of management under firm control is very important because without clear procedures and routines, teachers can be overwhelmed with problem-based lesson details.

Regulating Movement and Behavior outside the Classroom

When teachers encourage students to conduct investigations outside the classroom in such places as the library or the computer lab, they need to make sure that students understand schoolwide procedures for movement and use of these facilities. If hall passes are required, teachers must ensure that students use them appropriately. If movement in halls is regulated, students must understand the rules associated with this movement. Similarly, teachers must establish guidelines to govern student behavior when they are conducting their investigations in the community. For example, students should be taught the etiquette of interviewing and the need to obtain permission before looking at certain records or taking certain kinds of pictures. Ideas regarding the use of the Internet for problem-based learning were described earlier in this chapter's Enhancing Teaching and Learning with Technology box.

Assessment and Evaluation

Most of the general assessment and evaluation guidelines provided in earlier chapters also pertain to problem-based instruction. Assessment procedures must always be tailored to the goals the instruction is intended to achieve, and it is always important for teachers to gather reliable and valid assessment information. As with cooperative learning in which the instructional intents are *not* the acquisition of declarative knowledge, assessment tasks for problem-based lessons cannot consist solely of paper-and-pencil tests.

The trend has been away from paper-and-pencil testing and toward performance assessments, which allow students to show what they can do when confronted with real problem situations.

Assessing Understanding and Problem-Solving Skills

Problem-based learning goes beyond development of factual knowledge about a topic and aims instead at the development of rather sophisticated understandings of problems and the world that surround students. Some of the assessment and evaluation procedures described in Chapter 6 are the most appropriate ones for assessing student understanding and problem-solving skills. Essay and other written-response items work particularly well for assessing understanding of complex issues. Performance assessments, also described in Chapter 6, can be used to measure students' problem-solving potential as well as their ability to work collectively in groups.

Using Checklists and Rating Scales

Finding valid and reliable measurement techniques is one of the problems faced by teachers who want to use authentic assessment procedures. Some have turned to such fields as sports and the performing arts in which systems have been developed to measure complex performance tasks. Criterion-referenced checklists and rating scales are two devices that are often used in these fields. For example, individuals who judge diving or ice skating competitions use rating scales that compare individual performances to agreed-upon standards. Rating scales are similarly used to evaluate musical or dance performances.

Finding valid and reliable measurement techniques is a challenge faced by teachers who use PBL.

Teachers at Mark Twain Elementary School in Littleton, Colorado, have developed a series of units that require students to address such real-world questions as, "How are chimpanzees and people alike?" "How are wooden baseball bats made?" "How do parrots learn to talk?" After completing their investigations, students write a report or develop a Web site (artifact) about their topic; develop a visual representation (exhibit) of their topic; and deliver oral presentations to students, the principal, and a parent or community representative. The oral presentation is judged using the adapted rating scale illustrated in Figure 11.5.

Figure 11.5 *Sample Rating Scale for Oral Presentations*

Content		
Clearly describes the essential question or statement of problem.	Vague or incomplete statement of question or problem.	Inability to communicate question or problem.
Demonstrates breadth of understanding of the topic.	Partial understanding of the topic.	Lack of understanding of the topic confuses the audience.
Presentation is organized and flows in a way that is logical and easily understood by the audience.	Presentation has some organizational issues that detract or distract.	Presentation is disorganized and difficult for the audience to follow.
Visual Supports		
Technology, artwork, charts or graphs, artifacts, etc. are effectively used to describe and explain the content.	Some visual supports are present but not referred to, or do not enhance the presentation.	Visual supports are not present.
Verbal Presentation		
Presenter uses appropriate grammar, tone of voice, and varied and correct sentence structure.	Presenter makes some grammatical errors, and has some lapses in voice tone or sentence structure.	Presenter speaks in a monotone, or struggles with grammar.
Presenter is poised, calm, confident, and does not make mistakes.	Presenter is somewhat nervous, makes some mistakes, but recovers.	The presenter is visibly nervous, lacks confidence, and makes mistakes.
Nonverbal Presentation		
Presenter maintains appropriate eye contact with the audience.	Presenter sometimes loses eye contact to focus on notes.	Presenter avoids eye contact or focuses on notes throughout.
Presenter uses varied facial expressions appropriate to the topic, appropriate body language, and appears animated and engaged.	Presenter sometimes lacks gesture or animation.	Presenter does not vary facial expression or body language; appears disengaged or ill at ease.

Source: After Rothman (1995), pp. 12–13.

Assessing Adult Roles and Situations

Problem-based learning, as you read at the beginning of this chapter, strives to engage students in situations that help them to learn about adult roles and to perform some of the tasks associated with these roles. Adult situations that might be learned and how they might be assessed are listed below:

- *Physician:* Diagnose and effectively treat symptoms.
- *Dog groomer:* Provide grooming that adheres to breed standards and does not create injury or stress to the animal.
- *City planner/engineer:* Map a neighborhood; develop and recommend zoning policies to city council.
- *Online tech support:* Speak clearly, listen well, diagnose the problem, provide a solution in a timely manner, and remain cheerful and patient throughout.
- *Citizen:* Work effectively with a neighborhood group; provide clear and fair advocacy for a candidate.

Most of these situations can be assessed using the performance assessment tests, checklists, and rating scales described in the previous sections.

Assessing Learning Potential

Most tests, whether paper-and-pencil or performance-oriented, are designed to measure knowledge and skills at specific points in time. They do not necessarily assess learning potential or readiness to learn. Vygotsky's idea about the zone of proximal development, described earlier, has prompted measurement experts and teachers to consider how a student's learning potential might be measured, particularly potential that could be enhanced with the guidance of a teacher or more advanced peer. Readiness (learning potential) tests exist for reading and other language development areas. Assessment devices that present students with problem-solving tasks that diagnose their ability to benefit from particular kinds of instruction also exist. Assessment tasks that measure learning potential in most areas, however, are still in their infancy stage with much work yet to be done.

Assessing Group Effort

Chapter 10 on cooperative learning described assessment procedures used to assess and reward students for both individual and group work. These procedures can also be used for problem-based instruction. Assessing group effort reduces the harmful competition that often results from comparing students with their peers and makes school-based learning and assessment more like that found in real-life situations. At the same time, attempts to assess group effort should ensure that individuals' contributions are also recognized.

Student presentations are fun and also provide a rich source for assessment.

Problem-Based Learning: A Final Thought

The current interest in problem-based learning is quite extensive. The approach is based on solid theoretical principles, and a modest research base supports its use. In addition, there appears to be considerable teacher and student enthusiasm for using problem-based learning in a variety of subjects in both elementary and secondary schools. It provides an attractive alternative for teachers who wish to move beyond more teacher-centered approaches to challenge students with active learning. PBL also utilizes powerful Internet resources that make its use more practical than in pre-Internet times.

There is considerable teacher and student enthusiasm for PBL.

However, problem-based learning still has some obstacles to overcome if its use is to become widespread. The organizational structures currently found in many schools are not conducive to problem-based approaches. For instance, many schools lack sufficient library and technology resources to support the investigative aspect of PBL. The standard forty- or fifty-minute class period typical of most secondary schools does not allow time for students to become deeply involved in out-of-school activities. Additionally, because problem-based learning does not lend itself to coverage of a great deal of information or foundational knowledge, some administrators and teachers do not encourage its use. Drawbacks such as these cause some critics to predict that problem-based learning will fare no better than Dewey's and Kilpatrick's *project method* or the *hands-on, process-oriented* curricula of the 1960s and 1970s. That is for your generation of teachers to decide.

Check, Extend, Explore

Check
- What are the key features of the learning environment for problem-based learning?
- What are the unique management concerns for teachers using problem-based learning?
- What factors should teachers consider when they think about how to assess student learning in problem-based learning?

Extend
- Do you think problem-based learning will be embraced or discarded by your generation of teachers? Go to the "Extend Question Poll" on the Online Learning Center to respond.

Explore
- Go to Online Learning Center at www.mhhe.com/arends10e for links to Web sites related to *Problem-Based Learning Environments and Assessment*.
- Do a Google search on problem-based learning. You will find thousands of sites, many of them in the field of medicine. Find a site that discusses problem-based learning in medical education and compare it with sites that are more K–12 in orientation.

Reflections from the *Classroom*

Disappointment

You have just finished grading the history projects you assigned to your students. You sigh. Their work is very, very disappointing. Projects (research papers, video productions, Web sites, computer simulations) were supposed to be the result of a six-week, problem-based unit on local history in which students researched a variety of local historic problems, linked these to current problems, and produced interesting and engaging artifacts and exhibits. Yet, the products you have just graded are not very good. Most students prepared reports of the more traditional term paper variety. These are not carefully done; they lack depth of analysis, and they are filled with grammatical and punctuation errors. Artifacts and exhibits appear to have been done in haste. Almost all of them lack creativity.

As a beginning teacher, this is your first attempt at using problem-based learning. You are puzzled about why students didn't do better, and you start thinking about what has gone wrong. You ask yourself, "Did I provide sufficient directions to students about what they were supposed to do?" "Did I help them enough as they did their investigations?" "Did I provide sufficient motivation?" Reflect on your answers to these questions before you compare your thoughts to the following comments from experienced teachers. Approach this situation from the perspective closest to the grade level or subject area you are preparing to teach. Prepare your reflections as an exhibit in your professional portfolio.

Lynn Ciotti

Snyder-Girotti Elementary School, 6th Grade, Bristol Borough, PA

When assigning major projects to my sixth grade students I often ask myself, "Were the directions given clearly? Do the students know what is expected of them? Are the students excited and motivated to do their best work?" My main goal when assigning a major project is to give explicit details and examples so students know what is expected of them.

The first step I would take to ensure understanding is to administer detailed directions to each student with all pertinent information required to complete the project successfully. The second step would be to provide sample projects for students to review during class time. Examples of projects completed from previous year students would be beneficial so they have a concrete idea of what is expected of them.

The third step, and the most important step, would be to distribute a rubric on how the project will be evaluated. The rubric is a critical tool to show students what is expected on an assignment or project. If it is used correctly, it can be used as a checklist enabling students to verify whether they included all elements needed for a successful project. The rubric can also be used as a guideline to help students determine the grade they may receive for their project. The rubric must include ranges in effort for each domain required in the project. It is then up to the student to determine their level of effort.

If I found that projects were still done poorly after implementing these steps, I would re-teach and re-direct students in the appropriate areas. I would conference with students on an individual basis using the rubric provided to inform students of their areas of weakness. I would allow ample time for students to reflect and improve their projects making necessary corrections. Projects would then be re-evaluated and given a final grade.

Jennifer Patterson
Murdock Middle School, 8th Grade, Charlotte County, FL

When I am disappointed in the quality of work submitted by my students, I engage in the practice of self-reflection. I ask myself and reflect on the following questions: Did I set realistic expectations for my students and were they appropriate for their grade level? Were the objectives and desired outcomes clearly stated? Did I provide a clear and concise explanation and did I check to ensure that all students understood the task? Was there adequate time in and out of class for students to complete the activity? Did the assessment criteria correlate to the expectations and outcomes? In short, I ask myself whether I gave my students enough preparation and guidance, and whether I, as a teacher, was sufficiently prepared to ensure that students could complete the activity successfully.

I also encourage my students to reflect back on the project. I would ask them to discuss any problems or difficulties they encountered, and to offer suggestions that would have made the project more stimulating and meaningful. Student feedback is often as valuable as self-reflection. If necessary, I would then attempt to create an equitable solution, such as modifying the expectations and grading criteria accordingly. Another alternative is to allow students additional time to edit their work and resubmit.

There are many things a teacher can do to prevent this situation from occurring. Preparation is essential to making any student project successful. Check to make sure you fully understand the process and structure of the pedagogical strategy you employ. If you do not fully understand the nature of the strategy, do not expect your students to comprehend it either. Also, thoroughly review your expectations, objectives, and desired outcomes to make sure they are at the appropriate age and difficulty level.

Next, get your students involved and engaged in the project from the beginning. Try to pique their curiosity and interest, and make the task relevant and meaningful. Students respond best to activities and projects that are student-centered, so try to include them in setting goals and even the criteria for assessment. This gives students a stake in their learning and this ownership will serve to motivate them. Another way to motivate students is to show them examples of work from previous students—both exemplary and poor—which will provide students with a better understanding of what is expected of them. Many times, this practice will give them the impetus to outdo former students' work.

Also, all aspects or phases of a project must be addressed. For example, if students need to use primary sources, you must make sure they understand primary sources. If the assignment requires reports to be written in a specific format, you should model this format and provide examples.

Finally, if a project is lengthy or complex, it is important for the teacher to monitor students' progress. This can be accomplished by requiring a series of due dates or "check" points for different components of the project. Above all, teachers should provide guidance and direction, while simultaneously enabling students to become self-directed learners.

Summary

Provide an overview of problem-based learning and describe the special features that define this approach to teaching.

- Unlike other approaches to teaching in which the emphasis is on presenting ideas and demonstrating skills, in problem-based learning, teachers present problem situations to students and get them to investigate and find solutions on their own.
- The instructional goals of problem-based learning are threefold: to help students develop investigative and problem-solving skills, to provide students experiences

with adult roles, and to allow students to gain confidence in their own ability to think and become self-regulated learners.

- The general flow or syntax of a problem-based lesson consists of five major phases: orient students to the problem; organize students for study; assist with independent and group investigations; develop and present artifacts and exhibits; and analyze and evaluate work.
- The learning environment of problem-based learning is characterized by openness, active student involvement, and an atmosphere of intellectual freedom.

Describe the theoretical foundations of problem-based learning and summarize the research that supports its use.

- Problem-based learning has its intellectual roots in the Socratic method dating back to the early Greeks but has been expanded by ideas stemming from twentieth-century cognitive and social constructivist theories.
- The knowledge base on problem-based learning is rich and complex. Several studies done in the last few years provide strong evidence about some of the approach's instructional effects. However, other studies lead to the conclusion that effects are cloudy.
- Over the past three decades, considerable attention has been devoted to teaching approaches known by various names—discovery learning, inquiry-based teaching, higher-level thinking—all of which focus on helping students become independent, autonomous learners capable of figuring things out for themselves.

Explain how to plan and use problem-based learning, including how to adapt its use to students of differing backgrounds and abilities.

- Major planning tasks associated with problem-based learning consist of communicating goals clearly, designing interesting and appropriate problem situations, and organizing resources and planning logistics.
- During the investigative phase of problem-based lessons, teachers serve as facilitators and guides of student investigations.

Describe how to implement a learning environment conducive to using problem-based learning.

- Particular management tasks associated with problem-based learning include dealing with a multitask learning environment; adjusting to different finishing rates; finding ways to monitor student work; and managing an array of materials, supplies, and out-of-class logistics.

Describe and discuss appropriate ways to assess student academic and social learning consistent with problem-based learning goals.

- Assessment and evaluation tasks appropriate for problem-based learning necessitate finding alternative assessment procedures to measure such student work as performances and exhibits. These procedures go by the names of performance assessment, authentic assessment, and portfolios.

Speculate about the restraints for using problem-based learning and make predictions about its use in the future.

- Teachers who use problem-based learning face many obstacles such as inflexible school schedules and rules that restrict student movement. Will the current interest in PBL continue, or will the use of the learning approach be discontinued over time?

Key Terms

artifacts   423
discovery learning   411
exhibits   424

level of actual development   410
level of potential development   410
scaffolding   411

self-regulated learners   409
zone of proximal development   410

Interactive and Applied Learning

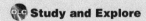 **Study and Explore**

- Access your Study Guide, which includes practice quizzes, from the Online Learning Center.

Observe and Practice

- Listen to audio clips on the Online Learning Center of Corine Marino and Ian Call (tenth-grade world history) talking about problem-based learning in the *Teachers on Teaching* area.

Complete **Practice Exercise 11.1,** Planning for Problem-Based Learning, including
- Write Objectives
- Design the Problem Situation
- Plan Logistics
- Conduct the Lesson
- Assess Student Learning
- Reflect on Planning for Problem-Based Learning

Complete the following additional **Practice Exercises** that accompany Chapter 11:
- Practice Exercise 11.2: Forming Student Learning Teams
- Practice Exercise 11.3: Out-of-School Investigations
- Practice Exercise 11.4: Generating Performance Assessment Ideas
- Practice Exercise 11.5: Teaching Dilemma: Complaints
- Practice Exercise 11.6: Reflection: Is Problem-Based Learning Worth the Time?

Portfolio and Field Experience Activities

Expand your understanding of the content and processes of this chapter through the following field experience and portfolio activities. Support materials to complete the activities are in the *Portfolio and Field Experience Activities* area on your Online Learning Center.

1. Complete the **Reflections from the Classroom** exercise at the end of this chapter and use the recommended reflective essay as an exhibit in your portfolio about your views on problem-based learning. **(InTASC Standard 8: Instructional Strategies)**

2. **Activity 11.1: Assessing My Skills for Using Problem-Based Learning.** Assess your current understanding and skills to plan and conduct problem-based learning lessons. **(InTASC Standard 8: Instructional Strategies)**

3. **Activity 11.2: Observing Problem-Based Learning in Microteaching or Classrooms.** Observe experienced teachers using problem-based learning. **(InTASC Standard 8: Instructional Strategies)**

4. **Activity 11.3: Interviewing Teachers about Their Use of Problem-Based Learning.** Interview experienced teachers about their use of problem-based learning and some of the barriers they perceive that keep them from using the model more fully. **(InTASC Standard 8: Instructional Strategies)**

5. **Activity 11.4: Portfolio: Designing Problem Situations.** Design two problem situations that could be used in a problem-based lesson. Arrange your work as an artifact in your portfolio. **(InTASC Standard 8: Instructional Strategies)**

Books for the Professional

Bellanca, J. (2010). *Enriched learning projects: A practical pathway to 21st century skills.* Bloomington, IN: Solution Tree.

Bender, N. (2012). *Project-based learning: Differentiating instruction for the 21st century.* Thousand Oaks, CA: Corwin Press.

Capraro, R., Capraro, M., & Morgan, J. (2013). *STEM project-based learning: An integrated science, technology, engineering, and mathematics (STEM) approach* (2nd ed.). Rotterdam: Sense Publishing.

Krauss, J., & Boss, S. (2013). *Thinking through project-based learning: Guiding deeper inquiry.* Thousand Oaks, CA: Corwin Press.

Richardson, W. (2010). *Blogs, wikis, podcasts, and other powerful Web tools for classrooms* (3rd ed.). Thousand Oaks, CA: Corwin Press.

Savin-Baden, M. (2008). *Problem-based online learning.* New York: Routledge.

CHAPTER 12
Classroom Discussion

Learning Goals

After studying this chapter you should be able to

Overview of Classroom Discussion	Provide an overview of classroom discussion and explain its appropriate use.
Theoretical and Empirical Support	Describe the theoretical foundations of classroom discussion and summarize the research that supports its use.
Planning and Conducting Discussion Lessons	Explain how to plan and use classroom discussion, including how to adapt its use for students of differing backgrounds and abilities.
Managing the Learning Environment	Describe how to implement a learning environment conducive to using classroom discussion.
Assessment and Evaluation	Describe appropriate ways to assess student learning consistent with the goals of classroom discussion lessons.
Classroom Discourse Patterns: A Final Thought	Speculate about why classroom discussion has not been embraced by large numbers of classroom teachers and make predictions about its use in the future.

 ## Reflecting on Classroom Discussion

Surely you have had teachers during your student career who made extensive use of discussion methods. Perhaps one was the type of teacher who came to class every day and presented you with provocative questions to talk about. Perhaps another started every class with a discussion about the previous night's homework.

Consider the discussions you have participated in as a student:

- Did you participate widely in classroom discussions? Or were you a student who didn't participate much? If you didn't participate, do you know why?

- Did you think your level of participation made any difference in how much you learned? Why or why not?

- Of the discussions you remember, which ones stand out in your mind? Which were most effective? Least effective?

- What features did the effective discussions have in common?
- What features did the ineffective discussions have in common?
- What do you think students learn during discussions? What don't they learn?

What do your answers to these questions have to say about you and your views on classroom discussion? What do they say about how you might use discussion once you have your own classroom? Will you be a teacher who uses discussions often? Or will you tend to stay away from discussions and use other approaches instead?

 Go to the Online Learning Center at www.mhhe.com/arends10e to respond to these questions.

Next to lecture, discussion and questioning have been fundamental to teaching as far back as Aristotle and Socrates, and as you read in previous chapters, today it is a required component of almost every type of lesson. For instance, teacher questioning comes toward the end of presentation and direct instruction lessons as an effort to check for understanding and to help students extend their thinking about particular ideas or skills. Discussion occurs mainly in small groups during cooperative learning lessons, whereas inquiry lessons and problem-based learning demand constant dialogue to accomplish the intended instructional goals.

This chapter focuses on *classroom discussion* in a more general way and describes its use as a stand-alone approach to teaching.

The chapter begins with an overview of classroom discussion, presents its theoretical and empirical support, and examines the specific procedures involved in planning, conducting, adapting, and assessing classroom discussions. The final section highlights the importance of teaching students how to become effective participants in the classroom discourse system and describes how teachers can change some of the unproductive communication patterns that have traditionally characterized many classrooms.

Discussion is a teaching procedure that is a crucial part of almost all approaches to teaching but can also stand alone.

Overview of Classroom Discussion

Classroom discussion and discourse are central to all aspects of teaching. Effective use of classroom discussion requires an understanding of several important topics pertaining to classroom discourse and discussion. The dictionary definitions of *discourse* and *discussion* are almost identical: to engage in a verbal interchange and to express thoughts on particular subjects. Teachers are more likely to use the term **discussion,** since it describes the *procedures* they use to encourage verbal interchange among students. Scholars and researchers are more likely to use the term **discourse,** because it reflects their interest in the *larger patterns* of exchange and communication found in classrooms. The term *discourse* is used to provide the overall perspective about

Recitations are question-and-answer exchanges in which teachers check how well students recall factual information or understand a concept.

classroom communication described in the section on theoretical support. The term *discussion* is used when specific teaching procedures are described.

Sometimes discussions are confused with *recitations.* As described in more detail later, discussions are situations in which teachers and students or students and other students talk with one another and share ideas and opinions. Questions employed to stimulate discussion are usually at a higher cognitive level. **Recitations,** in contrast, are those exchanges, such as in a direct instruction lesson, in which teachers ask students a series of lower-level or factual questions aimed at checking how well they understand a particular idea or concept.

Discussions are used by teachers to achieve at least three important instructional objectives, as shown in Figure 12.1. First, discussion improves students' thinking and helps them construct their own understanding of academic content. As described in previous chapters, telling students about something does not necessarily ensure understanding. Discussing a topic helps students strengthen and extend their knowledge of the topic and increase their ability to think about it.

Second, discussion promotes student involvement and engagement. Research, as well as the wisdom of experienced teachers, demonstrates that for true learning to take place, students must take responsibility for their own learning and not depend solely on a teacher. Using discussion is one means of doing this. It gives students public opportunities to talk about and play with their own ideas and provides motivation to engage in discourse beyond the classroom.

Third, discussion is used by teachers to help students learn important communication skills and to develop more effective thinking processes. Because discussions are public, they provide a means for a teacher to find out what students are thinking and how they are processing the ideas and information being taught. Discussions thus provide social settings in which teachers can help students analyze their thinking processes and learn important communication skills such as stating ideas clearly, listening to others, responding to others in appropriate ways, and asking good questions.

Most discussions follow a similar pattern, but variations do exist, depending on the teacher's goals for particular lessons and the nature of the students involved. Three variations will be described later in the chapter, but essentially, all three share the same five phases: explaining the aims of the discussion, focusing the discussion, holding the discussion, bringing the discussion to a conclusion, and debriefing the discussion.

The learning environment and management system surrounding discussion are incredibly important. The environment is characterized by open processes and active student roles. It also demands careful attention to the use of physical space. The teacher may provide varying degrees of structure and focus for a particular discussion, depending on the nature of the class and the learning objectives. However, in many ways, the students themselves control the specific, minute-to-minute interactions. This approach to teaching requires a large degree of student self-management and control, a topic that is explored more fully later in this chapter.

Figure 12.1 *Learner Outcomes for Discussion*

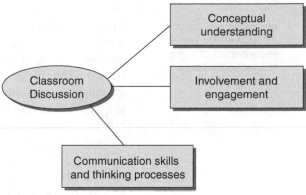

Check, Extend, Explore

Check
- What are the five phases of a classroom discussion?
- What are the major learner outcomes for classroom discussions?
- What type of learning environment works best for classroom discussions?

Extend
- Do you agree or disagree with the assertion that teachers can have effective discussions regardless of the nature of the learning environment? Go to the "Extend Question Poll" on the Online Learning Center to respond.

Explore
- Go to the Online Learning Center at www.mhhe.com/arends10e for links to Web sites related to *Classroom Discussion.*

Theoretical and Empirical Support

Much of the theoretical support for the use of discussion stems from the fields in which scholars study language, communicative processes, and patterns of exchange. These studies extend to virtually every setting in which human beings come together. To consider the role of language, think for a moment about the many everyday situations in which success depends largely on the use of language and communication. Friendships, for instance, are initiated and maintained mainly through language—friends talk and share experiences with one another. Families maintain their unique histories by building patterns of discourse, sometimes even in the form of secret codes, that are natural to family members but are strange to outsiders, such as new in-laws. Youth culture develops special patterns of communication that provide member identity and group cohesion. The secret codes used by gangs are an example of communication used to maintain group identity. It is difficult to imagine a cocktail party, a dinner party, a church social, or any other social event existing for very long if people could not verbally express their ideas and listen to the ideas of others. The popularity of radio talk shows, text messaging, Internet chat rooms, and social networks provides additional evidence of how central interaction through the medium of language is to human beings.

Discourse through language is also central to what goes on in classrooms. More than three decades ago Courtney Cazden (1986), one of America's foremost scholars on the topic of classroom discourse wrote that "spoken language is the medium by which much teaching takes place and in which students demonstrate to teachers much of what they have learned" (p. 432). Spoken language provides the means for students to talk about what they already know and to form meaning from new knowledge as it is acquired. Spoken language affects the thought processes of students and provides them with their identity as learners and as members of the classroom group.

Discourse and Cognition

A strong relationship exists between language and thinking, and both lead to the ability to analyze, to reason deductively and inductively, and to make sound inferences based on knowledge.

Discourse and Thinking. Discourse is one way for students to practice their thinking processes and to enhance their thinking skills. Mary Budd Rowe (1986) summarized this important point nicely.

> To "grow," a complex thought system requires a great deal of shared experience and conversation. It is in talking about what we have done and observed, and in arguing about what we make of our experiences, that ideas multiply, become refined, and finally produce new questions and further explorations. (p. 43)

In some ways, discourse can be thought of as the *externalization of thinking*; that is, exposing one's invisible thoughts for others to see. Through discussions, then, teachers are given a window for viewing the thinking skills and processes of their students and a setting for providing correction and feedback when they observe faulty, incomplete reasoning. Thinking out loud also provides students opportunities to "hear" their own thinking and to learn how to monitor their own thinking processes. Remember, learners don't acquire knowledge simply by recording new information on a blank slate;

instead, they actively build knowledge structures over a period of time as they interpret new knowledge and integrate it with prior knowledge.

Social Aspect of Discourse. One aspect of classroom discourse, then, is its ability to promote cognitive growth. Another aspect is its ability to connect and unite the cognitive and the social aspects of learning. Indeed, the classroom discourse system is central to creating positive learning environments. It helps define participation patterns and, consequently, has a great deal of impact on classroom management. The talk of teachers and students provides much of the social glue that holds classroom life together.

> **In addition to promoting cognitive growth, discussion can also be used to further a positive social environment in the classroom.**

The cognitive–social connection is most clear in the way social participation affects thinking and cognitive growth. Lauren Resnick and Leopold Klopfer (1989) observed, for instance, that the "social setting provides occasions for modeling effective thinking strategies":

> Skilled thinkers (often the instructor, but sometimes more advanced fellow students) can demonstrate desirable ways of attacking problems, analyzing texts, or constructing argument. . . . But most important of all, the social setting may let students know that all the elements of critical thought—interpretation, questioning, trying possibilities, demanding rational justification—are *socially valued.* (pp. 8–9)

Much of the work of Vygotsky and contemporary educators who hold cognitive-constructivist perspectives emphasizes the importance of social interaction in all aspects of human learning. It is through this interaction that students learn how to think and solve problems (see Craig, 2013; Hicks, 1996; Kosminsky & Kosminsky, 2003; Murphy, Wilkinson, & Soter 2011; Palincsar, 1986).

Traditional Classroom Discourse Patterns

Working from a variety of perspectives, researchers who study classrooms have found a discourse pattern that has remained consistent over a rather long period of time. They have also found that the traditional pattern is not necessarily the best for promoting full student participation and higher-level thinking.

> **Studies have repeatedly shown that teacher talk routinely constitutes about two-thirds to three-fourths of classroom discourse.**

We are all familiar with the basic pattern, labeled the *initiation-response-evaluation* (IRE) model by Cazden (1986, 1988, 2001), Burbules and Bruce (2001), and Reznitskaya (2012). This exchange takes place in a whole-class setting and consists of three phases:

- Initiation: Teacher asks a question about the lesson.
- Response: Students raise their hands and reply.
- Evaluation: Teacher evaluates the response with praise or corrects the response. Teachers often answer the question themselves with a short lecture.

As you will see later, the pace of this pattern is rapid—the teacher talks most of the time and only a few students participate.

Larry Cuban (1984, 2003) documented how this pattern emerged early in the history of formal schooling and how it has persisted to the present day at all levels of schooling and across all academic subjects. Ned Flanders documented teacher dominance of classroom communication in the late 1960s with numerous studies on teacher–student interaction. Flanders (1970) concluded that in most classrooms, two-thirds of the talk was by teachers. John Goodlad (1984), in his extensive study of schools years later, made essentially the same observation, as did Burbules and Bruce (2001) and Reznitskaya (2012).

Despite its potentially harmful effects and an endless effort to modify the IRE model of discourse, the pattern is still very much with us today (Burbules, 1993; Burbules & Bruce, 2001; Marzano, 2007; Murphy, Wilkinson, & Soter, 2011).

Teacher and Student Questioning

Studies have resulted in conflicting conclusions regarding the benefits of higher-order questioning over fact-based question-and-answer sessions.

Discussion and, particularly, recitation teaching rely on teachers asking questions. The types of questions teachers ask and the ways they ask them have been the focus of considerable inquiry and concern for quite some time (Craig, 2013; Cuban, 1993; Gall, 1970, 1984; Marzano, 2007). An obvious concern is what effect such details have on student learning. One line of inquiry has been the effect of factual and higher-order questions on student learning and thinking. For many years, the conventional wisdom held that asking higher-order questions led to greater cognitive growth than asking more concrete, factual questions. However, reviews of research in the early 1970s reported no clear evidence one way or the other (Dunkin & Biddle, 1974; Rosenshine, 1971). By 1976, Barak Rosenshine was prepared to challenge the conventional wisdom when he concluded that "narrow" (factual) questions actually seemed to be the most useful, particularly when teachers provided immediate feedback about the correct and incorrect answers. A few years later, Redfield and Rousseau (1981) challenged this conclusion and reported that asking higher-level and thought-provoking questions had positive effects on student achievement and thinking.

Whether teachers should ask more higher-order or lower-order questions depends on their instructional objectives and on the students being taught.

During the past two decades, researchers have continued to study the controversy over the effects of question types on student achievement and thinking. A consensus appears to be emerging that the type of questions teachers ask should depend on the students with whom they are working and the type of educational objectives they are trying to achieve (Gall, 1984; Marzano, 2007; Walberg, 1999).

- Emphasis on fact questions is more effective for promoting young children's achievement, which involves primarily mastery of basic understandings and skills.
- Emphasis on higher cognitive questions is more effective for students when more independent and higher-level thinking is required.

In addition to the types of questions teachers ask, researchers have also been interested in the questions' level of difficulty and in teachers' overall pattern of questioning. **Level of difficulty** refers to students' ability to answer questions correctly regardless of cognitive level. Research on this topic has also produced mixed results. However, after a thorough review of the research, Jere Brophy and Tom Good (1986) concluded that teachers should consider three guidelines when deciding how difficult to make their questions:

- A large proportion (perhaps as high as three-fourths) of a teacher's questions should be at a level that will elicit correct answers from students in the class.
- The other one-fourth of the questions should be at a level of difficulty that will elicit some response from students, even if the response is incomplete.
- No question should be so difficult that students will not be able to respond at all.

The overall pattern of questioning is also important. All too often, the unspoken classroom discussion rules are that the teacher should ask all the questions, students should respond with right answers, and the teacher should repeat the questions if the answers are wrong. Later, you will find that this kind of discussion pattern does not promote higher-level thinking or much real engagement.

A final concern about questioning has to do with the questions students ask or the lack thereof. The IRE pattern doesn't account for student questioning, and experienced

Traditional teacher questioning patterns may lead students to boredom and passivity.

teachers have made the observation that Dewey made many years ago about the scarcity of questions asked by students:

> No one has ever explained why children are so full of questions outside of school (they pester grown-up persons if they get any encouragement), and the conspicuous absence of display of curiosity [and questions] about the subject matter of school lessons. Reflection on this striking contrast will throw light upon the question of how far customary school conditions supply a context of experience in which [questions] naturally suggest themselves. (Boydston, 2008, as cited in McTighe & Wiggins, 2013, p. 81)

Wait-Time

A final, important line of research in relation to classroom discussion and discourse focuses on the pace of interchange and a variable known as *wait-time* (Rowe, 1974; Tobin & Capie, 1980). **Wait-time** is the pause between a teacher's question and the student's response and between the response and the teacher's subsequent reaction or follow-up question. This variable was first observed in the 1960s, when considerable effort was under way to improve curricula in almost all academic subjects. These new curricula, particularly in the sciences and the social sciences, were developed to help students learn how to inquire and discover relationships among social and/or natural phenomena. The recommended method for virtually all curricula was inquiry or discovery-oriented discussions. However, researchers found that these types of discussions were not occurring. The now classic study by Rowe on this important topic is highlighted in the Research Summary in this chapter for two reasons. Her investigations highlighted an important problem with classroom discourse and offered a cure. The Rowe study also is included here because it illustrated how research in education sometimes moves from observation of teacher behavior in regular classrooms to experimentation and the testing of new practices.

Wait-time is the pause between the teacher's question and the student's response and between the student's response and the teacher's reaction.

Classic

Research Summary
When Can Slowing Down Increase Learning?

Rowe, M. B. (1974). Wait-time and rewards as instructional variables, their influence on language, logic, and fate control. Part one: Wait-time. *Journal of Research in Science Teaching, 11,* 81–94.

Could it be that the absence of talk (pauses by the teacher) does more to influence discourse and complex thinking processes than its presence? That's what Mary Budd Rowe found in a series of interesting and important studies.

Problem and Approach: In Chapter 8, process-product research was introduced to show how researchers examine existing practices in a natural setting to discover relationships between teacher behavior and student learning. Other chapters, however, described how some knowledge has resulted from experiments and comparing the effects of innovative teaching practices. Sometimes a researcher may employ both observation in natural settings and experimentation with new practices. The classic study by Rowe and her colleagues on the discourse patterns of teachers is a good example of research that moved from observation of teachers in regular classrooms to experimentation with a new procedure.

Sample and Setting: This study actually progressed through two stages: (1) systematic observation of teachers in natural settings and (2) planned experiments in which the researchers attempted to change the natural behavior of teachers.

Natural Observations: Discussion patterns were initially analyzed from tapes made by teachers using a new science curriculum. By the end of the first stage of their inquiry, they had obtained over three hundred tapes from rural, suburban, and urban areas and from a variety of grade levels. Analysis of these lessons showed that the pace of instruction in most classrooms was very fast. In all but three classrooms, out of the hundreds studied, teachers displayed the following pattern:

- Teacher asked a question. Student had to respond within one second.
- If student did not respond in one second, teacher repeated, rephrased, asked a different question, or called on another student.
- When a student did respond, the teacher reacted or asked another question within an average of 0.9 second.

The investigators concluded that instruction in virtually all classrooms was very fast and without sufficient wait-time.

They also concluded that in a few classrooms where they did find students engaged in inquiry, sustained conversation, speculation, and argument about ideas, the average wait-time hovered around three seconds. With this information, the researchers planned and conducted a series of controlled studies to see (1) if teachers could be taught to slow down the pace of their discussions by using wait-time, and (2) if the slower pace had an impact on discourse and cognitive processes.

Procedures for the Microstudies: Ninety-six teachers from two locations were recruited and trained to employ wait-times of at least three seconds. From a pool of lessons prepared by the researchers, teachers were asked to teach six lessons to students who were assigned to four-member learning groups. Each lesson was recorded on audiotape. Tapes were transcribed and coded. The wait-time variables were measured using the following criteria:

- **Wait-time 1:** The time between when the teacher stops speaking and when either a student responds or the teacher speaks again
- **Wait-time 2:** The time between when a student stops speaking and when the teacher speaks

Pointers for Reading Research: The results of this study are descriptive and rather straightforward. However, Rowe's study is interesting in that it was conducted in stages. This illustrates how good research often moves from casual observations of phenomena in a natural setting to more systematic observation, and only then to intervention and manipulation of important variables in controlled settings for the purpose of seeing if things can be changed for the better.

Results: Teacher behavior changed as a result of training to use longer wait-times. Table 12.1 shows the number of questions asked and the typical distribution of question types by teachers before and after wait-time training.

Notice the sharp drop in the number of questions asked by teachers after wait-time training. Also note that the number of informational questions declined while the number of probing and thought-provoking questions increased rather dramatically.

The researchers hypothesized that if teachers could slow down their pace, this behavior would impact on the way their students responded. Table 12.2 displays the results of Rowe's wait-time studies on student outcome variables.

Table 12.1 *Number of Questions and Typical Distribution of Question Types before and after Wait-Time Training*

	Before Training	After Training
Mean number of questions per 15 minutes of transcript	38	8
Typical questions (%)		
Rhetorical	3	2
Informational	82	34
Leading	13	36
Probing	2	28

Table 12.2 *Student Outcome Variables: Contrasts between Tape 1 and Tape 6 of the Training Sequence for 76 of 95 Teachers Who Achieved Criterion Wait-Times of 3 Seconds or Longer*

Student Variable	Tape 1	Tape 2
Length of response		
Mean	8	27
Range	(3–12 words)	(14–39 words)
Number of unsolicited but appropriate responses		
Mean	5	17
Range	(0–17)	(12–28)
Number of failures to respond		
Mean	7	1
Range	(1–15)	(0–3)
Number of evidence-inference statements		
Mean	6	14
Range	(0–11)	(6–21)

Table 12.2 shows these results when teachers started to use longer wait-times:

- The length of student responses increased from eight words per response under the fast pace used by teachers to twenty-seven words. This signifies considerably longer statements by students after teachers are trained to use wait-time.
- The number of unsolicited but appropriate responses increased from a mean of five to a mean of seventeen.
- Failures to respond ("I don't know" or silence) decreased. In classrooms prior to training, the "no response" occurred as high as 30 percent of the time. This changed dramatically once teachers started to wait at least three seconds for students to think.

- When wait-time was lengthened, students provided more "evidence-type" statements to support the inferences they were making. They also asked more questions.

Discussion and Implications What is striking about this study is (1) teachers, left to their natural inclinations, pace instruction too fast to allow much careful inquiry or serious dialogue, and (2) a rather simple intervention can bring rather striking changes in discourse patterns. Learning to wait results in fewer and different types of questions by teachers and, most important, different student responses. Students in classrooms in which teachers use wait-time engage in inquiry-oriented and speculative thinking.

Planning and Conducting Discussion Lessons

Check, Extend, Explore

Check
• What relationships exist among language, discourse, and thinking abilities?
• Why is the cognitive-social connection important to the understanding of classroom discussions?
• How does the use of different kinds of questions impact different types of student thinking?
• Why is the concept of wait-time important to classroom dialogue?

Extend
• What might you do as a teacher to ensure an appropriate pace in your classroom discussions?
• How do you explain the persistence of the IRE pattern of classroom discourse?

Explore
• Go to the Online Learning Center at www.mhhe.com/ arends10e for links to Web sites related to *Theory and Research on Classroom Discussion.*

As with the approaches to teaching described in the preceding chapters, effective discussions require that teachers perform planning, interactive, management, adaptive, and assessment tasks. Planning and interactive tasks are described in this section, followed by a discussion of management and assessment tasks.

Planning for Discussion

Two common misconceptions held by many teachers are that planning for a discussion requires less effort than planning for other kinds of teaching and that discussions cannot really be planned at all because they rely on spontaneous and unpredictable interactions among students. Both of these ideas are wrong. Planning for a discussion necessitates every bit as much effort, perhaps more, as planning for other types of lessons, and even though spontaneity and flexibility are important in discussions, it is a teacher's planning beforehand that makes these actions possible.

Consider Purpose. Deciding that discussion is appropriate for a given lesson is the first planning step. Preparing the lesson and making decisions about what type of discussion to hold and specific strategies to employ are next. As described earlier, discussions can stand alone as a teaching strategy, they are, however, more frequently used in connection with other teaching models. Although the particular uses of discussion are practically infinite, teachers generally want their discussion to accomplish one of the three objectives: to check for student understanding of reading assignments or presentations through recitations, to teach thinking skills, or to share experiences.

Consider Students. Knowing about students' prior knowledge is just as important in planning a discussion as it is in planning other kinds of lessons. If students have no understanding of the topic under discussion, it is impossible for them to express an opinion or to render a reasonable idea. Experienced teachers know that they must also take into consideration their students' communication and discussion skills. They consider, for instance, how particular students in the class will respond differently to various kinds of questions or foci; they predict how some will want to talk all the time whereas others will be reluctant to say anything. When planning discussions, it is important to devise ways to encourage participation by as many students as possible, not just the bright ones, and to be prepared with questions and ideas that will spark the interest of a diverse student group. More is said about this aspect of discussion later.

Choose an Approach. There are several different kinds of discussions, and the approach chosen should reflect a teacher's purposes and the nature of the students involved. Three approaches are described here.

Recitations. Although recitation is often overused, it nonetheless has its place. One important use is when teachers ask students to listen to or read about information on a particular topic. A reading assignment in history may vary in length from a paragraph to a whole book. A teacher's talk on ecosystems may be as long as a full-hour

Brief question-and-answer or recitation sessions covering assigned materials are useful in checking student understanding.

lecture or as short as five or ten minutes. Either can cover a variety of topics. Teachers generally ask students to read or listen with a definite purpose in mind. Sometimes it is to glean important information about a topic, whereas at other times it is to become familiar with a particular author, a specific type of literature, or a point of view or particular interpretation. Brief question-and-answer sessions (recitations) about assigned reading materials or a lecture can provide teachers with a means of checking student understanding. They can also motivate students to complete their reading assignments or to listen carefully when the teacher is talking.

Inquiry or Problem-Based Discussion. Discussions are sometimes used to engage students in higher-order thinking and, thereby, to encourage their own intellectual investigation. Normally, such discussion is part of some type of problem-based teaching. Although a number of specific approaches have been developed, they all have a common syntax in which the teacher opens the lesson by presenting students with what Suchman (1962) labeled a *discrepant event* or what Palincsar and Brown (1989) called *mystery spots*. Both refer to puzzling situations that are not immediately explainable, such as water appearing to run uphill, metal changing shape when heated, and social data that confront conventional wisdom. Because these situations are puzzling to students and create **cognitive dissonance,** they provide a natural motivation to think. When using this approach, teachers encourage students to ask questions, to generate empirical data, and to formulate theories and hypotheses to explain the puzzling situation. In this type of discussion, teachers help students become conscious of their own reasoning processes and teach them to monitor and evaluate their own learning strategies.

> **Problem-based lessons centered on a discrepant event encourage discussion and help students become aware of their own reasoning processes.**

Sharing-Based Discussion. Often teachers hold discussions for the purpose of helping students develop shared meaning from common experiences or to confront one another with differences of opinions. Younger children may be asked to talk about what they learned from their visit to the zoo or the apple farm. Older students may be asked to talk about what they learned from a science experiment they performed or from a novel they read. Important current events such as a breakthrough in an arms treaty, new abortion legislation, or a natural disaster are often discussed in the classroom so that different points of view may be explored. Unlike recitations, during which teachers ask students *to recall* specific information, or problem-based discussions, in which teachers get students *to reason,* sharing-based discussions help students *to form and express thoughts and opinions independently.* Through dialogue about shared experiences and what these experiences mean, ideas are refined or expanded and questions are raised for future study.

Make a Plan. A lesson plan for a discussion consists of a set of objectives and a content outline. The plan should include not only the targeted content but also a well-conceived focus statement, the description of a puzzling event, and/or a list of questions. If the discussion is to follow a teacher presentation, it is likely that the teacher already has the content firmly in mind and has explored the important conceptual relationships. When the discussion follows assigned readings, experienced teachers know that they must have extensive notes not only about specific facts but, more important, about the main ideas, points of view, and key relationships highlighted in the reading.

Sometimes teachers find using the *conceptual web* technique a useful planning device. As described in Chapter 9, a web provides a visual image of the characteristics and relationships around a central idea. Remember, to make a conceptual web, you identify the key ideas associated with a particular topic and arrange them in some logical pattern.

Advance preparation and identification of questioning patterns can greatly improve the flow of a classroom discussion.

Develop a Questioning Strategy. For many types of discussions, asking students questions becomes a key feature. In preparing their questioning strategy, teachers need to consider both the cognitive level of questions and the level of difficulty. Several systems have been developed for classifying questions in regard to the cognitive processing they require of students. Most widely used is Bloom's *Revised Taxonomy of Educational Objectives,* which is described in Chapter 3. Table 12.3 illustrates how this taxonomy can be used to design questions for classroom discussions and provides examples of various levels of questions.

Notice that questions in the "remember" and "understand" categories require students to recall information (facts, events, principles) that they have learned and to explain what it means. "Apply" and "analyze" questions require more of students and ask them to focus on the "why" of some situation and/or to apply particular kinds of knowledge. These questions are sometimes called **convergent questions** because they ask students to focus on a single, best answer or conclusion and to explain known relationships. "Evaluate" and "create" questions, in contrast, require students to make judgments based on criteria or answer "what if" questions. These are called **divergent questions.** Divergent questions allow multiple answers, conclusions, and creativity on the part of students.

Pressley et al. (1992) and Marzano (2007) describe another type of question very similar to divergent questions. They label these **elaborative interrogation questions.**

Table 12.3 *Question Types according to Bloom's Revised Taxonomy*

Cognition Process	Examples of Questions	Type of Cognition Required to Answer
Remember	In which region of the United States is Ohio? What does H_2O stand for?	Retrieving factual knowledge
Understand	What is the difference between longitude and latitude?	Constructing meaning
	What is the book *The Old Man and the Sea* about?	
Apply	If John has 12 feet of lumber, how many 2-foot-long boards can he make?	Applying or using principles or procedures
	In which of the situations would Newton's second law apply?	
Analyze	Why do some trees lose their leaves in winter?	Explaining relationships or overall purposes
	How does Hemingway's view of war reflect the political ideology of his time?	
Evaluate	Which novel do you think is the best piece of literature?	Making judgments based on criteria and standards
	What do you think about the city's recycling program?	Generating hypotheses
Create	If the North had not won the Civil War, what would life be like in the United States today?	
	What if John Brown had succeeded at Harpers Ferry?	

They come after a student has answered a particular inferential question and include such follow-up questions as:

- Why do you believe what you said is true?
- Tell me why you believe that is so.
- What information do you have to support that statement?
- How would you test that idea?

Elaborative interrogation questions enhance student comprehension and help extend their thinking about particular topics. They also provide teachers with a window for observing the thinking and reasoning processes their students are using.

McTighe and Wiggins (2013) provide even another type of question, labeled **essential questions.** You perhaps remember this term described in Chapter 3 when it was used to help determine "what is important to teach." Here it is used to define a type of question that provokes student understanding and higher-level thinking. According to McTighe and Wiggins, essential questions have seven defining characteristics. An essential question:

1. Is open-ended.
2. Is thought-provoking and intellectually engaging.
3. Calls for higher-level thinking.
4. Points toward important, transferable ideas.
5. Raises additional questions.
6. Requires support and justification, not just an answer.
7. Recurs over time (adapted from p. 3).

But you may be asking, "What makes a question essential? How does it differ from a nonessential question?" Table 12.4 provides some examples offered by McTighe and Wiggins (2013).

Finally, there are questions that should be avoided in a discussion. Sandra Metts (2005) offered five types of questions that teachers should not ask:

- *The Dead-End Question:* A question requiring only a "yes/no" response. This question goes nowhere (e.g., "Can animals communicate?").
- *The Chameleon Question:* A question that begins in one direction and then switches to a different direction (e.g., "If language requires both symbols and rules, can animals have language? That is, if a chimpanzee can be taught to make a sign for banana, does it have language?").
- *The Fuzzy Question:* A question that is unclear or confusing (e.g., "What do you think about animals communicating?").

Table 12.4 *Essential vs. Nonessential Questions*

Essential Questions	Nonessential Questions
• How do the arts shape as well as reflect a culture?	• What common artistic symbols were used by the Incas?
• What do effective problem solvers do when they get stuck?	• What steps did you follow to get your answer?
• How strong is the scientific evidence?	• What is a variable in scientific investigations?
• Is there ever a "just" war?	• What key event sparked America's involvement in World War II?
• Who is a true friend?	• Who is Maggie's best friend in the story?

Note: Adapted from McTighe & Wiggins (2013), p. 1.

- *The Put-Down Question:* A question that is largely rhetorical, minimizes the legitimacy of a comment, and/or closes down additional discussion (e.g., "Can we all see why Mary's solution is not feasible?").
- *The Programmed-Answer Question:* A question that gives away the intended answer. "Many scholars say that animals can communicate with each other, but are they using signals or language?"

As described earlier, the research about the effects of using various types of questions is still somewhat unclear. However, beginning teachers should keep in mind one important truth; that is, different questions require different types of thinking and a good lesson should include both lower- and higher-level questions. One way to achieve this is to start by asking questions that require recall of factual or conceptual information to see if students have grasped the basic ideas under consideration. Follow with application and analysis questions ("why" questions) and then conclude with more thought-provoking evaluation and creating ("what-if") questions.

In preparing the lesson plan and questioning strategies, remember to think through the issues associated with question difficulty. Experience helps teachers to know their students and to devise questions of appropriate difficulty. Decisions about question type and difficulty can be better made during the quiet of advance planning than during the discussion itself.

Use Physical Space Appropriately. Another planning task involves making arrangements for appropriate use of physical space. Earlier chapters explained how different seating patterns affect communication patterns within the classroom. The best seating arrangements for discussion are the U-shape and the circle formations illustrated in Figures 12.2 and 12.3. Both seating patterns allow students to see each other, an important condition for verbal interaction. Both can be accommodated in most classrooms. Each, however, has some advantages and disadvantages that should be considered.

Figure 12.2 *U-Shaped Seating Arrangement*

Figure 12.3 *Circle Seating Arrangement*

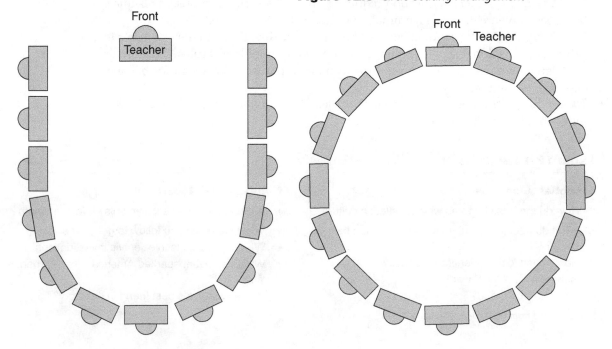

The **U-shaped seating pattern,** with the teacher situated in front at the open end of the U, gives a bit more authority to the teacher, an important feature when working with groups of students who lack discussion skills or where behavior management is a problem. The U-shape also allows freedom of movement for teachers. They have ready access to the chalkboard or flip charts, which may be important during the course of a discussion, and they can move into the U to make closer contact with particular students when necessary. The disadvantage of the U is that it establishes some emotional distance between the teacher, as discussion leader, and students. It also puts considerable physical distance between students who are sitting at the head of the U and those sitting at the end.

The **circle seating pattern,** in contrast, minimizes both emotional and physical distance among participants and maximizes opportunities for students to talk freely with one another. The disadvantage of the circle is that it inhibits the teacher from moving freely to the chalkboard or among students.

> **The best seating arrangement for a discussion is either a U-shape or a circle.**

Almost all elementary and secondary schools today have furniture and other features that make movement from one seating arrangement to another possible. In some instances, however, teachers will be confronted with situations that severely limit this possibility. For example, some science laboratories and shop classes have fixed tables that make moving furniture impossible. Some drama and English classes may be held in the school's theater with fixed seating. These conditions require special problem solving on the part of teachers. Some experienced science teachers have students stand in a U-shape during discussion sessions; drama teachers and some elementary teachers have their students sit on the floor. The specifics of the classroom space and the teacher's own personal preferences certainly are strong considerations when making planning decisions about use of the space prior to a discussion.

Conducting Discussions

For whole-class discussions to be successful, some rather sophisticated communication and interaction skills are needed on the part of both teachers and students. It also requires norms that support open exchange and mutual respect. The syntax for most discussions consists of five phases: establishing set, focusing the discussion, holding the discussion, bringing it to a close, and debriefing. These five phases are summarized in Table 12.5. As discussion leader, a teacher also is responsible for keeping the discussion on track by refocusing student digressions, encouraging participation, and helping to keep a record of the discussions. In some instances, teachers have students serve as discussion leaders. All of these behaviors are described in some detail in the following sections.

> **As discussion leader, a teacher should focus the discussion, keep it on track, encourage participation, and keep a visible record of it.**

Establish Set and Focus the Discussion. Many classroom discussions are characterized by talk and more talk, much of which has little to do either with the main aims of the lesson or with encouraging student thinking. An effective discussion, just like an effective demonstration, is clearly focused and to the point. At the beginning, teachers must explain the purposes of the discussion and get students set to participate. They should also pose a specific question, raise an appropriate issue, or present a puzzling situation associated with the topic. As described previously, essential questions are thought provoking and intellectually challenging and are those most likely to get students engaged. Stating the focus question or issue clearly is one key to getting a good discussion started. Another way to establish set and spark student interest is to relate the beginning discussion question or focus to students' prior knowledge or experiences. Notice how the teacher in Figure 12.4 focuses her discussion.

Table 12.5 *Syntax for Holding Discussion*

Phase	Teacher Behavior
Phase 1: Clarify aims and establish set.	Teacher goes over the aims for the discussion, gains students' attention, and gets them ready to participate.
Phase 2: Focus the discussion.	Teacher provides a focus for discussion by describing ground rules, asking an initial question, presenting a puzzling situation, or describing a discussion issue.
Phase 3: Hold the discussion.	Teacher monitors students' interactions, asks questions, listens to ideas, responds to ideas, enforces the ground rules, keeps records of the discussion, and expresses own ideas.
Phase 4: End the discussion.	Teacher helps bring the discussion to a close by summarizing or expressing the meaning the discussion has had for him or her.
Phase 5: Debrief the discussion.	Teacher asks students to examine their discussion and thinking processes and the meaning the discussion had for them.

Figure 12.4 *Focusing the Discussion*

"Today, let's focus our discussion on global warming. First, I would like you to recall what you remember from the video I asked you to view last night and the various points of view presented in that video. Then let's consider specifically how strong the scientific evidence is to support or negate the threat of global warming."

Hold the Discussion. As a whole-class discussion proceeds, many circumstances can get it off track. In some cases, students will purposely try to get the teacher off the topic, as, for instance, when they want to talk about last Friday's ball game instead of the causes of World War I. Talking about Friday's game is fine if that is the objective of the lesson, but it is not appropriate if the aim is to encourage student reasoning about military conflicts.

A second example of wandering is when a student expresses an idea or raises a question that has little or nothing to do with the topic. This happens often, particularly with students who have trouble concentrating in school. It is also likely to happen with younger students who have not been taught good listening and discussion skills.

In both instances, effective teachers acknowledge what students are doing—"We are talking about last Friday night's game" or, "You say your father had a good time in New York last weekend"—and then refocus the class's attention on the topic with a comment such as, "Talking about the game seems to be of great interest to all of you. I will let you do that during the last five minutes of the class period, but now I want us to get back to the question I asked you" or, "I know you are very interested in what your father did in New York, and I would love it if you would spend some time during lunch telling me more. Right now we want to talk about. . . ." There is fine line between keeping the discussion on track and providing needed flexibility to encourage student engagement and independent thinking.

> Effective discussion leaders acknowledge students' off-track remarks and then refocus their attention to the topic at hand.

Random Calling. Recall that the traditional IRE discourse pattern described earlier consisted of the teacher asking a question followed by a student raising his or her hand and responding. Several observers (Lemov, 2010; McTighe & Wiggins, 2013) recommend that sometimes teachers should abandon the practice of calling on students who have their hands raised and replace it with **random calling.** This communicates to students that everyone should be expected to be ready to answer a question. Several variations of this practice have been described and include:

- Drawing students' names from a hat or fishbowl.
- Jumping around the room, but making sure everyone is called on during the lesson.
- Having a student who has just responded to a question select the next student to respond.

Keeping Records. Verbal exchanges during a discussion proceed more orderly if teachers keep some type of written record of the discussion as it unfolds. Writing students' main ideas or points of view on the chalkboard, flip charts, or electronic devices provides this written record. Or it may consist of constructing conceptual webs that illustrate the various ideas and relationships.

A dilemma faced by beginning teachers in keeping a discussion record is how much detail to include and whether or not all ideas should be written down. These decisions, obviously, depend on the nature of the students involved and the purposes of the discussion. When a teacher is working with a group that lacks confidence in discourse skills, it is probably a good idea to write down as much as possible. Seeing many ideas on the chalkboard, flip chart, or interactive whiteboards provides a public display of the many good thoughts that exist within the group and can encourage participation. With a more experienced and confident group, the teacher may want to list only key words, thus affording a more open exchange of ideas and opinions.

> Discussion proceeds in a more orderly fashion if some type of visible written record is kept as the discussion unfolds.

If the teacher has asked students specifically for their theories or ideas about a topic, it is important to list all ideas and treat these equally, regardless of their quality. However, if questions focus on direct recall of right answers, then only right answers should be recorded.

Enhancing Teaching and Learning with Technology

Taking Your Discussions Online with Blogs and Social Networks

The emergence of the Internet and social media has made it possible for people to talk with one another in ways never before imagined. Every day, millions of people around the world, young and old, enter "Weblogs," "discussion forums," and "social networks" to talk and listen to one another. Sometimes this exchange is between people who know one another; sometimes it is between strangers. Regardless, the phenomenon highlights the centrality of discourse in human communities and the popularity of online interactions.

Teachers can use the popularity of online interaction among youth to accomplish some of the traditional goals for classroom discussions as well as to enrich their in-class discussions in ways not possible in pre-Internet times. Currently, the more technology-savvy teachers use e-mail, social networks, and Weblogs to help facilitate online discussions. Here are some examples. Rosen (2010) reported about trigonometry and humanity teachers who set up online discussion groups on Facebook and told students in their classes that they had to make at least one comment on the topic under consideration. These teachers were amazed at the amount of online discussion that took place, that so much of it occurred after midnight, and that it continued into the classroom the following day. Teachers who have developed personal or class Weblogs and then require students in their classes to respond to the blog in general or to provocative questions that have been posed have demonstrated similar results.

It seems that online interaction motivates some students to continue talking about important topics after the class is over. This increases learning time beyond the confines of the classroom. Online discussions can also increase participation, an important goal emphasized throughout this chapter. Some students, particularly those who are shy, say things online that they would never say in class (see Panza, Poytthast, & Cathey, 2006; Rosen, 2010; West, 2012). Finally, some students prefer this type of exchange because they don't have to respond immediately, as they do in face-to-face discussions. They can take time to think about a topic and compose their thoughts before responding. They can also engage more freely in topics that are controversial and require lively debate.

It is important to recognize that academic online discussions are different than the interactions students may be having with their friends on Facebook or Twitter and that effective discussion will not happen automatically. It is important for teachers to encourage, guide, and facilitate

"For more information on what I did this summer, be sure to check out my website at www.funinsun.com."

Copyright © Charles Almon. Reprinted with permission.

online discussions just as they do face-to-face discussions. To encourage and facilitate online discussions:

- *Teach students how to use online discussions.* Most students (even younger ones) are familiar with chatrooms, social networks, and other kinds of online interactions; some, however, are not. Just as with face-to-face discussions, students need to be taught requisite discussion skills and expectations for interacting online.

- *Deal with the logistics of online discussions.* For younger children, teachers may want to begin online discussions in their school's computer lab or in their own classrooms. This in-school effort then can expand slowly, perhaps with each student contributing to an online discussion at least once per week. It is reasonable to expect older students to use their own computers or those available at school or the public library and to contribute on a regular basis to discussion topics. Many teachers treat online discussions held out of class like they treat other types of homework.

- *Control the pace of online discussions and encourage broad participation.* Just as in face-to-face discussions, online discussions can become fast-paced and dominated by a few students. Reminding students to slow down and requiring those with comments to symbolize a raised hand with an asterisk are means to control pace and participation.

- *Use small groups.* Again, as with face-to-face discussions, teachers can divide the students into teams, have them work together on particular projects, and then have them communicate as a team with other teams through class Weblogs or social networks.
- *Keep track about what is going on.* Scan all the student comments, pick out one or two that bring up especially interesting issues, and respond to these. Then, send out a general communication to the whole class telling students to read particular comments and respond to them.
- *Use a student leader.* Sometimes teachers like to designate one or two students to facilitate and summarize the online discussion for the class. Create a topic with the directions "Student leader, please post topic here" and let the leader post his or her own original discussion question.

Teachers need to be aware that there may be some negative aspects to online discussions. When students engage each other face-to-face, they can attend to the nuances of body language and observe the emotions that many topics generate, particularly those that are controversial and sensitive. These constraints are absent in online discussions, thus

requiring "virtual etiquette." Shelia Harbet (2002) proposed the following simple rules for online discussions:

- Respect each other's viewpoints.
- Don't shout (ALL CAPS).
- Don't use profanity.
- Don't flame (put down someone or his or her ideas).

When teachers use social networks, such as Facebook, they need also to decide to what degree they should "friend" their students. Most observers (Hamblin & Bartlett, 2013; Richardson, 2010; Rosen, 2010) recommend a "no friend" policy or to proceed with caution. It is better to keep the online teacher–student relationship confined to academics and to remain outside the social aspect of students' lives. Some teachers, however, report that they cannot reach many students unless they enter into a close personal and authentic relationship with them.

Finally, teachers and parents must also be aware of the potential for students to hide behind their computer monitors, never acquiring the skills to be effective in face-to-face situations.

Listening to Students' Ideas. A favorite discussion technique used by many teachers at the high school and college levels is "playing the devil's advocate." Teachers using this technique purposely take the opposite point of view from that being expressed by individual students or groups of students. Even though this approach can create lively exchange between a teacher and a few of the more verbal students, it does not work well with younger students or with many older students who lack good verbal and communication skills. Debate and argument arouse emotions, and despite their motivational potential, may divert the students' attention from the topic. They also cause many less-articulate or shy students to shrink from participation. If the teacher's goal is to help students understand a lesson and extend their thinking, then the teacher should listen carefully to each student's ideas. In this case, the teacher should remain nonjudgmental and inquiry-oriented, rather than challenging or argumentative. Being authoritative, it seems, reduces dialogue and participation (Smith & Connolly, 2005).

Free and open discussion is enhanced when teachers listen carefully and nonjudgmentally to students' ideas.

Using Wait-Time. Earlier we discussed how some teachers do not give students sufficient time to think and to respond. There are probably several reasons for this. One is the strong cultural norm in our society against silence. Silence makes many people uncomfortable and, consequently, they jump in to keep the conversation moving. Another is that waiting for student responses can be perceived by teachers as threatening to the pace and momentum of a lesson. Additionally, silence or waiting can give uninvolved students opportunities to start talking or otherwise misbehave. Although many contextual conditions influence wait-time, the general recommendations are for teachers to practice waiting at least three seconds for a student's response, to ask the question again or in a slightly different way if there is no response, and never to move on to a second question without some closure on the first. The amount of wait-time

In most circumstances, teachers should practice waiting at least three seconds for a student's response.

Being responsive to student ideas encourages participation.

should probably be less for direct recall questions and more for questions aimed at higher-level thinking and more complex content. After a student response, teachers should also wait a sufficient time before moving on.

Responding to Student Answers. When students respond correctly to teachers' questions, effective teachers acknowledge the correct answer with brief affirmations such as, "That's right," "Okay," or "Yes." They do not spend time providing overly gushy praise. Most teachers learn these behaviors quite quickly. However, responding to incorrect or incomplete responses is a more complicated situation. The guidelines described in Chapter 8 are repeated here:

1. *Dignify* a student's incorrect response or performance by giving a question for which the response would have been correct. For example, "George Washington would have been the right answer if I asked you who was the first president of the United States."
2. Provide the student with an *assist,* or prompt. For example, "Remember, the president in 1828 was also a hero in the War of 1812."
3. Hold the student *accountable.* For example, "You didn't know President Jackson today, but I bet you will tomorrow when I ask you again."

Student thinking can be extended by teacher actions that review student ideas, ask for alternative ideas, and/or seek clarification or supporting evidence.

Responding to Student Ideas and Opinions. Although the art of questioning is important for effective discussions, other verbal behaviors by teachers are equally important, especially those for responding to students' ideas and opinions. These are responses aimed at getting students to extend their thinking and to be more conscious of their thinking processes. Statements and questions such as the following provide illustrations on how to do this:

• Reflect on student ideas:
  "I heard you say. . . ."
  "What I think you're telling me is. . . ."
  "That's an interesting idea. I have never thought of it in quite that way. . . ."
• Get students to consider alternatives:
  "That's an interesting idea. I wonder, though, if you have ever considered this as an alternative. . . ."
  "You have provided one point of view about the issue. How does it compare with the point of view expressed by . . . ?"
  "Evelyn has just expressed an interesting point of view. I wonder if someone else would like to say why they agree or disagree with her idea?"
  "Do you think the author would agree with your idea? Why or why not?"
• Seek clarification:
  "I think you have a good idea. But I'm a bit confused. Can you expand your thought a bit to help me understand it more fully?"

- Label thinking processes and ask for supportive evidence:
  "It sounds to me like you have been performing a mental *experiment* with these data."
  "You have made a very strong *inference* from the information given you."
  "Can you think of an *experiment* that would put that hypothesis to a good test?"
  "What if I told you (give new information)? What would that do to your *hypothesis?*"
  "That's an interesting position. What *values* led you to it?"
  "If everyone held the *judgment* you just expressed, what would the result be?"

Expressing Opinions. Many beginning teachers are uncertain about whether or not they should express their own ideas and opinions during a discussion. Although teachers do not want to dominate discussions or make it appear that they are the only ones with good ideas, expressing ideas appropriately can be beneficial. It provides opportunities for teachers to model their own reasoning processes and to show students the way they tackle problems. It also communicates to students that the teacher sees himself or herself as part of a learning community interested in sharing ideas and discovering knowledge. However, as described previously, talking too much or displaying too much authority and expertise can have the dynamic of dampening student participation.

Having Fun. Finally, teachers can keep students engaged by making discussions interesting and fun. Experienced teachers employ a variety of strategies for this purpose. Marzano (2007) has included the following:

- Demonstrate enthusiasm and passion toward the discussion topic.
- Engage students in friendly controversy, but remind students what "friendly" means as different ideas are expressed and debated.
- Provide opportunities for students to talk about themselves.
- Make question asking into a game such as the popular television show, *Jeopardy.*

End the Discussion. As with other types of lessons, discussions need to be brought to proper closure. Effective teachers do this in a variety of ways. In some instances, they may choose to summarize in a few sentences what has been said and try to tie various ideas together or to relate them to the larger topic being studied. In other instances, teachers may want to close the discussion with a short presentation highlighting new or previously studied information. Some teachers ask students to summarize the discussion by posing a final question such as, "What is the main thing you got from our discussion today?" or, "What do you think was the most provocative point made during our discussion?"

Debrief the Discussion. From time to time, discussions should be debriefed. Here, the focus is not on the content of the discussion but on the way the discussion proceeded. To conduct a successful **debriefing,** teachers must teach students the differences between the discussion itself and the debriefing and then pose questions such as: "How do you think our discussion went today? Did we give everyone a chance to participate? Did we listen to one another's ideas? Were there times when we seemed to get bogged down? Why? What can we all do next time to make our discussion more stimulating or provocative?"

Diversity and Differentiation

Adapting Discussions for Diverse Learners

Even under the best of circumstances, it is difficult to obtain good discussions characterized by open and honest communication. Student diversity presents a particular set of opportunities and challenges. On one hand, when students differ in their cultural backgrounds, experiences, gender, and outlooks, classroom discussions create opportunities for them to learn from one another. What could be better? On the other hand, differences among students can also lead to silence and unproductive misunderstandings. Effective teachers know that to be successful in classroom discussions, they must be sensitive to cultural and gender differences, and they must create alternatives to the traditional IRE discourse model.

Discourse Gender Differences. Gender accounts for important differences in discourse patterns in classrooms. Considerable research (Gilligan, 1982; Tannen, 1990, 1994) illustrates how men and women speak and listen in different ways and how they have different aims for their communicative acts. Males are socialized for public speaking, and females are socialized for private speaking (Tannen, 1990). Girls are socialized to be passive and caring and to defer to males in public discourse. Kramarae and Treichler (1990) illustrated how this socialization finds its way into mathematics classrooms. Young women in their study were more prone to listen and to make statements about the "learning process," whereas young men talked a lot and focused their comments on ideas. Young women placed importance on "mutual support" and "collaboration" as contrasted to young men who placed priority on individual expertise, debate, right answers, and elaboration of abstract concepts. Although gender differences may be changing, the traditional IRE discourse model, with its focus on competition and correct ideas, reflects the natural and socialized discourse patterns of males more than it does females and can make classrooms a "chilly climate" for females. It has also led to a situation wherein boys are called upon more often than girls, a practice that seems to persist regardless of teachers' good intentions. (See David's story on the Online Learning Center.)

Race and Class Differences. Race and class likewise account for significant differences in classroom discourse and communication. Individuals are socialized first in their families. Here, we are taught at a very early age the forms of communication politeness, the appropriateness and inappropriateness of particular gestures, as well as when and where to speak. The traditional IRE discourse pattern found in classrooms stems from middle-class values and it represents a discourse pattern incongruous to many Asians, African Americans, Native Americans, and students from low-SES backgrounds. Thus, many students who have been socialized with communication patterns different from the dominant form found in schools are disadvantaged and often choose to exclude themselves from the communication system altogether (see Burbules & Bruce, 2001; Delpit, 1988, 1995; Ladson-Billings, 1992, 1995a, 1995b). As with gender, teachers have been shown to interact differently with students who are culturally or socially different. They ask them fewer questions, give them less time to respond, and provide them with less praise and encouragement (Delpit, 1988; Good & Brophy, 2003; Ladson-Billings, 1995a, 1995b, 2010).

There are *no* simple solutions for adapting discussions to meet the diverse needs of all students, and warnings provided about cultural stereotyping in Chapter 2 need to be repeated here. Students are not just boys or girls, African Americans or Hispanic, affluent or poor. They are combinations of all these features. Remember this important fact when you consider the following guidelines:

Guideline 1: *Systematically monitor your own patterns of asking questions, using wait-time and providing praise.* This is very important because teachers have been shown to be unaware of the impact of their discourse patterns on students. Most teachers say they treat all students fairly and the same. Like the case of David, described in the *Action Research Resource* found on the Online Learning Center, teachers will continue to focus their attention in traditional ways even when confronted with data of differential treatment. Most do this *not* because they believe in differential treatment, but because they are unconscious of their actions.

Guideline 2: *Become familiar with students' backgrounds, customs, values, and dialects.* Every classroom is going to have a different mix of students, so there is no guideline to meet every situation. However, effective teachers learn about the culture of their students through study and by seeking ways of interacting in nonschool settings with parents and other adults in the school's community.

Guideline 3: *Explore with students what your communication and interactions mean to them.* Teachers can obtain valuable information about discourse patterns during debriefing sessions. Ask students, "What did you like and dislike about our discussion?" "Did our discussion allow you to participate on an equal footing with other students?" "What can I do to make you feel more comfortable the next time we have a discussion?" "More engaged?"

Guideline 4: *Help each student experience communication success.* Discussion and communication skills are learned through practice just like any other skill. Using techniques such as the "think-pair-share," "buzz groups," or "beach ball" (described later in this chapter) helps slow down the pace of discussion and allow every student practice opportunities for making contributions without having to compete with the students who are more dominant and verbal.

Guideline 5: *Create and foster alternative discourse patterns.* Unfortunately, the IRE discourse pattern is the primary contributor to teachers' differential treatment of students. Changing this traditional pattern through the use of such structures as "think-pair-share," "dyads," and "small group" will broaden participation and enhance the quality of discussions.

Check, Extend, Explore

Check
- What are the major planning tasks of preparing for classroom discussion?
- What are the five phases of a discussion? What kinds of teacher behaviors are associated with each?
- What significant variables should teachers consider when choosing a seating plan for discussion?
- What actions can teachers take when conducting discussions to facilitate cultural and gender differences?

Extend
- Do you agree or disagree that playing "devil's advocate" is an effective way to have good classroom discussions? Go to the "Extend Question Poll" on the Online Learning Center to respond.

Explore
- Go to the Online Learning Center at www.mhhe.com/arends10e for links to Web sites related to *Planning and Conducting Discussions.*

Managing the Learning Environment

Many of the management tasks described in previous chapters also apply to discussion lessons. For example, pacing the lesson appropriately and dealing quickly and decisively with misbehavior are both essential teacher management behaviors when conducting a discussion. However, the most important management tasks are those aimed at improving discussion and discourse patterns in the classroom: teaching students specific discussion skills and establishing classroom norms that support productive discourse patterns. Several skills and norms are critical. In this section, skills and strategies to broaden participation, to promote interpersonal regard, and to heighten classroom thinking are described. Underlying the presentation is the premise that if discussion and discourse are to improve substantially, and to improve student understanding and higher-level thinking. rather dramatic changes in the classroom discourse patterns must occur.

Slow the Pace and Broaden Participation

An often-heard statement of inexperienced teachers is, "I tried to hold a discussion, but no one said anything." It is not uncommon for discussions, even those led by experienced teachers, to follow a pattern in which the teacher's questions are all answered by less than a half dozen of the twenty-five to thirty students present. Remember the rapid discourse pattern described by Rowe earlier in this chapter? To broaden participation and get real discussions going requires substantial changes to this limited pattern of discourse. The pace must be slowed down and the norms about questioning and taking turns modified as well as using alternatives to whole class discussion formats. Following are strategies that work and are used by experienced teachers.

Think-Pair-Share. The **think-pair-share** strategy created by Lyman (1981) was described in Chapter 10 as a cooperative learning structure that increased student participation. It is also an effective way to slow down the pace of a lesson and extend student thinking. This is true because it has built-in procedures for giving students more time to think and to respond and can affect the pattern of participation. For a description of the three-step think-pair-share strategy, return to Chapter 10.

Buzz Groups. The use of **buzz groups** is another effective means of increasing student participation. When using buzz groups, a teacher asks students to form into groups of three to six to discuss ideas about a particular topic or lesson. Each group assigns a member to list all the ideas generated by the group. After a few minutes, the teacher asks the recorders to summarize for the whole class the major ideas and opinions expressed in their group. Buzz groups, like think-pair-share, allow for more student participation with the learning materials and make it difficult for one or a few class members to dominate discussions. Using buzz groups can change the dynamics and basic patterns of classroom discourse and are easy for most teachers to use.

Beach Ball. A third technique, *beach ball,* is particularly effective with younger students for broadening participation and promoting one person to talk at a time. The teacher gives the ball to one student to start the discussion with the understanding that only the person with the ball is permitted to talk. Other students raise their hands for the ball when they want a turn. *Time tokens* and *high talker tap out*, described in Chapter 10, are two other activities teachers can use to broaden classroom participation patterns.

Increase Interpersonal Regard and Understanding

An open and honest communication process is perhaps the single most important variable for promoting positive classroom discourse and discussion. Fortunately, the way discourse occurs in classrooms can be greatly influenced by a teacher's leadership, particularly if he or she teaches skills that promote worthwhile **interpersonal communication** as well as a positive regard for it among students.

Because communication is essentially a process of sending and receiving messages, effective communication requires the sender of a message to express clearly what he or she intends to communicate and the receiver to interpret that message accurately. In reality, however, the message a person intends to send often is not the one the other person receives. The meaning intended in the sender's mind may not be accurately expressed or may be expressed in a manner that does not fit the receiver's prior experiences. Whenever either of these conditions occurs, a *communication gap* develops.

Two simple, but important, communication skills can be taught to help reduce communication gaps. One, the paraphrase, promotes active listening on the part of message receivers; the other, the I-message, provides help to the senders of messages as they strive to communicate their ideas and feelings clearly.

Paraphrase. Paraphrasing is a skill for checking whether the intended receiver of a message understands the ideas being communicated. Paraphrasing is more than word swapping or merely saying back what another person says. It answers the question, "What exactly does the sender's message mean to me?" It asks the sender to verify the correctness of the receiver's interpretation. The sender's statement may convey specific information, an example, or a more general idea, as shown in the following examples:

Example 1
Sender: I'd sure like to own this book.
You: *(being more specific)* Does it have useful information in it?
Sender: I don't know about that, but the binding is beautiful.

Example 2
Sender: This book is difficult to use.
You: *(giving an example)* Do you mean, for example, that it fails to cite research?
Sender: Yes, that's one example. It also lacks an adequate index.

Example 3
Sender: Do you have a book on teaching?
You: *(being more general)* Do you just want information on that topic? I have several articles about it.
Sender: No, I want to find out about cooperative learning.

I-Message. The I-message is a communication skill consisting of a message sender describing the behavior of an event, particularly an event that has caused a problem, and expressing the feelings triggered by the event. The behavior should be reported without evaluation. Feelings should be described in words as accurately as possible and should be owned by the person experiencing the feeling, normally by starting with "I." Here are two examples:

Example 1
Behavior: You have asked us to *read two pages* of a passage in a five-minute time frame.
Feeling: I feel very *inept and overwhelmed* because I can't read the passage in the amount of time allowed.

Example 2

Behavior: Marvin, the last three times I tried to express my ideas, you *interrupted* me. Feeling: I feel very *anxious* when you do this and it makes me cautious about talking in class.

Teachers can learn and model these skills in their classrooms. They can also teach them directly to students, just as they teach many other skills. Direct instruction, described in Chapter 8, provides an appropriate strategy for teaching communication skills initially.

Use Tools That Highlight Discourse and Thinking Skills

Lyman and McTighe were particularly interested in the ways that visual tools and aids can be used by teachers.

Frank Lyman and James McTighe have written extensively about the use of teaching tools, particularly visual ones, that help teachers and students learn discourse and thinking skills (Lyman, 1986; McTighe & Lyman, 1988).

Visual Cues for Think-Pair-Share. The think-pair-share discussion strategy described previously is not easy for students to use at first. Old habits, such as responding to teacher questions before thinking or blurting out answers without waiting, are difficult to change. Lyman and teachers working with him have developed various ways of teaching students how to employ think-pair-share, particularly how and when to switch from one mode to another. A favorite strategy is to make and use **visual cuing** devices such as those illustrated in Figure 12.5.

Teaching specific discourse skills is no different from teaching content-specific skills or social skills. Direct instruction, which requires teachers to demonstrate and model the skill being taught and to provide time for students to practice the skill and receive feedback on how they are doing, is the best approach to use.

Figure 12.5 *Cues for Using Think-Pair-Share*

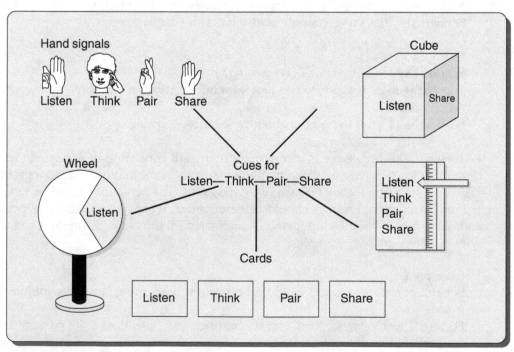

Source: After Lyman (1985), p. 2.

Assessment and Evaluation

As with the other teaching approaches, there are assessment and evaluation tasks for teachers to perform following a discussion. One is considering how a particular discussion should be followed up in subsequent lessons; the other is grading.

Follow-Up Discussions

Experienced teachers make both formal and mental notes for themselves following discussions. Sometimes these notes pertain to the content of the discussion and help determine subsequent lessons. For example, perhaps a discussion identifies some serious gaps in students' knowledge about a topic. Learning this might prompt a teacher to plan a presentation on a particular topic that came up in the discussion or to find suitable reading materials to assign students. A discussion can also identify aspects of a topic in which students are particularly interested. Teachers use the information they gain during discussions to plan lessons that will take advantage of this natural interest. The conduct of the discussion itself will give the teacher information about the strengths and weaknesses of students' thinking processes as well as the group's ability to engage in purposeful dialogue. Future lessons can then be planned to strengthen areas targeted for improvement.

Another aspect of following up a discussion is obtaining formal information from students about what they thought of the discussion and their role in it. The rating scale illustrated in Figure 12.6 can be an effective tool for gathering this type of assessment information.

Grading Classroom Discussions

Grading classroom discussion can pose a perplexing problem for many teachers. On one hand, if participation is not graded, students may view this part of their work as less important than work for which a grade is given. Remember the "work for grade exchange" concept described in Chapters 4 and 6? On the other hand, it is difficult to quantify participation in any satisfactory way. The questions teachers are

Two ways to grade a discussion are to award bonus points for student participation and to have students do a reflective writing assignment based on the discussion.

Figure 12.6 *Discussion Rating Scale*

What do you feel about the discussion we had today?

Directions: Make a √ in the space that best reflects your experiences.

Everyone participated

| _____Most of the time | _____Some of the time | _____Not very much |

My personal participation

| _____More than I wanted | _____About right | _____Less than wanted |

Quality of our discussion

| _____Excellent | _____Average | _____Poor |

Quality of my participation

| _____Excellent | _____Average | _____Poor |

confronted with when they try to grade discussions are, "Do I reward quantity or quality?" "What constitutes a quality contribution?" "What about the student who talks all the time but says nothing?" "What about the student who is naturally shy but has good ideas?"

There are two ways experienced teachers have confronted this grading dilemma. One is to give bonus points to students who consistently appear to be prepared for discussions and who make significant contributions. If this method is used, it needs to be discussed thoroughly with the class and opportunities provided that allow each student equal access to the bonus points available. This approach, however, should be used sparingly because, as described in Chapter 6, academic grades should *not* in most situations be tied to nonacademic factors such as good behavior or participation.

A second way to grade discussions is to use the discussion as a springboard for a reflective writing assignment. The grade in this instance is given not for participation but for the student's ability to reflect on the discussion and put in words what the discussion meant to him or her. When students know they are responsible for a post-discussion reflective essay, this approach, when properly conceived and managed, can heighten student attention during the discussion and extend student thinking about the discussion after it is over. The obvious disadvantage of using this type of assignment is the time required to read and assign grades to the essays. Another drawback is that teachers are never sure whether this type of assignment assesses what students learn in the discussion or just assesses their writing abilities.

Classroom Discourse Patterns: A Final Thought

Although most teachers agree that classroom discussions are an important part of the learning process, actual discussion time is often quite limited.

There is almost universal agreement among scholars, researchers, and many experienced teachers that for real learning to occur, a different discourse pattern than the one currently found in many classrooms must be established. When asked about how they are going to teach, most beginning teachers will attest to the importance of providing opportunities for students to discuss important topics and to exchange ideas with each other and with the teacher.

Yet, year after year, classroom observers say this is not happening. Teachers continue to dominate the talk that goes on in classrooms by presenting information and giving directions for students to follow. When they ask students questions, most of them are the kind that require direct recall rather than higher-level thinking. If students don't answer immediately, the teacher asks another question or calls on another student. All of this takes place at a very rapid pace. We know from research that teacher dominance of classroom discourse patterns and the rapid pace of this discourse are harmful. We also know that slowing down the pace of discourse and using different discourse patterns such as think-pair-share and asking essential questions will produce more and better student thinking and understanding.

If this is true, why is it so difficult to change the discourse patterns in classrooms? Are there some underlying causes for this phenomenon? Do students really want to participate in discussions? Perhaps it is easier to sit and listen. Do teachers really want to have discussions? Perhaps it is easier just to talk. Will your generation of teachers accomplish the changes so many have talked about?

Check, Extend, Explore

Check
- What are the key features of the learning environment for classroom discussions?
- What factors should teachers consider when they think about how to assess student learning in classroom discussions?

Extend
- Why do you think it has been so difficult to change discourse patterns in most classrooms?
- Do you think most students really want to participate in classroom discussions? Go to the "Extend Question Poll" on the Online Learning Center to respond. Do you think it is fair to factor participation in discussions into a student's report card grade?

Explore
- Go to the Online Learning Center at www.mhhe.com/arends10e for links to Web sites related to *Learning Environments and Assessment of Classroom Discussion.*
- Do a Google search on classroom discussion. Pick out a couple Web sites with guidelines for holding effective discussions. How do the recommendations differ from those in *Learning to Teach?*

Reflections from the *Classroom*

Why Won't They Talk?

For the third day in a row, you have begun your science lesson by tossing out a provocative and challenging question. It has been your hope that you would be able to get a lively discussion going. Instead, you are met with deadly silence. Two or three students try to respond, but the others just sit there staring at you or looking down at their desks. You are embarrassed by the silence, but, more important, you are frustrated because your favorite classes when you were a student were those in which you could participate in lively debate. You believe strongly that effective teachers are those who have lively discussions in their classrooms.

You ponder this situation and ask yourself, "What's wrong? Perhaps my students are just a bunch of kids who don't care about science and care even less about talking about it. Perhaps everyone in my class is shy. Or perhaps I am doing something wrong."

Spend some time reflecting on this situation and then compare your thoughts with the following comments from experienced teachers. Approach the situation from the perspective closest to the grade level or subject area you are preparing to teach. When you are finished, write up your reflections and include them as an exhibit in your professional portfolio.

Jason O'Brien
Sacred Heart Academy, 3rd through 5th Grades, Diocese of St. Petersburg, FL

Every student, whether they admit it or not, wants to feel like he or she has a voice. If I am not getting students to respond to my questions, I would rethink the questions that I am asking. If teachers start a discussion by asking very complex questions and nobody responds, they should try starting with easier questions and working toward higher-level questions. It also helps to ask questions that are relevant to the students' lives. If you are asking a science question about the polarity of the Earth, ask students about a compass that you are holding in your hand. Once students have had success answering simple questions and you have praised them for it, they will become comfortable and less afraid to take a chance answering more difficult questions. Body language is also very important. It is crucial for students to know that you care about their answers. Do not cut off student answers. Use simple prompts such as, "Can you elaborate on that?" to facilitate higher-level thinking. If you are still getting no response, model the behavior to the students. Have them write down school-related questions for you to answer. Demonstrate what an appropriate answer looks like. A technique I sometimes employ at the beginning of the year to ensure total class participation is to hand out a token to each student. Every time a student answers a question, I take his or her token. I tell the students that I expect everyone to have given me their token by the end of class. Or you can do the opposite and devise a system of rewards for good answers. The important thing is to keep trying. With a little hard work, you can have a class full of eager respondents!

Dennis Holt
Tampa Bay Technical High School, 11th and 12th Grades, Hillsborough, FL

Classroom discussion and debate can be among the liveliest teaching experiences that you will encounter. However, on occasion, the discussion will fall flat, or worse, not occur at all. To diminish this situation, there are several actions that you can take in advance and during the discussion. First, make sure your students are prepared to discuss the subject matter. Having students complete a graphic organizer or take a short set of notes on the key points brought up in the lesson should help them focus their thoughts and facilitate discussion. You can also provide students with speaking prompts that will allow them to overcome unfamiliarity with the subject matter or just plain nervousness.

I would suggest that you consider placing students in mixed ability pairs to smooth the progress of the discussion. Begin by posing fairly simple questions to the students. Allow them time to discuss the question with each other and frame a short written response. Next, call on pairs of students at random to share their answers with the entire class. Start with fairly basic questions and spiral upwards to increasingly more difficult concepts. This allows students time to build upon their own and shared knowledge in a step-by-step manner. This method is often commonly referred to as "think, pair, share." You may also wish to provide different pairs of students with conflicting or controversial information in order to spur debate.

Whether you are engaged in a science, math, language, or social studies lesson, you will often find that the "experts" in the field have disagreements over the subject (evolution comes to mind). Providing your students with this conflicting information allows them to discover for themselves that knowledge and understanding often progress out of differences of opinion. A word of caution: In advance of any discussion or debate, particularly when the subject is controversial, make sure that your students have had a chance to practice the art of listening to each other respectfully and exchanging ideas productively. Posting and modeling classroom rules for discussion and debate can spare hurt feelings and foster an atmosphere where everyone's opinions are important.

Summary

Provide an overview of classroom discussion and explain its appropriate use.

- Discourse and discussion are key ingredients for enhancing student thinking and uniting the cognitive and social aspects of learning.
- When experienced teachers refer to classroom discourse, they often use the label *discussion* to describe what they are doing. Classroom discussions are characterized by students and teachers talking about academic materials and by students willingly displaying their thinking processes publicly.
- Discourse can be thought of as externalization of thinking and has both cognitive and social importance.
- The primary instructional outcomes of a discussion lesson are to improve student thinking, to promote involvement and engagement in academic materials, and to learn important communication and thinking skills.
- The general flow or syntax for a discussion lesson consists of five major phases: provide objectives and set; focus the discussion; hold the discussion; end the discussion; and debrief the discussion.
- The structure of the learning environment for discussion lessons is characterized by open processes and active student roles.

Describe the theoretical foundations of classroom discussion and summarize the research that supports its use.

- Studies for a good many years have described how discourse patterns in most classrooms do not afford effective dialogue among students or promote much discovery or higher-level thinking.
- A substantial knowledge base exists that informs teachers on how to create positive discourse systems and to hold productive discussions. Studies also provide guidelines about the types of questions to ask and ways to provide appropriate pacing for students to think and to respond.
- Most classroom discourse proceeds at too rapid a pace. Teachers can obtain better classroom discourse by slowing down the pace and giving themselves and their students opportunities to think before they respond.

Explain how to plan and use classroom discussion, including how to adapt its use for students of differing backgrounds and abilities.

- An important planning task for a discussion lesson is deciding on which approach to use. There are several kinds of discussions. Major approaches include using discussion in conjunction with other teaching models; recitation discussions; discovery or inquiry discussions; and discussions to clarify values and share personal experiences.

- Other important planning tasks for teachers to consider include determining the purposes of the discussion; being aware of students' prior knowledge and discourse skills; making plans for how to approach the discussion; and determining the type of questions to ask.
- Placing students in circles or using U-shaped seating arrangements facilitates classroom discussions.
- Primary tasks for teachers as they conduct a discussion consist of focusing the discussion; keeping the discussion on track; keeping a record of the discussion; listening to students' ideas; and providing appropriate wait-time.
- Teachers should respond with dignity to students' ideas. They should help students extend their ideas by seeking clarification, getting students to consider alternative ideas, and labeling students' thinking processes.
- Teachers must be aware of gender discourse differences as well as those that stem from race and class. To be effective, they must adapt discussions to meet the diverse language patterns of their students.

Describe how to implement a learning environment conducive to using classroom discussion.

- In general, discussion and classroom discourse patterns can be improved if teachers slow the pace and use methods to broaden participation and if they teach students to try to understand one another and have high interpersonal regard for each other's ideas and feelings.
- Teaching students communication skills (paraphrasing and I-messages) can enhance the quality of classroom discourse and students' regard for each other.
- Specific visual tools such as the think-pair-share cuing device can help students learn discourse and thinking skills.
- For students to become effective in the discourse system and during specific discussions requires teaching students discourse skills just as directly as academic content and other academic skills are taught.

Describe appropriate ways to assess student learning consistent with the goals of classroom discussion lessons.

- Assessment and evaluation tasks appropriate for discussion consist of finding ways to follow up on discussions and to evaluate students for their contributions.
- Teachers use two ways to evaluate discussions: giving bonus points to students who consistently appear to be prepared and who make contributions and grading reflective writing assignments based on the content of the discussion.

Speculate about why classroom discussion has not been embraced by large numbers of classroom teachers and make predictions about its use in the future.

Key Terms

buzz groups 460	discussion 438	random calling 453
circle seating pattern 451	divergent questions 448	recitations 439
cognitive dissonance 447	elaborative interrogation questions 448	think-pair-share 460
convergent questions 448	essential questions 449	U-shaped seating pattern 451
debriefing 457	interpersonal communication 461	visual cuing 462
discourse 438	level of difficulty 442	wait-time 443

Interactive and Applied Learning

Study and Explore

- Access your Study Guide, which includes practice quizzes, from the Online Learning Center.

Observe and Practice

- Listen to audio clips on the Online Learning Center of Vickie Williams (K–8 reading specialist) and Ian Call (tenth-grade world history) talking about classroom discussion in the *Teachers on Teaching* area.

Complete **Practice Exercise 12.1**, Planning for a Discussion, including

- Write Objectives and Prepare a Questioning Strategy
- Plan for Implementation of the Discussion

- Differentiate for Two Students
- Assess Student Learning
- Reflect on Planning a Discussion Lesson

Complete the following additional **Practice Exercises** that accompany Chapter 12:

- Practice Exercise 12.2: Using Concept Maps to Plan a Discussion
- Practice Exercise 12.3: Using Various Levels of Questioning
- Practice Exercise 12.4: Use of Wait-Time
- Practice Exercise 12.5: Teaching Dilemma: Student Participation
- Practice Exercise 12.6: Teaching Dilemma: Discussions and Planning
- Practice Exercise 12.7: Reflecting on Classroom Discourse Patterns

Portfolio and Field Experience Activities

Expand your understanding of the content and processes of this chapter through the following field experience and portfolio activities. Support materials to complete the activities are in the *Portfolio and Field Experience Activities* area on your Online Learning Center.

1. Complete the **Reflections from the Classroom** exercise at the end of this chapter and use the recommended reflective essay as an exhibit in your portfolio about your views on classroom discussion. **(InTASC Standard 8: Instructional Strategies)**

2. **Activity 12.1: Assessing My Discussion and Discourse Skills.** Assess your current understanding and skills to plan and conduct classroom discussion lessons. **(InTASC Standard 8: Instructional Strategies)**

3. **Activity 12.2: Observing Classroom Discussions.** Observe experienced teachers using classroom discussion. **(InTASC Standard 8: Instructional Strategies)**

4. **Activity 12.3: Observing Student Participation in Discussion.** Observe a classroom discussion and keep track of patterns of student participation. **(InTASC Standard 8: Instructional Strategies)**

5. **Activity 12.4: Observing Teacher Use of Questions and Wait-Time.** Observe an experienced teacher and see how she or he asks questions during a discussion and uses wait-time. **(InTASC Standard 8: Instructional Strategies)**

6. **Activity 12.5: Portfolio: Demonstrating Executive Control of Questioning.** Develop a set of questions to guide a classroom discussion and practice using them with a small group of students. Arrange your work as an artifact in your portfolio. **(InTASC Standard 8: Instructional Strategies)**

Books for the Professional

Mayer, S. (2012). *Classroom discourse and democracy: Critical pedagogical perspectives.* New York: Peter Lang Publishing.

McTighe, J., & Wiggins, G. (2013). *Essential questions: Opening doors to student understanding.* Alexandria, VA: Association for Supervision and Curriculum Development.

Pagliro, M. (2011). *Exemplary classroom questioning: Practices to promote higher level thinking and learning.* Lanham, MD: Rowman and Littlefield.

Richardson, W. (2010). *Blogs, wikis, podcasts, and other powerful Web tools for classrooms.* Thousand Oaks, CA: Corwin Press.

Rothstein, D., & Santana, L. (2011). *Make just one change: Teach students to ask their own questions.* Cambridge, MA: Harvard Education Press.

Walsh, J., & Sattes, B. (2011). *Thinking through quality questioning: Deepening student understanding.* Thousand Oaks, CA: Corwin Press.

Zwiers, J., & Crawford, M. (2011). *Academic conversations: Classroom talk that fosters critical thinking and content understandings.* Portland, ME: Stenhouse Publishers.

Learning Goals

After studying this chapter you should be able to

Introduction and Rationale	Define what is meant by connecting and using multiple approaches to teaching and differentiating instruction and explain why each is important.
Connecting and Using Multiple Approaches	Explain how to use multiple approaches to instruction to accomplish particular learning goals, to provide variety, and to meet the needs of all learners.
Differentiated Instruction	Describe the rationale and major features of instructional differentiation, and discuss the strategies that support the differentiated classroom.
Management and Assessment in the Differentiated Classroom	Describe how to implement a learning environment conducive to instructional differentiation and explain special concerns about assessment and grading created by this type of classroom.

Reflecting on Multiple Approaches and Differentiation

Attending to the needs of all learners though differentiation and the use of various and multiple approaches to teaching is the topic of this chapter. As you prepare to read the chapter, think for a moment about your own experiences in K–12 or college classrooms.

* What type of learner were you? Were you more successful with some types of learning activities than others? Which approaches used by teachers did you like best? Least?

* Did you prefer teachers who used the same approach day after day? Or did you appreciate teachers who had a rich repertoire of approaches and who provided variety?

* Were you able to do all the activities and assignments pretty much as initially designed by the teacher? Or did you require some aspects of a lesson to be adapted for you and your learning needs?

Now think about your philosophy of education.

- Do you think it is best for most students to use the same book? Reach for the same goals? Experience the same curriculum? Or should students be given particular materials and activities based on their unique learning needs?
- Do you believe that students will learn in the same way and pretty much at the same rate as defined by grade-level placements, or will their pace vary?
- Is it important to provide choice for learners about what they should learn and how, or is it important for all learners to master a standard curriculum?

 Go to the Online Learning Center at www.mhhe.com/ arends10e to respond to these questions.

Introduction and Rationale

A major theme throughout *Learning to Teach* has been how best to attend to the needs of students and to help all learners succeed. This was a challenge for teachers in the nineteenth century when public education was conducted in rural, one-room schools where a single teacher was expected to teach reading, writing, arithmetic, history, and spelling to a group of students ranging in age from 6 to 16. It has remained a challenge into the twenty-first century, regardless of efforts to remove variations and to reduce heterogeneity by adopting age-graded classrooms, ability grouping, and a more standardized curriculum.

Teachers are expected to help all students learn, and strategies and tactics are available to make this possible.

Today, standard practices in most schools require teachers to follow a prescribed curriculum within the confines of traditional age and grade-level divisions. However, unlike earlier eras when teachers were minimally accountable for student learning and when many students were not in school or in regular classrooms, it is no longer acceptable to allow students to drop out or to tolerate low levels of achievement. As a society we expect all children and youth to be in school and to be placed in regular classrooms. We also hold teachers accountable for the success of every student. This is the unique challenge of teaching at the beginning of the twenty-first century and will likely remain so for most of your teaching career. Fortunately, a variety of strategies and tactics are available that provide teachers with opportunities and tools to meet this challenge.

Connecting and using multiple approaches is the practice of employing several different approaches to teaching over the course of a lesson or unit.

The aims of this chapter are threefold. First, a rationale for connecting and using multiple approaches to instruction will be provided, and specific examples about how teachers employ multiple strategies over the course of a unit of work will be described in some detail. Second, the rationale for instructional differentiation will be discussed, and strategies that support the differentiated classroom will be provided. Finally, the chapter concludes with a discussion of unique issues associated with classroom management and assessment posed in classrooms characterized by instructional variety and differentiation.

Differentiation is the practice of adapting instruction to meet the needs of particular students.

Connecting and Using Multiple Approaches

For many years, arguments raged among educators, as well as citizens and policymakers, about which approaches to instruction were the most effective—for example, lecture versus discussion or inductive versus deductive teaching. Today the debate about superiority of one approach over another continues as proponents in the so-called reading wars argue for phonics versus whole language or submersion versus bilingual approaches for English language learners. Teacher-centered as contrasted to student-centered models of instruction are also often debated by advocates on both sides. As pointed out in Chapter 1, this debate is futile and misdirected. No single approach is consistently better than another. The choice to use a particular approach depends on the goals teachers are trying to achieve, the characteristics of particular learners, and community values. This means that teachers must be ready to employ *multiple approaches of instruction* and to connect them in creative ways over the course of a lesson or unit of instruction.

In Parts 3 and 4 of *Learning to Teach,* six instructional approaches were introduced, and detailed descriptions were provided on how to plan for and use each model. These models can be used separately by teachers. More often, however, various strategies are used in tandem over a time span of several days or weeks and sometimes even within a particular lesson. This section begins by returning to a theme introduced in Chapter 1, the importance of repertoire for effective teaching. It then explores when and how to use various combinations of approaches to accomplish the goals and objectives of particular lessons and/or units. Finally, two examples are provided to illustrate how an elementary and a secondary teacher combine a variety of teaching strategies to provide instructional variety and to match their use to accomplish valued learning goals.

Repertoire and Choice

Repertoire refers to the number and variety of approaches and strategies teachers have at their command. A teacher's repertoire is similar to the number and different types of music pieces a pianist can play or how many tools a carpenter can use effectively. Two or three songs is an insufficient repertoire for an individual who plays in a piano bar, just as the ability to use only a screwdriver and a hammer is not enough to make a carpenter effective. The same is true for teaching; effectiveness (and satisfaction) is enhanced only when teachers can use a fairly large number of different approaches to teaching.

Effective teachers are able to use a variety of teaching approaches.

Check, Extend, Explore

Check
- Briefly contrast the expectations today for helping all students learn to those held for teachers in earlier eras.
- Define what is meant by "connecting and using multiple approaches to instruction."
- Define what is meant by "differentiating instruction."

Extend
- Thinking back to your own schooling, to what degree do you agree or disagree that teachers sufficiently differentiated instruction? To what extent were they committed to helping each student learn to his or her potential? Go to the "Extend Question Poll" on the Online Learning Center to respond.

Explore
- Go to the Online Learning Center at www.mhhe.com/arends10e for links to Web sites related to *Differentiation of Instruction.*

Effective teachers use a variety of approaches to teaching during the course of a lesson or unit of work.

A teaching repertoire consists of the number of approaches and tactics teachers have at their command that can be used to ensure every child will learn.

Even when teachers have command of a variety of approaches and strategies, making wise choices about which ones to use can be a complex undertaking. Remember that all the approaches described earlier were designed to increase student learning by accomplishing particular learning outcomes. For instance, presentation teaching is effective for helping students acquire and process declarative knowledge. Direct instruction aims at helping students learn important skills and procedural knowledge, whereas concept attainment supports conceptual development and higher-level thinking. The student-centered approaches of cooperative learning, problem-based learning, and classroom discussion can lead to academic learning. However, they are more effective in promoting problem solving and enhancing students' social skills. They also are good for helping students learn the importance of metacognition and for taking responsibility for their own learning.

The goals and objectives of particular lessons or units of work are the first factors to consider when selecting a particular approach. Context and the nature of the students are others. Sometimes the choice is rather straightforward because one instructional approach is clearly the most appropriate for a given purpose. For instance, it is hard to imagine students learning how to use a microscope through classroom discussion, whereas a lesson using direct instruction that includes guided practice would help them accomplish this important skill in a short period of time. However, presenting information on the attributes of a novel would not necessarily lead students to have positive attitudes toward literature or to apply situations in the novel to their own lives the way a classroom discussion would.

Choice of approaches becomes more difficult under certain circumstances. Sometimes several approaches can help achieve the same goals or purposes. For example, spelling can be taught using direct instruction (whole-class drill and practice), but the use of cooperative learning groups also has been shown to be effective. Direct and inductive approaches for teaching concepts have been shown to accomplish desired results, as has problem-based learning. Both small-group and whole-class discussions are effective ways to encourage students to share their ideas with others and to provide teachers with windows into their thinking processes. When several approaches can achieve the same outcome, choice often is made on the basis of teacher preference ("I like using classroom discussion") or on secondary purposes ("I think it is better for students to work together than alone").

A lesson's goals and student characteristics are major factors in selecting which teaching approach to use.

Choice of approaches or strategies is made even more complicated because students in any given classroom have diverse interests, learning styles, and abilities. Some students learn effectively from lecture and presentation, but may resist participation in cooperative learning groups or classroom discussions. Other students have great difficulty becoming engaged in teacher-centered lessons, but will spend endless hours engaged in a project of their own choosing.

Finally, like most things in life, variety adds spice to teaching and learning. Lack of variety causes students and their teachers to become bored and resistant to sustained engagement. You can conjure up instances of teachers or professors who did the same thing day after day—always lectured to you, always had you answer the questions at the end of the chapter, always held discussions that involved participation by a few, or always had you "get into groups." Using the same approach over and over often renders it ineffective. Accomplished teachers know to include two or three different approaches and activities in any given lesson and know variety can make a unit of work much more engaging and interesting.

> **Variety in instructional approaches keeps both students and teachers interested and engaged in learning.**

Connecting and Using Multiple Approaches: Two Classroom Scenarios

Let's now explore how a variety of approaches might be used by visiting two classrooms, one a sixth-grade science classroom, the other a tenth-grade classroom in American literature. Both classrooms are taught by accomplished teachers who have created effective learning communities and who have motivated their students to invest thoroughly in classroom tasks and activities. Both teachers have command of an extensive repertoire of teaching strategies.

Sixth-Grade Science Ecology Unit: Wetlands

This unit has been planned for a sixth-grade, mixed-ability classroom in the Midwest taught by Mr. Avi Ornstein. Mr. Ornstein, an experienced teacher, has considerable background in science and has been appointed by the principal to help coordinate science instruction in the school.

Context

The students in the class represent several racial and ethnic groups: 55 percent white, 23 percent African American, 13 percent Hispanic, and 9 percent Asian. This school is in a district that has implemented total inclusion. As a result, Mr. Ornstein has three students who have been identified as gifted and talented, two students who have learning disabilities, one who is visually impaired, and another who is confined to a wheelchair.

Overview

Wetlands are critical features of the environment. However, many adults and young people do not have a firm grasp of what wetlands really are and the important role they play in our lives. Wetlands are found in all parts of the United States, so a unit on this topic allows study of local environments as well as larger ecological issues. Study of wetlands, though normally considered a science curriculum, can also be integrated into units on civics, sociology, art, and literature. There are vast library and Internet resources available for teachers to use in a unit on wetlands.

Curriculum Standards

The Common Core Standards have not been fully developed and approved for science. The following standards have been adapted from the science standards for fifth to seventh grades in the state of Kansas (see Kansas State Science Standards).

1. *Standard 1: Science as Inquiry.* Student will develop abilities to do scientific inquiry, be able to demonstrate how scientific inquiry is applied, and develop understanding about scientific inquiry.
2. *Standard 6: Science in Personal and Environmental Perspectives.* Student will apply process skills to explore and

develop an understanding of personal health, population, resources and environment, and natural hazards.

Mr. Ornstein's Unit Objectives

1. Students will identify how questions can be answered through scientific investigations and show that they can conduct scientific investigations using appropriate tools and techniques to gather, analyze, and interpret data about wetlands.
2. Students will understand the impact of human activity on resources and on the environment, show that they can investigate the effects of human activity on wetlands, and make decisions based on knowledge of benefits and risks.
3. Students will recognize patterns of natural processes and human activities (channeling a stream, putting a shopping center on wetlands) that can contribute to natural hazards.

Resources

Collections of science and environmental materials housed in the school library, resource center, selected Internet sites, and the local prairie pothole wetlands.

Length of Unit

This unit will extend over thirteen days.

Day by Day

Now let's see how Mr. Ornstein approaches this unit on a day-to-day basis and how he uses multiple teaching strategies to meet state standards and his own unit objectives. Notice also how he adapts each lesson to meet the needs of particular students.

Lesson 1: PowerPoint Presentation on Local Wetlands Day (Presentation—1 Day)

Mr. Ornstein has chosen to begin his wetlands unit by helping students see what we mean when we refer to an area as wetlands.

Day 1: Mr. Ornstein points out that there are basically two types of wetlands: coastal (sometimes called tidal) and inland (nontidal or freshwater). Bogs, marshlands, prairie potholes, swamps, and fens are also words used to refer to different types of coastal and inland wetlands. This introduction is followed by a motivating and provocative PowerPoint presentation consisting of slides Mr. Ornstein has taken of past and present wetlands in the local region. The PowerPoint presentation also provides an overview of the unit and lists several questions for which answers will be sought:

1. How are wetlands defined and where do we find them? In the United States? In the Midwest?

2. Why are wetlands important?
3. How are the different types of wetlands similar? How do they differ?
4. How do wetlands protect the environment and affect wildlife?
5. What human activities in our local community over the past decade have affected wetlands and the wildlife that depend on this type of environment?

Adaptation of Lesson 1. A special assistant will visit the classroom and assist the student who is visually impaired. Mr. Ornstein will make available a handout on his presentation for his students with learning disabilities. They will go over the main ideas later in the day assisted by the special education teacher.

Lesson 2: Hopscotch Wetlands (Experiential Activity and Discussion—1 Day)*

Lesson Overview. An important understanding reflected in the state standards and Mr. Ornstein's objectives is the relationship between wetlands and certain kinds of wildlife and how human activity such as development can affect both. This lesson aims at getting students to see the relationship between wetlands and migratory birds. It makes use of a motivating outdoor activity followed by whole-class discussion.

Day 2: Outside Activity Procedures

1. Mr. Ornstein begins this lesson by taking students to the parking lot where he has drawn a large-sized hopscotch course.
2. He instructs students to line up at the beginning of the course and asks them to pretend they are migratory birds starting their journey northward. He tells students that each square represents a wetland between Texas and Canada.
3. All students are successful on their first migration. Now Mr. Ornstein tells students he is a developer. He has built condos on two wetlands areas. He puts an X on two squares. Students start another migration but cannot step foot on destroyed wetlands. He keeps repeating this procedure (eliminating wetlands) until most or all the students fail to make the migration.

Day 2: Whole-Class Discussion. Mr. Ornstein concludes this lesson with a whole-class discussion. He returns to the classroom and has students sit in a horseshoe seating

---

*The activity was adapted from one designed by the Columbia Education Science Center (http://ofcn.org/cyber.serv/academy/ace/sci/cecsci/cecsci045.html).

arrangement. He uses the following questions to guide the discussion:

1. Why did some birds die earlier than others? Why did the rest of the birds die?
2. How does this game represent or not represent real-life migration?
3. What might happen if wetlands were replaced?
4. Why is it important to save wetlands?

Adaptation of Lesson 2. Special arrangements were made to assist the participation of a student who is confined to a wheelchair.

Lesson 3: Wetland Investigations: Jigsaw (Cooperative Learning—3 Days)

Lesson Overview. The lesson uses cooperative learning groups and is spread across three days. This approach has been chosen because Mr. Ornstein wants students to work together and to conduct their own investigations in regard to different types of wetlands.

Day 3: Getting Started and Forming Teams. Mr. Ornstein introduces the lesson and gets students ready to learn by explaining that over the next three days they are going to work in cooperative learning groups and do a "Jigsaw" on wetlands. He reminds them of the Jigsaw approach (see Chapter 10) and how they will be involved with two teams: their "home" team and their "expert" team. He gives them the handout explaining what they are to do. The home teams listed in Figure 13.1 are heterogeneous groups.

Day 4. Students are instructed to work in expert groups to develop their understandings of the particular type of wetlands assigned to their group.

Day 5. Students return to their home teams and teach other students what they have learned in their expert groups.

Mr. Ornstein concludes the lesson by having each home team report to the whole class what the team has learned and to ask and discuss questions they may have about the four types of wetlands.

Adaptation of Lesson 3. Mr. Ornstein has grouped students heterogeneously, and he has taught students that each person should contribute according to his or her strengths. He has also made available special materials to assist students who have learning difficulties and to expand understanding of his gifted students.

Lesson 4: Wetlands Projects (Problem-Based Learning—7 Days)*

Lesson Overview. An important standard and objective for this unit is to help students develop their investigative and analysis skills. Problem-based learning is an excellent strategy to accomplish this objective.

Day 6. Mr. Ornstein begins this lesson by providing students with the problem-based learning assignment sheet found in Figure 13.2.
Day 7. Field trip to prairie potholes.
Days, 8, 9, and 10. Students work in teams and investigate their particular problem.
Days 11 and 12: Student presentations.

1. Presentations by zoologist and botanist teams, followed by whole-class discussion.

*This activity is adapted from lessons created by Aleida Perez and Patty Torres (Webquest titled Wet and Wild Woodlands; http://www.pavenet.org/FTP/Users/all_share/Cohort5/5319Project/TorresWebQuest/).

Figure 13.1 *Wetlands Jigsaw Activity*

Over the next three days we will be working in cooperative learning groups to learn more about wetlands. I have divided the class into four home teams.

Home Team 1	Home Team 2	Home Team 3	Home Team 4
Jack	Miguil	Sun Ho	Joan
Marsha	Marisa	Susie	Won
Jon	Avi	Sanford	Krista
Donnette	Kev	Maria	Judith
Amy	Kim	Christine	Anthony

Expert teams will be formed around the five topics described below. You will need to appoint one of your home team members to each of the expert groups.

Expert Group #1: Your job is to develop thorough understandings of bogs.
Expert Group #2: Your job is to develop thorough understandings of marshes.
Expert Group #3: Your job is to develop thorough understandings of prairie potholes.
Expert Group #4: Your job is to develop thorough understandings of swamps.
Expert Group #5: Your job is to develop thorough understandings of fens.

2. Presentations by surveyor and animal rights activist teams, followed by whole-class discussion.

Adaptation of Lesson 4. As with the Jigsaw, Mr. Ornstein has grouped most students heterogeneously and has taught students that each person should contribute according to his or her learning strengths. He has also made available special materials for students who have learning difficulties and for his gifted students. For this particular project, Mr. Ornstein has allowed three students who have special interests and abilities to work together and do an advanced Webquest on wetlands and associated issues. He also has made appropriate arrangements so all students can participate fully and safely in the field trip.

Lesson 5: Unit Assessment (Assessment—1 Day)

Day 13. Mr. Ornstein concludes the wetlands unit with a teacher-made test covering wetlands facts and concepts and the investigative topics associated with the unit. He also has included a performance assessment.

Adaptation of Lesson 5. Mr. Ornstein has designed two versions of his test, one for most students and another for students who have learning disabilities. The special education teacher is available to help the students who have learning disabilities, and an assistant reads the test to the student who is visually impaired. The students who worked on the Webquest are asked to write a short reflective essay on what they learned.

Figure 13.2 *Problem-Based Learning Project Assignment Sheet*

Your job over the next few days will be to work in teams to investigate various aspects of the Estes Prairie Potholes found in our area. You will work in one of four teams and each team will assume one of four different roles: zoologist, botanist, land surveyor, and animal rights activist.

Zoologist	Botanist	Land Surveyor	Animal Rights Activist

Zoologist: A zoologist is a specialist on animals. Your team's job is to become familiar with the different animals found in prairie potholes in general and specifically the ones in our area. Among other investigative tasks you should
- List the wildlife that inhabit prairie potholes.
- Illustrate at least two kinds of wildlife, perhaps one animal and one bird.
- Illustrate (visually or verbally) the relationships among the wildlife and the wetlands.

Botanist: A botanist is a person who is a specialist in plants and plant life. Your team's job is to become familiar with the different plants found in prairie potholes in general and specifically the ones in our area. Among other investigative tasks you should
- List the plants that inhabit prairie potholes.
- Illustrate at least two plants found in prairie potholes.
- Illustrate (visually or verbally) the relationships among the plants and the wetlands.

Surveyor: A land surveyor is a person who inspects land conditions to determine their environmental significance. Your team's job will be to inspect the physical characteristics of prairie potholes. Among other investigative tasks you should
- Research the common locations, landforms, and water types found in prairie potholes.
- Complete the data on the attached survey sheet.

Animal Rights Activist: An animal rights activist is a person who serves as an advocate for animal rights. Your team's job is to identify endangered species associated with all types of wetlands and suggest ways to protect them. Among other investigative tasks you should
- List endangered species associated with various types of wetlands.
- Create a banner or flyer that persuades the community to protect an endangered species in a particular wetland.

Once individuals have completed their investigations they should discuss what they have learned with their team members. Then combine the information and create a PowerPoint on a Web site to be shown to the whole class. Work will be assessed using the Wetlands PowerPoint Scoring Rubric.

High School Literature Unit: To Kill a Mockingbird

The following unit has been planned by Ms. DaSilva, an experienced and respected high school English teacher in a Riverside, California, suburb.

Context

Students in the school come mainly from middle-class homes but represent several racial and ethnic groups: 30 percent are white, 30 percent are Hispanic, and 25 percent are African American. Fifteen percent of the students are recent immigrants from Asia and Mexico.

Overview

Harper Lee's *To Kill a Mockingbird* became a favorite among high school literature teachers shortly after it won a Pulitzer Prize in 1960. The story is about a young girl, Scout, growing up in rural Alabama in the 1930s. Her idyllic childhood is challenged, however, when her father is assigned to defend a black man unjustly accused of rape. Use of the book has been challenged repeatedly by both the political right and left. However, it remains a favorite among English teachers and their students, because study of *To Kill a Mockingbird* allows analysis of many features of the modern novel (narrative voice, use of symbols, descriptive style, and the nature of the hero) as well as explorations of important and timeless social issues: conflict between children and adults, race and class, stereotyping, and intolerance.

Curriculum Standards

As this section of *Learning to Teach* is being revised, the English/Language Arts Common Core Standards have not been fully implemented across the country. The following standards used in the lesson have been adapted from the Common Core Standards for grades 9 and 10 as they are being designed and implemented by the state of California (see http://www.cde.ca.gov/index.asp). Note the overall standards being used as well as the specific learning objectives developed by the teacher for her unit on *To Kill a Mockingbird*.

Standard 3: Analyze how complex characters (e.g., those with multiple or conflicting motivations) develop over the course of a text, interact with other characters, and advance the plot or develop the theme.

>**DaSilva's Learning Objective 1.** Students will be able to describe characteristics of the main and subordinate characters in *To Kill a Mockingbird* and analyze their significant interactions.

Standard 5: Analyze how an author's choices concerning how to structure a text, order events within it (e.g., parallel plots), and manipulate time (e.g., pacing, flashbacks) create such effects as mystery, tension, or surprise.

>**DaSilva's Learning Objective 2.** Students will be able to explain how voice and choice of narrator affect the tone and plot in a novel.

>**DaSilva's Learning Objective 3.** Students will be able to recognize and discuss the importance of two literary devices: narrative voice and descriptive style.

Standard 4: Determine the meaning of words and phrases as they are used in the text, including figurative and connotative meanings; analyze the cumulative impact of specific word choices on meaning and tone.

>**DaSilva's Learning Objective 4.** Students will be able to discuss and express their own opinions on courage, prejudice, intolerance, justice, and discrimination. They will be able to relate these to actions in the novel and to their own lives.

Ms. DaSilva's Unit Objectives

1. Students will be able to describe characteristics of the main and subordinate characters in *To Kill a Mockingbird* and analyze their significant interactions.
2. Students will be able to explain how voice and choice of narrator affect the tone and plot in a novel.
3. Students will be able to recognize and discuss the importance of two literary devices: narrative voice and descriptive style.
4. Students will be able to discuss and express their own opinions on courage, prejudice, intolerance, justice, and discrimination. They will be able to relate these to actions in the novel and to their own lives.

Resources

Lessons will use the novel itself, information from Internet sites, and library resources.

Length of Unit

The unit will extend over twelve days.

Day by Day

Let's now see how Ms. DaSilva uses her repertoire of teaching strategies to translate her overall unit plans into daily lessons. It should be noted that students were asked to read the novel as homework the prior week, so they are somewhat familiar with the novel on the first day.

Lesson 1: Storytelling (Small-Group Activity and Whole-Class Discussion—2 Days)

Lesson Overview. Ms. DaSilva has chosen to launch her unit on *To Kill a Mockingbird* by getting students to consider the importance of common, everyday stories in literature and in their own lives.*

Day 1. To accomplish her objective, Ms. DaSilva has placed the following quotations from the novel at various locations around the room.

- "You're scared," he said. "You're too scared to even put your big toe in the front yard."
- "I realized I would be starting school in a week. I never looked forward more to anything in my life."
- "Lord, I thought, she's scared of a mouse."
- "Shut your eyes and open your mouth and I will give you a big surprise."
- "You never really understand a person until you consider things from his or her point of view."

1. Students are instructed to walk around the room until they find a quotation that "speaks" to them or one that is similar to something that has happened in their own lives.

2. Students who have gathered around the same quotation are instructed to work as a group. Each person tells his or her own story and then nominates one story to share with the whole class.

Day 2. After all groups have shared their stories, Ms. DaSilva holds a whole-class discussion focused with the following questions:

- What did the stories tell you about your own lives?
- Did we have similar stories as a class? Different?
- What do you anticipate about stories to be found in *To Kill a Mockingbird* from the quotations we considered today?

Adaptation of Lesson 1. All students participated in the group discussion; from past experiences Ms. DaSilva knows that some students are reluctant to participate in the group discussion. She makes special efforts to involve them and to make them feel comfortable speaking to the whole class.

*The lesson is adapted from English Online (http://english. unitecnology.ac.nz). Retrieved May 23, 2005.

Lesson 2: Narrative Voice (Cooperative Learning, Presentation, Discussion—2 Days)

Lesson Overview. The standards for this unit reflect the need to teach both the substance of *To Kill a Mockingbird* and particular literary features of the modern novel. Narrative voice is an important feature or device used by authors to let readers see the events and characters in a novel from a particular perspective. The following assignment and activity is aimed at helping students consider and understand "narrative voice."

Day 3: Ms. DaSilva begins this lesson by providing the following information to students on an overhead projector.*

Narrative Voice Activity

Because Harper Lee invites us to see the events of the novel and the people in it through Scout's eyes, a good deal is revealed about Scout by what she notices and reports, and the comments she makes as she tells her story. This puts the reader in an interesting position. We hear about what happens in such a way that we can form some opinions about the characters in the story but also about the narrator. By the end of Chapter 3, Scout has introduced the following people: Atticus, Dill, Boo, Chuck Little, Calpurnia, Mr. Radley, Caroline Fisher, Burris Ewell, Jem, Nathan, and Walter Cunningham.

Ms. DaSilva next asks students to work in four-member heterogeneous cooperative learning groups to accomplish the following tasks:

1. Put the list into order, according to which person Scout likes most, down to the person she likes the least.

2. Make another list of people whom Scout understands best down to those she understands the least.

3. Compare the lists and see in which ways they are different. How might the differences be explained? Some of the reasons will have to do with Scout's character; others may be due to her age.

4. Scout as narrator is a child, so we get a child's version of what is going on. Some events Scout cannot explain very well. As readers we are sometimes able to understand the meaning of certain events before Scout does. At other times we remain as confused as she is. How might the story and characters differ if Scout were 18 years old? How might that affect us as readers?

*Adapted from English Online (http://english.unitecnology.ac.nz). Retrieved May 23, 2005.

Figure 13.3
Descriptive Style

> The house was low, was once white with a deep front porch and green shutters, but had long ago darkened to the color of the slate gray yard around it. Rain rotted shingles dropped over the eaves of the verandah; oak trees kept the sun away. (p. 14)

> She appeals to a reader's sense of sight. Look at the number of words about color.

> The descriptions of actions (the verbs she uses) are really precise and vivid. The house is made to sound as if it's actively decaying ("dropped," "darkened" . . .)

> He was the filthiest human I had ever seen. His neck was dark gray, the backs of his hands were rusty, and his fingernails were black deep into the quick. He peered at Miss Caroline from a fist-sized clean space on his face. (p. 32)

> Burris is so dirty he has to "peer" as though the dirt makes it difficult for him to see.

Day 4

1. Cooperative learning groups are instructed to prepare short reports of the previous day's work that can be shared with the whole class.
2. Ms. DaSilva concludes this lesson with a brief presentation on "narrative voice" as a literary device and conducts a whole-class discussion on this topic. She stops intermittently and employs "think-pair-share" to encourage students to remain engaged in the presentation and to share their own ideas.

Adaptation of Lesson 2. Ms. DaSilva has grouped students heterogeneously into their cooperative learning groups and has taught students that each person should contribute according to his or her learning strengths. She has also made available special materials for students who have learning difficulties and for her gifted students. She has made handouts summarizing her presentation on Day 4 for students who need a little extra help.

Lesson 3: Descriptive Style (Cooperative Learning—1 Day)

Lesson Overview. Authors must give enough detail in a story so readers can see vividly what is going on. As with "narrative voice," it is important for students to understand this important literary feature.

Day 5. Ms. DaSilva begins this lesson by forming cooperative learning groups and asking group members to perform the following tasks:

1. Study the materials found in Figure 13.3.
2. Next, choose two other descriptions from the early chapters of *To Kill a Mockingbird* and make notes to explain what makes them vivid and memorable.

3. Write on newsprint a description of a person or place that your group knows well. Provide visual detail in three or four sentences and try to use Harper Lee's descriptive style as a model.

This lesson concludes with each group sharing its description with the whole class and a brief summary by Ms. DaSilva of descriptive style as a literary device.

Adaptations of Lesson 3. As with the previous cooperative learning activity, Ms. DaSilva has grouped students heterogeneously in their cooperative learning groups and has taught students that each person should contribute according to his or her capabilities.

Lesson 4: Discussion about the Novel (Whole-Class Discussion and Think-Pair-Share—3 Days)

Lesson Overview. Many literature teachers like to teach a particular novel by having students explore a variety of questions and issues by using whole-class discussions.

Days 6, 7, and 8. Over a period of three days, Ms. DaSilva poses questions similar to the ones listed below:*

1. In Scout's account of her childhood, her father Atticus reigns supreme. How would you characterize his abilities as a single parent? How would you describe his treatment of Calpurnia and Tom Robinson vis-à-vis his treatment of his white neighbors and colleagues. How would you typify his views on race and class in the larger context of his community and his peers?

*Source: Adapted from *To Kill a Mockingbird* Reading Guide (http://harpercollins.com/global_scripts/product_catalog/book_xml.asp?isbn=0060935464&tc=rg). Retrieved May 23, 2005.

2. *To Kill a Mockingbird* has been challenged repeatedly by the political left and right, who have sought to remove it from libraries for its portrayal of conflict between children and adults; ungrammatical speech; references to sex, the supernatural, and witchcraft; and unfavorable presentations of blacks. Which elements of the book—if any—do you think touch on controversial issues in our contemporary culture? In your community? Did you find any of those elements especially troubling, persuasive, or insightful?

3. What elements of this book did you find especially memorable, humorous, or inspiring? Are there individual characters whose beliefs, acts, or motives especially impressed or surprised you? Did any events in this book cause you to reconsider your childhood memories or experiences in a new light?

Adaptations of Lesson 4. All students participated in the whole-class discussion; from past experiences Ms. DaSilva knows that some students are reluctant to participate in the group discussion. She makes special efforts to involve them and to make them feel comfortable speaking to the whole class. She also uses "think-pair-share" (see Chapter 10) from time to time to make sure every student has discussion time.

Lesson 5: Exploring Timeless Social Issues (Group Investigation—3 Days)

Lesson Overview. *To Kill a Mockingbird* is a favorite novel among teachers not only because of its literary quality

but also because it addresses several themes and issues regarding the human condition that are as important today as they were nearly fifty years ago when the novel was written.

Days 9 and 10. Students are instructed to work in five cooperative learning groups. Each group will be asked to explore one of five themes and be prepared to share its interpretation with the whole group. Themes include *courage, prejudice, justice, intolerance,* and *discrimination.*

Students are instructed to create brief PowerPoint presentations of their interpretations and to include specific incidents from the novel and from their own lives that illustrate the theme. These PowerPoints will be used to guide group presentations.

Adaptations of Lesson 5. As with the previous cooperative learning activity, Ms. DaSilva has grouped students heterogeneously in their cooperative learning groups and has taught students that each person should contribute according to his or her learning strengths.

Day 11. Each group is asked to present and discuss its work to the whole class.

Lesson 8: Unit Assessment (Assessment—1 Day)

Day 12. Ms. DaSilva concludes her unit on *To Kill a Mockingbird* with a teacher-made open-response test covering particular features of the novel as literary form and specific aspects of Harper Lee's work.

Differentiated Instruction

This section is intended to introduce you to approaches of **differentiated** instruction. It will provide a perspective about instructional differentiation, define key characteristics of a differentiated classroom, and offer specific strategies that teachers can use to help reach all students.

Why Differentiate Instruction?

Two conditions prompt teachers to differentiate their instruction. One, society expects every child to be successful in classrooms characterized by diversity. Two, ability grouping, as traditionally practiced, has raised serious concerns.

Differentiating instruction consists primarily of adapting teaching to the abilities and needs of students who differ widely. They differ in their intellectual development and learning styles. They have multiple intelligences, and, as described in Chapter 2, within any single classroom teachers are likely to find a range of three to five years in ability differences along with widespread cultural and language diversity.

Grouping students by ability was the practice used traditionally for dealing with the diverse abilities and needs. In secondary schools classes were organized in particular subject areas for students, some of whom had more advanced abilities and others who had less. Tracking was and remains most prevalent in mathematics, but it also has been used in a variety of subject areas under the rubric of advanced placement. In elementary schools efforts to achieve more homogeneity sometimes resulted in creating whole classes of students grouped according to ability. More often, however, elementary teachers divided their students within a particular classroom into small instructional groups made up of different ability levels.

Ability grouping and tracking practices, however, came under attack in the 1970s and 1980s, mainly over concerns about equity and the negative effects ability grouping had on some students. Remember the "self-fulfilling prophecy" effects found in the Rist study (1970) described in Chapter 2. Several scholars and social justice advocates (Oakes, 1985; Rosenbaum, 1976; Slavin, 1987, 1990), among many others, argued that there was no clear evidence that ability grouping led to more effective learning, but more important, its use reinforced negative views about "race and class" and resulted in serious inequalities.

This criticism, according to Loveless (2013), led to a dramatic decline in the use of ability grouping between 1960 and 1990. In 1961, for example, 80 percent of elementary school teachers reported they grouped students by ability for reading instruction. By the 1990s, only 28 percent reported this practice. During the past decade, however, the trend toward *less* use of ability grouping seems to have been reversed and some types of ability grouping have regained favor among teachers. For instance, between 1998 and 2009 teachers reported that the use of ability groups for reading instruction increased significantly from 28 percent to 71 percent (see Yee, 2013; Loveless, 2013).

Currently the debate about grouping students by ability continues along the lines of *equity* and *effectiveness*. Social justice advocates continue to maintain that grouping and tracking practices stereotype students and are discriminatory, whereas many teachers report the need to group students by ability (at least some of the time) if they are to be *effective* in meeting the demands that every child will learn. It is likely that the use of ability grouping, in some form or another, will continue as you begin your teaching careers, particularly if teachers remain accountable for having every student master a prescribed curriculum within the confines of traditional age and grade-level divisions. The practice of differentiating instruction and flexible grouping as described below are attempts to minimize the negative effects of grouping while providing teachers with a means to provide meaningful instruction to a diverse range of students.

The Differentiated Classroom

Traditionally, many teachers taught all students the same subjects in the same way. Teachers in the differentiated classroom, however, strive to base instruction on student interests, needs, and readiness ("where the students are") and then use various teaching processes and instructional arrangements to ensure that students reach their potential. Table 13.1 compares processes and procedures in traditional and differentiated classrooms. These comparisons are helpful for understanding how curriculum and instruction in traditional and differentiated classrooms differ and the changes required of teachers who want to provide more differentiated instruction.

Essential Elements of Differentiation

To meet the challenges of diversity, teachers must find ways to differentiate their instruction so that each student can learn as much as possible. Carol Ann Tomlinson and her colleagues Jay McTighe (2010) and Marcia Imbeau (2013) have identified important elements of differentiation.

Check, Extend, Explore

Check
- Describe why it is important for teachers to have a rich repertoire of teaching practices.
- Discuss factors that should be considered when choosing a particular teaching practice or the use of multiple approaches to instruction.
- Provide examples for how particular approaches and strategies can be used over a unit of work to accomplish important standards and objectives.

Extend
- To what extent do you agree or disagree that teachers are more effective if they use multiple teaching practices as contrasted to sticking to one or two favorites? Go to the "Extend Question Poll" on the Online Learning Center to respond.

Explore
- Go to the Online Learning Center at www.mhhe.com/arends10e for links to Web sites related to *Adapting and Using Multiple Approaches to Instruction.*

Theories of multiple intelligences provide an important framework for thinking about ways for differentiating instruction.

In most regular classrooms, teachers are likely to find a range of three to five years in ability differences as well as differences in intelligences and learning styles.

Table 13.1 *Comparison of Key Features of Traditional and Differentiated Classrooms*

Traditional Classroom	Differentiated Classroom
Common assignments are the norm.	Multiple assignments are provided and used appropriately according to student needs and readiness.
Unitary view of intelligence exists.	Multiple intelligences are recognized.
Heavy reliance on textbooks and standard curriculum guides is followed.	A variety of print and nonprint resources are available within the confines of commonly accepted curriculum standards.
Common standards guide instruction and define mastery.	Standards are consulted but instruction is guided by student needs, readiness, and capabilities.
Assessment is used mainly to assess student achievement at end of lessons or segments of instruction; normally consists of a single form.	Assessment is frequent and ongoing and is an integrated aspect of instruction; a variety of assessment formats are used.

Source: Adapted from Danielson (1999, 2004).

Teachers who differentiate instruction know that it is important to focus on the essentials when deciding what to teach.

- **Focus on Essential Standards and Learning Objectives.** With time a very scarce resource as described in Chapter 3, it is crucial for teachers to focus on essential understanding and skills instead of covering many topics lightly.
- **Attend to Student Differences.** Students, as described previously, come to school with varying readiness, capabilities, interests, and needs. Teachers must remain aware of these differences and help each individual learn to his or her potential.
- **Integrate Instruction and Assessment.** For differentiation to be effective, assessment must be an integral part of instruction. As described in Chapter 6, it provides teachers with day-to-day information about what their students have learned and knowledge about when to move on to new content and skills.
- **Find Ways for All Students to Participate in Respectful Work.** Teachers should expect all students to meet essentials standards. However, assignments and work must be differentiated to fit the needs and readiness of particular learners. This type of differentiation should *not* result in watered-down or busy work, but instead in respectful work that is appropriately challenging.
- **Help Students Collaborate in Learning.** Effective differentiation can occur only in a classroom where planning and instruction is learner-centered, where students understand the importance of their input and their involvement in the planning process.
- **Balance Individual and Group Approaches to Learning.** As will be described in more detail in the next section, it is important for teachers to recognize both individual and group norms, needs, and approaches to learning.
- **Modify Content, Process, and Products.** Finally, Tomlinson (1999) and Shaklee and Castle (2008) have pointed out that there are three aspects of instruction that can be modified—content, process, and product—and that these modifications are based on students' interests, learning profiles, and abilities and their readiness (see Table 13.2).

Teachers can modify content, process, or product based on students' readiness, interests, and learning profiles.

Content in Tomlinson's model consists of the essential understanding and skills the teacher wants students to learn. *Process* describes the strategies and activities used to accomplish learning, and *products* are the assessments and artifacts students produce to

Table 13.2 *Ways to Modify Instruction*

Student Characteristics	Curriculum Elements		
	Content: Skills and Understandings	Strategies and Processes	Products and Assessments
Readiness to Learn			
Interests			
Learner Profile			

Source: This matrix was based on the work of Tomlinson (1999) and adapted by George Mason University professors Beverly Shaklee and Sharon Castle (2008).

demonstrate their learning. Student *readiness* to learn consists of their level of understanding in regard to particular content and/or their readiness to participate in certain kinds of activities. *Interest* stems from students' curiosity or passion for particular topics, whereas *learner profile* refers to their multiple intelligences and learning styles. Teachers can modify instruction on one or more of the curricular elements or student characteristics.

Instructional Strategies for Differentiating Instruction

A variety of instructional strategies are available for teachers who want to differentiate their instruction. Several of the major strategies are described below.

Differentiation Using Multiple Intelligences. As described previously, Howard Gardner has posited that intelligence is multiple rather than singular. Educators have applied his model in several ways. One way has been to design whole schools

Rich classroom environments facilitate the full range of human abilities.

around the model. These schools organize curriculum and teaching so that students are involved in a range of activities that involve them in the full range of human abilities.

A more modest application is when particular teachers design teaching strategies that help students build capacity in each of the eight intelligences. Examples of teaching strategies that might be used are listed in Table 13.3.

It is important that Gardner's theory of multiple intelligences not be misused.

Application of Gardner's multiple intelligence theory has the potential for helping differentiate instruction for a wider range of students and in turn helping develop a broader range of their abilities. It also helps teachers and educators personalize education by recognizing the array of human differences that exist. However, Gardner has cautioned educators about the misapplication of his theory (Gardner, 1998, as found in Woolfolk, 2013). He points out that every subject cannot be approached from the perspective of all the intelligences. Teachers who try to include every intelligence in every lesson are inappropriately using the model. He also observes that using a particular intelligence as a background for other classroom activities (playing music during math lessons) is a waste of time and can even distract from the main activity. He cautions against "grading" particular intelligences.

Curriculum Differentiation. For differentiation to work, often the curriculum itself must be modified. If students have different abilities, interests, and readiness to learn, content as found in textbooks and described in curriculum frameworks or common standards must be modified to match the needs of particular students. This may mean compacting the curriculum for some students while extending it for others. It also may mean providing some students more time to develop important understandings, while shortening time requirements for others. Teachers must focus on the essentials rather than covering everything lightly.

Curriculum differentiation poses challenges and dilemmas for teachers. On one hand, state legislative bodies have adopted common standards that all students are expected to meet. Teachers are held accountable for helping students meet these standards. On the other hand, experienced teachers and learning and developmental theorists know that students come to school with different life experiences and levels of development and different attitudes and dispositions for learning. So, what should teachers do? Should they teach to grade-level standards even though particular students in the class are not ready to learn what is being taught and others are ready for greater challenges? Or, should curricula be significantly modified for some students even if this means that they will not be prepared to meet predetermined standards? It is likely that issues associated with standardization versus differentiation will be with us for a long time. Effective teachers will find some type of integrated position—teach to the standards in a thinking environment but also be concerned that every student is making maximum progress given his or her background and unique learning characteristics.

Cooperative and problem-based learning allow students of varying abilities to contribute their own strengths to group efforts.

Cooperative Learning. Cooperative learning is an important strategy in the differentiated classroom. As discussed in Chapter 10, in cooperative learning, the teacher normally forms heterogeneous groups of students and provides for task differentiation within the various groups. Groups comprising various ability levels allow the full range of students to learn to work together, to use their varied learning strengths, and to contribute to the group as a whole on their own level. Cooperative learning

Table 13.3 *Teaching Strategies for Each of Gardner's Eight Types of Intelligences*

Intelligence	Teaching Strategies
Logical-mathematical	Play games of logic.
	Be on lookout for situations that inspire students to think about and construct understanding of numbers.
	Take students on field trips to computer labs, science museums, and electronic exhibits.
	Do math activities with students.
Linguistic	Read to children and have them read to you.
	Discuss authors of books with children.
	Visit libraries and bookstores.
	Have students keep journals.
Musical	Provide students with tape recorders.
	Give students opportunity to play musical instruments.
	Create opportunities for students to make music.
	Take students to concerts.
Spatial	Have a variety of creative materials for students to use.
	Have students navigate mazes and create charts.
	Take students to art museums.
	Go on walks with students and have them visualize where they are; draw maps of their experiences.
Bodily-kinesthetic	Provide students with opportunities for physical activity.
	Provide areas where students can play.
	Take students to sporting events or the ballet.
	Encourage students to participate in dance activities.
Interpersonal	Encourage students to work in groups.
	Help students develop communication skills.
	Provide group games for students to play.
	Encourage students to join clubs.
Intrapersonal	Encourage students to have hobbies and interests.
	Listen to students' feelings and give them sensitive feedback.
	Encourage students to use their imagination.
	Have students keep journals and scrapbooks of ideas and experiences.
Naturalist	Take students to science museums.
	Create a naturalist learning center in the classroom.
	Engage students in outdoor naturalist activities.
	Have students make collections of flora and fauna.

Source: Adapted from Santrock (2004, 2010).

Enhancing Teaching and Learning with Technology

Using Technology to Differentiate Instruction

Technology can be an enormous help for teachers who are striving to differentiate their instruction and to personalize learning. Many of the applications described here have been mentioned in previous chapters. They are repeated here but with a new focus.

The many and multiple modalities made available with computers and associated technologies can appeal to students with varying learning styles and preferences. For example, PowerPoint or smartboard presentations will appeal to students who are more visually oriented, whereas programs with interesting sound features may provide help for those who prefer getting their information through auditory channels. Technology can also be used to facilitate learning in the various multiple intelligences; for example, verbal skills can be enhanced by the ease with which computers allow revisions of written work, or interpersonal skills can be developed when students work on computers together in small groups or interact on social networks such as Facebook or Twitter.

For students with special learning needs, computers can assist teachers with record keeping often required by state, federal, or local agencies. An array of special programs can be found on the Internet that can be used for students who need a little extra help or who need lessons to be adapted into clearly defined steps or made more concrete. Many computer programs can be motivating for students who have trouble remaining engaged in other kinds of learning activities.

Similarly, computers and communication technologies can be a boon for working with gifted students. The Internet can connect talented students to university, museum, and research laboratory digital resources. Webquests afford inquiry in an endless array of topics. E-mail and social networks allow motivated students to share ideas with peers across the United States and around the world.

has also been a highly recommended strategy for teaching English language learners (ELLs) (Quiocho & Ulanoff, 2008; Slavin, 1990, 2012). In this context, cooperative learning provides ELL students with the opportunity to work with their peers to construct meaning and share understandings. This approach works because students involved in cooperative learning must engage in significant amounts of oral interaction while jointly negotiating meaning and solving problems.

Problem-Based Learning. Problem-based learning, described in Chapter 11, places students in active roles as they investigate puzzling situations and problems that lack clear answers. Students using this approach can investigate the problems in a variety of ways using their own approaches and resources. As with cooperative learning, problem-based learning allows students to contribute their own strengths, to use their own special talents, to identify problems of their own choosing, and to design projects that address these problems in authentic and challenging ways.

Compacting the Curriculum and Instruction. If students have a sound grasp of the knowledge and skills associated with particular lessons, teachers can compact the curriculum for these lessons. This normally means reviewing the content of the lesson quickly and then allowing some students to move on to more complex and higher-level ideas, concepts, and skills.

Tiered activities allow students with varying abilities to focus on essential understandings and skills but at different levels of complexity.

Tiered Activities. Teachers can also use what Tomlinson (2004) has called **tiered activities.** This allows all students to focus on the same understanding and skills, but at different levels of abstraction and complexity. When teachers use tiered activities, it is important that they increase the level of challenge for students who have special knowledge or skills in particular areas.

Dodge (2005) described how teachers can develop tiered assignments and proposes a three-step process:

Step 1: Develop an assignment for grade-level learners.

Step 2: Develop an assignment for students who are struggling and provide additional support to ensure their success in completing the assignment.

Step 3: Develop a challenging assignment for the more advanced learners. These assignments should stretch their level of functioning, not just add more work.

Independent Study and Learning Contracts. Independent assignments and learning contracts are additional strategies that challenge both gifted students and those with learning difficulties. The author used this strategy while teaching a course on the history of the Pacific Northwest to a group of ninth-graders. Two students in the class were incredibly bright. They had advanced analytical reasoning skills, were excellent writers, and were very well read in history. Instead of attending class, they went to the library at a local university a few blocks away. Their task, agreed upon in a learning contract, was to write their own version of the history of their community from the time the first settlers arrived in 1850 through 1900. They were to use only original sources. The product of their efforts was outstanding, and it was published in the local newspaper.

> **The use of learning contracts is an important strategy for challenging gifted students in the differentiated classroom.**

Use of Flexible Grouping in the Differentiated Classroom

One of the primary practices for differentiating instruction is the use of **flexible grouping.** Sometimes referred to as *within-class grouping* (Castle et al., 2007; Loveless, 2013; Tomlinson, 2004), this practice consists of keeping students in the regular classroom and putting them temporarily in smaller groups for specific subjects and activities, most often reading, writing, or mathematics.

> **Flexible grouping is the practice of putting students in smaller groups for specific subjects but keeping them within the same classroom.**

As described previously, the current popularity of flexible grouping has been in response to **ability grouping** practices of the past, where students were placed more or less permanently in special classes or small groups based on an initial assessment of their abilities. Teachers traditionally have supported this practice because they believe it helped them reduce diversity found in large classes and to better meet managerial challenges. The disadvantages of this type of ability grouping have been its negative effects on some students as well as teachers' tendencies to prepare lessons on the assumption of single abilities or readiness levels within the grouped classrooms.

> **Ability grouping is the practice of placing students in special classes or small groups based on an assessment of their ability to learn.**

For flexible grouping practices to be successful and not merely a return to ability grouping as practiced in the past, teachers must attend to several instructional and assessment matters.

1. *Accurate diagnosis of performance and prior knowledge.* It is critical that students be placed in small groups based on sound assessment data about performance and/or levels of prior knowledge. Misdiagnosis or information based on past performance will lead to many of the negative effects of more traditional ability grouping practices.

2. *Differentiation of curriculum and instruction.* Nothing is accomplished if teachers place students in small groups and then teach the same curriculum the same way to every group. Curriculum differentiation would include the type and amount of curriculum covered; instructional differentiation would include the pace of instruction and the models or teaching strategies used.

3. *Identification with the regular classroom learning community.* Students should be kept in their small groups for a limited amount of time so they keep their connections and relationship with all students in the regular classroom.

4. *Maintain temporary and flexible nature of the small groups.* Students should remain in particular groups only as long as needed to meet individual learning goals. Care should be taken not to have students in any group be stereotyped—known as the "smarties" or the "dummies," for example. The overall learning environment must help all students see that grouping practices are sensitive to individual needs and level of readiness to learn.

5. *Continuous assessment.* The key to successful placement and reassignment of students in small, flexible groups is the practice of continuous assessment. Student growth should lead to reassignment to a group doing more advanced work. Likewise failure to meet certain learning objectives should lead to reassignment to a small group where a student can find success.

6. *Meaningful and respectful work for students in all groups.* Some (Tomlinson, 2004) have observed that a classroom where flexible grouping is used requires a different type of classroom management. Teachers must be able to manage several groups involved with different learning activities simultaneously. It has been reported that some teachers accomplish this by providing students in the lower-level groups worksheets and drill and practice to keep them engaged. Although this may help solve the classroom management issue, it does not allow these students to engage in higher-level thinking activities, something they often need. The critical thing is that all students should be engaged in meaningful and respectful work.

Management and Assessment in the Differentiated Classroom

Classrooms where teachers are using a variety of approaches and where they are differentiating instruction require both minor and major adjustments in the ways these classrooms are managed and the ways student learning is assessed. These adjustments are the focus of this final section.

Classroom Management

Many of the general management guidelines described in Chapter 5 apply to the management of classrooms that are highly differentiated. For instance, it is always important for teachers to have a clear set of rules and routines, to keep lessons moving smoothly without disruption, and to deal with misbehavior quickly and firmly. Similarly, the guidelines for how to manage group work provided in Chapters 10 and 11 on cooperative learning and problem-based learning instruction also apply here. Some special management concerns for teachers who differentiate instruction are discussed below.

Managing a Multitask Environment. In differentiated classrooms, as in problem-based learning, multiple learning tasks occur simultaneously. Some student groups may be working on various subtopics in the classroom, others may be in the library, and still others out in the community or online. Students may be using interest centers where they work alone, in pairs, or in small groups on learning tasks tailored to their particular interests, abilities, and needs. To make a multitask environment work, students must be taught to work both independently and together. They must understand that they need to take responsibility for their own learning without the minute-by-minute supervision of the teacher and that the teacher always expects quality work from them.

Establishing Routines for Starting Work and for Making Transitions. Effective teachers develop routines for starting work and for making transitions from one learning task to another. Teachers should establish routines and instruct students on how to begin and end learning activities each day or period. This includes giving clear, concise directions to particular students to get them started and developing cuing systems to alert students and to assist them with the transition from one type of learning task to another. Clear rules are necessary to tell students when they are expected to talk with one another and when they are expected to listen. Charts and time lines on the chalkboard should specify tasks and deadlines associated with various assignments and projects. Routines are also required to monitor the progress of each student or group of students during multitask situations, a skill that requires a high degree of teacher with-itness, to use Kounin's term.

Adjusting to Differing Finishing Rates. One of the most complex management problems faced by teachers in the differentiated classroom is that students working on an array of learning activities are likely to finish at different times. Some may finish earlier than expected; others may lag behind. Rules, procedures, and downtime activities are needed for students who finish early and have time on their hands. These include high-interest activities such as making available special reading materials or educational games that students can complete on their own or (for older students) procedures for moving to special laboratories to work on other assignments or projects. Effective teachers also establish the expectation that those who finish early will assist others.

Late finishers present a different set of problems. In some instances, teachers may give lagging students more time. Of course, this action results in the early finishers having even more downtime. Teachers may alternately decide to get late finishers to put in extra time after school or on the weekend. However, this action is often problematic. If students are working in teams, it could be difficult for them to get together outside of school. Furthermore, students who are falling behind often are those who do not work well alone and who need a teacher's assistance to complete important tasks and assignments. The key to all of this, of course, is to have assignments and learning activities designed to provide the appropriate level of challenge for each student.

Monitoring Student Work and Managing Resources. Unlike some other types of instruction in which all students complete the same assignment at the same time, the differentiated classroom generates multiple assignments, multiple products, and often varying completion dates. Consequently, effective techniques for monitoring and managing student work are crucial. Three important management tasks are critical if student accountability is to be maintained and if teachers are to keep a degree of momentum in the overall instructional process: (1) work requirements for all students must be clearly delineated, (2) student work must be monitored and feedback provided on work in progress, and (3) careful records must be maintained.

Many teachers manage all three of these tasks through the use of *student project forms* (described in Chapter 11), and special *filing systems* maintained by students themselves. Today, electronic forms and grade books can also assist with the monitoring process.

Check, Extend, Explore

Check
- Discuss the rationale for differentiating instruction and describe theoretical perspectives that provide context for its use in classrooms.
- List the key features of the differentiated classroom and compare these to features found in traditional classrooms.
- Explain how teachers use the planning process to adapt and modify instruction to meet the needs of particular students.
- List and discuss instructional strategies that support differentiation.
- Define flexible grouping and list and discuss the factors teachers must consider if they are to use this practice successfully.

Extend
- To what degree do you agree or disagree with the use of ability grouping? With flexible grouping? Go to the "Extend Question Poll" on the Online Learning Center to respond.

Explore
- Go to the Online Learning Center at www.mhhe.com/arends10e for links to Web sites related to *Instructional Differentiation Ability Grouping*.

Home and School

Seeking Parent Understanding and Participation

The use of differentiated instruction poses new challenges and new possibilities for involving parents and caregivers in their children's education. Important steps teachers can take to help make home–school connections positive and productive include:

- Providing clear *communication about goals and processes* of differentiated instruction. Many parents will be unfamiliar with this approach. They may expect all students to be treated the same way, as perhaps they were treated when they were in school.
- Paying particular attention to explaining the concept of *appropriate student progress.* Many parents or caregivers will be disappointed if their child is not working at what they perceive as grade level.

- Justifying the *use of more able students* working with those who have learning difficulties. Remember from Chapter 10 that these actions are often believed to be exploitive.
- Justifying the grading system if *grading for growth* is being used. Again, this will be a new concept for many parents and not one they experienced when they were in school.
- Recruiting parents and family members to *assist in the differentiated classroom.* Many are willing to help manage the multitask environment by organizing and distributing materials, serving as tutors, and keeping files in order. Care must be taken, however, to protect student privacy. Also, it is important to recognize that work may prevent many parents from helping out. This situation should not be interpreted as not caring about their children's education.

Having organizational arrangements for student work and for managing materials is critical for remaining aware of what students are doing in the differentiated classroom.

Almost all teaching situations require some type of materials and equipment, and the management of these resources is always troublesome for teachers. A differentiated classroom places even greater demands on this aspect of management. Effective teachers develop procedures for organizing, storing, and distributing materials, and they require students to help with this process.

Assessing and Evaluating Student Work

Many of the assessment strategies and procedures described in previous chapters are those required in a differentiated classroom. Instead of assessment being a single event coming at the end of a lesson or unit of work or only as a means to evaluate what students have remembered, assessment must be ongoing and an integral part of instruction. It is designed to provide teachers with important diagnostic information on student readiness and information about how to modify content and choose particular instructional strategies. Multiple forms of assessments are used to ensure all aspects of student learning are assessed.

In the differentiated classroom students are given work and assigned learning activities appropriate to their abilities and needs. In this situation, teachers are interested in growth for particular students rather than normative comparisons. Traditional grading procedures and report cards are often inconsistent with instructional differentiation. Grading and report cards need to change to reflect individual growth, not just relative standing. Criterion grading on report cards aligned to particular competencies and standards as described in Chapter 6 is one way to report student growth and progress. Tomlinson (2001, 2004) has argued for redefining what letter grades on the report card mean. For example, A = excellent growth, B = good growth, C = some growth, D = little growth, and F = no growth. She also suggests that adding a number notation where 1 means working above grade level, 2 means working at grade level, and 3 means working below grade level would provide additional information for students and their parents. An example of this grade might be a B2 in reading, which means the student has made "good growth" and is working at "grade level," or A3, communicating that the student has made "excellent growth" but is still working below grade level. The aim of this approach is to evaluate growth and also to communicate to parents information about their child's overall standing in comparison to grade-level norms. Most important, assessment and grading practices must respect student differences and emphasize the individual growth of each student.

Check, Extend, Explore

Check

- Describe special classroom management concerns for the differentiated classroom.
- Provide the rationale for continuous assessment and integration of assessment with instruction.
- Explain why it is important to evaluate student progress and growth in the differentiated classroom rather than making just normative comparisons.

Extend

- To what extent do you agree or disagree that grading should reflect individual student growth? Go to the "Extend Question Poll" on the Online Learning Center to respond.

Explore

- Go to the Online Learning Center at www.mhhe.com/arends10e for links to Web sites related to *Differentiation, Classroom Management,* and *Grading to Reflect Individual Growth.*
- Do a Google search on ability grouping, differentiation, and flexible grouping. How does what you read on these sites inform your thoughts about these topics? How do some of the perspectives differ from those in *Learning to Teach*?
- Visit Carol Ann Tomlinson's Web site. Read about the author and check out two or three of the links to important Web sites on differentiated instruction.

Reflections from the *Classroom*

Overwhelmed and Frustrated in October

It is mid-October of your first year of teaching. You have taken seriously the expectations that you are responsible for helping every child learn, yet you are faced with twenty-six students with varying abilities, interests, and learning styles, including four special education students. To meet each student's needs you have strived diligently to create a "student-centered, differentiated classroom," one characterized by careful attention to student differences, modification of your curriculum and your instructional approaches, and a lot of attention to teaching individuals independently or in small, flexible learning groups. For all lessons and units of work, you create plans that call for differentiated activities and varying assignments tailored to particular students' abilities and interests. You

make sure you have a variety of resources available to facilitate the different points of readiness of your students.

More and more, however, things just aren't working. Lessons often get off track or break down when you can't seem to manage so much student movement and so many things going on at the same time. You believe every assignment should be carefully evaluated, yet there are piles of unread student work on your desk. A colleague has told you that she has heard that some of your parents reported being confused about what you are trying to do. In sum, you are tired, overwhelmed, and frustrated, and there are still eight long months before the end of the school year.

Reflect on this situation and consider what you would do. Do you want to reconsider your dedication to the differentiated, student-centered classroom? Are there steps you can take to bring things back under control? Are there ways to manage the multiple learning tasks going on in your classroom? Are there ways to monitor student work more effectively? Compare your thoughts with those provided below by experienced teachers who have faced or known about similar situations.

Samuel Barker
5th- and 6th-Grade Team

The best advice I can provide to this overwhelmed and frustrated beginning teacher is for him to start small and to go slow, because there are many demands on a first-year teacher and most responsibilities and activities are being assumed for the first time. You can start small in a number of ways. During a unit of work, select a small number of students (three or four) and adapt a particular assignment for them. Allow the remainder of the class to work on a common assignment. Another way to start small is to differentiate one lesson in a total unit of work for all students in the class. Teach the other lessons in more traditional or undifferentiated fashion.

Differentiating one subject in the total curriculum during the first three months of school, instead of all subjects at once, is a way to go slow. Using flexible grouping in reading or mathematics (not both) would be a good way to start. Another would be to spend a lot of time learning how to assess student interests and readiness, but waiting until later to fully implement differentiated processes and assignments. Learn to talk to students about their progress; observe them and take notes on what they can and cannot do; monitor which work they complete on time and which work comes in late or not at all.

Starting small and slow the first year can help beginning teachers build the understandings and skills about differentiating that will allow more complete implementation the next year.

Louise Foreman
10th-Grade Social Studies

I had the same problem when I began teaching four years ago. I tried to have a learner-centered, differentiated classroom from the first day. I, too, was overwhelmed at the end of the month. I found that I needed to scale back my efforts and concentrate on differentiating only a fraction of my curriculum, assignments, and teaching strategies. I started with "discussion lessons." I would have the whole class participate in the discussion, but from time to time ask students to discuss in pairs. I assigned particular students to these pairs to ensure that more effective discussants and less effective discussants would work together. I emphasized the importance of everyone getting a chance to express his or her ideas and points of view. Following discussion lessons, I asked students to reflect on the discussion in personal journals. This allowed students to write and express their ideas at levels of complexity most appropriate for them.

I also started to build my own skills for using informal and time-effective ways to assess student abilities. I chose three students, one below grade level, one at grade level, and another above grade level and started to observe their behavior such as homework completion, puzzling looks, and scores on quizzes. This allowed me to monitor their progress on a day-to-day basis. Only after I became confident in my assessment strategies did I start making assessment an integral part of my instruction and start differentiating assignments and teaching strategies based on these assessments.

I also found that I needed to discuss what I was trying to accomplish with both students and their parents. I called on parents' help, and I slowly established routines for students to take increasing responsibility for their own learning and to help other students in the class when appropriate.

Summary

Define what is meant by connecting and using multiple approaches to teaching and differentiating instruction and explain why each is important.

- Attending to the needs of all learners is one of the most important and difficult challenges facing teachers today.

- For over a century teachers have been admonished to attend to the individual needs of learners; however, they have also been expected to teach a prescribed curriculum to twenty to thirty students in age-graded classrooms.

- Today strategies and tactics exist that provide teachers with the tools to meet the challenges associated with adapting instruction to meet learner needs.

Explain how to use multiple approaches to instruction to accomplish particular learning goals, to provide variety, and to meet the needs of all learners.

- *Repertoire* refers to the number of models and strategies teachers have at their command. A wide repertoire allows a teacher to use multiple approaches to adapt instruction and make wise instructional choices for ensuring different types of student learning.
- Although the goals of particular lessons is one factor for deciding which models and strategies to use, the nature of the students is another very important factor.
- The need for variety is a third factor that helps teachers decide to use various and multiple instructional approaches during a lesson or unit of work.

Describe the rationale and major features of instructional differentiation, and discuss the strategies that support the differentiated classroom.

- Theories of human development and abilities help teachers understand the wide range of readiness and abilities found in all classrooms.
- Developmental theorists such as Piaget and Vygotsky provide a perspective on how children develop and grow and how development proceeds at differing rates.
- Sternberg and Gardner, among others, posit that intelligence is multiple rather than unitary. Sternberg has defined three types of intelligence; Gardner has described eight basic forms of intelligence.
- Differentiated classrooms are characterized by features where teachers focus on the essentials; attend to student differences; view assessment and instruction as inseparable; make modifications of content, process, and products; and provide all students with respectful work appropriate to their abilities and needs.

- Strategies that support differentiation of instruction include curriculum differentiation, cooperative learning, problem-based learning, curriculum compacting, tiered activities, and independent study and contracting.
- For much of the twentieth century, grouping students by ability was the major means to decrease the range of abilities found in classrooms.
- Over the past three decades, research has pointed out some of the negative effects of ability grouping and has led many educators to explore alternative practices, such as within-class "flexible grouping." These practice, unless used appropriately, can also have negative effects.
- A small knowledge base is beginning to show the positive effects of flexible grouping.

Describe how to implement a learning environment conducive to instructional differentiation and explain special concerns about assessment and grading created by this type of classroom.

- Differentiated classrooms, as with most learner-centered situations, place special demands on the teacher's management systems. They require systems for dealing with students when they are pursuing multiple learning tasks and ways to deal with differing finishing rates.
- Monitoring and managing student work is also more complicated in classrooms where students are working on various types of learning tasks and assignments.
- Assessment and instruction must be inseparable and fully integrated for differentiated instruction to be effective.
- Traditional approaches to assessment and grading can often inhibit efforts to adapt instruction to meet the needs of particular learners; emphasis should be on student growth rather than normative comparisons.

Key Terms

ability grouping   489
differentiation   472

flexible grouping   489
repertoire   473

tiered activities   488

Interactive and Applied Learning

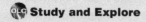 **Study and Explore**

- Access your Study Guide, which includes practice quizzes, from the Online Learning Center.

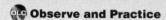 **Observe and Practice**

Complete the following **Practice Exercises** that accompany Chapter 13:
- Practice Exercise 13.1: Planning a Unit Using Multiple Models

- Practice Exercise 13.2: Considering Multiple Intelligences in Unit Planning
- Practice Exercise 13.3: Differentiating a Lesson
- Practice Exercise 13.4: Differentiating for Content, Process, and Product
- Practice Exercise 13.5: Differentiating a Unit Plan

Portfolio and Field Experience Activities

Expand your understanding of the content and processes of this chapter through the following field experience and portfolio activities. Support materials to complete the activities are in the *Portfolio and Field Experience Activities* area on the Online Learning Center.

1. Complete the **Reflections from the Classroom** exercise at the end of this chapter. The recommended essay will provide insights into your overall view about teaching repertoire and instructional differentiation. **(InTASC Standard 2: Learner Differences; InTASC Standard 5: Application of Content; InTASC Standard 8: Instructional Strategies)**
2. **Activity 13.1: Assessing My Repertoire and Differentiation Skills.** Check your level of understanding and skill to use multiple approaches to instruction and to differentiate instruction. **(InTASC Standard 2: Learner Differences; InTASC Standard 5: Application of Content; InTASC Standard 8: Instructional Strategies)**

3. **Activity 13.2: Interviewing Teachers about Differentiation.** Interview an experienced classroom teacher and get examples about how he or she differentiates instruction. **(InTASC Standard 2: Learner Differences; InTASC Standard 5: Application of Content; InTASC Standard 8: Instructional Strategies)**
4. **Activity 13.3: Observing Teacher Use of Multiple Approaches to Instruction. During a single lesson or over several days (InTASC Standard 2: Learner Differences; InTASC Standard 5: Application of Content; InTASC Standard 8: Instructional Strategies)**
5. **Activity 13.4: Interviewing Teachers about Flexible Grouping Practices.** Interview an experienced classroom teacher and get examples about how he or she uses flexible grouping. **(InTASC Standard 2: Learner Differences; InTASC Standard 5: Application of Content; InTASC Standard 8: Instructional Strategies)**

Books for the Professional

Gregory, G., & Chapman, C. (2012). *Differentiated instructional strategies: One size doesn't fit all.* Thousand Oaks, CA: Corwin Press.

Heacox, D. (2012). *Differentiating instruction in the regular classroom: How to reach and teach all learners.* Minneapolis, MN: Free Spirit Publishing.

Tomlinson, C. (2004). *How to differentiate instruction in mixed ability classrooms* (2nd ed.). Alexandria, VA: Association for Supervision and Curriculum Development.

Tomlinson, C., & Imbeau, M. (2010). *Leading and managing a differentiated classroom.* Alexandria, VA: Association for Supervision and Curriculum Development.

Tomlinson, C., & McTighe, J. (2013). *Integrating differentiated instruction and understanding by design: Connecting content and kids.* New York: Pearson Teacher Education/ASCD College Textbook.

PART 5 The Organizational Aspects of Teaching

Part 5 of *Learning to Teach* is devoted to the organizational aspects of teaching. Teachers, like other professionals, are expected not only to perform their primary responsibilities (in this case, providing instruction to students) but also to provide leadership to their school as a whole. For teachers, this means working alongside others in the school—colleagues, administrators, parents, and students—to help set schoolwide expectations, gain clarity of purposes and actions, and work toward needed reforms.

Chapter 14 focuses on four specific expectations for teachers: understanding schools as social organizations, providing leadership and working collaboratively with members of the school community, helping schools improve, and continuing to grow as a professional. To perform these functions effectively, teachers must understand the nature of the school not only as a place where children come to learn but also as a place where adults work and where society and policymakers have considerable influence. Teachers also need specific organizational skills aimed at making work with others in their school productive.

As you read about and study these topics, you will discover two reasons they are so important. One, there appears to be a certain synergy at work in schools where teachers and others have come together and made agreements about what is going to be taught. This synergy makes a difference in how much students learn. Two, your ability to provide leadership and to relate to and work with others within the school and larger professional community will have a significant impact on your career. Often it is in this arena that you will become known to others and will build your professional reputation. Teachers who grow and progress in their careers are those who can enter into professional and schoolwide dialogue about educational issues as they find ways to become accomplished teachers.

CHAPTER 14
School Leadership and Collaboration

Learning Goals

After studying this chapter you should be able to

Perspective on Schools as Workplaces	Describe the perspective on schools as social organizations and as places where teachers work. Explain the features of schools that are the same as and different from other organizations.
Theoretical and Empirical Support	Describe the theoretical foundations behind schools and the nature of teachers' work. Summarize the features of effective schools.
Organizational Skills for Teachers	Describe the workplace skills required of teachers and discuss ways teachers can work effectively and collaboratively with colleagues, administrators, and parents for the purpose of improving education for all students.

Reflecting on School Leadership and Collaboration

Before you read this chapter, consider the following situations, which are based on studies about what teachers do and how they spend their time.

Neil is a new third-grade teacher at Holbrook Elementary School. He usually arrives at school about 7:30 A.M. This particular morning, Neil opens his room, then joins other third- and fourth-grade teachers who are planning a field trip to the local airport. They discuss how each of them is going to integrate this experience into the social studies curriculum. Back in his room in time to start class at 8:35 A.M., Neil spends the rest of the morning with his third-graders. He is joined at several points by other adults. The principal drops in for a few minutes to observe and see if Neil needs any help. Two mothers join the class at 9:30 A.M. to assist Neil with his reading groups, and they stay through morning recess. The school's reading specialist comes by and tests a student who Neil thinks is having a severe word recognition problem. The special education resource teacher joins Neil's classroom to work for thirty minutes with two students with learning disabilities who are mainstreamed in Neil's room.

Over lunch, Neil talks with two second-grade teachers about students of his who were in their classrooms last year. Neil stops at the library on his way back to his classroom to pick up a video he plans to show as part of his social studies unit and to remind the librarian that he will be bringing a small group of students to the library next Tuesday. School lets out at 2:45 P.M.; Neil checks his e-mail and then drops by the reading specialist's office to discuss the results of her testing before heading to the central office to participate on a science textbook selection committee. Neil was appointed to this committee by his principal because the principal knew that he had a very strong background in science and had worked at the Marine Biology Research Center for the past two summers.

Helena teaches tenth-grade English at Cordoza High School. She, too, arrives at school about 7:30 A.M., and she meets with another new teacher to have a cup of coffee and discuss an exchange of teaching materials. Helena teaches three classes of sophomore English in the morning. Just before lunch, she is visited by her department chairperson, who is conducting one of his required formal observations of new teachers.

During her afternoon planning period, Helena and the department chair meet. He gives her feedback on her lesson, pointing out that her lecture was clear and had good examples, but that her students took a long time getting to work in the small-group exercise that followed her presentation.

After school, Helena meets for a few minutes with members of the school's debate team for whom she serves as advisor. On this day, Helena leaves her work with the debate team early because she wants to participate in the discussion on student advising planned for this week's faculty meeting. After the faculty meeting, Helena dashes home to have a quick dinner. The school's open house is this evening, and Helena has scheduled meetings with several 3s to discuss their children's work. Returning home at 10:00 P.M., Helena settled into her easy chair, put her feet up, and enjoyed a glass of wine.

Analyzing these typical days in the lives of two beginning teachers illustrates that they do many things in addition to interacting with students in classrooms. They meet with students about nonacademic tasks; they meet with fellow teachers and specialists within the school; they go to meetings; they work with parents; and they attend to their own learning. What do you think of these aspects of a teacher's work? How do you see yourself relating to the rapid pace and schedule of teaching? How do you see yourself relating to the noninstructional aspects of teaching? Working with fellow teachers? With parents? In the community?

 Go to the Online Learning Center at www.mhhe.com/arends10e to respond to these questions.

Teachers are members of an organization called *school*, a place where many diverse organizational responsibilities are performed.

Previous chapters described what teachers do as they plan for and deliver instruction and manage complex classroom settings. Providing leadership and teaching students in classrooms, however, are not the only aspects of a teacher's job. Teachers are also members of an organization called *school* and, as such, are asked to assume important leadership responsibilities at the school level, including working cooperatively with colleagues, serving on committees, and working with administrators and parents. The way these aspects of a teacher's job are performed makes a significant difference in the school's professional community, how students behave and what they learn. The way teachers carry out these responsibilities also makes a significant difference in their own professional careers.

A critical aspect of a teacher's work is working with other teachers.

This chapter describes the work environment of schools and the corresponding culture of teaching. Emphasis is placed on the idea that schools are not only places where students come to learn; they are also places where adults work. After providing a conceptual framework for viewing schools as workplaces, we summarize a sample of the knowledge base on the nature of teachers' work behavior and what makes some schools more effective than others. We conclude with a discussion of several important skills that beginning teachers need as they become fully involved in their first school and community.

Perspective on Schools as Workplaces

At this point in your career, it is likely that your view of schools stems mainly from many years of being a student. You are familiar with the classroom portion of the teacher's role, with the role of student, and with the way that students and teachers interact around academic tasks. However, you may not have had much chance to observe or reflect on schools from behind the teacher's desk or on the nonclassroom aspects of a teacher's job. In fact, many people (including those in the media) rarely view schools from the perspective of the complex social organizations they are. This is unfortunate because views of schools, stemming only from experiences as students, have caused misunderstanding on the part of many—teachers, parents, and policymakers—regarding school reform efforts. Also, unrealistic views have led to many beginning teachers' disillusionment. The section that follows provides a view of schools that extends beyond the classroom doors.

Schools Are Human Systems

In discussing schools, we take a perspective that schools are human systems that are influenced not only by the people who learn and work in them but also by the larger community and society. Schools are places where individuals do not act in totally free and disconnected ways but, instead, in more or less interdependent and predictable ways. Although individuals come together in schools to promote purposeful learning, each person does not chart his or her own course alone, nor do the actions of each have consequences only for that person. Also, the synergy developed by teachers and others acting in concert can have important consequences for student learning. To understand the human systems view of schools, think for a moment about the number of interdependent actions required to bring about a day's worth of instruction for students:

- Paper, pencils, and computers have been ordered.
- Rooms have been cleaned.
- Curriculum standards and frameworks have been prepared and textbooks ordered.
- Parents have chosen to send their children to school.
- Teachers have chosen to be professionally trained.
- Buses have been driven and breakfasts and lunches prepared and served.
- Schedules have been determined and children assigned to classes.
- Health services for students have been planned and managed.

This list could go on and on. The point, however, is that the contemporary school is a complex human system requiring its members to perform important functions in interdependent ways.

Schools Have Histories and Cultures

School culture consists of the ways members think about their actions and it reflects their beliefs, values, and history.

Schools, like other organizations, have histories and cultures consisting of values, beliefs, and expectations that have developed and grown over time. The history of a school provides traditions and a multitude of routines—some good and some not so good—that are taken for granted by organizational members. The *culture of a school* provides the organizational arrangements that hold it together and give it power as a social entity. Lortie (1975) referred to culture as the "way members of a group think about social action; culture encompasses alternatives for resolving problems in collective life" (p. 216). Others have provided similar definitions, although they sometimes use different labels. Rutter and his colleagues (1979), for example, refer to the common values, beliefs, and ways of doing things as the school's **ethos;** Glass (1981) has called it *tone;* Joyce and his colleagues (1993) and Sergiovanni (1996) prefer the word *community.* Schein (2010) labels this aspect *organiztional culture.* Regardless of how it is labeled, **school culture** greatly influences what goes on in schools and determines expectations and roles for beginning teachers.

Figure 14.1 *The School in Context*

Source: From Cole, Griffin, et al. (1987) and Gallego, Cole, et al. (2001).

Schools Exist in Context

Schools exist in a **social context** and context, is another lens for viewing schools. One way of thinking about context is to consider it as the background or environment in which teaching and learning take place. In complex educational systems, several important embedded contexts surround the total system, from the values expressed by the larger society, to the culture of the community, and the structures and norms found in particular homes and families. Figure 14.1 illustrates the relationships among various contextual features.

Notice how each activity in the concentric circles is embedded in a set of interlocking or reciprocal relationships. For instance, a particular learner task (at the center) is influenced by the teacher and particular lessons. This, in turn, is influenced by the principal and the school and ultimately by features of the home, community, and larger society. Beginning teachers will find considerable variability in the social context that influences their classrooms. Some communities may have many resources to provide their schools, whereas others have few. Some families will provide strong support for their children and provide them with safe environments in which to grow up. Other families will be deficient in support and children may come to school hungry or abused. Viewing schools through the context lens is important because it influences how teachers perform their work and what students learn in very fundamental ways.

Schools Have Features in Common with Other Organizations

In some ways, schools are similar to other organizations in society. For example, as in other organizations, members are directed toward the accomplishment of some goal. In a textile plant, the goal may be the production of men's shirts; Toyota's job is to make cars, and Apple serves up beautiful design and information. The overriding goal for schools is to provide *purposeful learning experiences* that enhance student learning. Members of schools—principals, teachers, and students—are rewarded, as are members in other organizations, when they strive for and accomplish common organizational goals. Similarly, they are punished when they fail. An example of a reward is experiments in some states in which teaching faculties are given merit increases if, as a group, they can lift achievement in their school above a set criterion. An example of punishment is instances in which teachers are dismissed if they cannot provide purposeful learning activities for their students or if their students do not learn. Another example is when schools are put on probation or reconstituted when they do not meet the standards prescribed by legislation such as No Child Left Behind, Race to the Top, or other current federal or state legislation.

> **The primary goal of schools is to provide a purposeful environment that enhances student learning.**

Another organizational feature of schools similar to that found in other organizations is that coordination of effort is required. In addition to teachers, school staffs include curriculum coordinators, administrators, nurses, counselors, janitors, and other support personnel. Most of the people in schools, however, are students, and they, too, must be considered organizational members. Because school roles are specialized, routines and structures are created to help members carry out their special tasks in ways that will more or less facilitate what others are doing. The reason coordination of effort is sometimes difficult to accomplish in schools is described later.

Schools Have Unique Features

Just as schools have features in common with other organizations, they also have features that are unique. It is the special features of schools that are most important for us to understand.

Ambiguous and Conflicting Goals. It has been stated several times in this book that the overriding goal of schools is to facilitate purposive learning for students. Stated at this level of abstraction, most people would readily agree with this goal. However,

> **Goal ambiguity and conflict are more prevalent in schools than in other organizations.**

when people speak more precisely about what purposive learning means, many of their statements may seem ambiguous and may conflict with the aims of one group or another in the community.

Goal ambiguity can be illustrated with reference to citizenship education. Most people in Western societies believe that the schools should socialize students as citizens who accept the values of democratic political systems and who embrace some degree of freedom in their own economic activities. However, how do school people, parents, and others know whether this goal is being accomplished? Parents, for example, are never sure their sons or daughters are embracing the values they desire for them. Teachers seldom know how their former students behave as adult citizens. Do they vote? Are they participating in their communities? Will they defend the rights of the minority?

As for goal conflict, do citizenship goals compete with academic learning goals? Which of the two is most important? How should time be allocated between the two? What constitutes good citizenship? For example, some argue that the most important aspect of citizenship education is the socialization of students into traditional values and beliefs. Some church-related and private schools are inclined toward this position. However, others argue that this approach to citizenship education is simply indoctrination and leads to narrowness and conformity. The good citizen, from this point of view, might be the critical thinker who questions existing values and structures and attempts to modify them.

Efforts by most states to find agreement on a set of common standards in mathematics and literacy on the surface appeared to be an effort to reduce goal conflict about what should be taught in these two important school subjects. However, as the new standards are being implemented and tests are being devised to measure student learning, several states have started to pull back from their earlier agreements. It seems that conflicts over important goals still exist.

The fact that students are compelled to attend school makes for a unique type of client relationship.

Compulsory Attendance. A second special feature of schools is that their clients (the students) are compelled to be there. All states have compulsory attendance laws that require parents to send their children to school, normally until age 16. Although most people support these laws because they guarantee a minimum education for all children and help prevent forced child labor, they do create the problem of keeping unmotivated students involved in school life. Schools with large numbers of academically unmotivated students are often schools where teachers choose not to work. Recent innovations in some school systems, such as the creation of alternative, magnet, and charter schools, attempt to combat the compulsory nature of schooling by giving students and their parents more choices in the type of school the students attend. The fact still remains, however: students *must* go to school.

Political Visibility. Schools have always been highly visible and political in most local communities. Many people take an active interest in their schools, and, given local control, schools offer one of the few places where people in complex societies can have their voices heard. For example, it is quite easy in most communities to stay informed about school events because large portions of the daily newspapers are devoted to school news, including the school's budget and students' test scores. It is also easy to attend local school board or council meetings and voice opinions, just as it is easy to walk directly into most principals' offices without an appointment. The whole system is open and permeable. Today, the quality of education is a major political issue not only at the local level but also at state and national levels. No Child

Left Behind, Race to the Top, and Common Core requirements have had and will continue to have considerable influence over what goes on in schools and in teachers' classrooms. Statewide testing dictates in large and significant ways what is taught and how.

Some aspects of this situation are positive. It is good that citizens locally and across the country have an interest in their schools. This is the way it should be in a democracy. It is also good when this interest helps maintain strong social and financial support for education. At the same time, this situation can leave the schools and those who work there vulnerable to the whims and unfair attacks by special interest groups and create conditions in schools that are not always conducive to student learning.

Schools Are Communities. According to some observers, schools also differ from other organizations in that they are more like communities than modern bureaucracies (Ancess & Darling-Hammond, 2003; Sergiovanni, 1996, 2004). Rather than being organizations governed by hierarchical control structures and formal systems of supervision, Sergiovanni (1996) argues, schools are communities built on shared purposes and mutual respect:

> Communities are collections of individuals who are bonded together by natural will and who are together bound to a set of shared ideas and ideals. This bonding and binding is tight enough to transform them from a collection of "I's" into a collective we. As a "we," members are part of a tightly knit web of meaningful relationships. (p. 48)

In some ways, schools are more like communities than they are like modern organizations.

Notice some of the words used by Sergiovanni: *bonded individuals, shared ideas,* and *collective we.*

Sergiovanni has argued that over the past hundred years modern organizations in business, the military, and the health fields have been constructed around formal and contractual arrangements rather than conditions of shared values found in earlier times. Schools, he says, have mistakenly adopted these inappropriate formal and contractual arrangements, and though these arrangements may make sense for businesses and hospitals, they do not work well for schools. Instead, they are the source of many of the problems found in today's school. Sergiovanni believes that schools are closer in character to the family, the neighborhood, and voluntary social groups—all organizations that have a special sense of shared values, belonging, and community.

The community metaphor for understanding schools is interesting and potentially powerful. And, as you will see later in this chapter, important research shows that schools where teachers share a common vision and shared values and have created a collaborative professional community characterized by a dialogue and sense of belonging produce higher student learning than schools in which relationships are more formal and contractual.

Schools are highly visible and political.

Norms, Roles, and the Culture of Teaching

Another way to think about schools is to think about the norms, roles, and social arrangements that exist for the purpose of getting work accomplished. These will have strong influences on the experiences that beginning teachers have during both internships and their first year of teaching.

The expectation that educators are virtually free to teach as they please within the confines of their classrooms is known as the autonomy norm.

Norms. **Norms** are the expectations that people have for one another in particular social settings. They define the range of social behaviors that are allowed in given situations. Some norms are informal, such as the norm that prescribes a swimsuit rather than a cocktail dress on the beach. Some norms, however, are formal. For example, a person might not be arrested if he wore a tuxedo to the beach, but he would be if he broke a local ordinance that restricts bathing in the nude.

In schools, many formal and informal norms exist that affect teachers and students. For example, in some schools, new teachers will find norms supporting friendliness and openness that will make them feel welcome. In other schools, people may act toward one another in more reserved ways. In some schools, norms to encourage experimentation may make beginning teachers feel comfortable in trying out new ideas, whereas in other schools, few risks will be encouraged. Two important norms associated with schools and the culture of teaching need highlighting, because they affect the lives of beginning teachers most directly.

Autonomy Norm. In some ways, teachers have relatively little power and influence in the larger school system. However, they do have a great deal of influence in their own classrooms, supported by what has been labeled the **autonomy norm.** Teachers, including beginning teachers, do pretty much what they want to once they are in their classrooms and their doors are closed. In many schools, they alone are responsible for the day-to-day curricula and make almost all instructional decisions for themselves. Recently, Schmoker and Allington (2007) and Lieberman and her colleagues (2011) have observed that teacher autonomy—the lack of interaction among teachers, as well as the lack of channels to observe each other's teaching—interferes with effective teaching and, in turn, with student learning.

The hands-off norm is the expectation in schools that teachers will not interfere in the work of other teachers.

The Hands-Off Norm. Closely paralleling the autonomy norm is a norm observed and labeled by several as the **hands-off norm** (Goodlad, 1984; Lortie, 1975; Sarason; 1982). Not only are teachers given autonomy in their classrooms, but strong sanctions exist against interfering with other teachers in any but the most superficial ways. It is not appropriate for teachers to ask for help, for example. Such a request suggests that the teacher is failing, and it is often not permissible for teachers to tell a peer what to do or to suggest that he or she teach something differently.

This is not to suggest to beginning teachers that colleagues within a particular school will be unfriendly or unsupportive. Teachers socialize a great deal with one another and on an emotional level are concerned and supportive of one another. Even so, teachers often avoid talking about instructional practices. It is important to point out that many contemporary school reform projects aim at breaking down the autonomy and hands-off norms by encouraging and helping teachers to work together. Indeed, the traditional norms governing teachers' behavior may be changing as more and more teacher recognize the positive effects of working with their colleagues in collaborative ways. We return to this idea later in the chapter.

Roles. Organizations and organizational culture also describe a teacher's role. The teacher's role, for example, includes norms about how teachers should behave toward students and students toward them, how teachers should interact with each other and with the principal, and how much teachers should participate in schoolwide problem solving and decision making. People in schools learn roles through interacting with each other.

Some aspects of the teacher's role are clear and straightforward. For example, it is clear that teachers should teach academic content to students and evaluate their students' progress. Some aspects of the teacher's role, however, are not so clear and sometimes provide contradictory expectations. Contradictions in role expectations cause anxiety and trouble for beginning teachers as they enter the school for the first time.

> **Contradictions in aspects of the teacher's role often cause anxiety for beginning teachers.**

One of the most basic contradictions in the teacher's role stems from strong expectations that teachers should treat each child as an individual even though schools are organized so that teachers must deal with students in groups. This conflict is particularly acute with secondary teachers, who face as many as 150 to 180 students a day for rather brief periods of time. This role conflict, according to Lieberman and Miller (1999, 2008), is what makes teaching so personal, because to deal with the contradictory demands of individualization and group instruction requires the development of a teaching style that is "individual and personal."

A second basic contradiction in the teacher's role involves the degree of distance between teacher and students. On one hand, teachers are expected to maintain a certain social distance from students so authority and discipline can be maintained. In fact, as described in Chapters 4 and 5, control is often an overriding concern for beginning teachers, because they know they are being heavily judged on this score. On the other hand, most teachers know that they must form some type of bond with students in order to motivate them and help them to learn. Beginning teachers manifest the tensions of this role contradiction in a number of ways. They worry about whether or not they should allow students to call them by their first name or how friendly they should become with a particular student they really like and so on. A more recent tension has been whether to "friend" a student on Facebook. Such tensions are quite normal, and only experience, it seems, provides the means for dealing with the many contradictions built into the teacher's role.

> **School organizations are called cellular because teachers are independently responsible for organizing leadership and teaching functions within the "cells" of their own classrooms.**

Cellular Organizational Structure. Compared to most other organizations, schools are rather flat organizations. In elementary schools, there are mainly teachers and a principal, and in most secondary schools, one additional role, the department chair, is added. Some (Joyce et al., 1993; Lortie, 1975) have called this arrangement "cellular"; that is, each classroom can be regarded as a cell within which the teacher is responsible for organizing the students, managing discipline, and teaching academic content. This arrangement, coupled with the hands-off norm, often creates an isolated work situation for teachers. They make independent decisions about when and how to teach each subject, and they do not ask other teachers for help. This professional isolation has led some observers to refer to teaching as a "lonely profession." With the addition of many new roles in schools over the past few years, such as special teachers and lead teachers of one kind or another, and new approaches for organizing curricula, it may be that the *cellular structure* of schools is changing. Currently, it remains a common arrangement.

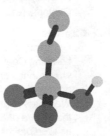

Cellular Structure

Loosely Coupled

Check, Extend, Explore

Check

- What is meant by the saying "the school is a social system"? A community?
- How do culture, history, and ethos define many important functions and characteristics of a school?
- What features of schools make them different from other formal organizations?
- What norms tend to exist in schools that beginning teachers should anticipate?
- What aspects of a teacher's role are clear? Which tend to be more complex and contradictory?

Extend

- Teaching has been called the "lonely profession." How much will this description affect your decision to stay in teaching? Go to the "Extend Question Poll" on the Online Learning Center to respond.

Explore

- Go to the Online Learning Center at www.mhhe.com/arends10e for links to Web sites related to the *Nature of Schools as Workplaces.* Visit the Web sites for the American Federation of Teachers and the National Education Association to explore how they see the teacher's role.

Loosely Coupled Structure. The school's cellular structure also causes an organizational arrangement that has been labeled **loosely coupled** (Peterson & Deal, 2002; Weick, 1976). This means that what goes on in classrooms is *not* very tightly connected to what goes on in other parts of the school. Teachers can and do carry out their own instructional activities independent of administrators and others. The central office may initiate new curricula or new teaching procedures, but if teachers choose to ignore these initiatives, they can. An example of teachers choosing to ignore a centrally imposed initiative occurred recently in the Seattle Public Schools. The district's school board had established a policy that all students through grade 10 would be required to take a particular district-sanctioned standardized test. Results from this test were used to provide feedback on student progress and also to serve as a component of a teacher's yearly evaluation. A group of English teachers at one of the high schools refused to administer the test, arguing that it did not measure what they were teaching and that it took too much time away from instruction, thus harming student learning. The boycott soon spread to other schools. A lengthy debate ensued, and ultimately the district changed its policy to the teachers' liking, illustrating the loose connections between those who make policies for schools and those who carry them out. On the positive side, loose coupling allows considerable room for individual teacher decision making in situations where a substantial knowledge about "best" teaching practice is lacking. Conversely, loose coupling can stymie efforts to establish common goals and coordinated activities, something that is important for effective schooling, as you will see later.

Theoretical and Empirical Support

For many years, educators have thought about the school as a formal organization. In fact, a very important book written many years ago by Waller (1932) on the sociology of teaching provided many important insights into the nature of schools and of teaching. However, it is only in the last three decades that educators and educational researchers have started to highlight the importance of schools as workplaces and the importance of the *organizational aspects of teaching.* This section provides examples from fairly recent research about the nature of the work teachers do in schools and how the way this work is done can affect what students learn.

Nature of Teachers' Work

Some people think that teachers' hours match those of the children they teach. Others think that teachers' work consists mainly of working with students. Experienced teachers do not agree with these perceptions. They know that teachers do many other things in addition to directly working with students. They also know that the time demands of teaching are quite great. Over the years, studies have supported this view.

Since 1961, the National Education Association (NEA) has surveyed teachers every five years and asked them to report the number of hours per week they spend on various teaching responsibilities. For more than forty years, the findings of the reports (NEA, 2007) have remained pretty consistent.

- Teachers reported spending on average 50.3 hours per week on all teaching duties. This was an increase from 47 hours in 1961.
- The actual in-school time required stayed at 37 hours for the forty-year period.

- Some regional and school size differences have been reported. Teachers in small schools and those in the middle states and the west reported working more hours than those in large school systems and in the northeast or southeast.

Other studies conducted over the years have tended to validate the NEA's findings about teachers' work. For example, in one particularly interesting study, Cypher and Willower (1984) shadowed five secondary teachers to find out precisely what kind of work they did and for how long. They found that teachers averaged a 48.5-hour work-week, spending approximately 38 hours in school and 10.5 hours in after-school work. A Metropolitan Life Survey of Teachers in 1995 produced similar results (Metropolitan Life, 1995). In 2011, Scholastic and the Bill and Melinda Gates Foundation (*Primary Sources,* 2012) surveyed a nationwide sample of 10,000 teachers representing all grade levels. Teachers reported working about 10 hours per day. Table 14.1 shows how their time is distributed among various aspects of the work. Note that about half of this time was spent with direct instruction of students. A sizable portion of their work consisted of grading, planning, and exchanges with other adults such as parents, the principal, and professional colleagues.

Research on School Effectiveness

There is a growing body of evidence that the overall culture of a school and what teachers do in concert contribute to what students learn as much as the performance of individual teachers. Sometimes this research is called **school effectiveness research;** other times it is referred to as *organizational context research.* Some aspects of this research have been controversial; nonetheless, over time it has pretty consistently found that school culture and community, and the collective behavior of teachers, administrators,

Table 14.1 *How Teachers Spend Their Time during the School Day and At Home*

Instruction	**4 hours, 49 minutes**
In-class instruction	4 hours, 29 minutes
Providing student tutoring and help	20 minutes
Student supervision/discipline	**36 minutes**
Discipline	18 minutes
Supervision: hall, lunch, recess	18 minutes
Planning, preparing, and collaboration with colleagues	**55 minutes**
Lesson planning/prep	40 minutes
Collaborating with colleagues	15 minutes
Grading, documenting/analyzing student work	**34 minutes**
Grade student work/prepare reports	19 minutes
Professional paperwork and analysis	15 minutes
E-mailing, speaking, or meeting with parents	**14 minutes**
Free time/lunch/personal time	**23 minutes**
Working at home	**1 hour, 42 minutes**

Source: Summarized from *Primary sources: America's teachers on the teaching profession* (2012), pp. 13–14.

Helping the community is also part of a teacher's work.

and parents, can make an important difference in how much students learn. It points toward the importance of participants coming together and making schoolwide agreements about what should be taught, how it should be taught, and how people should relate to one another. It seems that there is a certain **synergy** working in schools that produces results that cannot be achieved when a teacher works alone on particularistic goals.

School effectiveness research tries to uncover features that make some schools more effective than others.

Additionally, this research emphasizes the people aspect of schooling. The quality of the school's social capital and how people relate to one another have been found to be more important than the amount of money spent on concrete, books, or paper. That does not mean that resources are not required for good schools; it just means that the amount of money spent on the school's library collection or the physical plant takes a backseat to the community that people within the school create.

Several groundbreaking studies in the late 1970s provided the first evidence on the importance of organizational features and processes. One study was done by an English child psychiatrist and his colleagues who studied twelve secondary schools in London (Rutter et al., 1979). Over a number of years, Rutter and his colleagues collected information about student behavior and achievement in and organization processes of a sample of high schools. The researchers found that student behavior and achievement varied markedly from school to school but that students were more likely

Synergy is at work in the school, which produces results that exceed what a teacher working alone could achieve.

to show good behavior and higher achievement in some schools than in others. Better behavior and higher achievement were strongly related to aspects of the school's social organization, such as the degree to which a common ethos existed, the extent to which teachers held common attitudes, and the degree to which they behaved in consistent ways toward their students.

Behavior and achievement are strongly related to aspects of a school's social organization.

Since Rutter's study, many other researchers have conducted similar studies with elementary and secondary schools in the United States (Brookover et al., 1979; Firestone & Rosenblum, 1988; Hindin et al., 2007; Lee & Smith, 1996; Rosenholz, 1989).

Almost all of these studies have produced similar results and conclusions; namely, that some schools develop cultures and communities that support student learning whereas other schools do not. A recent study by Carrie Leana (2011) and her colleagues at the University of Pittsburgh highlighted in the Research Summary for this chapter is an excellent example of research that illustrates the importance of the social aspects of schools. It shows the gains that can be achieved when teachers take collective responsibility for their students' learning and where the school culture supports trust and closeness among teachers and between teachers and their administrators.

Features of Effective Schools

The schools-effects research has demonstrated that several school-level factors contribute significantly to student learning. Those who have summarized this research (Fullan, 2007; Goodlad, 1984; Joyce et al., 1993; Marzano, 2003; Shannon & Bylsma, 2007) have reported a particular set of organizational and instructional features found in some schools that consistently produce high levels of student learning. These features are listed in Table 14.2.

In sum, effective schools, those that make a difference in student learning, have high expectations for students, which are communicated clearly to students and their families. The school has developed a safe environment with strong administrative leadership and community support. Teachers in these schools are empowered, they feel trust and closeness, and they are in possession of a rich and varied repertoire of teaching strategies. They are supported by administrators and by their community. They know how to work together for the purpose of designing a relevant and coherent curriculum. Most important, teachers work in collegial ways and develop learning communities that are learner centered and where the cultural traditions and language practices of all students are respected.

Effective school features are divided into two categories: those that deal with the social organization and those that deal with instructional and curriculum patterns.

Unfortunately, not all beginning teachers will end up in schools that possess the features just described. This will require efforts to help improve these conditions, a process that is described in the next sections.

Table 14.2 *Key Features of Effective Schools*

Organizational Features	Curriculum & Instructional Features
Environment where students feel safe and where teachers have trust	Clear and challenging goals
Schoolwide high expectations for every student	Relevant and coherently organized curriculum
Teacher collegiality and efficacy	Opportunities for students to assume responsibility
Respect and pervasive caring for all students	Rich repertoire of teaching strategies
Strong collegial administrative leadership	High proportion of time devoted to learning
Family and community support and involvement	Frequent monitoring of homework and provision of feedback
Collective focus on student learning	Teachers as a group highlight the importance of student learning over everything else.

Research Summary

The Benefits of Teacher Collaboration

Leana, C. R. (2011, Fall). The missing link in school reform. *Stanford Social Innovation Review*, p. 20.

The media often portray effective teachers through characters such as Jaime Escalante, of *Stand and Deliver* fame, who against great odds taught his East Los Angeles, low-academic students advanced calculus, or David Holland of *Mr. Holland's Opus*, who over a lifetime defended music education in his school and inspired his students through his singular devotion to their education and to their personal lives. Or, as in *Waiting for Superman*, the filmmaker attributed the failure of education to the lack of competence and skills of individual teachers. It is true that individually inspiring teachers are effective, and we all remember them. It is also true that teachers who lack competence can be devastating to the lives of their students. At the same time, the *collective*, rather than *individual*, responsibility of teachers seems also to be crucial and provided the focus for a study by Carrie Leana and her colleagues at the University of Pittsburgh.

Problem and Approach: The researchers started by building on previous findings that the interactions among teachers who focus on student learning have a considerable positive effect on student achievement. Further, they made an important distinction between two types of capital found in organizations—human capital and social capital (see Leana & Pil, 2009).

- **Human capital** consists of such factors as the qualifications and experiences of teachers and their abilities, knowledge, and skills.
- **Social capital** consists of the types of interactions that teachers have with their peers that focus on instruction and the amount of trust and closeness among teachers and between teachers and their administrators.

Sample and Setting: Leana and her colleagues conducted studies on human and social capital in several school districts. The study reported here is a research project conducted in the New York City Public Schools. Over a full year, researchers followed "over 1,000 fourth- and fifth-grade teachers in a representative sample of 130 elementary schools across the city" and studied the effects of human and social capital on student achievement in mathematics.

Procedures: Researchers studied the one-year changes in students' achievement in mathematics, specifically how much gain each student made under a particular teacher. They took into account and controlled for the economic background, attendance patterns, and special education status of students in the study.

- Measures of *human capital* consisted of the teacher's educational background, experiences, and classroom competence as measured by a performance test of ability to "instruct children in the logic of mathematics."
- Measures of *social capital* consisted of self-reports about the degree of trust, communication, and collaboration among teachers and between teachers and their principal. Examples of questions were: "Who do you talk to when you have a question or need advice?" and "How much do you trust the source of the advice?"

Results: When teachers in the study reported frequent conversations with peers that centered on math and a feeling of trust and closeness with other teachers, students showed significantly higher gains that did students in classrooms where teachers did not trust or collaborate with each other. Leana reported, "If a teacher's social capital was just one standard deviation [see the Research Handbook for the definition of standard deviation] higher than the average, her students' math scores increased by 5.7 percent."

The researchers also interviewed teachers to find out how social capital worked in their schools. Below is what one teacher reported:

Teaching [in my school] is not an isolated activity. If it's going to be done well, it has to be done collaboratively over time. Each of us sets our own priorities in terms of student outcomes. For example, one teacher might emphasize students' knowing all the facts and operational skills. Another might think that what's most important is to develop a love of learning in students. Still another might want to develop students to be better critical thinkers and problem solvers. . . . A good teacher needs to help students develop all these things; it's easy to get stuck in your own ideology if you are working alone. With collaboration, you are exposed to other teachers' priorities and are better able to incorporate the to broaden your own approach. (p. 4)

The researchers also found teachers with low-abilities (low human capital) did much better and could perform quite well if they were in settings with strong social capital.

Discussion and Implications Leana and her colleagues report that the results of their New York study and other studies of this type have two important implications for education policy and teaching practices:

1. Focusing on enhancing human capital (more skillful and competent teachers) will not alone bring the desired results of more student achievement. Instead, ways must be found to enhance "collaboration and information sharing" among teachers.
2. The conventional wisdom about the importance of the "principal as instructional leader" and helping individual teachers improve should be questioned. Instead of spending time evaluating and helping individual teachers gain competence, time might be better spent collaborating with people and helping teachers build trust and closeness with each other.

Leana reports that when she describes results of her research to teachers, they agree with her findings. However when she describes results to school administrators and policymakers she often is faced with skepticism. What do you think of the results of her study?

Organizational Skills for Teachers

The perspectives and research on organizational context and effective schools are important for beginning teachers for several reasons. First, they can provide a lens for understanding schools as social organizations, and second, they can serve as a reminder that your own classroom will be but part of a larger school effort. This research also draws attention to several contradictions that stem from the way schools have been organized. On one hand, it appears that effective schools are places where people have common goals, teachers have organized their curriculum coherently, and common rules and norms guide teachers' expectations for students, homework policies, and discipline. On the other hand, the cellular structure of many schools and traditional norms that support teacher autonomy make it difficult for people in a school to create the conditions that will make their school a better place for students.

The remainder of this chapter looks at specific organizational skills that will be of concern to beginning teachers. These are organized according to the other major *role holders* in schools with whom teachers are expected to work. As you read about these organizational skills, keep in mind the main idea from the effective schools research: namely, collective effort schoolwide can produce important conditions for student learning.

Working with Colleagues

Establishing good working relationships with colleagues is an important challenge for a beginning teacher. Being successful in this endeavor requires an understanding of important norms governing collegiality and specific actions that can be taken.

Norms. When beginning teachers enter their first school, they should be aware of the norms that will govern many of the relationships between them and their colleagues. The hands-off and autonomy norms, which allow colleagues within the school to be friendly and supportive but discourage specific suggestions about instructional practices, has already been described. The beginning teacher is likely to be included in lunchroom talk about school politics and the personalities of individual students but will not find much talk about curriculum or teaching methods. Beginning teachers will find they can ask colleagues to provide assistance in finding a place to live or locating

Check, Extend, Explore

Check

- How does a teacher's typical workday differ from that perceived by the general public?
- What types of work do teachers do in addition to direct instruction of students? What percentage of their time is spent outside the classroom?
- What overall findings have been demonstrated by school effectiveness research?
- How does research such as Carrie Leana's illustrate the importance of a cohesive school culture and collaborative action on the part of teachers?

Extend

- Teachers working together has been shown to influence student learning in significant ways. To what degree are you the type of person who will enjoy working with other teachers? Go to the "Extend Question Poll" on the Online Learning Center to respond.

Explore

- Go to the Online Learning Center at www.mhhe.com/arends10e for links to Web sites related to *School Effectiveness and School Reform.* Visit the Web sites for the Annenberg Institute for School Reform and for the Gates Foundation.

New teachers can attempt to overcome autonomy norms in schools by observing, discussing, and meeting with colleagues.

a good doctor; they may not be able to ask for help (at least not very directly), however, if they are having a classroom management problem.

The cellular structure in many schools means that beginning teachers may be expected to work alone. They will not be observed by other teachers, nor will they be invited to observe their peers.

Possible Actions. All schools will not reflect the norms described in exactly the same way. Some schools, in fact, may have norms that support professional collegiality, and this situation is becoming much more common as teachers and administrators recognize that student learning can be enhanced if everyone works together. Regardless of the situation, beginning teachers do have some latitude for working with colleagues in open and constructive ways. However, it may require well-planned initiatives on their part. The following activities are usually possible.

Observing Other Teachers. This book has stressed the importance of focused observation and reflection in the process of learning to teach. This process should continue for first-year teachers. In fact, many of the observation schedules provided on the Online Learning Center can be used again and again—during early field experiences, during student teaching, and in the beginning years.

Beginning teachers who want to observe other teachers should inquire early about whether or not classroom visits and observations are acceptable practice in their schools. If they are, principals, department chairs, or lead teachers can facilitate observation opportunities. If norms prevent collegial observations, it is still likely that these can be done in other schools where the beginning teacher is not known. These visits may have to be arranged by principals or by system-level curriculum specialists because they will require substitute teachers.

Discussing Educational Issues with Colleagues. Even if school norms prevent widespread collegial interaction concerning the problems of teaching, most schools have at least a handful of teachers who like more discussion and collegiality. A beginning teacher can take the initiative in seeking out these teachers and promoting this type of exchange. Initial discussions may eventually lead to exchanges of materials and perhaps exchanges of classroom visits and observations.

Finally, beginning teachers can seek out other beginning teachers who have not yet been socialized into the hands-off norm and who are probably suffering from many of the same problems and concerns. It has happened that beginning teachers have established their own weekly study and support group where mutual concerns and teaching strategies are shared.

Working in Small Groups and at Meetings. It will be a rare school where a beginning teacher will not find at least a few meetings at which teachers come together for the purpose of mutual planning. Some beginning teachers may not feel comfortable speaking up at faculty assemblies, but they can seek out membership within numerous small groups in the school. In these small-group settings, they can promote collegial norms through modeling good group behavior, such as open communication and effective problem solving and decision making.

Participating in Lesson Study. According to Danielson (2006), lesson study is a process used quite widely among teachers in Japan, the United States, and many developed countries. Here is how it works.

A group of teachers who work at the same grade level or in the same subject area meet and plan a lesson jointly. One member then teaches the lesson while others observe. Members of the lesson-study group critique the lesson and together they revise it. Another member of the group then teaches the revised lesson. This process can continue until the group agrees that the lesson is about as good as it can be. Beginning teachers have been known to initiate this process and benefit greatly from joint planning and from professional discourse with peers.

Working with Administrators and Leadership Personnel

A second group of people beginning teachers need to relate to is the leadership personnel within the school. School norms govern these relationships also, and specific actions are required.

Norms. Most careful observers of teachers' relationships with principals and other school leaders have pointed out that norms governing these relationships are somewhat ambiguous. On one hand, the school's professional ethos supports the concept of the principal serving as the school's instructional leader and as a role model for teachers. On the other hand, the hands-off norm applies to principals and other leadership personnel as well as to other teachers. Often this norm inhibits direct participation by principals in matters of curriculum or teaching strategies. It seems that traditionally teachers wanted their principal to act as a buffer between them and outside pressures, but did not want too much interference with what was going on in the classroom. However, norms surrounding the principal's involvement are changing, and today beginning teachers will likely find many principals who assume some direct responsibilities for curriculum and instruction.

> New teachers can take several steps to build positive communication channels with the principal.

Possible Actions. Obviously, principals vary greatly in their educational beliefs and management styles. Some are very supportive, and some are not. Some have excellent organizational and interpersonal skills, and some don't. One principal's priorities and values will differ from another's. In some instances, these values and priorities will be consistent with the values and beliefs of a beginning teacher; in other cases, they will be diametrically opposed.

Several specific actions can be taken by beginning teachers to gain the support of the principal and to establish a positive working relationship, regardless of the type of person he or she turns out to be. These actions include the following:

- Initiate regular weekly meetings with the principal during the first few weeks to discuss expectations for teacher and student behavior, academic goals, and other features of the school. Find out the principal's thoughts on the attributes of effective schools and effective teaching.
- Keep the principal informed in writing about what you are doing in your classroom, particularly on such topics as special successes you have had, such as a good lesson; a complimentary note from a parent; any conflicts with students or parents; special events such as guest speakers, field trips, or parties you are planning.
- Invite the principal to your classroom, particularly for a lesson that is unique or special, and for parties in elementary schools or special celebrations in secondary schools.
- Write complimentary notes to the principal when he or she does something you like or something that is particularly helpful to you or one of your students.

All of these suggestions fall under the category of building positive communication channels between the beginning teacher and the principal. They are efforts by beginning teachers to get clear about the principal's expectations on one hand and, on the other, to make sure the principal understands their instructional program and activities.

Other School Leaders. In many schools, beginning teachers work with other school leaders as well as the principal, including counselors, reading specialists, special education resource teachers, librarians, media specialists, curriculum specialists, and department chairs. A beginning teacher should remember that roles within organizations are governed by norms that role holders shape as they interact with each other. This means that beginning teachers will have some latitude in their interactions with leadership personnel. These interactions could range from ignoring them completely to actively seeking out their support and assistance. The latter is recommended in most instances.

Beginning teachers should strive, in the very early weeks of school, to build positive working relationships with school leaders and specialists for several reasons. First, unlike teacher colleagues, leadership personnel often are expected to help beginning teachers and to provide help in confidential ways free of evaluation. Second, most counselors and resource teachers got to their current positions because they were effective classroom teachers who received advanced training. This means they probably possess important knowledge they can pass along to beginning teachers if appropriate relationships are established. Finally, resource personnel have more time to provide assistance and support than principals or other teachers in the school do. Beginning teachers should set up regular meetings with resource personnel to discuss roles and expectations, and they should try to keep these individuals informed of their classroom programs and activities.

Working with Families

Parents and primary caregivers are another important group in a teacher's work and professional life. For many years, researchers have known that out-of-school factors, such as family and community, have strong effects on children and youth's school-related attitudes and learning. Teachers themselves also recognize the important role parents and families play in the education of their children. For instance, when they were asked in the Scholastic and Bill and Melinda Gates Survey (*Primary Sources,* 2012) what they believed to be the "efforts" that had the best chance of improving student learning, "gaining parent engagement and involvement" was highest on their list. Indeed, the importance of families led to our inclusion of the Home and School feature in *Learning to Teach* as well as this update and expansion of the working with families section of Chapter 14.

As early as 1966, Coleman and his colleagues identified the importance of family and found that family characteristics were strong predictors of student success in school. Many subsequent studies have been conducted over the past thirty years and were summarized by Honig, Kahne, and McLaughlin (2001). One strong conclusion stands out: *Families matter.* In general, this research demonstrates that children's opportunities to learn and be successful in school are enhanced by the support and encouragement that parents (or other primary caregivers) provide them. This has led many experts in the field (Boulfard, Bridgall, Gordon, & Weiss, 2009; Epstein, 2010; Molnar, 2013) to argue that parent and family involvement is one of the most important actions schools and teachers can take to improve student achievement in both the short and the long term.

Working with parents and others in the community, however, is not easy for several reasons. First, the traditional norms governing parent–teacher relationships are somewhat contradictory. Teachers want their relationships with parents to include both concern for the child and support for their instructional program. At the same time, some teachers do not want parents to interfere with their classrooms. Some teachers tend to keep a good distance between themselves and parents and, in fact, have little interaction with them.

Second, many schools exist in communities that are very different from the way they were a century ago, when schools as we know them were established. Communities have changed and workplace demands on parents are far greater than in earlier times. Families have been reconfigured, and the nuclear family, as once defined, is no longer the norm. In many, many families today, in both affluent and impoverished neighborhoods, all of the adults work outside the home.

Copyright © Pedro Molina. Reprinted with permission.

Finally, as described in Chapter 2, there is often a discontinuity between the school and the home. Many times the school represents a cultural background quite different from that of the parents. In general, teachers and administrators are middle class, Anglo, and monolingual speakers of English. Many students and their parents, however, are working class, members of minority groups, and speak English as a second language. Further discontinuities or mismatches between home and school exist in regard to linguistic features and value orientations. Several of these differences were identified by Corno (1989) and are listed in Table 14.3.

Corno (1989) observed that the differences between the home and the school, particularly the language and value differences, made communication between home and school difficult even under the best of circumstances.

Thus, working with parents, regardless of the difficulties, is important. These actions will not only affect student learning but also create a strong support system for beginning teachers in the community. It can also be a very rewarding aspect of a teacher's work. Following are several ways beginning teachers can build positive, supportive relationships with parents or other significant adults in students' lives. Remember that guidelines for working with parents, as with other aspects of teaching, will vary from one context to another. You need to remain sensitive to the fact that in many communities, the two-parent home may no longer be the norm. You also need to recognize that even when two parents or adults live in the same home, it is likely that both are working outside the home.

Table 14.3 *Differences between Culture of the Home and Culture of the School*

Culture of the Home	Culture of the School
Oral language tradition	Written language tradition
Natural	Unfamiliar
Casual	Formal
Low child–adult ratio	High child–adult ratio
Adults as nurturers	Adults as leaders or managers

Source: Adapted from "What It Means to Be Literate in Classrooms" by L. Corno (1989), in Bloom (ed.), *Classrooms and Literacy.* Norwood, NJ: Ablex.

Possible Actions. Teacher–parent interactions can take several forms. For example, in the previously described Scholastic and Bill and Melinda Gates Survey (*Primary Sources*, 2012) teachers reported the following kinds of interactions with families and parents:

- Communicate with students' parents by e-mail.
- Attend and talk to parents at students' school and non-school-related extracurricular and sporting events.
- Have parent–teacher conferences in the student's home.
- Provide a phone number where they can be reached to parents and students.

For our discussion here, parent or family activities have been categorized into the following actions: reporting to parents, holding conferences with parents, and enlisting parents' help in school and at home.

Reporting to Parents. Remember the idea described in Chapter 6 that parents of children at any age want to know how their children are doing in school. The traditional report card is one means of giving parents this information. Experienced teachers, however, often use additional means to keep parents informed, because the formal report card is only issued quarterly and only summarizes progress in general terms.

Some teachers, particularly of younger children, try to make weekly or biweekly contact with parents through notes, telephone calls, or e-mail. Such contacts allow teachers to explain what is going on in their classrooms and how the parent's child is doing on specific lessons. Such frequent and regular contact provides the teacher with a natural means for communicating children's successes, not just their deficiencies, which often dominate more formal reports.

Another means of parent communication—one that works well for middle and high school teachers who have many students—is the use of a weekly or monthly newsletter or Weblog (blog). The use of these devices was described in Chapter 10. Following are suggestions to guide the production and circulation of classroom or schoolwide parent newsletters/blogs adapted from Dietz and Whaly (2005), Epstein (2001, 2010), and Mathews (2007):

- Newsletters/blogs can be formal or informal. They should reflect a newspaper format with headings, and they should always be neatly and carefully done.
- The language of the newsletter/blog should be suitable for the community and chosen with the parents' backgrounds in mind.
- Newsletters/blogs should be sent home consistently. Once a month is best in most situations. They can also be shared with other teachers and with the principal.
- Newsletters/blogs should be designed to provide information parents are interested in, such as what the class is studying; changes in formats or schedules; new goals and directions for the class; new rules; routines and expectations; and upcoming projects, programs, and events.
- A portion of the newsletter/blog should be devoted to recognitions, such as for students or teams who have done good work, for parent helpers who have made significant contributions, and for others in the community who have visited or contributed to the class.
- Newsletters/blogs should contain samples of students' work, such as writings, poems, or projects. Make sure every student's work is included eventually.
- Newsletters/blogs can be used as a way to involve parents by inviting them to participate in class activities or to serve as classroom or school helpers.

Margin notes:

Teacher–parent interactions may include written reporting, conferencing, and requesting parent help when needed.

Newsletters/blogs are a means of providing written updates to parents regarding activities in the classroom.

Conferences provide a valuable opportunity for parents and teachers to develop a positive working relationship.

Holding Conferences with Parents. Most beginning teachers will be involved with parent conferences sometimes in school and sometimes in the student's home. Teachers of younger children are sometimes required to make a home visit early in the school year and to hold quarterly in-school meetings with parents. Teachers of older students are normally given more latitude to initiate conferences as needed or when parents request them. In either event, holding parent conferences is an important organizational responsibility of teaching and can provide valuable experiences for the teacher and the parents if done properly. This is also a function that some beginning teachers feel somewhat nervous about.

Preconference preparations include the following:

1. **Notify:** Purpose, place, time, length of time allotted. Consider the parent's schedule and availability; offer choices of time whenever possible.
2. **Prepare:** Review child's folder, gather examples of work, and prepare materials. Be very familiar with the student's performance and progress before the parent arrives.
3. **Plan agenda:** List items for discussion and/or presentation.
4. **Arrange environment:** Have comfortable seating, eliminate distractions. The parent is at an immediate disadvantage by being on your "turf." To help avoid power implications, arrange the environment so that you and the parent are on equal planes (same-sized chairs), sitting side-by-side at a table, as opposed to face-to-face across your desk.

The actual conference includes the following:

1. **Welcome:** Establish rapport.
2. **State:** Purpose, time limitation, note taking, options for follow-up. This is where you share information and present data. You may find note taking during the conference useful in recording your interactions—particularly the parent's feedback and responses. In addition, discuss various avenues you (each) may follow in future dealings with the student, including directions for your instruction and expectations.
3. **Encourage:** Information sharing, comments, questions.
4. **Listen:** Pause once in a while. Look for verbal and nonverbal cues. The previous two recommendations support the concept of a conference being an *exchange* between the teacher and the parent.
5. **Summarize.**
6. **End** on a positive note.

Postconference steps and recommendations include the following:

1. **Review** conference with child, if appropriate.
2. **Share** information with other school personnel, if needed.
3. **Mark** calendar for planned follow-up.
4. **Send** follow-up notes specifying any agreements or later actions to be taken by the teacher or the parents.

Finally, some schools and teachers have found that involving students in parent or family conferences can increase communication among all parties and help develop stronger school–family relations.

Enlisting Family Members' Help in School and at Home. Another way that beginning teachers can work with parents is by involving them as teachers and assistants, both in school and at home. This practice is more common in elementary and middle schools than in high schools. It is also easier in communities where *not all* the parents hold jobs. Regardless of the situation, beginning teachers will always find some parents or parent surrogates willing to help if proper encouragement is given. Parents can help

- **To assist with small groups.** Conducting small-group activities is difficult for teachers because there are so many simultaneous demands in the classroom. Effective teachers sometimes find parents who will come to the school and help on a regular basis. If beginning teachers choose to use parents in this way, they should consider the parents' schedules and plan some training so that parents know what is expected of them.
- **To assist with field trips and other special events.** Field trips and many other special events such as parties or celebrations take an extra set of hands. Again, with proper encouragement and training, parents can be most useful during these times.
- **As teacher aides.** Some teachers have found ways to use parents as aides in their classrooms, thus getting valuable assistance in correcting papers, writing and publishing class newsletters, organizing parties, and the like.
- **To help with homework.** Most parents feel a responsibility for helping their children with homework. Unfortunately, many do not know how to be helpful. Effective teachers teach parents how to teach their own children. This can also be done on a schoolwide basis. This generally requires holding special evening sessions

Planning conference topics in advance can relieve the stress that beginning teachers may experience at meeting time.

Teachers can develop positive relationships with parents by asking them for assistance at work or home.

during which the teacher explains to parents what the homework is trying to accomplish, shows them how to help students practice, and provides them with guidelines for giving students feedback. Many of the skills described in this book can be taught to parents. Teaching parents teaching skills may be time-consuming, but it can extend the teacher's influence over student learning, perhaps more than any other single action.

Many districts, particularly those with large populations of students who are at risk, are adopting family involvement programs that require teachers to behave in new and different ways. Working with parents and caregivers can be difficult, but it can also be a very rewarding aspect of a teacher's work. It can help break down the discontinuities between the home and the school and it can greatly enhance children and youth's opportunity to participate and be successful in school.

Providing Leadership for School Improvement

Helping schools improve, as with other aspects of school leadership and collaboration, will not be the major concern of beginning teachers. It is, however, an area that beginners should know about. Making classrooms and schools better is a responsibility of teachers, and involvement, if only in a very small way, should start early in one's career.

Why Improvement? Schools, as they exist today, assumed their basic design in the late 1800s. Curiously, people are ambivalent about this design. Many citizens are comfortable with the familiar patterns of the schools they experienced as children, and they get upset with changes that challenge these basic patterns. For example, efforts to get rid of the "neighborhood school" concept, for whatever reasons, meet severe resistance in most communities. At the same time, citizens are quick to find fault with the schools when they fail to live up to contemporary expectations. A number of years ago Bruce Joyce and his colleagues (1993) caught the essence of this paradox when they wrote:

> Throughout history . . . [critics] . . . have found [the school] both too backward and too advanced. It falls behind the times and fails to keep us in simultaneous cadence. . . . Most citizens are cautious about educational innovation. People like the familiar old schoolhouse as much as they criticize it. They tend to believe that current problems in education are caused by changes (perceived as "lowering of standards") rather than because the old comfortable model of the school may be a little rusty and out-of-date. In fact, our society has changed a great deal since the days when the familiar and comfortable patterns of education were established, and many schools have become badly out of phase with the needs of children in today's world. (pp. 3–4)

Joyce and his colleagues were right. The world has changed considerably since the idea of formal schooling was first conceived. As you know, many aspects of people's lives and of their social institutions have transformed dramatically over the past quarter of a century. As described in Chapter 1, a shrinking world produced by new communication and transportation technologies has replaced older parochial views with more cosmopolitan outlooks and interests. Shifting population patterns have made diverse, multicultural communities the norm and have greatly increased social sensitivity. New information technologies that include telecommunication satellites, word processors, microcomputers, and the Internet have substantially changed the way information can be thought about and used. The printing technologies that came into being only during the last two hundred years, making possible the current system of schools and libraries, must now compete with electronic communications. Today, every classroom and most homes have electronic access to the information and wisdom stored in the major libraries of the world. These changes provide the context in which education and schools must operate. They also influence the values and interests of the youth found in classrooms, as well as the values and beliefs you have about teaching and about schools.

Social changes are also accompanied by changes in childhood and adolescence. Youth mature sooner than in earlier times, and each generation is confronted with a different set of questions and priorities that must be addressed. Some years ago, American sociologist James Coleman (1972) illustrated this problem in an article titled "The Children Have Outgrown the Schools." In this article, he argued that schools fail students because they are pursuing the wrong goals with inappropriate experiences. Schools were created at a time when the society, according to Coleman, was "information poor and action rich." This meant that people, including youth, had plenty of things to do but little information to assist them. Over time, however, society has become "information rich but action poor"—people now have access to all kinds of information but fewer opportunities for applying and acting on the information. Coleman suggested that modern curricula should require more opportunities for active learning and involvement rather than merely providing exposure to more and more information. Almost forty years later many still agree with Coleman and believe that schools remain out of touch with the needs of today's youth. Today, we hold high expectations for all students, yet many continue to drop out prior to graduation. Today, we believe that students should construct knowledge in student-centered classrooms, yet transmitting information from a standardized curriculum prevails. Today, we believe in providing realistic links between education and daily living, yet many students of the "net generation" report being more involved with their home computers than with school (Tapscott, 1998; Trotter, 2007; West, 2012). How to change schools to meet these new realities is a difficult and perplexing problem and a challenge to your generation of teachers. Here are some ways beginning teachers can get started.

Possible Actions. As a beginning teacher encountering your first classroom, you likely will be faced with many dilemmas and unanswered questions. You also will likely be troubled by some of the discrepancies between your professional ideals and the realities you find. Some beginning teachers have been known to accept these realities with a sense of resignation or defeat. Others have faced the complexities of teaching with a desire for improvement. There are some concrete things teachers can do, even in their beginning years, that will establish healthy patterns and contribute to school improvement.

Working at the School Level. A beginning teacher's role in schoolwide improvement efforts at first involves being a thoughtful participant in proposals that come from others. Such proposals may involve policies for beginning teacher evaluation created by the state legislature, a new science curriculum adopted by the school district, or perhaps new approaches for classroom management offered by the principal. In all these instances, beginning teachers will be primarily on the receiving end. According to Fullan (1992, 2001, 2009), when teachers are faced with proposals for reform, they

Enhancing Teaching and Learning with Technology
A Look to the Future

All major innovations have both positive and negative consequences. The automobile increased individual mobility, but it also led to highway deaths, urban sprawl, and inadequate mass transit systems. The airplane has helped turn the world into a global village; it has also caused pollution and been used as a tool of terrorism and mass destruction. Twenty-first-century computers and related technologies hold great potential for positive effects on student learning. As described in previous chapters, research supports the use of computers and has shown how they and related technologies can not only enhance teacher-centered instruction but also provide very strong support for activity and student-centered approaches. However, negative consequences may also occur. This final technology box discusses some societal-wide technology issues of which beginning teachers should be aware as well as some issues that pertain to your own growth as a professional in using technology to enhance student learning.

Technology-Related Issues

As described in Chapter 1, the perspective taken in *Learning to Teach* is that technology will not in the immediate future take over education, replace teachers, or drastically change some of the more traditional ways we have organized schooling and learning. Most students will continue to go to neighborhood schools and will likely be taught by a single teacher in an age-graded classroom. However, beginning teachers can expect the use of technology at all grade levels to become more sophisticated and for technology to have an increasing presence in their students' lives. There will also be some important societal issues for tomorrow's educators to worry about.

Information-age technologies have, in Collins and Halveson's (2009) words, created their own *imperatives* that include "customization, interaction, and learner control" (p. 5). Regardless of what schools do, youth will have their computers, tablets, iPods, and smartphones, and these devices will allow them to pursue their own interests and goals and to access and interact with knowledge wherever they are and on just about any topic. The Internet will allow them "to control what they do, whom they communicate with, and even who they are" (p. 5). This condition will require your generation of educators to rethink the role and purposes of education in a technological world. More and more learning will be interactive with peers and will occur outside of school. Support for student learning will come not only from guidance professionals but also from an array of individuals connected through social networks.

What is important to learn will also have to be examined. Traditional academic subjects—mathematics, language, history, and the sciences—dominate prescribed standards and curriculum frameworks found in today's schools. In the years, ahead, teachers and the larger society will have to wrestle with whether this is the best curriculum for a technological age and answer questions such as: Is the current curriculum too narrow? Should it be expanded to include a new set of literacy and critical-thinking understandings and skills? Should these new skills reflect the shift from the dominance of text to the dominance of visual images? What understandings and skills are required to prepare students to be visually literate and to be effective consumers of Internet information? What does this mean for literacy instruction? For mathematics?

Many teachers and parents believe that technology will have a negative impact on children and youth. Hours spent staring at computer monitors and playing electronic games distract youth from other endeavors—reading books, spending time with family, playing and socializing with friends. Frequent media reports of youth engaged in mass killings and bullying who were addicted to violent games and Web sites heighten concerns about potentially negative aspects of computers and related technologies.

What are the schools' responsibilities to these larger social issues? What can individual teachers do?

Similarly, educators and parents worry about the content of many Web sites and what children may be watching or to whom they may be talking. Although schools have taken steps to filter out inappropriate content, filters are not often used in home computers and filtering practices raise a host of privacy and freedom issues. Finally, parents and educators are concerned about the rise and popularity of social networking sites such as Facebook, Twitter, and YouTube. What kinds of dangers do these types of interactions present? How do these networking features facilitate "bullying"? What is lost if youth are getting their strong needs for affiliation satisfied online? What is gained?

Again, what are the schools' and teachers' responsibilities for addressing the negative aspects of social media?

A Final Word about Technology

Most observers agree with Rosen (2010), Trotter (2007), and West (2012) that technological change in the larger society will continue at a rapid pace and that these changes will demand responses by our educational institutions and by teachers. Schools will be required to move technology from the periphery into the mainstream of their core academic and social practices. Teachers will be required to stay abreast of technological change and continue to upgrade their skills for using technology.

Any new field presents many opportunities for optimism and vision. Technology is no different. It can provide yet unknown opportunities for making education a more promising experience for all students and for enhancing student learning. Fullan (2011), however, warns us that technology *alone* will not remake the schools or get us the kind of student learning we want. He writes that "the notion of having a computer or hand-held device for every student will make her or him smarter, or even more knowledgeable is pedagogically vapid" (p. 13). Instead what is required is a new generation of teachers who are pedagogically adept, grounded in instruction, technologically literate, and who can figure out with their students how "best to engage technology" in the pursuit of learning.

should consider individually and as a faculty several issues before deciding to commit themselves to the change effort. These issues include the following:

1. *Assess the nature of the proposed change.* Teachers need to give the proposed change careful study. They need to determine if it addresses an important need and if it has been successful elsewhere. They also need to assess their own priorities. Teachers are faced with many changes all the time, and they can only put their energy into a few. In most instances, a faculty can only work on one or two improvement efforts at a time, and these are best accomplished when they are connected to the overall direction and vision of the school.

2. *Assess administrative support.* Some form of active support by administrators (superintendents and principals) is usually required for reform efforts to be successful. Although teachers may decide to go it alone, independent of their administrators, they should do so only after careful consideration of the risks involved with this type of action.

3. *Assess support by other teachers.* Most school improvement efforts require the support of most, if not all, the teachers in a school. If a single or a few teachers choose to initiate a project, it is wise to check out colleague support first and to stimulate support if it does not already exist before moving forward. School improvement is easier in schools in which teachers have a collaborative work culture.

4. *Move beyond the conventional wisdom.* Many times teachers reject new ideas and innovations because they go against the traditional ways of doing things. Beginning teachers can bring fresh perspectives to educational problems and give new ideas a chance.

Exhibiting Leadership. First impressions affect the way beginning teachers are received by professional colleagues both inside and outside school. One way that beginning teachers can become known among colleagues and win their regard is to exhibit leadership potential within the school or school system. Following are some examples, reported by principals and colleagues, of what several successful beginning teachers did to exhibit leadership during their first year:

- Elaine taught on a fifth- and sixth-grade teaching team that had a weak science curriculum. Elaine had majored in biology in college and had more science background than the other, more experienced teachers on the team. She volunteered to revise the science curriculum for the team and found suitable materials for teachers to use. This leadership was applauded by team members and made Elaine a highly valued and respected team member.

- Valerie, a high school English teacher, was upset about the hall behavior of the students in the building wing where she had been assigned. After getting things off to a good start in her own class, she began discussing the hall problem with other teachers in the wing. Under her leadership, they established a set of rules for hall behavior and together agreed on ways to monitor student behavior between classes.

Obviously, beginning teachers should not overextend themselves by assuming too many leadership responsibilities. However, it is important to pick at least one project that has the potential for schoolwide attention and devote energy to getting successful results. Meeting the leadership challenges of teaching can be among the most rewarding accomplishments of a teacher's career.

Check, Extend, Explore

Check

- What actions can beginning teachers take to facilitate positive working relationships with their colleagues?
- What actions can beginning teachers take to facilitate positive working relationships with their principals?
- What are some common parent–teacher interactions? What can a teacher do to promote optimal relationships?

Extend

- Do you agree or disagree that families should be closely involved in everything that goes on in schools? Go to the "Extend Question Poll" on the Online Learning Center to respond.

Explore

- Go to the Anneburg Institute of School Reform Web site. Review two or three of the tools educators can use in school improvement efforts. How useful are they? Review the "School Improvement Guide." Compare the ideas to those in *Learning to Teach*.
- Go to the National Coalition of Parent Involvement In Education Web site. What are the major goals of the organization? What kinds of tools and resources does it provide to help increase parent and family involvement?

Reflections from the *Classroom*

Teacher's Work

At the beginning of this chapter, you read about the busy work lives of two beginning teachers. Both are highly involved, not only with their students, but also with schoolwide activities.

Think about all aspects of a teacher's work and write a reflective essay on school leadership and collaboration. Consider the following questions: What are your views on the noninstructional aspects of a teacher's work? Are these aspects important? Or do they take valuable time that could be spent with students? What about the effective school research? Do you believe that synergy can be created

and student achievement enhanced when teachers work together? Or do you believe that the best way to improve student learning is to allow maximum autonomy for teachers? When you begin your teaching career, which aspects of a teacher's work will you value the most? Which aspects will you find most troublesome? Do you look forward to working with colleagues and parents? Or do you think you will resent this type of work because it takes time away from your students? You may wish to illustrate your reflections with photographs of schools, videos, papers, and other artifacts that will demonstrate your understanding of the school as a place where teachers work and the features that make some schools more effective than others. Approach the situation from the perspective closest to the grade level you are preparing to teach. Finally, place this work in your professional portfolio and compare it with the following views of two experienced teachers.

Amy Callen
Lyndon Pilot School, 4th and 5th Grade Loop, Boston, MA

Whether you are a first-year teacher or have twenty years of experience, the day does not end when the last child steps on the school bus. There are papers to correct, bulletin boards to design, new units to research, parents to call, conferences to facilitate, meetings to attend, etc. Becoming involved in your school community is vital to your survival as a teacher. There are many ways to become involved.

However, one of the most common mistakes I have seen is taking on too many responsibilities that are not connected to your everyday work in the classroom. When I began my teaching career, I volunteered for everything I could. I joined the School Site Council. I was a member of the Hiring and Evaluation Committee. I regularly attended PTO meetings, started an after-school math club, and often found myself still at school at ten o'clock at night. Because of these activities, added to my everyday classroom responsibilities, I became too busy and had no life of my own.

Teachers at the beginning of their careers should spend time outside of the classroom focusing on their practice. Attending school and districtwide professional development programs, joining study groups, observing other teachers, being observed, and attending common planning sessions are all experiences that will enhance your performance in the classroom. Allow yourself time to get comfortable with who you are as a teacher, and begin to balance that with who you are outside of school. Do not forget that there is a life outside the school walls.

After a few years, your classroom responsibilities will seem automatic to you. You will know your curriculum inside and out, and you will be ready to share your knowledge and time with the community. This is the time to join the PTO, to start a school newspaper, write a grant, or take on a student teacher. People will appreciate your knowledge and time, and you will not become frustrated or overwhelmed with all of your responsibilities.

It is extremely tempting to involve yourself in opportunities that arise during your first year, but be patient. You have a lifetime of teaching ahead of you. Your first year is for you. Be selfish and choose only those opportunities that will support you and your growth as an educator. Also make sure you let your colleagues know that you are part of the school team.

Angela Adams
Jacksonville Middle School, 7th and 8th Grades, Jacksonville, TX

Teaching is a profession that fulfills many aspects of my life. Unfortunately, for many teachers, teaching is simply a job they think about only when inside the classroom. They rarely get involved in schoolwide activities. During my first year, I wanted to be involved with everything, from science club to supporting the cheerleaders, from the band to the sports teams. I quickly realized that I had overextended myself. Now, I choose one or two activities that I feel I can devote an adequate amount of time to and volunteer for events, depending on my schedule. When my students are involved, I also try to attend concerts, games, and plays. This is an excellent way to build positive, rewarding relationships with students and show that you support their efforts.

In addition to being involved with students, teachers should also be involved with other teachers in their school. My school allows an extra planning period so teachers can meet in departments to plan collaborative projects and lessons each day. Working with other teachers provides me with fresh ideas and new angles in which to view my subject. And, don't forget parents!

Summary

Describe the perspective on schools as social organizations and as places where teachers work. Explain the features of schools that are the same as and different from other organizations.

- Schools are social organizations and, as such, are adult workplaces as well as places where students come to learn.

- People in schools act not in totally free and disconnected ways but in more or less interdependent and predictable ways.

- Schools have individual histories and cultures (tone, ethos) with norms and roles that influence school goals and processes and the way people work to achieve them.

- Although schools, like other organizations, are characterized by goals and control structures, they also have special features, such as goal ambiguity, compulsory attendance, political visibility, limited resources, and sense of community.

- Two important norms that regulate the culture of teaching and behavior in schools are the autonomy norm and the hands-off norm. The autonomy norm allows teachers to do pretty much what they want inside their classrooms. The hands-off norm sanctions teachers who try to interfere with other teachers' teaching methods or processes.
- Roles also define how teachers do their work. Some aspects of a teacher's role are contradictory: for example, the need to provide individual attention to students in group settings and the need to maintain a certain amount of social distance from students.

Describe the theoretical foundations behind schools and the nature of teachers' work. Summarize the features of effective schools.

- Research on teachers' work lives has documented that teachers carry out many organizational functions in addition to working directly with students and that the time demands on teachers are quite extensive.
- A moderately strong knowledge base exists that helps explain why some schools are more effective than others. Some aspects of this research are still controversial.
- Research on schools has illustrated that while teaching performance in individual classrooms is important, the way that principals, teachers, parents, and students all come together to define common goals, expectations, and procedures and the way teachers take collective responsibility for student learning have substantial impact on what students learn.
- More effective schools have processes and procedures characterized by clear goals, high expectations, pervasive caring, strong leadership, community support, high academic learning time, frequent monitoring of student progress, coherent curricula strong family involvement, and variety in the methods used by teachers.

Describe the workplace skills required of teachers and discuss ways teachers can work effectively and collaboratively with colleagues, administrators, and parents for the purpose of improving education for all students.

- Teachers contribute to effective schools by successfully working with colleagues; working with school leaders, such as the principal; working with parents; and providing leadership for school improvement.
- Establishing good working relationships with colleagues is very important and can be enhanced by observing other teachers in the school, volunteering to work on committees and task forces, and seeking out colleagues for discussion of educational issues.
- Teachers build good working relationships with principals and other leadership personnel by meeting with them regularly, keeping them informed about what they are doing in their classrooms, and participating in school-wide activities.
- Parents and caregivers will become partners in the teacher's classroom if they are kept informed about what is going on, made to feel welcome in the school and at conferences, and enlisted to help in their child's education at home and in school. Family involvement can have very strong, positive effects on how well students do in school.
- Helping to improve classrooms and schools is an important aspect of the teacher's job.
- Improvement is needed because schools, in many instances, are out of phase with the needs of today's youth and do not live up to rising expectations people have for education.
- Teachers who choose to work toward school improvement can do so by becoming thoughtful and informed about change initiatives proposed by others and by helping to create and provide leadership for improvement projects.

Key Terms

autonomy norm   506
ethos   502
hands-off norm   506
human capital   512

loosely coupled   508
norms   506
school culture   502
school effectiveness research   509

social capital   512
social context   502
synergy   510

Interactive and Applied Learning

Study and Explore

- Access your Study Guide, which includes practice quizzes, from the Online Learning Center.

Observe and Practice

- Listen to audio clips on the Online Learning Center of Kendra Ganzer (fifth grade) and Amy Callen (fourth/fifth grade) talking about nonclassroom work in the *Teachers on Teaching* area.

Complete the following **Practice Exercises** that accompany Chapter 14:
- Practice Exercise 14.1: Writing a Letter to a Parent or Family Member
- Practice Exercise 14.2: Generating Action Research Questions
- Practice Exercise 14.3: Getting to Know Your School as a Workplace

Portfolio and Field Experience Activities

Expand your understanding of the content and processes of this chapter through the following field experience and portfolio activities. Support materials to complete the activities are in the *Portfolio and Field Experience Activities* area on the Online Learning Center.

1. Complete the **Reflections from the Classroom** exercise at the end of this chapter. The recommended essay will provide insights into your overall view about the work of teachers, particularly that work that focuses on schoolwide leadership. **(InTASC Standard 10: Leadership and Collaboration)**
2. **Activity 14.1: Assessing Your Workplace Skills.** Check your level of understanding and skill to provide leadership and to work on schoolwide issues and concerns. **(InTASC Standard 10: Leadership and Collaboration)**

3. **Activity 14.2: Interviewing Teachers about Involving Parents and Caregivers.** Interview experienced teachers to find out how they strive to work and build partnerships with parents. **(InTASC Standard 10: Leadership and Collaboration)**
4. **Activity 14.3: Charting the Characteristics of a School's Boundary.** Gather information about the neighborhood of a school in your area. **(InTASC Standard 10: Leadership and Collaboration)**
5. **Activity 14.4: Portfolio: My Platform for Effective Schools.** Create a platform on teachers' work and effective schooling. Place this artifact in your portfolio to show your understanding of this aspect of teaching. **(InTASC Standard 10: Leadership and Collaboration)**

Books for the Professional

Danielson, C. (2008). *Enhancing professional practice: A framework for teaching* (2nd ed.). Alexandria, VA: Association for Supervision and Curriculum Development.

Epstein, J. (2010). *School, family, and community partnerships: Preparing educators and improving schools.* Boulder, CO: Westview Press.

Fullan, M. (2009). *The challenge of change: Start school improvement now!* (2nd ed.). Thousand Oaks, CA: Corwin Press.

Kohn, A. (2000). *The schools our children deserve.* New York: Houghton Mifflin.

Lieberman, A., & Miller, L. (2008). *Teachers in professional communities: Improving teacher and learning.* New York: Teachers College Press.

Ravitch, D. (2011). *The death and life of the great American school system: How testing and choice are undermining education.* New York: Basic Books.

Sahlbergol, P. (2011). *Finnish lessons: What can the world learn from educational change in Finland?* New York: Teachers College Press.

Resource Handbook

Contents

Handbook 1 *Reading and Using Research*

Chapter 1 of *Learning to Teach* described the importance of the knowledge base on teaching and learning and how educational research supports the practice of teaching and frees teachers from an overreliance on commonsense and rule-of-thumb approaches. As with other complex human activities, research has its own rules and specialized language, which can be very confusing to the novice. Learning to learn from research requires some understanding of the methods and language used by researchers and an awareness of where to go for research information. A broad understanding of educational research is obviously beyond the scope of this book, but certain key concepts that are important for reading and understanding research are presented in this special resource section. The aim of this section is to help beginning teachers to use research, to read research reports with a critical eye, and to locate research that may be needed to inform the practice of evidence-based teaching.

Key Research Ideas

Several basic features of research are important to understand in order to read and use it properly. These include the way researchers state problems, the overall conception or model that guides their research, and the way they seek to find relationships among variables.

Research Questions and Problems

Researchers and educational practitioners often pose their questions and problems in different ways. A problem, from the researcher's perspective, normally has three ingredients: (1) It is clearly stated in question form; (2) it focuses on relationships between two or more variables; and (3) it implies the possibility of testing from a scientific perspective. Practical problems, however, although sometimes stated in question form, rarely focus on relationships that can be clearly tested. Instead, they generally strive to state a discrepancy between the "way things are" and the way the problem solver would like them "to be." To show the difference between a practical problem faced by teachers and a researchable problem posed by researchers, consider two types of questions that might be asked about student motivation. A teacher might ask a practical question such as, "How can I get my unmotivated students to do their homework each night?" A researcher, however, might ask a researchable question such as, "What are the effects of two different reward systems (free time in school versus parental praise) on time devoted to homework by unmotivated students?" Both problems are clearly stated in question form and are important, but only the latter focuses on relationships among variables and has a built-in procedure for investigation.

Model for Research on Teaching

Educational researchers try to make sense of the world of education they study. Essentially, they try to find out what influences the very complex environment of teaching and learning. To do this, they have theories about how teaching and learning occur, and they try to arrange various characteristics (variables) of this world into models that can explain teaching and learning more fully. An educational research **variable** is a characteristic, element, or feature of a person (teacher, student, parent) or some aspect of the environment (classroom, strategy, home, school, government) that can vary. Much of the research on teaching and learning during the last few decades has come from researchers who have been guided by what Robert Floden (2001) has called the "effects of teaching" model. The goal and defining characteristic of this research has been to identify the links and relationships among teachers, students, environments, and student outcomes (Floden, 2001; Gage, 1963; Groschner, Seidel, & Shavelson, 2013; Schulman, 1986; Seidel & Shavelson, 2007). The "effects of teaching" model has been expanded over the years, and many interesting and important variables have been added. For the most part, however, the basic model has remained the same, as illustrated in Figure R1.1.

Figure R1.1 *Model for Thinking about Teaching and Research on Teaching*

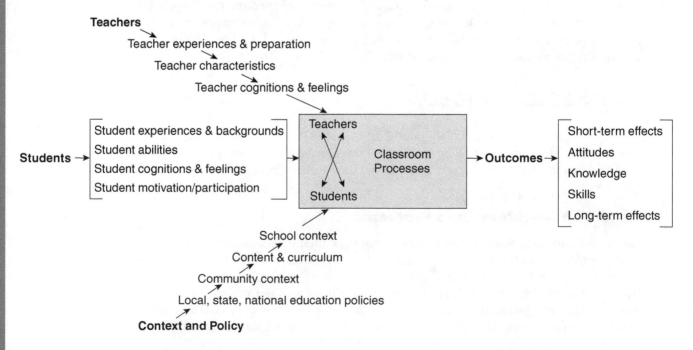

As you can see, the "effects of teaching" model organizes variables into five classes: students, teachers, context and policy, classroom, and outcomes.

1. *Student variables*—the characteristics students bring with them to the classroom, including their experiences, abilities, motivation, cognitions, and feelings.
2. *Teacher variables*—the characteristics of teachers; namely, their experiences, their training, and special properties they have such as skills, motivations, cognition, and feelings.
3. *Context and policy variables*—the larger environment to which teachers and students must adjust, such as characteristics of the community, the school and its curriculum, and local, state, and national policies.
4. *Classroom process variables*—the activities and procedures that occur in classrooms. These variables are associated with what teachers and students do. These classroom process variables are those of most concern in *Learning to Teach*.
5. *Outcome variables*—the outcomes of teaching and classroom interaction, including knowledge, skills, and attitudes. These variables can be divided into more short-term or immediate outcomes as well as long-term effects.

Notice the arrows in the model in Figure R1.1. These show the presumed causative relationships among the variables. It is important to point out that the arrows are only predictions and are not necessarily always accurate. When discussing the model some time ago, Dunkin and Biddle (1974) explained the complexity of discovering what causes what in teaching and learning:

> For example, let us assume that teachers who come from middle-class backgrounds are known to approach pupils somewhat differently than those with lower-class backgrounds. Does this mean that social class "causes" differential classroom behavior? Indeed this interpretation might be correct. But it might also be true that teachers who come from middle- and lower-class backgrounds are more likely to attend different colleges and thus to have had different experiences in teacher training; this latter factor, then, would be the actual cause of their different behaviors in the classroom. (p. 37)

Other researchers (Schulman, 1986) have taken the position that rather than assuming a causation that flows from the teacher to the learner, we should conceive of teaching as an activity involving teachers and students working jointly. Teachers learn and students teach, so the arrows in the model could go both ways. Researchers using the "effects on teaching" model strive to find relationships primarily between teacher behavior and subsequent student outcomes or they may focus on a wider array of variables and explore multiple relationships, including the cognitions and feelings of students and their teachers, as well as the multiple interactions found in classroom settings.

More recently, other models have been developed to provide conceptual maps for the research on teaching. Although each has been constructed from its own point of view, all are attempts to show important relationships in the complex world of teaching and learning. Over the past decade, the "effects of teaching" model has been challenged. For example, some postmodern theorists have argued that any "search for firmly supported knowledge is bound to be fruitless, because all human observation and understanding are mediated by language and context" (Floden, 2001, p. 5; see also Lyotard, 1987). Hamilton and McWilliam (2001) have written that they believe the model to be "moribund." Others (Gilligan, 1982; Noddings, 1992, 2001) have argued that the dominant "effects of teaching" model has been flawed because it was conceived from the vantage point of advantaged white males and neglected views of the less privileged, such as the poor and women. For example, Nel Noddings argued that schooling and research on schooling have held that "feminine" traits such as "caring" are inferior while holding masculine traits up as models.

This brief Resource Handbook on Reading and Using Research reflects mainly the "effects of teaching" perspective. However, as you read this handbook and as you read and use research, you should remain aware that the field of educational research today represents many scholarly traditions. Like any other human endeavor, it will change and evolve significantly over your professional lifetime.

Independent and Dependent Variables

When you read the research on teaching summarized in this book and elsewhere, you will often come across words such as *independent* and *dependent variable*. These are words used by researchers to describe a particular aspect of the variables they are studying. Strictly speaking, **independent variable** refers to a property that is the presumed *cause* of something, whereas **dependent variable** is the *consequence*. In the study of teaching, variables associated with teacher behavior (causes) are normally important independent variables, and student attitude or achievement (consequences) are important dependent variables.

Knowledge about teaching is really knowledge about the relationships between the many independent and dependent variables in the models displayed in Figure R1.1. Many of the relationships that appear to exist are only tentative and are always open to alternative interpretations. It is important to remember that an enterprise as complex as teaching does not always fall neatly into the models devised by researchers.

Approaches to Educational Research

Educational researchers use several different approaches to study problems related to teaching and learning. The critical differences among the various approaches include the assumptions researchers make about the nature of scientific knowledge and the ways they design their studies, collect information, and interpret results.

Assumptions about Scientific Knowledge

Today, researchers make different assumptions about the nature of the social world of education and about the nature of knowledge, and these assumptions influence the type of research they do. Some researchers, for instance, assume that the social world, in our case the world of schools and classrooms, has an *objective reality*. These researchers believe that schools, classrooms, teachers, and students exist independent of the researcher and that they are available for study in an objective, unbiased manner. Researchers who hold this perspective focus their research mainly on observable behaviors that can be measured. This perspective is often referred to as **positivism.** Much of the research that has been done in education over the past century rests on positivistic assumptions.

Constructivism is a different perspective about the social world and the nature of knowledge that has gained favor among the educational research community during the past thirty years. Researchers with this perspective believe that the social world does *not* exist independently but is instead constructed by the participants, mainly students, their teachers, and often the researcher himself or herself. This view of the social world is consistent with the constructivist principles of teaching and learning discussed elsewhere in *Learning to Teach.* However, as with other aspects of education where positivist and constructivist views differ, actions in the real world of research most often do not progress from views of either one or the other but instead in ways where both views inform research design and method.

These perspectives about the social world and scientific knowledge are important because they influence the type of studies researchers conduct and the manner in which they analyze and report their results. Positivists, for instance, are more likely to conduct what has been labeled **quantitative research,** an approach to research that assumes an objective reality, that studies behavior in an objective fashion, and that uses statistical methods to analyze data. Constructivists, in contrast, are more likely to conduct **qualitative research,** an approach that relies on holistic observations, reports data in narrative rather than quantitative form, and conducts the whole research process in a more personalized and interpretative fashion.

Over the years, considerable debate has occurred among researchers using these two approaches. Today, however, many of the issues have been resolved and most researchers would say that both the quantitative and qualitative methods should be used, sometimes together, in the same study. Together they can provide valuable insights into the world of teaching and classroom practice and uncover important complexities that neither can reveal when used alone.

Types of Research Studies

Let's now look more closely at some of the specific types of research used in education and reported in this book.

Descriptive Research

Most of you can readily cite examples of **descriptive research,** not only in the field of education but in other fields as well. On any given day, you can pick up a newspaper and read the results of a survey someone has done. A survey is one type of descriptive research. Researchers adopting this approach commonly use questionnaires or interviews to gather information about the characteristics of some phenomenon or to measure people's opinions or attitudes on some subject.

Although it is difficult to do "good" survey research, the results of such research are easily understood. In most cases, the results are presented numerically and describe the number and percentage of people who have a specific characteristic or who believe in a particular way. The well-known yearly surveys conducted to get citizens' opinions about the schools is a good example of survey research, as is the constant surveying done to get opinions about political preferences.

Sometimes researchers using the descriptive approach are interested in a type of problem that can best be studied using qualitative methods through direct observation of a single case or a small number of cases. These approaches take the form of case studies or, in some instances, ethnographies. **Ethnography** is a word that comes from the field of anthropology and means an extensive study of an intact group of people, such as a culture, a society, or a particular role group. Normally, what a researcher does when conducting this type of research is to select from many possibilities what might be called a typical case and then to conduct in-depth observations of that single case. The aim of a case study, or an ethnography, is to collect extensive information so that a rich description and an in-depth understanding of the research problem will result. Famous early examples of this type of research include the work of anthropologists such as Margaret Mead, who lived with and studied the people in Samoa to discover some of the important underlying patterns of that culture, and the work of Jean Piaget, who conducted in-depth case studies of children to discover how a young child's mind develops and grows.

As a rule, researchers using observational techniques must get quite close to the subjects they are studying. In fact, some become participants themselves and try to influence the problems they are studying.

As contrasted to collecting information using questionnaires or interviews, observation allows the researcher to study the point of view of a group or person and, in turn, construct a more complete picture of the situation. A weakness of this type of research, however, is that the researcher is only studying a single case or a small number of cases. Readers or users of this research must always ask how typical or representative the researcher's case was and whether the researcher's conclusions would hold up in other cases or other settings.

Experimental Research

A second approach to research in education is the *experiment*. This is the traditional approach based on positivistic assumptions. Most readers are already familiar with the basic logic and procedures of this approach through their high school and college psychology, social science, and science classes. The results of this type of research are also frequently reported in the mass media.

The experimental study of teaching involves procedures in which the researcher, instead of describing or studying variables as they exist naturally in the world, sets up conditions so specified variables can be manipulated. Although there are over a dozen variations of educational experiments, the classical approach is for the researcher to perform three important acts: (1) to establish two groups believed to be the same; (2) to give one group (the **experimental group**) a special treatment and withhold the treatment from the other (the **control group**); and (3) to compare some measurable feature of the two groups to see if the treatment made any difference. The most well-known experimental studies are those done in medicine to determine positive and possible unintended effects of particular drugs used to treat a variety of illnesses.

True experiments are difficult to do in education because many of the problems teachers and researchers are interested in are not amenable to experiments for either logistical or ethical reasons. When they can be done, however, experiments produce powerful results because they allow the researcher to draw conclusions about cause-and-effect relationships among variables. The educational problems most amenable to experimental manipulations are those associated with particular models and methods of teaching. The "bowling study" described in Chapter 10 is a good example of a cleverly constructed experiment.

Correlational Research

Because so many aspects of teaching and learning cannot be studied experimentally, a third major research approach is often employed. **Correlational research** is used when the researcher explores the relationships between two or more variables that exist naturally and tries to sort out what goes with what. This approach is also familiar to most of you. Take, for example, the now well-known correlational studies showing strong relationships between cigarette smoking and certain diseases. Over many years, medical researchers have shown that people who smoke have a higher incidence of lung cancer and heart attacks than nonsmokers have. Nonetheless, the cause-and-effect relationship remains experimentally unproven because of the ethics of setting up a true experiment in which members of one group would be given a treatment (i.e., smoking) that might lead to their deaths. Much of the research on effective teaching is also correlational research. For example, the many studies that show strong relationships between certain features of classroom management and student learning, such as Kounin's classical study described in Chapter 5, are nearly all correlational.

In the study of teaching, the researcher is usually interested in finding relationships between some type of teacher behavior and student learning. Although very useful in education, it is important to keep in mind that correlational research does not establish cause and effect among variables, only relationships. More is said about this later.

Causal-Comparative Research

Many times in education, variables of interest to the researcher cannot be manipulated experimentally, and data must be used from already defined groups. A method used to explore causal relationships in this situation is the **causal-comparative** method. In this type of research, unlike experimental research, the independent variable is not manipulated by the researcher because it already exists. Researchers compare two groups: subjects (normally in already existing groups) for whom a particular trait or pattern exists and similar subjects for whom it is absent. Two examples are given here. In both examples, the researcher studied variables that already exist and groups (classrooms) already defined.

- A researcher believes teachers are more critical toward Hispanic students than toward Anglo students. The researcher records teacher behaviors and then compares the teachers' interactions with the two groups. The independent variable in this case is ethnic origin—a trait in students that obviously already exists and is not manipulated.
- A researcher is interested in the attitudes of students toward school in two classrooms—one in which the teacher is using cooperative learning strategies, the other in which the teacher relies mainly on direct instruction. Attitudes are measured in the two classrooms and compared. Again, the independent variable (cooperative learning versus direct instruction) is a condition that already exists in the classroom and is not one the researcher manipulated.

In causal-comparative studies, differences between means are most often observed. The statistical tests employed are similar to those used in experimental research. This differs from correlational studies, in which the correlation coefficient is observed. Like correlational research, the results from causal-comparative studies are limited and must be interpreted with care because it is not clear whether the variables observed are a cause or a result or whether some third factor is present that may be influencing both the independent and dependent variables.

Statistical Concepts and Research Conventions

The vast majority of educational research involves measuring individual or group traits that produce quantitative data. Over the years, researchers have developed statistical procedures to help organize, analyze, and interpret their data. To read and to use research requires an understanding of some of the basic procedures and agreed-on conventions used by researchers. There is nothing magical about statistics or about symbols used by researchers. They are merely a means to communicate clearly and objectively. They may, however, appear mysterious to the novice. Brief descriptions of several key ideas can help beginning teachers understand research and perhaps motivate further study.

Sampling

Because it is obviously impossible to study all teachers or all students, educational researchers must, out of necessity, confine their studies to a small portion, or **sample**, of a total population. An example of this technique is the *sampling* done by market researchers to find out which TV shows people watch. From the millions of viewers at a given programming hour, researchers poll as few as fifteen hundred to two thousand persons selected from known segments of the viewing population. Users of market research ratings accept the results because they know that what the sample is watching represents (more or less) the habits of the total viewing audience.

The way a sample is selected is very important—if it does not accurately represent the intended larger population, the results will obviously be biased. A famous mistake in sampling occurred in the 1948 presidential election when a sample of citizens drawn from telephone directories across the country the night before the election indicated that Thomas Dewey, the Republican candidate, would be elected. The next day, however, Harry Truman, the Democratic candidate, was elected. Upon analysis, the polling firm discovered that in 1948, many voters still did not have telephones, and those without phones, who could not be included in the sample, were more prone to vote Democratic. Drawing a sample from the telephone directory was not appropriate if the pollsters wanted to know what the total population of voters was going to do. Today, concerns have been expressed about how representative samples are when they are drawn from people who have land telephones during an era when many people use only wireless. When reading reports of educational research, it is important to study carefully the sampling techniques used by the researcher.

Randomness

The concept of **randomness** is also very important in educational research. Usually random sampling or random assignment to groups means that individuals in any population have an equal chance of being selected for study. In survey research, this means that the researcher strives to define the total population of people he or she is going to study and then decides by chance which ones will be chosen for study. In experiments in which one group is to receive a special treatment and the other to serve as a control, the researcher is careful that subjects are assigned to one of the two groups on a random basis. The logic behind random sampling or random assignment to groups is that by using this procedure, the sample or the groups under investigation will have the same characteristics. This, however, is not always the case. For example, just as there is a chance, although very small, of flipping heads in a coin toss one hundred times in a row, there is also always a chance that a random sample will indeed not represent the total population or that two groups assigned at random will differ from one another in important ways.

Numbers and Conventions

Researchers also use certain conventions to organize and report the results of their work to others.

Mean Scores. In many of the research studies summarized in this book as well as elsewhere, researchers report mean scores that allow comparison of one group with another. A **mean score** is nothing more than an average score and is calculated by adding all scores and dividing by the number of cases. The reporting convention of researchers is to use the symbol or M to designate the mean score and the symbol N to communicate to readers the number of cases used to compute a particular mean. Mean scores are used to perform many of the statistical tests employed in educational research.

Standard Deviation. Standard deviation (SD) is another statistic that provides information about a set of scores. This statistic, found in many data tables, indicates the spread of a particular set of scores from the mean. Differences in means as well as differences in standard deviation are used to compute tests of statistical significance. The symbol SD is the most common convention for reporting standard deviation.

Correlation and Correlation Coefficients. Correlation expresses the degree to which a relationship exists between two or more variables. Familiar examples are the relationship between student IQ and student achievement, and the relationship between particular teaching behaviors (keeping students on task) and student achievement. Another is the relationship between a person's height and his or her performance on the basketball court.

To express these relationships in mathematical terms, researchers use a statistic called the **correlation coefficient.** A correlation coefficient can range from $+1.00$ through .00 to -1.00. The sign does not have the traditional mathematical meaning. Instead, a plus sign represents a positive relationship, a minus sign a negative relationship. Thus, .00 means no relationship exists, $+1.00$ means a perfect relationship exists, and -1.00 means a perfect reverse relationship exists. As observed in many of the studies summarized in this book, few instances are found in education (or any other aspect of human behavior) where perfect positive or negative relationships exist.

As described earlier, an important thing to remember about correlational studies and correlational coefficients is that even though they may show relationships among variables, they do not explain cause and effect. As an example, many studies show a positive relationship between students' time on task and academic achievement. Consequently, it is assumed that teachers who can keep students on task more will produce superior scores on achievement tests. Although this may be true, the time-on-task principle could be turned on its head. It could be logically argued that it is not time on task that produces achievement, but instead it is high-achieving students who produce high time-on-task ratios.

Tests of Significance. In any empirical research on human behavior, there is always the possibility that a specific outcome is the result of chance instead of some presumed relationship that is being studied. Researchers have developed a procedure called the *test of statistical significance* to help decide whether research results are indeed true or perhaps a matter of chance. Several different tests of significance are observed in the research reports found in this book. The main idea to remember is that when researchers use the word *significance*, they are using it differently than in common usage, where it normally means *important.* In the language of researchers, **statistical significance** means the degree of truth rather than chance that they assign to their results. In general, researchers agree that differences between two sets of scores are statistically significant if they could occur by chance only one to five times out of one hundred. When you read the research reports in this text you will often see the notation $p < .01$ or $p < .05$. This means that the probability (p) of such results occurring by chance is less than (<) one time out of one hundred (.01) or five times out of one hundred (.05).

Effect Size. Finally, a convention labeled effect size has been used recently as an alternative to the more traditional "test of significance." Most often it is used when the results of a number of studies are synthesized. **Effect size** (Glass, 1982) shows how much larger or smaller one can expect an average score to be when a particular experimental method (teaching strategy, curriculum, technology) is used as compared to a situation where some type of control group does not use the method. There are various approaches to measuring and using effect size. For our purposes here, effect size is computed by dividing the difference between two means (experimental and control) and then dividing it by the standard deviation (described previously) of the control group. According to Cohen (1988), effect sizes can also be interpreted in terms of the percent of nonoverlap of the experimental group's scores with those of the control group (pp. 21–23). An ES of 0.0 indicates that the distribution of scores for the experimental group overlaps completely with the distribution of scores for the control group. In contrast, an ES of 1.7 indicates a nonoverlap of 75.4 percent in the two distributions. Thus, research that reports a more positive effect size tells the reader that a particular strategy or method has a tendency to enhance student learning.

Value Added. As described previously in Chapter 6, the concept of **value added** (normally attributed to Sanders & Rivers, 1996) is a procedure of analyzing student achievement data so that the contributions of particular teachers or schools can be determined. Students are tested initially in particular subjects, such a reading, writing, and/or mathematics. Each student's achievement is then tracked from grade to grade. The gains made by a particular student or classes of students are then compared to gains expected from a normative sample for the same subjects and/or the same grades. As a result of this type of analysis, a gain for a particular student or group of students can be identified as an average amount of gain or above or below expectations. The more traditional analysis of achievement test data shows a student score at a particular point in time. Value-added analysis shows the amount of student growth or gain as compared to a normative group and helps answer the question about how much "value" a particular teacher or school added to students' growth. Some have questioned the statistical methods used in value-added approaches; however, it remains in fairly wide use and has been built into the concept of "Annual Yearly Progress" (AYP) used in both federal and state school reform initiatives.

Reading and Keeping Abreast of Research

Reading Research with a Critical Eye

Most research in education today is subjected to a review process before it is published. Nonetheless, a teacher who is reading and using the results of research should learn to approach studies with a critical eye. Some things to look out for, as summarized from Bracy (2006) and Gall, Gall, and Borg (2006, 2014), are:

- *Look for deliberate bias.* Although the goal of research is to discover truth, sometimes research is done to convince others of a point of view or of the effectiveness of a particular educational program. Readers of research look to see whether the researcher has anything to gain if the results turn out in a particular way. If so, the possibility of bias is greatly increased, and the study has to be examined very carefully. This does not mean, however, that all inventors of new programs or approaches who also conduct research on their inventions will deliberately bias the results.
- *Look for nondeliberate bias.* Sometimes bias enters into research without the researchers being aware of it. As with many other aspects of life, distortion can exist and influence us without our knowing it.
- *Consider the possibility of sampling bias.* Sampling bias is something that plagues educational research because it is so difficult to get random samples from total populations. However, as you learned in a previous section, if a sample contains bias, results can be spurious. Studies in which volunteers have been used, where many subjects have been lost from the sample, or in which intact groups have been used for convenience purposes should raise red flags for readers and users of research.
- *Strive to uncover how variables are constructed and manipulated.* Try to see if the researcher has made errors in logic or if the way variables have been manipulated has been politically motivated.
- *Watch for observer and measurement bias.* Human beings have a tendency to see what they want to see, hear what they want to hear, and remember what they want to remember. Even though researchers go to great lengths to guard against observer bias, they are always open to subtle error. Looking at observation instruments or protocols to see if the researcher has included features to ensure objectivity and looking at interview questions for leading or threatening questions are means to check whether observer bias has influenced the results of a study.
- *Analyze how conclusions are drawn in the study.* Readers should study very carefully and decide whether or not the conclusions of a piece of research are consistent with the data presented.

Reading a Research Report: An Example

It is time now to see if you can apply these research concepts to an actual research report. Read the research summary in Chapter 10 and then consider the following questions:

1. What assumptions about the nature of scientific knowledge are embedded in the study?
2. Is the study an example of descriptive, experimental, correlational, or causal-comparative research?
3. What variables were studied? Which variables are the independent variables? Which are the dependent variables?
4. Where would these variables fit in the model described in Figure R1.1?
5. How did the researchers use the mean statistic? From studying the scores and frequencies and tests of significance, what conclusions would you draw?
6. Based on your conclusion, what might you say about the impact of cooperative learning?

7. Which forms of bias do you find in the study? Deliberate bias? Nondeliberate bias? Observer bias? What about the sample? Is it biased?
8. What are the strengths of the study? What are the limitations?

Keeping Abreast of Research

Once one starts teaching full time, it is sometimes difficult to keep up with research. There are just so many other things to do. Fortunately, there are special services available to teachers that can cut down the time needed to keep abreast of the research on teaching and learning. Beginning in the mid-1960s, the federal government became more interested in educational research and created several services to encourage the dissemination of educational research to classroom teachers. Two of these services can be useful to the beginning teacher.

Regional Educational Laboratories. Knowing that most research and research centers were not directly applicable to classroom teachers, regional educational laboratories were created in 1964 to translate research into classroom materials and strategies and to disseminate the results to teachers. Even though their budgets do not allow direct assistance in every classroom in their region, laboratory staffs hold many useful workshops and are eager to have classroom teachers visit their labs and learn about the work they are doing. These laboratories also provide opportunities for the more energetic teachers to participate in ongoing research and development projects. Information about each of the Regional Educational Laboratories (REL) can be obtained from the REL Web sites. (See http://ies.ed.gov/ncee/edLabs/regions.)

Educational Research Information Centers. In the mid-1960s, the federal government began to put together a network of educational research information centers called ERICs, sponsored by the U.S. Department of Education. ERIC clearinghouses or centers are charged with three major tasks: (1) collecting the available knowledge on topics associated with various specialized areas of education; (2) organizing this information so it can be retrieved via computers from any place in the United States; and (3) summarizing these data in short bulletins and papers on topics of particular interest to teachers and other educators.

The heart of the ERIC system is the ERIC database, which contains over 1.4 million abstracts and documents on educational research and practice. This database can be accessed online via the Internet and through abstract journals available in libraries. All libraries in major universities and many large school districts or intermediate educational agencies have direct computer connections to ERIC. To get started, you may want to contact a person in your library who can show you how to access ERIC and conduct online searches. That person will discuss the type of topic about which you would like research information and then perform an online search to give you an example of the types of articles and reports that are available. The Web site for ERIC is www.eric.ed.gov.

Journals That Report Research in Education. There many journals that report on research in education that can help teachers keep abreast of research. Several of the most prominent ones are listed in Table RH.1.

Table RH.1 Journals in Education

Subject Area	Journal	Web Sites
Child Development	*Child Development*	www.srcd.org
Early Childhood	*Early Childhood Research Quarterly*	www.naeyc.org
Educational Research (general)	*American Educational Research Journal*	ww.aer.sagepub.com
Educational Psychology	*Journal of Educational Psychology*	www.apa.org/pubs/journals/edu
Elementary Education	*The Elementary School Journal*	www.journals.uchicago.edu
English/Language Arts	*English Journal*	www.ncte.org/journals/ej
Foreign Language	*Foreign Annals Annuals*	www.actfl.org/publications/all/ foreign-language-annals
Practitioner Oriented	*Educational Leadership*	www.ascd.org
	Phi Delta Kappan	www.pdkintl.org/publications
Mathematics	*Journal of Research in Mathematics Education*	www.nctm.org
	Mathematic Teacher	www.nctm.org/publications
Science	*Journal of Research on Science Teaching*	www.onlinelibrary.wiley.com/journal
	Science Teacher	www.nsta.org
Social Studies	*Social Education*	ww.socialstudies.org/publications
Teaching	*Teaching and Teacher Education*	www.elsevier.com

Library Digital Resources. Today all university libraries as well as many public libraries provide users with an array of digital resources. These include e-journals and full-text availability from many resource providers such as EBSCOhost, LexisNexis, and Academic Search Premier. To get started using digital resources, contact library personnel or visit your library's Web site.

Glossary

ability grouping Practice of placing students in special classes or small groups based on an assessment of their abilities or readiness to learn.

academic learning Type of learning normally associated with basic school subjects and the type of thinking processes required to understand them.

academic learning time (ALT) The amount of time a student is engaged in a particular subject or learning task at which he or she is successful.

accommodation Process of developing new concepts or schemata to understand a situation that is new and can be made to fit existing schemata.

accountability Holding teachers responsible for their teaching practices and for what their students learn.

achievement motives Desires and impulses that lead one to take action and to excel for the purpose of experiencing success and feeling competent.

advance organizer A statement made by teachers before a presentation or before having students read textual materials that provides a structure for new information to be linked to students' prior knowledge.

affiliative motives Desires and impulses that lead one to take action for the purpose of experiencing friendship and close relationships with others.

alternate-form reliability The degree to which two different forms of a test over the same topics can produce consistent results.

analogies Statements or phrases that compare two things.

analytical intelligence Defined by Robert Sternberg as the kind of intelligence that involves an individual's cognitive processes.

analyze One of the six types of cognitive processes in Bloom's revised taxonomy, defined as being able to break materials into constituent parts and show how parts relate to one another.

apply One of the six types of cognitive processes in Bloom's revised taxonomy, defined as being able to apply particular knowledge and carry out and implement particular procedures in a given situation.

artifacts The products produced by students in problem-based instruction, such as reports, videos, computer programs.

art of teaching A degree of accomplishment that allows basing complex decisions more on the teacher's experience than on research and scientific evidence.

assertive discipline An approach to classroom management that emphasizes teachers asserting their right to teach by insisting on appropriate student behavior and by responding assertively to student infractions.

assessment Process of collecting a full range of information about students and classrooms for the purpose of making instructional decisions.

assessment as learning Classroom situations that help students assess their own learning and the learning of their peers.

assessment for learning Ongoing formative assessment used to diagnose students' prior knowledge and interests and to monitor their learning progress.

assessment of learning Summative assessments of students used to determine grades, placements, graduation, and college admission.

assimilation Process of understanding something new by adapting it to what is already known.

assistive technologies Special tools, mainly computer-related, to assist individuals who have special needs.

attribution theories View of motivation that emphasizes the way individuals come to perceive and interpret the causes of their successes and failures.

authentic assessment Assessment procedures that have students demonstrate their abilities to perform particular tasks in real-life settings.

authentic relationships Relationships teachers build with their students in which both teachers and students treat each other as real and significant people.

autonomy norm The expectation in many schools that teachers can do pretty much what they want within the confines of their classroom.

behavioral objective A form for writing an instructional objective that emphasizes precision and careful delineation of expected student behaviors, the testing situation, and a performance criterion.

behavioral theory Approach to motivation emphasizing that external events, positive or negative, direct behavior.

behaviorism School of psychology emphasizing the importance of behavior and the external environment as a determinant of human behavior and learning.

benchmarks Designated checkpoints or the degree to which a particular instructional standard has been mastered.

best practice Teaching methods, processes, and procedures that have been shown to be effective for helping students learn.

bullying Persistent physical and/or verbal abuse (including teasing and goading) by one person toward a less powerful person aimed at causing harm.

buzz groups A small-group technique to help broaden student participation in discussion.

causal-comparative research Research that explores causal relationships when the independent variable cannot be manipulated.

challenged A term used to refer to individuals who have special needs or disabilities.

checking for understanding Technique used by teachers to see if students have grasped newly presented information or skills.

circle seating pattern A seating arrangement used in discussion that places the teacher and students in a circle; maximizes free interchange among participants.

classroom activities Things students are expected to do in the classroom, such as listening, discussing, completing worksheets, and taking tests.

classroom management The ways teachers organize and structure their classrooms for the purposes of maximizing student cooperation and engagement and minimizing disruptive behavior.

classroom meetings An approach to classroom management in which the teacher holds regular meetings for the purpose of helping students identify and resolve problem situations.

classroom processes Interpersonal and group processes that help classroom participants deal with issues of expectations, leadership, attraction, norms, communication, and cohesiveness.

classroom properties Distinctive features of classrooms, such as multidimensionality, simultaneity, immediacy, unpredictability, publicness, and history, that shape behavior of participants.

classroom structures The ways classrooms are organized around learning tasks and participation, and the ways goals and rewards are defined.

cluster seating A seating arrangement that puts desks in groups to facilitate cooperative learning and small-group lessons.

cognitive-constructivist perspective A view of learning that posits that learning occurs when learners are actively involved in the process of acquiring and constructing their own knowledge.

cognitive dissonance Discrepancies or contradictions between what an individual believes to be accurate or true and what is present in a current situation or simultaneously held belief.

cognitive process dimension The dimension in Bloom's revised taxonomy that identifies the cognitive processes or thinking required of particular learning tasks.

cognitive processes The thinking engaged in by teachers and students.

Common Core State Standards A set of curriculum standards adopted by most states aimed at standardizing what students should know and be able to do.

communication skills Interpersonal skills that help facilitate the transmission and reception of verbal and nonverbal messages.

competitive goal structure Situation that occurs when one person is successful in reaching his or her goals when others are unsuccessful.

concept attainment An inductive approach to teaching concepts by which students derive the meaning and attributes of a concept from examples and nonexamples of the concept given by the teacher.

concepts Ways of organizing knowledge and experiences in categories within which items have common attributes.

concept teaching Approaches to teaching in which the emphasis is on helping students learn how to make and label categories of ideas, objects, and experiences.

conceptual knowledge One of four types of knowledge in Bloom's revised taxonomy, defined as knowing about the interrelationships among basic elements and knowing about principles, categories, theories, and models.

conceptual mapping A technique of visually organizing and diagraming a set of ideas or concepts in a logical pattern so relationships can be readily observed. Also called *webbing*.

conditional knowledge Knowledge about when it is appropriate to use particular declarative or procedural knowledge.

conjunctive concept A concept that has a constant rule structure.

constructed-response items Type of traditional test items such as essay or short answer that require students to provide their own responses.

constructivism A perspective of teaching and learning in which a learner constructs meaning from experience and interaction with others and the teacher's role is to provide meaningful experiences for students.

constructivist perspective A view that knowledge is often personal and that humans construct knowledge and meaning through experience.

control group Group of subjects that receives no special treatment during experimental research.

convergent questions Type of question that focuses on relationships and analysis of cause and effect; calls for finding single, best answer.

cooperative goal structure Situation that occurs when students perceive they can obtain their goal if, and only if, the other students with whom they work also obtain their goals.

corrective feedback Information given to students about how well they are doing.

correlation A term used to express how two or more variables are related.

correlational research A type of research that investigates relationships between variables that exist naturally.

correlation coefficient Numbers ranging from +1.00 to −1.00 that describe the numerical relationship between variables.

create One of the six types of cognitive processes in Bloom's revised taxonomy, defined as being able to combine elements together for a coherent whole and/or reorganize elements into a new pattern.

creative intelligence Defined by Robert Sternberg as the type of intelligence that involves having insight to cope with new situations or experiences.

criterion-referenced test A test that evaluates a particular student's performance against a preestablished standard or criterion.

critical attribute Feature of a concept that distinguishes it from all other concepts.

critical thinking Thinking directed toward analyzing arguments and detecting bias and fallacious reasoning.

cuing A signal from teachers to alert or to set up situations for students in order to help them get ready to make an appropriate response.

cultural competence A situation where individuals are aware of their own culture and the assumptions they make about human behavior and values and where they attempt to understand and respect the worldview of culturally diverse populations.

cultural deficit theory The now-discredited theory that accounts for the low achievement of minorities by postulating some defect in their culture or race.

cultural difference theory The currently accepted theory that accounts for the low achievement of minorities by postulating that the discontinuity between home culture and school culture interferes with learning.

culturally relevant curriculum Teaching practices where teachers connect the world of their students and their cultures to the world of the school and the classroom.

cultural pluralism An ideology encouraging minority cultures to maintain their distinctive identities within the larger culture and to value cultural diversity within societies.

culture A group's total way of life; the way group members think about social action and ways to resolve issues in social collective life.

curriculum mapping A technique for charting what is taught (curriculum) across grade levels and among various subjects.

cyberbullying Form of bullying using the Internet and social media with the aim of causing harm or embarrassment of a person.

dangle When a teacher starts an activity and then leaves it in midair.

debriefing Way to assess the effectiveness of a classroom discussion by asking students what they thought of the discussion.

declarative knowledge Knowledge about something or that something is the case; knowledge of facts, concepts, or principles.

deductive reasoning Process of determining particular instances from more general rules or principles.

dependent variable In research, the variable that may change as a result of the independent variable; the consequences of the independent variable.

descriptive research Research aimed at gathering detailed information about some phenomenon.

desist behavior A teaching behavior aimed at stopping disruptive student behavior.

desist incidence A classroom incident serious enough that if not dealt with will lead to widening management problems.

differential treatment The difference in the educational experiences of the majority race, class, culture, or gender and those of minorities; that is, differences in quality of curriculum, instruction, classroom interaction, funding, enrollment, etc. and so on.

differentiation Practice of adapting instruction to meet the needs of particular students.

direct instruction An approach to teaching basic skills and sequential material in which lessons are highly goal-directed and learning environments are tightly structured by the teacher.

direct presentation One of several approaches to concept teaching.

disability A term used to refer to individuals who have special needs or challenges; the inability to do something such as hear, walk, or learn.

discontinuity A term used to describe a situation where the beliefs, values, and ways of communicating are different between one setting and another (e.g., the home and the school).

discourse The larger patterns of verbal exchange and communication that occur in classrooms.

discovery teaching or learning An approach to teaching that emphasizes encouraging students to learn concepts and principles through their own explorations and to solve problems on their own.

discrepant event A puzzling situation that sparks curiosity and motivates inquiry into cause-and-effect relationships; used by teachers to engage students.

discussion A teaching method that relies on verbal exchange of ideas among students and the teacher.

disjunctive concept A concept that contains alternative sets of attributes.

dispositions Attitudes and inherent qualities of mind. Used to designate attitudes toward thinking.

distributed practice Practice assigned to students to be done for brief periods spread over several sessions or periods of time.

divergent questions "What-if" questions that allow multiple answers and solutions and promote creativity.

downtime Time in classrooms when lessons are completed early or when students are waiting for upcoming events, such as moving to another class or going home.

Ebonics A term used to refer to a dialect used by some African Americans.

ecological system A view of classrooms in which inhabitants (teachers, students, and others) interact within a highly interdependent environment.

economy Term used by Bruner to describe ways to limit the amount of material to be taught at any one time.

effect size A statistic that shows how much larger or smaller an expected effect may be of an experimental method as compared to a more traditional method used in a control group.

elaborative interrogation questions Questions that follow up on other inferential questions and require students to support and expand their ideas.

e-learning Term used to define learning that takes place using the Internet. Also referred to as virtual and distance learning.

ELLs See *English language learners.*

emotional intelligence Defined by Goleman as an individual's ability to recognize and monitor one's emotions and be aware of the emotions of others.

enacted curriculum The curriculum that is planned and carried out (enacted) by classroom teachers.

enduring understandings The big ideas of a subject that every student should learn because the ideas have enduring value.

engaged time The amount of time students actually spend on a particular subject or learning activity; also called *time on task.*

English language learners (ELLs) Students for whom English is a second language.

enthusiasm See *teacher enthusiasm.*

equity Refers to making conditions for everyone impartial, fair, just, and equal.

essay test An approach to testing in which students are required to express their thoughts in writing.

essential questions Questions that reflect big ideas in any subject and serve as the heart of the curriculum.

establishing set Procedure teachers use at the beginning of a lesson aimed at getting students ready to learn. See also *anticipatory set.*

ethnicity Refers to groups that have common identities such as language or nationality.

ethnography Term from the field of anthropology to describe an extensive descriptive study of a single culture, society, or particular phenonemon.

ethos Common set of values, beliefs, and ways of doing things found in particular classrooms or schools. See also *school culture.*

evaluate One of the six types of cognitive processes in Bloom's revised taxonomy, defined as being able to make judgments based on criteria or standards.

evaluation Process of judging, assigning value, or deciding on the worth of a particular program or approach or of a student's work.

evidence-based practices Teaching practices in which evidence from research has shown them to be effective in producing student learning.

exceptionality Term used to define students who have special social, mental, emotional, or physical needs.

exhibits Displays of artifacts (products) students present that show their work from a problem-based lesson.

experimental group A group of subjects that receives a special treatment in experimental research.

expert teachers Experienced teachers who have mastered the art and science of teaching.

explaining links Prepositions or conjunctions used in a presentation that indicate the cause, result, means, or purpose of an event or idea.

extrinsic motivation Behavior caused by external factors such as rewards, punishments, or social pressures.

factual knowledge One of four types of knowledge in Bloom's revised taxonomy, defined as the basic elements, facts, and vocabulary of a topic or subject.

FAIR approach A process used to deal with behavioral situations caused by troubled students. Process includes understanding the cause of the student's behavior, making accommodations, developing interactive strategies, and finding ways to de-escalate the situation.

fairness The degree to which a test is free from bias and does not discriminate against a particular group of students because of race, ethnicity, or gender.

feedback Information given to students about their performance. Same as *knowledge of results.*

feeling tone The degree to which a learning environment or a particular learning task is perceived as pleasant or unpleasant.

field dependent Refers to individuals who tend to perceive situations "as a whole."

field independent Refers to individuals who tend to perceive the separate parts of a situation rather than the whole.

flexible grouping Teaching practice where students within the same classroom are temporarily grouped by ability for particular subjects, such as reading, writing, or math.

flip-flop Occurs when a teacher starts an activity, then stops and starts another one, and finally returns to the original activity.

flipped classroom Approach to teaching where teacher creates videos or other multimedia presentations for student to view as homework, thus freeing up class time to provide individual help and to hold discussions.

flow experience State when individuals feel total involvement and concentration and strong feelings of enjoyment as a result of a particular experience.

formal curriculum The curriculum that is planned by educational agencies, normally state departments of education and/or local school districts.

formative assessment Assessment that occurs before or during instruction and is used to assist with planning or making adaptations.

fragmentation Occurs when a teacher breaks a learning activity into overly small units.

full bilingual program A program in which instruction is carried out equally in two languages and the goals are full oral proficiency and literacy in both.

Gantt chart A planning technique to show pieces of work in relationship to one another and when each piece is expected to start and to finish.

gender bias Views of or actions toward males and females that often favor one gender over the other.

gifted and talented Students who are identified as being very bright, creative, and/or having special talents.

goal structures The way that goals specify the degree of interdependence sought among students. There are three different types of goal structures: individualistic, competitive, and cooperative.

grading on a curve A practice of assigning grades so they will follow a normal curve.

grading to criterion Practice of assigning grades according to how well students do on a predefined set of objectives or standards.

graphic organizer A visual image presented to students to provide structure for new information about to be presented. Similar to an *advance organizer.*

group development Stages classroom groups go through in the process of developing into a cohesive and effective group.

group processes See *classroom processes.*

group skills Skills students have to participate effectively in groups.

guided practice Practice assigned to students to be completed under the guidance or watchful eye of the teacher.

handicapped A term used to refer to individuals who have special needs or challenges. Some believe it carries a negative connotation and projects a negative image toward those with special needs or challenges.

hands-off norm Expectation in many schools that teachers will not interfere in other teachers' work.

higher-level thinking Abstract intellectual process that involves analyzing, criticizing, and reaching conclusions based on sound evidence.

high-stakes tests Tests used to make important decisions about students, such as placement or admissions to particular programs or educational institutions.

holistic scoring Technique for grading essay questions or other written work that emphasizes looking at the work as a whole rather than at its individual parts.

homework Independent practice and academic work performed outside the classroom.

human capital Factors in an educational organization such as the qualifications and experiences of teachers who work there, including their abilities, knowledge, and skills.

inclusion Practice of including students, regardless of their disabilities, in regular classrooms.

in-context learning style Refers to the learning style where individuals acquire understanding and skills as they are needed in real-life situations.

independent practice Practice given to students to accomplish on their own without the teacher's guidance.

independent task A situation where a learning task can be accomplished by individuals working alone.

independent variable In research, the variable that is treated and presumed to cause some change in the dependent variable.

individualistic goal structure A situation where a goal can be accomplished by individuals working or performing by themselves.

individualistic reward structure Occurs when achievement of the goal by one student is unrelated to the achievement of the goal by other students.

individualized education plan (IEP) A learning plan specifying long- and short-term educational goals for students who are disabled and agreed on by teachers, parents, and special educators.

inductive reasoning Process of coming up with general rules or principles based on information from specific examples or data.

influence motives Desires and impulses that lead one to take action for the purpose of having more control over learning or having more say in how schools are run.

information processing The process used by the mind to take in, store, and retrieve information for use.

infusion strategies Approach to teaching thinking that infuses the teaching of thinking into regular subject matter lessons.

iGeneration Term coined to refer to the current generation of students who have grown up using computers and digital technologies.

instructional aspects of teaching Those aspects of teachers' work during which they are providing face-to-face instruction to students in classrooms.

instructional objective Statements that describe a teacher's instructional intents.

intelligence Ability individuals have for solving problems and adapting to one's environment.

intelligence quotient (IQ) A score that compares chronological and mental ages.

interaction patterns A term used to refer to the patterns of the verbal and nonverbal communication in classrooms.

interdependent task A situation where a learning task can only be accomplished by two or more individuals working together.

interpersonal communication skills Skills that promote honest communication and positive regard among students.

intrinsic motivation Occurs when people behave because an act brings personal satisfaction or enjoyment.

Jigsaw An approach to cooperative learning in which students work in mixed-ability groups and each student is responsible for a portion of the material.

knowledge base Information, accumulated over time from research and the wisdom of experienced teachers, that informs teaching practices.

knowledge dimension The dimension in Bloom's revised taxonomy that defines what learners know or are expected to know.

knowledge of results Feedback given to students about their performance.

leadership aspects of teaching Aspects of teachers' work, such as providing motivation and coordinating and controlling learning environments and activities.

learner-centered planning Planning that involves students in the process.

learning abilities Abilities individuals have for acquiring new knowledge and skills and for adapting to one's environment.

learning goal orientation An orientation toward learning wherein students are motivated by internal factors and compete mainly with themselves.

learning preferences Preferred environments or modalities learners have toward learning and studying.

learning progression A tool that specifies a set of subskills and enabling knowledge that must be learned prior to mastering a more complex curriculum standard or learning outcome.

learning strategies Plans or strategies learners have for approaching particular learning tasks or studying.

learning styles Particular approaches learners have toward learning or studying.

Learning Together An approach to cooperative learning developed by Roger and David Johnson consisting of students working on assignments interdependently in heterogeneous teams.

least restrictive environment The placement situation for students with disabilities that is the most normal and least confining based on the student's particular needs and problems.

lesson plan Organization for instruction for a particular lesson or period.

level of actual development A concept attributed to Lev Vygotsky that identifies a learner's level of current intellectual functioning.

level of difficulty Refers to how difficult a question asked of students is to answer.

level of potential development A concept attributed to Lev Vygotsky that identifies the level at which a learner could function intellectually with the assistance of a teacher or more advanced peer.

logical consequences Punishments administered for misbehavior that are directly related to the infraction.

long-term memory Place in the mind where information is stored, ready for retrieval when needed.

loosely coupled systems An organizational arrangement in which what goes on in one part of an organization is not very connected to what goes on in other parts of the organization.

mainstreaming Placing children with special needs in regular classes full time or part time.

massed practice Practice assigned to students to be done during a single extended period of time.

mean score The arithmetic average of a group of scores.

melting pot Ideology of education that believes the strengths of minority cultures should be blended into a new, single, superior culture.

mental abilities Phrase used to define abilities individuals have as measured by performance on particular cognitive tasks.

mental age Score in intelligence testing that designates average mental ability for a particular age group.

mental planning Planning done by teachers as they think and reflect about their teaching; these plans are not always committed to paper.

metacognitive knowledge One of four types of knowledge in Bloom's revised taxonomy, defined as knowledge and awareness of one's own cognition.

metaphors A figure of speech where one thing is applied to something else.

momentum Term used by Kounin to describe how teachers pace instruction.

motivation The process by which behavior is directed toward important human goals or toward satisfying needs and motives.

multicultural education An approach to teaching aimed at helping students recognize and value cultural diversity.

multiple intelligences Gardner's theory that states intelligence is more than a single ability and instead consists of eight different types of abilities.

needs theory Theory of motivation positing that people are motivated to take action to satisfy basic and higher-level needs.

negative reinforcer A stimulus such as punishment intended to eliminate or reduce undesirable behavior.

Net generation generation born in the late 1970s and the 1980s characterized by their familiarity and use of computers and digital technologies.

noncritical attributes Features found in some but not all members of a category.

nonlinear model An approach to planning in which planners start with actions or activities deemed important and later attach goals to the action to help explain what happened.

norm-referenced test A standardized test that evaluates a particular student's performance by comparing it to the performance of some other well-defined group of students.

norms The shared expectations students and teachers have for classroom behavior.

novice teacher A teacher who is just beginning and is still learning the art and science of teaching.

numbered heads together Small group strategies that encourage cooperation and participation.

objectivist perspective A view that knowledge consists of "truths" and an objective reality that humans have access to and can learn through discovery and inquiry.

observational learning Learning that occurs by observing others.

opportunity to learn The amount of time a teacher actually spends on academic tasks or activities.

organizational aspects of teaching Those aspects of teachers' work involving interactions with other adults in the school setting for the purpose of schoolwide planning and coordination.

out-of-context learning style Learning that is not necessarily connected to real or immediate needs—the typical kind of learning required of students in schools.

overdwelling Situation that occurs when a teacher goes on and on after a subject or a set of instructions is clear to students.

overlappingness The ability of teachers to spot disruptive behavior and to deal with it without interrupting the flow of the lesson.

overlearning Working or practicing a task or skill until it is learned completely and can be performed automatically.

participation structures The established rules and processes that determine who can say what, when, and to whom during classroom discourse.

pedagogy The study of the art and science of teaching; also refers to the methods and approaches to instruction.

performance assessment Assessment procedures that have students demonstrate their abilities to perform particular tasks in testing situations.

performance criteria The standards used for judging the quality of a student's performance.

performance goal orientation An orientation toward learning in which students strive to reach externally imposed standards and to better their own performanceas compared to the performance of others.

performance indicators Assessment items that measure student mastery of a specified benchmark or curriculum standard.

performance standards Recommendations about what should be taught that define what students should know or be able to do and at what level they are expected to perform in various subjects.

performance task Activities students are asked to undertake so a performance can be judged.

positive reinforcer A stimulus such as a reward intended to get individuals to repeat desirable behavior.

positivism View that knowledge is somewhat fixed and can be studied best through direct observation of behavior.

power Term used by Bruner to describe the process of selecting only the most important (powerful) ideas and concepts to teach to students.

practical arguments Reasoning based on knowledge and beliefs that is used by teachers as they make pedagogical decisions.

practical intelligence Defined by Robert Sternberg as the kind of abilities individuals have to adapt and reshape their environments.

praise Positive verbal and nonverbal statements offered by teachers as reinforcers to encourage and strengthen desirable student behaviors.

presentation teaching model An approach to teaching wherein the primary emphasis is on explaining new information and ideas to students.

preventative management Perspective that effective classroom management can be achieved through good planning, interesting lessons, and effective teaching.

prior knowledge Information and knowledge held by students before they receive instruction.

procedural knowledge Knowledge about how to do something. Can pertain to specific behavioral skills or to complex *cognitive strategies.*

procedures Systems established by teachers for dealing with routine tasks and coordinating student talk and movement.

punishments Penalties imposed by teachers to discourage undesirable behaviors.

qualitative research An approach to research that relies on more holistic observations and reports data in narrative rather than quantitative form.

quantitative research An approach to research that studies behavior in an objective fashion and uses traditional statistical procedures to analyze data.

race A term used to refer to a group of people who share common biological traits.

random calling Approach used during a discussion or a question and answer session where students are called at random rather than called after having their hands raised.

randomness Term used to denote random sampling or random assignment to a group in a research experiment.

rational-linear model An approach to planning that focuses on setting goals and objectives first and then on selecting particular strategies or activities to accomplish these predetermined goals.

recitation An approach to teaching in which a teacher provides bits of information, asks questions, gets students to respond, and then provides feedback by praising or correcting.

reflection Careful and analytical thought by teachers about what they are doing and the effects of their behavior on their instruction and on student learning.

reinforcement Consequences administered by teachers to encourage and strengthen certain desirable behaviors.

reinforcement principles Psychological principles holding that reinforced behaviors tend to be repeated; behaviors that are not reinforced tend to disappear.

relational concept A concept whose rule structure depends on its relationship to other concepts.

reliability The degree to which a test produces consistent results over several administrations.

remember One of the six types of cognitive processes in Bloom's revised taxonomy, defined as being able to recognize and recall relevant knowledge from long-term memory.

repertoire The number of teaching approaches and strategies that teachers are able to use to help students learn.

responders Electronic devices that allow students to respond to teachers' questions during a presentation or discussion.

response to intervention A process designed to provide services to students who are struggling and who have special needs as early as possible. The process involves early screening, use of evidence-based intervention strategies, and precise monitoring and documentation of progress.

reward structures The ways in which rewards can be distributed within a classroom. There are three types: *individualistic, competitive,* and *cooperative.*

rule-example-rule technique A technique used when explaining something whereby the general principle or rule is given first, then elaborated on with specific examples, and finally summarized by a restatement of the rule.

rules for behavior Statements that specify expected classroom behaviors and define behaviors that are forbidden.

sample A group of subjects drawn from a larger population for the purpose of research.

scaffolding The process in which a learner is helped by a teacher or more accomplished person to master a problem or skill slightly beyond his or her current developmental level.

schema, schemata An individual's (teacher or student) knowledge structure or the way information has been organized and stored in memory.

school culture The ways members of a school think about social action; the embedded beliefs, values, and attitudes of members of a school. *Ethos, tone,* and *community* are often used to describe the same phenomenon.

school effectiveness research Research that tries to uncover features that make some schools more effective than others.

scientific basis of teaching Teaching in which decisions are based on research and scientific evidence.

scientific thinking Reasoning associated with scientific inquiry that involves drawing conclusions based on evidence.

scoring rubric A detailed description of some type of performance and the criteria that will be used to judge it.

seatwork Independent practice and academic work performed in the classroom.

selected-response items Type of traditional test items such as multiple choice and true-false that allow students to select responses from provided alternatives.

self-fulfilling prophecy A situation in which teachers' expectations and predictions about student behavior or learning cause it to happen.

self-regulated learner A learner who can diagnose a learning situation, select an appropriate learning strategy, monitor the effectiveness of the strategy, and remain engaged in the learning task until it is accomplished.

sensory memory Part of the memory system that first notes and does the initial processing of stimuli.

short-term working memory The place in the mind where conscious mental work is done; also called *working memory.*

smoothness The smooth flow and pacing of instructional events.

social capital Factors in an educational organization such as the interactions that teachers have with their peers that focus on instruction and the amount of trust and closeness among teachers and between teachers and their administrators.

social context The surrounding environment within which something (teaching and learning) exists and which influences what happens.

social cognitive theory Theory of learning that emphasizes learning through observation and the importance of learner beliefs about self and learning situations.

socially just classroom Classrooms where students are engaged in the struggle for social justice in the larger society as well as in the classroom itself.

social skills Skills or abilities individuals have to work or interact effectively in social and group settings.

sociocultural theory Theory that human motivation is influenced not only from factors within the individual, such as needs, goal orientations, and expectancies, but also from the expectations and behaviors of groups that the individual identifies.

socioeconomic status (SES) Variations among peoples based on income, family background, and relative prestige within the society.

split-half reliability The degree of consistency a test can produce when it is divided into two halves and student performance is compared for each half.

stages of teacher development A theory explaining how growth in teaching expertise occurs over time, progressing from one stage to the next stage in sequence.

standard deviation (SD) A measure that shows the spread of a set of scores from the mean.

standardized tests Tests that are normally designed by professional test makers for nationwide use and commercially distributed.

standards Statements about what students should know and be able to do. Often used today instead of *goals* and *objectives.*

statistical test and significance Procedures used to determine whether results from research are indeed true or a result of chance.

structural approach Approach to cooperative learning attributed to Spencer Kagan.

student portfolios Collection of a sample of student work used to evaluate accomplishments over time

Student Teams Achievement Divisions (STADs) An approach to cooperative learning in which students work in mixed-ability groups and rewards are administered and recognized for both individual and group effort.

submersion approach The now-illegal practice of simply placing limited English proficiency students in the classroom and expecting them to pick up English on their own without any formal teaching or other support from the school.

successful intelligence Robert Sternberg's label for a set of abilities possessed by an individual that make it possible to attain success in life.

summative assessment Assessment done after instruction to determine program effectiveness or the worth of students' work.

sustaining expectation effect Occurs when teachers do not change their previous expectations about a student, even after the student's performance has improved or regressed.

swing seating Seating plan that allows easy movement of seats during cooperative learning lessons.

synergy Positive results achieved from working together or through combined action.

syntax The overall flow, sequence, or major steps of a particular lesson.

task analysis A process for breaking down complex learning tasks into fundamental parts or subdividing complex skills into specific subskills so they can be mastered one at a time.

task structures The way lessons are arranged and the learning demands that lessons place on students.

taxonomy A classification system or device that helps arrange and show relationships among objects and ideas.

teacher clarity Phrase used to describe the process of teachers giving presentations that are clear and free of ambiguity.

teacher effectiveness research Refers to research that aims at finding relationships between teaching behavior and student achievement.

teacher enthusiasm A set of behaviors employed by teachers, such as using uplifting language and dramatic body movements, to make students interested in learning materials.

teacher expectations Beliefs, attitudes, and perceptions teachers hold about the capabilities of particular students—may or may not be accurate.

test anxiety Phenomenon that occurs when students experience undue stress while taking a test and do poorly as a result.

test blueprint A tool used in constructing a test so it will have a balance of questions representing various forms of knowledge and cognitive processes.

test-retest reliability The degree to which a test shows consistent results when administered to the same student at different times.

thinking routines Routines and structures that provide scaffolding to help make thinking processes visible to students.

think-pair-share A technique used by teachers to slow down the pace of discourse and to increase student participation.

tiered activities A strategy for getting all students, regardless of abilities, to focus on the same understanding or skill but at different levels of abstraction or complexity.

time on task See *engaged time*.

time-tabling Chronological mapping of time relationships among various instructional activities.

tone See *ethos* and *school culture*.

transitional bilingual programs Programs in which limited English proficiency students are initially provided instruction in their native language, with gradual increases in English until proficiency is achieved.

transitions The times during a lesson when the teacher is moving from one type of learning activity to another.

understand One of the six types of cognitive processes in Bloom's revised taxonomy, defined as being able to interpret, exemplify, classify, summarize, infer, compare, and explain knowledge.

unit plan An integrated plan for instruction covering several days and including several lessons aimed at a common set of goals and objectives.

U-shaped seating pattern A seating arrangement used for discussions in which students' chairs form a U and the teacher is seated at the open end of the U.

validity The degree to which a test measures what it claims to measure.

value-added assessments Assessments that show the amount of learning gain made by students as a result of particular instruction situations, such as being in a teacher's classroom for the school year.

variable A characteristic of a person or a physical or social situation that can change or vary from one instance to the next.

verbal signposts Statements made by teachers when explaining something that tells the students what is important or alerts them to important points coming up.

visual cuing Use of visual devices, such as hand signals, to inform students about what they should be doing.

wait-time The time a teacher waits for a student to respond to a question and the time a teacher waits before responding back.

webbing See *conceptual mapping*.

with-itness The ability of teachers to spot disruptive student behavior quickly and accurately.

working memory See *short-term memory*.

zone of proximal development A concept attributed to Lev Vygotsky that represents the area between a learner's level of actual development and his or her level of potential development.

References

A *broader, bolder approach to education*. (2008). Retrieved January 2010 from http://www.boldapproach.org

Achievement gap. (2011). *Education Week*. Retrieved March 21, 2013, from http://www.edweek.org/ew/issues/achievement-gap/

Adventure Learning Foundation. Retrieved May 25, 2005, from http://www.questconnnect.org

Airasian, P., & Russell, M. (2007). *Classroom assessment* (6th ed.). New York: McGraw-Hill.

Albanese, M., & Mitchell, S. (1993). Problem-based learning: A review of literature on its outcomes and implementation issues. *Academic Medicine, 68*, 52–81.

Allen, V. (1991). Teaching bilingual and ESL children. In J. Flood, J. M. Jensen, D. Lapp, & J. R. Squire (eds.), *Handbook of research on teaching the English language arts*. New York: Macmillan.

Alliance for Children. (2004). *Tech tonic: Towards a new literacy of technology*. College Park, MD: Author.

Alschuler, A. S., Tabor, D., & McIntyre, J. (1970). *Teaching achievement motivation: Theory and practice in psychological education*. Middletown, CT: Education Ventures.

American Association of University Women (AAUW). (1992). *Shortchanging girls, shortchanging America*. Washington, DC: Author.

American Educational Research Association, American Psychological Association, & National Council on Measurement in Education. (1985). *Standards for educational and psychological testing*. Washington, DC: American Psychological Association.

A nation at risk. (1983). Washington, DC: National Commission on Excellence in Education.

Ancess, J., & Darling-Hammond, L. (2003). *Beating the odds: High schools as communities of commitment*. New York: Teachers College Press.

Anderman, E., & Anderman, L. (2009). *Classroom motivation*. New York: Prentice Hall.

Anderson, L. (1989). Classroom instruction. In M. Reynolds (ed.), *Knowledge base for beginning teachers*. New York: Pergamon.

Anderson, L. M. (1985). What are students doing when they do all that seatwork? In C. Fisher & D. Berliner (eds.), *Perspectives on instructional time*. New York: Longman.

Anderson, L. M., & Smith, E. L. (1987). Teaching science. In V. Richardson-Koehler (ed.), *Educator's handbook: A research perspective*. New York: Longman.

Anderson, L. W., & Krathwohl, D. R. (eds. with P. W Airasian, K. A. Cruikshank, R. E. Mayer, P. R. Pintrich, J. Raths, & M. C. Wittrock). (2001). *A taxonomy for learning, teaching, and assessing: A revision of Bloom's taxonomy of educational objectives*. New York: Longman.

Anyon, J. (1980). Social class and the hidden curriculum of work. *Journal of Education, 162*, 67–69.

Apple, M. (1990). *Ideology and the curriculum*. New York: Routledge.

Arends, R., & Kilcher, A. (2010). *Teaching for student learning: Becoming an accomplished teacher*. New York: Routledge.

Armstrong, T. (2012). First, discover their strengths. *Phi Delta Kappan, 70*(2), 10–17.

Aronson, E., & Patnoe, S. (1997). *The Jigsaw classroom*. New York: Addison-Wesley/Longman.

Aronson, E., & Patnoe, S. (2010). *Cooperation in the classroom: The jigsaw method* (3rd ed.). London: Pinter & Martin Ltd.

ASCD whole child. Retrieved August 27, 2007, from http://www.wholechildeducation.org

Ash, K. (2008). Promises of money meant to heighten student motivation. *Education Week Online*. http://www.edweek.org/ew/articles/2008/02/13/23cash_ep

Ashcraft, M., & Radvansky, G. (2009). *Cognition* (5th ed.). Boston: Pearson.

Atkinson, J., & Feather, N. (1966). *A theory of achievement motivation*. New York: Wiley.

Audet, R., & Jordon, L. (2005). *Integrating inquiry across the curriculum*. Thousand Oaks, CA: Corwin Press.

Ausubel, D. P. (1960). The use of advance organizers in the learning and retention of meaningful verbal material. *Journal of Educational Psychology, 51*, 267–272.

Ausubel, D. P. (1963). *The psychology of meaningful verbal learning*. New York: Grune & Stratton.

Baker, D. (1986). Sex differences in classroom interaction in secondary science. *Journal of Classroom Interaction, 22*, 212–218.

Bandura, A. (1977). *Social learning theory*. Englewood Cliffs, NJ: Prentice-Hall.

Bandura, A. (1986). *Social foundations of thought and action*. Englewood Cliffs, NJ: Prentice-Hall.

Bangert, R., Kulik, C., Kulik, J., & Morgon, M. (1991). The instructional effects of feedback on test-like events. *Review of Educational Research, 61*(2), 213–238.

Bangert-Drowns, R. L., Kulik, C. C., & Kulik, J. A. (1991). The instructional effects of feedback in testing events. *Review of Educational Research, 61*, 213–238.

Banks, J. (1993). *Introduction to multicultural education*. Boston: Allyn & Bacon.

Banks, J. (1998, October 16). Reliance on technology threatens the essence of teaching. *Chronicle of Higher Education*, p. B5.

Banks, J. (2007). *Introduction to multicultural education* (4th ed.). Boston: Allyn & Bacon.

Banks, J. (ed.). (1995). *The handbook of research on multicultural education*. New York: Macmillan.

Banks, J., et al. (2005). Teaching diverse students. In L. Darling-Hammond & J. Bransford (eds.), *Preparing teachers for a changing world*. San Francisco: Jossey-Bass.

Barell, J. (2003). *Developing more curious minds*. Alexandria, VA: Association for Supervision and Curriculum Development.

Barker, R. G. (1968). *Ecological psychology*. Stanford, CA: Stanford University Press.

Barnett, B. (2011). *Teaching 2030: What we must do for our students and our public schools—now and in the future*. New York: Teachers College Press.

Barrett, T. (2010). The problem-based learning process as finding and being in flow. *Innovations in Education and Teaching International, 47*(2), 165–174.

Barsalou, L. W. (2000). Concepts: An overview. In A. E. Kazdin (ed.), *Encyclopedia of psychology*. New York: Oxford University Press.

Barth, P. (2013). Virtual schools: Where's the evidence? *Educational Leadership, 70*(6), 32–36.

Bazelon, E. (2013). *Defeating the culture of bullying and rediscovering the power of character and empathy*. New York: Random House.

Beals, K. (2013). Are grading trends hurting social awkward students? The Atlantic, www.theatlantic.com/national/archive/2013. Retrieved March 22, 2013.

Beauchamp, M. (2013). Face to faith: Teaching global citizenship. *Phi Delta Kappan, 93*(4), 24–27.

Beaulieu, R. P., & Utecht, K. M. (1987). Frequently administered formative tests and student achievement. *Journal of Instructional Psychology, 14,* 195–200.

Bellanca, J. (2007). *A guide to graphic organizers: Helping students organize and process content for deeper learning* (2nd ed.). Thousand Oaks, CA: Corwin Press.

Bellanca, J. (2010). *Enriched learning projects: A practical pathway to 21st century*. Bloomington, IN: Solution Tree.

Bellanca, J., Fogarty, R., & Pete, B. (2012). *How to teach thinking skills within the Common Core: 7 key student proficiencies of the new national standards*. Bloomington, IN: Solution Tree.

Bender, N. (2012). *Project-based learning: Differentiating instruction for the 21st century*. Thousand Oaks, CA: Corwin Press.

Benjafield, J. G. (1992). *Cognitions*. Englewood Cliffs, NJ: Prentice-Hall.

Benjamin, A. (2002). *Differentiated instruction: A guide for middle and high school teachers*. Larchmont, NY: Eye on Education.

Bennett, S., & Kalish, N. (2006). *The case against homework: How homework is hurting our children and what we can do about it*. New York: Crown.

Bennett, W., Finn, C., & Cribb, J. (1999). *The educated child: A parent's guide to preschool through eighth grade*. New York: Free Press.

Berger, K. (2004). *The developing person through the life span* (6th ed.). New York: Worth.

Berninger, V., & Richards, T. (2002). *Brain literacy for educators and psychologists*. San Diego, CA: Academic Press.

Beyer, B. (2001). Practical strategies for direct instruction in thinking skills. In A. Costa (ed.). *Developing minds: A resource for teaching thinking* (3rd ed.). Alexandria, VA: Association for Supervision and Curriculum Development.

Biklen, D. (1985). *Achieving the complete school*. New York: Teachers College Press.

Biklen, S. K., & Pollard, D. (2001). Feminist perspectives on gender in the classroom. In V. Richardson (ed.), *Handbook of research on teaching* (4th ed.). Washington, DC: American Educational Research Association.

Black, P., Harrison, C., Lee, C., Marshal, B., & Wiliam, D. (2004). Working inside the black box: Assessment for learning in the classroom. *Phi Delta Kappan, 86*(1), 8–21.

Black, P., & Wiliam, D. (1998a). Assessment and classroom learning. *Assessment in Education, 5*(1), 7–73.

Black, P., & Wiliam, D. (1998b). Inside the black box: Raising standards through classroom assessment. *Phi Delta Kappan, 80*(2), 139–148.

Bloom, B. S. (1976). *Human characteristics and school learning*. New York: McGraw-Hill.

Bloom, B. S. (ed.). (1956). *Taxonomy of educational objectives. Handbook 1: Cognitive domain*. New York: David McKay.

Bluestein, J. (1982). *The beginning teacher's resource handbook*. Albuquerque, NM: Instructional Support Services.

Blythe, T. (1997). *The teaching for understanding guide*. San Francisco: Jossey-Bass.

Bobbitt, F. (1918). *The curriculum*. Boston: Houghton Mifflin.

Bohn, C., Roehrig, A., & Pressley, M. (2004). The first days of school in the classrooms of two more effective and four less effective primary-grade teachers. *The Elementary School Journal, 104*(4), 269–287.

Bonney, C., & Sternberg, R. (2011). Learning to think critically. In R. Mayer & P. Alexandria (eds.), *Handbook of research on learning and instruction*. New York: Routledge.

Borg, W. R., & Gall, M. D. (1993). *Educational research: An introduction* (4th ed.). New York: Longman.

Boulfard, S., Bridgall, B., Gordon, E., & Weiss, H. (2009). *Reframing family involvement in education*. Cambridge, MA: Harvard Family Research Project.

Boydston, J. A. (2008). *The middle works, 1899–1924, John Dewey*. Carbondale: Southern Illinois University.

Bozeman, M. (1995). *Signaling in the classroom* (mimeographed). Salisbury, MD: Salisbury State College.

Bradley, R., Danielson, L., & Doolittle, J. (2005). Response to intervention. *Journal of Learning Disabilities, 38,* 485–486.

Brandt, R. S. (2000). *Education in a new era*. Alexandria, VA: Association for Supervision and Curriculum Development.

Brannon, L. (2007). *Gender: Psychological perspectives* (5th ed.). Boston: Allyn & Bacon.

Bransford, J., Brown, A., & Cocking, R. (eds.). (2000). *How people learn*. Washington, DC: National Academy Press.

Bransford, J., Darling-Hammond, L., & LePage, P. (2005). Introduction. In L. Darling-Hammond & J. Bransford (eds.), *Preparing teachers for a changing world: What teachers should learn and be able to do*. San Francisco: Jossey-Bass.

Bredderman, T. (1983). Effects of activity-based elementary science on student outcomes: A quantitative synthesis. *Review of Educational Research, 53,* 499–518.

Brenton, Myron (1970). *What's happened to teacher?* New York: Coward-McCann.

Brody, N. (2001). Personal communication found in Santrock, J. W. (2004). *Education psychology* (2nd ed.). New York: McGraw-Hill.

Brookhart, S. (2004). *Grading*. Upper Saddle River, NJ: Pearson.

Brookhart, S., & Nitko, A. (2007). *Assessment and grading in classrooms*. Boston: Pearson.

Brookhart, S. (2008). *How to give effective feedback to your students*. Alexandria, VA: Association for Supervision and Curriculum Development.

Brookhart, S. (2010). *How to assess higher-order thinking skills in your classroom*. Alexandria, VA: Association for Supervision and Curriculum Development.

Brookhart, S. (2012). Preventing feedback fizzle. *Educational Leadership, 70* (1), 24–29.

Brookhart, S. (2013). *How to create and use rubrics for formative assessment and grading*. Alexandria, VA: Association for Supervision and Curriculum Development.

Brookhart, S. M. (1997). A theoretical framework for the role of classroom assessment in motivating student effort and achievement. *Applied Measurement in Education, 10,* 161–180.

Brookhart, S. M., & Durkin, D. T. (2003). Classroom assessment, student motivation, and achievement in high school social studies classes. *Applied Measurement in Education, 16*(1), 27–54.

Brookover, W., Beady, C., Flood, P., Schweitzer, J., & Wisenbaker, J. (1979). *School social systems and student achievement: Schools can make a difference.* New York: Praeger.

Brophy, J. (2004). *Motivating students to learn* (2nd ed.). Hillsdale, NJ: Erlbaum.

Brophy, J. E. (1981, Spring). Teacher praise: A functional analysis. *Review of Educational Research,* 5–32.

Brophy, J. E., & Good, T. L. (1974). *Teacher-student relationships: Causes and consequences.* New York: Holt, Rinehart & Winston.

Brophy, J. E., & Good, T. L. (1986). Teacher behavior and student achievement. In M. C. Wittrock (ed.), *Handbook of research on teaching* (3rd ed.). New York: Macmillan.

Brophy, J. E., & Putnam, J. (1979). Classroom management in the early grades. In D. L. Duke (ed.), *Classroom management.* Chicago: University of Chicago Press.

Brown, A. (1987). Metacognition, executive control, self-regulation, and other mysterious mechanisms. In F. Weinert & R. Kluwe (eds.), *Metacognition, motivation, and understanding.* Hillsdale, NJ: Erlbaum.

Brown, A., & Palincsar, A. (1985). *Reciprocal teaching of comprehension strategies.* Technical Report no. 334. Champaign–Urbana: University of Illinois.

Bruner, J. (1960). *The process of education.* Cambridge, MA: Harvard University Press.

Bruner, J. (1961). The art of discovery. *Harvard Education Review, 31,* 21–32.

Bruner, J. (1962). *On knowing: Essays for the left hand.* Cambridge, MA: Harvard University Press.

Bruner, J. (1966). *Toward a theory of instruction.* Cambridge, MA: Harvard University Press.

Bruner, J. (1990). *Acts of meaning.* Cambridge, MA: Harvard University Press.

Bruner, J. (1996). *The culture of education.* Cambridge, MA: Harvard University Press.

BSCS 5E Instructional Model. Retrieved January 2009 from http://www.bscs.org

Bulgren, J., Marquis, J., Lenz, B., & Deshler, D. (2011). The effectiveness of a Question-Exploration Routine for enhancing the content learning of secondary students. *Journal of Educational Psychology, 130*(3), 578–593.

Burbules, N. C. (1993). *Dialogue in teaching: Theory and practice.* New York: Teachers College Press.

Burbules, N. C., & Bruce, B. C. (2001). Theory and research on teaching as dialogue. In V. Richardson (ed.), *Handbook of research on teaching* (4th ed.). Washington, DC: American Educational Research Association.

Burden, P. (2012). *Classroom management: Creating a successful K–12 learning community* (5th ed.). Indianapolis, IN: Wiley.

Burmark, L. (2002). *Visual literacy: Learn to see, see to learn.* Alexandria, VA: Association for Supervision and Curriculum Development.

Bush, J., & Wise, B. (2010). *Digital learning now.* Washington, DC: Foundation for Excellence in Education.

Cangelosi, J. (2007). *Classroom management strategies: Gaining and maintaining student cooperation* (6th ed.). Indianapolis, IN: Wiley.

Canner, J., et. al. (1991). Regaining trust: Enhancing the credibility of school testing programs. A report from the National Council on Measurement in Education Task Force. National Council on Measurement in Education. Mimeo.

Canter, L. (2005). *Classroom management for academic success.* Bloomington, IN: Solution Tree.

Canter, L. (2009). *Assertive discipline: Positive behavioral management in today's classroom.* Bloomington, IN: Solution Tree.

Canter, L., & Canter, D. M. (2002). *Assertive discipline: Positive behavior management for today's classroom.* Santa Monica, CA: Canter & Associates.

Carnegie Corporation. (1986). *A nation prepared: Teachers for the twenty-first century.* New York: Author.

Casoli-Reardon, M., Rappaport, N., Kulick, D., & Reinfeld, S. (2012). Ending school avoidance. *Educational Leadership, 17*(2), 50–55.

Castle, S. (2002). "Learning Centers." Working Document. Fairfax, VA: George Mason University.

Cavanagh, S. (2008). Since NCLB law, test scores on rise. *Education Week, 27*(43), 3.

Cazden, C. (2001). *Classroom discourse: The language of teaching and learning* (2nd ed.). Portsmouth, NH: Heinemann.

Cazden, C. B. (1972). *Child language and education.* New York: Holt, Rinehart & Winston.

Cazden, C. B. (1986). Classroom discourse. In M. C. Wittrock (ed.), *Handbook of research on teaching* (3rd ed.). New York: Macmillan.

Cazden, C. B. (1988). *Classroom discourse.* Portsmouth, NH: Heinemann.

Census Bureau. (2007). U.S. Department of Commerce. Current Population Survey (CPS). 1979 and 1989 November Supplement 1992, 1995, and 1999 October Supplement and American Community Survey (ACS) 2000–2007.

Census Bureau. (2007). U.S. Department of Commerce. Current Population Survey (CPS). October Supplement, selected years 1972–2007.

Chappuis, J. (2012). How am I doing? *Educational Leadership, 70* (1), 36–41.

Chappuis, J., Stiggins, R., Chappuis, S., & Arter, J. (2011). *Classroom assessment for student learning: Doing it right-using it well.* (2nd ed.). Boston: Pearson.

Charney, R. S. (1992). *Teaching children to care: Management in the responsive classroom.* Turner Falls, MA: Northeast Foundation for Children.

Chartock, R. (2009). *Strategies and lessons for culturally responsive teaching: A primer for K–12 teachers.* Boston: Allyn & Bacon.

Children's Defense Fund. (2010). *The state of America's children.* Washington, DC: Author.

Chomsky, N. (2002). *Understanding power: The indispensable Chomsky.* New York: New Press.

Claiborn, W. L. (1969). Expectancy effects in the classroom: A failure to replicate. *Journal of Educational Psychology, 60,* 377–383.

Clark, C. M., & Lampert, M. (1986). The study of teacher thinking: Implications for teacher education. *Journal of Teacher Education, 37,* 27–31.

Clark, C. M., & Yinger, R. J. (1979). *Three studies of teacher planning.* East Lansing: Institute for Research on Teaching, Michigan State University.

Coffield, F., Moseley, D., Hall, E., & Ecclestone, K. (2004). *Learning styles and pedagogy in post-16 learning: A systematic and critical review.* London: University of New Castle Upon Tyne.

Cognition and Technology Group at Vanderbilt. (1990). Anchored instruction. Unpublished paper. Nashville, TN: Vanderbilt University.

Cognition and Technology Group at Vanderbilt. (1996a). Looking at technology in context: A framework for understanding technology and educational research. In D. Berliner & E. R. Calfee (eds.), *Handbook of educational psychology.* New York: Wiley.

Cognition and Technology Group at Vanderbilt. (1996b). Designing environments to reveal, support, and expand our children's potentials. In S. A. Soraci & W. McIlvane (eds.), *Perspectives on fundamental processes in intellectual functioning.* Greenwich, CT: Ablex.

Cohen, E. (1988). *Statistical power analysis for the behavioral sciences* (2nd ed.). Mahwah, NJ: Erlbaum.

Cohen, E. (1994). *Designing groupwork: Strategies for the heterogeneous classroom.* New York: Teachers College Press.

Cohen, E., & Lotan, R. (2004). Equity in heterogeneous classrooms. In J. Banks & C. Banks (eds.), *Handbook of research on multicultural education* (2nd ed.). San Francisco: Jossey-Bass.

Coiro, J. (2005). Making sense of online text. *Educational Leadership, 63*(2), 30–35.

Cole, M., Griffin, P., & Laboratory of Comparative Cognition. (1987). *Contextual factors in education.* Madison: Wisconsin Center for Educational Research.

Coleman, J. (1961). *The adolescent society.* New York: Free Press.

Coleman, J. (1972, February). The children have outgrown the schools. *Psychology Today, 72*–82.

Collins, A., & Halveson, R. (2009). *Rethinking education in the age of technology: The digital revolution and schooling in America.* New York: Teachers College Press.

Collins, C., & Gan, L. (2013). Does sorting students improve scores? An analysis of class composition. *NBER Working Paper Series,* 18848, http://www/nber.org/papers/w18848

Collins, M. L. (1978). Effects of enthusiasm training on preservice elementary teachers. *Journal of Teacher Education, 29,* 53–57.

Collins, R. (2009). Taking care of one another. *Educational Leadership, 66*(8), 81–82.

Columbia Education Science Center. Retrieved May 19, 2005, from http://ofcn.org/ciber.serv/academy/ace/sci/cecsci/eewcsci045.html

Colorado district scraps traditional teachers pay schedule. (2010). *Education Week.* Retrieved May 10, 2010, from http://www.edweek.org/ew/articles/2010/05/12/31pay/

Comer, J. P. (1988). Educating poor minority children. *Scientific American, 259*(5), 42–48.

Common Core State Standards Initiative. Retrieved November 2013 from http://www.corestandards.org

Condition of education. (2000). Washington, DC: National Center for Education Statistics.

Condition of education. (2001). Washington, DC: National Center for Education Statistics.

Condition of education. (2004). Washington, DC: National Center for Education Statistics.

Conditions of education. (2005). Washington, DC: National Center for Education Statistics.

Conditions of education. (2006). Washington, DC: National Center for Education Statistics.

Conditions of education. (2007). Washington, DC: National Center for Education Statistics.

Conditions of education. (2009). Washington, DC: National Center for Education Statistics.

Conditions of education. (2011). Washington, DC: National Center for Education Statistics.

Conditions of education. (2012). Washington, DC: National Center for Education Statistics.

Constantino, P., & De Lorenzo, M. (2009). *Developing a Professional Teaching Portfolio: A Guide for Success.* (3rd ed.). Boston: Pearson.

Conway, P., & Clark, C. (2003). The journey inward and outward: A re-examination of Fuller's concerns-based model of teacher development. *Teaching and Teacher Education, 19,* 465–482.

Cooper, H. (1989). *Homework.* New York: Longman.

Cooper, H., Jackson, K., Nye, B., & Lindsey, J. J. (2001). A model of homework's influence on the performance evaluation of elementary school students. *Journal of Experimental Education, 69*(2), 181–200.

Cooper, H., Robinson, J., & Patall, E. (2006). Does homework improve academic achievement? A synthesis of research, 1987–2003. *Review of Educational Research, 76*(1), 1–62.

Cooper, H., & Valentine, J. (2001). Using research to answer practical questions about homework. *Educational Psychologist, 36,* 143–153.

Cooper, H. M. (2006). *The battle over homework: Common ground for administrators, teachers, and parents.* Thousand Oaks, CA: Corwin Press.

Corbett, L. Hill, C., & St. Rose, A. (2008). *Where the girls are: The facts about gender equity and education.* Washington, DC: American Association of University Educational Foundation.

Corno, L. (1989). What it means to be literate in classrooms. In D. Bloome (ed.), *Classrooms and literacy.* Norwood, NJ: Ablex.

Corno, L. (1996). Homework is a complicated thing. *Educational Researcher, 25*(8), 27–30.

Corno, L. (2001). Using research to answer practical questions about homework. *Educational Psychologist, 36,* 143–153.

Costa, A. (2011). *Developing minds: A resource book for teaching thinking* (3rd ed.). Alexandria, VA: Association for Supervision and Curriculum Development.

Costa, A. (ed.). (2001). *Developing minds: A resource book for teaching thinking* (3rd ed.). Alexandria, VA: Association for Supervision and Curriculum Development.

Costantino, P., De Lorenzo, M., & Tirrell-Corbin, C. (2008). *Developing a professional teaching portfolio: A guide for success* (3rd ed.). Boston: Pearson.

Cotton, K. (1995). *Effective school practices: A research synthesis, 1995 update.* Portland, OR: Northwest Regional Educational Laboratory.

Council for Chief State School Officers. (2011). *InTASC, model core standards: A resource guide for state dialogue.* Washington, DC: Author.

Craig, S., Sullins, J., Witherspoon, A., & Gholson, B. (2006). Deep-level reasoning questions effects: The role of dialogue and deep-level reasoning questions during vicarious learning. *Cognition and Instruction, 24,* 565–591.

Crater High School Rogue River Project. (1999). Retrieved May 25, 2005, from http://www.mind.net/dlmark/greenway/up&down.htm

Crawford, J. (1997). *Best evidence: Research foundations of the Bilingual Education Act.* Washington, DC: National Clearinghouse for Bilingual Education.

Cronback, L., & Snow, R. (1977). *Aptitudes and instructional methods: A handbook for research on interactions.* New York: Irvington.

Crooks, T. J. (1988). The impact of classroom evaluation practices on students. *Review of Educational Research, 58*(4), 438–441.

Cruickshank, D., & Metcalf, K. (1994). Explaining. In T. Husen & T. N. Postlewaite (eds.), *International encyclopedia of education* (2nd ed.). Oxford: Pergamon Press.

Csikszentmihalyi, M. (1990). *Flow: The psychology of optimal experience.* New York: Harper & Row.

Csikszentmihalyi, M. (1998). *Creativity: Flow and the psychology of discovery and invention.* New York: HarperCollins.

Cuban, L. (1982). Persistent instruction: The high school classroom, 1900–1980. *Phi Delta Kappan, 64,* 113–118.

Cuban, L. (1984). *How teachers taught: Constancy and change in American classrooms, 1900–1980.* New York: Longman.

Cuban, L. (1993). *How teachers taught: Constancy and change in American classrooms 1890–1990* (2nd ed.). New York: Teachers College Press.

Cuban, L. (2001). *Oversold and underused: Computers in the classroom.* Cambridge, MA: Harvard University Press.

Cuban, L. (2003). *Why is it so hard to get good schools?* New York: Teachers College Press.

Cullen, F. T., Cullen, J. B., Hayhow, V. L., & Plouffe, J. T. (1975). The effects of the use of grades as an incentive. *Journal of Educational Research, 68,* 277–279.

Curriculum mapping. Retrieved March 2013 from http://ok.gov/sde/curriculum-mapping

Cushner, K., McClelland, A., & Safford, P. (2008). *Human diversity in education: An integrative approach* (6th ed.). New York: McGraw-Hill.

Cushner, K., McClelland, A., & Safford, P. (2011). *Human diversity in education: An intercultural approach* (7th ed.). New York: McGraw-Hill.

Cypher, T., & Willower, D. J. (1984). The work behavior of secondary school teachers. *Journal of Research and Development, 18,* 17–24.

Danielson, C. (1996). *Enhancing professional practice: A framework for teaching.* Alexandria, VA: Association for Supervision and Curriculum Development.

Danielson, C. (2006). *Teacher leadership that strengthens professional practice.* Alexandria, VA: Association for Supervision and Curriculum Development.

Darling-Hammond, L. (2000). Reforming teacher preparation and licensing. Debating the evidence. *Teachers College Record, 102*(1), 28–56.

Darling-Hammond, L. (2004). What happens to a dream deferred? The continuing quest for equal educational opportunity. In J. Banks & C. Banks (eds.), *Handbook of research on multicultural education* (2nd ed.). San Francisco: Jossey-Bass.

Darling-Hammond, L. (2010). *The flat world and education: How America's commitment to equity will determine our future.* New York: Teachers College Press.

Darling-Hammond, L., Amrein-Beardsley, A., Haertel, E., & Rothstein, J. (2012). Evaluating teacher evaluation. *Phi Delta Kappan, 93* (6), 8–15.

Darling-Hammond, L., & Bransford, J. (eds.). (2005). *Preparing teachers for a changing world: What teachers should learn and be able to do.* San Francisco: Jossey-Bass.

Darder, A. (1991). *Culture and power in the classroom.* New York: Bergin & Garvey.

Davidson, C. N. (2012). *Now you see it: How technology and brain science will transform schools and business for the 21st century.* New York: Penguin Books.

Davies, D. (1991). Schools reaching out: Family, school, and community partnerships for student success. *Phi Delta Kappan, 72,* 376–382.

Dean, C., Hubbell, E., Pitler, H., & Stone, B. (2012). *Classroom instruction that works: Research-based strategies for increasing student achievement.* Alexandria, VA: Association for Supervision and Curriculum Development.

deCharms, R. (1976). *Enhancing motivation.* New York: Irvington.

Deci, E., & Ryan, R. (1985). *Intrinsic motivation and self-determination in human behavior.* New York: Plenum.

Deci, E., & Ryan, R. (2002). The paradox of achievement: The harder you push, the worse it gets. In J. Aronson (ed.), *Improving academic achievement: Impact of psychological factors on education.* San Diego: Academic Press.

Delpit, L. (1988). The silenced dialogue. *Harvard Educational Review, 58,* 280–298.

Delpit, L. (1995). *Other people's children: Cultural conflict in the classroom.* New York: The New York Press.

Dempster, F. N. (1991). Synthesis of research on reviews and tests. *Educational Leadership, 48,* 71–76.

Dempster, F. N. (1992). Using tests to promote learning: A neglected classroom resource. *Journal of Research and Development in Education, 20,* 197–203.

Dewey, J. (1909). *How we think.* Boston: D.C. Heath.

Dewey, J. (1916). *Democracy and education.* New York: Macmillan.

Dewey, J. (1933). *How we think* (rev. ed.). Lexington, MA: Heath.

Dewey, J. (1938). *Experience and education.* New York: Macmillan.

Dietz, M., & Whaley, J. (2005). *School, family, and community.* Mississauga, ON, Canada: Jones and Bartlett.

Diller, D. (2008). *Space and places: Designing classrooms for literacy.* Portland, ME: Stenhouse.

Dilworth, M. E., & Brown, C. E. (2004). Consider the difference: Teaching and learning in culturally rich schools. In V. Richardson (ed.), *Handbook of research on teaching* (5th ed.). Washington, DC: American Educational Research Association.

Dodge, J. (2005). *Differentiation in action.* New York: Scholastic.

Dolezal, S. E., Welsh, L. M., Pressley, M., & Vincent, M. M. (2003). How nine third-grade teachers motivate student academic engagement. *Elementary School Journal, 103*(3), 239–269.

Donovan, M. S., & Bransford, J. D. (2005). *How students learn: Science in the classroom.* Washington, DC: National Academies Press.

Doyle, W. (1979). Classroom tasks and students' abilities. In P. L. Peterson & H. J. Walberg (eds.), *Research on teaching: Concepts, findings and implications.* Berkeley, CA: McCutchan.

Doyle, W. (1986). Classroom organization and management. In M. C. Wittrock (ed.), *Handbook of research on teaching* (3rd ed.). New York: Macmillan.

Doyle, W. (1990). Themes in teacher education research. In W. R. Houston (ed.), *Handbook of research on teacher education.* New York: Macmillan.

Doyle, W. (2006). Ecological approaches to classroom management. In C. Evertson & C. Weinstein (eds.), *Handbook for classroom management: Research, practice, and contemporary issues.* Mahwah, NJ: Erlbaum.

Doyle, W., & Carter, K. (1984). Academic tasks in classrooms. *Curriculum Inquiry, 14,* 129–149.

Dreikurs, R. (1968). *Psychology in the classroom: A manual for teachers* (2nd ed.). New York: Harper & Row.

Dreikurs, R., & Grey, L. (1968). *A new approach to discipline: Logical consequences.* New York: Hawthorne Books.

Dreikers, R. (with Grunwald, B. B., & Pepper, F. C.). (1998). *Maintaining sanity in the classroom: Classroom management techniques* (2nd ed.). New York: Behavioral Science Press.

Duchastel, P. C., & Brown, B. R. (1974). Incidental and relevant learning with instructional objectives. *Journal of Educational Psychology, 66,* 481–485.

Duckworth, E. (1987). *The having of wonderful ideas and other essays on teaching and learning.* New York: Teachers College Press.

Duckworth, E. (1991). Twenty-four, forty-two, and I love you: Keeping it complex. In K. Jervis & C. Montag (eds.), *Progressive education for the 1990s: Transforming practice.* New York: Teachers College Press.

Duffy, G., & Kear, K. (2007). What is the real message about research-based practice? *Phi Delta Kappan, 88*(8), 579–581.

Dunn, K., & Dunn, R. (1978). *Teaching students through their individual learning styles.* Reston, VA: National Council of Principals.

Dunn, K., & Dunn, R. (1987). Dispelling outmoded beliefs about student learning. *Educational Leadership. 47*, 50–58.

Dunn, R., & Dunn, K. (1993a). *Teaching secondary students through their individual learning styles*. Boston: Allyn & Bacon.

Dunn, R., & Dunn, K. (1993b). *Teaching young children through their individual learning styles*. Boston: Allyn & Bacon.

Eamon, M. K. (2002). Effects of poverty on mathematics and reading achievement of young adolescents. *Journal of Early Adolescents, 22,* 49–74.

Earl, L. (2003). *Assessment as learning: Using classroom assessments to maximize student learning*. Thousand Oaks, CA: Corwin Press.

Eccles, J. S. (1989). Bringing young women to math and science. In M. Crawford & M. Gentry (eds.), *Gender and thought: Psychological perspectives*. New York: Springer-Verlag.

Education Trust. (1998). *Education watch, 1998*. Washington, DC: Author.

Eisner, E. (2003, May). Questionable assumptions about schooling. *Phi Delta Kappan,* 648–657.

Elias, M., & Schwab, Y. (2006). From compliance to responsibility: Social and emotional learning and classroom management. In C. Evertson & C. Weinstein (eds.), *Handbook for classroom management: Research, practice, and contemporary issues*. Mahwah, NJ: Erlbaum.

Eliot, L. (2010). The myth of pink and blue brains. *Phi Delta Kappan, 69*(3), 32–36.

Elliott, P. (2013). Schools find a niche for digital bookcases. *Seattle Times,* March 7, A8+.

Ellis, W., Dumas, T., Mandy, J., & Wolfe, D. (2012). Observations of adolescent peer group interactions as a function of within-and between-group centrality status. *Journal of Research on Adolescence, 22*(2), 252–266.

Emmer, E., & Evertson, C. (2012). *Classroom management for middle and high school teachers* (9th ed.). Boston: Allyn & Bacon.

Emmer, E., Evertson, C., Clements, B., & Worsham, W. E. (2002). *Classroom management for secondary school teachers* (6th ed.). Englewood Cliffs, NJ: Prentice-Hall.

Emmer, E. T., Evertson, C., & Anderson, L. M. (1980). Effective classroom management at the beginning of the school year. *Elementary School Journal, 80,* 219–231.

Emmer, E. T., Evertson, C. M., & Worsham, M. E. (2005). *Classroom management for middle and high school teachers* (7th ed.). Boston: Allyn & Bacon.

English Online. Retrieved May 23, 2005, from http://english.unitecnology.ac.nz

Englund, M., Luckner, A. E., Whaley, G., & Egeland, B. (2004). Children's achievement in early elementary school: Longitudinal effects of parental involvement, expectations, and quality of assistance. *Journal of Educational Psychology, 96*(4), 723–731.

Epstein, J. (2001). *School, family, and community partnerships*. Boulder, CO: Westview Press.

Epstein, J. (2005). A case study of the partnership schools comprehensive school reform model. *Elementary School Journal, 106*(2), 151–170.

Epstein, J. (2010). *School, family, and community partnerships: Preparing educators and improving schools* (2nd ed.). Boulder, CO: Westview Press.

Epstein, J., Sanders, M., et al. (2002). *School, family and community partnerships. Handbook for action* (2nd ed.). Thousand Oaks, CA: Corwin Press.

Epstein, J. L. (1988). How do we improve programs for parent involvement? *Educational Horizons, 66,* 58–59.

Epstein, J. L. (1995). School/family/community partnerships: Caring for children we share. *Phi Delta Kappan, 76,* 701–712.

Epstein, J. L. (2001). School, family, and community partnerships. In M. H. Bornstein (ed.), *Handbook of parenting* (2nd ed). Mahwah, NJ: Erlbaum.

Epstein, J., and Associates (2009). *School, family, and community partnerships.* (3rd ed.).Thousand Oaks, CA: Corwin.

Equity and race relations: What is cultural competence? (2010). Retrieved May 2010 from http://www.seattleschools.org/area/equityandrace/culturalcompetence.xml

Erickson, H. L. (2007). *Concept-based curriculum and instruction for the thinking classroom*. Thousand Oaks, CA: Corwin Press.

Erickson, H. L., & Tomlinson, C. A. (2002). *Concept-based curriculum and instruction: Teaching beyond the facts*. New York: Corwin Press.

Ervin, K., & Long, K. (2013). Seeking an even hand at discipline. *The Seattle Times,* March 10, pp. 1, 13.

Evaluating web pages: Techniques to apply and questions to ask. Retrieved July 8, 2007, from http://www.lib.berkeley.edu/Teaching Lib/Guides/Internet/Evaluate

Evans, R. (2002). *The human side of school change: Reform, resistance, and the real-life problems of innovation*. San Francisco: Jossey-Bass.

Evans, R. (2002, May 22). Family matters: The real crisis in education. *Education Week,* 48–50.

Evertson, C., & Emmer, E. (2008). *Classroom management for elementary teachers* (8th ed.). Boston: Allyn & Bacon.

Evertson, C., & Emmer, E. (2012). *Classroom management for elementary teachers* (9th ed.). Boston: Allyn & Bacon.

Evertson, C. M., Emmer, E. T., & Worsham, M. E. (2005). *Classroom management for elementary teachers* (7th ed.). Boston: Allyn & Bacon.

Evertson, C. M., Emmer, E. T., Sanford, J. P., & Clements, B. S. (1983). Improving classroom management: An experiment in elementary classrooms. *Elementary School Journal, 84,* 173–188.

Feiman-Nemser, S. (1983). Learning to teach. In L. S. Shulman & G. Sykes (eds.), *Handbook of teaching and policy*. New York: Longman.

Feiman-Nemser, S., & Floden, R. E. (1986). In M. C. Wittrock (ed.), *Handbook of research on teaching* (3rd ed.). New York: Macmillan.

Felman, J. L. (2001). *Never a dull moment*. New York: Routledge.

Fenstermacher, G. D. (1986). Philosophy of research on teaching: Three aspects. In M. C. Wittrock (ed.), *Handbook of research on teaching* (3rd ed.). New York: Macmillan.

Fenton, E. (1966). *Teaching the new social studies in secondary schools: An inductive approach*. Washington, DC: International Thomson.

Feriazzo, L., & Hammond, L. (2009). *Building parent engagement in schools*. Santa Barbara, CA: Linworth.

Feriazzo, L. (2011). *Helping students motivate themselves: Practical answers to classroom challenges*. Fitchburg, MA: Eye on Education.

Finkelstein, D., & Samsonov, P. (2007). *PowerPoint for teachers: Dynamic presentations and interactive classrooms*. San Francisco: Jossey-Bass.

Firestone, W. A., & Rosenblum, S. (1988). Building commitment in urban high schools. *Educational Evaluation and Policy Analysis, 93,* 285–299.

First look at PISA 2012: Performance of U.S. 15-year-old students in mathematics, science, and reading literacy in an international context (2013). Washington, DC: National Center of Education Statistics.

Fischer, K. (2009). Mind, brain, and education: Building a scientific groundwork for learning and teaching. *Mind, Brain, and Education, 3,* 1–16.

Fisher, C. W., Berliner, D., Filby, N., Marliave, R., Cahen, L., & Dishaw, M. (1980). Teaching behavior, academic learning time, and student achievement: An overview. In C. Denham & A. Lieberman (eds.), *Time to learn*. Washington, DC: National Institute of Education, Department of Education.

Fisher, D., & Frey, N. (2007). *Checking for understanding: Formative assessment techniques for your classroom.* Alexandria, VA: Association for Supervision and Curriculum Development.

Fisher, D., & Frey, N. (2010). *Guided instruction: How to develop confident and successful learners.* Alexandria, VA: Association for Supervision and Curriculum Development.

Fisher, T. (2007). Unwrapping the gifted: More than meets the eye. Retrieved November 12, 2007, from http://www.edweek.org

Flanders, N. A. (1970). *Analyzing teaching behavior.* Reading, MA: Addison-Wesley.

Flavel, J. (1985). *Cognitive development* (2nd ed.). Englewood Cliffs, NJ: Prentice-Hall.

Fleener, A. (1989). *Sample lesson plan format* (mimeographed). Minneapolis, MN: Augsburg College.

Flipped Learning Network Ning. Flipped learning network for teachers to discuss how to flip classrooms. Retrieved November 2013 from http://www.flippedclassroom.org

Floden, R. E. (2001). Research on effect of teaching: A continuing model for research on teaching. *Handbook of research on teaching* (4th ed.). Washington, DC: American Educational Research Association.

Fogarty, R., & Stoehr, J. (2007). *Integrating curricula with multiple intelligences: Teams, themes, and threads.* Thousand Oaks, CA: Corwin Press.

Ford, G. W., & Pugno, L. (eds.). (1964). *The structure of knowledge and the curriculum.* Chicago: Rand McNally.

Friedman, T. L. (2005). *The world is flat: A brief history of the twenty-first century.* New York: Farrar, Straus and Giroux.

Friend, M., & Bursuck, W. (2002). *Including students with special needs* (3rd ed.). Boston: Allyn & Bacon.

Friend, M., & Bursuck, W. (2012). *Including students with special needs: A practical guide for classroom teachers* (6th ed.). Boston: Allyn & Bacon.

Fuchs, L. S., Fuchs, D., Kazdan, S., Karns, K., Calhoon, M. B., Hamlett, C. I., & Hewlett, S. (2000). Effects of workgroup structure on size and student productivity during collaborative work on complex tasks. *Elementary School Journal, 100*(3), 183.

Fullan, M. (1992). *The new meaning of educational change* (2nd ed.). New York: Teachers College Press.

Fullan, M. (2001). *The new meaning of educational change* (3rd ed.). New York: Teachers College Press.

Fullan, M. (2007). *The new meaning of educational change* (4th ed.). New York: Teachers College Press.

Fuller, F. (1969). Concerns of teachers: A developmental conceptualization. *American Educational Research Journal, 6,* 207–226.

Fuller, M. L., & Olsen, G. (1998). *Home–school relations: Working successfully with parents and families.* Boston: Allyn & Bacon.

Fulton, K. (2012). 10 reasons to flip. *Phi Delta Kappan, 94*(2), 20–24.

Gage, N. L. (ed.). (1963). *Handbook of research on teaching.* Chicago: Rand McNally.

Gage, N. L. (1978). *The scientific basis of the art of teaching.* New York: Teachers College Press.

Gage, N. L. (1984). *An update of the scientific basis of the art of teaching* (mimeographed). Palo Alto, CA: Stanford University.

Gagné, E. D. (1985). *The cognitive psychology of school learning.* Boston: Little, Brown.

Gagné, E. D., Yekovick, C. W., & Yekovick, F. R. (1993). *The cognitive psychology of school learning* (2nd ed.). New York: HarperCollins.

Gagné, R. M. (1977). *The conditions of learning and theory of instruction* (3rd ed.). New York: Holt, Rinehart & Winston.

Gall, M. (1984). Synthesis of research on teachers' questioning. *Educational Leadership, 42,* 40–47.

Gall, M. D. (1970). The use of questions in teaching. *Review of Educational Research, 40,* 707–721.

Gallagher, J. J., & Gallagher, S. A. (1994). *Teaching the gifted child* (4th ed.). Boston: Allyn & Bacon.

Gallego, M. A., Cole, M., & The Laboratory of Comparative Cognition. (2001). Classroom cultures and cultures in the classroom. In V. Richardson (ed.), *Handbook of research on teaching.* Washington, DC: American Educational Research Association.

Garcia, R. (1992). *Teaching in a pluralistic society. Concepts, models, and strategies.* New York: HarperCollins.

Gardner, H. (1983). *Frames of mind.* New York: Basic Books.

Gardner, H. (1985). *The mind's new science.* New York: Basic Books.

Gardner, H. (1991). *The unschooled mind: How children think and how schools should teach.* New York: Basic Books.

Gardner, H. (1993). *Multiple intelligences: The theory in practice.* New York: Basic Books.

Gardner, H. (1994). Multiple intelligences: The theory in practice. *Teacher's College Record, 83,* 501–513.

Gardner, H. (1998). Multiple intelligences: Myths and messages. In A. Woolfolk (ed.), *Reading in educational psychology* (2nd ed.). Boston: Allyn & Bacon.

Gardner, H. (1999, February). Who owns intelligence? *Atlantic Monthly,* 67–75.

Gardner, H. (2002). The pursuit of excellence through education. In M. Ferrari (ed.), *Learning from extraordinary minds.* Mahwah, NJ: Erlbaum.

Gardner, H. (2006). *Multiple intelligences: New horizons in theory and practice.* New York: Basic Books.

Gardner, H. (2009). *Five minds for the future.* Cambridge, MA: Harvard Business School Press.

Gardner, H. (2011). *Frames of mind: The theory of multiple intelligences* (3rd ed.). New York: Basic Books.

Gay, G. (2010). *Culturally responsive teaching* (2nd ed.). New York: Teachers College Press.

Gay, Lesbian, and Straight Education Network (GLSEN). (2011). National School Climate Survey. Retrieved November 2013 from http://www.glsen.org

Gazzaniga, M. S. (2005). *The ethical brain.* Chicago: University of Chicago Press.

Gersten, R. (1996). Literacy instruction for language-minority students: The transition years. *The Elementary School Journal, 96,* 241–242.

Gerwertz, C. (a) (2013). Common-Core tests to take students up to 10 hours. *Education Week, 32* (20), 10.

Gerwertz, C. (b) (2013). Teachers say they are unprepared for Common Core. *Education Week, 32* (22), 1, 12.

Genesee, F., Lindholm-Leary, K., Saunders, W., & Christian, D. (2010). English language learners in U.S. schools: An overview of research findings. *Journal of Education of Students Placed at Risk, 10*(4) 363–385.

Getzels, J. W., & Thelen, H. A. (1960). The classroom group as a unique social system. In N. Henry (ed.), *The dynamics of instructional groups.* Chicago: National Society for the Study of Education, 59th Yearbook, Part 2.

Gewertz, C. (2001, August 8). Study estimates 850,000 U.S. children schooled at home. *Education Week,* 12.

Gewertz, C. (2007). Outside interests. In *Technology Counts 2007: A Digital Decade, Education Week, 26*(30), 24–27.

Gewertz, C. (2008). Consensus on learning time builds. *Education Week, 28*(5), 12.

Giant, N. (2013). *E-safety for the I-generation: Combating the misuse and abuse of technology in Schools.* Philadelphia, PA: Jessica Kingsley Publications.

Gijbels, D., Bossche, P., & Loyens, S. (2013). Problem-based learning. In J. Hattie & E. Anderman (eds.), *International guide to student achievement.* New York: Routledge.

Gijbels, D., Dochy, F., Van den Bossche, P., & Segers, M. (2005). Effects of problem-based learning: A meta-analysis from the angle of assessment. *Review of Educational Research, 75*(1), 27–61.

Gillies, R. (2007). *Cooperative learning: Integrating theory and practice.* Thousand Oaks, CA: Sage.

Gilles, R. M. (2002). The residual effects of cooperative learning experiences: A two-year follow-up. *Journal of Educational Research, 96*(1), 15–21.

Gilligan, C. (1982). *In a different voice: Psychological theory and women's development.* Cambridge, MA: Harvard University Press.

Glass, G. (1981). Effectiveness of special education. Paper presented at Wingspread Conference, Racine, WI.

Glass, G. (1982). Meta-analysis: An approach to the synthesis of research results. *Journal of Research in Science Teaching, 19*(2) 93–112.

Glass, G., & Welner, K. (2011). *Online K–12 schooling in the U.S.: Uncertain private ventures in need of public regulation.* National Education Policy Center. Retrieved November 2013 from http://nepccolorado.edu/publication/online-k-12-schooling

Glasser, W. (1969). *Schools without failure.* New York: Harper & Row.

Glasser, W. (1986). *Control theory in the classroom.* New York: Harper & Row.

Glasser, W. (1990). *The quality school: Managing students without coercion.* New York: Harper & Row.

Glasser, W. (1998a). *Choice theory in the classroom.* New York: Harper Paperbacks.

Glasser, W. (1998b). *The quality school teacher.* New York: Harper.

Glasser, W. (1999). *Choice theory: A new psychology of personal freedom.* New York: Harper Paperbacks.

Glasser, W. A. (1992). *The quality school.* New York: HarperCollins.

Glynn, G. (2007). The teaching with analogies model: Build conceptual bridges with mental models. *Science and Children, 44*(8), 52–55.

Goeke, J. (2008). *Explicit instruction: Strategies for meaningful direct teaching.* Boston: Allyn & Bacon.

Gold, R. M., Reilly, A., Silberman, R., & Lehr, R. (1971). Academic achievement declines under pass-fail grading. *Journal of Experimental Education, 39,* 17–21.

Goldenberg, C. (2008). Teaching English language learners. What the research does—and does not say. *American Educator, 32*(2), 8+.

Goldman, C. (2012). *Bullied: What every parent, teacher, and kid needs to know about ending the cycle.* New York: HarperCollins.

Goleman, D. (1995). *Emotional intelligence.* New York: Bantam.

Goleman, D. (2006). *Emotional intelligence: Why it can matter more than IQ* (10th ed.). New York: Bantam Books.

Goleman, D. (2011). *The brain and emotional intelligence: New insights.* Northampton, MA: More Than Sound LLC.

Goleman, D., McKee, A., & Boyatzis, R. E. (2002). *Primal leadership: Realizing the power of emotional intelligence.* Cambridge, MA: Harvard Business School.

Good, T., & Brophy, J. (2007). *Looking in classrooms* (10th ed.). Boston: Allyn & Bacon.

Good, T., & Brophy, J. (2008). *Looking in classrooms* (10th ed.). New York: Allyn & Bacon/Longman.

Good, T. L., & Grouws, D. A. (1977). Teaching effect: A process-product study in fourth grade mathematics classrooms. *Journal of Teacher Education, 28,* 49–54.

Good, T. L., & Grouws, D. A. (1979). The Missouri mathematics effectiveness project: An experimental study in fourth-grade classrooms. *Journal of Educational Psychology, 71,* 355–362.

Good, T. L., Grouws, D. A., & Ebmeier, H. (1983). *Active mathematics teaching.* New York: Longman.

Good, T. L., & Weinstein, R. (1986). Teacher expectations: A framework for exploring classrooms. In K. Zumwalt (ed.), *Improving teaching.* Alexandria, VA: Association for Supervision and Curriculum Development.

Goodlad, J. (1984). *A place called school: Prospects for the future.* New York: McGraw-Hill.

Goodlad, J. (2004). *Romances with schools.* New York: McGraw-Hill.

Goodwin, B., & Miller, K. (2013). Evidence on flipped classrooms is still coming in. *Educational Leadership, 70*(6), 78–80.

Gore, A. (2007). *The assault on reason.* New York: Penguin Press.

Gould, S. J. (1996). *The mismeasure of man* (2nd ed.). New York: Norton.

Graham, S., & Weiner, B. (1996). Theories and principles of motivation. In D. Berliner & R. Calfee (eds.), *Handbook of educational psychology.* New York: Macmillan.

Grant, C. A., & Sleeter, C. E. (1989). Race, class, gender, exceptionality, and education reform. In J. Banks & C. McGee Banks (eds.), *Multicultural education: Issues and perspectives.* Boston: Allyn & Bacon.

Grants, C. D., & Sleeter, C. (2011). *Doing multicultural education for achievement and equity* (2nd ed.). New York: Routledge.

Greeno, J. G., Collins, A. M., & Resnick, L. B. (1996). Cognition and learning. In D. C. Berliner & R. C. Calfee (eds.), *Handbook of educational psychology.* New York: Simon & Schuster.

Gregorc, A. (1982). *Inside styles: Beyond the basics.* New Haven, CT: Gregorc Associates.

Gregory, G. (2008). *Differentiated instructional strategies in practice* (2nd ed.). Thousand Oaks, CA: Corwin Press.

Gregory, G., & Chapman, C. (2002). *Differentiated instructional strategies: One size doesn't fit all.* Thousand Oaks, CA: Corwin Press.

Grigoroenko, E., Meier, E., Lipka, J. Mohatt, G., Yanez, E., & Sternberg, R. (2004). Academic and practical intelligence: A case study of the yup'ik in Alaska. *Learning and Individual Differences, 14,* 183–207.

Grissmer, D., et al. (2000). *Improving student achievement: What state NAEP test scores tell us.* Santa Monica, CA: Rand.

Grolnick, W., Friendly, R., & Bellas, V. (2009). Parenting and children's motivation in school. In K. Wentzel & A. Wigfield (eds.), *Handbook of motivation in school.* New York: Routledge.

Gronlund, N., & Brookhart, S. (2009). *Gronlund's writing instructional objectives* (8th ed.). Columbus, OH: Pearson.

Gronlund, N. E. (2005). *Assessment of student achievement* (8th ed.). Boston: Allyn & Bacon.

Gronlund, N. E., Linn, R. L., & Davis, K. (2000). *Measurement and assessment in teaching* (8th ed.). Englewood Cliffs, NJ: Prentice-Hall.

Grothe, M. (2008). *I never met a metaphor I didn't like: A comprehensive compilation of history's greatest analogies, metaphors, and similes.* New York: HarperCollins.

Gunter, M. A., Estes, T. H., & Schwab, J. (2003). *Instruction: A models approach.* Boston: Allyn & Bacon.

Gurian, M. (1996). *The wonder of boys: What parents, mentors, and educators can do to shape boys into exceptional men.* New York: Putnam.

Gurian, M. (2002). *Boys and girls learn differently.* San Francisco: Jossey-Bass.

Gurian, M., & Stevens, K. (2005). *The minds of boys: Saving our sons from falling behind in school and life.* San Francisco: Jossey-Bass.

Guskey, T. R., & Bailey, J. M. (2001). *Developing grading and reporting systems for student learning.* Thousand Oaks, CA: Corwin Press.

Guskey, T. R., & Gates, S. L. (1986). Synthesis of research on mastery learning. *Educational Leadership, 43,* 73–81.

Guthrie, G. P., & Guthrie, L. F. (1991). Streamlining inter-agency collaboration for youth at risk. *Educational Leadership, 49*(1), 17–22.

Haberman, M. (1991). The pedagogy of poverty versus good teaching. *Phi Delta Kappan, 72,* 290–294.

Hale, J. (2007). *A guide to curriculum mapping.* Thousand Oaks, CA: Corwin Press.

Hale, J., & Fisher, M. (2013). *Upgrade your curriculum: Practical ways to transform units and engage students.* Alexandria, VA: Association for Supervision and Curriculum Development.

Hale, M., & City, E. (2006). *The teacher's guide to leading student-centered discussions: Talking about texts in the classroom.* Thousand Oaks, CA: Corwin Press.

Hallinan, M. (2003). Ability grouping and student learning. In D. Ravitch (ed.), *Brookings papers on educational policy.* Washington, DC: Brookings Institution.

Hallinan, M. T., & Sorensen, A. B. (1983). The formation and stability of instructional groups. *American Sociological Review, 48,* 838–851.

Halpern, D. F. (2007). The nature and nuture of critical thinking. In R. Sternberg, H. Roediger III, & D. Halpern (eds.), *Critical thinking in psychology.* Cambridge, England: Cambridge University Press.

Halpern, D. F., & LaMay, M. L. (2000). The smarter sex: A critical review of sex differences in intelligence. *Educational Psychology Review, 55,* 47–86.

Hamblin, D., & Bartlett, M. (2013). Navigating social networks. *Educational Leadership, 70*(6), 44–47.

Hammerness, K., Darling-Hammond, L., Bransford, J., Berliner, D., Cochran-Smith, M., & McDonald, M. (2005). How teachers learn and develop. In L. Darling-Hammond & J. Bransford (eds.), *Preparing teachers for a changing world.* San Francisco: Jossey-Bass.

Hart, B., & Risley, T. (1995). *Meaningful differences in the everyday experience of young American children.* Baltimore, MD: Brookes.

Hart, P. (2006). *Report findings based on a survey among California ninth and tenth graders.* Washington, DC: Peter D. Hart Research Associates. Available at http://www.connectedcalifornia.org/downloads/irvine_poll.pdf

Harvard Family Research Council. (1995). *Raising our future: Families, schools, and communities joining together.* Cambridge, MA: Author.

Hatfield, S. (1996). *Effective use of classroom computer stations across the curriculum.* ERIC Document No. ED-396704.

Hattie, J. (2008). *Visible learning: A synthesis of over 800 meta-analyses relating to achievement.* New York: Routledge.

Hattie, J., & Anderman, E. (2013). *International guide to student achievement* (Eds.). New York: Routledge.

Hattie, J., & Timperley, H. (2007). The power of feedback. *Review of Educational Research, 77* (1), 81–112.

Hawley, W., & Nieto, S. (2010). Another inconvenient truth: Race and ethnicity matter. *Phi Delta Kappan, 69*(3), 66–71.

Haycock, K. (2006). *Promise abandoned: How policy choices and institutional practices restrict college opportunities.* Washington, DC: Educational Trust.

Haynes, C. (2013). Getting religion right in public schools. *Phi Delta Kappan, 93*(4), 8–14.

Heath, S. B. (1983). *Ways with words: Language, life and work in communities and classrooms.* Cambridge, England: Cambridge University Press.

Heider, E. R., Cazden, C. B., & Brown, R. (1968). *Social class differences in the effectiveness and style of children's coding ability* (Project Literacy Reports, No. 9). Ithaca, NY: Cornell University.

Heitin, L. (2012). Project-based learning helps at-risk students. *Education Week,* April, 8–9.

Herrnstein, R. J., & Murray, C. (1994). *The bell curve: Intelligence and class structure in American life.* New York: Free Press.

Heyck-Merlin, M., & Atkins, N. (2012). *The together teacher: Plan ahead, get organized, and save time.* San Francisco: Jossey-Bass.

Heyman, R. (2003). *How to say it ® to boys.* Englewood Cliffs, NJ: Prentice Hall.

Hickey, D., Moore, A., & Pellegrino, J. (2001). The motivational and academic consequences of elementary mathematics environments: Do constructivist innovations and reforms make a difference? *American Educational Research Journal, 39*(3), 611–653.

Hicks, D. (ed.). (1996). *Discourse, learning and schooling.* New York: Cambridge University Press.

Hiller, J. H., Gisher, G. A., & Kaess, W. (1969). A computer investigation of verbal characteristics of effective classroom lecturing. *American Educational Research Journal, 6,* 661–675.

Himmele, W., & Himmele, P. (2012). How to know what students know. *Educational Leadership, 70* (1), 58–63.

Himmele, W., & Hummele, P. (2011). *Total participation techniques: Making every student an active learner.* Alexandria, VA: Association of Supervision and Curriculum Development.

Hindin, A., Morocco, C., Mott, E., & Aquilar, C. (2007). More than just a group: Teacher collaboration and learning in the workplace. *Teachers and Teaching, 13*(4), 349–376.

Hirsch, L., Lowen, C., & Santorelli, D. (2012). *Bully: An action plan for teachers, parents, and communities to combat the bullying crisis.* New York: Weinstein Books.

Hmelo, C., Horton, D., & Kolodner, J. (2000). Designing to learn in complex systems. *Journal of the Learning Sciences, 9*(3), 247–298.

Hmelo-Silver, C. E. (2004). Problem-based learning: What and how do students learn? *Educational Psychology Review, 16,* 235–266.

Hmelo-Silver, C. E., & Barrows, H. S. (2006). Goals and strategies of a problem-based learning facilitator. *Interdisciplinary Journal of Problem-based Learning, 1,* 21–39.

Hmelo-Silver, C. E., & Eberbach, C. (2012). Learning theories and problem-based learning. *Innovation and Change in Professional Education, 8,* 3–17.

Hodgkinson, H. L. (1983). Guess who's coming to college? *Higher Education, 17,* 281–287.

Hodgkinson, H. L. (1992). *A demographic look at the future.* Washington, DC: Institute for Educational Leadership.

Hofstadter, D., & Sander, E. (2013). *Surfaces and essences: Analogy as the fuel and fire of thinking.* New York: Basic Books.

Hollingsworth, J., & Ybarra, S. (2008). *Explicit direct instruction (EDI): The power of the well-crafted, well-taught lesson.* Thousand Oaks, CA: Corwin Press.

Honeycutt, B. (2013). Looking for "flippable moments" in your class. *Faculty Focus.* Retrieved March 25, 2013, from http://www.facultyfocus.com

Honig, M. I., Kahne, J., & McLaughlin, M. W. (2001). School-community connections: Strengthening opportunity to learn and opportunity to teach. In V. Richardson (ed.), *Handbook of research on teaching* (4th ed.). Washington, DC: American Educational Research Association.

Housner, L. D., & Griffey, D. C. (1985). Teacher cognition: Differences in planning and interactive decision making between experienced and inexperienced teachers. *Research Quarterly for Exercise and Sport, 56,* 45–53.

Houston, B., & Miller, H. (2011). *Academic learning time: The most important educational concept you've never heard of.* Waterford Institute Early Education and Technology for Children. Retrieved October 15, 2013, from http://www.waterford.org

Howard, T. C. (2003). Culturally relevant pedagogy: Ingredients for critical teacher reflection. *Theory into Practice, 42*(3), 195–203.

Howard, T. (2010). *Why race and culture matters in school: Closing the achievement gap in America's classrooms.* New York: Teachers College Press.

Hunt, D. (1974). *Matching models in education.* Toronto: Ontario Institute for Studies in Education.

Hunter, M. (1995). *Enhancing teaching.* New York: Macmillan.

Hunter, M. C. (1982). *Mastery teaching.* El Segundo, CA: TIP Publications.

Husband, T. (2012). Why can't Jamal read? *Phi Delta Kappan, 93*(5), 23–27.

Income, poverty, and health insurance coverage in the United States. (2010). Washington, DC: U.S. Bureau of the Census.

Irvine, J. J., & York, D. E. (1995). Learning styles and culturally diverse students: A literature review. In J. Banks & C. Banks (eds.), *Handbook of research on multicultural education.* New York: Macmillan.

Jackson, L. (1999). Doing school: Examining the effect of ethnic identity and school engagement in academic performance and goal attainment. Paper presented at the annual meeting of the American Educational Research Association, Montreal.

Jackson, R. (2010). *How to plan rigorous instruction.* Alexandria, VA: Association for Supervision and Curriculum Development.

Jacobs, G. M., Power, M. A., & Loh, W. I. (2002). *Teacher sourcebook for cooperative learning: Practical techniques, basic principles, and frequently asked questions.* Thousand Oaks, CA: Corwin Press.

Jacobs, H., & Johnson, A. (2009). *The curriculum mapping planner: Templates, tools, and resources for effective professional development.* Alexandria, VA: Association for Supervision and Curriculum Development.

Jacobs, H. H. (2004). *Getting results with curriculum mapping.* Alexandria, VA: Association for Supervision and Curriculum Development.

Jacobs, T. (2011). How to stop bullying. ASCD Express, 6, (13), www.ace.org/ascdexpress.

James, M., & Gronlund, N. (2005). *Focused observation: How to observe children for assessment and curriculum planning.* St Paul, MN: Redleaf Press.

Jensen, A. R. (1969). How much can we boost IQ and scholastic achievement? *Harvard Education Review, 2,* 79–83.

Jensen, E. (2005). *Teaching with the brain in mind* (2nd ed.). Alexandria, VA: Association for Supervision and Curriculum Development.

Jeynes, W. (2011). Help families by fostering parental involvement. *Phi Delta Kappan, 93*(3), 38–39.

Jha, J., & Kelleher, F. (2007). *Boys' underachievement in education: An exploration in selected countries.* London: Commonwealth Secretariat.

Johnson, D., & Johnson, F. (2013). *Joining together: Group theory and group skills* (10th ed.). Boston: Pearson.

Johnson, D., Johnson, R., & Holubec, E. (1998). *Cooperative learning in the classroom.* Alexandria, VA: Association for Supervision and Curriculum Development.

Johnson, D. W., & Johnson, F. P. (2003). *Joining together: Group theory and group skills* (8th ed.). Boston: Allyn & Bacon.

Johnson, D. W., & Johnson, F. P. (2006). *Joining together: Group theory and group skills* (9th ed.). Englewood Cliffs, NJ: Prentice-Hall.

Johnson, R., Rynders, J., Johnson, D. W., Schmidt, B., & Haider, S. (1979). Interaction between handicapped and nonhandicapped teenagers as a function of situational goal structuring: Implications for mainstreaming. *American Educational Research Journal, 16,* 161–167.

Johnson, S. (2011). *Digital tools for teaching: 30 e-tools for collaborating, creating, and publishing across the curriculum.* Gainesville, FL: Maupin House.

Jolliffe, W. (2007). *Cooperative learning in the classroom: Putting it into practice.* Thousand Oaks, CA: Sage.

Jones, V., & Jones, L. (2009). *Comprehensive classroom management: Creating communities of support and solving problems* (9th ed.). New York: Prentice Hall.

Jordan, J. (1988). Nobody means more to me than you and the future life of Willie Jordan. *Harvard Educational Review, 58,* 363–374.

Joyce, B., Hersh, R., & McKibbin, M. (1993). *The structure of school improvement* (2nd ed.). New York: Longman.

Joyce, B., Weil, M., & Calhoun, E. (2006). *Models of teaching* (7th ed.). Boston: Allyn & Bacon.

Jung, L., & Guskey, T. (2010). Grading exceptional learners. *Educational Leadership, 67*(5), 31–35.

Jussim, L., Robustelli, S., & Cain, T. (2009). Teacher expectations and self-fulfilliing prophecies. In K. Wentzel & A. Wigfield (eds.), *Handbook of motivation in school.* New York: Routledge.

Kafele, B. (2012). Empowering young black males. *Educational Leadership, 70*(2), 67–70.

Kagan, L., & Kagan, S. (2006). *Structures for success.* San Juan Capistrano, CA: Kagan.

Kagan, S. (2001, Spring). Kagan structures: Research and rationale. *Kagan Online Magazine.*

Kagan, S., & Kagan, M. (2008). *Kagan cooperative learning.* San Juan Capistrano, CA: Kagan.

Kanazawa, S. (2010). Evolutionary psychology and intelligence research. *American Psychologist, 58,* 209–215.

Kansas State Science Standards. Retrieved May 23, 2005, from http://www.ksde.org/outcomes/science.html

Kaplan, A., Gheen, M., & Midgley, C. (2002). Classroom goal structure and student disruptive behavior. *British Journal of Educational Psychology, 72*(2), 191–212.

Keller, F. S. (1966). A personal course in psychology. In T. Urlich, R. Stachnik, & T. Mabry (eds.), *Control of human behavior.* Glenview, IL: Scott, Foresman.

Keller, M., Neuman, K., & Fischer, H. (2013). Teacher enthusiasm and student learning. In J. Hattie & E. Anderman (eds.), *International guide to student achievement.* New York: Routledge.

Killermann, S. (2012). Retrieved from http://www.itsPronounced Metrosexual.com

Kilpatrick, W. (1918). The project method. *Teachers College Record, 19,* 319–333.

Kirschner, P., Sweller, J., & Clark, R. (2006). Why minimal guidance during instruction does not work: An analysis of failure of constructivist, discovery, problem-based, experiential, and inquiry-based learning. *Educational Psychologist, 41*(2), 75–86.

Kissen, R. M. (ed.). (2003). *Getting ready for Benjamin: Preparing teachers for sexual diversity in the classroom.* Lanham, MD: Rowman and Littlefield.

Klahr, D., & Nibam, M. (2004). The equivalence of learning paths in early science instruction: Effects of direct instruction and discovery learning. *Psychological Science, 15,* 661–667.

Klausmeier, H. (1980). *Learning and teaching concepts.* New York: Academic Press.

Klausmeier, H. (1992). Concept learning and concept teaching. *Educational Psychologist, 27,* 267–286.

Kleinfeld, J. (1999). Student performance: Males versus females. *The Public Interest, 134,* 3–20.

Klingberg, T. (2012). *The learning brain: Memory and brain development in children.* New York: Oxford University Press.

Klotz, M., & Canter, A. (2007). Response to intervention: A primer for parents. Retrieved March 25, 2013, from http://www.nasponline.org/resources/handouts/revisedPDFs/rti-primer.pdf

Kohn, A. (1995). *Punishment by rewards: The trouble with gold stars, incentive plans, A's, praise and other bribes.* Boston: Houghton Mifflin.

Kohn, A. (1996). *Beyond discipline: From compliance to community.* Alexandria, VA: Association for Supervision and Curriculum Development.

Kohn, A. (2000). *The schools our children deserve: Moving beyond traditional classrooms and tougher standards.* New York: Marilner Books.

Kohn, A. (2002, November 8). The dangerous myth of grade inflation. *The Chronicle of Higher Education*, pp. B7–B9.

Kohn, A. (2004, November). Challenging students—and how to have more of them. *Phi Delta Kappan*, 184–194.

Kohn, A. (2006). The trouble with rubrics. *The English Journal*, 95 (4), 12–15. Retrieved from www.alfiekohn.org. April 10, 2013.

Kohn, A. (2006a). *Beyond discipline: From compliance to community* (10th Annual Edition). Alexandria, VA: Association for Supervision and Curriculum Development.

Kohn, A. (2006b). The truth about homework: Needless assignments persist because of widespread misconceptions about learning. *Education Week*. Retrieved September 8, 2006, from http://www.edweek.org/ew/articles/2006/09/02/o2kohn

Kohn, A. (2006c). *The homework myth: Why our kids get too much of a bad thing*. Cambridge, MA: Da Capo Press.

Kohn, A. (2007). *The homework myth: Why our kids get too much of a bad thing*. Cambridge, MA: Capo Lifelong Books.

Kohn, A. (2011). *Feel-bad education: And other contrarian essays on children*. Boston: Beacon Press.

Kohn, A. (2012). Homework: New research suggests it may be an unnecessary evil. *HuffPost Education*. Retrieved April 16, 2013, from http://bit.ly/9dXqCJ

Kosminsky, E., & Kosminsky, L. (2003). *Improving motivation through dialogue*. *Educational Leadership*, 61, 150–154.

Kotulak, R. (1996). *Inside the brain: Revolutionary discoveries of how the mind works*. Kansas City, MO: Andrew McMeel.

Kounin, J. S. (1970). *Discipline and group management in classrooms*. New York: Holt, Rinehart & Winston.

Krajcik, J., & Blumenfeld, P. (2006). Project-based learning. In R. Sawyer (ed.), *The Cambridge handbook of the learning sciences*. Cambridge, England: Cambridge University Press.

Krajcik, J. S., Blumenfeld, P. C., Marx, R. W., & Soloway, E. (1994). A collaborative model for helping middle grade science teachers learn project-based instruction. *Elementary School Journal*, 94, 483–497.

Krajcik, J. S., Czerniak, C., & Berger, C. (2003). *Teaching children science: A project-based approach* (2nd ed.). Boston: McGraw-Hill.

Krauss, J., & Boss, S. (2013). *Thinking through project-based learning: Guiding deeper inquiry*. Thousand Oaks, CA: Corwin Press.

Kryza, K., Stephens, S., & Duncan, A. (2007). *Inspiring middle and secondary learners. Honoring differences and creating community through differentiated instructional practices*. Thousand Oaks, CA: Corwin Press.

Kuiper, E., Volman, M., & Terwel, J. (2005). The Web as an information source in K–12 education: Strategies for supporting students in searching and processing information. *Review of Educational Research*, 75(3), 285–328.

Kulik, J. A. (2003). Grouping and tracking. In N. Colangelo & G. Davis (eds.), *Handbook of gifted education*. Boston: Allyn & Bacon.

Kumar, D. (1991). A meta-analysis of the relationship between science instruction and student engagement. *Education Review*, 43(1), 49–66.

Kumashiro, K. (2012). *Bad teacher ! How blaming teachers distorts the bigger picture*. New York: Teachers College Press.

Kunzman, R. (2012). How to talk about religion. *Educational Leadership*, 69(7), 44–48.

LaBrec, S. (1994). *How to respond to culturally diverse student populations*. Alexandria, VA: Association for Supervision and Curriculum Development.

Ladd, G., Herald-Brown, S., & Kochel, K. (2009). Peers and motivation. In K. Wentzel & A. Wigfield (eds.), *Handbook of motivation in school*. New York: Routledge.

Ladson-Billings, G. (1992). Culturally relevant teachers: The key to making multicultural education work. In C. A. Grant (ed.), *Research and multicultural education*. London: Falmer Press.

Ladson-Billings, G. (1994). *The dreamkeepers: Successful teachers of African American children*. San Francisco: Jossey-Bass.

Ladson-Billings, G. (1995a). But this is just good teaching! The case for culturally relevant pedagogy. *Theory into Practice, 34*, 161–165.

Ladson-Billings, G. (1995b). Toward a theory of culturally relevant pedagogy. *American Education Research Journal, 32*, 465–491.

Ladson-Billings, G. (2009). *The dreamkeepers: Successful teachers of African-American children* (2nd ed.). San Francisco: Jossey-Bass.

Lake, S. (1988). *Equal access to education: Alternatives to tracking and ability grouping* (Practitioner's Monograph No. 2). Sacramento: California League of Middle Schools.

Lake, R., & Berliner, D. (2013). *Dear Nel: Opening the circles of care (letters to Nel Noddings)*. New York: Teachers College Press.

Lampert, M. (2001). *Teaching problems and the problems of teaching*. New Haven, CT: Yale University Press.

Landsburg, M. (2008, June 21). Graduation rates declining in L.A. Unified despite higher enrollments. *Los Angeles Times*, p. B1.

Landsman, J. (2004). Confronting the racism of low expectations. *Educational Leadership, 62*(3), 28–32.

Leahy, S., Lyon, C., Thompson, M., & Wiliam, D. (2005). Classroom assessment: Minute-by-minute and day-by-day. *Educational Leadership, 63*(3), 18–24.

Learner-Centered Work Group. (1997). *Learner-centered psychological principles: A framework for school reform and redesign*. Washington, DC: American Psychological Association.

Learning Expeditions. Retrieved August 10, 2005, from http://www.cosi.org/progress/learningExpeditions/index.html

Lee, H. (1960). *To kill a mockingbird*. Philadelphia: Lippincott.

Lee, V. E., & Smith, J. B. (1996). Collective responsibility for learning and its effects on gains in achievement of early secondary school students. *American Journal of Education, 104*, 1103–1146.

Leinhardt, G. (1989). Math lessons: A contrast of novice and expert competence. *Journal for Research in Mathematics Education, 20*, 52–75.

Leinhardt, G. (1992). What research on learning tells us about teaching. *Educational Leadership, 49*(7), 20–25.

Leinhardt, G. (2001). Instructional explanations: A commonplace for teaching and location for contrasts. In V. Richardson (ed.), *Handbook of research on teaching* (4th ed.). Washington, DC: American Educational Research Association.

Lemov, D. (2010). *Teach like a champion: 49 techniques that put students on the path to college*. San Francisco: Wiley.

Leonard, J. (2000). How group composition influenced the achievement of sixth-grade mathematics students. *Mathematical Thinking and Learning, 3*(2&3), 175–200.

Lessow-Hurley, J. (2003). *Meeting the needs of second language learners: An educator's guide*. Alexandria, VA: Association for Supervision and Curriculum Development.

Lewin, K., Lippitt, R., & White, R. (1939). Patterns of aggressive behavior in experimentally created social climates. *Journal of Social Psychology, 10*, 271–299.

Lieberman, A. (1995). Restructuring schools: The dynamics of changing practice, structure and culture. In A. Lieberman (ed.), *The work of restructuring schools: Building from the ground up*. New York: Teachers College Press.

Lieberman, A., & Miller, L. (1984). *Teachers, their world, and their work*. Alexandria, VA: Association for Supervision and Curriculum Development.

Lieberman, A., & Miller, L. (1992). *Teachers—their world and their work: Implications for school improvement*. New York: City College Press.

Lieberman, A., & Miller, L. (1999). *Teachers: Transforming their world and their work*. New York: Teachers College Press.

Lieberman, A., & Miller, L. (2004). *Teacher leadership*. San Francisco: Jossey-Bass.

Lieberman, A., & Miller, L. (2008). *Teachers in professional communities: Improving teacher and learning.* New York: Teachers College Press.

Linn, M. C., & Hyde, J. S. (1989). Gender, mathematics, and science. *Educational Researcher, 18*(8), 17–27.

Lippitt, R., & White, R. (1963). An experimental study of leadership and group life. In E. E. Macoby, T. M. Newcomb, & F. L. Hartley (eds.), *Readings in social psychology.* New York: Holt, Rinehart & Winston.

Lippman, P. (2010). *Evidence-based design of elementary and secondary schools: A responsive approach to creating learning environments.* Hoboken, NJ: Wiley.

Little, J. W. (1990). The persistence of privacy: Autonomy and initiative in teachers' professional relations. *Teachers College Record, 91,* 509–536.

Lobato, J., Clarke, D., & Burns, A. B. (2005). Initiating and eliciting in teaching: A reformulation in telling. *Journal of Research in Mathematics Education, 36*(2), 101–112.

Lortie, D. C. (1975). *School-teacher: A sociological study.* Chicago: University of Chicago Press.

Loveless, T. (2013a). *The resurgence of ability grouping and persistence of tracking.* Brookings Institution's Brown Center on American Education. Retrieved March 18, 2013.

Loveless, T. (2013b). The Common Core initiative: What are the chances for success? *Educational Leadership, 70*(4), 60–63.

Loyens, S., & Rikers, R. (2011). Instruction based on inquiry. In R. Mayer & P. Alexandria (eds.). *Handbook of research on learning and instruction.* New York: Routledge.

Luiten, J., Ames, W., & Aerson, G. (1980). A meta-analysis of advance organizers on learning and retention. *American Educational Research Journal, 17,* 211–218.

Lundy, K., & Swartz, L. (2011). *Creating caring classrooms: How to encourage students to communicate, create and be compassionate to others.* Ontario, Canada: Pembroke.

Lyman, F. (1983). *Journaling procedures* (mimeographed). College Park: University of Maryland.

Lyman, F. (1985). *Think-pair-share* (mimeographed). College Park: University of Maryland.

Lyman, F. (1986). *Procedures for using the question/response cues* (mimeographed). College Park: University of Maryland and the Howard County Public Schools.

Lyotard, J. (1987). The postmodern condition. In K. Baynes, J. Bohman, & T. McCarthy (eds.), *After philosophy: End or transformation?* Cambridge, MA: MIT Press.

Lytton, H., & Romney, D. M. (1991). Parents' sex-related differential socialization of boys and girls: A meta-analytic review. *Psychological Bulletin, 109,* 267–295.

Macbeth, D. (2000). On an actual apparatus for conceptual change. *Science Education, 84*(2), 226–234.

Macias, J. (1990). Scholastic antecedents of immigrant students: Schooling in a Mexican immigrant-sending community. *Anthropology and Education Quarterly, 21,* 291–318.

Maehr, M., & Zusho, A. (2009). Achievement goal theory: The past, present, and future. In K. Wentzel & A. Wigfield (eds.), *Handbook of motivation in school.* New York: Routledge.

Mager, R. F. (1962). *Preparing instructional objectives.* Palo Alto, CA: Fearon.

Mager, R. F. (1997). *Preparing instructional objectives: A critical tool in the development of effective instruction* (3rd ed.). Los Angeles: Center for Effective Instruction.

Magnusson, S., & Palincsar, A. (1995). The learning environment as a site of science reform. *Theory into Practice, 34*(1), 43–50.

Maltese, A., Tai, R., & Fan, X (2012, October/November). When is homework worth the time? Evaluating the association between homework and achievement in high school science and math. *The High School Journal,* 52–72.

Marchand-Martella, N., Slocum, T., & Martella, R. (2004). *Introduction to direct instruction.* Boston: Allyn & Bacon.

Marzano, R. (2006). *Classroom assessment and grading that works.* Alexandria, VA: Association for Supervision and Curriculum Development.

Marzano, R. (2007). *The art and science of teaching: A comprehensive framework for effective instruction.* Alexandria, VA: Association for Supervision and Curriculum Development.

Marzano, R. (2009). Teaching with interactive whiteboards. *Educational Leadership, 67*(3), 80–82.

Marzano, R., & Haystead, M. (2008). *Making standards useful in the classroom.* Alexandria, VA: Association for Supervision and Curriculum Development.

Marzano, R., & Pickering, D. (2007). Errors and allegations about research on homework. *Phi Delta Kappan, 88*(7), 507–513.

Marzano, R., & Pickering, D. (2007). The case for and against homework. *Educational Leadership, 64*(6), 74–79.

Marzano, R., Pickering, D., & McTighe, J. (1993). *Assessing student outcomes.* Alexandria, VA: Association for Supervision and Curriculum Development.

Marzano, R. J. (1992). *A different kind of classroom: Teaching with dimensions of learning.* Alexandria, VA: Association for Supervision and Curriculum Development.

Marzano, R. J. (2000). *Transforming classroom grading.* Alexandria, VA: Association for Supervision and Curriculum Development.

Marzano, R. J. (2003). *What works in schools: Translating research into action.* Alexandria, VA: Association for Supervision and Curriculum Development.

Marzano, R. J. (2004). *Building background knowledge for academic achievement: Research on what works in schools.* Alexandria, VA: Association for Supervision and Curriculum Development.

Marzano, R. (2012). The many uses of exit slips. *Educational Leadership, 70* (2), 80–81.

Marzano, R. J., Marzano, J. S., & Pickering, D. J. (2003). *Classroom management that works: Research-based strategies for every teacher.* Alexandria, VA: Association for Supervision and Curriculum Development.

Maslow, A. (1970). *Motivation and personality* (2nd ed.). New York: Harper & Row.

Mathews, J. (2007, January 21). Tips for building a stronger parent-school relationship. *Chicago Tribune Online Edition.* Retrieved January 26, 2007, from http://www.chicagotribune.com

Mathis, W. (2013). *English language learners and parental involvement.* Boulder, CO: National Education Policy Center. Available at http://nepc.colorado.edu

Mayer, R., & Massa, L. (2003). Three facets of visual and verbal learners: Cognitive ability, cognitive style, and learning preferences. *Journal of Educational Psychology, 95*(40), 833–846.

Mayer, R. E. (1979). Can advance organizers influence meaningful learning? *Review of Educational Research, 49,* 371–383.

Mayer, R. E. (2003). *Learning and instruction.* Upper Saddle River, NJ: Merrill.

Mayer, R. E. (2011). *Applying the science of learning.* Boston: Pearson.

Mayer, S. (2012). *Classroom discourse and democracy: Critical pedagogical perspectives.* New York: Peter Lang.

McCaffrey, D. F., Koretz, D. M., Lockwood, J. R., & Hamilton, L. S. (2004). *Evaluating value-added models for teacher accountability.* Santa Monica, CA: Rand Cooperation.

McClelland, D. C. (1958). Methods of measuring human motivation. In J. W. Atkinson (ed.), *Motives in fantasy, action and society.* New York: Van Nostrand.

McClelland, D. C. (1985). *Human motivation*. New York: Scott, Foresman.

McCombs, B. L. (2001). What do we know about learners and learning? The learner-centered framework. Paper presented at the annual meeting of the American Educational Research Association, Seattle.

McCombs, G., & Miller, L. (2007). *Learner-centered classroom practices and assessments*. Thousand Oaks, CA: Corwin Press.

McCown, R. R., & Roop, P. (1992). *Educational psychology and classroom practice: A partnership*. Needham Heights, MA: Allyn & Bacon.

McCutcheon, G. (1980, September). How do elementary teachers plan? *Elementary School Journal*, 4–23.

McCutcheon, G., & Milner, H. R. (2002). A contemporary study of teacher planning in a high school English class. *Teachers and Teaching: Theory and Practice, 8*(1), 81–94.

McDonald, E., & Hershman, D. (2010). *Classrooms that spark!: Recharge and revive your teaching*. San Francisco: Jossey-Bass.

McGarry, R. (2013). Build a curriculum that includes everyone. *Phi Delta Kappan, 84*(5), 27–31.

McLaughlin, D. (1996). Personal narratives for school change in Navajo settings. In D. McLaughlin & W. Tierney (eds.), *Naming silenced lives: Personal narratives and processes of school change*. London: Routledge.

McLaughlin, M., & Talbert, J. (2001). *Professional communities and the work of high school teaching*. Chicago: University of Chicago Press.

McMillan, J. (2010). *Classroom assessment: Principles and practice for effective standards-based instruction* (5th ed.). Boston: Allyn & Bacon.

McTighe, J., & Lyman, F. T. (1988). Cueing thinking in the classroom: The promise of theory-embedded tools. *Educational Leadership, 45*, 18–24.

McTighe, J., & O'Connor, K. (2005). Seven practices for effective leadership. *Educational Leadership, 62*(3), 13–19.

McTighe, J., & Wiggins, G. (2013). *Essential questions: Opening doors to student understanding*. Alexandria, VA: Association for Supervision and Curriculum Development.

Mendler, A. (2006). *Motivating students who don't care: Successful techniques for educators*. Bloomington, IN: Solution Tree.

Mergendoller, J., Bellisimo, Y., & Maxwell, N. (2000). Comparing problem-based learning and traditional instruction in high school economics. *Journal of Educational Research, 93*(6), 374–383.

Merrill, M. D., & Tennyson, R. D. (1977). *Teaching concepts: An instructional design approach*. Englewood Cliffs, NJ: Educational Technology.

Merrow, J. (2009, September 30). When roads diverge: Where will the charter movement take education? *Education Week*, 32.

Mertler, C. A. (2001). Designing and scoring rubrics for your classroom. *Practical Assessment, Research and Evaluation, 7*(25). Retrieved April 1, 2005, from http://PAREonline.net/getvn.asp?v=7&n=25

MetLife survey of the American teacher (1995–2006). Retrieved December 10, 2007, from http://www.metlife.com

Metropolitan Life survey of the American teacher. (1995). New York: Louis Harris & Associates.

Metts, S. (2005). Suggestions for classroom discussion. Retrieved August 10, 2005, from http://www.cat.ilstu.edu/teaching-tips/handouts/classdis.shtml

Meyer, E. (2010). *Gender and sexual diversity in schools: Explorations of educational purpose*. New York: Springer.

Meyer, R. (2004). Should there be a three-strike rule against discover learning? A case for guided methods of instruction. *American Psychologist, 59*, 14–59.

Meyer, R. (2011). *Applying the science of learning*. Boston: Pearson.

Meyer, R. (2011). Instruction based on visualization. In R. Meyer & P. Alexandria (eds.), *Handbook of research on learning and instruction*. New York: Routledge.

Miller, P. (2011). *Theories of developmental psychology* (5th ed.). New York: Worth.

Mills, L., Tyler-Wood, T., & Knezek, G. (2011). Understanding student attitudes towards school: A literature review. In M. Koehler & P. Mishra (eds.), *Proceedings of the Society for Information Technology & Teacher Education International Conference*. Chesapeake, VA: AACE. Retrieved from http://www.editlib.org/p/36521

Milman, N. (2008). *What every teacher should know about creating digital portfolios*. Boston: Pearson.

Milman, N., & Kilbane, C. (2008). *What every teacher should know about: creating digital teaching portfolios*. Boston: Pearson

Milton, O., et al. (1986). *Making sense of college grades*. San Francisco: Jossey-Bass.

Minahan, J., & Rappaport, N. (2012). *The behavior code: A practical guide to understanding and teaching the most challenging students*. Cambridge, MA: Harvard Education Press.

Minke, K. M., & Anderson, K. J. (2003). Restructuring routine parent-teacher conferences. The family-school conference model. *Elementary School Journal, 104*(1), 13–34.

Minner, D., Levy, A., & Century, J. (2010). Inquiry-based science instruction—what it is and does it matter? Results from a research synthesis years 1985–2002. *Journal of Research in Science Teaching, 47*(4), 474–496.

Mishel, L. (2006, March 8). The exaggerated dropout crisis. Civic Enterprise Report as cited in *Education Week*, 30.

Mitchell, S. N., Reilly, R., Bramwell, F. G., Lilly, F., & Solnosky, A. (2004). Friendship and choosing groupmates: Preferences for teacher-selected vs. student-selected grouping in high school science classes. *Journal of Instructional Psychology, 31*(1), 20–33.

Mitzel, H. (1960). Teacher effectiveness. In C. W. Harris (ed.), *Encyclopedia of educational research* (3rd ed.). New York: Macmillan.

Moll, L., & Gonzalez, N. (2004). Engaging life: A funds of knowledge approach to multicultural education. In J. Banks & C. Banks (eds.), *Handbook of research on multicultural education* (2nd ed.). San Francisco: Jossey-Bass.

Molnar, M. (2013). Home and community involvement can play key part in school success. *Education Week, Quality Counts, 32*(16), 28–31.

Monitoring the future, 12th grade study: 1983, 1990, 1995, and 2000. (2000). Ann Arbor: University of Michigan Institute of Social Research.

Moore, S. (2006). *Workplace matters: Workplace conditions*. Best Practices NEA Research. Retrieved December 10, 2007, from http://www.nea.org/assets/docs/

Moss, C., & Brookhart, S. (2012). *Learning targets: Helping students aim for understanding in today's lesson*. Alexandria, VA: Association for Supervision and Curriculum Development.

Murphy, C., & Lick, D. (2005). *Whole-faculty study groups: Creating professional learning communities that target student learning* (3rd ed.). Thousand Oaks, CA: Corwin Press.

Murphy, P., Wilkinson, I., & Soter, A. (2011). Instruction based on discussion. In R. Mayer & P. Alexandria (eds.), *Handbook of research on learning and instruction*. New York: Routledge.

Murphy, P. K., Delli, L. M., & Edwards, M. N. (2004). The good teacher and good teaching: Comparing beliefs of second-grade students, preservice teachers, and inservice teachers. *Journal of Experimental Education, 72*(2), 69–92.

Narvaez, L., & Brimijoin, K. (2010). *Differentiation at work, K–5: Principles, lessons, and strategies*. Thousand Oaks, CA: Corwin Press.

National Center for Children in Poverty. Retrieved October 2013 from http://www.nccp.org/topics/childpoverty.html

National Center for Education Statistics, U.S. Department of Education. (2004). Condition of education. Retrieved March 15, 2005, from http://nces.ed.gov/programs/coe/2004/section1/index.asp

National Home Education Research Institute. (2005). Retrieved February 2005 from http://www.nheri.org

NEA survey of teachers 1961–2001. Retrieved December 10, 2007, from http://www.nea.org

Nettles, S. M. (1991). Community involvement and disadvantaged students: A review. *Review of Educational Research, 61,* 379–406.

Neu, T., & Weinfeld, R. (2006). *Helping boys succeed in school.* Austin, TX: Prufrock Press.

Newcomb, T. M. (1961). *The acquaintance process.* New York: Holt, Rinehart & Winston.

Nickerson, R. (1987). Why teach thinking? In J. Baran & R. Sternberg (eds.), *Teaching thinking skills: Theory and practice.* Boston: Harvard University Press.

Nichols, S., & Berliner, D. (2007). *Collateral damage: How high stakes testing is corrupting American schools.* Boston: Harvard University Press.

Noblit, G. (1995). In meaning: The possibilities of caring. *Phi Delta Kappan, 77,* 682.

Noddings, N. (1984). *Caring: A feminine approach to ethics and moral education.* Berkeley: University of California Press.

Noddings, N. (1995). Teaching themes of care. *Phi Delta Kappan, 77,* 676.

Noddings, N. (2001). The caring teacher. In V. Richardson (ed.), *Handbook of research on teaching* (4th ed.). Washington, DC: American Educational Research Association.

Noddings, N. (2005). *The challenge to care in schools: An alternative approach to education* (2nd ed.). New York: Teachers College Press.

Noddings, N. (2013). *Education and democracy in the 21st century.* New York: Teachers College Press.

Noguera, P. (2011). A broader and bolder approach uses education to break cycle of poverty. *Phi Delta Kappan, 93*(3), 8–13.

Noguera, P. (2012). Saving black and Latino boys. *Phi Delta Kappan, 93*(5), 8–12.

Noll, B. (2013). Seven ways to kill RTI. *Phi Delta Kappan, 94*(6), 55–59.

Nosich, G. (2011). *Learning to think things through: A guide to critical thinking across the curriculum* (4th ed.). New York: Prentice Hall.

Novak, J. D. (2004, January). Reflections on a half-century of thinking in science education and research: Implications from twelve-year longitudinal study of children's learning. *Canadian Journal of Science, Mathematics, and Technology,* 23–41.

Novak, J. D. (2013). Concept mapping. In J. Hattie & E. Anderman (eds.), *International guide to student achievement.* New York: Routledge.

Novak, J. D., & Musonda, D. (1991). A twelve-year longitudinal study of science concept teaching. *American Educational Research Journal, 28,* 125–130.

Oakes, J. (1985). *Keeping track: How schools structure inequality.* New Haven, CT: Yale University Press.

Oakes, J. (1992). Can tracking research inform practice? Technical, normative, and political considerations. *Educational Researcher, 21*(4), 12–21.

Oakes, J. (2005). *Keeping track.* New Haven, CT: Yale University Press.

Oakes, J., Joseph, R., & Muir, K. (2004). Access and achievement in mathematics and science: Inequalities the endure and change. In J. Banks & C. Banks (eds.), *Handbook of research on multicultural education* (2nd ed.), San Francisco: Wiley.

Oakes, J., & Lipton, M. (2003). *Teaching to change the world* (2nd ed.). New York: McGraw-Hill.

Oakes, J., & Lipton, M. (2006). *Teaching to change the world* (3rd ed.). New York: McGraw-Hill.

Oakes, J., Lipton, M., Anderson, L., & Stillman, J. (2012). *Teaching to change the world* (4th ed.). St. Paul, MN: Paradigm.

Oakes, J., & Saunders, M. (2002). *Access to textbooks, instructional material, equipment, and technology: Inadequacy and inequality in California's public schools.* Los Angeles: University of California at Los Angeles.

Ogbu, J. U. (1995). Understanding cultural diversity and learning. In J. Banks & C. Banks (eds.), *Handbook of research on multicultural education.* New York: Macmillan.

Ogbu, J. U. (1997). Understanding the school performance of urban blacks: Some essential background knowledge. In H. Walberg, O. Reyes, & R. P. Weissberg (eds.), *Children and youth: Interdisciplinary perspectives.* Norwood, NJ: Ablex.

Ogle, D. (1986). K-W-L: A teaching model that develops active reading of expository text. *Reading Teacher, 39*(6), 564–570.

Oja, S. N., & Smulyan, L. (1989). *Collaborative action research: A developmental approach.* New York: Falmer Press.

Okagaki, L. (2000). Determinants of intelligence: Socialization of intelligence. In A. Kazdin (ed.), *Encyclopedia of psychology.* Washington, DC: American Psychological Association.

Ormrod, J. (2008). *Educational psychology: Developing learners* (6th ed.). Upper Saddle River, NJ: Prentice Hall.

Ormrod, J. E. (2000). *Educational psychology: Developing learners* (3rd ed.). Upper Saddle River, NJ: Merrill.

Pagliro, M. (2011). *Exemplary classroom questioning: Practices to promote higher level thinking and learning.* Lanham, MD: Rowman and Littlefield.

Palincsar, A. (1998). Social constructivist perspectives on teaching and learning. In J. Spence, J. Darley, & D. Foss (eds.), *Annual review of psychology.* Palo Alto, CA: Annual Reviews.

Palincsar, A., & Brown, A. (1989). Instruction for self-regulated reading. In L. Resnick & L. Kloper (eds.), *Toward the thinking curriculum: Current cognitive research.* Alexandria, VA: Association for Supervision and Curriculum Development.

Palincsar, A. S. (1986). The role of dialogue in providing scaffolding instruction. *Educational Psychologist, 21,* 73–98.

Palincsar, A. S., & Herrenkohl, L. R. (2002). Designing collaborative learning contexts. *Theory into Practice, 41,* 26–32.

Pallas, A., Natriello, G., & McDill, E. (1989). The changing nature of the disadvantaged population: Current dimensions and future trends. *Educational Researcher, 18,* 16–22.

Panza, C., Poytthast, A., & Cathey, C. (2006). Thinking outside the room: Enhancing philosophy courses with online forums. *Teaching Philosophy, 29*(4), 279–297.

Pape, L. (2012). *Online education and virtual schooling.* Boston: National School Boards Association.

Papert, S. (1980). *Mindstorms: Children, computers, and powerful ideas.* New York: Basic Books.

Pardini, P. (2013). Having allies makes a difference. *Phi Delta Kappan, 94*(5), 14–20.

Patrick, B., Hisley, J., & Kempler, T. (2000). What's everybody so excited about? The effects of teacher enthusiasm on students' intrinsic motivation and vitality. *Journal of Experimental Education, 68*(3), 217–237.

Paullio, H. R. (1985). A tiger examines his stripes. *Teaching-Learning Issues,* No. 55. Knoxville: University of Tennessee Press.

Paullio, H. R. (1992). Learning new materials is fun—yes, but will it be on the test? *Teaching-Learning Issues,* No. 72, Knoxville: University of Tennessee Press.

Pawak, P. (2009). *Common characteristics and classroom practices of effective teachers of high-poverty and diverse students.* Doctoral dissertation, Claremont University.

Pedulla, H., et al. (2003). *Perceived effects of state-mandated testing programs on teaching and learning.* Boston: National Board on Education Testing and Public Policy.

Pelech, J., & Pieper, G. (2010). *The comprehensive handbook of constructivist teaching: From theory to practice.* Charlotte, NC: Information Age.

Perelman, L. (1992). *School's out. Hyperlearning, the new technology and the end of education.* New York: William Morrow.

Perkins, D. N. (1992). *Smart school: From training memories to educating minds.* New York: Free Press.

Perkins, D. N. (1995). *Outsmarting IQ: The emerging science of learnable intelligence.* New York: Free Press.

Perna, D., & Davis, J. (2007). *Aligning standards and curriculum for classroom success.* Thousand Oaks, CA: Corwin Press.

Perry, W. (1969). *Forms of intellectual and ethical development during the college years.* New York: Holt, Rinehart & Winston.

Peterson, K., & Deal, T. (2002). *The shaping of school culture fieldbook.* San Francisco: Jossey-Bass.

Peterson, P. L., Marx, R. W., & Clark, C. (1978). Teacher planning, teacher behavior and student achievement. *American Educational Research Journal, 15,* 417–432.

Phillips, S. (1972). Participant structures and communicative competence: Warm Springs children in community and classroom. In C. Cazden & D. Hymes (eds.), *Functions of language in the classroom.* New York: Teachers College Press.

Piaget, J. (1954). *The construction of reality in the child.* New York: Basic Books.

Piaget, J. (1963). *Psychology of intelligence.* Paterson, NJ: Littlefield Adams.

Pintrich, P. R. (2003). A motivational science perspective on the role of student motivation in learning and teaching contexts. *Journal of Educational Psychology, 95*(4), 667–686.

Pintrich, P. R., & Schunk, D. H. (2002). *Motivation in education: Theory, research, and applications* (2nd ed.). Englewood Cliffs, NJ: Prentice-Hall.

Pogrow, S. (1990). Challenging at-risk students: Findings from the HOTS program. *Phi Delta Kappan, 71,* 389–397.

Pogrow, S. (1999). Systematically using powerful learning environments to accelerate the learning of disadvantaged students in grades 4–8. In C. Reigluth (ed.), *Instructional design theories and models.* Hillsdale, NJ: Erlbaum.

Pollard, D. S. (1998). The contexts of single-sex classes. In *Separated by sex: A critical look at single-sex education.* Washington, DC: American Association of University Women Education Foundation.

Popham, J. (2008). *Transformative assessment.* Alexandria, VA: Association for Supervision and Curriculum Development.

Popham, W. (2011). *Classroom assessment: What teachers need to know.* (6th ed.). Boston: Allyn & Bacon.

Popham, J. (2013). *Classroom assessment: What teachers need to know* (7th ed.). Boston: Pearson.

Popham, W. J. (2001). *The truth about testing: An educator's call to action.* Alexandria, VA: Association for Supervision and Curriculum Development.

Poplin, M., Rivera, J., Durish, D., Hoff, L. Kawell, S., Pawlak, P., Hinman, , I., Straus, L., & Veney, C. (2011). She's strict for a reason: High-performing teachers in low-performing schools. *Phi Delta Kappan, 92*(5), 39–43.

Poverty in the United States. National Poverty Center. Retrieved March 2013 from http://www.npc.umich.edu/poverty/

Prensky, M. (2013). Our brains extended. *Educational Leadership, 70* (6). 22–27.

Pressley, M., et al. (1992). Encouraging mindful use of prior knowledge: Attempting to construct explanatory answers to facilitate learning. *Educational Psychologist, 27,* 91–109.

Pressley, M., Roehrig, A., Raphael, L., Dolezal, S., Bohn, K., Mohan, L., Wharton-McDonald, R., & Bogner, K. (2003). Teaching processes in elementary and secondary education. In W. M. Reynolds & G. E. Miller (eds.), *Comprehensive handbook of psychology: Vol. 7. Educational psychology.* New York: Wiley.

Putnam, J. (2005). *Organizing and managing the learning community.* New York: McGraw-Hill.

Rappaport, N. (2013). www.nancyrappaport.com. Retrieved March 14, 2013.

Rappaport, N., & Minahan, J. (2012). Cracking the behavior code. *Educational Leadership, 70*(2), 18–25.

Ravitch, D. (2010). *The death of and life of the great American school system: How testing and choice are undermining education.* New York: Basic Books.

Ravitch, D. (2013). *Reign of error: The hoax of the privatization movement and the danger to American public schools.* New York: Random House.

Redfield, D., & Rousseau, E. (1981). A meta-analysis of experimental research on teacher questioning behavior. *Review of Educational Research, 51,* 237–245.

Reeves. A. (2011). *Where great teaching begins: Planning for student thinking and learning.* Alexandria, VA: Association for Supervision and Curriculum Development.

Resnick, L. (1987a). Learning in school and out. *Educational Researcher, 16,* 13–20.

Resnick, L. B. (1987b). *Education and learning to think.* Washington, DC: National Academy Press.

Resnick, L. B., & Klopfer, L. E. (eds.). (1989). *Toward the thinking curriculum: Current cognitive research.* Alexandria, VA: Association for Supervision and Curriculum Development.

Reynolds, M. C. (ed.). (1989). *Knowledge base for the beginning teacher.* New York: Pergamon.

Reznitskaya, A. (2012). Dialogic teaching: Rethinking language use during literature discussions. *The Reading Teacher, 66*(7), 446–456.

Richardson, V. (ed.). (2001). *Handbook of research on teaching* (4th ed.). Washington, DC: American Educational Research Association.

Richardson, V., & Placier, P. (2001). Teacher change. In V. Richardson (ed.), *Handbook of research on teaching* (4th ed.). Washington, DC: American Educational Research Association.

Richardson, W. (2010). *Blogs, wikis, podcasts, and other powerful Web tools for classrooms.* Thousand Oaks, CA: Corwin Press.

Richardson-Koehler, V. (ed.). (1987). *Educators' handbook: A research perspective.* New York: Longman.

Richert, A. E. (2002). Narratives that teach: Learning about teaching from the stories teachers tell. In N. Lyons & V. LaBoskey (eds.), *Narrative knowing in teaching: Exemplars of reflective teaching, research, and teacher education.* New York: Teachers College Press.

Riddle, J. (2009). *Engaging the eye generation: Visual literacy strategies for the K–5 classroom.* Portland, ME: Stenhouse.

Ringstaff, C., Sandholtz, J. H., & Dwyer, D. C. (1995). Trading places: When teachers utilize student expertise in technology-intensive classrooms. In *Apple education research reports.* Eugene, OR: International Society for Technology in Education.

Ripley, A. (2010). Is cash the answer? *Time,* April, 41–47.

Rist, R. C. (1970). Student social class and teacher expectations: The self-fulfilling prophecy in ghetto education. *Harvard Education Review, 40,* 411–451.

Ritchhart, R. (2002). *Intellectual character: What it is, why it matters, and how to get it.* San Francisco: Jossey-Bass.

Ritchhart, R. (2005). The seven cultural forces that define our classrooms. Unpublished paper.

Ritchhart, R., Church, M., & Morrison, K. (2011). *Making thinking visible: How to promote engagement, understanding, and independence of all learners.* San Francisco: Jossey-Bass.

Ritchhart, R., Palmer, P., Church, M., & Tishman, S. (2006). Thinking routines: Establishing patterns of thinking in the classroom.

Paper presented at the annual meeting of the American Educational Research Association, San Francisco, April.

Ritchhart, R., & Perkins, D. (2008). Making thinking visible. *Educational Leadership, 65*(5), 57–61.

Robertson, C. (2012). Interactive whiteboards on the move. *TechTrends, 56*(6), 15–17.

Robinson, A., & Clinkenbeard, P. (1998). Giftedness: An exceptionality examined. In J. Spence, J. Darley, & D. Foss (eds.), *Annual review of pyschology*. Palo Alto, CA: Annual Reviews.

Robinson, A., Shore, B., & Enersen, D. (2006). *Best practices in gifted education: An evidence-based guide*. Austin, TX: Prufrock Press.

Roeser, R., Urdan, T., & Stephens, J. (2009). School as a context for student motivation and achievement. In K. Wentzel & A. Wigfield (eds.), *Handbook of motivation in school*. New York: Routledge.

Rolstad, K., Mahoney, K., & Glass, G. (2005). The big picture: A meta-analysis of program effectiveness research on English language learners. *Educational Policy, 19*(4), 572–594.

Rosen, L. (2010). *Rewired: Understanding the iGeneration and the way they learn*. New York: Palgrave Macmillan.

Rosenholz, S. (1989). *Teacher's workplace: The social organization of schools*. New York: Longman.

Rosenshine, B. (1970). Enthusiastic teaching: A research review. *School Review, 78,* 499–514.

Rosenshine, B. (1979). Content, time and direct instruction. In P. L. Peterson & H. J. Walberg (eds.), *Research on teaching*. Berkeley, CA: McCutchan.

Rosenshine, B. (1980). How time is spent in elementary classrooms. In C. Denham & A. Lieberman (eds.), *Time to learn*. Washington, DC: U.S. Department of Education.

Rosenshine, B. (2002). Converging findings on classroom instruction. In A. Molner (ed.), *School reform proposals: The research evidence*. Tempe: Arizona State University Research Policy Unit.

Rosenshine, B. (2009). The empirical support for direct instruction. In S. Tobias & T. Duffy (eds.), *Constructivist instruction: Success and failures*. New York: Routledge.

Rosenshine, B. (2012, Spring). Principles of instruction. Research-based strategies that all teachers should know. *American Educator,* 12–19+.

Rosenshine, B., & Furst, N. (1973). The use of direct observation to study teaching. In R. M. W. Travers (ed.), *Second handbook of research on teaching*. Chicago: Rand McNally.

Rosenshine, B., & Stevens, R. (1986). Teaching functions. In M. C. Wittrock (ed.), *Handbook of research on teaching* (3rd ed.). New York: Macmillan.

Rosenthal, R., & Jacobson, L. (1968). *Pygmalion in the classroom*. New York: Holt, Rinehart & Winston.

Rothstein, D., & Santana, L. (2011). *Make just one change: Teach students to ask their own questions*. Cambridge, MA: Harvard Education Press.

Rothstein, R. (2004, October). A wider lens on the black-white achievement gap. *Phi Delta Kappan,* 105–110.

Rothstein-Fisch, C., & Trumbull, E. (2008). *Managing diverse classrooms: How to build on cultural strengths*. Alexandria, VA: Association for Supervision and Curriculum Development.

Rowe, M. B. (1974a). Relation of wait-time and rewards to the development of language, logic, and fate control. Part II: Rewards. *Journal of Research in Science Teaching, 11,* 291–308.

Rowe, M. B. (1974b). Wait-time and rewards as instructional variables, their influence on language, logic, and fate control. Part I: Wait-time. *Journal of Research in Science Teaching, 11,* 81–94.

Rowe, M. B. (1986). Wait time: Slowing down may be a way of speeding up. *Journal of Teacher Education, 37,* 43–50.

Rugg, H. (1926). Curriculum-making and the scientific study of education since 1910. In H. Rugg (ed.), *Twenty-sixth yearbook of the national society for the study of education, Part I*. Bloomington, IL: Public Schools.

Russell, M., & Airasian, P. (2011). *Classroom assessment: Concepts and applications*. (7th ed.). New York: McGraw-Hill.

Rutter, M., Maughan, B., Mortimore, P., Ouston, J., & Smith, A. (1979). *Fifteen thousand hours: Secondary schools and their effects on children*. Cambridge, MA: Harvard University Press.

Ryan, R., & Brown, K. (2005). Legislating competence: The motivational impact of high stakes testing as an educational reform. In C. Dweck & A. Elliot (eds.), *Handbook of competence*. New York: Guilford.

Ryan, R., & Deci, E. (2009). Promoting self-determined school engagement: Motivation, learning, and well-being. In K. Wentzel & A. Wigfield (eds.), *Handbook of motivation in school*. New York: Routledge.

Ryan, R. M., & Deci, E. L. (2000). Self-determination theory and the facilitation of intrinsic motivation, social development, and well-being. *American Psychologist, 55,* 68–78.

Ryle, G. (1949). *The concept of mind*. London: Hutchinson's University Library.

Sabers, D., Cushing, K. S., & Berliner, D. C. (1991). Differences among teachers in task characterized by simultaneity, multidimensionality, and immediacy. *American Educational Research Journal, 28*(1), 63–88.

Sadker, M. (1985). *Women in educational administration*. Washington, DC: Mid-Atlantic Center for Sex Equity.

Sadker, M., Sadker, D., & Klein, S. (1991). The issue of gender in elementary and secondary education. *Review of Research in Education, 17,* 269–334.

Sams, A., & Bergmann, J. (2013). Flip your student's learning. *Educational Leadership, 70*(8), 16–21.

Sanders, W. L., & Rivers, J. C. (1996). *Cumulative and residual effects of teachers on future student academic achievement* (unpublished paper). Knoxville: University of Tennessee.

Santrock, J. (2005). *Child development* (14th ed.). New York: McGraw-Hill.

Santrock, J. (2012). *Life-span development* (14 ed.). New York: McGraw-Hill.

Santrock, J. W. (1976). Affect and facilitative self-control. Influence of ecological setting, cognition, and social agent. *Journal of Educational Psychology, 68*(5), 529–535.

Sarason, S. (1982). *The culture of school and the problem of change* (2nd ed.). Boston: Allyn & Bacon.

Sarason, S. D. (1995). *Parental involvement and the political principle*. San Francisco: Jossey-Bass.

Savin-Baden, M. (2003). *Facilitating problem-based learning*. Philadelphia: Open University Press.

Savin-Baden, M. (2008). *Problem-based online learning*. New York: Routledge.

Sax, L. (2009). *Boys adrift: The five factors driving the growing epidemic of unmotivated boys and underachieving young men*. New York: Basic Books.

Schafer, W. D. (1991). Essential assessment skills in professional education of teachers. *Educational Measurement: Issues and Practices, 10*(1), 3–6.

Schafer, W., & Lissitz, R. (1987). Measurement training for school personnel: Recommendations and reality. *Journal of Teacher Education, 38,* 57–63.

Schalock, D., et al. (2007). *Working in standards-based environments*. Monmouth, OR: Teaching Research.

Schell, J. Flipped classrooms. Retrieved April 23, 2013, from http://www.flippedclassroom.org

Schmidt, W., & Burroughs, N. (2013). How the Common Core boosts quality and equality. *Educational Leadership, 70*(4), 54–58.

Schmoker, M. (2011). *FOCUS: Elevating the essential to radically improve student learning.* Alexandria, VA: Association for Supervision and Curriculum Development.

Schmoker, M. (2012). The stunning power of good traditional lessons. *Phi Delta Kappan, 93*(4), 70–71.

Schmoker, M., & Allington, R. (2007). The gift of bleak research: How the Pianta classroom study can help schools improve immediately. *Education Week,* May 16, 27+.

Schmuck, R. (1997). *Practical action research for change.* Arlington Heights, IL: Skylight Professional Development.

Schmuck, R., & Schmuck, P. (2001). *Group processes in the classroom* (8th ed.). New York: McGraw-Hill.

Schmuck, R. A., & Schmuck, P. A. (1992). *Small districts, big problems.* Newbury Park, CA: Corwin Press.

Schön, D. A. (1983). *The reflective practitioner.* San Francisco: Jossey-Bass.

Schön, D. A. (1987). *Educating the reflective practitioner.* San Francisco: Jossey-Bass.

Schmidt, H. (1983). Problem-based learning rationale and description. *Medical Education, 17,* 11–16.

Schmidt, H., Van der Molen, H., Winkel, W., & Wijen, W. (2009). Constructivist problem-based learning does work: A meta-analysis of curricular comparisons involving a single medical school. *Educational Psychologist, 44,* 1–23.

Schuck, R. (1981). The impact of set induction on student achievement and retention. *Journal of Educational Research, 74,* 227–232.

Schuh, K. L. (2003). Knowledge construction in the learner-centered classroom. *Journal of Educational Psychology, 95*(2), 426–443.

Schulman, L. S. (1986). Paradigms and research programs in the story of teaching: A contemporary perspective. In M. C. Wittrock (ed.), *Handbook of research on teaching* (3rd ed.). New York: Macmillan.

Schute, V. (2008). Focus on formative feedback. *Review of Educational Research, 78*(1), 154–189.

Schwab, J. (1966). *Biological science curriculum study: Biology teacher's handbook.* New York: Wiley.

Schwert, G., & Wupperman, A. (2010). Is traditional teaching really all that bad? A within-student between-subject approach. *Economics of Education Review, 30*(2), 365–379.

Segro, G. (1995). Meeting the needs of all students: Making ability grouping work. *NASSP Bulletin, 79*(56), 18–26.

Serbin, L., & O'Leary, D. (1975, January). How nursery schools teach children to shut up. *Psychology Today,* 56–58.

Sergiovanni, T. (1996). *Leadership for the schoolhouse.* San Francisco: Jossey-Bass.

Sharan, S. (1999). *Handbook of cooperative learning methods.* New York: Praeger.

Sharan, S., Kussell, P., Hertz-Lazarowitz, R., Bejarano, Y., Raviv, S., & Sharan, Y. (1984). *Cooperative learning in the classroom: Research in desegregated schools.* Hillsdale, NJ: Erlbaum.

Sharp, V. (2002). *Computer education for teachers* (4th ed.). New York: McGraw-Hill.

Shepard, L., et al. (2005). Assessment. In L. Darling-Hammond & J. Bransford (eds.), *Preparing teachers for a changing world.* San Francisco: Jossey-Bass.

Shui-fong, Lam, & Pui-shan, Yim. (2004). The effects of competition on achievement motivation in Chinese classrooms. *British Journal of Educational Psychology, 74*(2), 281–297.

Shulman, L. S. (2004). *The wisdom of practice: Essays on teaching, learning, and learning to teach.* San Francisco: Jossey-Bass.

Shute, V. (2008). Focus on formative feedback. *Review of Educational Research, 38,* 153–189.

Silver, H., & Perini, M. (2010). *The interactive lecture: How to engage students, build memory, and deepen comprehension.* Alexandria, VA: Association for Supervision and Curriculum Development.

Silver, H., & Strong, R. (2000). *So each may learn: Integrating learning styles and multiple intelligences.* Alexandria, VA: Association for Supervision and Curriculum Development.

Simkins, M., Cole, K., Tavalin, F., & Means, B. (2002). *Increasing student learning through multimedia projects.* Alexandria, VA: Association for Supervision and Curriculum Development.

Sizer, T. (1984). *Horace's compromise: The dilemma of the American high school.* Boston: Houghton Mifflin.

Skinner, B. F. (1956). *Science and human behavior.* New York: Macmillan.

Skowron, J. (2006). *Powerful lesson planning: Every teacher's guide to effective instruction* (2nd ed.). Thousand Oaks, CA: Corwin Press.

Slavin, R. (1983). *Cooperative learning.* New York: Longman.

Slavin, R. (1986). *Student team learning* (3rd ed.). Baltimore: Center for Research on Elementary and Middle Schools, Johns Hopkins University.

Slavin, R. E. (1987). *Ability grouping and student achievement in elementary schools: A best-evidence synthesis.* Baltimore: Johns Hopkins University Press.

Slavin, R. E. (1990). Achievement effects of ability grouping in secondary schools. *Review of Educational Research, 57*(3), 293–336.

Slavin, R. (1994). *Using student team learning* (4th ed.). Baltimore: Johns Hopkins University.

Slavin, R. (1995a). *Cooperative learning* (2nd ed.). Boston: Allyn & Bacon.

Slavin, R. (1995b). Cooperative learning and race relations. In J. Banks & C. Banks (eds.), *Handbook of research on multicultural education.* New York: Macmillan.

Slavin, R. (1996). *Every child, every school: Success for all.* Thousand Oaks, CA: Corwin Press.

Slavin, R., & Madden, N. (2000). *One million children: Success for all.* Thousand Oaks, CA: Corwin Press.

Slavin, R., & Madden, N. (2001). *Success for all: Research and reform in elementary education.* New York: Routledge.

Slavin, R., Madden, N., Dolan, L., & Wasik, B. (1992). *Success for all.* Arlington, VA: Educational Research Services.

Slavin, R., Madden, N., Dolan, L., & Wasik, B. (1994). Roots and wings: Inspiring academic excellence. *Educational Leadership, 52,* 10–14.

Slavin, R., Sharan, S., Kagan, S., Hertz-Lazarowitz, R., Webb, C., & Schmuck, R. (eds.). (1985). *Learning to cooperate, cooperating to learn.* New York: Plenum Press.

Slesaransky-Poe, G. (2013). Adults set the tone for welcoming all students. *Phi Delta Kappen, 94*(5), 40–44.

Smith, D. (2006). *Introduction to special education: Teaching in an age of challenge* (3rd ed.). Boston: Allyn & Bacon.

Smith, H. (1995). Rogue eco-system project. *Educational Connection, 1,* 3–4.

Smith, M., & Connolly, W. (2005). The effects of interpretative authority on classroom discussion of poetry: Lessons from one teacher. *Communication Education, 54*(4), 271–288.

Sorensen, A. B., & Hallinan, M. T. (1986). Effects of ability grouping on growth in academic achievement. *American Educational Research Journal, 23,* 519–542.

Sousa, D. (2006). *How the brain learns* (3rd ed.). Thousand Oaks, CA: Corwin Press.

Spady, W., & Schwahn, C. (2010). *Learning communities 2.0: Educating in the age of empowerment.* Lanham, MD: Rowman & Littlefield Education.

Sparks, S. (2013). Remedial placements found to be overused. *Education Week, 32*(21), 1, 21.

Spaulding, C. L. (1992). *Motivation in the classroom.* New York: McGraw-Hill.

Spencer, J. (2013). I'm a better teacher when students aren't testing. *Phi Delta Kappan, 94*(5), 72–73.

Sprick, R. (2008). *Discipline in the secondary classroom: A positive approach to behavior management* (2nd ed.). San Francisco: Jossey-Bass.

Stahl, S. (2002). Different strokes for different folks? In L. Abbeduto (ed.), *Taking sides: Clashing on controversial issues in educational psychology*. Guilford, CT: McGraw/Duskin.

Stallings, J., & Kaskowitz, D. (1974). *Follow-through classroom observation evaluation 1972–1974* (SRI project URU-7370). Stanford, CA: Stanford Research Institute.

Starch, D., & Elliot, E. C. (1912). Reliability of grading high school work in English. *Scholastic Review, 20,* 442–456.

Starch, D., & Elliot, E. C. (1913). Reliability of grading high school work in history. *Scholastic Review, 22,* 676–681.

Starkey, D. (1980). *The origins of concept formation: Object sorting and object preference in early infancy.* (ERIC No. ED 175555: Resources in Education).

Steele, C. M. (1992, April). Race and the schooling of black Americans. *Atlantic Monthly,* 68–78.

Steffe, K., & Gale, J. (eds.). (1995). *Constructivism in education.* Hillsdale, NJ: Erlbaum.

Sternberg, R., & Grigorenko, E. (2004). Successful intelligence in the classroom. *Theory into Practice, 43*(4), 274–280.

Sternberg, R., Jarvin, L., & Grigorenko, E. (eds.). (2009). *Teaching for wisdom, intelligence, creativity, and success.* Thousand Oaks, CA: Corwin Press.

Sternberg, R., Nokes, C., Geissler, P., Prince, R., Okatcha, F., & Bundy, D. (2001). The relationship between academic and practical intelligence: A case study in Kenya. *Intelligence, 29*(5), 401–418.

Sternberg, R., Torff, B., & Grigorenko, E. (1998). Teaching for successful intelligence raises school achievement. *Phi Delta Kappan, 79*(9). pp. 667–669

Sternberg, R. (2009). Teaching for wisdom, intelligence, and creativity. *School Administrator, 66*(4), 2–4.

Sternberg, R., & Williams, W. (2009) *Educational psychology* (2nd ed.). Boston: Pearson.

Sternberg, R. J. (1985). *Beyond IO: A triarchic theory of human intelligence.* New York: Cambridge University Press.

Sternberg, R. J. (1994). Answering questions and questioning answers. *Phi Delta Kappan, 76*(2), 136–138.

Sternberg, R. J. (1999a, Spring). Ability and expertise: It's time to replace the current model of intelligence. *American Educator,* 10–13.

Sternberg, R. J. (1999b). Myths, countermyths, and truths about intelligence. In A. Woolfork (ed.), *Readings in educational psychology.* Boston: Allyn & Bacon.

Sternberg, R. J. (2002a). *Cognitive psychology* (3rd ed.). Belmont, CA: Wadsworth.

Sternberg, R. J. (2002b). Intelligence: The triarchic theory of intelligence: Toward a theory of successful intelligence. In M. Bennett (ed.), *Encyclopedia of education* (2nd ed.). New York: Macmillan.

Stevens, D., Levi, A., & Walvoord, B. (2012). *Introduction to rubrics: An assessment tool to Save grading time, convey effective feedback, and promote student learning.* Sterling, VA: Stylus.

Stevens, R., & Slavin, R. (1995). The cooperative elementary school: Effects on students' achievement, attitudes, and social relations. *American Educational Research Journal, 32*(2), 321–351.

Stiggins, R. (2007). *Introduction to student-involved assessment for learning* (5th ed.). Englewood Cliffs, NJ: Prentice-Hall.

Stiggins, R., Arter, J., Chappuis, J., & Chappuis, S. (2006). *Classroom assessment for student learning: Doing it right—using it well.* Portland, OR: ETS Assessment Training Institute.

Stiggins, R. J. (2004). *Student-involved assessment for learning* (4th ed.). Englewood Cliffs, NJ: Prentice-Hall.

Stiggins, R., Arter, J., Chappuis, J., & Chappuis, S. (2009). *Classroom assessment for student learning: doing it right,-using it well.* Boston: Allyn & Bacon.

Stiggins, R., & Chappuis, J. (2011) *An Introduction to Student-Involved Assessment.* Boston: Pearson.

Stiggins, R., & Chappuis, J. (2012). *An Introduction to Student-Involved Assessment FOR Learning.* (6th ed.). Boston: Pearson.

Stipek, D. J. (1996). Motivation and instruction. In D. Berliner & R. Calfee (eds.), *Handbook of educational psychology.* New York: Macmillan.

Stipek, D. J. (2002). *Motivation to learn: Integrating theory and practice* (4th ed.). Boston: Allyn & Bacon.

Stout, M. (2007). Critical thinking, imagination, and new knowledge in education research. In K. Egan, M. Stout, & K. Takaya (eds.), *Teaching and learning outside the box: Inspiring imagination across the curriculum.* New York: Teachers College Press.

Strauss, V. (2006). As homework grows, so do arguments against it. *Washington Post.* Retrieved September 12, 2006, from http://www.washingtonpost.com/wp-dyn/content/article/2006/09/11/

Strauss, V. (2008, May 20). No crisis for boys in school. *Washington Post.* Retrieved from http://www.washingtonpost.com/wp-dyn/content/article/2006/09/11/

Stronge, J. (2007). *Qualities of effective teachers* (2nd ed.). Alexandria, VA: Association for Supervision and Curriculum Development.

Stronge, J. H., Tucker, P. D., & Hindman, J. L. (2004). *Handbook for qualities of effective teachers.* Alexandria, VA: Association for Supervision and Curriculum Development.

Suchman, R. (1962). *The elementary school training program in scientific inquiry.* Report to the U.S. Office of Education. Urbana: University of Illinois.

Sue, D., & Sue, D. (2007). *Counseling the culturally diverse: Theory and practice* (5th ed.). Hoboken, NJ: Wiley.

Sullo, B. (2007). *Activating the desire to learn.* Alexandria, VA: Association for Supervision and Curriculum Development.

Swanson, T. (2005). Providing structure for children with learning and behavior problems. *Intervention in School and Clinic, 40,* 182–187.

Swartz, R. (1987). Teaching for thinking: A developmental model for the infusion of thinking skills into mainstream instruction. In J. Baron & R. Sternberg (eds.), *Teaching thinking skills: Theory and practice* (pp. 106–126). New York: W.H. Freeman.

Tannen, D. (1990). *You just don't understand: Women and men in conversation.* New York: William Morrow.

Tannen, D. (1994). *Gender and discourse.* New York: Oxford University Press.

Tapscott, D. (1998). *Growing up digital: The rise of the Net generation.* New York: McGraw-Hill.

Tapscott, D. (2000). The digital divide. *Jossey-Bass reader on technology and learning.* San Francisco: Jossey-Bass.

Tapscott, D. (2008). *Grown up digital: How the Net generation is changing the world.* New York: McGraw-Hill.

Tapscott, D. (2010). Changing the pedagogy for the Net generation. ASCD Inservice. Retrieved March 7, 2010, from http://www.typepad.com/services

Taylor, R. (1949). *Basic principles of curriculum and instruction.* Chicago: University of Chicago Press.

Technology Counts 2007: A Digital Decade, Education Week, 26(30).

Tennenbaum, H., & Ruck, M. (2007). Are teachers' expectations different for racial minorities than for European American students? *Journal of Educational Psychology, 99,* 253–273.

Tennyson, R. (1978). Pictorial support and specific instructions as design variables for children's concept and rule learning. *Educational Communication and Technology: A Journal of Research and Development, 26,* 291–299.

Tennyson, R., Youngers, J., & Suebsonthi, P. (1983). Concept learning by children using instructional presentation forms for prototype formation and classification-skill development. *Journal of Educational Psychology, 75,* 280–290.

Terrell, S., & Rendulic, P. (1996). Using computer-managed instructional software to increase motivation and achievement in elementary school children. *Journal of Research on Computing in Education, 26*(3), 403–414.

Thelen, H. A. (1954). *Dynamics of groups at work.* Chicago: University of Chicago Press.

Thelen, H. A. (1960). *Education and the human quest.* New York: Harper & Row.

Tieso, C. L. (2003). Ability grouping is not just tracking anymore. *Roeper Review, 26*(1), 29–37.

Tileston, D. W. (2007). *Teaching strategies for active learning.* Thousand Oaks, CA: Corwin Press.

Timpson, W. M., & Tobin, D. N. (1982). *Teaching as performing.* Englewood Cliffs, NJ: Prentice Hall.

Timperly, H. (2013). Feedback. In J. Hattie & E. Anderman. *International guide to student achievement.* (Eds.). New York: Routledge.

Tishman, S., Perkins, D., & Jay, E. (1995). *The thinking classroom.* Boston: Allyn & Bacon.

Tobey, C., & Goldsmith, L. (2013). The critical role of Feedback. *ASCDExpress, 8,* (11), Retrieved March 15, 2013.

Tobias, S., & Duffy, T. (eds.). (2009). *Constructivist instruction: Success or failure?* New York: Routledge.

Tobin, K., & Capie, W. (1980). The effects of teacher wait time and questioning quality in middle school science achievement. *Journal of Research in Science Teaching, 17,* 469–475.

Tobin, K., Kahle, J. B., & Fraser, B. J. (eds.). (1992). *Windows into science classrooms: Problems associated with higher-level cognitive learning.* New York: Falmer Press.

Tollefson, N. (2000). Classroom applications of cognitive theories of motivation. *Educational Psychology Review, 12*(1), 63–83.

Tomlinson, C. (2004a). *The differentiated classroom: Responding to the needs of all learners.* Alexandria, VA: Association for Supervision and Curriculum Development.

Tomlinson, C. (2004b). *How to differentiate instruction in mixed ability classrooms* (2nd ed.) Alexandria, VA: Association for Supervision and Curriculum Development.

Tomlinson, C., & Imbeau, M. B. (2010). *Leading and managing a differentiated classroom.* Alexandria, VA: Association for Supervision and Curriculum Development.

Tomlinson, C., & McTighe, J. (2006). *Integrating differentiated instruction and understanding by design.* Alexandria, VA: Association for Supervision and Curriculum Development.

Tomlinson, C. A. (1995). *How to differentiate instruction in mixed-ability classrooms.* Alexandria, VA: Association for Supervision and Curriculum Development.

Tomlinson, C. A. (1999). *The differentiated classroom: Responding to the needs of all learners.* Alexandria, VA: Association for Supervision and Curriculum Development.

Tomlinson, C. A. (2001). Grading for success. *Educational Leadership, 58*(6), 12–15.

Tomlinson, C. A., & Germundson, A. (2007). Teaching as jazz. *Educational Leadership, 64*(8), 27–31.

Toppo, G. (2013). More teachers are grouping kids by ability. *USA Today,* March18.RetrievedMarch18,2013,fromhttp://www.usatoday.com/story/news/nation/2013/03/18/elementary-teachers-grouping-reading-ability/1990917/

Tovani, C. (2011). *So what do they really know? Assessment that informs teaching and learning.* Portland, ME: Stenhouse

Travers, R. M. (ed.). (1973). *Second handbook of research on teaching.* Chicago: Rand McNally.

Trotter, A. (2007). Getting up to speed. In *Technology Counts 2007: A Digital Decade, Education Week 26*(30), 10–16.

Tuckman, B. (1995). Assessing effective teaching. *Peabody Journal of Education, 70*(2), 127–138.

Tuckman, W. B. (1992). Does the length of the assignment or the nature of grading practices influence the amount of homework students are motivated to produce? *Journal of General Education, 41,* 190–199.

Turnbull, A., Turnbull, H., & Wehmeyer, M. (2010). *Exceptional lives: Special education in today's schools* (6th ed.). Upper Saddle River, NJ: Prentice Hall.

Turnbull, A., Turnbull, H., Wehmeyer, M., & Shogren, K. (2012). *Exceptional lives: Special education in today's schools* (7th ed.). Boston: Pearson.

Tyack, D., & Cuban, L. (2000). Teaching by machine. *The Jossey-Bass reader on technology and learning.* San Francisco: Jossey-Bass.

Tyler, R. W. (1949). *Basic principles of curriculum and instruction.* Chicago: University of Chicago Press.

Tyre, P. (2006, January 30). The trouble with boys: They're kinetic, maddening and failing at school. Now educators are trying new ways to help them succeed. *Newsweek.* Retrieved from http://www.newsweek.com/id/47522

Tyre, P. (2008). *The trouble with boys: A surprising report card on our sons, their problems at school, and what parents and educators must do.* New York: Three Rivers Press.

U.S. Census Bureau Documents on Poverty. (2002). Retrieved from http://www.census.gov/hhes/www/poverty.html

U.S. Department of Education. (1999). *To assure the free appropriate public education of all children with disabilities: Twenty-first century report to Congress on the implementation of the Individuals with Disabilities Act, A-2.* Washington, DC: Author.

U.S. Department of Education. (2004). Secretary Paige announces new policies to help English language learners. Retrieved February 2005 from http://www.ed.gov/news/pressrelease/2004/02/02.02192004.html

U.S. Department of Education. (2010). *Revised classification system.* Washington, DC: Author.

U.S. Department of Education, Office of Bilingual Education and Minority Language Affairs. (1998). *Facts about limited English proficient students.* Washington, DC: U.S. Government Printing Office.

VanSledright, B. A. (2002). Fifth graders investigating history in the classroom: Results from a researcher-practitioner design experiment. *Elementary School Journal, 103*(2), 131–160.

Vedder, P., & Veendrick, A. M. (2003). The role of task and reward structure in cooperative learning. *Scandinavian Journal of Educational Research, 47*(5), 529–543.

Veenman, S. (1984). Perceived problems of beginning teachers. *Review of Educational Research, 54,* 143–178.

Viadero, D. (2007). Collecting evidence. In *Technology Counts 2007: A Digital Decade, Education Week, 26*(30), 30–33.

Viadero, D. (2008). Research yields clues on the effects of extra time on for learning. *Education Week, 28*(5), 16–18.

Viadero, D. (2009). Research hones focus on ELLs. *Education Week,* January 8, 22, 25.

Villegas, A. M. (1991). *Culturally responsive teaching.* Princeton, NJ: Educational Testing Service.

Vygotsky, L. S. (1978). *Mind in society. The development of higher psychological processes.* Cambridge, MA: Harvard University Press.

Vygotsky, L. S. (1994). The problem of environment. In Rene van der Veer & J. Valsiner (eds.), *The Vygotsky reader.* Cambridge, England: Blackwell.

Walberg, H. (1999). Productive teaching. In H. C. Waxman & H. J. Walberg (eds.), *New directions for teaching practice research.* Berkeley, CA: McCutchen.

Walberg, H. J. (1986). Syntheses of research on teaching. In M. C. Wittrock (ed.), *Handbook of research on teaching* (3rd ed.). New York: Macmillan.

Walker, H., Colvin, G., & Ramsey, E. (1995). *Antisocial behavior in schools: Strategies and best practices.* Pacific Grove, CA: Brooks/Cole.

Walker, J. E., Shea, T. M., & Bauer, A. M. (2003). *Behavior management: A practical approach for educators* (8th ed.). Englewood Cliffs, NJ: Prentice-Hall.

Waller, W. (1932). *The sociology of teaching.* New York: Russell & Russell.

Wallis, C., & Steptoe, S. (2006, December 18). How to bring our schools out of the 20th century. *The New Times,* 50–56.

Walsh, J., & Sattes, B. (2011). *Thinking through quality questioning: Deepening student understanding.* Thousand Oaks, CA: Corwin Press.

Walsh, S. (2011). *Exploring classroom discourse: Language in action: Introductions to applied linguistics.* New York: Routledge.

Wang, M. C., Reynolds, M., & Walberg, H. (1995). Serving students at the margin. *Educational Leadership, 52,* 12–17.

Wang, M. C., Walberg, H. J., & Reynolds, M. C. (1992). A scenario for better—not separate—special education. *Educational Leadership, 50,* 35–38.

Wapner, S., & Kemick, J. (1991). *Field-dependence-independence: Cognitive styles across the life span.* Hillsdale, NJ: Erlbaum.

Watkins, C. (2005). *Classrooms as learning communities. What's in it for schools?* New York: Routledge.

Waugh, C., & Gronlund, N. (2012). *Assessment of Student Achievement.* (10th ed.). Boston: Pearson.

Webb, N. M., Farivar, S. H., & Mastergeorge, A. M. (2002). Productive helping in cooperative groups. *Theory into Practice, 41*(1), 13–20.

Weick, K. E. (1976). Educational organizations as loosely coupled systems. *Administrative Science Quarterly, 21,* 1–19.

Weiner, B. (1986). *An attributional theory of motivations and emotion.* New York: Springer.

Weiner, B. (1992). *Human motivation: Metaphors, theories, and research.* Newbury Park, CA: Sage.

Weiner, B. (ed.). (1974). *Achievement motivation and attribution theory.* Morristown, NJ: General Learning Corporation.

Weinstein, C. (2007). *Middle and secondary classroom management: Lessons from research and practice* (3rd ed.). New York: McGraw-Hill.

Weinstein, C., & Mignano, A. (2007). *Elementary classroom management: Lessons from research and practice* (4th ed.). New York: McGraw-Hill.

Weinstein, C., & Novodvorsky, I. (2010). *Secondary classroom management: Lessons from research and practice* (5th ed.). New York: McGraw-Hill.

Weinstein, C., Romano, M., & Mignano, A. (2010). *Elementary classroom management: Lessons from research and practice* (5th ed.). New York: McGraw-Hill.

Weinstein, C. S., & Mignano, A. J. (2004). *Elementary classroom management: Lessons from research and practice* (3rd ed.). New York: McGraw-Hill.

Weissbourd, R., & Jones, S. (2012). Joining hands against bullying. *Educational Leadership, 17*(2), 26–31.

Weisz, D. (n.d.) *Action research project: Equitable distribution of questioning and feedback in the classroom* (mimeographed). College Park: University of Maryland.

Wenger, E. (1998). *Communities of practice: Learning meaning and identity.* New York: Cambridge University Press.

Wenglinsky, H. (2002). The link between teacher classroom practices and student academic performance. *Educational Policy Analysis Archives, 10*(12).

Wenglinsky, H. (2005/06) Technology and achievement: The bottom line. *Educational Leadership, 63*(4), 29–32.

Wentzel, K. R., Barry, C. M., & Caldwell, K. A. (2004). Friendship in middle school: Influences on motivation and school adjustments. *Journal of Educational Psychology, 96*(2), 195–204.

West, D. M. (2012). *Digital schools: How technology can transform education.* Washington, DC: Brookings Institution.

Wigfield, A., & Eccles, J. (2002). *Development of achievement motivation.* San Diego: Academic Press.

Wiggins, G., & McTighe, J. (1998). *Understanding by design.* Alexandria, VA: Association for Supervision and Curriculum Development.

Wiggins, G. (2012). Seven keys to effective feedback *Educational Leadership, 70* (1), 10–17.

Wiggins, G., & McTighe, J. (2005). *Understanding by design* (2nd ed.). Alexandria, VA: Association for Supervision and Curriculum Development.

Wiggins, G. P. (1997). *Assessing student performance.* San Francisco: Jossey-Bass.

Wiggins, G. P. (1998). *Educative assessment: Designing assessments to inform and improve student performance.* San Francisco: Jossey-Bass.

Wilde, S. (2012). *Care in education: Teaching with understanding and compassion.* New York: Routledge.

Wiliam, D. (2007). Content then process: Teacher learning communities in the service of formative assessment. In D. Reeves (ed.), *Ahead of the curve: The power of assessment to transform teaching and learning.* Bloomington, IN: Solution Tree.

Wiliam, D. (2011). *Embedded Formative Assessment.* Bloomington, IN: Solution Tree.

Wiliam, D. (2012). Feedback: Part of a system. *Educational Leadership, 70* (1), 30–35.

Willard-Holt, C. (2003). Raising expectations for the gifted. *Educational Leadership, 61*(2), 72–75.

Williams, R. (2007a). *Cooperative learning: A standard for high achievement.* Thousand Oaks, CA: Corwin Press.

Williams, R. (2007b). *Higher order thinking skills: Challenging all students to achieve.* Thousand Oaks, CA: Corwin Press.

Williams, W., et al. (1996). *Practical intelligence in schools.* New York: HarperCollins.

Williams, W., Blythe, T., White, N., Li, J., Sternberg, R., & Gardner, H. (1996). *Practical intelligence for school.* New York: HarperCollins.

Willingham, D. (2010). *Why don't students like school: A cognitive scientist answers questions about how the mind works and what it means.* San Francisco: Jossey-Bass.

Wilson, D., & Conyers, M. (2013). *Five big ideas for effective teaching: Connecting mind, brain, and education research to classroom practice.* New York: Teachers College Press.

Winger, T. (2009). Grading what matters. *Educational Leadership, 67*(3), 73–75.

Winner, E. (2000). The origins and ends of giftedness. *American Psychologist, 55,* 159–169.

Wise, A. (1995). NCATE's emphasis on performance. *NCATE Quality Teaching, 5,* 1–12.

Wittrock, M. C. (ed.). (1986). *Handbook of research on teaching* (3rd ed.). New York: Macmillan.

Wolfe, P. (2001). *Brain matters: Translating research into classroom practice.* Alexandria, VA: Association for Supervision and Curriculum Development.

Wolk, R. (2011, March 9). The high stakes of standards-based accountability. *Education Week, 26,* 24.

Wolk, R. (2012, December). Common Core vs. common sense. *Education Week,* 40+.

Wolk, S. (2007). Why go to school. *Phi Delta Kappan, 88*(9), 648–654.

Women on Words and Images. (1975). *Dick and Jane as victims: Sex stereotyping in children's readers.* Princeton, NJ: Unpublished manuscript.

Wood, B. (2009). *Lecture-free teaching: A learning partnership between science educators and their students.* Washington, DC: National Science Teachers Association.

Woolfolk, A. (2005). *Educational psychology, active learning edition* (9th ed.). Boston: Allyn & Bacon.

Woolfolk, A. (2007). *Educational psychology* (10th ed.). Boston: Allyn & Bacon.

Woolfolk, A. (2010). *Educational psychology* (11th ed.). Upper Saddle River, NJ: Merrill.

Woolfolk, A. (2013). *Educational psychology* (12th ed.). Boston: Pearson.

Woolfolk, A. (ed.). (1998). *Readings in educational psychology* (2nd ed.). Boston: Allyn & Bacon.

Wormeli, R. (2006). *Fair isn't always equal: Assessing and grading in the differentiated classroom.* Portland, ME: Stenhouse.

Yazzie-Mintz, E. (2006). *Voices of student engagement: A report on the 2006 high school survey of student engagement.* Available at http://www.ceep.indiana.edu/hassse/pdf/HSSSE_Report.pdf

Yinger, R. (1980). A study of teacher planning. *Elementary School Journal, 80,* 107–127.

Zahorik, J. (1970). The effects of planning on teaching. *The Elementary School Journal, 71,* 143–151.

Zambo, R., & Hess, R. K. (1996). The gender differential effects of a procedural plan for solving mathematic word problems. *School Science and Mathematics, 96,* 362–370.

Zeichner, K., & Noffke, S. (2001). Practitioner research. In V. Richardson (ed.), *Handbook of research on teaching* (4th ed.). Washington, DC: American Educational Research Association.

Zoller, K., & Landry, C. (2010). *The choreography of presenting: The 7 essential abilities of effective presenters.* Thousand Oaks, CA: Corwin Press.

Zull, J. E. (2002). *The art of changing the brain: Enriching the practice of teaching by exploring the biology of learning.* Sterling, VA: Stylus.

Zumwalt, K. (1989). The need for curricular vision. In M. Reynolds (ed.), *Knowledge base for the beginning teacher.* New York: Pergamon Press.

Zwiers, J., & Crawford, M. (2011). *Academic conversations: Classroom talk that fosters critical thinking and content understandings.* Portland, ME: Stenhouse.

Credits

Photo Credits

Chapter 1

Opener: © Digital Vision/Getty Images; **p. 5** Library of Congress Prints and Photographs Division [LC-USZ62-90603]; **p. 12** Blend Images/Ariel Skelley/Getty Images; **p. 17** © amana images inc./Alamy; **p. 28** Ryan McVay/Getty Images

Chapter 2

Opener: McGraw-Hill Companies, Inc. Lars A. Niki, photographer; **p. 44** PhotoLink/Getty Images; **p. 57** SW Productions/Brand X Pictures/Getty Images; **p. 86** Nicole Hill/Getty Images

Chapter 3

Opener: Ingram Publishing; **p. 97** Decisive Images/Alamy; **p. 101** Purestock/SuperStock; **p. 123** Getty Images/Mark Thornton

Chapter 4

Opener: © Ocean/Corbis; **p. 140** BananaStock/PictureQuest; **p. 146** © BananaStock/PunchStock; **p. 157** BananaStock/AGE Fotostock; **p. 163** BananaStock/PictureQuest; **p. 168** UpperCut Images/Getty Images

Chapter 5

Opener: BananaStock/AGE Fotostock; **p. 179** Stockbyte/PunchStock; **p. 196** BananaStock/AGE Fotostock

Chapter 6

Opener: Blend Images/Ariel Skelley/Getty Images; **p. 230** © image 100 Ltd; **p. 244** Eric Audras/Photoalto/PictureQuest; **p. 248** © Tim Pannell/Corbis; **p. 253** © Image Source/PunchStock

Chapter 7

Opener: Comstock Images/Jupiterimages; **p. 282** © Ariel Skelley/Blend Images/Getty Images; **p. 284** Stock 4B RF; **p. 295** BananaStock/AGE Fotostock; **p. 297** Photodisc/Getty Images

Chapter 8

Opener: © image 100 Ltd./Corbis; **p. 304** © Digital Vision/Getty Images; **p. 317** BananaStock/AGE Fotostock; **p. 325** BananaStock/AGE Fotostock

Chapter 9

Opener: Monashee Frantz/Getty Images; **p. 352** © Stockbyte/PunchStock; **p. 353** © BananaStock/PunchStock

Chapter 10

Opener: franckreporter/Getty Images; **p. 373** Library of Congress Prints and Photographs Division [LC-USZ62-51525]; **p. 376** © Corbis; **p. 388** © Creatas Images/PunchStock; **p. 393** © David Ashley/Corbis

Chapter 11

Opener: Peter Muller/Getty Images; **p. 408** Creatas Images/PunchStock; **p. 418** © Pixland/PunchStock;

p. 425 Ariel Skelley/Getty Images; **p. 426** © Randy Faris/Corbis; **p. 431** Rebecca Emery/Getty Images

Chapter 12

Opener: © Bananastock/AGE Fotostock; **p. 443** Corbis/PictureQuest; **p. 456** BananaStock/AGE Fotostock

Chapter 13

Opener: Jupiterimages/Brand X/Alamy; **p. 473** dynamicgraphics/Jupiterimages; **p. 474** Creatas Images/PunchStock; **p. 485** © Creatas/PunchStock

Chapter 14

Opener: © Chris Ryan/AGE fotostock; **p. 501** © Image Source/PunchStock; **p. 505** Nigel Sawtell/Alamy; **p. 510** Jupiterimages; **p. 519** Comstock Images/Getty Images

Text and Illustrations

Fig. 1.7, Fig. 1.8: Copyright © 2004 From "The Good Teacher and Good Teaching: Comparing Beliefs of Second-Grade Students, Preservice Teachers, and Inservice Teachers" by Murphy, P. K., Delli, L. M., and Edwards, M. N. in *The Journal of Experimental Education*. January 1, 2004. Reprinted by permission of Taylor & Francis Group, LLC., http://www.tandf.co.uk/journals;3; **p. 53:** © Adam Stoller. Reprinted with permission; **Table 3.7, Table 3.8:** Anderson, Lorin W.; Krathwohl, David R.; Airasian, Peter W.; Cruikshank, Kathleen A.; Mayer, Richard E.; Pintrich, Paul R.; Raths, James; Wittrock, Merlin C., *A Taxonomy for Learning, Teaching and Assessing: A Revision of Bloom's Taxonomy of Educational Objectives, Complete Edition.* 1st, ©2001. Printed and Electronically reproduced by permission of Pearson Education, Inc., Upper Saddle River, New Jersey; **Table 4.3, Table 4.4:** Dolezal, S.E., L.M. Welsh, M. Pressley and M.M. Vincent, "How Nine Third-Grade Teachers Motivate Student Academic Engagement" in *Elementary School Journal, 103:* 3, pp. 239–269. Copyright ©2003 The University of Chicago. Reprinted with permission of The University of Chicago Press via Copyright Clearance Center; **Table 5.10:** Kohn, Alfie in *Beyond Discipline: From Compliances to Community.* Copyright ©1996 Alfie Kohn. Adapted by permission of the author; **Fig. 6.2:** Individual Profile report reprinted from *TerraNova, The Second Edition*, Individual Profile Report, by permission of the publisher. CTB/McGraw-Hill LLC, a subsidiary of The McGraw-Hill Companies, Inc. Copyright ©2000 by CTB.McGraw-Hill LLC. All rights reserved; **Table 7.3:** Bulgren, J., Marquis, J., Lenz, B., & Deshler, D. (2011). The effectiveness of a Question Exploration Routine for enhancing the content learning of secondary students. *Journal of Educational Psychology*, 130 (3), 578–593. Published APA. Reprinted with permission; **p. 314:** Reprinted by permission of Glen Dines/KAPPAN; **Fig. 8.2:** Lazaroff, Michael J. Vieira, *The Complete Idiot's Guide to Anatomy and Physiology*, ISBN 1-59257-203-0. Reprinted with permission; **p. 391:** Weinstein, C.F. and A.J. Migano in *Elementary Classroom Management: Lessons from Research and Practice.* Copyright ©1993 McGraw-Hill. Reprinted by permission of The McGraw-Hill Companies; **p. 420:** Adams' Apples. Copyright 2007, James R. Adams. Reprinted with permission; **p. 454:** Copyright Charles Almon. Reprinted with permission; **Fig. 13.1:** Torres, Patricia D. and Aleida Pérez-Sánchez. Reprinted by permission of the authors, Patricia D. Torres, M.Ed. and Aleida Pérez-Sánchez, M.Ed., both Instructional Technologists, Northside ISD, San Antonio, Texas; **Fig. 13.2:** This activity is adapted from lessons created by Aleida Perez and Patty Torres (Webquest titled Wet and Wild Woodlands; http://www.pavenet.org/FTP/Users/all_share/Cohort5/5319Project/TorresWebQuest/); **Table 13.3:** Santrock , John W. Table, "Teaching Strategies for each of Gardner's eight types of intelligences," in *Educational Psychology*, 2nd ed. Copyright © 2006. McGraw-Hill. Reprinted by permission of The McGraw-Hill Companies; **Fig. 14.1:** Gallego and Cole in *Handbook of Research on Teaching*, 4th ed., Virginia Richardson, ed. Reprinted with permission; **p. 517:** Copyright © Pedro Molina. Reprinted with permission.

Name Index

Subject Index